*Mark Twain*

# UNSANCTIFIED NEWSPAPER REPORTER

MARK TWAIN
AND HIS CIRCLE
SERIES

· · · ·

*Tom Quirk, Editor*

# *Mark Twain*

## UNSANCTIFIED NEWSPAPER REPORTER

JAMES E. CARON

UNIVERSITY OF MISSOURI PRESS

COLUMBIA AND LONDON

Copyright © 2008 by
The Curators of the University of Missouri
University of Missouri Press, Columbia, Missouri 65201
Printed and bound in the United States of America
All rights reserved
5 4 3 2 1    12 11 10 09 08

Library of Congress Cataloging-in-Publication Data

Caron, James Edward, 1952–
    Mark Twain, unsanctified newspaper reporter / James E. Caron.
        p.   cm.
    Includes bibliographical references and index.
    Summary: "A fresh perspective on the early years of Samuel Clemens's
career as a writer and newspaper reporter. Caron examines Clemens's
developing comic voice in his journalism in Nevada and San Francisco, then
in the travel letters from Hawaii and letters chronicling his trip from
California to New York City"—Provided by publisher.
    ISBN 978-0-8262-1802-5 (alk. paper)
    1. Twain, Mark, 1835-1910—Criticism and interpretation.  2. Twain,
Mark, 1835-1910—Knowledge—Journalism.  3. Twain, Mark, 1835–
1910—Correspondence.  4. Authors, American—19th century—
Correspondence.  5. Humorists, American—19th century  6. Humorists,
American—19th century—Biography.  7. Twain, Mark, 1835-1910—Travel.
8. Twain, Mark, 1835-1910—Knowledge—America.  9. United States—
Description and travel.  I. Title.
    PS1338.C37 2008
    818'.409—dc22
                                                                    2008011961

♾ This paper meets the requirements of the
American National Standard for Permanence of Paper
for Printed Library Materials, Z39.48, 1984.

Designer: Foley Design
Typesetter: BookComp, Inc.
Printer and binder: Thomson-Shore, Inc.
Typefaces: Minion, Carpenter ICG, American Typewriter, and
            EngraversDRom

Acknowledgment is made for permission to quote from *Mark Twain's
Letters, Volume 1: 1853–1866,* ed. Edgar M. Branch, Michael B.
Frank, and Kenneth M. Sanderson, © 1988 by
The University of California Press.

FOR LOU BUDD AND HENRY NASH SMITH

they showed the way

**Mark Twain's early literary training was that of a writer for newspapers,** where news was scarce and hard to get, and the public demanded their intellectual fare dressed with the hottest, strongest condiments. Is it not natural that we should see distinct and powerful traces of this method in all his later work?

GEORGE T. FERRIS
*APPLETON'S JOURNAL*
JULY 4, 1874

# CONTENTS

vii

*Act Four*

## CORRESPONDENT ON ASSIGNMENT

*Act Five*

---

## CORRESPONDENT AT LARGE

# Acknowledgments

$\mathbf{I}$t is a cheerful thing to acknowledge debts, because they list the friends and supporters one has for projects like this one. The Mark Twain Circle of scholars has always provided a congenial and stimulating environment to pursue thoughts and ideas, however tenuous they may be at the outset. Thanks to Tom Quirk, editor of the Mark Twain and His Circle Series, for his interest in and enthusiasm for the project. To Lou Budd and Bruce Michelson I owe a particularly hearty thanks for braving the thickets of a much earlier draft: they both provided suggestions for needed improvement and encouragement to make it happen. I also want to thank my University of Hawai'i colleague Bob McHenry, who read early material too, but who also listened patiently over the years as I spun out my argument and who asked questions to help me stay on track. Finally, I want to thank my wife, Michelle, who has lived with me and Mark Twain since graduate school days, for her unfailing humor. And for my children, Will and Camille: now you can see what Dad has been trying to build all those years in his study.

Parts of Act One have been published in earlier versions and are reprinted with permission by the original publishers: "Backwoods Civility; or, How the Ring-Tailed Roarer Became a Gentle Man for David Crockett, Charles F. M. Noland, and William Tappan Thompson" appeared in M. Thomas Inge and Ed Piacentino, eds., *The Humor of the Old South* (Lexington: University Press of Kentucky, 2001), 314–58; and "Playin' Hell: Sut Lovingood as Durn'd Fool Preacher" appeared in James E. Caron and M. Thomas Inge, eds., *Sut Lovingood's Nat'ral Born Yarnspinner: Essays on George Washington Harris* (Tuscaloosa: University of Alabama Press, 1996); 272–98. Part of Act Two was published as "Washoe Mark Twain," *Nevada Historical Society Quarterly* 46 (2003): 77–88.

# Abbreviations

*Mark Twain*

# UNSANCTIFIED NEWSPAPER REPORTER

# Prologue for a Comic Performance

S am Clemens was not Mark Twain. Sam Clemens scribbled stories and jokes, signed them "Mark Twain," and marketed them to periodicals, not Mark Twain. Sam Clemens married an heiress and fathered four children, not Mark Twain. Sam Clemens bankrupted both his wife's and his own fortune and then recouped it all, not Mark Twain. And yet the clean distinction insisted upon by biographical facts misses the complexity of Sam Clemens as a writer with a genius for comic statement. Using a discourse of modern scholarship may move us closer to capturing the elaborate process that defines the career of Mark Twain. However, saying that Sam Clemens wrote comic texts complicated by a multifaceted implied author misses the essential theatricality of "Mark Twain." A man from the frontier region of Missouri had created an alternative and comic identity through the device of a pseudonym, and he had performed it so well for his readers and audiences that the literary presentation of Mark Twain and the physical appearance of Sam Clemens fused completely, leaving no seams for evidence. The performance was so artful, the illusion of comic singularity was so complete, that William Dean Howells's memoir had to be titled *My Mark Twain;* writing *My Sam Clemens* was impossible, even for such a close friend. Sam Clemens became Mark Twain.

Moreover, the artful performance ensured that the historical circumstance of Sam Clemens's being from a border state simply did not register on a literary scale, even though Clemens launched the career of Mark Twain in the midst of the Civil War. By the time *The Innocents Abroad* was published in 1869, the erasure of his southernness was so thorough that Clemens in the book's preface claimed the comic perspective of Mark Twain as a national mode of seeing the world, and the American public reacted by making the book a best seller. The divisions of the war, symbolized by the border status of Missouri, had not just been masked by a comic pseudonym, but in a measurable way had been transcended through a literary character's humor, a humor identifiable as American rather than frontier or urban, a humor dosed with stringent satire.

This study examines the first part of the professional writing career of Samuel Langhorne Clemens, when he invented Mark Twain and explored different ways to use the literary device to create comic laughter in his readers and audiences. Clemens began his career in September 1862 as a local editor for the *Virginia City Territorial Enterprise,* which featured the first extant appearance of "Mark Twain" on February 3, 1863. Scholars have neglected this initial period since two extended analyses were published in 1950: Gladys Bellamy's *Mark Twain as a Literary Artist* and Edgar Branch's *Mark Twain's Literary Apprenticeship.* Even the unpublished manuscripts of Sam Clemens's later life have received more attention. Subsequent scholarship, such as Paul Fatout's *Mark Twain in Virginia City* (1964) or Edgar Branch's *Clemens of the "Call"* (1969), have focused on shorter time periods, while landmark studies of Mark Twain, such as Kenneth Lynn's *Mark Twain and Southwestern Humor* (1959) and Henry Nash Smith's *Mark Twain: The Development of a Writer* (1962), have used only a small selection from the 1860s material. More recent studies, such as Everett Emerson's *The Authentic Mark Twain* (1984), Randall Knoper's *Acting Naturally: Mark Twain in the Culture of Performance* (1995), Lelend Krauth's *Proper Mark Twain* (1999), or Joseph Coulombe's *Mark Twain and the American West* (2003), have followed the same pattern—when the initial period is considered at all. Almost nothing has been written about the travel letters from Hawai'i as a group. Equally neglected are the letters chronicling Clemens's trip to New York City from California. No one has connected these two sets of travel letters with the comic materials Clemens had previously published in New York, California, and Nevada periodicals. This study makes those connections by considering all known items from the first phase of Sam Clemens's professional writing career, including the virtually forgotten writings from his stint as a reporter on the *San Francisco Morning Call* during the summer of 1864.

*Mark Twain, Unsanctified Newspaper Reporter* traces the arc from an obscure newspaperman on a regional paper to a national author with a best-selling travel narrative, *The Innocents Abroad.* The book charts Sam Clemens's early writing career within the context of mid-nineteenth-century American periodical publication, for the success of Mark Twain in the 1860s signaled the maturing of funny, popular writing in periodicals. That maturation necessitated leaving regional attitudes and backwoods settings behind in favor of a more urbane perspective on important subjects, subjects treated with a myriad of comic strategies. The book also traces the literary ways in which a comic character with a habit of lampooning assumes the role of a cultural critic whose acerbic tongue-lashings express what he observes with his satirist's eye. Treating Mark Twain as a comic character wholly separated from an implied author, a comic character who tells laughable stories, focuses an examination of how Sam Clemens initially developed his talent as a comic writer. Examining Sam Clemens's comic art requires bracketing Mark Twain as a comic character separate from a historical author as well. The dazzling performance of comic singularity must not blind one to its essential illusion. Sam Clemens was never Mark Twain. Sam Clemens became Mark Twain. These contradictory statements suggest the fundamentally comic meaning behind the pseudonym. Mark Twain was no more—and no less—than the vehicle by which Sam Clemens expressed his comic genius.

As a literary vehicle, Mark Twain allowed Sam Clemens to make a living as a professional comic writer and to dramatize a comic vision of the world. Mark Twain enacts that comic vision by "playin' hell," that is, by embodying what proper society might call social "sins." Clemens expressed a sense of these comic transgressions by referring to himself as "an unsanctified newspaper reporter." By playing hell, by dramatizing variations on the trope "unsanctified" with his Mark Twain character, Clemens found a comic process adaptable to the circumstances of periodical publishing. Moreover, dramatizing Mark Twain's "unsanctified" status provided Sam Clemens enough maneuvering room to develop a cultural depth for his comic depiction of the world.

"Unsanctified" expresses first the humor of raillery that characteristically defined Mark Twain throughout this initial period of Sam Clemens's professional writing career. Portraying Mark Twain as comically choleric not only helped Clemens to establish a distinctive profile for his literary alter ego, but the tactic also epitomized the tumultuous and sometimes subversive quality of Mark Twain as a comic character. This potentially subversive element most often manifested itself as a disruption of normative middle-class thinking about what constituted respectability. A good example of this symbolic disruption comes from Clemens's tenure as a reporter in Nevada for the *Territorial Enterprise*. In a one-paragraph newspaper item, Mark Twain reverses a cultural stereotype and deflates the pretension upheld by its assumption of superiority. When early Nevada settlers organized themselves into a pioneer association called the "Pah-Utes" to designate their first-family status, Mark Twain delivered a mock encomium ridiculing their pride as the people who settled in the territory before the mining rush in May 1860. Organized by a series of left-handed compliments about the Pah-Utes camping and eating and sleeping together in the wild, the newspaper item uses their name for the cleverest part of its ironic praise. Because the club names itself after the indigenous people of the region (the Paiute), Mark Twain can acknowledge his own inferiority by calling himself a "poor but honest half-breed," a phase that accedes to the association's claim of superior status. He can also make fun of the pioneers by calling them "blasted old patriarchs banding together like a decaying tribe," a reference to the degraded state of the native "Pi-Utes." Mark Twain delivers the "snapper" when he refers to the members of this exclusive club as "happy, and lousy and contented" (ETS 1:170). Pretending that Pah-Utes are really Pi-Utes, Clemens attributes a stereotypical view of Native American hygiene to the white settlers, deflating the pride of place implied in their club's existence.

The irony is particularly just, for the erasure of the name "Pi-Utes" by "Pah-Utes" symbolizes the appropriation of land by white settlers, an act that points to their second-family status and the racist denial of the true first-family status for the indigenous folk. Mark Twain's mock encomium pretends to take the claim to be first in Nevada as total and absolute by making a joke about lice and the Pah-Utes, erasing the difference between whites and Native Americans entailed in the stereotype about hygiene as well as erasing the Pah-Utes' assertion of superiority to all other white settlers. By satirizing the claim of first-family respectability, Clemens engages his literary creation in a deep form of play called *paidia*. Roger Caillois characterizes *paidia* as "an almost indivisible principle, common to diversion, turbulence, free improvisation, and carefree gaiety." Such play carries a metamessage—"This is uncertainty"—and thus has a dangerous potential "to meddle with, to disturb, and perhaps dissolve, centres of social gravity": in vernacular terms, to play hell.[1] This deep play energizes the engagement with his society that Mark Twain represented for Sam Clemens during the 1860s, for Mark Twain's satiric attacks and humorous antics drafted Clemens into the role of cultural critic.

Understanding Mark Twain as a comic phenomenon that playfully disrupts its cultural milieu necessitates an analysis of Clemens's writings within their popular culture context and history. Louis Budd makes the basic point that reading Mark Twain requires the context of contemporary periodical writing.[2] Sam Clemens began his professional writing career as a newspaperman and then became a freelance writer. His reports, sketches, and travel letters were commodities situated within a mass-produced commodity, periodicals. From the perspective of high culture enshrined in the humanist tradition of belles lettres, mass-producing popular cultural artifacts guarantees their lack of artistic merit. Cultural artifacts created for a market are merely entertainment vehicles, items to be consumed and forgotten, like last year's fashions. Cultural artifacts created

---

1. Roger Caillois, *Man, Play, and Games,* 13; Don Handelman, "Precariousness in Play," 70.
2. Louis J. Budd, "Mark Twain and the Magazine World."

to induce laughter seemed particularly ephemeral to contemporary intellectuals, as transitory as the laughter itself. This elite perspective employed a standard of transcendent quality in order to maintain a division between high culture and "low-brow" culture. Certainly editors of periodicals during, before, and after the 1860s who adhered to this dominant tradition of belles lettres in America saw themselves as defenders of serious art. They waged their aesthetic battle within a democratic society that increasingly refined the mass production of cultural artifacts in ways now recognized as thoroughly modern.

Mark Twain provides one of the few examples in which literary material clearly written for a popular culture market has garnered enduring critical accolades. The long process that repositioned Sam Clemens's periodical work, travel books, and fictions from pop culture commodities to literary canon began by evaluating his comic talent against the belletristic model. Contemporary nineteenth-century periodical editors were a crucial first audience for Sam Clemens to impress. Moreover, critical debate about Mark Twain since the late nineteenth century has often continued to be about evaluating the art and comic talent of Sam Clemens within or against the belletristic model, which uses a binary opposition of marketplace versus artistry to discriminate lasting merit. The fundamental division of culture into high and low, elite and popular modes structured the Van Wyck Brooks/Bernard DeVoto controversy about Mark Twain during the 1920s and 1930s. Branch and Bellamy in their 1950 analyses of the early Mark Twain both insisted on excavating the "literary" aspects of the materials, a high-culture perspective that looks forward to masterworks already declared and turns individual items into milestones on the road toward them. Recent books, such as Knoper's *Acting Naturally* and Krauth's *Proper Mark Twain,* emphasize links to either side of this broad division of cultural production. My investigation redeploys with a different purpose the belletristic assumption that culture fractures into "high" and "popular" domains. Even though I use divisions of aesthetic taste that map readily onto socioeconomic strata in order to describe Sam Clemens's comic style, I do not have discernment of the "Literary" (with a capital *L*) qualities of Mark Twain as a goal. I employ the belletristic model operating in the 1860s only as a tactic to assist in discovering cultural significance for Mark Twain.

Probing for cultural significance, I have followed the lead of anthropologists like Edward Bruner, Clifford Geertz, and Victor Turner, who have advocated approaching a culture through a study of its own homegrown expressions. In their theoretical models, cultural artifacts—whether categorized as "elite" or "folk," "literary" or "popular"—function as units of expression that structure everyday experience. Some units of expression—such as plays and poems and novels—are potentially more intense, complex, and revealing of experience than

others (certainly that is the privileging view of literary critics and literary historians). However, an anthropological approach makes no theoretical distinction
among units of expression and establishes no hierarchy based upon prejudged
standards. Units of cultural expression both "literary" and "popular" expose
social presuppositions and express values, despite contrasting connotations.[3]
Thus, no a priori difference exists between a poem of Henry Longfellow and the
autobiography of David Crockett as potential expositors of social values and
presuppositions.

This initial theoretical position does not mean that literature as a category
disappears; rather, it necessarily rests within the larger cultural context. "Since
literature as a medium has been with us more or less since the beginning of
recorded time, its presence must presumably meet certain anthropological
needs."[4] Furthermore, placing literature within the larger realm of "anthropological needs" does not erase a special status for literature, as Wolfgang Iser's
work shows. And yet, however marked as special, the fictional units of cultural
expression that Iser tracks in his literary anthropology should not be privileged
over others, such as travel books or the reportage of Sam Clemens as he observes
and writes about Virginia City, San Francisco, and Honolulu. From this anthropological perspective, the problem of the literariness of the early Mark Twain
taken up by Bellamy and Branch does not exist. Nevertheless, I evaluate and
explain how Clemens crafted his work, how he improved it as he aimed for a successful career writing funny items for various periodicals. Most of all, I explain
the early writings of Sam Clemens as *comic* writings, interpreting the reports,
sketches, and travel letters signed "Mark Twain" through the cultural work they
accomplish. This interpretation requires the elaboration of multiple contexts.

Because "Mark Twain" signified a popular comic writer, the marketplace for
publishing newspapers and literary weeklies in the 1860s assumes a vital interpretive role. To understand Mark Twain when the pen name first appeared in the
*Virginia City Territorial Enterprise,* and when it subsequently appeared in a number of other periodicals on both the East and West coasts of the United States,
one must comprehend these publications, the marketplace in which they operated, and the historical reading public they reached. Because newspapers
remained the chief outlet for the writing efforts of Sam Clemens throughout the
1860s, Mark Twain the narrator and comic character was very much a creature
of newspaper headlines and deadlines. The genre initially the most important to
the invention of Mark Twain, therefore, is the local items column. Also, whatever

3. Edward M. Bruner, "Experience and Its Expressions," 10.
4. Wolfgang Iser, "Toward a Literary Anthropology," 263–64.

culturally significant satire Sam Clemens developed with his narrator and comic character during the 1860s happened largely in response to specific newspaper assignments. Clemens first covered the Nevada Territorial legislature as well as the local beat in Virginia City, and then worked the police station, courthouse, and theater circuit in San Francisco. He followed these assignments with a brief tour of the Hawaiʻian kingdom, a stint in New York City and Washington, D.C., and a correspondent's participation in the first luxury cruise for tourists to Europe and the Holy Land.

Given the exigencies of his trade, Clemens had no master plan for what would become his masterful literary invention. Of course, he wanted to make readers and audiences laugh, but his efforts were necessarily constrained by contemporary taste. To an extent, the kind of periodical in which a comic sketch might appear signaled how high or low on a scale of taste one could expect to rate the piece, with newspapers usually marked lower than literary weeklies. Though Clemens achieved his first big success in newspapers, by 1864 he also aimed for the more sophisticated readership of the literary weeklies. Compared to the typical newspaper's reader, these historical readers had more education and thus a more refined taste. Readers of literary weeklies did not necessarily dislike broad humor and the easy horselaugh, but they enjoyed vigorous wit more than coarse buffoonery. This desire for a more sophisticated reader did not cause Clemens to forget that his main customer was always middle-brow and middle-class—that was, after all, the biggest segment of the marketplace. Clemens, aspiring to be popular with a readership as broad as possible and at the same time as sophisticated as possible, inevitably created a tension in his writing, replicating the belletristic model that splits culture into elite and popular levels. This tension played out in several ways for Clemens. No literary material is more sensitive to a reader's expectations than that which falls within the domain of the laughable, and Clemens, exploring the possibilities of his comic invention Mark Twain, experimented with high and low registers on a contemporary scale of taste. Also, insofar as Clemens wished to use Mark Twain as a vehicle for satire, he had to be very aware of his readership. If the biggest target for satire is also the biggest market, a comic writer has to decide how he can cause laughter to be directed at his chosen victims without losing them as customers.

A second necessary context is composed of the contemporary writers with whom Clemens competed for publication space and against whom he would be compared by consumers of periodicals. My study of Sam Clemens as a periodical writer proceeds by reading his work as Mark Twain along with the work of certain other periodical writers. The picture of Mark Twain that emerges from those comparisons differs significantly from the one outlined in previous scholarship. No one has included Charles Webb in a discussion about the comic abilities of

Sam Clemens, for instance, and no one has compared comic techniques among Clemens, Bret Harte, Charles Farrar Browne (Artemus Ward), and William Wright (Dan De Quille). Yet Clemens had each of these writers at hand as literary models—and as competitors. Reading them alongside Sam Clemens is imperative to achieve an understanding of how the Mark Twain pseudonym impacted the periodical world of the 1860s.

*Mark Twain, Unsanctified Newspaper Reporter* also briefly examines comic predecessors of Mark Twain to understand the popular culture background that enabled the figure's creation and success. In earlier considerations of these predecessors, scholars have created and elaborated lineages for Sam Clemens as a comic writer. However, when one concentrates on just the initial phase of Sam Clemens's career, from 1862 to 1869, to depict Mark Twain, the portrait again diverges significantly. A thorough examination of the contemporary context undermines long-accepted tenets of Mark Twain scholarship. For example, established links to the comic tradition of the Old Southwest become overstated or misstated, as does the significance of "Jim Smiley and His Jumping Frog." Not only as evidence of Clemens's debt to the Old Southwest comic tradition but also as a milestone in Clemens's career, that tale diminishes in significance when assessed in its immediate context. Also, Mark Twain's affinity with other comic writers usually grouped together as "Literary Comedians" has been obscured or simply overlooked, with one notable exception: David E. E. Sloane's *Mark Twain as Literary Comedian* (1979). During the 1860s, when Clemens first develops Mark Twain, his work resembles that of the Literary Comedians more than it does the work of the Old Southwest writers in his repeated use of literary burlesque as a basic comic technique.

This study will also argue that the links among Clemens and his comic predecessors are not so much due to a display of the vernacular found in "Jumping Frog" as it is in the way that the character of Mark Twain replicates the comic ambiguity of an earlier generic figure, the "Gentleman Roarer." This comic figure is a significant variation of a popular antebellum comic stereotype, the Ring-Tailed or Backwoods Roarer. The Gentleman Roarer is part of a panoply of representations that embody an important theme in the American comic tradition: the laughably improper or plainly uncivilized behavior of *dēmos,* the common folk. While the Backwoods Roarer personifies the bestial potential of people, especially the untutored common man and woman, the Gentleman Roarer models a positive though comic view of plain folks. The Backwoods Roarer is an uncouth lubber at best and a ruffian at worst, capable of eye-gouging in a rough-and-tumble fight. The Gentleman Roarer may not have parlor manners, but he is morally virtuous, a comic image of the sturdy pioneer. The Mark Twain first invented in Nevada, which I call Washoe Mark Twain, is an avatar of the Gentleman Roarer and the first manifestation of what Sam Clemens meant by calling himself "unsanctified." The significance of the Gentleman Roarer figure, however, goes beyond providing a new way to connect the Mark Twain Clemens had fashioned in Nevada with other comic figures popular before the Civil War. Because the Gentleman Roarer comically embodies a theme of socially improper or even uncivilized behavior, the figure also provides a way to track how Clemens transformed Washoe Mark Twain during his stay in San Francisco.

In addition to insisting that understanding Mark Twain requires the context of periodical writing, Louis Budd emphasizes that Clemens was "incorrigibly a humorist."[5] Understanding the comic aspects of texts signed "Mark Twain" is a fundamental goal of this study, and I begin with the notion that the signature functions as a play frame licensing comic antics. On a formal level, Clemens employs parody as a consistent tactic. His tall-tale local items and newspaper hoaxes from his Comstock days, as well as his comic travel letters, parody their form. On a broad thematic level, the signature "Mark Twain" signifies a comic pleasure, its play frame bracketing out everyday concerns and opposing workday behavior. "Mark Twain" also signifies a middling comic style. Especially in San Francisco, Mark Twain the narrator and comic character possesses a voice slangy at times but never speaking in vernacular dialect, a voice capable of elevated effects of rhetoric without being choked by genteel sentiment, a voice that in its comic phases can be lighthearted—even whimsical—or sardonic.

The comic aspects of Mark Twain also operate at deeper levels. As narrator and comic character, Mark Twain playfully questions social values. This play inevitably has the tumultuous quality of *paidia,* expressed foremost by his habit of raillery. In both the figure's Washoe and San Francisco phases, the raillery can by turns be aggressive or good-natured, and it can be directed at either people or social institutions. Clemens uses Mark Twain's comic raillery to dispute the conventional boundary between centric and eccentric behaviors and their informing values. Disputing conceptual boundaries that organize behavior into centric or normative patterns characterizes a fundamental effect of Mark Twain. Sometimes Clemens questions these boundaries through the literary and cultural criticisms uttered by a Mark Twain catering to the readers of literary weeklies, reminding them of a value they profess but fail to practice. Sometimes Clemens highlights the boundaries for a newspaper audience through the negative example of the loud and extravagant manners, or even the violent behavior displayed by Washoe Mark Twain. The social norm thus can be known because an unsanctified Mark Twain has once again and in laughable ways transgressed it. Mark Twain in particular dramatizes differences between merely eccentric and clearly

---

5. Budd, "Magazine World," 35.

disreputable behavior. Unsanctified Mark Twain's comic evocation of the boundary between the respectable and the disreputable can be traced back to the figure of the Gentleman Roarer. Drawing attention in a playful manner to arbitrary boundaries can theoretically generate laughter in readers or audiences, even if they adhere to a centric perspective. However, the very act of exposing the socially constructed nature of behavior to laughter continually runs the risk of arousing disapproval as well.

In Nevada, Clemens used Mark Twain to question centric or normative values by burlesquing the conventions of newspaper reporting. That focus on journalism widened to an aesthetic perspective about good and bad writing when Clemens moved to San Francisco. The genres of the local item and the news report, essential to Washoe Mark Twain in Nevada, take a backseat in San Francisco to sketches in which Mark Twain becomes a cultural critic. These cultural critiques evince a decidedly Bohemian perspective, that is, an opposition to bourgeois, middle-class and middle-brow, centric norms. Honoré de Balzac's young and impecunious artists in "Un Prince de la Bohème" implied this opposition, signifying an alternative aesthetic to mainstream views on art as well as a denial of the marketplace as an arbiter of art. Though not comic per se, the anti-bourgeois quality of a Bohemian aesthetic provided a congenial space for comic eccentricities. That space allowed Clemens's literary alter ego to dramatize new versions of "unsanctified" behavior. Though comic sketches based on a news item are still employed in San Francisco, burlesques of literary genres or a particular feature in a literary weekly, such as an "Answer to Correspondents" column, become prevalent. The news report often becomes a "special" report on aspects of urban living, of people in San Francisco and their behavior, or of the sights to be seen. These special reports functioned as the domestic equivalent of travel letters, telling not of some exotic place but rather of what might be intriguing at home. This man-about-town pose becomes an opportunity for Clemens to recast Mark Twain into a comic version of what French periodical writers earlier in the nineteenth century had called a *flâneur*. Writing about his voyages to Hawai'i and back to New York City, Clemens combines laughable *flânerie* with eccentric Washoe behavior in Mark Twain to produce travel letters unprecedented in their comic quality.

Sam Clemens was not Mark Twain. And yet the illusion of comic singularity persists. While contextual elaborations can reveal Mark Twain's cultural significance, piercing the illusion to reveal the complexity of Clemens's literary invention also requires a textual focus that begins with the implied author. What complicates the experience of reading Mark Twain goes beyond the distinction between author and implied author to which a pseudonym loudly draws the reader's attention. That complication exists because Mark Twain is both a represented narrator and a comic character in the stories he tells. At first glance, this status seems nothing more than that of any first-person narrator who tells funny stories about himself. Merely noting that common trait, however, underestimates the craft with which Sam Clemens represents his narrator and comic character, for the elaborate and artful nature of these textual representations "perform" Mark Twain. This trope accounts for the several ways Sam Clemens has manipulated the possibilities of a first-person narrator woven as comic character into certain types of narratives.

Yet another twist to the complication of reconstructing Mark Twain as a literary experience must be noted. Mark Twain the comic character provided Sam Clemens the author with the same literary possibilities of any fictional creation. That slide over to fiction within a first-person narration distinguished Sam Clemens among his newspaper brethren and made his early travel letters popular. However, in addition to exploiting Mark Twain as a fictional comic character whenever it suited him, Sam Clemens also maintained the fiction that he was Mark Twain. The exemplary moment for that fiction occurred when Clemens first performed Mark Twain in a mock lecture in the fall of 1866. However, even before Clemens had ascended the lecture platform, performing Mark Twain had quickly become the modus operandi for public speeches in 1863 and 1864 once newspaper sketches and out-of-town letters had been signed with the pseudonym. For Clemens to create an expectant and attentive audience, a discernibly specific comic attitude in speeches and lectures as well as written work was necessarily present, but dramatizing the attitude through the fiction of Sam Clemens being Mark Twain dazzled contemporaries—when it did not just plain confuse them.

Readers today remain bedazzled by Sam Clemens's fictions and artful performances; they remain confused, too, because talking about the narrator and comic character Mark Twain easily becomes talking about Sam Clemens the man—and vice versa. Most people, even biographers, say "Mark Twain" at times when they mean "Sam Clemens." Clemens so obviously poured his own personality into the character of Mark Twain that it seems natural to conflate one with the other. Sam Clemens was not Mark Twain, but in order to puzzle out the significance of "Mark Twain," one must sometimes proceed as though he were. One must both employ and ignore a division into private and public domains implied by separating the author from his pseudonym. Moreover, one must also both respect and transgress the boundary between historical and fictional narratives that "author" and "pseudonym" imply, and thereby contemplate how a writer performs a comic character. These conceptual oppositions acknowledge difference and enable analysis, but they can also obscure the achievement of comic singularity that "Mark Twain" signifies. Sam Clemens acted as if he were someone called Mark Twain. This fiction precedes all others, enables all others signed with the pseudonym. Clemens early in his career used Mark Twain to fictionalize his life and times in a manner unprecedented for a writer, comic or otherwise. In doing so, Clemens did not write genuine autobiography, but neither did he write a fictional autobiography distinct from his own life. Rather, his first-person narrations occupy a place in-between.[6] "Mark Twain" therefore does not just indicate a pseudonym, but neither does it exactly signify a comic character wholly separate from its author, as Don Quixote exists apart from Miguel Cervantes. Though "Mark Twain" names a comic character, one remarkably similar to comic characters invented by and wholly separate from other, earlier American authors, the pseudonym also uniquely entangles the man.

To uncover and examine the entanglement of Sam Clemens the author with his character Mark Twain, to fathom their comic singularity, requires an analysis that, at times, alternates between the historical man and the textual figure, employing historical facts to provide a focus for textual details. I do not simply mean that biography can assist textual explication. Rather, fiction invades biography and transforms it, even as biography informs a fiction. Ovid Bolus, a character created by the antebellum comic writer Joseph Baldwin, anticipates Mark Twain in this respect because he "had long torn down the partition wall between his imagination and his memory."[7] Having no partition between memory and imagination enables the dazzling illusion of comic singularity created by Sam Clemens acting as though he were Mark Twain. Not only does Sam Clemens invent Mark Twain because news stories become yarns, but Mark Twain also exists because Clemens let his imagination infiltrate his memory. Sam Clemens became Mark Twain by behaving as Ovid Bolus did, which meant that a man had refashioned his experiences to become a comic character similar to other fictional creations.

Nevertheless, *Mark Twain, Unsanctified Newspaper Reporter* shows what can be learned by insisting that "Mark Twain," first and foremost, signifies a textual figure, a comic character within various narratives. Louis Budd has detailed Clemens's lifelong talent for posturing. Bruce Michelson has claimed that "to be Mark Twain truly is to affirm above all a privilege of imposture."[8] With them, I would assert the *fictional* quality of Mark Twain as well as the *performative* quality of Sam Clemens's modes of presenting Mark Twain to a reading and a listening public. Remembering these qualities is crucial to understanding the complications Mark Twain presents as a literary experience. Remembering them is also important to understanding how Mark Twain's quirky humors and satiric

6. See William Riggan, *Picaros, Madmen, Naifs, and Clowns: The Unreliable First-Person Narrator,* 27.
7. Joseph Glover Baldwin, *Flush Times in Alabama and Mississippi,* 3.
8. Bruce Michelson, *Mark Twain on the Loose: A Comic Writer and the American Self,* 24. See also Louis J. Budd, "A 'Talent for Posturing': The Achievement of Mark Twain's Public Personality."

statements become tools to express Sam Clemens's sense of the world he encountered in the 1860s. Michelson's project seeks the postmodern in the comic laughter of Mark Twain's audience—how an anarchic humor suggests unconscious motives and resists stable meanings and clear identity. My project reconstructs the contemporary to reveal the symbolic, showing how social and economic as well as literary circumstances of the day enabled a comic laughter that dramatizes communal attitudes about cultural values.

Treating Mark Twain first as a textual figure, as a comic character within various narratives, requires elaborated distinctions. These textual distinctions are necessary because Samuel Langhorne Clemens, the historical author, created layers of fictional agents within his literary alter ego, "Mark Twain." First, Sam Clemens writing as Mark Twain creates at the level of implied author the fiction of a reliable correspondent, one capable of literary polish. This implied author should be understood as a member in good standing of a community of respectable citizens in which the implied reader also necessarily partakes. Whatever satiric and moral force Clemens demonstrates in his writing through the fiction of "Mark Twain" flows from the implied author's ultimately proper character. At the level of narrator, however, Mark Twain may or may not match the implied author's ideal character and its projection of proper behavior and respectability. Nevertheless, the implied author always claims membership in an ideal community of the respectable. This ideal community constitutes a baseline of behavior against which Clemens can satirically measure everyone, including those readers who are only nominally proper and respectable. This implied author, in other words, allows Clemens to project his fundamental writerly self, namely, a competent journalist always ready to assume a comic perspective.

Wayne Booth and other critics have proposed and elaborated such textual differences.[9] Mark Twain presents a particularly complicated instance of the theoretical difference between narrator and implied author because Clemens assigns two master roles to his narrator and then manifests both roles with several poses, all with appropriate voices. In effect, the master narrators put on and take off a variety of masks—personae—as though Mark Twain were an actor on stage in ancient Rome. More precisely, Mark Twain as narrator changes his personae as though he were a character within a play whose signature behavior entails the adoption of multiple disguises. As a narrator of newspaper reports as well as of comic sketches, Mark Twain speaks through his personae

---

9. Wayne C. Booth, *The Rhetoric of Fiction*. Other critics who proved helpful in sorting out the relationships among Sam Clemens, Mark Twain, and their audiences include Wolfgang Iser, *The Implied Reader: Patterns of Communication in Prose Fiction from Bunyan to Beckett;* William Nell, "Historical and Implied Authors and Readers"; and Peter Rabinowitz, *Before Reading: Narrative Conventions and the Politics of Interpretation.*

to a potential variety of "narratees."[10] These various personae alternate and blend together comic and serious perspectives on events. This alternation and blending did not always sit well with Sam Clemens's contemporaries, but its dynamic fueled his success as a comic writer, enabling Clemens to breach at will the conventional partition between literature and journalism, and thus to obscure the boundary between fiction and nonfiction narratives. That obscuring contributed significantly to an initial reputation worthy of an "unsanctified newspaper reporter."

The two master roles of Mark Twain the narrator are reversed images: the respectable newspaperman who efficiently and accurately reports, recounts, and summarizes the events he observes or about which he interviews eyewitnesses; the unsanctified newspaperman who distorts and ignores the conventions of journalism by dramatizing what he observes and hears, or who subverts the conventions by inserting wholesale fictionalizing into the newspaper story. Sam Clemens manipulated these polar opposites virtually from the beginning of his invention of Mark Twain, with sophisticated comic effects. That playful manipulation complicates the relationship between narrator and implied author. Mark Twain's voice for one master narrative role—the respectable newspaperman who reports events faithfully—is apparently the same as the implied author: a competent journalist. Presenting the doubled image of a competent journalist, both at the level of narrator/narratee as well as implied author/implied reader, creates options for Clemens when he wishes to explore comically what competent journalism means. Keeping the images identical at both levels implies a reader who takes Mark Twain the newspaper reporter seriously. Splitting the images by creating mockery of the competent journalist on the level of narrator/narratee, however, allows for degrees of laughter at Mark Twain the unsanctified newspaper reporter and/or the serious business of journalism without giving up the fundamental effort to project and maintain the presence of journalistic competence on the level of implied author/implied reader. Splitting this doubled image also allowed Sam Clemens to

---

10. Don Florence, *Persona and Humor in Mark Twain's Early Writings,* is also concerned with making and elaborating this point. However, Florence's discussion of "persona" is based on a Derridean idea of language's irreducible play. For Florence, this play authorizes a transcendence of on-the-ground realities, as well as a freedom from history itself, that provides an enabling mechanism for an endless reinvention of Mark Twain's identity built on comic confidence games. My idea of "persona" emphasizes the texts, but the voices and masking that constitute Mark Twain are always tied to audiences, implied and historical, and the realities of periodical journalism and its marketplace. For Florence, Mark Twain's humor is a personalized adventure the ultimate moment of which is either an epistemological void or an aura of transcendence (5, 11). In my view, Sam Clemens's primary comic role of clowning is a socially embedded tactic meant to affect its specific milieu. The ultimate sign of the clown's role would not be an aura of transcendence, but the limelight of performing Mark Twain on stage.

manufacture his most famous hoaxes while working for the *Virginia City Territorial Enterprise.*

By presenting Mark Twain the competent journalist as a narrative role with various personae, as though the figure were a comic character within a fictional story, rather than as a pen name merely signifying a historical writer, Clemens maneuvered adroitly within the conventional constraints of narrative reporting. The fiction of "Mark Twain" licensed Sam Clemens to imagine laughable ways to narrate the world he observed, and thus imagine laughable ways to write fiction from within the precincts of journalism. There was a drawback, however. This strategy easily allowed a contemporary reader to interpret anything signed "Mark Twain" as though the pen name merely signified a newspaper reporter. Reading "Mark Twain" in this manner guarantees missing all the play and fun the fictional name generates. Readers today would not misread Mark Twain in this way. Most readers of the 1860s did not make this mistake either, but the doubled image of competent newspaper reporter meant that, even when Clemens deliberately exposed the difference between Mark Twain the ostensibly respectable reporter and the implied author, some readers nevertheless insisted on conflating them and charging Clemens with incompetence or deliberate falsehood. Understanding how the fiction of "Mark Twain" in its various personae engendered implied readers explains why certain historical readers reacted as they did to particular writings.

In addition, understanding the various kinds of implied readers engendered by the personae of "Mark Twain" will uncover how Clemens imagined the changeable interaction between his writings and their historical readers, that is, how he calculated his market. Constructing an implied reader can help to infer how a historical reader reacted to a particular text because the abstraction of an implied reader inevitably reflects and represents some of the values, beliefs, and attitudes current in an actual population during a given period of history. Because of this metonymic relationship, the elaborate textual fiction of Mark Twain that begets various implied readers can be read as a calculus designed to measure what would sell in the periodical market of the 1860s. Similarly, the comic elements of Mark Twain can be read as a set of tactics designed to manipulate the various comic tastes of historical readers of the 1860s. Moreover, values, beliefs, and attitudes in Sam Clemens's contemporary readers can be inferred when the comic laughter of an implied reader is discriminated into a corrective satiric mode and a tolerant humorous mode. A brief look at the attitudes expressed by these different comic modes will show their potential for revealing cultural norms.

Robert Elliott's anthropological study of satire shows how teasing and oral raillery exist on one end of a formal spectrum of comic utterance and writing that has a basic motivation of playful aggression, of making fun of someone or something. Literary satire sits at the other end of this spectrum of the ridiculous. Elliott demonstrates how forms of verbal teasing in traditional societies are related to curses and magic as well as how such verbal abuse underpins literary techniques like caricature. Within a range of "verbal tickling," artful formalization creates differences between oral and printed forms of raillery, between spontaneous teasing and crafted satire. Teasing, because spontaneous, is likely to be brief and loosely organized. Games of raillery like "the dozens" or the rap battles featured in the movie about singer Eminem, *8 Mile,* possess more structure. Some cultures, like the ancient Greek and ancient Irish, or West African Ashanti and Greenland Eskimo, institutionalize contests of raillery like "the dozens," implying that even more effort can be put into the artfulness of the utterances.[11] Kenneth Reckford shows how such raillery *(aischrologia)* in Athenian festivals is linked to comedy *(kōmōidia).*[12] The purpose of comic teasing or raillery creates another important difference. Insofar as someone dishes out such mock abuse for personal pleasure in a premeditated way, making fun of someone and his or her habits, foibles, or vices can rise beyond spontaneity to the level of a lampoon. When such artful mock abuse makes fun of an individual or a type of individual for the benefit of a community, comic raillery acquires the full force of a satiric intent, that is, ridicule delivered with a putative hope of reform. Ridicule can also be directed at social institutions or art forms, such as literary genres. One can also make fun of someone or something without an intent to reform. Rather than laugh at the object, one laughs with it. This distinction between tolerant and scornful comic laughter—between humorous laughter and satiric laughter—provides a crucial insight into how the textual layers of Mark Twain create implied readers.

The more sophisticated humorous reaction, however, bypasses a traditional function of laughter. Debates about the function of laughter and about what subjects were legitimately comic as well as what elements factor into the nature of laughter were important topics of intellectual discussions during the ancient, medieval, and Renaissance periods of Western history—as well as in the present time. Up to at least the eighteenth century, comic art needed justifying because much of it was deemed harmful—scurrilous, abusive, scandalous—and because laughter too often seemed only to signify childishness, vulgarity, or even madness. My division of comic laughter into a satiric laughter and a humorous laughter draws upon the way Western intellectuals—mostly philosophers and literary critics—have conceptualized the function of cultural artifacts that make people laugh. In that tradition, comic laughter functions primarily to reinforce what a society defines as proper behavior by ridiculing improper behavior. By

---

11. Robert C. Elliott, *The Power of Satire: Magic, Ritual, Art,* 66–81. In a game of "the dozens," two or more contestants trade witty insults on a specific topic—"mothers," for instance.

12. Kenneth J. Reckford, *Aristophanes' Old-and-New Comedy,* 449–51, 461–67.

the nineteenth century, this function was a premise for any discussion about comic material: to correct the defects, foibles, faults, vices, iniquities, eccentricities, and follies of mankind.

The virtual unanimity on the question of what constituted the fundamental function for comic artifacts and comic laughter established a second premise: a laughable, comic character or person appears so because a reader, audience, or observer perceives some lack in the character or person, a lack defined by what constitutes proper behavior for a particular group or society. Plato called that lack an ignorance of one's true self. The lack or fault therefore is mocked or ridiculed, not the character or person. When Aristotle delineated the subjects *kōmōidia* may lawfully ridicule, he also began with lacks or faults, what he called deformities. For both philosophers, the laughable *(to geloion)*, what Cicero and Quintilian called *ridiculūm,* had to be harnessed to an ethical purpose.[13]

The moralistic theory about comic art continued to be uppermost in the numerous accounts of comedy that flooded Renaissance Italy in the wake of the discovery of Aristotle's *Poetics.* From comedies "one learns what is useful in life and what on the contrary is to be avoided."[14] Comedies chastised evildoers "as with a public whip."[15] Most Italian analyses of the laughable during the fourteenth and fifteenth centuries were fundamentally rhetorical because they sought to explain how a comedy persuaded its audience to laugh or because the critic sought to justify comedy on moral grounds.[16] Similar points are made by English writers like Martin Bucer, Thomas Elyot, and Nicolas Udall in the late medieval period.[17]

An important distinction running throughout Western commentary on the ethical purpose of comic laughter claims that not all faults are ridiculous. Plato says that faults in powerful people are detestable or dangerous, not ridiculous. For Aristotle, some faults are too grave or painful for laughter, and Cicero notes that while deformity is the source of the laughable, great vice or great misery require "a weapon rather more formidable" than ridicule.[18] My theoretical distinction between satiric laughter and humorous laughter imagines not faults too serious for laughter but rather lesser faults, faults trivial enough that the laughter does not signify the ridicule of a satiric attitude with its underlying corrective intent. Thus two differing degrees of fault exist within comic characters (or actual people): 1) vice and folly, which elicit the ridicule of satiric laughter, and 2) foibles and eccentric-

---

13. Plato, "Philebus," 438–39; Aristotle, *Poetics,* 2319; Cicero, *De Oratore,* Book II (liv.217–lxxi.290); Quintilian, [Laughter, Wit, and Humour].

14. Donatus, "A Fragment on Comedy and Tragedy," 27.

15. John Tzetzes, *First Proem to Aristophanes,* 34.

16. Paul Lauter, ed., *Theories of Comedy,* 37.

17. Martin Bucer, "De Honestis Ludis"; Thomas Elyot, *The Book Named the Governor;* Nicholas Udall, prologue to *Ralph Roister Doister.*

18. Plato, "Philebus," 439; Aristotle, *Poetics,* 2319; Cicero, *De Oratore,* 375.

ities, which elicit the tolerance of humorous laughter. This theoretical distinction between a reader's, audience's, or observer's satiric and humorous laughter expands the realm of the laughable *(to geloion)* to name comic foibles that could be tolerated by a social body. The realm of the laughable, or "the Comic," thus can be divided into two modes, "the ridiculous," and something more playful, "the ludicrous," to indicate the complexity of how people laugh.

The important implication of this distinction is its admission that comic laughter and comic artifacts need not be concerned with correcting faults. This admission departs radically from traditional Western thought on the subject. Plato certainly did not make the distinction. Evoking laughter against an actual person (lampooning), even done playfully, was forbidden because his world-view did not include the notion of a tolerant laughter.[19] Nevertheless, a basis exists within Western thought for the use of *humorous* to signify tolerance toward oddities of behavior. This conception emerged from writings about the term *humor* among English men of letters—including Thomas Hobbes, Richard Steele, Joseph Addison, and Henry Fielding; its roots, however, were in the sixteenth-century dramatic practice of the playwright Ben Jonson.[20] By the nineteenth century, the notion that a humorous laughter tolerates rather than corrects faults would have been easily recognized in discussions such as William Thackeray's public lecture on English humorists.

Following Addison and Steele, Thackeray mixed satiric laughter and the corrective function of laughter with a conception of amiable humor. In addition, his focus was not on humorous characters but on the temperament of the writers as humorists. For Thackeray, being a humorist was about more than possessing the power to make people laugh: "The humourous writer professes to awaken and direct your love, your pity, your kindness—your scorn for untruth, pretension, imposture—your tenderness for the weak, the poor, the oppressed, the unhappy. To the best of his means and ability he comments on all the ordinary actions and passions of life almost. He takes upon himself to be the week-day preacher, so to speak."[21] Two notable elements in this description are the moral dimension of humor implicit in the comparison to a preacher and Thackeray's emphasis on benevolent emotions that accompany any laughter. Instead of conceiving the humorist to be someone whose temperament is faulty and whose behavior is there-

---

19. Plato, "Laws," 1587.

20. The key documents are Joseph Addison and Richard Steele, *Spectator,* nos. 23, 35, 47, and 249; and Addison and Steel, *The Tatler,* nos. 63 and 242. These arguments about the nature of laughter took place within larger philosophic debates. See Stuart Tave, *The Amiable Humorist: A Study in the Comic Theory and Criticism of the Eighteenth and Early Nineteenth Centuries;* and R. S. Crane, "Suggestions toward a Genealogy of the 'Man of Feeling.'"

21. William Thackeray, "The English Humourists of the Eighteenth Century," 4.

fore in need of correction for the good of society, a notion strongly expressed in the work of Ben Jonson, Thackeray's humorist is someone who does society good because his writings induce others to have proper moral feelings. For Ben Jonson, a humorist needs a sermon read to him; for William Thackeray, a humorist delivers the sermon. Thackeray's presentation of English humorists illustrates the usefulness of conceptualizing humor and humorous laughter in opposition to satire and satiric laughter. Humorous laughter signifies a markedly different attitude on the part of an audience or reader toward a comic character than satiric laughter, one that does not insist upon correction. This difference theoretically allows for important distinctions when analyzing comic characters like Mark Twain. Cultural and social contexts provide metrics to gauge what might be tolerated or ridiculed by a historical reader from a particular time period. These contexts provide clues to an author's comic intent when an implied reader can be shown to be significantly at odds with actual readers from the time period in question.

The difference between the ludicrous and ridiculous modes of the Comic, with their respective humorous and satiric perspectives, underscores the essentially social nature of comic laughter. Both humor and satire induce comic laughter because they point out to an audience or reader a salient difference in the object from the customs or norms of a social group. Thus all possible differences are potentially ex-centricities, that is, they exist conceptually outside the normative center of a group's social behavior. As long as eccentricities remain relatively small or harmless, or perhaps even charming in their difference, their comic presentation will elicit the tolerant laughter of a humorous perspective. As the eccentricities move farther from the group's normative behavior, however, the group recognizes their potential harm, and its comic laughter changes to the scorn of satire. Humor and the ludicrous perceive foibles of character yet are comfortable with them. Satire and the ridiculous expose character foibles as a way to express the normative concerns of the social group, and they move beyond mere exposure to attack when the targets are vice and social wrongs.

Sam Clemens's creative talent finds expression in his manipulation of Mark Twain as a narrator and comic character who embodies eccentricities both humorous and satiric. With Washoe Mark Twain, Clemens created a comic figure characterized by a penchant for raillery so strong that it constitutes a humor in Ben Jonson's sense, that is, a defining habit of behavior that traces a thin line between deserving an implied audience's approbation or scorn. Because this humor of raillery ridicules, its verbal abuse can be made to serve a satiric purpose. Clemens braids into this aggressive personality of Washoe Mark Twain a disarmingly foolish or whimsical aspect that can elicit the tolerance of humorous laughter. As Sam Clemens developed Mark Twain while living in San Francisco and in travel letters written during and after his stay there, the humorous side of the narrator and character came to be used most effectively when it masked the habit of aggressive raillery yet still allowed the corrective purpose of satire to be conveyed.

Sam Clemens alluded to a comic intent to correct the body politic when in his famous 1865 letter to his brother Orion he acknowledged his "'call' to literature of a low order—*i.e.* humorous." "*You* see in me a talent for humorous writing," he says. The religious rhetoric that turns a writing career into a "call" and his ability into a "talent" echoes Thackeray's conception of humorists as "week-day preachers." The letter to Orion deliberately invokes the parable of the talents given to each person by God (Matthew 25:14–30) and clearly shows Sam ready to begin "seriously scribbling to excite the *laughter* of God's creatures." His considerable talent for exciting the laughter of God's creatures is most interesting when Clemens combines the tolerant laughter elicited by quirky humors with the scornful laughter created by the inevitable moral purpose of satire. The comic career during the 1860s of Mark Twain as an unsanctified newspaper reporter can be characterized as one long exploration by Sam Clemens of how to exploit a mixture of the ridiculous and the ludicrous. Like Thackeray's definition of "humorist," Clemens's religious turn of phrase implies the role of a comic preacher. Clemens in the letter may lament his inability to succeed in an earlier ambition of becoming a respectable Sunday preacher, but all of his better comic efforts demonstrate how he indirectly succeeded by becoming the unsanctified weekday variety.

The metaphor of comic ministry again underscores the essentially social nature of comic laughter. Mark Twain the unsanctified newspaper reporter tends to his flock of readers in laughable ways meant to improve the body politic. This communal function suggests a symbolic cultural role for Mark Twain: the Citizen Clown. Analogous to sacred clowns performing ritually within traditional societies, the Citizen Clown dramatizes what ought to be done in his modern democratic society by behaving in ways that transgress social norms, thus comically highlighting communal values by disrupting them. Ritual clowns protect social customs "while at the same time they are burlesquing them."[22] Barbara Babcock calls ritual clowning "sanctioned disrespect" and "a sophisticated form of socio-cultural self-commentary." Henry Nash Smith captures the paradox of sacred clowns when he says that Mark Twain was a "moralist and social critic as well as buffoon" (1990, 252).[23] Smith focuses on the celebrity of Mark Twain,

22. N. Ross Crumrine, "Capakoba, the Mayo Easter Ceremonial Impersonator: Explanations of Ritual Clowning," 1, 20–21.

23. Barbara A. Babcock, "Arrange Me into Disorder: Fragments and Reflections on Ritual Clowning," 107; Henry Nash Smith, "Mark Twain, Ritual Clown." For overviews of ritual clowning, see Vilsoni Hereniko, *Woven Gods: Female Clowns and Power in Rotuma;* and William E.

especially later in Clemens's life, to discuss the relationship to a mass audience. I use the sacred clown analogy to uncover Mark Twain's relationship to a series of symbolic communities and to examine how the figure enables social satire.

In traditional societies, sacred clowns perform their antics within a ritual drama that reinforces mythic cultural narratives. The Citizen Clown must discover and reveal to his audience the cultural narratives that function as myth and then perform his own comic drama of disruption. For Sam Clemens in the 1860s, the most compelling cultural narrative spelled out the genteel difference between the sanctified and the unsanctified. Satirically exposing the narrative's inconsistencies became his theme. In this exposure, Mark Twain behaves as a comic preacher, and like an antebellum forerunner, Sut Lovingood, delivers comic sermons by playing hell with genteel notions of propriety.[24]

This deep play of *paidia,* with its drama of comic disruption, can refocus the body politic upon how it defines the boundary between social propriety and impropriety. Forcing the question of definition through symbolic disruption can create conceptual instability, however. While that instability can measure the power of a comic writer, disruption as a basic strategy has its dangers. Sam Clemens is practically expelled from Virginia City for attempting to fight a duel. That event represents an initial culmination of his fiction of being Mark Twain the unsanctified newspaper reporter. The event also measures how a comic character's habit of mixing fact and fiction engulfed the career of the local editor for the *Enterprise.*

Explaining the comic singularity of Mark Twain will begin by demonstrating, in Act One, the links between Mark Twain and comic predecessors via the generic figure of the Gentleman Roarer. "Washoe Mark Twain" names Clemens's Nevada version of the Gentleman Roarer in Act Two. Acts Three, Four, and Five respectively encompass Sam Clemens in San Francisco, Hawai'i, and New York City and show him reshaping Washoe Mark Twain while retaining the essential comic unruliness of the unsanctified newspaper reporter. Act Five also has analysis of Sam Clemens performing Mark Twain the Citizen Clown during his first lecture, "Our Fellow Savages from the Sandwich Islands."

Mitchell, "Introduction: Mother Folly in the Islands." For a bibliography of the widespread phenomenon of sacred clowns, see Kimberly A. Christen, *Clowns and Tricksters: An Encyclopedia of Tradition and Culture.*

24. George Orwell called Mark Twain a "licensed jester," but he used the role as a way to discuss not the potential subversiveness behind the pseudonym but instead Sam Clemens's "inability to despise success" ("Mark Twain—Licensed Jester," 328).

# Act One

## THE COMIC LINEAGE OF WASHOE MARK TWAIN

# Scene One

BACKWOODS CIVILITY; OR,
HOW THE ROARER BECAME A GENTLEMAN

## Washoe Mark Twain and the Old Southwest Writers:
## Comic Violence and Cultural Barbarism

Mark Twain was trained as a writer in the old Southwest during the days of the flowering of its humor.

———

Walter Blair, *Native American Humor* (1937)

In 1869, while working on the *Buffalo Express,* Sam Clemens published a burlesque of frontier newspapers entitled "Journalism in Tennessee." Its violent action exaggerates a journalism replete with personal attacks that was widespread before the Civil War. The sketch's theme of comic barbarity offers a starting point for understanding Mark Twain when the pseudonym first appeared in the pages of the *Virginia City Territorial Enterprise.* Because it also encompasses earlier comic figures, that theme reveals a new way to conceptualize Mark Twain's lineage.

"Journalism in Tennessee" dramatizes for its central joke the stereotype of the hot-blooded Southerner. Told to go to a better climate for his health, Mark Twain takes an assistant editor's position on a small Tennessee newspaper, the *Morning Glory and Johnson County War-Whoop.* The editor of the *War-Whoop* caricatures the Southern gentleman occupying a newspaper editor's chair: well-dressed and well-mannered but engaged in the most vituperative style of personal journalism. Anticipating the behavior of the Shepardsons and Grangerfords in *Adventures of Huckleberry Finn,* the editor maintains a perfectly polite demeanor as he foments and participates in all manner of mayhem. Indeed, comic horror pervades the sketch partly because of the gentlemanly behavior of the editor and others in the town, notably Colonel Blatherskite Tecumseh, who act as though the bloodshed portrayed is as routine in a day as reading a newspaper. Mortally wounded by the editor after exchanging gunfire in the newspaper office, the Colonel "remarked, with a fine humor, that he would have to say good morning now, as he had business up town. He then inquired the way to the undertaker's and left" (SNO 47).

In addition to ridiculing the stereotypical Southern temperament, the sketch comically presents the often contentious world of newspaper editors, especially in small-town or frontier settings. Clemens brilliantly uses the traditional tactic of the tall-tale, deadpan exaggeration, to satirize the journalistic excesses of the editor and his blackguard style of writing. The tactic is best seen in Mark Twain's polite and matter-of-fact understatement while retailing the wounds he receives during the violence of the day's work. Struck by a brick, dinged with a piece of stove sent flying by a bomb, nicked several times by bullets, cowhided by one "customer" and thrown out a window by another, Mark Twain consistently notes these outrages without emotion or in polite terms that match those of the editor or the Colonel. The exaggerated mayhem and the exaggerated polite reactions to the mayhem render the brutality fantastic and laughable.

Though the deadpan creates enough distance from the mayhem to allow for comic laughter, its satire never lets go of the historical reality behind the sketch. Clemens makes sure that the attentive reader cannot forget that reality by providing in an epigraph what purports to be an actual example of the kind of personal attacks that "Journalism in Tennessee" satirizes. Mark Twain's quote from an editor of the *Memphis Avalanche* refers to a statement by a rival as "saturated with infamy and reeking with falsehood." Clemens has Mark Twain characterize the attack as "swooping *mildly* down" upon the rival (emphasis added), not just to contrast with the exaggerated attacks made in the sketch by the *War-Whoop*'s editor, but also because he had witnessed worse attacks while reporting for the *Virginia City Territorial Enterprise*. Editors in the Nevada Territory routinely indulged in the calumny and name-calling featured in the sketch. Moreover, bloody consequences of such verbal abuse were not unknown. During Sam Clemens's employment on the *Enterprise*, the editor-in-chief, Joe Goodman, fought a duel that resulted in the rival editor walking with a limp thereafter.

Though Sam Clemens in fact left Virginia City as a direct result of nearly fighting his own duels, his more typical responses to the frequently violent world of newspapers while working on the *Enterprise* featured burlesque and parody. The mock combats of subeditors like Clemens parodied the literal combat of dueling as well as the war of words by chief editors on serious civic and political issues. For example, shortly after Clemens joined the *Enterprise* staff, he was assigned to cover the territory's legislative session. When he was ridiculed for mistakes by a veteran reporter of the legislature, Clement Rice of the *Virginia City Union*, Clemens retaliated by pretending that only Rice made mistakes, calling his rival the "Unreliable" while dubbing himself the "Reliable."

Clemens first participated in an editor's war of words when he was only seventeen and substituting for his brother Orion as editor on Orion's paper, the *Hannibal Journal*. Young Sam mercilessly ridiculed a rival editor for supposedly failing to kill himself after being jilted in a love affair. Sam attacked with more than words, using homemade woodcuts that depicted the rival editor as a dog. One reply from the editor hinted at a duel, but he backed off when he discovered how young his assailant was. Orion apologized in print when he returned to the paper, but the incident suggests how deeply rooted in experience is the comic violence of "Journalism in Tennessee."

Although the *War Whoop*'s editor illustrates comic barbarity, the satire in "Journalism in Tennessee" is not just directed at choleric behavior. The chief editor's writing style epitomizes pernicious editorial practices. His language embodies a mistaken idea about the virtue of vigorous prose, one that subverts the ethical principles of proper journalism and tramples its civic duty. Clemens ironically emphasizes the point by having the editor state the true purpose of journalism in the midst of an extended attack on a rival:

> We observe that the besotted blackguard of the Mud Spring *Morning Howl* is giving out, with his usual propensity for lying, that Van Werter is not elected. The heaven-born mission of journalism is to disseminate truth; to eradicate error; to educate, refine, and elevate the tone of public morals and manners, and make all men more gentle, more virtuous, more charitable, and in all ways better, and holier, and happier; and yet this black-hearted scoundrel degrades his great office persistently to the dissemination of falsehood, calumny, vituperation, and vulgarity. (SNO 46)

"Journalism in Tennessee" thus shows a concern for journalistic standards as well as a fondness for parodying the kind of journalism that Sam Clemens had practiced even before his time in the Territory of Nevada. The narrator Mark Twain takes a satiric swipe at the behavior of newspapermen who fail to live up to their own professed standards, as the chief editor does. The character Mark Twain, however, plays a different role, that of a comic victim whose resignation speech to his boss displays marvelous restraint, despite his maimed body. The comic victim is one of the personae Clemens fashions for Mark Twain.

This maneuvering between narrator and character typifies Clemens's use of Washoe Mark Twain, a haphazard literary invention, born from the exigencies of the newspaper business and the circumstances of Sam Clemens's temperament. As a reporter, Clemens was responsible for providing facts and information to Virginia City and to the other mining towns in the Nevada Territory. The job made him a respectable member of his community. However, the community of Virginia City during the 1860s was itself not altogether respectable. The manner in which journalism was practiced all along the Comstock was not respectable either, with slanders, sensationalism, mock feuds, and real duels all part of a newspaper staff's repertoire. "Journalism in Tennessee" could have been titled "Journalism in the Nevada Territory." Nominally respectable as an *Enterprise* reporter, Sam Clemens nevertheless created Washoe Mark Twain as a bantering newspaperman who could best his mock-combat rivals.[1]

Washoe Mark Twain was more than an alter ego by which Sam Clemens could practice his version of Nevada's rough-and-tumble journalism. The figure

1. Washoe is the name of the indigenous people whose traditional lands surrounded Lake Tahoe (Russell R. Elliott, *History of Nevada*, 24–31). The Comstock Lode was named after Henry Comstock, who was connected with the original discoverers of the first major silver vein in Nevada, the Grosch brothers (Hubert Howe Bancroft, *History of Nevada, Colorado, and Wyoming*, 96–99).

unleashed Clemens's sardonically comic perspective on people and society, as well as his considerable talent for transmuting what he saw and heard into fiction. Inciting laughter and spinning yarns were ultimately at cross-purposes with the duties of a reporter. However, this conflict did not deter Clemens from taking a comic approach to his job by inventing Washoe Mark Twain, neither respectable in adhering to conventional expectations nor irresponsible in refusing to acknowledge a journalist's duty to serve the community. This curious in-between status laid the foundation for Sam Clemens's meteoric success. This foundation in turn rested upon a tradition of comic writing in the United States well-known by 1863 when Mark Twain first appeared in print.

Literary scholarship has shown that the American comic tradition in the nineteenth century has a major investment in depicting the common man and woman. Focused on literary techniques, however, this scholarship has not explored how these comic representations embody issues concerned with the social history of the Old Southwest and with popular culture in the antebellum United States, with the recent exception of James Justus's *Fetching the Old Southwest*. Fundamental misunderstandings have been the result, beginning with the conception of Southern society upon which comic images of the common folk were usually based. On the popular culture side, literary critics have emphasized the negative aspects of one particular comic image of the common man, the Backwoods Roarer. In doing so, they have failed to grasp the complexities of this image's presentation and to comprehend how that complex presentation can aid in investigating Mark Twain's comic lineage.

Kenneth Lynn's *Mark Twain and Southwestern Humor* stands as the classic exposition on Mark Twain's relationship to the comic writers of the Old Southwest. The book also remains as the chief disseminator of misunderstandings about antebellum Southern society and about the Backwoods Roarer. These problems begin with employing the frame story technique as a *"cordon sanitaire"* that symbolizes antagonism between the two narrators, the Self-Controlled Gentleman and the Clown. Lynn uses the frame story's separation of a well-spoken gentleman from a dialect-speaking backwoodsman to generate a false image about society in the antebellum South. Lynn posits a society with only two classes of whites: the planters and the poor. The *cordon sanitaire* concept also allows Lynn to generalize about the social and political attitudes of the Old Southwest writers. Ultimately, Lynn's two-tiered image of Southern society can be traced back to the publication of Frederick Law Olmsted's *The Cotton Kingdom* in 1861.[2]

2. The firmly entrenched false image of Southern culture can also be found in E. B. Seabrook's "The Poor Whites of the South" (1867). Critics who followed in Lynn's wake include Florence, *Persona and Humor*; Pascal Covici Jr., *Mark Twain's Humor: The Image of a World*; Thomas McHaney,

Though influential, Lynn's analysis has been challenged on both historical and literary grounds. A counterimage of Southern society has been presented by Frank Owsley, Clement Eaton, and John Q. Anderson, one that insists upon a more complex set of classes among white Southerners. Such a complex view had been originally promulgated in Daniel H. Hundley's *Social Relations in Our Southern State* (1860), which differentiated between poor whites and different classes of plain folks. Recent historical scholarship has confirmed Hundley's view. To comprehend antebellum Southern society, one must distinguish between poor whites and plain folks.[3] The challenge to Lynn on literary grounds consists of different interpretations of the frame story technique. The most widespread alternative has followed from the position of James Cox, who argues that the frame signifies a collaboration between the gentleman who speaks a proper English and the backwoodsman who speaks a dialect form.[4] The ambivalence toward the backwoodsman on the part of the gentleman implied by Cox's analysis has become a significant alternative to Lynn's dynamic of antagonism.

Some scholars have pushed this alternative further, asserting that literary images of the plain folk include positive elements within a complex attitude.[5] That comic portraits of the common folk can be measurably positive, that one can laugh with, not merely at *dēmos*, are ideas crucial to understanding both the intricate nature of the comic tradition of the Old Southwest and Washoe Mark

---

"The Tradition of Southern Humor"; J. V. Ridgely, "The Southern Way of Life: The 1830s and '40s"; and William C. Spengemann, *Mark Twain and the Backwoods Angel: The Matter of Innocence in the Works of Samuel L. Clemens.*

3. Frank Owsley, *Plain Folk of the Old South;* Clement Eaton, "The Humor of the Southern Yeoman" and "The Southern Yeoman: The Humorist's View and the Reality"; John Q. Anderson, "Scholarship in Southwestern Humor—Past and Present." See also Merrill Maguire Skaggs, "The Beginning: Southwest Humor"; and M. Thomas Inge, introduction to *The Frontier Humorists: Critical Views.* For overviews of historical scholarship, see Randolph B. Campbell, "Planters and Plain Folks: The Social Structure of the Antebellum South"; and Lacy K. Ford, "Popular Ideology of the Old South's Plain Folk: The Limits of Egalitarianism in a Slaveholding Society." Tommy W. Rogers, "D. R. Hundley: A Middle-Class Thesis of Social Stratifications in the Antebellum South," discusses Hundley's class analysis in sociological terms.

4. James Cox, "Humor of the Old Southwest."

5. For example, Sonia Gernes, "Artists of Community: The Role of Storytellers in the Tales of the Southwest Humorists"; and Richie Devon Watson Jr., "Southwest Humor, Plantation Fiction, and the Generic *Cordon Sanitaire.*" Some critics—Lorne Fienberg, "Laughter as a Strategy of Containment in Southwestern Humor"; J. A. Leo Lemay, "Origins of the Humor of the Old South"; and Michael Pearson, "Pig Eaters, Whores, and Cowophiles: The Comic Image in Southern Literature," for example—lump these classes together, like Lynn, yet find ambivalence. To the extent that poor whites and plain folks have been differentiated (e.g. Sylvia Jenkins Cook, "The Development of the Poor White Tradition"; Michael Fellman, "Alligator Men and Cardsharpers: Deadly Southwestern Humor"; Robert D. Jacobs, "*Tobacco Road:* Lowlife and the Comic Tradition"), Lynn's idea of *cordon sanitaire* works well for representations of the poor folk.

Twain's relation to it. In Lynn's view, Mark Twain "solves" the problem of the conflict of the Self-Controlled Gentleman and the Clown by combining the two voices of the frame story.[6] This solution, however, can be achieved only by positing conflict in the frame story, conflict resulting from an upper-class attitude toward the vernacular voice featured within the frame. Yet that superior satiric attitude should be understood as only one among a variety of comic representations. Moreover, if this variety already includes a more complex humorous attitude toward the vernacular character, such as the one implied by combining the voices, then Clemens through Mark Twain did not create a hitherto unheard-of solution. Rather, the Old Southwest tradition already contained such a combination, a variant of the Backwoods Roarer. Significantly, this variation of the Backwoods Roarer stereotype does not take years to develop. Instead, it exists in early writings of the tradition. Charles F. M. Noland and William Tappan Thompson, for example, do not portray the gentleman's antagonistic perspective insisted on by Lynn and his followers, and their work was published at the same time as Augustus B. Longstreet's and Johnson J. Hooper's. Since 1901, when William Trent suggested linking Mark Twain with Longstreet and Hooper,[7] their writings have remained the standard evidence for the majority opinion expressed in the epigraph by Walter Blair about the intimate relationship between Mark Twain and comic writers from the Old Southwest.

The complexity of the Old Southwest comic tradition missing from Kenneth Lynn's analysis reflects the representations in nineteenth-century popular culture of backwoods settlers, hunters, and keelboatmen. Well before the Old Southwest writers began about 1830 to sketch their comic views of the common man, the customs and manners of such men had contributed to the first widespread comic stereotype of the poor white, the Ring-Tailed or Backwoods Roarer. Based on frontier conditions found even in colonial times, this image by the beginning of the nineteenth century had captured the popular imagination of America and established the tradition of a "comic barbarian."[8] The image fomented a swirl of ridiculing laughter that caught up the real David Crockett and created his popular culture counterpart, Davy Crockett of the almanacs. To the extent that writers like Augustus Longstreet perceived the Roarer stereotype in poor whites and plain folk alike, their satiric condescension is clear. The stories written about such wild comic figures provide some of the best evidence for Kenneth Lynn's thesis about Mark Twain and the comic tradition of the Old Southwest.

6. Kenneth S. Lynn, *Mark Twain and Southwestern Humor*, 148.
7. William P. Trent, "A Retrospect of American Humor."
8. Walter Blair, "Traditions in Southern Humor."

The impromptu duel between the editor and the Colonel in "Journalism in Tennessee" could therefore be understood as one instance in a long series of comic representations of the violence endemic in backwoods areas and frontier settlements, representations embodied in the Backwoods Roarer. These fictional presentations also crystalized into a favored scene, a comic confrontation between two men who often battle with fists instead of guns. In *Letters from the South* (1817), James Paulding penned what would become the *locus classicus* of such scenes, two Backwoods Roarers who duel verbally before engaging in rough-and-tumble fisticuffs. Clemens in 1852 had written a variation of the stereotyped battle, "The Dandy Frightening the Squatter," and he would return to it in elaborate fashion with the raftsmen's passage, originally written for *Huckleberry Finn* but published in *Life on the Mississippi.*

Despite the popularity of such tales and their comic figures in the antebellum period, they were less noteworthy than work by other comic writers, like Noland and Thompson, work that reshaped the Roarer stereotype into a roughneck who nevertheless behaved remarkably like a gentleman. By thus transforming the theme of the comic barbarian, with its easy laughter of condescension, to a theme of backwoods civility, some antebellum comic writers from the Old Southwest could elicit from their readers a more complex laughter. Washoe Mark Twain should be understood as an avatar not of the Backwoods Roarer, but of its variation that for so long had effectively combined Lynn's categories, the Self-Controlled Gentleman and the Clown, a figure I call the Gentleman Roarer. The link between Mark Twain and comic writers from the Old Southwest, though indisputable, has been misconstrued.

"Journalism in Tennessee" offers a comic view of frontier violence, echoing writers from the Old Southwest and anticipating later material, in *Roughing It* as well as in *Huckleberry Finn.* Equally important, the sketch taps into a comic theme that runs deep throughout the antebellum United States: the seemingly inherent cultural barbarism of American society. If even ostensible gentlemen, like the editor of the *War-Whoop,* reduce all discourse to a violent and not always symbolic battle, what can be said for the uneducated masses? That concern was most prominently represented in comic writings, such as Paulding's, which are structured by the confrontation scene between two Roarers. The Roarers' competitive boasts foreshadow the combat figured in the violent language of the *War Whoop*'s editor. The boasts trumpet the oral equivalent of his editorial. The Roarer in the antebellum period enabled the ultimate satiric comment on the potentially negative behavior of *dēmos,* embodying fear and loathing from the respectable viewpoint of the elite.

Clemens's presentation of the *War Whoop*'s editor (and Colonel Blatherskite Tecumseh), however, also satirizes those maintaining that respectable viewpoint for the same casual violence perpetrated by the Backwoods Roarer. While the Mark Twain character presented in "Journalism in Tennessee" does not act violently, Washoe Mark Twain has his part in the theme of cultural barbarism highlighted by the comic stereotype. Reminiscent of previous comic figures created by writers from the frontier regions of the Old Southwest, Washoe Mark Twain has a profile comically beyond the social pale, rough and rambunctious in his behavior, far too aggressive to be consistently respectable, and far too disdainful of important social conventions to be consistently trustworthy. Glimpsing the distinctive behavior of the Gentleman Roarer presented through earlier comic figures provides the background for understanding Mark Twain's place within a tradition of popular comic writings. Knowing that place helps explain the astonishingly swift success of Sam Clemens in Nevada.

## DAVID CROCKETT MEETS NIMROD WILDFIRE

MRS. FREEMAN: THIS MAN [COLONEL WILDFIRE] IS A SAVAGE.
MR. FREEMAN: MARY, YOU ARE PREJUDICED. YOU WILL NOT UNDER-
STAND THE REAL CHARACTER OF THE KENTUCKIANS. ALL THIS WHIM-
SICAL EXTRAVAGANCE OF SPEECH RESULTS FROM MERE EXUBERANCE
OF SPIRITS, AND HIS TOTAL IGNORANCE OF CONVENTIONAL RESTRAINT
HE OVERBALANCES BY A HEART WHICH WOULD SCORN TO DO A MEAN
OR DISHONEST ACTION.

————

JAMES K. PAULDING, *THE LION OF THE WEST* (1831)

In December 1833, a remarkable encounter took place in the nation's capital at Washington Theater. James Hackett, a famous comic actor, came out on stage to portray Nimrod Wildfire, a caricatured backwoodsman whose chief occupations apparently were drinking, bragging, and fighting. In the audience was David Crockett, a congressman from a western Tennessee district. The performance that night was a one-man show composed of Hackett's original comic characters. Hackett had been playing Nimrod Wildfire to appreciative crowds since April 1831, when the character debuted in James K. Paulding's *The Lion of the West*. Before the actor began his show, he walked downstage toward the seated congressman and bowed. To cheers and applause from the audience, Crockett stood up and returned the bow. This unusual exchange was remarkable because by then Hackett's character was widely understood to be not just an instance of the stereotypical and popular Backwoods Roarer but a lampoon of Crockett as well. Until Crockett returned the bow, the audience was in the dark about how he would react to the ridicule in Hackett's performance.[9]

Though initially he had taken offense at the perceived connection between him and Nimrod Wildfire, Congressman Crockett realized that the character had boosted his popularity, enhancing his image as an irreverent representative of the common folk, without his being completely defined as a loutish Backwoods Roarer. Crockett was an old hand at shaping a public image since his days in the Tennessee legislature ten years earlier, and he must have recognized long before the bow from Hackett that Wildfire's backwoods dialect and the foolish image it helped create could not harm him politically. Sometime in the same month Crockett attended Hackett's show, he wrote his son that he was preparing his autobiography. When published in April 1834, *A Narrative of the Life of Colonel David Crockett* featured a tailored image of Crockett the man and the politician. David Crockett's bow was as much theater as James Hackett's.[10]

The theater of that polite exchange remains noteworthy because it demonstrates a fascinating entanglement of politics, history, and popular images about antebellum common men that results from mythmaking by and about David Crockett. This skein of representations tangles two competing ideologies about *dēmos*. One rendered an individual as a bestial man in the wilderness; the other pictured a pastoral world inhabited by a natural gentleman, a cross between *le bon sauvage* and an Arcadian shepherd.[11] An overlooked aspect of American antebellum comic writers is the curious way that some of their characters amalgamate these two ideological, apparently irreconcilable, images of *dēmos*. James K. Paulding could therefore take the stereotypical Backwoods Roarer and create *The Lion of the West*, a popular play featuring a relatively tame version of the figure, despite the fact that the Roarer stereotype was largely based on a very brutal behavior, rough-and-tumble fighting. The clichéd boast of the Backwoods Roarer was his claim to be half horse, half alligator, with a little touch of snapping turtle. The corresponding boast of the comic composites of *dēmos* such as

9. Paulding wrote the play to win a cash prize Hackett had offered for a new drama featuring an original American character. Apparently, Paulding did not think of Wildfire as a lampoon of Crockett. He wrote Crockett shortly after *The Lion of the West* opened in New York to disavow any intention of lampooning him, and Crockett supposedly wrote a friendly letter in reply. See Richard Boyd Hauck, "Making It All Up: Davy Crockett in the Theater," 121nn9, 10.

10. See Joseph J. Arpad, introduction to *A Narrative of the Life of Colonel David Crockett;* and Richard Boyd Hauck, "The Man in the Buckskin Hunting Shirt: Fact and Fiction in the Crockett Story." Arpad mentions Crockett's letter to his son (26).

11. See James E. Caron, "Laughter, Politics, and the Yankee Doodle Legacy in America's Comic Tradition."

Nimrod Wildfire would be that they are half horse, half alligator, with a little touch of aspiring gentleman. They are Gentleman Roarers.

The David Crockett of the *Narrative* as well as the Davy Crockett of the almanacs encapsulate this oxymoronic Gentleman Roarer figure. In his analysis of comic writers from the Old Southwest, Kenneth Lynn uses the narrative device of the framed story to draw a sharp distinction between the urbane narrators and the vernacular, clownish characters. In this view, the narrator is a literary hero who embodies conservative Whig values while the clownish characters embody the violence of Jacksonian Democrats: the Self-Controlled Gentleman versus the Clown or its historically famous stereotype, the Backwoods Roarer.[12] The Gentleman Roarer, however, confounds Lynn's distinction, suggesting it is far too neat for a significant portion of the comic writing from antebellum America, beginning with the material by and about David Crockett.

Lynn distorts the historical man, depicting him as merely ruthless and hard, full of rage and revenge despite his gift for humor. Because he portrays Crockett with a savage nature, Lynn expresses surprise that Paulding fashions Nimrod Wildfire as a natural gentlemen as much as a lampoon of the congressman. *The Lion of the West*, Lynn declares, deviates from Paulding's Southern sympathies and aristocratic politics. Joseph J. Arpad, however, renders a very different David Crockett, a man who fought for squatters' rights and who also had a rare sympathy for Native Americans' rights. Moreover, Crockett possessed a gentility that was "basic, something inherent in his nature, whereas his backwoods eccentricity was superficial, a masquerade." Richard Boyd Hauck demonstrates that the masquerade functioned for political as well as for comic purposes, noting that Crockett humorously cultivated an image of "the gentleman from the cane" in the 1822 session of the Tennessee legislature. Crockett also designed his 1827 electioneering tactics to play up a contrast between new settlers or squatters and the rich, educated politicians who then controlled Tennessee politics.[13]

Arpad bases his rendition of Crockett on the experience of John Chapman, a painter who in 1834 over a period of a month and a half executed two oil portraits of the congressman. Given Chapman's testimony about Crockett's natural civility, Arpad concludes that Nimrod Wildfire's character captures the essential David Crockett, a man possessing an inner goodness masked by the crudities of being a backwoods bear hunter. Given Lynn's analysis, one might see Wildfire as an echo of Jonathan Swift's bestial Yahoo, although the Whigs' propaganda to set up Crockett as their political counterpart to Andrew Jackson partially refutes the comparison. For Arpad, Nimrod Wildfire evokes Roger de Coverly, Uncle

12. Lynn, *Southwestern Humor*, 58, 61.
13. Ibid., 32–36, 40; Arpad, introduction, 12–14, 16, 18–19; Hauck, "Buckskin," 3–7.

Toby, and Deidrich Knickerbocker.[14] David Crockett did not mind drinking whiskey, did his share of bragging about his prowess as a hunter, and admitted to a fight in which he attacked his opponent "like a wild cat [and] scratched his face all to a flitter jig"—the requisite credentials for a Backwoods Roarer. Nevertheless, Chapman, who had a six-week close-up view, underscores the gentleman.[15] This contradiction distinguishes the strand of antebellum comic writing I offer as the comic lineage of Mark Twain, one exemplified by a Roarer who is nevertheless capable of gentlemanly behavior. The contradictory attitudes that created this Gentleman Roarer can be found everywhere in antebellum culture. The mythic force of David Crockett draws much of its strength from his embodiment of those attitudes.

According to Catherine Albanese, the oxymoron also informs the literary representations of Crockett in the autobiography and pseudo-biographies as well as the almanacs. These representations at their core depict a civilized savagery that resonated with the collective mental world of Crockett's contemporary Americans. Crockett figures both the man from the woods, representative of wilderness, and the man from Congress, representative of *polis* and politics, of civilization and civility. The almanacs present this contradiction in a caricatured manner, but one that nevertheless encapsulates an important cultural debate about the definitions of savage and civilized while reflecting antebellum Americans' fear and fascination with the wildness of the frontier. Americans first of all feared the lack of civilized refinement found in their culture when compared to Europe, a lack emblemized by frontier wilderness but discernible even in cities. Nevertheless, Americans were fascinated by an ideology of pristine newness that transformed the untamed natural world into a democratic antidote against a decadent Europe. Crockett, in his *Narrative,* but especially in the almanacs, expressed both sides of the question, providing an opportunity for Americans to identify ambiguously with wildness. Given the popularity of the *Narrative* (at least seven editions in the first year) and other stories supposedly written by Crockett, the identification was widespread. The almanacs alone made the identification widespread, for they contain the first prose fiction with mass appeal in the United States. Printed for twenty years in several editions, the almanacs commanded an audience that knew no boundaries, encompassing adults and juveniles, middle-class city and rustic dwellers, yeoman farmers and mechanics, eastern seaboard as well as western frontier folk.[16]

14. Arpad, introduction, 25.
15. David Crockett, *A Narrative of the Life of Colonel David Crockett,* 30; Curtis Carroll Davis, "A Legend at Full-Length: Mr. Chapman Paints Colonel Crockett—and Tells about It," 171–72.
16. See Catherine Albanese, "Davy Crockett and the Wild Man; or, The Metaphysics of the *Longue Durée,*" 81, 83; and Catherine Albanese, "King Crockett: Nature and Civility on the American

In Albanese's analysis, the Davy Crockett of the almanacs exhibits a mastery of nature, a control that symbolizes the order of civilization, but the power of that mastery comes from a union with the wildness he ultimately tames. By becoming more savage than the savages he encounters in the wilderness, Davy Crockett ironically ensures the triumph of civilized values and behavior. He embodies both cultural degeneracy (the ultimate backwards man from the backwoods) and cultural progress (the pioneer trailblazing for civilization). The crudities attributed to Crockett therefore can be read either as a loss of civility or as merely the rough manners that necessarily mediate the prospective wilderness and the subsequent civilization.

J. A. Leo Lemay demonstrates that the contradiction Albanese finds in the popular Crockett literature has its roots in the historical realities of the eighteenth century and in Enlightenment conceptions of history. During the eighteenth century, city dwellers looked unfavorably upon folk living in back settlements within the eastern seaboard colonies. These rural people, who usually engaged in subsistence farming but often lived on what they could shoot in the woods or catch in the streams, had no education and were generally thought to have few manners and even fewer morals. However, up until the early part of the nineteenth century, such folk were not thought to be the worst of the lot. That distinction was reserved for the "frontier man," an individual who had largely adopted "Indian" ways and was therefore a traitor to his culture.[17] The wilderness and the Native Americans who inhabited it posed a psychological threat to the colonists who would become citizens of the new republic in part because they feared a transformation to the wild ways of the "frontier man." Fear and loathing of the "frontier man" lasted at least until the Lewis and Clark Expedition of 1803–1806. One scholar argues that the "frontier man" did not become a positive popular culture figure until the "Kentucky" riflemen proved decisive at the Battle of New Orleans (1815), an assertion that finds confirmation in the immensely popular song celebrating the victory, "The Hunters of Kentucky," performed on stages as late as 1822 by a buckskin-clad actor, Noah Ludlow.[18]

Lemay articulates the intellectual context within which these historical and cultural events enabled a positive reevaluation of the frontiersman. This new

Frontier," 249, 230–31. For publication information, see James A. Shackford and Stanley J. Folmsbee, introduction to Crockett, *Narrative,* ix–x. For publication of the almanacs, see John Seelye, "A Well-Wrought Crockett; or, How the Fakelorists Passed through the Credibility Gap and Discovered Kentucky."

17. J. A. Leo Lemay, "The Frontiersman from Lout to Hero," 187, 191.

18. Jules Zanger, "Frontiersman in Popular Fiction, 1820–1860." Stuart W. Hyde, "Ring-Tailed Roarer in American Drama," discusses "The Hunters of Kentucky." For the difference between a comic image of Crockett and the other famous historical man from the woods, Daniel Boone, see Michael Lofaro, "From Boone to Crockett: The Beginnings of Frontier Humor."

interpretation of the figure is founded on a theory that envisions civilization developing in progressive stages. Within intellectual circles of the Enlightenment, the existence of Native Americans had provided fuel for a debate centered on two versions of the history of mankind: one that imagined them as people who had degenerated from known standards of civilization, and one that imagined them as representative of an earlier, heroic stage of civilization. If Native Americans were conceptualized not as degenerate but as examples of earlier civilizations, then the frontiersman, who had in some ways become like them, was not a traitor to his culture. Instead, the frontiersman could be understood as a mediator between the early stage of civilization that Native Americans represent and the later stages of farming and commerce that marked Euro-American culture. Thus, the frontiersman could be fitted into a "stage theory" of civilization, not as a traitor but as a pioneer, not as an uncouth vagabond but as the rough-and-ready vanguard of civilized behavior. In Lemay's analysis, the pivotal document for effecting this change in American culture is Hector St. John de Crèvecoeur's *Letters from an American Farmer* (1782).

Kenneth Lynn's reading of Old Southwest comic writers of the 1830s to mid-1850s and Catherine Albanese's reading of the Crockett almanacs in the 1830s to mid-1850s both suggest that despite the positive view of the common man largely enabled by Crèvecoeur's *Letters,* Americans remained very unsure about the settlers along the border areas in the trans-Appalachian region throughout the antebellum period. An image of a pioneering and progressive frontiersman did not easily replace an image of a violent and backwards backwoodsman. Tracing the historical career of what might be taken as the epitome of the backwoodsman, the rough-and-tumble fighter, demonstrates this uncertainty. The major antebellum comic American writers manipulated stereotypes of actual frontier folk, like the rough-and-tumble fighter, to create comic figures. The Backwoods Roarer undoubtedly embodies the most enduring literary representation of the stereotyped backwoodsman. Certainly, he is the most dramatic. That dramatic force distorts Lynn's analysis of Old Southwest comic writers because he narrowly conceives of the voice of what he calls "the Clowns" as the voice of the Roarer, the stereotype of the actual rough-and-tumble fighter.[19]

The historical basis for the Backwoods Roarer comes from two broad geographical areas where rough-and-tumble fighting was typical within two time frames. The first instance can be located along the eastern seaboard and in the eighteenth century, generally fitting with the paradigm shift about people in back settlements that Lemay describes. These people were not viewed as pioneers, but

19. See Hennig Cohen and William B. Dillingham, who claim that the Roarer figure "provided the origins of Old Southwest humor" (introduction to *Humor of the Old Southwest*, xvi).

as examples of what William Byrd derisively called "lubbers." The no-holds-barred style of fighting often called "rough-and-tumble" created such a problem among these lower classes in the backwoods settlements of Virginia and the Carolinas that officials enacted regulations to curb the custom. Virginia's legislators amended an 1748 statue against barbarous forms of fighting in 1772 explicitly to discourage men from "gouging, plucking, or putting out an eye, biting or kicking or stomping upon" their opponents.[20] From the viewpoint of respectable folks like those legislators, the frontier man betrayed his culture by assimilating to the ways of Native Americans, and the backwoods bully who resorted to such tactics apparently betrayed all civilization. No wonder Benjamin Franklin stated once that, "Our Frontier People are yet greater Barbarians than the Indians."[21]

Constance Rourke has noted the second germane instance of rough-and-tumble fighting, in the trans-Appalachian region after the American Revolution. The custom of rough-and-tumble fighting continued in the frontier settlements. Some men engaging in this style of combat had fought native tribes before becoming keelboatmen. Starting out from Pittsburgh in western Pennsylvania, these boatmen established before the end of the eighteenth century the Ohio River valley and the lower Mississippi River as the territory for the Backwoods Roarer, the cultural primitive who used teeth and fingernails like a bird of prey to rend opponents.[22] Such men also came from settlements in Kentucky and Tennessee to populate the newer frontiers farther west. In the winter of 1803, Captain Meriwether Lewis, camped near St. Louis before his Corps of Discovery made its ascent of the Missouri River, recognized the type at a horse race near the city: "almost entirely emegrant from the fronteers of Kentuckey & Tennessee, [they] are the most dessolute and abandoned even among these people."[23]

A dispute exists among scholars about just how often actual examples of Backwoods Roarers might have been found in the frontier territories. Yet the historical reality of such men is far less important than their psychological reality or emblematic depiction.[24] Emblematic depiction certainly had much to do with the creation of a story cycle about Mike Fink, the most famous historical instance of a Backwoods Roarer. Fink exemplified behavior that formed the basis for the stereotype. Fink started his career in the West as a scout for Fort Pitt

20. Quoted in Elliott J. Gorn, "'Gouge and Bite, Pull Hair and Scratch': The Social Significance of Fighting in the Southern Backcountry," 19.

21. Quoted in Lemay, "Frontiersman," 190.

22. Constance Rourke, *American Humor: A Study of the National Character,* 38–43; see also Fellman, "Alligator Men," 311.

23. Quoted in Stephen E. Ambrose, *Undaunted Courage: Meriwether Lewis, Thomas Jefferson, and the Opening of the American West,* 122, with Lewis's spelling.

24. Fellman, "Alligator Men," 321–22n2.

during the border wars with native tribes along the Ohio River during the 1780s and 1790s. In this capacity, Fink acquired a reputation for courage, daring, and skilled shooting with his "Kentucky" rifle. Once the hostile tribes were decisively defeated at the battle of Fallen Timbers (1794), these scouts were no longer needed. By then unsuited for farming, many turned to the river for a living. These scouts, said a historian in 1845, "had imbibed in their intercourse with the Indians a . . . contempt as well as a disrelish for regular and steady labor. . . . A boatsman's life was the very thing for such individuals. From the nature of their movements, they felt themselves scarcely responsible to the laws, as indeed they were not, except at New Orleans."[25] Mike Fink became one of these frontier scouts turned keelboatman.

Though the backwoodsman in his horrific incarnation as the Backwoods Roarer might be found in almost any frontier setting, such as the horse race near St. Louis witnessed by Captain Lewis, circumstances surrounding keelboating made this form of river commerce a focal point for rough-and-tumble fighting. The difficulty in bringing a keelboat back up river meant that its crew were among the hardiest to be found anywhere in the frontier areas. However, the "best" man in backwoods slang meant more than mere strength. Fights to maintain the pecking order among river boats, with rafts at the bottom and keelboats at the top, necessitated physical prowess. Just as important, however, the "best" man embodied the courage to fight no-holds-barred. The backwoods view of "best" spawned rivalries among the keelboat crews to establish preeminence, sometimes one champion bully meeting another in a wrestling match with no rules. Travelers' books describe the brutality of these fights. Once the keelboatman's habits of excessive drinking and boasting were added, those descriptions helped create the brutal profile upon which the literary figure of the Backwoods Roarer was predicated.[26]

Mike Fink encapsulates the quasi-folkloric process from actual frontiersman to emblematic backwoodsman. Oral tales about Fink circulated during his lifetime, and after his death in 1823 tales continued to be told as written accounts added to the image. The written tales transformed the historical Mike Fink into the stereotypical Roarer—always full of fight and homemade whiskey while roaring his boast of being the best man. The key motif of Mike Fink as a literary image is his status as the "champion of the unrestrained and unrestrainable."[27]

25. Quoted in Walter Blair and Franklin J. Meine, "Mike Fink in History, Legend, and Story," 7.
26. Despite the plausibility that circumstances added to the portrait of the typical keelboatman being a Roarer, the image is assuredly more invented than real. Even contemporaries objected that the Backwoods Roarer was far from typical within the western population (Walter Blair, *Native American Humor*, 31).
27. Blair and Meine, "Mike Fink," 25.

This process of the actual becoming the emblematic worked for the Backwoods Roarer, too, as the figure was shaped into a comic stereotype of the common man west of the Appalachians. Oral stories circulated about Roarer figures even before 1800, though 1808 marks the earliest date for a written account of a Backwoods Roarer's boast. Within five years, however, eastern newspapers were printing the most common boast—the claim to be half horse, half alligator, with a little touch of snapping turtle—without any explanation for the reader, indicating that the stereotype was already in place.[28] Other early written notices of the figure occur in Washington Irving's *A History of New York by Deidrich Knickerbocker* (1809) as well as the previously noted *Letters from the South* by James K. Paulding. Paulding's version places a fictional sketch of the Roarer within a travel book, combining the two most prominent narrative genres in which the Roarer appears. Paulding's sketch suggests that by 1817 the Backwoods Roarer's emblematic function had made him perfect for literary uses.

While accounts written after 1825 cemented Mike Fink's personal reputation,[29] the literary version of the Backwoods Roarer was headed for national prominence on the stage. Alphonse Wetmore's *The Pedlars* (1821) marks the first theater appearance of a fight between two boasters. By 1831, the stock situation of two Backwoods Roarers fighting with fists after they have figuratively fought with their boasts forms a literary trope familiar enough to eastern audiences that Paulding includes it in *The Lion of the West*. James Hackett's one-man show witnessed by David Crockett in 1833 featured Nimrod Wildfire's monologue of boasting and fighting, suggesting that this behavior was the most popular feature of the backwoodsman's character. Moreover, the fight story trope from *The Lion of the West* inspired the early Crockett almanacs: the general outlines of the story were thoroughly literary in origin.[30]

The Backwoods Roarer in Paulding's play figures most importantly here because the character, despite its basis in horrific reality, was by 1831 already sufficiently literary so that it could be successfully rendered as a relatively genteel comic image of the common man. Like David Crockett in his *Narrative*, Nimrod Wildfire leavens the Backwoods Roarer stereotype with gentlemanly behavior. Paulding accomplishes this modification mainly by confining Wildfire's Roarer aspect to words: he merely relates his tall-tale encounter with another Roarer. His onstage actions fall more in line with the image of the natural-born gentleman, for though Wildfire's manners are comically uncouth and the character clearly should be played as slapstick, his behavior also depicts

28. Blair, *Native American Humor,* 30n4.
29. See Mody Boatwright, *Folk Laughter on the American Frontier,* 103.
30. Joseph J. Arpad, "The Fight Story: Quotation and Originality in Native American Humor"; Seelye, "Well-Wrought Crockett."

a fearless soldier who helps expose the true villain's evil nature. Despite his loutish manners, Wildfire functions as an agent of sentimental comedy too, generously offering to establish the romantic couple, Caroline and Percival, on his land in Kentucky. In the end, this loud-mouthed but well-off landowner resembles Henry Fielding's Squire Western more than the genuine Backwoods Roarer who gouges out eyes in a rough-and-tumble fight. By containing Wildfire's Roarer aspect in anecdote rather than expressing it in action, Paulding evokes the backwoods stereotype while suggesting Wildfire's good-hearted nature. Wildfire does not win a lady's love in the process, which would have completely placed the figure within a domestic narrative, but the colonel nevertheless plays the comic hero. He is the Gentleman Roarer, tamed just enough for the drawing room. Like the image of Crockett in the *Narrative* and the almanacs, Wildfire comically symbolizes a civilized savagery.

---

## CHARLES F. M. NOLAND ON THE DEVIL'S FORK

PETE WHETSTONE . . . IS NOT ONLY THE MOST ABLE SPEAKER IN THE STATE LEGISLATURE, BUT CAN OUT-SHOOT, DANCE, SING, FIDDLE, ANY MAN IN THE STATE; WHILE AT RACING, PREACHING, OR TELLING A STORY, NOBODY THERE IS A HUCKLEBERRY TO HIS PERSIMMION.

———

WILLIAM PORTER, *NEW YORK SPIRIT OF THE TIMES*, FEBRUARY 17, 1838

The theme of civilized savagery embodied by the Gentleman Roarer provides the clue for linking Washoe Mark Twain with the antebellum tradition of comic writing. Two other well-known comic characters from the 1830s and 1840s demonstrate that the Gentleman Roarer was a comic figure long established by the time Sam Clemens invented Mark Twain: Charles Noland's Colonel Pete Whetstone and William Tappen Thompson's Major Joseph Jones. Noland's and Thompson's comic characters establish a trajectory toward gentility and respectability begun by Paulding's Nimrod Wildfire.[31]

What makes Pete Whetstone most interesting is Noland's willingness to portray him as a Backwoods Roarer capable of learning gentlemanly behavior. Pete

31. For a more complete discussion of Whetstone and Jones, as well as Crockett, see James E. Caron, "Backwoods Civility; or, How the Ring-Tailed Roarer Became a Gentle Man for David Crockett, Charles F. M. Noland, and William Tappan Thompson."

is unafraid in a backwoods encounter with a bear but naturally polite to women, capable of wielding a knife in a melee or learning a cotillion for a society ball. Colonel Pete Whetstone and Colonel David Crockett would have been bosom friends. The composite image of a Gentleman Roarer gains a sharper outline when the Pete Whetstone letters telling about fights and near-fights over horses and politics are considered.[32] These accounts of brawling imply that Arkansas folks in any dispute resort to fisticuffs and worse. Because they out-roar him, Pete's friends Jim Cole and Dan Looney and Bill Spence are crucial to the composite image. Though belligerent at times, Pete never starts a fight. The two fights that involve him begin with either Dan Looney or Jim Cole. Pete draws his knife only after another man has drawn his and stabbed one of Pete's compatriots. In addition, Noland never depicts Pete Whetstone using no-holds-barred tactics. The same is true for his brother-in-law Jim Cole, though he almost loses an eye when he gets into a brawl because he drinks too much (49). However, Dan Looney, from Raccoon Fork, participates in two fights where he eye-gouges (40, 63). Noland distances Pete, his family, and all of Devil's Fork from this quintessential bestial act of the backwoods.

Perhaps the ultimate example of Charles Noland's ambivalence toward the vernacular-speaking folk of his day occurs in his use of Dan Looney to defend against talk by abolitionists about breaking up the union, for Dan vanquishes his opponent when he gouges his eyes (63). With the ultimate gesture of frontier violence, a Backwoods Roarer ironically defends a moderate political position, a structure that echoes Albanese's view that Davy Crockett embraces savagery to tame savages and the wilderness.

Though Noland's depiction of violence in the Pete Whetstone letters more realistically evokes a fight between Backwoods Roarers than Paulding's sanitized version in *The Lion of the West,* neither can match the realism of Augustus B. Longstreet's "The Fight," a sketch from *Georgia Scenes.* In this telling of the stock encounter of two rough-and-tumble fighters, Longstreet makes a great effort to detail the horror of such contests, highlighting the physical perfection of the two men before the fight so that the reader will all the more feel disgust at their mutilation as the match proceeds: "I looked, and saw that Bob had entirely lost his left ear, and a large piece from his left cheek. His right eye was a little discoloured, and the blood flowed profusely from his wounds. Bill presented a hideous spectacle. About a third of his nose, at the lower extremity, was bit off, and his face so swelled and bruised that it was difficult to discover in it anything of the

---

32. Fights and disputes are shown in Charles F. M. Noland, *Cavorting on the Devil's Fork: The Pete Whetstone Letters,* letters 7, 9, 13, 15, 19, 23, 40, 42, 49, 60, 63. Citations will hereinafter appear in the text and refer to this edition of Noland's sketches.

human visage, much more of the fine features which he carried into the ring."[33] The difficulty discovering "anything of the human visage" in Bill's battered face symbolizes the stakes in such fights when they are presented seriously: the difference between human and animal behavior. The identification with beasts at the heart of the Roarer's clichéd boast—his claim to be half horse and half alligator with a little touch of the snapping turtle—seems literally true as the two men's human features disappear. As the fight continues, Bill bites off one of Bob's fingers, though finally Bill gives up the battle when Bob begins to grind a handful of dirt and sand into his eyes. Longstreet's tale has no eye-gouging, but it does end the fight in stereotypical fashion, with an assault on the eyes meant to blind. Whether actual men engaged in such fights for fun or for honor, the literary characters who fight no-holds-barred in these tales represent the worst fears about *dēmos* that upper-class gentlemen might have. In these cases, the Backwoods Roarer embodies the darkest of antebellum satires on the American experiment with democracy.

As Elliott Gorn shows, Longstreet's battle between Backwoods Roarers is itself tame compared to what actual travelers recorded.[34] Editing occurred even in the modest literary pretensions of a newspaper sketch, and the Pete Whetstone letters demonstrate how a frontier writer had a range of omission from which to choose when presenting events beyond the pale of civilized society. The difference between Longstreet and Noland on the one hand, and Paulding on the other, however, is more than which gruesome details should be left out. When Nimrod Wildfire tells of his fight, not only is there no mention of blood from bitten fingers, ears, and lips, nor any frightful narration of how eyes are lost, but also the blows delivered are described in language so absurdly extravagant that realism nearly disappears. Moreover, Paulding lavishes much more description on the competitive exchange of verbal boasts than on the exchange of physical blows.

> Mister, says he, I'm the best man—if I ain't, wish I may be tetotaciously exflunctified! I can whip my weight in wildcats and ride strait through a crab apple orchard on a flash of lightning—clear meat axe disposition! And what's more, I once back'd a bull off a bridge. Poh says I [Wildfire], what do I keer for that? I can tote a steam boat up the Mississippi and over the Allegheny mountains. My father can whip the best man in old Kaintuck, and I can whip my father. When I'm good natured I weigh about a hundred and seventy, but when I'm mad, I weigh a *ton*. . . . I put it to him mighty droll—tickled the varmint till he squealed like a young colt.[35]

33. Augustus Baldwin Longstreet, *Georgia Scenes*, 62.
34. Gorn, "Gouge and Bite," 25, 26.
35. James K. Paulding, *The Lion of the West*, act 2, scene 2.

This instance of two Backwoods Roarers contesting to determine the best man exhibits a radical combination of comic fantasy and brutal realism, a combination that creates the quintessential American ambivalence in the literary representations of antebellum comic common man. The combination can still be found in Mark Twain's 1869 sketch "Journalism in Tennessee." The violent encounter of two Backwoods Roarers boasting and then fighting acknowledges the worst fear about the frontier's effects on people: it turns them into beasts, into "natural men," into savages. At the same time, the comic presentation happens in outlandish terms as a sign of an astonished admiration for the physical and mental qualities needed to transform the wilderness. The mighty punches may indicate hardy bodies, but the witty punchlines indicate shrewd minds, too. These fantastic renditions of the Backwoods Roarer were not depicting *dēmos* as natural gentlemen, but the fusion of horror and admiration in these renditions presents only the extreme form of the odd notion that the best of the common men were a combination of Roarer and Gentleman.

---

## WILLIAM TAPPAN THOMPSON'S DOMESTIC ROARER

THUNDER! HOW MY BLOOD DID BILE UP ALL OVER ME, AND I FELT LIKE I COULD KNOCK MATTHEW MATIX INTO A GREAS-SPOT, IF HE'D ONLY BEEN THAR.

———

*MAJOR JONES'S COURTSHIP* (1844)

The Gentleman Roarer represents the most intriguing part of antebellum, Old Southwest humor because the figure embodies an ambivalence in American culture about *dēmos* that creates a necessary condition within popular culture for the first appearance of Mark Twain. The work of William Tappan Thompson provides a final instance of this proposition. Pete Whetstone's character suggests that the faults of the vernacular-speaking folk might be remedied by education; Thompson's Major Joseph Jones demonstrates it. Major Jones completes a movement from the civilized savagery of Davy Crockett in the almanacs toward a backwoods figure of gentility, for the Major, in comic country fashion, wins his lady love. Though domesticated, even to the point of abjuring tobacco and whiskey, the Major nevertheless does not lose all of the Backwoods Roarer's features. Instead, Major Jones suggests an idealized image of frontier *dēmos,* losing the Roarer's brutality but not his courage, transforming hardiness into an ethic of hard work, displaying as much common sense as naïveté and bumptiousness. Though an implied audience laughs satirically at Major Jones as a slapstick figure, country oaf, and lovesick swain, it also laughs humorously with his homespun philosophy about education, people, politics, fashions, and manners. Thompson makes him admirable as much as he renders him ridiculous, his character a comic compound of book learning and common sense.

Moreover, the Major exemplifies the behavior of a Gentleman Roarer. Hints of the Major's pugnacity readily surface in connection with his courtship. He is ready to kick one rival in the pants (Letter 8) or knock another into "a greas-spot,"[36] and cousin Pete only has to be rude to Mary to be bodily picked up and thrown into a creek (Letter 5). The quick temper of the Major and his physical strength recall the Roarer stereotype. After his marriage, however, an incident occurs demonstrating that Thompson's conception of Major Jones, though decidedly civil and proper, includes typical Roarer behavior. Cousin Pete again stirs up trouble, this time by trumping up a warrant for the Major's arrest that charges him with harming young women from Macon with his book of letters. When Jones rides into town to rectify the situation, Pete and a crowd led by a man named Snipe attempt to arrest the Major, literally, by tying him up with a rope:

> That was more'n I could stand from [Pete], and I jest brung my hand round and tuck him spang in the mouth. I spose it must [have] been pretty much of a lick, for it sounded jest like hittin a piece of raw beef with the flat side of a meet-axe, and it drawed considerable blood and a tooth or two. Peter kivered his mouth with his hand and sort o' backed out of the crowd. But little Snipe stood off and hollered "help! rescue! help!" as loud as he could, and the fellers grabbled hold of me like they was gwine to tear me to pieces. My dander was up and I couldn't help slingen 'em a little, and after I piled five or six of 'em on top of one another and put two or three of their noses out of jint, I told Snipe I was ready to go.[37] (140–41)

Given the Major's ability in a fight, the restraint with cousin Pete shown in earlier letters is noteworthy. The Major thus contents himself with a simple ducking of Pete when he is rude to Mary, and he refrains completely from acting when Pete, under cover of a parlor game, more than once hits Joe hard with a book. Restraint is noticeable, too, in the above quotation: Pete whips everyone

---

36. William Tappan Thompson, *Major Jones's Courtship*, 17. Citations will hereinafter appear in the text and refer to this edition.

37. Bartlett's *Dictionary of Americanisms* calls "dander" "scruff" or "dandruff" and says the phrase "To get one's dander up" means to "get into a passion" (108). The first quotation for the phrase is from *An Account of Col. Crockett's Tour to the North and Down East* (1835); the third is from Thompson's *Courtship*. The phrase echoes Crockett's *Narrative* (73, 89), and dander linked to scalp and hair suggests animal fur—more hints of Major Jones's link to the boast of the Roarer.

and then surrenders. All of this restraint suggests that Major Joseph Jones has the strength and courage of the Backwoods Roarer tempered with the civility of what Kenneth Lynn would call a Self-Controlled Gentleman. His readiness to defend Mary's character forms part of his natural-born gentleman's behavior, and so too does his restraint with Pete during the parlor game, for Joe defers to Mary's plan of revenge. No full-fledged Backwoods Roarer would have restrained himself after realizing Pete's cowardly trick with the book, and when the Major does punch Pete during the attempted arrest, clearly Joe has been pushed beyond a reasonable man's limit. Jones had shown the same balance at a militia muster that ends in a drunken brawl. Ready beforehand to fight at the muster if the men attempt to play practical jokes on him as they did on the previous commanding officer, Joe nevertheless stays out of the senseless fray once it begins on a political pretext.

While Major Jones represents vernacular-speaking *dēmos,* he is very far from Lynn's conception of how the Old Southwest writers portrayed their vernacular characters. Retaining the bumptiousness of the Jacksonian folk and even a significant measure of the Roarer's fighting ability, Major Jones is nevertheless held up by Thompson for the admiration of the implied reader as well as for its ridicule. The height of admiration for the Major comes with his speech at a liquor-free Fourth of July celebration. The speech focuses on the inferior behavior of contemporary men compared to the founding fathers, a standard antebellum rhetorical theme on such occasions. Major Jones, however, should be taken as an exception to that decline and more like the mythical founding fathers: a sober and loving husband, hardworking, with enough education not to act foolish yet not to take on aristocratic airs, too. Major Jones is a republican in the generic sense of the word; like Colonel Pete Whetstone, he advocates Whig politics, naming his son Henry Clay in a symbolic gesture. Major Jones thus portrays an idealized yet comic image of *dēmos.* The curious mixture found in the Gentleman Roarer also extends to the major's political partisanship when he declares that he goes for Clay "tooth and toenail" (189), evoking the rough-and-tumble fight in defense of sober Whig principles, as Dan Looney does in the Pete Whetstone letters. Finally, no frame exists around the major's letters to contain his bumptiousness in the name of a gentleman's point of view.[38]

38. Frank Owsley uses tax records to divide antebellum society into no fewer than nine groups. The non-slaveholders plus small slaveholding farmers are the groups Owsley calls "plain country folk" (*Plain Folk of the Old South,* 8). Though in his first letter Major Jones implies that his farm is a "plantation" (12), in a subsequent letter Thompson pictures him working in the fields with his slaves (letter 19), which suggests that the Major is either a small planter or a small slaveholding farmer in Owsley's taxonomy. Joseph Jones, as successful author and farmer, married to a woman with a college education, represents a rising middle class.

In his analysis of the influence of the Old Southwest writers on Mark Twain, Kenneth Lynn sees all the writers as representative of a Whig, upper-class perspective, what might be called the view of the "sporting crowd." The sporting crowd pursued horse racing, hunting, and the theater as pastimes. Individuals would subscribe to the *New York Spirit of the Times.* People who either were from or aspired to the planter class composed the crowd. The monolithic publishing world that Lynn and Pascal Covici invoke as part of their analyses of popular comic authors mirrors the Whig values of this sporting crowd.[39] However, their analyses ignore the variety within historical readers, a variety reflected by what sold in all segments of the book-buying market, not just the one defined by the sporting crowd. Thompson's work rivaled the popularity of the Colonel Pete Whetstone letters, the Crockett materials, and *The Lion of the West,* indicating penetration throughout the market. The enormous popularity of all these comic works suggests that Lynn's argument only accounts for the intent of some Old Southwest writers.

Lynn's term "Self-Controlled Gentlemen" focuses the problem. The comic frontier writers from the Old Southwest are better described not as "gentlemen," with that term's connotations of the upper-class planter, but rather as "men of moderation." Literary equivalents include Molière's *homme raisonnable* or Joseph Addison's persona in *The Spectator.* The distance from certain characters found in the voices of the Old Southwest writers and in their framing technique is therefore more one of behavior, attitude, or temperament than of economic class or political affiliation. These writers directed their satire at excess, no matter who practiced it—gentleman, yeoman, or poor white. Historians have shown that the excessive drinking, fighting, and boasting that coalesce into the Backwoods Roarer figure informed all social strata in the Old Southwest. The comic "Gentleman Roarer" figure thus satirized a masculine ideal gone awry. To call the narrators of frame stories "Self-Controlled Gentlemen" because they ridicule excessive behavior in the lower orders and to assume that those narrators should be aligned with the upper classes against the lower classes is to misunderstand the social dynamics of the Old Southwest. Intemperance was endemic in backwoods settlements, not confined solely to the lower classes of people.[40]

Thompson's original historical readers in middle Georgia were "chiefly the hard-working, half-educated, rough-and-ready Scotch-Irish cotton farmers,"[41]

---

39. See Blair, "Traditions," 137–41.

40. Joan E. Cashin, *A Family Venture: Men and Women on the Southern Frontier,* 109; see also Dickson D. Bruce Jr., *Violence and Culture in the Antebellum South;* and Ian Tyrrell, *Sobering Up: From Temperance to Prohibition in Antebellum America, 1800–1860.*

41. Henry Prentice Miller, "The Background and Significance of *Major Jones's Courtship,*" 269.

a group Thompson, throughout his career, courted in his books and in his own newspaper and from which he received approval over the years.[42] Using Major Jones, Thompson could gently make fun of those folks but also praise them, too. Thompson's historical readers actually wrote half-literate letters to the *Southern Miscellany,* with poor spelling and bad grammar, and thus the Major Jones letters parodied real letters, while simultaneously idealizing the people who wrote them.[43] Sam Clemens can be linked with Thompson, as well with Noland, because, like the characters created by the two earlier comic writers, his initial Mark Twain represents a symbolic community based on actual readers. The Mark Twain in Nevada, "Washoe Mark Twain," is as much an emblem of the territory—a compelling image even though it distorts reality by magnifying certain aspects—as the Backwoods Roarer had been for the frontier in the antebellum period.

Washoe Mark Twain symbolizes his community through his clowning. Insofar as practical joking and bantering and raillery represented the frontier spirit of a male-centered democracy and its rough-mannered insistence on egalitarianism, Washoe Mark Twain occupied a symbolic social center: he was king of the jokers, the best of "the boys," a comic champion. The defining quality of "the boys" in Virginia City—as implied audience and as symbolic community—is found in the structure that Catherine Albanese identifies with Davy Crockett of the almanacs: "civilized savagery." That contradiction marks "the boys" in Nevada as respectable and yet not respectable. The steps between the starkness of "civilized savagery" and the ambiguity of the social status of "the boys" that Sam Clemens knew can be traced in the theme of backwoods civility. Pete Whetstone represents the idea that common folks, though uncouth and even at times violent, can transform themselves. Like Washoe Mark Twain, Pete also represents a community of "the boys," capable of rough-and-tumble fights but also capable of learning how to become well-mannered. Joseph Jones represents what "the boys" in Devil's Fork, Arkansas, or Virginia City, Nevada Territory, might evolve into: sober and loving husbands, hardworking, educated enough not to act merely as the foolish country clown, and possessed also of enough common sense not to take on aristocratic airs. The theme of backwoods civility and its representative figure, the Gentleman Roarer, are thus the most portentous aspects of the Old Southwest comic tradition, the fabric from which Sam Clemens tailors the Nevada phase of Mark Twain.

42. Carl R. Osthaus, "From the Old South to the New South: The Editorial Career of William Tappan Thompson of the *Savannah Morning News*," 240.

43. Miller, "Background," 270.

# SCENE TWO

THE BACKWOODS ROARER
AND THE "LITERARY COMEDIAN"

## CHARLES FARRAR BROWNE'S ARTEMUS WARD:
## SCALAWAG AND SPOKESMAN

I HISTID IN SO MUCH [DRINK] THAT I DIDENT ZACKLY KNOW WHARE
BOWTS I WAS. I TURND MY LIVIN WILD BEESTS OF PRAY LOOSE INTO
THE STREET & OPSOT MY WAX WURKS. I THEN BET I COOD PLAY HOSS.
SO I HARNIST MYSELF TO A KANAL BOTE.

———

ARTEMUS WARD, "ON FORTS," *VANITY FAIR,* NOVEMBER 17, 1860

Defining Mark Twain within a context of previous comic writers, Kenneth
Lynn argued for the preeminence of the Old Southwest tradition, as Walter Blair had done before him. However, the figure of the Gentleman Roarer suggests a different way to understand the nature of the link between Mark Twain
and the writers of the Old Southwest. David Sloane argued for a very different
grouping of comic writers as the answer to the question of Mark Twain's comic
antecedents by examining the influence of the so-called "Literary Comedians."
With these writers, "a minor literary tradition appears to have become a major
visionary phenomenon through a combination of literary and historical events
that are generally ignored in interpreting Twain's work."[44] Sloane's argument, in
effect, claims Mark Twain as the best of his comic contemporaries, rather than
repeating Blair's and Lynn's insistence upon a defining connection to the earlier
writers of the Old Southwest.

Other critics have also recognized an important connection between Mark
Twain and the Literary Comedians, writers who did their best work mostly in the
Northeast and mostly after the Civil War had started.[45] In his 1964 overview of
the American comic tradition, Willard Thorp notes that in a "span of seven years,
Mark Twain established himself as the best of the literary comedians." Even Wal-
ter Blair, so conspicuous a witness for the paramount importance of the Old
Southwest school, admitted that Mark Twain rose to international fame as a

44. David E. E. Sloane, *Mark Twain as a Literary Comedian,* 198.
45. Over the years, the term *Literary Comedian* has been applied loosely by different critics to
various groupings of writers that, more or less, overlap. The lists of the critics consulted: Fred
Lewis Pattee, "The Laughter of the West," 26; Jennette Tandy, *Crackerbox Philosophers in American
Humor and Satire,* chapters 5 and 6; Blair, *Native American Humor,* 102–4; Walter Blair, introduction to *The Mirth of a Nation: America's Great Dialect Humor,* viii; Willard Thorp, *American
Humorists,* 17; Jesse Bier, "Literary Comedians: The Civil War and Reconstruction," 78; Brom
Weber, "The Misspellers," 131; Walter Blair and Hamlin Hill, *America's Humor: From Poor Richard
to Doonesbury,* 289–90; Sloane, *Literary Comedian,* chapter 2; David E. E. Sloane, ed., *The Literary*

"Funny Fellow," a variant designation for these writers.[46] *Mark Twain as a Literary Comedian,* however, examined the connection more comprehensively than any other effort. Though Sloane carefully does not assert that the Literary Comedians are *the* most important influence on Mark Twain, his examination elaborates an alternative critical view about the influence of other comic American writers on Sam Clemens. The hallmark of the Literary Comedians, according to Sloane, is their infusion of a subject with significant social viewpoints. Ethical considerations thus bulk large in their comic material, and their literary antecedents can be found in the comic political criticism of Seba Smith and James Russell Lowell. In addition, Sloane notes three other significant features: the ethical engagement with serious issues takes place in urban settings; an approval of democratic egalitarianism always exists, at least implicitly; and a rejection of violence is prominent.[47] Because my study focuses exactly on the "span of seven years" in which Sam Clemens achieved his first fame, the claim that Mark Twain's comic genealogy can be traced to the Literary Comedians merits consideration. As with the Old Southwest writers, however, the Gentleman Roarer figure best illuminates a link to the most prominent of the Literary Comedians, Charles Farrar Browne.

The Gentleman Roarer has shown that writers from the Old Southwest tradition could depict an optimistic view of *dēmos.* This view insists that the common man, though rustic, was not maliciously rude; though simple and unpretentious, was not simple-minded; and though undereducated and practically unlettered, was nevertheless possessed of common sense and mother wit. He could be an American-style gentleman. Browne's semiliterate showman Artemus Ward represents the comic but positive view of *dēmos* with an angle different from the Old Southwest examples because his being an American-style gentleman is a self-proclaimed status. His boast of providing virtuous and moral

---

*Humor of the Urban Northeast, 1830–1890,* 21; David Kesterson, "Those Literary Comedians," 167; and David Kesterson, "The Literary Comedians: A Review of Modern Scholarship," 167. Blair says the term referred to burlesque lectures (introduction, xix). Thorp says the term was used as early as 1890 but gives no specifics (*American Humorists,* 17). He may have been referring to Henry Clay Lukens, who in 1890 wrote "American Literary Comedians" for *Harper's,* but Lukens uses the term to describe all comic American writers, starting with the colonial period.

46. Thorp, *American Humorists,* 19; Blair makes the statement in his introduction to *Mirth of a Nation* (xxi). The variant ("Funny Fellows") used in that 1983 anthology can be read as Blair's late acknowledgment of the inadequacy of "Literary Comedians" as a referent to a stable set of writers with a clearly definable tradition. Jennette Tandy in 1925 had used "The Funny Men" to designate some of her representative writers. Blair had used "Phunny Phellows" in 1978 in *America's Humor* as a nod to the fractured orthography favored by some "Literary Comedians" but had started out in 1937 with "Literary Comedians" in *Native American Humor,* which he kept for its 1960 revision. Brom Weber also referred to fractured orthography by entitling his essay "The Misspellers." I found no use of the term *Literary Comedians* before the misleading 1890 article by Lukens.

47. Sloane, *Literary Comedian,* 22, 8; Sloane, *Literary Humor,* 40, 19.

entertainment is therefore merely part of the show, an obvious facade for his low-brow manners and dubious profession, like the tawdry posters for his traveling menagerie. Nevertheless, Artemus Ward can reinforce status quo respectability. The difference from his Old Southwest brethren, especially Joseph Jones, lies in the way that the admirable portion of their natures are dramatized. Pete Whetstone's behavior signifies the potential for plain folks in a frontier setting to acquire the habits of the middle class. Joseph Jones embodies middle-class habits and values, an embodiment tantamount to an endorsement of democratic egalitarianism. Charles Farrar Browne's tactic for comically endorsing middle-class values involves set speeches by Artemus Ward. The declamatory quality of the endorsement fits a ringmaster's character; it also makes explicit and impossible to miss a surprisingly positive side of the usually rascally showman.

The decade after the popularity of Pete Whetstone and Joseph Jones, the 1850s, witnessed an unprecedented rise of the middling classes into a recognizable middle class in the United States. This background fact translates into an important emphasis on the values and perspectives of the middle classes in the work of many Literary Comedians, an emphasis usually not made with the Old Southwest writers due to the often inchoate quality of the middling classes along frontiers in the 1830s and 1840s. The endorsement of middle-class values found in Artemus Ward's set speeches, so much more explicit than the Old Southwest examples, symbolizes the emphatic presence of the new middle class in the 1850s. Nevertheless, an emphasis on a middle class in response to social circumstances should not be conceived as a rupture from the practices of the Old Southwest when discussing what is different about the Literary Comedians as the next generation of comic writers. Old Southwest writers portrayed the lower classes becoming the middling classes as well as the middling classes themselves. Indeed, Noland's and Thompson's Gentleman Roarers might have served as reminders to middle-class audiences of their humble origins. Thus David Sloane's emphasis on the role played by the middling classes is a difference of degree rather than kind.

Sloane also distinguishes the Literary Comedians by insisting on their rejection of the violence endemic to the Old Southwest tradition. However, that claim creates an overly neat distinction, too. Although the explicit linkage of aggression and laughter that the Old Southwest writers often represented has been generally eschewed by the Literary Comedians, they all did not genteelly eliminate comic uses of violence. Notably, Brown's best-selling comic character, Artemus Ward, fits into the theme of backwoods civility associated with the Gentleman Roarer.

As a local editor on the *Cleveland Plain Dealer* turned comic writer, editor of a well-known New York comic periodical called *Vanity Fair,* and a burlesque lecturer, Charles Farrar Browne could have been the perfect role model for Sam

Clemens as he aspired to be a professional funnyman. Several years before Clemens invented his wild and witty Mark Twain in Nevada, Browne's Artemus Ward had proved the feasibility of creating a comic figure who could both repel a mainstream audience and elicit its humoring approval. Browne also plays a particularly important role in understanding the comic background for Mark Twain because Artemus Ward so starkly portrays the oxymoron that organizes the features of the Gentleman Roarer. Browne relied on the technique of creating a dramatic encounter for his best work in *Artemus Ward: His Book*. A crude device, the technique induces two opposing responses from an implied reader, encouraging an oscillation from obvious ridicule of to clear identification with the character. As a showman, Artemus Ward bears a suspicious resemblance to Phineas T. Barnum, but the lampooning of Barnum remains a secondary comic effect. Despite lowbrow, even scandalous, behavior that includes an overt love of the bottle and a foolish eagerness for a fight, Artemus Ward serves as a mouthpiece for middle-class values. The simple formula of combining scalawag and spokesman made the showman enormously popular, allowing Browne to entertain the less discerning without completely giving up an attempt to hold the attention of the more demanding reader.

David Sloane's argument that Mark Twain should be placed into the camp of the Literary Comedians takes Charles Farrar Browne as the preeminent example of the group. Sloane's reading of the sketch, "Artemus Ward Sees the Prince of Wales," emphasizes the intelligent side of the showman, a figure who mirrors moderate American politics—democratic and genteelly idealistic, though conservative—politics virtually the same as Abraham Lincoln's.[48] Artemus Ward (and by extension the American people) can accept the prince as a good man because His Highness expresses a basic humanity and sense of egalitarianism that the showman has already dramatized in his encounter with the prince's snobbish bodyguard. In many ways, the Prince of Wales sketch best supports Sloane's contention that the Literary Comedians, in contrast to the Old Southwest writers, always engage with social issues.[49]

Nevertheless, there is more to the sketch. For instance, it begins by highlighting Artemus Ward's Barnum-like capacity for humbug and commercial fraud. The showman has been following the Prince of Wales through Canada and not

48. Sloane, *Literary Comedian,* 26, 28.

49. For the analysis of Browne's comic figure, I have consulted the original printings of his sketches in the *Cleveland Plain Dealer* and *Vanity Fair* as well as the revisions printed in his first book, *Artemus Ward: His Book.* Titles will be from the original periodical printings unless the title for the book has been significantly altered, when I will note both. Quotations are from the original printing unless the sketch was revised for the book or was written especially for the book. Then page numbers from an 1887 printing of the book are given.

making much money, despite playing British tunes like "Rule Britannia" and altering a wax figure to resemble the Governor General of Canada, Sir Edmund Head. When people complain that the figure does not look like Sir Edmund any more than it does anyone else, the waxworks owner replies, "That's the pint.... It looks like Sir Edmun Hed or any other man. You may kall it what you pleese.... *I* kall it Sir Edmun Hed."[50] Artemus Ward brags that he has exhibited the same statue as Napoleon, the Duke of Wellington, the Benicia Boy (James Heenen, a famous prize-fighter of the day), Mrs. Cunningham,[51] and "varis other notid persons." The comic cynicism of this expediency echoes a joke added to the initial Artemus Ward letter when it was revised for Browne's first book, a joke revealing the showman's habit of trimming morals to fit circumstances: "My perlitercal sentiments agree with yourn exackly. I know thay do, becawz I never saw a man whoos didn't."[52] If Artemus Ward mirrors the politics of moderate citizens on the eve of the Civil War, would those Americans feel comfortable being represented by the showman when he demonstrates, brags even, that he is devoid of scruples?

The answer would seem to be both yes and no, for Browne, in the Prince of Wales sketch, marvelously jumbles the best and worst of American morality. When the colonel who leads the prince's bodyguards calls Artemus Ward "audacious" for thinking he could simply walk up to the prince and say "hello" and then demands to know who he is, the answer both adumbrates democracy and hints at adultery: "'Sir,' sez I, drawin myself up & puttin on a defiant air, 'Ime a Amerycan sitterzen. My name is Ward. Ime a husband & the father of twins, which Ime happy to state they look like me. By perfeshun Ime a exhibiter of wax works & sich.'"[53] By first calling attention to his citizenship rather than giving his name, Artemus Ward emphasizes how democracy creates an identity for Americans. By identifying himself as a husband and father before revealing his profession, Artemus Ward emphasizes the middle-class values of a happy domestic life. However, the implication that not all husbands are equally happy with their children's appearances daringly undercuts that picture of domestic tranquillity by hinting at marital infidelity.

Though David Sloane mentions the burlesque quality of the sketch repeatedly and notes the vulgarity of the showman too, the stress in his analysis falls on Browne's ability to use Artemus Ward to symbolize a middle-class, egalitarian, American point of view about how people should behave. That symbolizing con-

50. "Artemus Ward Sees the Prince of Wales," 5.

51. Probably Augusta Cunningham, who was notorious for her association with a Dr. Burdell. See "Letter from a Side Showman," 5.

52. *Artemus Ward: His Book*, 38.

53. "Prince of Wales."

stitutes the serious intent behind whatever buffoonery animates the sketch, the satire against monarchy found when one peels off the burlesque wrapping. With this showman-as-spokesman role for Artemus Ward, Charles Browne can obtain for his character the approval of humorous laughter from an implied reader. Though Sloane's reading of the sketch is persuasive, it leaves out the kind of details represented by the versatile wax figure and the ambiguous comment on parentage, details that contribute to the scalawag aspect of the showman and thus would direct satiric laughter at the character. Moreover, even though other sketches support the point about Artemus Ward as a spokesman engaged with social issues, much more of the presentation of the showman, in the *Plain Dealer* as well as *Vanity Fair* phases of Browne's career, stresses vulgarity, dubious business ethics, and slapstick silliness. Spokesman for centric ideas and mainstream sentiments yet rascal businessman and low-class purveyor of humbug—Artemus Ward does not embody a straightforward ethical engagement with social issues.

The Artemus Ward character had first appeared in January 1858 in the *Cleveland Plain Dealer*. Browne held the local editor's post, responsible for a column entitled "City Facts and Fancies." Browne had come to the *Plain Dealer* from the *Toledo Commercial* late in 1857, where he had made a reputation as a jovial fellow and a genial wit. Frank Luther Mott has shown that, from the first, Browne's comic inclination enlivened the *Plain Dealer*'s columns.[54] A look through the paper even as the Artemus Ward letters are being published reveals a variety of comic efforts. For example, Browne spins a yarn about a butchered cow walking away from the butcher.[55] Another tale tells about an escaped hyena, and then, in the following weeks, Browne retracts the fantastic tale bit by bit.[56] The result was a local column that strongly foreshadowed the one Sam Clemens would later produce for the *Virginia City Territorial Enterprise*.

Creating Artemus Ward was apparently a spur-of-the-moment idea. Browne from time to time inserted letters from readers into his column, sometimes genuine and sometimes obviously not.[57] The latter includes a mock letter in tall-tale style from "Noggs Gogstopple" about the local problem with swill milk,[58] a scandal that the publisher Frank Leslie uncovered and had been pursuing in his New York newspaper for some time. Artemus Ward, "proprietor of the well-known sideshow," writes a letter to Browne the editor asking for a favorable notice of his show. The first letter signed "Artemus Ward," then, appeared to the contemporary

54. Frank Luther Mott, "The Beginnings of Artemus Ward."
55. "City Facts and Fancies: Remarkable Incident," 5.
56. "Hyena Loose in Paulding County," 5; "The Hyena—A Correction," 5; "Bad End," 5; "The Hyena," 5. All from the "City Facts and Fancies" column.
57. For an example of a "genuine" letter, see "City Facts and Fancies: Dear Local," 5.
58. "City Facts and Fancies: Swill Milk in the Country," 5.

reader in disguise, masquerading as a real letter to the local editor asking for help "to git up a grate blow" about his waxworks.[59]

This pretense allows Browne to create dramatic irony. Instead of editing the words of Artemus Ward, Browne allows the showman to speak. Printing the whole letter generously allows the supposedly real showman to deliver his own puff without restraint. That lack of restraint, however, also reveals the venality and hypocrisy of the showman's business practices. Those practices include promising to have his handbills printed at the newspaper in exchange for the puff: "Now mr. Editor scratch off [a] few lines and tel me how is the show bisness in your good city i shal have hanbils printed at your offis you scratch my back & i will scratch your back."[60]

Browne's irony cuts two ways. First, he satirizes unprincipled businessmen, a favorite target for ridicule by comic writers who used the figure of the Yankee peddler. Artemus Ward also clearly lampoons Phineas T. Barnum, the ultimate Yankee peddler and consummate showman, whose autobiography had been a publishing success only a few years before in 1855. In addition, the letter manages to satirize implicitly the unprincipled newspaperman, one who writes a glowing notice of a local event or coming attraction, a play or novel perhaps, as though his opinion were sincere, but who in fact has been paid. One editor reveals his venality by touting the show until Artemus Ward has his handbills printed elsewhere, when the showman becomes "a horery heded itinerunt vagerbone."[61]

Though Browne is willing to present the fact that some editors are as unscrupulous as the showman, Artemus Ward persists as the sharpest sharpster. A refrain throughout the first third of the original twenty-two letters to the *Plain Dealer,* as the showman supposedly wends his way toward Cleveland, is his promise to give the newspaper his handbill business in exchange not only for advertisement but even information about renting halls in town and rooms at local taverns. Artemus Ward repeats the promise so often one begins to suspect that it will come to naught. At least one of Browne's newspaper colleagues read the comic presentation of the showman as one that made such unethical behavior probable. By March 1858, Artemus Ward was so popular that someone impersonated the showman at a big masquerade ball in Cleveland. Commenting on the party the next day, the local for the *Toledo Times* joked that Artemus Ward "turned his back on the Plain Dealer Office, and got his handbills printed somewhere else." Browne reprints the joke in his local column for March 19, 1858.[62] The next day, Browne's column features the sixth Artemus Ward letter,

59. "Side Showman."
60. Ibid.
61. "Letter from Artemus Ward," 5 [February 15].
62. "City Facts and Fancies: The Masquerade," 5.

in which the showman complains about his "virtoo and repytashun" being endangered, though he blames a secret organization in Cleveland for any trouble.[63] Perhaps such "attacks" are why Artemus Ward suddenly bypasses Cleveland for Chicago, though he claims his change of itinerary happens because Cleveland does not appreciate the fine arts. The showman says he knows that the *Plain Dealer* editors will be disappointed about losing his business, but he also cleverly slides out of his commitment with flattery, saying the editors "hav soles abuv a few poltry hanbills."[64]

The local reporter of the *Toledo Times*, then, seems correct: Artemus Ward is perfectly capable of reneging on his business promises when it suits him. Indeed, the showman displays constant concern for his own welfare. Repeated even more often than his promises about giving his printing business to the *Plain Dealer* is the catalog of his show's attractions, his claim that they are a huge success wherever he is at the time, and his statement that he has been in the sideshow business for nearly twenty-two years. Like a Dickensian character identified with stock phrasing, Artemus Ward spouts one or more of these "facts" throughout his letters, regardless of whether their insertion is apropos. They complete the running joke about printing the handbills, for they turn all of the letters into handbills, free of charge. Browne wishes his implied reader to laugh at Artemus Ward the unsavory businessman, capable, like his lampooned model P. T. Barnum, of hoodwinking the unsuspecting, but he also complicates the ridicule through Artemus Ward's laughable compulsion to advertise himself. That compulsion constitutes the showman's "business humor," the basic comic element of the original letters. As a humorous exaggeration of the developing need for all businessmen to advertise, Artemus Ward might even draw a sympathetic identification from the businessmen in the historical audience, allowing them both to acknowledge the satiric element in the character and to humor his compulsion with a tolerant chuckle.[65]

Whatever tolerance Browne's readers had for Artemus Ward's business humor, however, the showman's behavior often undermines his role as a spokesman for middle-class folks. Browne has from the first pictured the showman as someone ready to manipulate the very idea of morality. The claim that wax figures and circus animals could furnish "moral" entertainment—a claim Artemus Ward constantly makes—is itself ridiculous and serves to point out

63. "Our Ward Correspondence," 5.
64. "Letter from Artemus Ward," 5 [April 17].
65. Stephen Fox says that advertising in antebellum America was considered "an embarrassment [like] the wastrel relative. . . . A firm risked its credit rating by advertising; banks might take it as a confession of financial weakness" (*The Mirror Makers: A History of American Advertising and Its Creators*, 15). Suspect patent medicines extensively used advertising in the 1850s. Pamela Walker Laird shows how that negative attitude had changed dramatically by the end of the 1860s (*Advertising Progress: American Business and the Rise of Consumer Marketing*).

that the fundamental humor of Artemus Ward is the business of making a buck. Establishing this humor as Artemus Ward's basic comic feature is Browne's chief strategy for creating a lampoon of Barnum, who made money with the same claims. This lampoon of Barnum also creates a running joke on a public that routinely proved its gullibility by patronizing Barnum's American Museum, where the theater shows "moral lectures" instead of plays.

As he first appeared to the reading public, then, Artemus Ward presented a figure of questionable morals. In his profession as a showman, he embodies suspicious business practices and promulgates entertainment of the lowest order, without moral uplift. His constant misrepresentation of historical figures in his show illustrates both his ignorance and his cynicism. His every utterance, with fractured spelling and grammar, demonstrates his low background. His misquotations of poetry and his use of stock "poetical" rhetoric not only exhibit his poor education, they also reveal his vanity about his small store of knowledge. Artemus Ward admits, even boasts, that he has no principles, yet he insists repeatedly that his show is a "moral" one. He is a confirmed scalawag.

In addition to being on the wrong side of the ethical equation, Artemus Ward appears in contexts that prevent any opportunity to be a sober spokesman on serious issues. The broad fun of the first several letters indicates that Browne's initial conception of Artemus Ward not only included venality and vulgarity. The showman is also plain silly. This slapstick side of Browne's early sketches involve the show's waxworks. In one letter, a member of the audience believes that the likeness of Judas Iscariot is alive, so he "made a lunge cross the table and seised Judus by the neck an dragged him out inter the middel of the haul and kommensed a poundin him."[66] In another, local wags break into the exhibit hall and rearrange and reclothe the waxworks so that, among other outrages, Washington resembles a working man and several apostles look like drunken sailors.[67] The wildest antics of the original *Plain Dealer* letters, however, occur in a sketch not reprinted in *Artemus Ward: His Book,* entitled "Our Local Heard From." Browne in this sketch imagines himself as a character in one of the showman's misadventures. The premise of the sketch's joke is Artemus Ward hiring Browne to impersonate a waxwork of Ben Franklin, but the local editor proves to be a poor employee. First, Artemus Ward tells about the problems he had boarding the train with Browne, problems that included the two of them mixing up and wearing each others' pants, then losing both pairs when a mob chases them as they are about to correct their mistake. Both without pants, they escape by riding underneath the railroad cars to reach the showman's hometown. Artemus

66. "Letter from Artemus Ward," 5 [February 27].
67. "Artemus Ward," 5.

Ward then relates how Mr. Browne has, since that fiasco, been an unsatisfactory substitute for the destroyed waxwork of Franklin because Browne starts "snickering every time any 1 sez 'franklin looks natral.'"[68] Through the slippery morality of Artemus Ward's business humor, and through the slapstick misadventures of the showman, Browne creates a comic figure fit for the ridicule of all.

And yet, as David Sloane argues, Artemus Ward can function as a voice for middle-class values. The crucial point, however, is that Artemus Ward performs as a *clownish* mouthpiece for middle-class values. One might grace the showman with the appellation "gentleman" in the newer American sense of the word because he articulates serious opinions held by mainstream folks, but Artemus Ward fits into a comic genealogy for Mark Twain because he consistently manages to subvert whatever respectable status he might claim. Several "dramatic encounter" sketches explicitly demonstrate this comic subversion. In them, Browne uses the showman both to portray behavior beyond respectable norms and to enunciate mainstream values. In each sketch, Artemus Ward encounters deviant behavior, triggering a speech in which he advocates behavior representative of social status quo.

Browne's reiterated advocacy of the value of hard work clearly underscores the mainstream nature of his satire in the encounter sketches. For example, the central criticism against a spirit rapper is his lack of bourgeois values, especially his refusal to work: "He dont do nobody no good & is a cuss to society and a pirit on honest peple's corn beef barrils."[69] In another example, the showman meets Lincoln, and Browne presents the reader with a comic exhortation about honest work. The satiric premise of the sketch revolves around the hordes of office seekers besieging President-elect Lincoln in his home. Browne pictures crowds so thick both in and out of the house that one enterprising man slides down the chimney to approach Lincoln while others already press in so close that they would have knocked him down if not for the intervention of Artemus Ward. After the showman prevents the president-elect from being knocked down, he clears the office seekers out of the house by threatening them with his boa constrictor. Before they leave, however, the showman gives them this advice:

> Go home, you miserable men, go home & till the sile! Go to peddlin tinware—go to choppin wood—go to bilin sope—stuff sassengers—black boots—git a clerkship on sum respectable manure cart—go round as original Swiss Bell Ringers—becum "orignal and only" Campbell Minstrels—go to lecturin at 50 dollars a nite—imbark in the peanut bizniss—*write for the Ledger*—saw off your legs and go round givin concerts,

68. "Our Local Heard From," 5.
69. "Artemus Ward among the 'Spirits,'" 5.

with techin appeals to a charitable public, printed on your handbills—anything for a
honest living, but don't come round here drivin Old Abe crazy by your outrajis cut-
tings up.[70]

In sketches satirizing free lovers and spirit rappers, Browne uses laughable clashes
between his showman character and these groups to dramatize their eccentric
nature.[71] In the Abe Lincoln sketch, the selfish office seekers receive the same treatment because they are people who do not represent the behavior of regular folks.

Browne also follows this basic strategy in a sketch on the Shakers. The oblig-
atory values speech that finishes the dramatic encounter sketch starts off by talking about the good points of the Shakers. Unlike the treatment given the free
lovers and women's rights advocates and spirit rappers, Browne allows the showman to acknowledge that the Shakers are honest and hardworking people. Nevertheless, he summarizes his judgment of the sect by saying that their life is
"unnatral, onreasonable and dismal."[72] The Shakers' basic fault is their denial of
"Human Nater," for the religion insists that there be no relationships between
men and women, including marriage.

The showman's sensible comments on the Shakers' repression of sexuality
have a particular force because of the manifest hypocrisy of Uriah, a Shaker elder.
During the course of the showman's overnight stay with the Shakers, Uriah
repeatedly calls Artemus Ward a man of sin, and near the end of the sketch Uriah
refers to Ward as a "base exhibiter of depraved monkeys and onprincipled wax
works." While the showman does display the base quality of his business humor,
asking what the wages of an elder are and how much his waistcoat costs,
"incloodin trimmins," his inevitable interest in money nevertheless remains but
a minor device to create a funny conversation. Moreover, the amorality of
exhibiting dubious waxworks fades when Artemus Ward discovers, upon coming downstairs to the breakfast table, Uriah and a female Shaker, "Huggin and
kissin like young lovers in their gushingist state." When the showman suggests a
suspension of Shaker rules in favor of a marriage, both Uriah and the woman
deny their desires: "'You must excoos Brother Uriah,' sed the female; 'he's sub-
jeck to fits and hain't got no command over hisself when he's into 'em.' 'Sartainly,'
Sez I, 'I've bin took that way myself frequent.' 'You're a man of sin!' sed the
Elder."[73] Uriah as an elder loses whatever moral authority he might command

70. *Artemus Ward: His Book,* 112, emphasis in the original; originally published as "Artemus
Ward on His Visit to Abe Lincoln."
    71. "Letter from Artemus Ward: He Visits Berlin Heights and Encounters the Free Lovers," 5;
"Artemus Ward among the 'Spirits,'" 5.
    72. "Artemus Ward on the Shakers," 95.
    73. Ibid., 95

over an itinerant showman when he repeats his formulaic charge against Artemus Ward. Uriah's hypocrisy is so well dramatized that a reader might be quite
ready to forgive the showman's attempts to kiss the young serving women immediately after this exchange.

If a contemporary reader can view Artemus Ward's business humor and sexual peccadillo in the Shaker sketch with humorous tolerance, he or she would
react even more favorably when the showman meets President-elect Lincoln.
The Shaker sketch allowed Browne a chance to move beyond the admonitions
of hard work he had made in the other encounter sketches to a consideration of
human nature. Similar to the encounter with the Prince of Wales, when Artemus
Ward meets Lincoln, Browne moves beyond specific social values and comments
upon the larger topic of democracy. The sketch with Lincoln makes its most
powerful statement about democracy by dramatizing the ridiculous nature of
the spoils system. Accepted by all parties as a natural consequence of a new
administration, the spoils system in 1861 was not only corrupt but also a dangerous distraction for a new president trying to hold the union together. The
selfish absurdity of the office seekers who crowd into Lincoln's house and the
help that Artemus Ward gives him endow the showman with a moral stature
rarely found in the letters. Any sense of the showman's usual foibles disappear
as he replies to Lincoln's question of how he can repay his kind help: "By givin
the whole country a good, sound administration. By poerin' ile upon the troubled waturs, North and South. By pursooin' a patriotic, firm, and just course."[74]
These sentiments could be endorsed by all who, in the spring of 1861, hoped for
a peaceful resolution of the constitutional crisis. The showman's advice to Lincoln culminates his spokesman role.

However, without denying the sometimes commonsense, even shrewd,
spokesman, one must also recognize Artemus Ward's disruptive behavior that
places him outside the social pale. The earlier analysis of the Prince of Wales
sketch outlined how Artemus Ward illustrates the mixture of satiric and humorous elements characteristic of the Gentleman Roarer. The spokesman for
middle-class, democratic values has a clear presence. And yet, not only does the
sketch open with an extended presentation of the showman's business humor,
but also Browne presents a buffoonish clash between Artemus Ward and the
prince's bodyguard that ends with a decidedly ambiguous assertion of domestic
tranquillity: "I'm a husband & the father of twins, which I'm happy to state they
look like me." The hint of his wife's possible infidelity undercuts the showman's
claim of being happily ensconced in domestic tranquillity. That hint represents

74. *Artemus Ward: His Book,* 112–13.

the less savory aspects of the Artemus Ward letters, which a second look at the encounter sketches reveals.

A list of darker characteristics could begin with comic violence and a fondness for liquor, but Browne also shatters domestic tranquillity with other hints at sexual transgression. Like Major Joseph Jones, Artemus Ward is married, but unlike Major Jones, no pastoral aura envelopes his household. Instead, Browne often includes comic scenes that reinforce the potential disruption of domestic bliss demonstrated by the comment on the paternity of the showman's twins. His sketch about the "Free Lovers," for example, portrays a woman who espouses free love behaving outrageously. When she sees the showman, she claims him as her "affinity," a term associated with the free lovers and used to indicate a natural soulmate. To the conventionally minded, "free love" and "affinity" also connoted illicit sex.[75] Artemus Ward protests that he is a married man, but the woman grabs him violently by the collar and swings her umbrella over his head, clutches at his arm, and shouts, "'You air mine, O you air mine.'" The showman shoves the woman away from him, and when the observing crowd of free lovers begins to shout "'shame'! 'beast,' etsettery, etsettery," Ward says, "'I was very much riled, and fortifyin myself with a spare tent stake, I addrest them as follers."[76] The image of the showman exhorting the free lovers to act morally and respectably while angrily brandishing a tent stake encapsulates the way that Browne's presentation of Artemus Ward delivers an ambiguous engagement with the social issues raised by the sketch. Moreover, the encounter is too brief for Browne to explore why the free lovers are wrong. The comic result includes as much simple burlesque and slapstick as satire, and within the overall farcical tone, Artemus Ward with his hysterical violence personifies a wild man as much as he represents a spokesman for the status quo. The showman's becoming "riled" may be justified, yet his violent reaction disrupts mainstream values.

The Shaker sketch features the most complex presentation of disrupted domestic tranquillity. Probably the most famous aspect of the group was their prohibition against marriage. In theory, no sexual activity exits in a Shaker community. This background allows Browne the opportunity to underscore the

75. Though the term *free lovers* had multiple meanings for various free-thinking groups, all rejected marriage (Joanne E. Passet, *Sex Radicals and the Quest for Women's Equality,* 2), which implied licentiousness for traditionalists (John C. Spurlock, *Free Love: Marriage and Middle-Class Radicalism in America, 1825–1860,* 158). Thomas Cook, who advocated his own alternative to marriage, the "love principle," defined *free love* as promiscuous sexual indulgence (Passet, *Sex Radicals,* 43). See Passet (*Sex Radicals,* 83–88) for reaction to the free lovers' community established in Berlin Heights during 1857–1858. Browne also ridiculed radical thinkers in his regular column when he judged the "Age of Freedom," which advocates women's rights, as stupid rather than morally harmful ("City Facts and Fancies: Berlin Heights," 5).

76. *Artemus Ward: His Book,* 70, 71.

ARTEMUS WARD'S
INNOCENT KISSES.
*VANITY FAIR,* 1861,
VOL. 3, P. 94.

hypocrisy of Uriah the elder while making his kissing a spinster the sketch's comic highlight. However, a second highlight to complement this older Shaker couple kissing is Artemus Ward kissing not one but two young Shaker women. The women agree to the showman's request for kisses after playing parlor games with him, the first hint that the Shakers' policy of repression did not work. The showman's flirtations may not be morally defensible, but at least he admits his weakness, and so a reader might agree with the showman characterizing the kisses as "innersent." In any case, when *Vanity Fair* printed·this sketch, the accompanying illustration shows Artemus Ward with an arm around each of the two women, kissing one on the lips as the other waits her turn. For *Vanity Fair,* the comic highlight clearly was the showman's "innersent" kisses.

The most notable part of the sketch, however, is the manner in which Browne dramatizes Artemus Ward's guilt about the kisses. After his dalliance, the showman retires for the night and dreams about running off with the young Shaker women. This frank admission of sexual desire has a comically violent end. Ward dreams that his elopement is discovered by his wife, who treats him to "a panfull of Bilin water" as punishment. A dream provides the perfect mechanism both to acknowledge the beast within and to dramatize Artemus Ward's ultimate conformity: he wants to run away with not one but two young women; he knows that he deserves to be punished for the wish. The violence of Betsy Jane's reaction completes the image of a domestic tranquillity disrupted.

The violence within that image dramatizes a struggle with the darker side of human nature symbolized by the Backwoods Roarer, with the figure's propensity to fight savagely. David Sloane differentiates the Old Southwest's from the Northeast's comic tradition by stressing the latter's disavowal of the violence endemic in the former. Taking Charles Farrar Browne as representative of the Literary Comedians, however, one must note how often that vow is broken. In a number of places in the sketches, Artemus Ward shows himself to be just as ready to fight as any Backwoods Roarer from the frontier of the Old Southwest. For instance, when Ward meets a man in a train car who will shortly prove to be a con man, the showman invokes the famous prizefighter James Heenan, known as the Benicia Boy. Ward stands ready to trade blows when the con man calls him obtuse: "'I kan . . . kave in enny man's hed that calls me a obtoos,' with whitch remarks I kommenst fur to pull orf my extry garmints. 'Cum on,' sez I,—'Time! hear's a Beniki Boy fur ye!' & I darnced round like a poppit."[77] When an editor denounces his show in print, Artemus Ward again declares himself ready to "pollish him orf ar-lar the Beneki Boy" before he thinks better of the idea.[78] In "Artemus Ward on Forts," the showman takes up a challenge from a man who tried to sneak into his tent, only to be thrashed. Browne even depicts the showman in a rough-and-tumble fight, complete with biting and kicking.[79] Artemus Ward wins the fight when he tosses his antagonist forty feet down a ravine. The shadow of the Backwoods Roarer even falls across "Artemus Ward Sees the Prince of Wales" when the showman alludes to eye-gouging in a rough-and-tumble fight, saying that the pompous bodyguard "puts on as many airs as tho he was the Bully Boy with the glass eye."

Browne portrays his showman as not always in control of his temper, and he also does not flinch from portraying the character as one who enjoys drinking, even though Artemus Ward often claims that circumstances force him. Origi-

77. "Artemus Ward Encounters the Octoroon," 5.

78. *Artemus Ward: His Book,* 79. Entitled "The Press" in Browne's book, this sketch is reworked from its original version, "Another Letter from Artemus Ward," the second in the series from the showman. The sketch's first half is the same as the original while the rest is new in the book. The pugnacious quotation comes from the second half, suggesting that Browne had no qualms about adding instances to the showman's violent behavior.

79. "Artemus Ward in the South: His Trials and Adventures," 251. The parody of the rough-and-tumble fight in this sketch was made famous by George Horatio Derby years before: "We held 'the Judge' down over the Press by our nose (which we had inserted between his teeth for that purpose), . . . while our hair was employed in holding one of his hands" (*Phoenixiana; or, Sketches and Burlesques,* 113–14).

ARTEMUS WARD DRUNK.
*VANITY FAIR*, 1860,
VOL. 2, P. 243.

nally in the *Plain Dealer* simply as "Artemus Ward,"[80] and retitled "Scandalous in Pittsburg" for the book collection, this sketch provides a good example of the comic tactic. The scandal is not drinking. Rather, "scandal" captures the showman's perspective when a set of young wags rearrange the wax figures and cause merriment among the customers. The outrage and humiliation are too much, driving Ward to drink in order to soothe his feelings, a parody of sentimentality. Similarly, the showman is riding in a railroad car when, "bein seized with a sudden faintness, [he] called for a drop of suthin to drink." Riled up by a temperance man who admonishes him, though not ready to take off his coat and invoke the Benicia Boy, Artemus claims that, "I never take anythin only when I really need it."[81] The illustration for another *Vanity Fair* sketch once again demonstrates the scandalous behavior the showman could embody: Artemus Ward sports a nose clearly discolored by drink.[82]

80. "Artemus Ward," 5.
81. "Artemus Ward on His Travels," 15.
82. "Artemus Ward on Forts," 243.

Details in other sketches add to the disreputable portrait of habitual drinking. Artemus is shown in his hometown of Baldwinsville, drinking in the tavern and yarning, while Mrs. Ward is having a baby.[83] When news of the birth reaches the tavern, the resultant chaotic reactions by various people provide the amusement for the rest of the sketch. In another, Browne had already made it clear that the showman enjoys his bottle. Ward's rum-soaked comments on New England women displace comic cynicism about patriotism and voting. The showman claims to drink infrequently but then launches into hilarious details about what happens to him after each of several glasses. If he seldom drinks, he apparently makes the most of the occasion.[84] One sketch has the showman talking as well as drinking like a Backwoods Roarer. Ward gets drunk because his organ grinder has died, acts like Sut Lovingood's daddy playing "hoss"—but with a canal boat—and ends up being kicked into the canal by the other horses pulling the boat, "yellin like a tribe of Cusscarorus savvijis."[85] While the portrayals of drinking reveal a showman as immoderate with liquor as he is with his anger, Artemus Ward's comment about admiring New England women—they "set my Buzzim on fire to look at 'em"—returns again to the struggle to control sexual desire seen in the sketch on the Shakers.[86] In the context of his disreputable behavior, the showman's drunken admission of sexual desire reinforces the theme of disrupted domestic tranquillity and suggests the repressed natural man.

The clearest picture of Artemus Ward speaking for mainstream values can be found in the dramatic encounter sketches, but within that picture, as shadows provide contrast, significant details contradict the role. As a lampoon of P. T. Barnum, Artemus Ward embodies a satire on ethically dubious business practices. Moreover, with his constant bragging about the superior nature of his show, its value as art and moral entertainment, and his frequent drinking and fighting, Artemus Ward evokes the Backwoods Roarer. And yet the showman upholds middle-class values by articulating egalitarian attitudes and moderate political principles, a contradiction that ultimately aligns him with the Gentleman Roarer. Claiming to be moral, the showman frequently dramatizes the opposite: "i startid out with the idear of makin my show a grate Moral Enter-

---

83. "Joy in the House of Ward," 5.

84. "Fourth of July Oration Delivered at Weathersfield, Connecticut," 5. Browne signaled his own fondness for drink with his famous reply to San Francisco's opera house owner Thomas Maguire, who had invited him to lecture in the West by asking, "What will you take for forty nights in California?" Browne telegraphed, "Brandy and water." When Browne lectured in Virginia City, his spree literally encompassed the town. The binge was legendary, according to reminiscences by Joseph T. Goodman ("Artemus Ward: His Visit to the Comstock") and William Wright ("Artemus Ward in Nevada").

85. "Artemus Ward on Forts," 243.

86. "Oration," 5.

tanement, but im kompeled to sware so much at that air infurnal Cangeroo that im frade this desine will be flustratid to some extent."[87] The showman's clownish defense of the status quo, simultaneously supporting and undercutting it with his positive and negative behaviors, demonstrates his comic affinity with David Crockett, Nimrod Wildfire, Pete Whetstone, and Joseph Jones. Linking these comic figures together as instances of the generic Gentleman Roarer exposes the arbitrary nature of the standard scholarly categories for organizing antebellum comic writers, "Old Southwest" and "Literary Comedians." The similarity of the examples and their existence before the appearance of Mark Twain reveal a ready-made comic stratum within antebellum popular culture upon which Sam Clemens could build his own laughable character. Moreover, the deeper theme expressed in this comic stratum, a backwoods (or backwards) civility, entailed cultural values and issues that still resonated when Clemens wrote "Journalism in Tennessee."

87. "Letter from Artemus Ward," 5 [July 10].

# Scene Three

THE COMMUNAL FUNCTION OF COMIC VIOLENCE

## SUT LOVINGOOD "PLAYIN' HELL"

"SUCKIT-RIDERS AM SURJESTIF THINGS TU ME. THEY PREACHES AGIN
ME, AN' I HES NO CHANCE TU PREACH BACK AT THEM. EF I CUD I'D
MAKE THE INSTITUSHUN BEHAVE HITSEF BETTER NUR HIT DUS."

GEORGE WASHINGTON HARRIS, "SICILY BURNS'S WEDDING," 1858, 1867

The affinity of the characters discussed thus far establishes a comic ancestry for
the initial version of Sam Clemens's literary alter ego, Washoe Mark Twain,
that could not be predicted by previous scholarship. The next candidate for this
surprising comic genealogy is George Washington Harris's Sut Lovingood. Like his
comic brethren, Sut Lovingood displays centric values ironically: in each case, a
lowbrow, even disreputable, figure can signify respectability. The expression of
respectability by Artemus Ward, the semiliterate, unethical showman, happens
directly, though in a very circumscribed manner, during his declamatory set
speeches. For the other characters in the genealogy, a "natural" gentleman's backwoods civility dramatizes respectability. Sut Lovingood not only replicates this last
tactic, but also dramatizes with his behavior what Artemus Ward speciously claims
as a showman of a "grate Moral Entertainment": a dissemination of morality. Sut's
comic antics thus function as a satiric force in his community.[88]

Like Pete Whetstone, Sut Lovingood occupies the lower end of the social scale
within his community. Raised in the lawless mountains near town, Sut has no
steady job and seems to spend all his time drinking whiskey and spinning yarns
about his own misadventures or about the practical jokes he plays on others. For
the respectable town folks, Sut embodies the unsanctified. Despite these Backwoods Roarer overtones, Sut can occupy the moral center of his community by
assuming the role of a preacher. However, Sut plays the role in comic fashion, as
"a nat'ral born durn'd fool," in his own words.

The symbolic center of authority in Sut's east Tennessee community is evangelical Christianity. As "a nat'ral born durn'd fool," Sut playfully evokes and
revokes this authoritative center with mock-preacher performances. To perform
his comic "sermons," he appropriates religious discourse.[89] The sermons' abiding

---

88. All the parenthetical page insertions in the following analysis refer to George Washington
Harris, *"Sut Lovingood. Yarns": A Facsimile of the 1867 Dick and Fitzgerald Edition.*

89. Compare to Milton Rickels's idea about Sut's relation to religion: "Sut exists outside Christianity" (*George Washington Harris,* 100). For background on religion in the antebellum South, see
John B. Boles, "Evangelical Protestantism in the Old South: From Religious Dissent to Cultural

theme centers on human nature, as he finds it both in himself and in his neighbors. However, this "preaching" does not represent a definable moral order, because a pursuit of freedom motivates everything Sut does. For him, license always trumps the law. Yet Sut weaves into his pleasure principle a notion of proper behavior, a notion that, while falling short of a true ethic, establishes a right and a wrong way to act. Thus all the tales in *Sut Lovingood: Yarns Spun by a "Nat'ral Born Durn'd Fool"* are about the creation or maintenance of community according to his foolish notion of proper conduct.[90]

An obvious example of Sut as comic preacher occurs in "Sut Lovingood's Sermon—'Ye Cat Fishe Tavern.'" When Sut rails against innkeepers as a herd of rascals, he frames his diatribe within the conventions of a church sermon, by announcing his text and by repeating it as a refrain. Very much aware he is acting the role of preacher, Sut jokes about his credentials by noting five "facts": he has no soul, he is a lawless fool, he has the longest pair of legs of any creature, he can drink more whiskey without falling over than anyone else, and he can get into and out of more scary scrapes faster than anyone else. This list parodies the boast of the Backwoods Roarer, but Sut is also ridiculing the lack of formal training that usually characterized Methodist and Baptist preachers of the antebellum period: "ef these . . . pints ove karactar don't gin me the right tu preach ef I wants tu I wud like tu know whar sum preachers got *thar* papers frum" (172–73). Sut's negative credentials comically comment on an age when any man with a religious turn of mind who felt the "call" would claim a right to preach. Sut demonstrates the requisite religious mind-set with biblical phrasing and direct references to the Holy Book, as he calls it (35). Appropriate to evangelical Christianity, nearly all the allusions refer to the Old Testament. Sut even mentions one of the most famous of the early evangelical preachers, Whitefield (262), showing a sense of history about the typical style of Christianity in antebellum east Tennessee.

Despite this apparent religious background, Sut has not "joined meeting," and he expounds anything but orthodox doctrine. His parodic fool's religion is as much folkish superstition as Christian tenet. Sut does acknowledge a basic division of sinners and saints, the unregenerate and the sanctified, but he does not

---

Dominance"; David Edwin Harrell Jr., "The Evolution of Plain-Folk Religion in the South, 1835–1920"; Donald G. Mathews, *Religion in the Old South;* and Wade Clark Roof, "Religious Change in the American South: The Case of the Unchurched."

90. Rickels (*Harris,* 78, 83, 86, 96) and Lynn (*Southwestern Humor,* 135–36) express a similar view about Sut's relationship to community and authority, one very different from mine. For a view much closer to mine, see David C. Estes, who not only names Sut as part of his community but also conceptualizes him as a "true pastor" ("Sut Lovingood at the Camp Meeting: A Practical Joker among the Backwoods Believers," 64). For a discussion of Sut's public role that uses the notion of playing hell in a different context, see John Wenke, "*Sut Lovingood's Yarns* [*sic*] and the Politics of Performance."

believe in the sense that he has experienced God's grace. His spiritual status in the community is summarized by the wanted poster Parson Bullen posts after Sut had interrupted his preaching by releasing lizards up his pant leg: "fur the raisin ove the devil pussonely, . . . an' a-makin the wickid larf" (48). Sut's willingness to mock, parody, and otherwise abuse religious discourse illustrates the nature of his belief in Christian doctrine: he believes as the blasphemer believes, negatively. Nevertheless, Sut's fundamental tenet matches identically with his community's orthodox Christianity: "univarsal onregenerit human nater" (245), people's arbitrary and mean-spirited enmity for each other. Antithetical to community, this enmity represents the basic transgression against Sut's idea of proper behavior. Against this manifestation of the unregenerate, Sut directs the force of his comic sermons, which usually consist of practical jokes.

Such scapegoating, however, does not constitute a morality, for Sut does not believe people will change. Rather, an impulsive desire to expose someone's pretense of being outside the basic fact of unregeneracy motivates him, for the postulate about human nature most emphatically includes Sut and provides the basic meaning of his constant reference to himself as a "nat'ral born durn'd fool."[91] When Parson Bullen says that Sut is "a livin proof ove the hell-desarvin natur ove man" (59), no one understands that better than Sut. What galls Sut is when people like Bullen act as though they are clearly exempt from the same statement. "Well, durn my rags ef gittin ove religun ain't the city ove rayfuge now-a-days; yu jis' let a raskil git hissef cotch, an' maul'd, *fur his dam meanness,* an' he jines chuch jis' es soon es he kin straitch his face long enuf tu fill the pius standurd" (274, emphasis added). Sut's "sermons" against meanness, however, do not erase his own obviously mean acts; comic sermons and mean practical jokes together illustrate the complexity of his role as fool, someone who both threatens and maintains the fundamental bond of community.

George Washington Harris provides the foundation to Sut's role as comic preacher by giving him the habit of using biblical allusions and by making the concept of universal unregeneracy a theme of several tales. Two other theological concepts are also prominent in Harris's tales and round out Sut's "religion":

91. In medieval and Renaissance traditions, a "natural" fool is someone who is mentally defective, an idiot. Sut is not an idiot in this sense, which makes him an "artificial" fool, acting foolishly for the entertainment and possible edification of others. See Heather Arden, *Fool Plays: A Study of Satire in the "Sottie";* Sandra Billington, *A Social History of the Fool;* Barbara Swain, *Fools and Folly during the Middle Ages and Renaissance;* Enid Welsford, *The Fool: His Social and Literary History;* and William Willeford, *The Fool and His Scepter: A Study in Clowns and Jesters and Their Audiences.* Rickels sees Sut as closest to this artificial or court fool (*Harris,* 105), yet he also thinks Sut personifies "mindlessness" (98). Noel Polk criticizes Rickels, saying, "Sut is not mindless and he is no fool" ("The Blind Bull, Human Nature: Sut Lovingood and the Damned Human Race," 150–51). See also M. Thomas Inge, "Sut Lovingood: An Examination of the Nature of a 'Nat'ral Born Durn'd Fool.'"

tribulation on earth and retribution in the hereafter.[92] In *Yarns*, retribution from God often means evoking the devil. For Sut personally, Satan is never far away, and when he dreams of things that frighten him, the list includes the devil and hell (69, 299). Sut's profound belief in the nearby presence of the devil matches the evangelical emphasis on the necessary justice of God. His attitude toward the devil, however, is more complicated than most. When Sheriff Doltin says Sut has "'play'd hell,'" and Sut replies, "'Folks generrlly sez that's my trade'" (259), clearly all concerned believe Sut to be a first-rate hell-raiser. Nevertheless, he can also sound so much like a true preacher, invoking hellfire and brimstone, that he loses his parodic function and occupies the symbolic center of his community.

One yarn in particular dramatizes this switching between the center and the margin of a community. In "Frustrating a Funeral," Sut demonstrates most completely his ability to play hell yet uphold traditional values, mimicking a preacher who invokes demons in a sermon to bring sinners to an awareness of their ways. Sut finds himself an uninvited mourner at the wake of a slave because one of the town doctors wants the cadaver for dissection. Sut wants to avoid digging up the grave, so he plans to substitute a drunk mourner for the corpse. However, a simple swap will not satisfy. He disguises Major, the drunken slave, to look like "a purfeck dogratype ove the devil, tuck while he wer smokin mad 'bout sum raskil . . . jinin meetin on his death-bed, an' 'scapin" (212–13). Complete with snakes and a pitchfork, the mortal remains of Seize also resemble the Evil One. With Major installed in the coffin, Sut commences his exhortation of sinners, using Seize.

First, he victimizes Simon, known for preaching among his fellow slaves. At the moment Simon sees the "skeer makin mersheen" (213) Sut has made of Seize, Sut "imitates" the devil's voice and accuses Simon of stealing corn, which Sut had witnessed. In a panic, Simon falls out the door, faints, and then runs off. More victims follow, including Mr. Hunnicut and Mrs. Loftin, symbolically figured as adulterers when Sut, via Seize, tells Mrs. Hunnicut he saw the two "way up in the air, ridin a-straddil ove a burnin ladder" (218). Both Mrs. Hunnicut and her cook believe the sign, the cook saying that she "know dis tree munf Missis Loftin fotch de debil heah" (219). When Major wakes up in the coffin on the way to the cemetery, he frightens not only all those in the procession but also (with the help of Sut's voice) the doggery keeper and the sheriff. The doctor Sut supposedly helped becomes a special case in Sut's list of sinners because, Sut says, a look at Seize "wud take away [the doctor's] appertite fur grave-yards . . . an' mout even

92. The example here focuses on Sut's version of retribution only. For a more complete discussion of Sut as a comic preacher, see James E. Caron, "Playin' Hell: Sut Lovingood as Durn'd Fool Preacher."

make him jine meetins. I cudn't tell how much good hit mout du the onb'lever" (214). "Frustrating a Funeral" reads like a deliberate effort on Sut's part to "preach a sermon," in this case using artful representations of hellfire to chastise sinners. Nevertheless, Sut does not lose an essentially playful attitude about his own behavior. Finishing up the grotesquely comic tale, Sut says he performed two Christian duties: one, he buried Seize; two, he "minister'd ontu Wright's doggery, an' run hit till . . . hit went dry" (226). This presentation of religious discourse typifies Sut as mock preacher, for the joke enwrapping the pious sentiment undercuts any sense of moral intent. Sut is not a parson *manqué* but a parson *malgré lui*.

As comic fool, Sut has a license to flout order, and his antics target secular as well as sacred law. Throughout *Yarns* this flouting produces ironic results because Sut's role as comic preacher functions to maintain community values. However, such improper maintenance would not be necessary if officials, such as preachers and sheriffs, behaved properly. In Sut's mind, phony sheriffs are indistinguishable from phony parsons. The intertwining of sacred and secular law occurs in a number of places in *Yarns*. The issue is hypocrisy, or the *appearance* of respectability. Stories told about preachers and sheriffs emphasize their hollow respectability and undeserved pride. Pride threatens a democratic community because it stresses a holier-than-thou attitude. This theme is evident in "Rare Ripe Garden-Seed," the first in a trio of stories (also including "Contempt of Court Almost" and "Trapping a Sheriff") that collectively narrates the downfall of the local sheriff, John Doltin, unmasked as an adulterer.

Sut's homespun backwoods dialect rewrites the religious discourse of *Yarns*. Thus tribulations become "skeers," while original sin and the consequent unregeneracy of human nature become "dam meanness." The enmity entailed in meanness and pride threatens community by emphasizing strife and separateness. Because these sins epitomize human nature, *Yarns* apparently argues against the existence of grace, which Sut would define as a neighborly attitude that binds people into a community. The numerous examples of adulterous couples justifies this gloomy conclusion. How authentic can a community be when its backbone—the family—is represented by so many shams? Though *Yarns* emphasizes negative behavior for comic purposes, an example of an admirable family does exist in the persons of Susan and Wirt Staples. The Stapleses represent grace and salvation, the possibility of people who transcend mean-spirited behavior and unneighborly pride.

My use of theological vocabulary, especially transcendence, seems to make Susan and Wirt saints. They are of course as unorthodox an example of a worthy family as Sut is a preacher. A whiskey-soaked boast by Wirt makes clear that he is a Backwoods Roarer (250–51). Susan proves to be as fun-loving and as eager to unmask damn meanness as Sut, given her role as the architect of Sheriff Doltin's punishment. As comic saints, Wirt and Susan do not stretch their faces to fit the dour mold of what passes for piety, nor do they pretend to abjure the body while in fact indulging it illicitly. Instead, descriptions of them suggest their physical beauty, Wirt with the strength typical of the Roarer (253) and Susan "es purty es a hen canary" (260). Significantly, Susan's good looks are accompanied by a good nature that contrasts with the other beautiful woman of *Yarns*, Sicily Burns, a good nature manifested in Susan's demeanor, especially toward Wirt: "She aint one ove yure she-cat wimmin, allers spittin an' groanin, an' swellin thar tails 'bout thar vartu. She never talks a word about hit, no more nor if she didn't hev eny; an' she hes es true a heart es ever beat agin a shiff hem, . . . a-smilin an' a-flashin her talkin eyes lovingly at her hansum husbun" (260, 262).

Susan and Wirt's love represents the ties that bind not just family life but the neighborly life of a true community. Sheriff Doltin's adulterous behavior cuts those ties, for he only pretends to live as a neighbor, a pretense dramatized by his answer when Wirt asks what Doltin is doing trying to kiss Susan: "'Yer—yer wife got her coatail tangled in the briars, an' I wer jis' in a neighborly way *ontangling her*'" (264–65). Doltin revises the rule "love thy neighbor" to "love thy neighbor till her husband comes home."

When parsons and sheriffs, pillars of communal law and order, enact disorder, the chaotic punishment that Sut constructs for them represents just deserts. The license of the fool is especially effective at revealing licentious behavior, and as self-proclaimed fool, Sut comically inverts what is already inverted when he appropriates the role of these so-called upholders of the law by righteously dol-ing out justice for their transgressions. This inversion becomes obvious in Sut's use of comic deadpan to mimic piety, for example, in a retort to Mrs. Rogers, who implicitly accuses Sut and his friends of stealing her eggs and butter by sarcasti-cally noting that their presence near her springhouse is not the holding of meet-ing. In a mock-pious fashion, Sut claims that Hen Baily has been poisoned by Mrs. Rogers's dairy products (thus confirming her worst fears) when in fact he has swallowed turpentine and a live lizard: "Sez I, mouns'us solimn, straitenin mysef up wif foldid arms, 'Missis Rogers, . . . take a look at sum ove yu're work. That ar a-dyin feller bein; let jis' a few ove yer bowils melt, an' pour out rite yere in pity an' rey-morse'" (205). Sut not only uses deadpan to counter her reference to the crowd's unsanctified status, but he also implies a rebuke for her notorious habit of feeding her workhands with buttermilk so sour "hit wud eat hits way outen a yeathen crock in wun nite" (206). Always conscious of such mean-spirited acts, Sut stands ready to chastise their perpetrators, which confirms what Sicily Burns's mother says when she claims that Sut is not "one half es durn'd a fool es ole Burns, an' ten times more ove a Cristshun than [Parson] Clapshaw" (105).

When Susan prepares a supper for Wirt and Sut after they have planned how to trap Sheriff Doltin, the three at table become a community of comic saints. Sut refers to the meal as "a rale suckit-rider's supper, whar the 'oman ove the hous' wer a rich b'lever" (261). In laughable fashion, the dinner provides that exact scenario. Sut assumes the role of the preacher, served a lavish repast by a household that believes in his comic dogma, which states that the mean-spirited and hypocritical shall be punished or, as Sut puts it, initiated "intu the seekrit ove home-made durnashun" (263). The supper, lovingly recounted by Sut in copious detail, constitutes meeting for the "saints" Susan and Wirt and Sut. In keeping with the comic principle of reducing spiritual and moral values to a material plane, the supper functions as a parodic communion supper, celebrating not what bread and wine might symbolize but celebrating instead the material symbols themselves, food and drink.

"He who would become wise must persist in his folly." William Blake's proverb of hell is particularly apt for Sut Lovingood, who dispenses his own kind of perverse wisdom when he demonstrates that his self-proclaimed epithet, "a natural born damned fool," applies to everyone. As Blake in *The Marriage of Heaven and Hell* sought to overturn conventional wisdom about how to lead a spiritual life, Harris uses *Sut Lovingood: Yarns Spun by a "Nat'ral Born Durn'd Fool"* to challenge those who are complacent about their rectitude. Sut playing hell as a comic preacher reminds his community that the apparently obvious boundary between the respectable and the disreputable is not so clear as convention would claim. Sut's comic sermons expose the facade of the nominally respectable, as Sheriff Doltin's manifest hypocrisy and the doctor's attempted desecration testify.

Apparently acting as nothing more than a trickster agent of the pleasure principle, Sut playfully disrupts communal order. The disruption, however, ultimately upholds communal values. In so doing, Sut Lovingood's "sermons" parallel Artemus Ward's set speeches on middle-class values. Symbolizing the center of his community as a preacher while living on its margin as a wild mountaineer, Sut manifests the oxymoronic nature of the Gentleman Roarer, rooted in the contradictory dynamic of comic barbarity. Moreover, by comically dramatizing the requirements for maintaining a community true to its own principles, Sut Lovingood demonstrates his affinity with traditional sacred clowns.

## WILLIAM WRIGHT'S DAN DE QUILLE AS CITIZEN CLOWN

I TRUST SUCH OF MY SILVER CITY FRIENDS AS MAY FIND SOME OF THEIR
LITTLE PECULIARITIES TOUCHED AT [IN THIS SKETCH] WILL TAKE IT ALL
AS GOOD-NATUREDLY AS IT IS MEANT—THAT I WOULD, ON NO ACCOUNT,
KNOWINGLY WOUND THEIR FEELINGS THEY CAN REST ASSURED.

———

DAN DE QUILLE, "ANOTHER STRIKE," *GOLDEN ERA*, MARCH 24, 1861

Sam Clemens's review of *Sut Lovingood: Yarns*, written in 1867 during a visit
to New York City, demonstrates his familiarity with Harris's comic creation
before and after his time on the West Coast. However, Clemens also had a more
readily available model in his *Enterprise* colleague, William Wright, whose work
at times foreshadows the porous boundary between serious reporting and comic
fictionalizing found in sketches signed "Mark Twain." Wright's character and
alter ego, "Dan De Quille" is the final candidate for Mark Twain's comic genealogy. Unlike the other predecessors, Dan De Quille does not display centric values and dramatize respectability ironically as a lowbrow, even disreputable,
figure. His status as a newspaper reporter instead endows him at the outset with
a gentleman's profession. However, when the base desire of greed gains an upper
hand, the resultant comic antics, like Sut Lovingood's, function as a satiric force
in his community. Exhibiting a feverish desire for mining stocks, Dan De Quille
demonstrates how Sut's behavior as "a nat'ral born durn'd fool" can be transferred to Comstock mining communities.

William Wright exemplifies the frontier style of journalism favored in the
mining districts of California and the Nevada Territory. A reporter first, yet ready
to employ the fictional techniques of scenes and dialogue, Wright blurred the
genre boundaries between newspaper report and comic sketch. The "breeziness"
of this style, that is, its willingness to personalize the news and to be playful about
objectivity, signified not a disinterest in accurate information on the part of his
readers, but rather a willingness to tolerate newspapermen who were indulging
their humors. Nowhere is this breezy frontier journalism better manifested than
when Wright inspected a mine and reported on its operations and prospects.
Though few subjects could be more important to their readers than the current
state of a well-known mine or the latest details of a new discovery, Wright could
deliver his reporting on the subject not only with the intimacy of personal correspondence, but also with the flourishes of a comic sketch, complete with scenes
and dialogue. Wright's "The Wealth of Washoe: A Day in the Silver Mines" illus-

trates how he could transform the role of newspaper reporter by projecting a sharply etched character defined in part by comic techniques.

Dan De Quille resembles a comic narrator from Augustus Longstreet's *Georgia Scenes*. Like Longstreet's Baldwin, Dan De Quille maintains a distance from the plain folks he visits, the miners in the report. His walking stick symbolizes a gentlemanly demeanor, but his status and its consequent social distance is most readily apparent from a use of high-culture language, including several instances of French phrasing, archaisms such as "anon," and Latinate words such as "perambulating" and "procured." Quotation marks also signify social distance, bracketing miners' slang (such as "keep a doin' of it")[93] and rendering their speech as dialogue separated from the narrative voice.

Also like Longstreet's Baldwin, Dan De Quille does not have the gentleman's aloofness entailed in the *cordon sanitaire* concept. The more cultured status of both narrators, signaled by a facility with elevated language, may allow for laughter at the uneducated, but the narrators are also capable of participating in the ruder world. For example, Dan De Quille employs descriptions using western comparisons: someone has "grizzly hair, standing erect as the bristles of an ireful coyote" (124). Moreover, Dan De Quille employs self-directed jokes about his fear when descending ladders, and the best comic scene happens at Dan's expense. He and his companion stow themselves into a mining car on tracks in order to descend deeply and swiftly into another part of the mine. Packed "as a pair of sardines [complete with] my chin *hooked* over his head" (129), the two men at the conclusion of the ride remain "lying as still as a pair of pet kittens" for so long that the miners watching explode into "loud laughter" (130). Dan De Quille, then, has a gentlemanly exterior and literate vocabulary, yet nevertheless can joke about his fear of being in the mines and can use everyday language, too. The change in status of Dan's walking stick represents the unexpected complexity of this portrait, so correct when he meets the publisher of the *Golden Era* early in the piece, yet so awkward— an actual impediment—when investigating the mines later. Throughout all, Wright's character gives clear details of mining operations and pertinent information about its management. Shareholders and potential investors could learn much from the report. Casual readers would be pleasantly entertained.

Despite his reputation as the *Enterprise* reporter adept with "figures, measurements and solid facts," as the writer ready for "cast-iron" items, William Wright could also match Sam Clemens with his comic fancy. Wright shows how extravagant that fancy can be in one of the first sketches he published after returning to Nevada late in the summer of 1863 from a vacation. Entitled "Petrified! or, The

93. Richard A. Dwyer and Richard E. Lingenfelter, *Dan De Quille, the Washoe Giant: A Biography and Anthology,* 126. Other references will hereinafter appear in the text.

Stewed Chicken Monster," the sketch has as its premise everyone back home in Iowa feeding Dan De Quille nothing but stewed chicken after he confessed that he "felt a hankering after stewed chicken and crab apple sauce" (158). Comically echoing the gothic psychology of an Edgar Allan Poe tale, Wright has Dan De Quille so anxiously obsessed by all the stewed chicken everyone wants to feed him that he dreams every night about tunneling mines into mountains made of stewed chicken. Dan then dreams that his invariable diet of chicken and apple-sauce has petrified him. Buried, discovered a thousand years later, and exhibited Barnum-style as a curiosity, Dan becomes so incensed by a lecture about him that his anger revives him. He then violently grabs the professor by the hair. The cli-max comes when he is awakened by his wife, whom he has attacked in his sleep, dreaming she is a member of the professor's audience whom he has kicked into a chandelier.

As a reporter transformed into a narrator of comic sketches and fantasies, Dan De Quille provided a model for Washoe Mark Twain. As a comic character, Dan De Quille fits into the gallery of Gentleman Roarers that form a comic genealogy for Mark Twain. Most notably, in three sketches Wright composed for the *Golden Era,* Dan De Quille does for Silver City what Sut Lovingood does for his locale, Ducktown: demonstrating to members of his community through his foolish behavior that they are foolish, too.

The initial example forms a large section of the first letter Wright sent to the *Golden Era* after returning to the West Coast from his vacation in Iowa. The let-ter has some account of Dan De Quille's journey to Washoe from San Francisco, but that factual aspect is overshadowed by the satiric scenario Wright creates when Dan, hearing about the mining boom during the summer, imagines him-self rich from stock holdings in his Pewterinctum mine: "Yes, we gave ourself up to pleasing thoughts of the probable value of our full, whole 'undivided interest' in said favorably located vein of mineral bearing rock." When the president of the mine greets Dan as he descends from the stagecoach in Silver City, the images of wealth assume a grandiose proportion: "Our full and undivided interest has made us a Rothchild, an Astor, a Vanderbilt, a Sam Brannan—in short we are a Pewterinctum nabob! All our late visions [of] mills and glittering bars flashed up again and danced in dazzling array before our eyes. Our whole frame appeared to be rapidly expanding. We felt at least twelve inches taller than our usual altitude." When the president, who sways enough while walking to doubt his sobriety, opens his mouth to speak, he talks not of fabulous wealth found but of assessments owed. Dan De Quille declares his amazement to be beyond words: "We hasten to bid adieu to the subject."[94]

94. "Our Washoe Correspondence: Letter from Dan De Quille," 1 [September 20].

In an earlier sketch for the *Era,* entitled "Washoe Pictures: Another Strike," Wright had already used Dan De Quille to satirize a miner's unquenchable dream of suddenly becoming rich. In this instance, Wright spins an exaggerated and fictional account of what must have been typical behavior in the Nevada and California mining districts, making fun of the crazed behavior caused by the overpowering thought of striking it rich. The basic joke in the sketch comes from the contrast between Dan De Quille and his friend Jones. Though Dan pretends to be calm in the face of the mining prospects on the Comstock, while he claims that Jones remains in a constant state of excitement, their behavior is exactly the opposite. Jones remains calm, even laconic, in his conversation as well as restrained in his actions, while Dan De Quille cannot stop talking and cannot sit still for very long in his cabin, just thinking about what the latest news might be from the mines. Because a torrent of words from Dan De Quille dominates the sketch, Jones can barely squeeze in two sentences. Wright masterfully uses dramatic irony, Dan De Quille revealing his true impetuous nature by constantly talking while at the same time asserting that the staid Jones is "too easily excited" (137) and should emulate Dan's supposed composure. The effect is a comic equivalent of Robert Browning's "My Last Duchess."

Because he is so skittish, Dan De Quille rushes to town when Jones tells him about the latest claim of a rich strike because he hopes to buy or trade for a few "feet" (shares) in the discovery. Dan meets several of his friends, who all have feet in the new mine, but they all respond negatively to the repeated inquiry, "*A—m I i—n?*" Increasingly desperate, Dan tries to acquire shares in the new strike by offering to trade shares from older mines, but no one will accommodate him, so captivated are they by the sensation and prospects of the new discovery. The sketch establishes a strong sense that the mine's novelty, its mere prospect of rich ore instead of proven quality, drives people to hold onto shares in it. Dan practically admits as much when he says that he is ready to trade shares in his best mine "just that I may say I'm in" (142). Even meeting another friend, Spudder, who scorns the new strike as a "Little ticky upstart, new-fangled gimcrack" (143), cannot assuage Dan's fear that he is the only one left out of the dazzling new prospect. Spudder's drunken state and his touting of another mine, however, only suggest how unreliable all offhand mining reports are and therefore how foolish it is to rush about buying or trading shares in them before any real work has been done. The implied moral of sensible behavior in the midst of general folly clearly appears when Dan De Quille returns home defeated. Jones then tells him that he has a full share in one section of the new mine and intended to give Dan half before he rushed off, blinded by a vision of riches.

In another fictional sketch, Wright had also ridiculed the feverish quality of people under the influence of a new strike, but in this instance he also uses Dan

De Quille to comment on the violence routinely exhibited in the mining districts. The violence at the end of "Petrified! or, The Stewed Chicken Monster" pales compared to "Our Washoe Correspondence," a comic extravaganza that begins with Dan De Quille so bored that he has been kicking everything in his cabin for a week: "if something in the line of news don't transpire shortly, you will hear of *some man* getting badly whipped—I *won't* stand it much longer and I *will* kick some feller" (114, original emphasis).

The desire to have anything happen to break his boredom transforms into a comically savage need for violence. The desire escalates past a hope for a fight that will produce "six, at least, shot or cut to pieces" and engulfs Dan De Quille's tender feelings for a young lady. Meeting her as he heads to town, he projects his exasperation onto her in a fashion worthy of Mark Twain in "Those Blasted Children" or in his more savage moments in the American travel letters or in his later "Facts Concerning the Recent Carnival of Crime in Connecticut." "She now comes running out to meet me—I feel for my revolver but haven't got it; so I give her a look so savage as to cause her hair to stand straight up on her head, and hurry on" (115). The news from a friend that Dan's Pewterinctum mine has struck a rich vein is not enough to relieve his emotion. Instead, it causes more rage because he had hoped to hear about a fight. Even tossing his friend out of the saloon plus throwing a Chinese man and his laundry basket over an embankment and through a canvas roof does not calm him down: Dan picks up a rock and waits in the street for the young lady to reappear. When she does not, he returns to his cabin and stands on his head in the corner for three days and nights. Then he feels better. However, only starting a fire in the mouth of a mining tunnel the next day finally purges his need for violence. The sketch ends with the whole town of Silver City in chaos because a new strike causes people to stake mining claims on every street in town. Dan defends his portion of the new strike by building a fort and procuring muskets. After two days, he sells out to a man from San Francisco for cash. Satirizing the Comstock mining towns' reputation for violence and the crazed speculation in mines by their populations could not be more outrageously funny. Dan De Quille in these sketches embodies the controlling humors of the community of Comstock miners that William Wright wants to ridicule. In doing so, Wright reminds readers in his community of their excessive behaviors and their need to do better.

As a writer with a solid West Coast reputation well before Sam Clemens joined the staff of the *Enterprise,* William Wright produced all manner of work in many genres. As a seasoned correspondent for newspapers and literary periodicals, Wright was an obvious model Clemens could use to help evaluate the scope available to him once he joined the staff. Similarities between the work of William Wright and Sam Clemens are striking, especially when they are writing out-of-town correspondence for periodicals other than their home base, the *Territorial Enterprise*. Both men moved easily along a spectrum of writing newspaper correspondence from straight factuality to wildly comic sketches. Wright invented a comic sidekick, Spudder, well before Clemens created Mark Twain and his first partner in laughs, "the Unreliable." Specific comic tricks, such as interrupting himself or digressing from the main subject, as well as specific comic targets of Wright's, such as bad musicians that deserve a thrashing (119), all suggest how much Sam Clemens might have "borrowed" from William Wright to build his comic character Washoe Mark Twain.

Like Sut Lovingood, Dan De Quille functions as would a traditional sacred clown, comically dramatizing improper behavior to remind his mining community how it ought to behave. In a democratic and modern society, one might call such figures "Citizen Clowns." The satire embedded in this role necessarily includes a self-deprecating humor because its foundation, the Gentleman Roarer, structures the Citizen Clown as oxymoron, both fool and fool killer. By ridiculing his participation in the community's foolish behavior about mining, Dan De Quille, like Sut Lovingood, knows he is a natural born damned fool and thus no better than his fellow citizens.

Breathing Virginia City's semiurbanized, semi–mining camp atmosphere, Sam Clemens manifested the generic Gentleman Roarer in a form similar to Dan De Quille, as an apparently responsible newspaper reporter who often behaved like an uncouth Comstock miner. As an unsanctified newspaper reporter, Washoe Mark Twain also played hell with communal values, enacting the symbolic drama of a Citizen Clown.

# Act Two

## WASHOE MARK TWAIN

# Scene One

SAM CLEMENS CLOWNING ON THE COMSTOCK

## FIGHTING WORDS

WE ARE TO BLAME FOR GIVING "THE UNRELIABLE" AN OPPORTUNITY
TO MISREPRESENT US, AND THEREFORE REFRAIN FROM REPINING TO
ANY GREAT EXTENT AT THE RESULT. WE SIMPLY CLAIM THE RIGHT TO
*DENY THE TRUTH* OF EVERY STATEMENT MADE BY HIM IN YESTERDAY'S
PAPER, TO ANNUL ALL APOLOGIES HE COINED AS COMING FROM US,
AND TO HOLD HIM UP TO PUBLIC COMMISERATION AS A REPTILE
ENDOWED WITH NO MORE INTELLECT, NO MORE CULTIVATION, NO
MORE CHRISTIAN PRINCIPLE THAN ANIMATES AND ADORNS THE
SPORTIVE JACKASS RABBIT OF THE SIERRAS. WE HAVE DONE.

MARK TWAIN, "[AN APOLOGY REPUDIATED]," *VIRGINIA CITY ENTERPRISE,*
AUGUST 4, 1863

On Sunday morning, May 29, 1864, Sam Clemens boarded a stagecoach leaving Virginia City, Nevada Territory, destination San Francisco. He had quit his job as a reporter for the *Virginia City Territorial Enterprise* only days earlier. By his own account, Clemens was leaving but two quick steps ahead of the law, wanted for violating a statute about dueling. Should Clemens have been arrested, no doubt exists that he would have been found guilty of violating at least the spirit of the law, for a challenge had been issued more than a week before by Samuel L. Clemens to James Laird, editor-in-chief of a rival newspaper, the *Virginia City Daily Union.* Evidence to prove the violation would have been easy to obtain. Clemens had permitted his newspaper to publish, on Tuesday May 24, his reiterated challenge, along with Laird's persistent refusal. By posting him as a coward in so public a manner, Clemens had hoped to force Laird onto the field of honor. The duel never happened, so Clemens technically was not a fugitive. He and his friend Steve Gillis, a foreman and compositor for the *Enterprise* who had acted as his second, left in the light of day, accompanied by Joe Goodman, editor-in-chief and part owner of the *Enterprise.* No real danger of arrest probably ever existed; the statute against dueling was honored mostly in the breach. Goodman was himself an example of lax enforcement, having fought a duel the previous fall with another editor of the *Daily Union,* Tom Fitch. Goodman had wounded Fitch in the leg, giving him a lifelong limp. Goodman's recollection of Sam Clemens's departure from Virginia City clearly indicates that the mood on the stagecoach was anything but apprehensive. Goodman had only intended to ride "a little way out on the Geiger Grade; but the company was too good and I kept clear on to San Francisco."[1]

When Sam Clemens quit Virginia City, never again to make his home there, he was leaving behind not one but probably three aborted duels. How did he manage such a feat? By being a master of raillery. He had first joked in his local column about a rumor that money raised by prominent Carson City women for the Sanitary Commission Fund (the forerunner of the American Red Cross) was being diverted to "a miscegenation society in the east." The next day he ribbed the staff of the *Virginia City Daily Union* by wondering in an editorial if their pledges to the Sanitary Fund would ever be redeemed. Such behavior in itself was not remarkable. For more than a year, Sam Clemens had established a reputation in the Nevada Territory, as well as in California, by aggressively teasing and ridiculing folks, mostly in the columns of the *Territorial Enterprise,* under the pseudonym "Mark Twain." Several people this time around, however, were insulted, not amused. Perhaps one could not joke about issues related to the Civil War, especially in the West, where the populace remained deeply divided about the war's prosecution. Perhaps the problem came from the fact that, for some people, the gibes about the Sanitary Fund were only the latest outrage perpetrated for laughs by Mark Twain, who functioned as literary alter ego to Sam Clemens but who could also metamorphose into a fictional comic character. In any case, the rejoinders to his raillery were clearly intended as insult, were taken so by Clemens, and the formal challenge followed (CL 1:287–301).

In approximately fifteen months of Mark Twain's print existence, so much of his comic personality had consisted of teasing people that an eighteenth-century English writer like Joseph Addison would have said he had a "humor for raillery." By May 1864, Clemens, in the guise of his comic alter ego, had made fun of nearly all of the important men in the Nevada Territory and California. Sam Clemens had also used his Mark Twain pseudonym to give a fellow newspaper reporter a derisive nickname, "The Unreliable," and then proceeded to fabricate comic stories about his uncouth behavior. These tales were immensely popular and did much to propel Mark Twain's career on the West Coast. The humor of teasing and raillery had been evident even before Clemens began signing his newspaper work "Mark Twain." A well-known instance of his early comic pieces, "The Petrified Man," had as a principal target for laughter a coroner, G. T. Sewall. Also, the most well-known of his writings after inventing Mark Twain and before the

---

1. Quoted in Chester L. Davis, "Goodman's Assistance on the Biography," 4. For versions of the events, see Samuel L. Clemens, "How I Escaped Being Killed in a Duel"; MTA, 1:350–60; Tom Fitch, "Fitch Recalls Mark Twain in Bonanza Times"; and Leland Krauth, "Mark Twain Fights Samuel Langhorne Clemens's Duel."

Sanitary Fund imbroglio, "A Bloody Massacre near Carson City," worked in some teasing jabs at individuals along with its main satiric attack on the crooked business habits of mining companies. Baiting the *Union* staff about their Sanitary Fund pledges and the Carson City ladies about the disposition of their money for the fund thus constituted standard behavior for Sam Clemens, also known as Mark Twain. Clemens the *Enterprise* reporter could claim to be a nominally respectable and reliable member of his Virginia City community. His behavior as the unsanctified Washoe Mark Twain had shown otherwise. Moving to San Francisco would not deter his humor of raillery, but why did it derail Sam Clemens's career at the *Enterprise*?

Fighting duels was not the sufficient condition for what amounted to an expulsion from Virginia City. The relentless nature of the raillery must also be factored into the equation. For readers of the *Enterprise,* Washoe Mark Twain's humor of raillery meant that Clemens's literary alter ego resembled an uncouth miner and behaved as an irresponsible journalist. Both figures were enough to disturb a respectable social order. In addition, Washoe Mark Twain's raillery acquired its force from the theme of backwoods civility, with its comic violence and cultural barbarity, that had complicated antebellum popular culture. The symbolic violence entailed in the humor of raillery evoked a wild frontier. Symbolic comic violence inevitably draws strength to offend and to disrupt from literal forms of violence, like dueling. Civilized communities circumscribe or forbid both symbolic and literal violence, yet Virginia City had previously tolerated duels and laughed frequently at the antics of Washoe Mark Twain, no doubt because the town routinely behaved in uncivilized ways, flaunting a carnival license without an expiration date. The civic but not always civil atmosphere of Virginia City was thus also a factor.

## VIRGINIA CITY CARNIVAL

"WHAT DISEASES DO [THE PEOPLE IN NEVADA] DIE OF MOSTLY?"
WELL, THEY USED TO DIE OF CONICAL BALLS AND COLD STEEL, MOSTLY,
BUT HERE LATELY ERYSIPELAS AND THE INTOXICATING BOWL HAVE
GOT THE BULGE ON THOSE THINGS, AS WAS VERY JUSTLY REMARKED BY
MR. RISING LAST SUNDAY. I WILL OBSERVE, FOR YOUR INFORMATION,
WILLIAM, THAT MR. RISING IS OUR EPISCOPAL MINISTER, AND HAS
DONE AS MUCH AS ANY MAN AMONG US TO REDEEM THIS COMMUNITY
FROM ITS PRISTINE STATE OF SEMI-BARBARISM.

———

MARK TWAIN, "WASHOE—INFORMATION WANTED," *VIRGINIA CITY
ENTERPRISE,* MAY 1864

Comic laughter vocalizes what Plato called playful malice. When an individual laughs, he or she expresses the aggression of that playful malice, redirected within a play domain.[2] Framed by the play domain's boundaries, mock aggressive behaviors like tickling and teasing simultaneously curb and allow the expression of potentially dangerous aggression. The same dynamic of containment and license structures carnival on a social level. Any society expects its members to behave in general conformity with its customs, rules, and laws. This ordinary behavior manifests society's status quo and indicates that the individual wishes to be considered a serious member of the group. "Carnival" in an abstract sense expresses a desire of a very different sort, a desire to be free from the necessity of conformity, a desire to exchange the stasis of ordinary life for the flux of some extraordinary existence. Many cultures have institutionalized this carnival desire, hedging it within the temporal boundaries of a festival. During this festive time, expressions of dangerous behaviors are given license. In effect, carnival creates a frame around itself that signifies pleasure and play. The sense of relaxation from the customs of ordinary life created by a carnival-style festi-

2. Plato's phrase is also translated as "comic malice"; see "Philebus," 436–40. Reckford, *Old-and-New Comedy,* 449–51, 461–67, shows how ancient Greek *kōmōidia* (comedy) is linked to such behaviors. Ethological studies of animals discuss "smiles" in relation to aggressive, bared-teeth displays and the complex of behaviors called "agonistic" (Owen Aldis, *Play Fighting;* Klaus Immelman, *Introduction to Ethology*). Insofar as comic laughter is concerned, its implied aggression is always playful. Playful aggression is practically the same as aggressive play. The link to other animals suggests how deep-seated is the tendency for humans to be playful and aggressive (see James E. Caron, "From Ethology to Aesthetics: Evolution as a Theoretical Paradigm for Research on Laughter, Humor, and Other Comic Phenomena," 251–57).

val is conducive to comic laughter. For Mikhail Bahktin, comic laughter virtually signified carnival.[3] That sense of relaxation also often spawns excessive displays of behaviors that are usually strictly controlled. Eating becomes feasting, and drinking alcoholic beverages becomes debauched revelry. Often the sense of temporary liberation created within the carnival play frame results from simple inversions of ordinary social forms and behaviors, transforming the usual social world into its reversed image.[4] In industrial societies since the nineteenth century, such deliberate efforts of re-creation have been weakened, their traditional communal excesses tamed and diluted to the simple leisure time of an individual's family.

Somewhere between cultures that officially sanction carnival license and cultures that have replaced such license with the diluted modern form known as leisure existed the relatively unrestrained frontier culture of Virginia City, as well as other mining towns along the Comstock Lode during the boom time of the 1860s. Mark Twain, in his earliest phase, Washoe Mark Twain, embodies the aggressive playfulness of that frontier mining culture.[5] The frontier community represented by Mark Twain was based on who was eligible for citizenship, not on an opposition of indigenous people versus Euro-American pioneers or on a notion of "ethnicity" (such as Chinese laborers versus white settlers). Ideas about citizenship within the newly created Territory of Nevada were modeled on states already in the union, which meant that the frontier community of citizens along the Comstock was de facto overwhelmingly white and male. "The boys," a phrase appearing in Mark Twain sketches and in the correspondence of Sam Clemens, is a colloquial designation for this sense of the Virginia City community. Given the fact that "the boys" living in Virginia City were often less than respectable, the unsanctified behavior of Mark Twain compromising the ostensible respectability of Sam Clemens mirrored civic dynamics.

Started as a mining camp on the Comstock lode, Virginia City in 1860 boasted about 2,500 permanent residents. By the fall of 1862, the population was nearly 4,000, but during the boom year of 1863, inhabitants numbered 25,000, earning

3. Mikhail Bakhtin, *Rabelais and His World.*

4. Barbara A. Babcock, ed., *The Reversible World: Symbolic Inversion in Art and Society;* Robert Dirks, *The Black Saturnalia: Conflict and Its Ritual Expression on British West Indian Slave Plantations;* John G. Kennedy, "Bonds of Laughter among the Tarahumara Indians: Towards a Rethinking of Joking Relationship Theory"; Emmanuel Le Roy Ladurie, *Carnival in Romans;* Arthur R. Radcliff-Brown, "On Joking Relationships."

5. I use "frontier" here in a relatively narrow sense, one that acknowledges but moves away from a larger debate among historians between a Turnerian construct and a less Anglo-centric narrative of continental conquest suggested by the term *borderland.* For the recent debate about frontier, see Jeremy Adelman and Stephen Aron, "From Borderlands to Borders: Empires, Nation-States, and the Peoples in between in North American History."

Virginia City the title "Queen of the Comstock."[6] Clemens during that boom year notes five stone and eighty-seven brick houses to accompany nearly three thousand wooden structures (MTCall no. 2). When Clemens lived in Virginia City from September 1862 to May 1864, the town boasted a combination of frontier and cosmopolitan living made extravagant by the silver and gold mines tunneled beneath it. Paved with low-grade refuse rock, the streets literally spangled with gold and silver.[7] Only San Francisco could rival Virginia City as the preeminent metropolis in the far west. Ubiquitous reminders of wealth transformed Virginia City into a place where disregard of the usual boundaries for behavior flourished, a place where wild-eyed speculation and incessant practical joking blended with routine violence and rampant vice to produce an ambience of intoxicating freedom. According to one historian, Virginia City at night possessed "an atmosphere more reminiscent of gaudy carnival than of a stable industrial community."[8]

This characterization applied to Virginia City's daytime atmosphere as well. The fabulous wealth created by the gold and silver mines allowed conditions of living unmatched in other frontier environments. Whereas the usual pioneering efforts of farmers and merchants required years of steady industry to succeed, the ever-present possibility of becoming rich overnight created a mood of giddy speculation and feverish haste in which the virtue of sober work seemed all but lost.[9] Charles Putnam, who worked on the *Enterprise* with Clemens, recalled that during the boom of 1863 everyone was "flush" and all mining ventures were financed.[10] The story of Sandy Bowers and Eilley Orrum, the Comstock's first millionaires, provides a legendary example of striking it rich. Eilley was given ten "feet," or shares, in the Gold Hill section of the Comstock lode as payment from a customer in her boardinghouse. When the mine struck it rich in 1863, Eilley joined her shares with ten more owned by a boarder, miner Sandy Bowers, when she married him. Their shares paid out $10,000 a month for three years, with a peak of $20,000 a month.[11] Mr. and Mrs. Bowers decided to make a grand tour of Europe while at the same time building a mansion near Washoe Lake that would eventually cost $400,000. The farewell banquet for the couple at the International Hotel in Virginia City was legendary for its munificence.[12] With such a

6. Grant H. Smith, "The History of the Comstock Lode, 1850–1920," 28; Bancroft, *History*, 168; Richard G. Lillard, *Desert Challenge: An Interpretation of Nevada*, 211; George D. Lyman, *The Saga of the Comstock Lode: Boom Days in Virginia City*, 219.

7. Paul Fatout, *Mark Twain in Virginia City*, 57; Effie Mona Mack, *Mark Twain in Nevada*, 183.

8. Elliott, *History of Nevada*, 147.

9. Sam P. Davis, ed., *The History of Nevada*, 238; Arthur McEwen, "In the Heroic Days," 15.

10. Charles A. V. Putnam, "Dan De Quille [William Wright] and Mark Twain," 3.

11. Lillard, *Desert Challenge*, 212; Lyman, *Comstock Lode*, 252.

12. Bancroft, *History*, 171n69; Mack, *Nevada*, 198–200.

good luck story as a goad, thousands of miners could always believe their turn would come with the next day's dawn.

In mining camps, the de facto laxity of a frontier invites every species of violence, chicanery, and vice to flourish. William Wright once made much of the dangerous presence of derringers in a letter to his hometown. Rollin Daggett, another *Enterprise* colleague, remembered Virginia City as a rough camp and "the boys [as] pretty wild fellows." A William Wright sketch portrays the boredom of his comic character Dan De Quille because no one has been killed recently. However, Virginia City was relatively peaceful before the boom year 1863 when the level of violence dramatically escalated. Grant Smith says that the number of homicides in 1863 equaled the total of the previous four years—thirteen—as well as the subsequent four years. Killings in the town then became so frequent they gave rise to the slang expression, "having a man for breakfast," that is, reading about the event while taking the morning repast. The *Gold Hill News* editorialized: "the past few months have been a season of murders and other heinous crimes, almost without parallel in the experience of even the blood-accustomed people of California, who form the great mass of our community."[13]

The *News* in the same issue reprints an item stating that "ruffianism runs rampant in this community."[14] Despite this hand-wringing, many citizens appeared indifferent to murder. When a man in Virginia City was killed in a billiard saloon about four o'clock in the morning, the corpse remained where it fell until nearly noon, the billiard players continuing to play by stepping around the body.[15] In April 1863, Clemens interrupts a letter he is writing to his mother in order to investigate "five pistol shots down [the] street," and he reports the fatal results for two police officers (CL 1:246). Later, the *Gold Hill News* reprints an item from the *Enterprise* about a thirteen-year-old boy stabbing a Chinese man with a bowie knife. The item also tells of a ten-year-old boy with a derringer. William Wright referred to such events as "the devil at large." On December 3, 1863, the *News* again reprints the *Enterprise,* this time about robberies: "So many robberies have occurred on the Carson road, between the New York House and Empire City, that it is with no great feeling of security that the bravest men nowadays travel that part of the highway." The day before, the *Gold Hill News* quotes Mark Twain on the crime wave: "The Carson reporter for the *Enterprise* [Clemens was in Carson reporting the Constitutional Convention], speaking of recent robberies and murders on the road, says: 'Our energetic officers are growing incensed at these

13. William Wright, "Utah Correspondence," 4; Rollin M. Daggett, "Daggett's Recollections," 15; William Wright, "Our Washoe Correspondence," 8 [February 24]; Smith, "Comstock Lode," 35; *Gold Hill News,* "Popular Discontent," 2.

14. *Gold Hill News,* "More Complaining," 2.

15. Mack, *Nevada,* 189.

repeated outrages in sight of town.'"[16] Virginia City obviously contributed to the image of a Wild West that the popular press created for the inhabitants of the settled United States.

With violence as endemic background, chicanery and vice occupied the middle perspective in a portrait of the frontier Comstock. Anything approaching the steadiness and order of family life in Virginia City constantly competed with the town's carnival behavior. Especially during the 1863 boom, various forms of licit and illicit industry composed Virginia City's commerce. An assortment of saloons, gambling houses, poolrooms, and hurdy-gurdy dance halls coexisted with a Chinese district infamous for opium dens and with an extensive red-light district where "prostitution flourished openly."[17] As a whole, Virginia City manifested "every form of vice, and all kinds of degrading amusements."[18] Nevertheless, "in back of the carnival city was another community of churches, schools, fraternal organizations, and homes, where family life was probably not much different from that experienced in communities of similar size elsewhere in the United States."[19] A letter published shortly after Sam Clemens's death made the same point: "It was always a sore point with Nevada people that [Mark Twain] should represent them as wearing pants in their boots, pistols in their belts, and using the most fearful and unheard-of slang; when in the Bonanza mining days Nevada was filled with cultured and refined people."[20]

The geography of the town literally replicated this division between the respectable social world (given voice by the shocked *Gold Hill News* editorial quoted above) and the demimonde. Starting with the commercial center on C Street, everything up the slope of Mount Davidson remained respectable, while the area below C Street did not.[21] The division could also be seen in the difference between daylight activities and what transpired between dusk and dawn when "hundreds of miners, underground all day, emerged from their holes to line the bars and clump over dance floors in small hot cellars with hurdy-gurdy girls."[22] In 1863, William Wright asserted that two hurdy-gurdy houses known to breed trouble routinely "should be shut up."[23] The clear boundary between the respectable and the scandalous suggested by daylight versus nightlife activities

16. *Gold Hill News,* "Social Improvement," 2; William Wright, "Our Washoe Correspondence: Letter from Dan De Quille," 8 [September 27]; *Gold Hill News,* "Rumored Murder and Robbery," 3; Samuel L. Clemens, [Energetic Officers], 3.

17. Elliott, *History of Nevada,* 146; see also Mack, *Nevada,* 185.

18. Bancroft, *History,* 172.

19. Elliott, *History of Nevada,* 147.

20. George Wharton James, "Mark Twain and the Pacific Coast," 132.

21. Lillard, *Desert Challenge,* 211; Mack, *Nevada,* 183–84.

22. Fatout, *Virginia City,* 73.

23. Wright, "Letter from Dan De Quille," 8 [September 27].

was illusory, however. Excessive drinking, for instance, happened without constraint.[24] The town's geographic containment of the disreputable proved no less illusory, with the Sazerac Saloon on South C Street functioning as an unofficial headquarters for leading citizens.[25] Pete Hopkins's Magnolia Saloon in Carson City, which shows up in "A Bloody Massacre near Carson," functioned similarly for the territory's politicians.[26]

However, one activity above all blurred the distinction between sober and carnivalesque behavior: speculation in shares of mining stocks. Hubert Bancroft states that wild speculation accompanied the opening of the first Comstock mines. Even working miners often owned stock so that the madcap frenzy typifying stock exchanges during a boom and bust cycle engulfed nearly all the white male population.[27] A letter in a newspaper at the height of the 1863 boom said: "The streets of Virginia City are literally crammed with crazy people who talk incoherently about 'feet' when most of them have no other feet than those they stand on." The *San Francisco Journal* in October 1863 notes that San Franciscans are also mad with speculating.[28] One minister prayed during a service that a certain stock's price might rise so that the church could pay its debts.[29] The previous chapter showed how William Wright ridiculed even his own propensity for mad speculation. He characterized its psychology in his retrospective account of the so-called Big Bonanza: "When the people *en masse* start in to buy stocks they—to use a very elegant illustration—shut their eyes and rush in like a hog going into battle. They exhibit startling vigor, activity, and enthusiasm for a short time, but the moment they stop to 'get their wind,' that moment they are in a fit condition for a panic. The least thing now startles them, and they . . . turn tail with a snort and make for the canebrakes."[30]

The second result of the Comstock mines opening, Bancroft says, was "endless litigation."[31] Lawyers like William Stewart made fortunes from lawsuits against mining companies, such as *Chollar v. Potasi*, which lasted from 1861 to 1865 at a cost of $1,300,000.[32] The *Gold Hill News* once suggested that inquiring about pending litigation would be a cagey strategy for finding good stocks: if none existed, the stock was worthless.[33] Bancroft might well have added a third result: endless

---

24. McEwen, "Heroic Days," 15.
25. Mack, *Nevada*, 182, 194–96; Fatout, *Virginia City*, 72–74, 141.
26. Mack, *Nevada*, 194–95.
27. Bancroft, *History*, 121, 130.
28. Fatout, *Virginia City*, 57, 58.
29. *Gold Hill News*, "Another 'Feet' Story," 4.
30. William Wright, *The Big Bonanza*, 367.
31. Bancroft, *History*, 121.
32. Lillard, *Desert Challenge*, 223.
33. *Gold Hill News*, "A Sure Indication," 3.

manipulation of mining companies' stock. A favorite tactic was "freezing out" small investors by assessing them with fees so often they are forced to sell.[34] Freezing out stock owners enabled bigger players to buy at a lower price, which translated to instant profit if a new strike in the mine was imminent but only certain people knew about it—not an unusual situation. Mine owners were known to keep the men in the tunnels overnight when a new strike was made so that the owners could buy up stock before the word got out. One story told about the lengths to which people would go concerns a stockbroker who took a job as a miner and always carried a bottle of emetic. When a strike occurred and the miners were held below ground, he took the emetic and was sent home. His wife, under cover of going for a doctor, went instead to the telegraph office and bought stock.[35]

Another favorite tactic was "cooking" the stock's dividend, that is, issuing a false dividend to inflate the worth of the stock.[36] At times the cooking was done with plenty of "salt," which meant loading a barren mine with melted bullion. An early Nevada joke about such "salting" told of a claim buyer who, after seeing the assay report, remarked that the ore was as good as that of the Comstock lode. The seller replied: "It ought to be. I got it from there."[37] Another bogus method of inflating the value of a mine was assaying the richest ore dug from one section of a mine and then declaring its value representative of the entire mine. In all these maneuvers, once the stock climbs sufficiently to make a big profit, the manipulators sell.

The *San Francisco Dramatic Chronicle* reported on an Englishman disgusted with Virginia City because he had been cheated by stockbrokers there. At one of the town's restaurants, when the waiter suggested sage hen, the Englishman turned it down, saying, "D—n anything with wings that will stay in such a country."[38] Chicanery entangled with routine business practices brought forth the following diatribe from another visitor to Virginia City in 1863. Writing home to San Francisco, he suggested that if California could be called the vestibule to hell, Nevada should be considered the throne room of Pluto himself:

> I have seen more rascality, small and great, in my brief forty days' sojourn in this wilderness of sagebrush, sharpers, and prostitutes, than in a thirteen years' experience of our squeamishly moral State of California.
>
> The principal occupation of the denizens of this God forsaken angle of creation seems to be the administering to one another of allopathic doses of humbug, which

34. Bancroft, *History,* 122.

35. Lillard, *Desert Challenge,* 222–23; see also Fatout, *Virginia City,* 54, 58.

36. Lyman, *Comstock Lode,* 246.

37. Lillard, *Desert Challenge,* 221; see also *Gold Hill News* articles on salting mines and freezing out investors: "Salting," 2; "Freeze Out," 2; "The Old Thing," 2.

38. Lillard, *Desert Challenge,* 37.

are received with an air of gravity and relish which betokens an abiding and universal faith in their virtue. God help me! I have never seen such a land before. . . . Mammon is the god of their idolatry, and slavishly submissive to the behests of their demon-lord are all his wretched worshippers. . . . If I resided here six months I should turn out a consummate rascal.[39]

Aided by few regulations on stockbrokers or exchanges and abetted by court-room practices that routinely included tampered juries, bribed judges, manu-factured evidence, and false witnesses, business with Comstock mining companies often consisted of "giving the business" to suckers.[40] Moreover, the plenitude of warnings issuing from newspapers did not deter people from becoming victims.[41] The allure of striking it rich proved too strong. Like a new hat deliberately tossed in the midst of an uproarious carnival celebration, cau-tion was thrown to the wind by otherwise sedate folks.

The ubiquitous nature of stock speculation and its accompanying giddiness had a curious parallel behavior: people developed the habit of playing practical jokes. Late in his life, Clemens mentions the boyish quality of practical joking and its approbation in the Nevada mining camps (MTA 2:305–6). Effie Mack suggests that no people enjoy playing jokes on one another as much as those liv-ing on the frontiers. "In the absence of organized amusement, they had to make their own fun, and particularly did they enjoy horseplay."[42] "The boys" in Nevada mining camps indulged often. After a battle with Native Americans in 1860, one of the men returned to Virginia City with an arrow in his rifle's muzzle from which dangled a scalp. Everyone gave the man all the whiskey he wanted for his part in the fray until they learned he had taken the souvenirs from a dead brave.[43] One evening, when a drunk stripped off his shirt in the street and began holler-ing for Bill to "come out," individuals in the crowd that quickly gathered took turns calling out, "Here he is," and spinning the would-be boxer about, much to everyone's amusement.[44] The boys working for the *Enterprise* typified this imp-ish joking. Just before Sam Clemens joined the newspaper, it was being pub-lished on A Street, a shed attached to the main building serving as kitchen, dining room, and bunkhouse. The cook at the time became so neglectful of keeping the food free from bugs and mouse hair that he was finally fired, and when other cooks proved unsatisfactory too, the men scattered to different boardinghouses.

39. Fatout, *Virginia City,* 90, 93; Lillard, *Desert Challenge,* 224.
40. Lillard, *Desert Challenge,* 223; Davis, *History of Nevada,* 238.
41. Fatout, *Virginia City,* 18–19, 59–60.
42. Mack, *Nevada,* 144.
43. Lyman, *Comstock Lode,* 118.
44. *Gold Hill News,* "Ludicrous," 3.

Before that dispersal, however, the *Enterprise* staff often invited a friend or acquaintance to dinner to see if his stomach could stand—not the food itself and what might be found in it—but the yarns about what had been supposedly found at previous meals.[45]

All types of jokes were rife. *Enterprise* colleague Alf Doten would pretend to new acquaintances that "Mark Twain" meant ordering two drinks on credit, which Clemens supposedly did frequently. Some months after William Wright had returned to Nevada from a vacation, he and Sam shared rooms, and their *Enterprise* visitors were always ready to play a joke, rigging buckets of water to fall on them when the door opened or setting up bells to ring in the middle of the night. One evening Clemens and Wright returned to their rooms, opened the door, and were startled to see a huge man menacing them with a sword. When they called on him to surrender and received no answer, they suddenly realized the "man" was a dummy holding Sam's Japanese sword.[46] *Enterprise* printers supposedly hid Sam's lamp shade whenever possible just to hear him swear.[47] A favorite tale often repeated involves a fake meerschaum pipe. In one account, Sam was told that the staff wanted to give him a new pipe, and the joke turned on having Sam pretend surprise at the gift and deliver an "extempore" speech; in another version, the goal was to have him discard his favorite pipe, one so odoriferous it was called "the remains."[48] Perhaps the most outrageous joke played on Clemens involved a fake robbery, staged after Sam had delivered a comic lecture in Virginia City and was given a fancy gold watch.[49]

Of course, Clemens had his moments on the other end of the joke. Calvin Higbie, to whom Clemens dedicated *Roughing It* and who was a partner in a mining venture with Sam and Orion Clemens before Sam became a newspaper writer, relates the joke Sam played on him the day they met. Returning home from a day's work on another mining claim, Higbie said that "a total stranger rushed up and began shaking hands cordially," declaring that he was moving in with him.[50] Clemens managed to talk Higbie into letting him stay without mentioning Orion's letter of introduction, which explained that Sam would help

45. Mack, *Nevada*, 208.

46. William Wright, "Salad Days of Mark Twain," 13. The tale from Doten is printed in Joseph Goodman, "Joseph Goodman's Memories of [Mark Twain the] Humorist's Early Days," in a separated space on page 2 entitled, "Recollections of His [Sam Clemens's] Life Here." The Doten story should be compared with the one Paul Fatout found in the *Nevada City (Calif.) Transcript* of February 22, 1866, which has the same idea of two drinks marked down on credit (*Virginia City*, 36).

47. McEwen, "Heroic Days," 15.

48. William Wright, "Reporting with Mark Twain," 174; Alf Doten, "Early Journalism in Nevada, Part II," 183; James, "Pacific Coast," 118.

49. Wright, "Reporting," 178; Doten, "Journalism, Part II," 182.

50. Michael J. Phillips, "Reminiscences of Mark Twain by His Partner, Calvin Higbie," 69.

Higbie work on their joint mining claim. Perhaps the ultimate joke was the fact that Clemens never did any work on their claim.

Remarkably, this habit of joking behavior pervaded the highest levels of government in Nevada. Before Charles Farrar Brown, the most popular comic writer and performer of the day, left the Comstock after a stop on his 1863 western tour, Governor Nye signed a document, complete with official seal, appointing the funnyman "Speaker of Pieces to the People of the Nevada Territory."[51] However, the Nevada Territory's best claim to having the most jokers per capita must rest on the strength of its unique institution, the so-called "Third House":

> This strange institution of Carson City appeared in 1862 and lasted at least seven years. It is, apparently, without a parallel in American history. Intended by its prankster founders to burlesque the processes and results of popular legislation, it met informally, in rear rooms, saloons, the schoolhouse, the Presbyterian Church, the Assembly itself. Legislators, lawyers, hangers-on, and townsmen made up the membership [who] made fun of governors' messages, proposed absurd bills, told lies, punned, played tricks, baited prominent politicians, and "elected" state officials.[52]

During the final shenanigans of the Third House for the 1864 legislative session, Sam Clemens helped present a giant wooden comb to an elected official, William Claggett, who was famous for his unruly hair.[53]

Extravagant behavior to accompany extravagant wealth—the Comstock way of life meant that much of the Virginia City community did not mind blurring the ordinary boundaries of morality. The mines' potential for enormous wealth encouraged an extravagance of gesture, as the Eilley Orrum and Sandy Bowers story illustrates. Hard work in the mines translated into equally hard play. The prodigality of the miners at their play established a community tolerant of vice on a scale out of proportion to the respectable population. Thus the background for Sam Clemens inventing his earliest version of Mark Twain featured an unspoken carnival license for playing in all manner of ways at all hours—not just nighttime gambling and whoring, drinking, and opium smoking, but also the day-and-night mania for becoming rich that unhinges reason and opens a Pandora's box of trickery. Without this atmosphere of reckless carnival, Washoe Mark Twain with his penchant for aggressive comic raillery could not have flourished.

Like tickling and the teasing of raillery, carnival behavior properly takes place within a play domain, its otherwise antisocial aspect licensed by that domain.

51. Richard G. Lillard, "Studies in Washoe Journalism and Humor," 83.
52. Ibid., 11; see also CL 1:272–73.
53. Dave Basso, ed., *Mark Twain in the "Virginia Evening Bulletin" and "Gold Hill News,"* 62.

Unlike tickling and teasing, true carnival also has a sanctioned time frame. If carnival had no specific time frame, its excessive but playful behaviors would be forbidden by community leaders, fearful of unlimited disruption to social order. The same antipathy could apply to any person whose clowning and foolish behavior embodied the carnival spirit. Unless a community perceived such a figure as operating within a sanctioned play frame and bounded by a specified time period, he could not be consistently understood as comic. The respectable portion of a community would not laugh at such a clown but would instead inevitably fear and loathe him, as a child cringes from the approach of a stranger who wishes to tickle. What happens to norms of respectability in a community that does not have carnivals designated by the official calendar, yet nevertheless routinely tolerates the excess of carnivalesque behaviors? What happens to an individual who creates a comic figure embodying a carnival spirit but who has no official, sanctioned place in the community to express it? This situation intensifies the already powerful ambiguity of joking behaviors like comic raillery. In such a community and situation, Mark Twain first appeared.

---

## BREWING WASHOE MARK TWAIN

WHAT DO YOU THINK OF THAT EFFORT . . . FOR AN UNSANCTIFIED
NEWSPAPER REPORTER . . . ? DOESN'T IT STRIKE YOU THAT THERE ARE
MORE BRAINS AND FEWER OYSTERS IN MY HEAD THAN A CASUAL
ACQUAINTANCE WITH ME WOULD LEAD ONE TO SUPPOSE?

———

MARK TWAIN, "MARK TWAIN—MORE OF HIM," *GOLDEN ERA*,
SEPTEMBER 27, 1863

The carnival atmosphere of Virginia City provided the first indispensable background factor for the creation of Mark Twain; the second came from the style of journalism practiced by the Washoe newspapers. Myron Angel, himself a newspaperman of the day, said that "The spirit of the Nevada Press has always been of an exaggerated character."[54] Americans in the nineteenth century were a newspaper-reading people, and the Nevada Territory proved no different. As a contemporary noted, "when not drinking every citizen of Virginia [City]

---

54. Myron Angel, ed., *History of Nevada with Illustrations and Biographical Sketches,* 292.

would be found reading a newspaper."[55] As in other parts of the United States at the time, publishing a newspaper in the Nevada Territory first meant editing and printing items from outside sources. Editors either scissored these items from copies of other periodicals (the "exchange system," which had no copyright restrictions) or took them from telegraph dispatches, if the newspaper could afford to buy them. Letters from correspondents could also be printed, often with news from other mining camps. Advertisements would take up a large share of space, of course, and in Nevada columns of assessment fees levied on owners of mining companies' stocks were also printed daily. After filling all these categories, a newspaper's staff would turn its attention to the areas that called for its own writing talents—editorials and local items.

The editorials in the Washoe papers addressed the civic issues of the day, which might be municipal or territorial, or concerned with California as well as Nevada. However, editorials might also be written on issues of greater scope—New York financial matters, the weakness of the present English government, the future of the South, Henry Ward Beecher's Thanksgiving sermon, and especially the prosecution of the Civil War.[56] The local items column, by contrast, focused solely on local matters—the weather, the conditions of the streets, the latest word from the mines, the events in the police station, the proceedings in the courthouse, and social affairs. While the editorials maintained a serious tone, the local items were chatty—even gossipy—and written informally, sometimes with humor. Feature stories or imaginative writing were both rare, but the genre of the local column was elastic enough to accommodate the impulse toward either if the reporter had the talent to produce them and the editor-in-chief had the temperament to allow them.

In Nevada, both kinds of in-house writing, editorials and local items, shared one thing: a spirited effort went into abusing other newspapers' staffs. With editorials, the abuse was earnest, sometimes harsh when serious charges such as corruption were involved, and these accusations could lead to duels. With the local items, the abuse was generally the mock feud of raillery—making fun of another reporter's errors or accusing him of plagiarism in a good-natured fashion.[57] "The inventive genius of those [Comstock] reporters was not always satisfied with its

---

55. Quoted in Lillard, "Washoe Journalism," 51.
56. Ibid., 54.
57. See Basso, *Bulletin and News,* for the following examples of the more serious charges that editors leveled at one another: taking bribes; always arguing, boasting, and misrepresenting facts; having political aspirations; switching sides on the proposed state constitution; being disloyal; printing false stories (*Gold Hill News,* December 1, 28, 31, 1863; January 8, 13, 15, June 13, 1864). The charge about taking bribes apparently had the *Virginia City Union* and *Virginia City Evening Bulletin* editors on the verge of dueling. Although these examples are all taken from a file of the *Gold Hill News,* in some cases the *News* is reprinting attacks made by the other leading Virginia

prey [*sic*] upon and hoaxing of the outside world, but kept constantly at play upon each other."[58] This playful abuse made lively copy and entertained the resident population, many of whom knew the principals on sight and all of whom were familiar with the pervasive Washoe spirit of teasing and practical jokes. Nevertheless, the local editor had to exercise care because no managing editor existed to review the copy before it was set in type and printed.[59] William Wright once wrote a comic story illustrating the troubles a local reporter can stir up when careless about what he publishes.[60] This atmosphere led Sam Davis, a Nevada newspaperman and historian, to declare that the two essentials for a successful Washoe newspaper editor were the abilities to fight well and to write well, evoking Clemens's 1869 sketch "Journalism in Tennessee."[61]

The *Virginia City Territorial Enterprise* epitomized Washoe journalism: "It was the nerve-centre of Washoe, the brainiest sheet on the Coast. It was privy to all of the Mountain's secrets both above and below the earth's crust. It had acquired enormous prestige. It could make or break any man in the Territory. It was honest and fearless. . . . It was Comstock to the core—the mirror of her astounding personality—the sounding-board of her buoyant, virile young life."[62] Started in Genoa, the *Enterprise* was the Nevada Territory's first newspaper. When the Comstock lode was discovered, the paper's founders followed the rush to Virginia City in October 1860. However, the paper did not enjoy success until Joseph T. Goodman and Denis E. McCarthy bought partnerships in March 1861 and turned it into a daily in September. Before year's end, they were clearing between six thousand and ten thousand dollars a month.[63] By late 1863, the paper's staff was huge by Washoe standards: Joe Goodman wrote the editorials, assisted by Rollin Daggett, Captain Joe Plunkett, and George Dawson; William Wright and Sam Clemens wrote the local columns; Steve Gillis and Charles Putnam edited the exchanges and telegraph dispatches;[64] between twenty and

---

City papers: the *Enterprise, Union,* and *Evening Bulletin.* Basso's collection also provides examples of more jocular verbal abuse: drinking too much, making awful puns, misquoting, misstating a fact (*Gold Hill News,* October 26, November 14, 1863; March 5, 26, 1864), stealing local items, stealing in general, being a poor reporter, eating too much, and lying (*Virginia City Evening Bulletin,* July 10, 11, 25, 31, November 10, 1863). When the locals from the *News* and the *Bulletin* have a friendly argument over a mining claim and exchange names—"Greenie" and "Smarty"—William Wright of the *Enterprise* encourages them to fight, parodying the ever-present danger of funny words turning into fighting words (*Gold Hill News,* November 6, 1863).

58. Angel, *History of Nevada,* 292.
59. Lillard, "Washoe Journalism," 55.
60. Quoted in Davis, *History of Nevada,* 461–62.
61. Ibid., 463; see also Fitch, "Fitch Recalls."
62. Lyman, *Comstock Lode,* 205; see also McEwen, "Heroic Days," 15.
63. Richard E. Lingenfelter and Karen Rix Gash, *The Newspapers of Nevada: A History and Bibliography, 1854–1979,* 254.
64. William Wright, "Reminiscences of the Comstock," 15.

twenty-five of the fastest printers on the Comstock set the type.[65] In 1864, the paper rolled off two steam presses, and Joe Goodman could claim a circulation twice that of all other dailies combined and six times that of any one of them.[66] At times, the *Enterprise* had a larger circulation than any paper in San Francisco, and for years it was the most successful and influential newspaper in Nevada.[67] Goodman recalled that the *New York Herald* had a subscription to the *Enterprise* though it refused to exchange with other "country" papers, suggesting that the influence of the *Enterprise* was not simply regional.[68]

With a large corps of writers, the *Enterprise* could afford more feature-length articles than its rivals. Given the high spirits of its editor-in-chief, Joe Goodman, it also printed imaginative material, encroaching on the province of San Francisco's literary periodicals, the *Golden Era* and *Mercury.* Spirited and fun-loving, at home in the rough-and-tumble world of practical jokes in print as well as political diatribes, and equally adept at the war of words involved in both cases, the *Enterprise* did mirror the folks that read it. When the second rush to the Comstock peaked at the end of June 1863, the population in Virginia City and the surrounding mining towns in the territory of Nevada overwhelmingly consisted of young, single men seeking their fortunes. To the owners of the *Territorial Enterprise,* Joe Goodman and Denis McCarthy, that demographic fact meant that the bulk of their readership were "the boys," mostly miners who wanted a lively newspaper capable of printing a comic sketch as well as a rousing editorial on the serious issues of the day. Better yet, "the boys" wanted a newspaper also capable of publishing, side by side with the editorial, burlesques on how the serious issues of the day were being seriously discussed. "The boys" had long before 1863 proven their sophistication for such mock-serious items (as well as for fashionable literature) by making a literary weekly, the *San Francisco Golden Era,* a financial success.[69]

Goodman and McCarthy had already made the *Enterprise* successful with this formula of vigorous editorializing and clear reporting as well as an occasional comic tale well told when, in April 1862, they received an unsolicited sketch from one of the boys in the mining camps who signed the piece "Josh." When the *Enterprise* printed the sketch, the miner was evidently encouraged to send more, one probably lampooning the oratorical style of George Turner, chief justice of the territory (ETS 1:17n35), another burlesquing the oratory of a generic Fourth of July speech. Some time after the *Enterprise* had printed these efforts as well,

---

65. Daggett, "Recollections," 15; Goodman, "Memories," 3.
66. Lillard, "Washoe Journalism," 76.
67. Wright, "Salad Days," 13; Daggett, "Recollections," 15; see also Lillard, "Washoe Journalism," 71.
68. Goodman, "Memories," 3.
69. Franklin Walker, *San Francisco's Literary Frontier,* 14, 117.

the miner revealed himself as Sam Clemens and applied for a job as correspondent to the paper. Possibly, some members of the *Enterprise* staff remembered
Sam as the brother of the secretary of the territory, Orion Clemens. The previous fall, Sam Clemens had served as the secretary's clerk in the first territorial
legislature. Andrew J. Marsh, who covered the constitutional convention with
Sam Clemens in the fall of 1863, notes the political connection to Orion in his
account of the hiring (CL 1:232n1). While such a political connection would be
obviously useful, Goodman recalled that the "Josh" sketches were "so funny" he
immediately offered Clemens a job as local editor, temporarily replacing the current man in the post, William Wright, while he went on an extended vacation to
visit his family in Iowa.[70]

As funny as the "Josh" letters were, in the very first phase of his career as a professional writer, before he signed anything "Mark Twain," Sam Clemens fur-
nished mostly straight reportorial writing. Reporting used two formats. The first
was the standard, daily column of local items. For the first few months as an
*Enterprise* employee, Clemens undoubtedly wrote scores of ordinary local items,
though no archive of the period is extant. As a local editor and reporter,
Clemens's first duty was to be informative, to report in these items what actually
happened in and around Virginia City. The other format allowed for longer
items that today might be called feature articles. Henry Nash Smith suggests
(MTEnt 34) that when Clemens covered the legislature in November 1862, he
submitted both a daily column about proceedings and a more expansive weekly
letter, similar to a feature article but more personal in tone. "The Spanish Mine,"
published in October 1862, provides a good example of this second format (ETS
1:164–66). As with the local items, Clemens in his feature articles needed to be
informative, yet he also sought to be entertaining without sacrificing credibility.
"The Spanish Mine" describes an actual descent into a mine in personal terms,
presenting the event as a tourist excursion and "how-to" for the curious. Despite
no extant complete file of the *Enterprise,* the popularity of these longer, more
personal articles can be surmised because reprinting in other papers has preserved many examples, whereas the bulk of the daily columns were not judged
worthy of reprinting. Were the record complete, the overall impression of the
writing done during the first few months of Sam Clemens's employment at the
*Enterprise* would probably not differ greatly from that of many other newspapermen at the time.

Nevertheless, merely being a reporter of facts did not suit the temperament of
Sam Clemens. Reminiscences by Calvin Higbie, Sam and Orion's mining partner
before Clemens joined the *Enterprise* staff, make it clear that Sam above all was a

---

70. Goodman, "Memories," 3; see also Daggett, "Recollections," 15.

gregarious soul who loved to talk and tell stories. So good was Clemens at yarn-ing that he could charm Higbie into doing all the housework and cooking while they lived together, or swap yarns for food at the local grocery store during daily visits.[71] Alf Doten tells of being in the town of Como with Clemens when Sam was supposed to report on the mines there, and Sam constantly postponing his work for visits to the brewery instead.[72] Along with most of "the boys," Sam Clemens enjoyed playing practical jokes, but he also indulged in more elaborate playful-ness, acting as impromptu entertainer, for instance, when he and Higbie attended a dance: "Sometimes [Sam] would act as though there were no use in trying to go right or in trying to dance like other people and would rush off into another set with his eyes half closed, declaring to everybody that he never dreamed there was so much pleasure to be had at a ball. Then, with a maybe-you-think-I-can't-dance air he would do a hoedown or a double shuffle all by himself. This caused great amusement and many laughed so heartily that they nearly broke up several sets."[73] Sam Clemens's acting propensity could also be discerned in his famous drawl, often consciously exaggerated, according to William Wright.[74]

Another fellow staff writer, Charles Putnam, thought Clemens possessed of an irresistible "quaintness," by which he seems to have meant that Sam was a character. That judgment could also refer to the way that Sam Clemens the yarn spinner overshadowed Sam Clemens the reporter. For Putnam, William Wright in "the proper journalistic sense . . . greatly outranked" Sam Clemens. Alf Doten, who worked for several Washoe newspapers, also thought Wright was the "most reliable reporter" for the *Enterprise,* while Clemens's forte was "humorous sketches and special reports." To Wright, Clemens was earnest, industrious, and enthusiastic in "such work as suited him . . . but when it came to 'cast-iron' items, he gave them 'a lick and a promise.'" After "Mark Twain" had become a pseudo-nym worthy of note, the *Golden Era,* advertising its best writers, boasted of his audacious freedom with reporting the news: "he manufactures more items in one year than happen in ten—beat him, if you can."[75]

Sam Clemens's propensity for fun and ability to yarn can be found in the first extant example, dated October 1, 1862, of the *Enterprise*'s local column that can reasonably be attributed to him (ETS 1:389). The column has three items. Two

71. Phillips, "Reminiscences" 69, 70; Ida L. Brooks, "Did Mark Twain's Laziness Cost Him a For-tune? Calvin H. Higbie, to Whom *Roughing It* Is Dedicated, Tells the Other Side of 'When We Were Millionaires for Ten Days,'" 1; see also Goodman, "Memories," 3.

72. Doten, "Journalism, Part II," 184.

73. Phillips, "Reminiscences," 72.

74. Wright, "Reporting," 178.

75. Putnam, "Dan and Mark Twain," 3; Alf Doten, "Early Journalism in Nevada, Part I," 52; Wright, "Reporting," 171; *Golden Era,* "The Golden Era" [Our Contributors], 4.

describe troubles immigrant wagons are having with native tribes. These stories bristle with facts: peoples' names and place-names; numbers of wagons, of assailants, of attacks. Clemens lets the inherent drama of the attacks organize these two news items, and his tone remains matter-of-fact throughout both, with one exception. When he describes the damage done to several wagons, he says that their "sides and covers had been transformed into magnified nutmeg-graters by Indian bullets" (ETS 1:390). Describing the peril these travelers had experienced, Clemens employs the comic by offering to the mind's eye Brobdingnagian graters. The third item, entitled "A Gale," reports the strong wind the town experienced the day before but relates the wind's force in tall-tale fashion, claiming that "a shooting gallery, two lodging houses and a drug store" were all picked up and moved "some ten or twelve feet." The image created has just as much visual impact as the one used for the covered wagons, but the statement's absurdity guarantees that no one will believe it. Despite the hint at laughter in the nutmeg grater image, the reader is expected to believe in the implied fierceness of the attack, an implication that well suits the sobering tenor of both items about the immigrants.

Writing his local columns, Clemens must have continually faced the question of how he could indulge his comic propensities without jeopardizing his obligations as a reporter. Another local column for the *Enterprise*, this one from late December 1862, suggests how he often answered the question (ETS 1:175, 393). The column has nine items in it. The first, entitled "Our Stock Remarks," is pure fiction, Clemens inventing a reporter who jumbles his notes on stock prices with the words from a wedding vow because he got drunk at the wedding. The fictionalizing extends to a slurred sentence from the reporter: "S(hic)am, just 'laberate this, w(hic)ill, yer?" Of the eight items that follow, four are completely serious, while each of the others contains merely one comic sentence or phrase. One reports a severe wind again, sidling up to a tall-tale narrative with "the face of heaven was obscured by vast clouds of dust all spangled over with lumber, and shingles, and dogs and things." Another item refers to amending a legislative bill for assessing and collecting revenue as a "thrilling romance" and pretends that the *Enterprise* will be printing this "admirable story" in the future, burlesquing literary periodicals' habit of serializing popular romance tales. A third makes fun of items reporting accidental deaths and the inevitable verdicts by the coroner: "SAD ACCIDENT.—We learn from Messrs. Hatch & Bro., who do a heavy business in the way of supplying this market with vegetables, that the rigorous weather accompanying the late storm was so severe on the mountains as to cause the loss of life in several instances. Two sacks of sweet potatoes were frozen to death on the summit, this side of Strawberry. The verdict rendered by the coroner's jury was strictly in accordance with the facts." These examples are not strictly in accordance with their facts. The list of things airborne because of the wind is clearly not factual. The items about the legislative bill and the frozen potatoes each present only their main fact—the *Enterprise* will print the amendment to the legislative bill and a vegetable dealer lost some of his goods—but the presentation dresses up these mundane events as burlesques of two genres well-known to Comstock readers, the serialized romance and the coroner's report. In these instances, Clemens successfully makes his comic points about the predictability of serialized novels and the stupidity of coroner's juries without obscuring the factual basis of the item.

Clemens's ability to burlesque familiar genres demonstrates the literary attitude in his extraordinary comic talent. Discussed in the introductory section, another early piece entitled "The Pah-Utes" reveals a gift for bold and clever satire. Clemens refers to members of an exclusive club for pioneer Nevadans as "happy, and lousy and contented" (ETS 1:170). By pretending that they are really Paiutes, Clemens attributes a stereotypical view of Native American hygiene to the white settlers, deflating the pride of place implied in their club's existence. Richard Lillard, in his study of Washoe journalism, notes that William Wright, famous for his ability to deliver "cast-iron" accounts of mining news, was also capable of improvising,[76] and a number of hoaxes and comic tales grace Wright's nom de plume, "Dan De Quille." Clemens, no doubt, had congenial company when he enlivened factual local items with witty phrasing or slang or humorous incident. Sam Clemens's initial efforts to be funny in his local column for the *Enterprise* thus fit the tenor of journalistic practice in carnivalesque Virginia City. Indeed, such practice was not confined to Virginia City in the 1860s, as Charles Farrar Browne demonstrated in his column entitled "City Facts and Fancies," written for the *Cleveland Plain Dealer* in 1858 and 1859.

Although Clemens apparently would not sign a piece "Mark Twain" until almost six months after starting with the *Enterprise,* the two examples of his local column exhibit capable reporting and sly yarn spinning, the twin forces that create the master roles for Mark Twain the narrator in his early phases and guarantee the success of *The Innocents Abroad.* Though Clemens throughout the 1860s shaped and reshaped Mark Twain, the single most important strategy in those efforts was his playing with the opposition of fact and fiction inherent in the two kinds of narration, reporting and yarn spinning. His play sometimes blurs those narrative boundaries, a deliberate confounding that created controversy among those who thought the most important duty of reporters was to be informative and creditable. Deliberately blurring fact with fiction suggests a primary reason why Clemens described himself as "an unsanctified newspaper reporter." Moreover, blurring or dissolving the fact/fiction boundary reveals a primary affinity

---

76. Lillard, "Washoe Journalism," 56.

of Mark Twain with sacred clowns: "the sacred clown can be said to subsume a border, or boundary, within itself, which it straddles, or through which it moves, back-and-forth in a never-ending pattern, for so long as it is true to type."[77]

In the local columns cited above, the logic of Mark Twain's playfulness with the commonsense boundary between fact and fiction begins narrowly, with metaphors or turns of phrase meant to capture vividly some aspect of what is being described. This level of play still legitimately serves the needs of a good reporter. However, play harnessed in the service of vivid description can also easily engender comic possibilities, some of which can approach the fantastic, undermining the factual basis of reporting. The image of covered wagons so scarred with bullets that they resemble giant nutmeg graters provides a good example of how the comic possibility in an image moves a vivid but realistic description toward wholesale fantasy. The description in "A Gale" operates differently in its blurring of fact and fiction, offering not a comic metaphor but rather an absurdity meant to be taken as a comic rendition of the habitually strong wind that besets Virginia City. Having routinely experienced just how strong the wind can be, residents would appreciate the joke, especially because local usage referred ironically to the wind as the "Washoe Zephyr." The topic was a safe one to lie about in a local column without jeopardizing its integrity; apparently such fantasies were routine.[78] Even readers from outside Virginia City would not accept the story as true, despite being printed side by side with two factual items as though it were their equal. The obvious absurdity about the wind's force protects all from confusion about the truth, in effect providing the frame necessary to discern playful intent.

Nevertheless, mixing fact and fantasy within a local column can become a dangerous exercise. Presenting a facetious yarn as though it were fact effectively burlesques the function of a local column. Moreover, such mixing mocks an expectation that a story printed in a newspaper signifies truth. This play with journalistic conventions has a paramount importance for the reception of Washoe Mark Twain. Once invented, Clemens installs Mark Twain within the sober columns of a respectable newspaper as a comic character who disrupts the orderly processes of journalism, inverting and subverting them in carnival fashion, even as he ostensibly maintains them. The disruption from simultaneously being a reporter and mocking that role will at times be calculated for maximum confusion, as the *Carson City Independent* acknowledged on February 13, 1864: "Our friend, Mark Twain, is such a joker that we cannot tell when he is really in earnest" (MTEnt 159). The effect approximates teasing someone with a deadpan

77. Don Handelman, "The Ritual Clown: Attributes and Affinities," 330.
78. Lyman, *Comstock Lode*, 119; Mack, *Nevada*, 180.

face—and remains just as problematic in determining intent. Finally, compounding the facetious with the serious enables literary hoaxes, the underlying cause in the hasty exit of Sam Clemens from the Comstock. From the start of his professional career as a writer, Clemens experimented with this volatile brew.

To the extent that Sam Clemens, after joining the *Enterprise,* quickly established a recognizable figure that stood apart from his contemporaries, he did so with his own comic version of the local reporter—by turns witty, clever, whimsical, or audacious. Other ingredients necessary to concoct Washoe Mark Twain included an out-of-town letter format to provide scope for comic embellishment, a foolish voice to alternate and contrast with the standard reporter's voice, and a comic sidekick to engage in mock feuds. Remarkably, Sam Clemens's professional writing efforts displayed all these basic elements by the end of 1862, only four months after he joined the *Enterprise* staff, and well before he unveiled Mark Twain. That rapid development depended on Clemens taking full advantage of the possibilities that the longer feature article gave him for creating comic effects, especially when those longer pieces were letters from out of town. The letter format played to a strength, not just because Clemens had written similar letters since 1853 when he made his first trip away from home. Clemens also at times wrote letters home knowing they would be published. Before he joined the *Enterprise,* Clemens wrote approximately thirty letters while in the Nevada Territory, some sent to the *Keokuk (Iowa) Gate City* for publication. Many are still readable, with their judicious mix of accurate description worthy of a reporter and comic perspective worthy of a humorist.[79]

This practice at writing letters both funny and informative served Clemens well when he first has a chance to send letters to the *Enterprise* as a staff member. From November 11 until December 20, 1862, the second Nevada territorial legislature held its session in Carson City, and for much of this time, Clemens reported on the proceedings. In three of the longer extant pieces written during this period, dated December 5, 12, and 23, 1862, another comic element to fashion Washoe Mark Twain appears: cloddish behavior that caricatures common folks. This behavior has its roots in the Thomas Jefferson Snodgrass character Clemens had created for comic letters written in 1856. The December 12 letter portrays a legislator from Virginia City named Colonel Williams eating an eighteen-pound raw turnip with his feet up on his desk during a legislative session (MTEnt 39). More important than depicting Williams in a way reminiscent of Snodgrass, however, is Clemens portraying himself similarly, as he does in the

79. The relationship between this letter writing and Clemens's professional efforts for the *Enterprise* is highlighted by Edgar M. Branch's analysis of the letters when discussing Clemens's Nevada days (*The Literary Apprenticeship of Mark Twain,* 63–73). Some of the Keokuk letters will be discussed later in Act Four, Scene One, "Writing Travel Letters."

December 5 letter, which uses a foolish voice portraying a common man who, for instance, becomes entangled in a simple legal sentence (MTEnt 35).

While this voice anticipates the humorous foolishness Washoe Mark Twain will later exhibit, the real comic discovery enabled by these letters from Carson City can be found in the one dated "Midnight, December 23rd," when Clemens provides an uncouth, Snodgrass-like companion for his own cloddish behavior. Like Colonel Williams, the companion lampooned an actual person, Clement T. Rice, the legislative reporter for the *Virginia City Union*. The lampoons of Williams and Rice provide good examples of Mark Twain's humor of raillery. Clemens, however, presents Rice under the cover of a nickname: the "Unreliable." The Unreliable and Sam have supposedly attended the "Grand Bull Drivers' Convention" in Washoe City, and the Unreliable, though attended by two constables, manages to drink "until he lost all sense of etiquette" so that Sam found himself "in bed with him with my boots on."[80] The raillery implied in the nickname for Rice had a history. Paine's biography recounts that Clement Rice ridiculed Sam Clemens's initial reports of the legislative proceedings, which were filled with errors. However, Clemens quickly learned the ropes, and returned the favor by claiming that Rice's reports were so filled with errors that he deserved the epithet the "Unreliable." He also dubbed himself the "Reliable."[81] Those Comstock readers in the know undoubtedly laughed at Clemens's ironic reversal of his greenhorn and Rice's veteran status.

In any case, the reversal initiated a mock feud with Rice. The mock feuds created among themselves by the local reporters of the Washoe press provided newspapers with a source of homemade comic fun.[82] As part of the local humor, these mock feuds reflected communal values. The wit displayed during these mock feuds was mediocre, but scintillating bon mots were probably never the goal. Rather, amid the rough-and-tumble, intensely democratic frontier conditions of the mining town, the objective was to test the individual's status in the community. As long as someone could take a ribbing, he remained one of "the boys." Teasing expressed equality, the frontier folks' insistence on everyone's right to associate freely with anyone else. Well-connected men like William Stewart and men in power like Governor James Nye both enjoyed political success partly because they demonstrated their willingness to exchange jests; each acted as one of "the boys."

The newspaper writers' mock feuds exhibited these values to the larger community too, though the writers' conscious motivation was to create interest in their newspapers and police each other's professional standards in a relatively

80. Mack, *Nevada*, 227.
81. Albert Bigelow Paine, *Mark Twain, A Biography*, 1:220.
82. Lillard, "Washoe Journalism," 59ff.

light-hearted way. The joke about accuracy implied in Clemens's nicknames for himself and Rice, "the Reliable" and "the Unreliable," folds itself into routine ridicule about factual errors, and the joke therefore takes its place amid other gibes about plagiarism, printer's errors, grammar, and writing styles. Applying unflattering sobriquets was also standard. Adair Wilson, a local reporter for the *Virginia City Union* until October 1863, was dubbed "the Unimportant." Charles Parker, local for the *Virginia City Evening Bulletin,* was called "the Obese." Parker and the local for the *Gold Hill Daily News,* Charles Sumner, called each other "Smarty" and "Greenie." Such epithets were mild compared to the hard names editors called each other in earnest over serious issues. Moreover, such comic epithets parodied the earnest name-calling. Clemens's abusing Rice fit nicely with Washoe's wild frontier standards for journalism.

The comic raillery between the "Reliable" and the "Unreliable" probably began early in the legislative session, judging by the headnote to a reprinting of the December 23 letter in the *Placer (CA) Weekly Courier* (January 17, 1863), which takes for granted the sobriquet "Reliable" for Clemens: "The Reliable of the *Enterprise* gives that paper a lively account of a trip he made to Washoe City, and what he saw there."[83] If Clemens and Rice carried out their mock combat in print throughout the legislative session, the December 23 letter may represent an initial climax, inventing comic incidents involving both men that were understood as fictional. Using the Unreliable and Reliable "characters" for an extended period of time developed Clemens as a comic writer because it allowed him to elaborate his humor of raillery. In addition, the series of legislative letters allowed Clemens to explore how to embed that humor of raillery in fictional events. Calling each other names and attributing bad habits to a rival were standard scurrilities for Washoe newspapermen. Inventing comic incidents and attributing them to real people raised the ante because the tactic obscured the boundary between fact and fiction in a potentially libelous way. The expanded length and the personal tone of the out-of-town letter format therefore facilitated the development of Sam Clemens as a comic writer in a way that was impossible by merely fooling with local items.

In the January 10, 1863, *Enterprise* local column, Clemens's propensity to fictionalize all but takes over in the item entitled "The Sanitary Ball" (ETS 1:185–87). The column implies that the earlier weekly letters from Carson City during the legislative session took the first big step toward the appearance of Mark Twain. The local item effectively has become a feature-length article minus the Mark Twain signature, for the basic comic character already exists, one month prior to the first extant letter signed "Mark Twain." The foolish common-man

83. Mack, *Nevada,* 224.

voice, briefly glimpsed in the letter of December 5, 1862, can be found in two passages. Because the incidents in these passages start out portraying the narrator as silly and end up making him sound sensible, however, the comic figure Clemens creates resembles William Tappan Thompson's Major Jones more than Clemens's own earlier comic character, Thomas Jefferson Snodgrass.

Presenting a pair of comic figures, however, would seem to be the final element needed for the appearance of Mark Twain: the first three letters signed "Mark Twain" and published in the *Enterprise* on February 3, 5, and 8, 1863, depend upon the scenario used in "Letter from Carson City, December 23." By juxtaposing the comic figure found in "The Sanitary Ball" with the Unreliable presented in that scenario, Clemens has in these first signed Mark Twain letters the conditions for fiction, automatically allowing for comic dialogue and greatly expanding the opportunities for comic incidents. These first Mark Twain letters are all written from Carson City, when Clemens was on a short holiday, probably to attend the weddings he mentions in the second and third letters. The reporting of the weddings underscores the way Clemens habitually erected his comic structures on the foundations of actual events. The best yarn spinning depends upon imaginative reworking of facts. The three letters also reveal how Clemens reworked earlier material by again featuring ballroom dancing as an occasion for laughter (see MTEnt 40; ETS 1:185–86) and by again mixing up wedding ceremonies with mining operations (see ETS 1:176). Finally, these three letters begin a series of misadventures for Mark Twain and the Unreliable that foreshadows comic sketches involving Mark Twain and Mr. Brown when Clemens writes his travel letters about the Kingdom of Hawai'i.

Remarkably, Clemens initially makes Mark Twain's behavior similar to the Unreliable's. In the first letter, both characters apparently crash the party described, and both look foolish in separate incidents, Mark Twain confessing to his "girlish passion" for looking into mirrors and the Unreliable pressing his face against a parlor window. Later, both guard the supper table and punch bowl "until the punch entirely evaporated," whereupon both rejoin "the hazy dance" (ETS 1:195, 196). In the second letter, Mark Twain again jokes about the drinking of the Unreliable, but when the description of the wedding follows, Mark Twain becomes "confused" by all the "shampain" (ETS 1:203). Having another comic figure at Mark Twain's side to kick around allows Clemens to project the figure as foolish but not in the same league as the inanities of the Unreliable. This dynamic can be found in the mildly funny way the first letter reports how Washoe Mark Twain sings a song while the Unreliable sings his song grotesquely. As a group, the three letters stress comic incident over attempts to report news; they center on the bad manners and vulgarity of the Unreliable, whose antics overwhelm potential news, despite the mention of real people encountered or the reports of actual events—for example, weddings and mining incorporations. The Unreliable blithely wears other people's clothes, tipples so much that drinking a glass of water is nearly fatal, acts like a coward about fighting a duel, pesters the bride and groom "like an evil spirit," and steals silver spoons along with a New Testament (ETS 1:209). During the wedding reception in the third letter, however, the behavior of the Unreliable reaches a climax of fantastic repugnance, making all else seem forgivable:

> he carried away a codfish under one arm, and Mr. Curry's plug hat full of sour-krout under the other. He posted himself right where he could be most in the way, and fell to eating as comfortably as if he were boarding with Trumbo by the week. . . . I believe he would have eaten a corpse last night, if he had one. Finally, Curry came and took his hat away from him and tore one of his coat tails off and threatened to thresh him with it, and that checked his appetite for a moment. Instead of sneaking out of the house, then, as anybody would have done who had any self-respect, he shoved his codfish into the pocket of his solitary coat tail (leaving at least eight inches of it sticking out), and crowded himself into a double quadrille. He had it all to himself pretty soon; because the order "gentlemen to the right" came, and he passed from one lady to another, around the room, and wilted each and every one of them with the horrible fragrance of his breath. Even Trumbo, himself, fainted. Then the Unreliable, with a placid expression of satisfaction upon his countenance, marched forth and swept the parlors like a pestilence. When the guests had been persecuted as long as they could stand it, though, they got him to drink some kerosene oil, which neutralized the sour-krout and codfish, and restored his breath to about its usual state, or even improved it, perhaps, for it generally smells like a hospital. (ETS 1:208–9)

In this climax to his "report" on the Unreliable, Clemens allows his comic imagination its greatest scope since the Thomas Jefferson Snodgrass letters by portraying a character whose manners are beyond belief. One can only wonder what Clement Rice thought of this elaborate lampoon.[84]

However conscious Clemens may have been about the possibilities for fiction writing that lay within his pair of nascent comic characters, his job ostensibly focused on reporting local events. Nevertheless, the Washoe newspapermen's habit of creating mock feuds, which had obviously been the starting point for turning Clement Rice into the Unreliable, allowed Clemens to do his job *and* to

84. Clemens possibly encountered Clement T. Rice during the first territorial legislature, which met from October 1 to November 29, 1861, when Rice was covering the session for the *Carson City Silver Age*. The *Silver Age* would become the *Virginia City Union* in November 1862, with Rice still as one of its reporters. Clemens and Rice were probably friends long before that date. A letter to Jane Clemens dated October 25, 1861, tells of Sam's interest in a mining claim owned by Rice, and another to Orion, dated May 12, 1862, takes note of more mining claims involving Rice. See CL 1:131; 135n5; 206; 211n5.

write comic fiction too: once he had invented the Unreliable, Clemens apparently made a habit of including him in his columns of local items, as he did on February 25, March 7, and August 4 in the *San Francisco Illustrated Press*. The Unreliable in 1863 also appears in out-of-town letters published on February 3, 5, 8; in mid-May; on June 21, in the first version of a burlesque of fashions at the Lick House in San Francisco, which was reprised in September; and on August 25. Feature articles in the *Enterprise* with the comic sidekick are printed on February 19 and 26 as well as on April 12.

The fortunate preservation of Clemens's entire local column for February 25, 1863, affords an opportunity to examine how he used the Unreliable to enliven his routine reporting. The column consists of nine items, the first one presenting the Unreliable's comic appearance at a Fireman's Ball, where his voracious appetite "accounts for the scarcity of provisions" (ETS 1:225). The third item is headed "The Fireman's Ball" and provides many details of the event, including the fact that those hired to provide food failed to do so properly. In the first item, Clemens reports the basic fact of too little food but turns it into a comic fantasy at Rice's expense, attributing the actual lack of food at the ball to him. Confirming that the joke on Rice fuels their ongoing mock feud, the first item also contains a complaint by Clemens that Rice's write-up of the ball contained a disparaging description of Clemens's outfit. The comic "battle" begins the column to pique the reader's interest, and the standard reporting that follows makes sure the public has all the facts. Clemens scribbles the remaining items in a mostly serious fashion, with comic phrasing here and there. Two other extant Unreliable items in local columns display the same elements of mock feud and comic fantasy built on a single fact (ETS 1:240, 269).

As a comic duo, the Unreliable and Washoe Mark Twain, also known as the Reliable, regularly allowed Clemens to elaborate their own mock-feud drama beloved by Washoe newspapermen. However, the fictionalizing of Mark Twain and the Unreliable evident in the first three extant Mark Twain letters transforms the standard mock feud of the reporters, for the feuding assumes a secondary comic role. Rather than focusing on two reporters kidding about each other's local columns, these letters present two comic characters bumbling along in a string of imaginary episodes loosely based on actual events. The difference is enormous. Clemens's other extant writings from the month of February 1863 show how he continued to depart from his normal reporting duties to imagine more comic episodes. During that month, Clemens published sketches using the comic sidekick format to create burlesques of literary targets: "Ye Sentimental Law Student" (ETS 1:217–19) makes fun of the sentimental language found in popular fiction; "Reportorial [Demise of the Unreliable]" (ETS 1:227–28) mocks the obituary genre; and a piece possibly titled "Advice to the Unreliable about Church-Going"

(ETS 1:242–43) imitates the answers-to-correspondents column, full of advice to readers on a myriad of subjects. In the last piece, Mark Twain continues to present the Unreliable as a boor, advising him about manners and proper behavior while in church.[85] As pretenses to chronicle further outrages supposedly perpetrated by the Unreliable, these sketches indicate that the misadventures of Sam Clemens's new comic characters had become popular: Joe Goodman published the pieces as "feature" comic articles, that is, items printed while Clemens is in Virginia City as local reporter but separated from the columns of local items and signed "Mark Twain." Goodman remembered "Ye Sentimental Law Student" as the "first special article" for the *Enterprise* signed with the pseudonym, and "Reportorial [Demise of the Unreliable]" evidently was the second special article signed with the newly minted pen name that the editor decided to publish (ETS 1:215, 226). Goodman obviously saw profit in promoting "Mark Twain" by allowing Clemens space beyond the local column to indulge his humor.

The character of the Unreliable does not change in any of the February items in which he appears. Said to have oysters instead of brains (ETS 1:167), he becomes an exemplar of dim-witted people, one capable of writing love notes mixed with legal jargon (ETS 1:217–19). His appetite sweeps through a firemen's ball like a famine (ETS 1:225), and he becomes drunk after rising up in the coffin at his own funeral, unreliable even in death (ETS 1:228). While the tall-tale motif of coming back from the dead continues the absurd quality of the Unreliable's character, the clash of inappropriate rhetoric—sentimental and legal—found in "Ye Sentimental Law Student" expands the earlier version of this comic device when a wedding vow tangles with jargon from the stock market. The tactic creates incongruities easily exploited for comic laughs, but the second instance strengthens the underlying contrast between love and commerce because Clemens does not merely adhere to the wedding vow formula for representing the rhetoric of love. Attributing the whole thing to the Unreliable freshens up the recycled device as it advances Clemens's yarn-spinning efforts.

In the second round of comic pieces published mostly in February 1863, Washoe Mark Twain's comic character also remained fixed. Compared to the Unreliable's, Washoe Mark Twain's behavior is mildly foolish, despite some additional characteristics exploited for comic purposes. He remains fond of drinking (ETS 1:213), more or less admits he does not go to church much (ETS 1:222), and reveals his pursuit of ladies (ETS 1:191). In short, the earliest version of Mark Twain on the Comstock comically replicates a stereotypically uncouth

85. The text for this last piece comes from a reprinting in Kate Milnor Rabb's *The Wit and Humor of America,* so one cannot be sure that the title she has given it is the original (ETS 1:241). One also cannot be sure that the piece was indeed a featured article, but its length suggests it was not part of the column of local items (indeed, Rabb may not have printed all of the piece).

miner. Fond of women and whiskey and not much given to religion, Washoe Mark Twain takes his place with "the boys." Add to that profile the habit of railing at Clement Rice, exemplary of joking behavior in the mining camps and towns, and Mark Twain's instant success in what I am calling his "Washoe" incarnation seems inevitable—as well as Joe Goodman's immediate willingness to devote newspaper space to the character.

The momentum toward fiction that the comic pair generated predictably continued when Clemens and Rice in early May began a two-month vacation together in San Francisco, and Clemens sent back a letter about their excursion. Being away from Virginia City and writing a feature-length letter for the *Enterprise* replicated the situation that had enabled the first appearance of Mark Twain and the Unreliable back in February, and with Rice in San Francisco too, Clemens seized the opportunity to fictionalize their stay. A notice in the *Enterprise* of May 3, the day after Clemens and Rice left Virginia City for San Francisco, announced their departure and joked about reasons for leaving. Written by Joe Goodman and entitled "Mark Twain," the notice not only indicates that the pen name was already recognized as a comic "personality" but also offers evidence that the *Enterprise* staff acted in concert to promote the comic feud. Goodman talked about Mark Twain's stock "mania" and his "self-conceit" about teaching the Unreliable manners. The latter comment alluded to the earlier item, "Advice to the Unreliable about Church-Going," while providing an invitation to continue the topic.

Clemens of course exploited the invitation, sending back a letter dated May 16 that expanded the fictional elements seen in earlier Unreliable items, elements that were transforming the standard mock feud into comic sketches. Completing his efforts to promote the newest sensation from the *Enterprise,* Goodman published the missive as "Letter from Mark Twain," the first time in the extant record that the pen name appears in a title. Two paragraphs in the letter deliver news in the witty reporter's style. One mentions the wedding of a Virginia City man and jokes that so many people from Carson City and Virginia City were in San Francisco that "provisions are scarce" and that only a few more such citizens would "carry this election" (ETS 1:252). The second paragraph reports on mining stocks, noting that official sales have slowed while private sales remain lively. The rest of the letter would have been familiar by now to regular *Enterprise* readers, for in a series of comic scenes it recounts the venality and bad manners of the Unreliable.

The remarkable development in this particular faux recounting of the Unreliable's misdeeds is Clemens's expanded use of dialogue, the Unreliable addressing "Mark" at some length in two places. This dramatic device indicates how the strategy of employing two comic figures continued to encourage Clemens to write fiction. A new difference between the manners of the two comic figures also marks a development. Perhaps this emphasis resulted from Goodman's comment about Mark Twain's "self-conceit . . . , [lecturing] the Unreliable on manners till he fancied himself a Chesterfield" (ETS 1:248). In any case, rather than continuing the role of the clown who is only somewhat better, found in the first three Mark Twain letters in February, Washoe Mark Twain assumes a genteel pose, sharpening the contrast with the Unreliable. Not only appalled at the Unreliable's gauche manners in the hotel and at his unscrupulous scheme not to pay his bill, Washoe Mark Twain also professes his discomfort about the moral tone of the entertainment at the Bella Union Melodeon, which the Unreliable had insisted they visit. The Melodeon is supported "entirely by Washoe patronage" (ETS 1:252), which implies that Mark Twain's taste is superior to that of his compatriots on the Comstock. At the end of the letter, however, the Unreliable scorns this genteel taste. Moreover, when Mark Twain wants to say something "poetical" about the weather, the Unreliable interrupts: "don't write any of those infernal, sick platitudes about sweet flowers, and joyous butterflies, and worms and things, for people to read before breakfast" (ETS 1:253). With his pair of comic figures, Clemens creates a complicated joke about aesthetics, implying the lowbrow nature of the miners' taste, yet dramatizing the miners' scorn for the pretensions of a genteel taste. As Edgar Branch notes in his introduction to the first volume of Clemens's early tales and sketches, Mark Twain's genteel pose as a contrast to the Unreliable foreshadows his relationship with Mr. Brown in the Sandwich Islands letters (ETS 1:249).

The genteel pose in "Letter from Mark Twain" is unique in the first few weeks of Washoe Mark Twain's appearance, contrasting with his more typical rendition of the uncouth behavior of "the boys." As a comic example of miners' behavior, Washoe Mark Twain possesses shortcomings that must have had multiple effects on his contemporary readers. In contrast to the more outlandish actions of the Unreliable, Mark Twain's defects fall more on the side of foibles than vices, making the character more ludicrous than ridiculous. The laughter created by Mark Twain in his most sympathetic readers, "the boys," would therefore have a humorous tolerance to leaven the scorn of satire. From "the boys'" point of view, Washoe Mark Twain and the Unreliable together probably amounted to a humorous self-deprecation of a stereotypical miner's boorish behavior. To the more settled and respectable elements in Virginia City, the characters would signify a warning that even carnivalesque Virginia City has limits for its tolerance. Both figures clearly make fun of the semicivilized behavior of the mining camps. Insofar as the Unreliable behaves in ways beyond the pale, he provides a laughable counterexample of proper manners. Washoe Mark Twain cuts essentially the same satiric figure, displaying behavior to be eschewed rather than imitated. The character will become more complicated, however, adding a wise fool pose to this cautionary role. Like his comic ancestors, Washoe Mark Twain presents a figure who initially appears as merely uncouth or dim-witted, with oysters for brains, but who turns out to be much more than a casual acquaintance would lead one to suppose.

---

## MARK TWAIN'S HUMOR OF RAILLERY

IF THAT FACETIOUS SINNER, BLUNDERER, AND *SAGE-BRUSH PAINTER,* "MARK TWAIN," HAD THUS LIBELLED ME, I COULD FORGIVE HIM; BUT TO BE THUS MISREPRESENTED (THOUGH UNDESIGNEDLY) BY [SAM CLEMENS] THE "INTELLIGENT" REPORTER OF THE *ENTERPRISE* IS, AS MRS. PARTINGTON WOULD SAY, ASSOLUTELY INSEPARABLE.

JUDGE CORNELIUS BROSNAN, DECEMBER 1863

IT IS HIGHLY IMPROPER FOR GENTLEMEN OF THE PRESS TO DESCEND TO PERSONALITIES, AND I NEVER PERMIT MYSELF TO DO IT.

MARK TWAIN, "ANSWERS TO CORRESPONDENTS," *CALIFORNIAN,* JULY 1, 1865

Using his standard local column, sketches that functioned as feature articles, and the out-of-town letter, Sam Clemens brewed his initial Mark Twain character from a series of comic experiments. The second letter from Mark Twain chronicling Clemens's stay in San Francisco with Clement Rice suggests the experimental nature of the comic pieces Clemens wrote when he debuted Mark Twain. Despite the popularity of the Unreliable/Mark Twain pairing, this next effort, entitled "All About the Fashions," includes only a mention of the Unreliable (WG 39). Instead of employing the sidekick for Mark Twain as a contrast, Clemens in this piece folds the Unreliable into the newly concocted Washoe Mark Twain, who pays hotel bills erratically and happily borrows not only expressions from the Unreliable but clothes to attend a ball, just as earlier letters had shown the Unreliable doing. However, the central joke of the letter, a burlesque of typical items about such social events in newspapers, turns on Washoe Mark Twain's foolish vanity, rooted in a false gentility, which asserts a competence to describe the attire of the women at the ball. A set of wonderfully crazy descriptions results, generated by mixing fabrics and clothing styles with wildly inappropriate things like sagebrush, sardines, and radishes. The reader's laugh centers on the character's pretending to have a genteel taste. In an earlier instance, Washoe Mark Twain had affected a taste for entertainment better than that of the Bella Union Melodeon and for poetical effusions about the weather, a taste mocked by the Unreliable. In "All About the Fashions," Clemens uses Washoe Mark Twain solo to dramatize the clash of highbrow and lowbrow aesthetics. The tactic attains a much greater comic sophistication than the earlier example because Washoe Mark Twain's own words deflate his supposed gentility and reveal the true "sagebrush" quality of his taste. If one agrees with Edgar Branch that the first example foreshadows Clemens's use of Mark Twain and Mr. Brown in the travel letters from Hawai'i, "All About the Fashions" foreshadows Mark Twain in *The Innocents Abroad.*

Mining this vein of comic pretension while in San Francisco, Clemens apparently discovered that Washoe Mark Twain did not need a comic sidekick to provoke complex laughter. After May 1863, the Unreliable virtually disappears from Clemens's extant featured work. The great popularity of "All About the Fashions" also probably helped Clemens make this discovery, which can be inferred by the way he pursued the topic of fashions in the next few months. While in California, Clemens arranges with the *San Francisco Morning Call* to furnish the kind of quasi-comic, quasi-reportorial letters for which he is already well-known. In the very first *Call* letter after he returns to Virginia City (MTCall no. 1), Mark Twain says he wants to write about the fashions on the Comstock, implying a deliberate follow-up to "All About the Fashions." Moreover, when Clemens returns to San Francisco later in the year, Mark Twain again mentions a desire to write on fashions at the end of his letter to the *Enterprise* dated September 13 (MTEnt 80). Shortly afterward, Clemens contributes four sketches to the literary weekly the *Golden Era,* and the second and third ones again burlesque write-ups of social events ("How to Cure a Cold," "Mark Twain—More of Him: All About the Fashions," "The Lick House Ball," and "The Great Prize Fight"). In fact, the first of these burlesques merely reprints "All About the Fashions," the repetition explained by a frame device consisting of a request from a fictional character to copy the original piece.

In the midst of this experimenting with topics, comic figures, dialogue, and scenes, Clemens maintained his fundamental teasing attitude, implied in his earlier pen name, "Josh," by which he was informally known until "Mark Twain" replaced it.[86] The bantering implied in such an attitude routinely found expression in Washoe Mark Twain's humor of raillery, which Clemens directed toward many people in the Nevada Territory. As "Josh," Clemens supposedly had made fun of the territory's chief justice. In his extant work as a reporter before inventing Mark Twain, Clemens had railed at individuals he knew in the legislature as early as December 5, 1862. No doubt, he could get away with this ribbing because

86. Wright, "Reporting," 170.

he had known the individuals since the previous legislative session, when he clerked for his brother Orion. The raillery against Clement Rice begins about the same time. Sustained raillery among Comstock newspapermen was common, and though Rice as the Unreliable was the favored rival for mock battle, another *Virginia City Union* reporter, Adair Wilson, was also a frequent target, as well as Charles A. Parker, reporter for the *Virginia City Evening Bulletin* (ETS 1:276). As Washoe Mark Twain, Clemens spared no one. For the people of Nevada in general, Mark Twain jokingly says they are mostly "thieves" (ETS 1:260). Other individuals Clemens made fun of early in his career include his boss, Joe Goodman (ETS 1:194, 405); R. W. Billet, a member of the Washoe Stock and Exchange Board and leader in the Nevada Democratic party (ETS 1:295); Virginia City Marshal Jack Perry (ETS 1:235–38; MTEnt, 68);[87] and the attorney general of the Nevada Territory, General Bunker (ETS 1:280–81). In one piece, the last of the four original sketches contributed to the *Golden Era* in 1863, "The Great Prize Fight," Washoe Mark Twain ridicules the governor of California, Leland Stanford; the governor-elect of California, Frederick F. Low; William M. Stewart, prominent attorney and future U.S. senator from Nevada; a judge of the California Supreme Court, Stephen J. Field; Brigadier General Wright, commander of all U.S. forces in the West; and John B. Winters, president of the Yellow Jacket mine, assemblyman from the second Nevada territorial legislature, and candidate for congressman (WG, 25–31; see also ETS 1:252, 255–56, 267–68). Washoe Mark Twain's controlling humor was truly one of raillery.

With such prominent targets singled out by name, perhaps Clemens should not have worried about teasing the well-known socialites he identified only by initials in his burlesque fashion pieces. Nevertheless, the burlesques themselves, which ask for indulgence, betray his concern, as does his next *Call* letter, which toys with the idea of describing fashions on the Comstock ("'Mark Twain's' Letter," ETS 1:258). Clemens's worry reflects a gentleman's attitude toward women that complements his bantering attitude toward men. Railing at "the boys" or playing practical jokes were expected in an atmosphere of physical roughhousing. Making fun of a respectable woman—especially the way she dressed—put Clemens instead on shaky ground. A story told by Effie Mack confirms this difference. When some of the women mentioned in "The Lick House Ball" were not pleased with the ridiculous part they played in the burlesque, their husbands sought revenge with a practical joke—overturning a stage in which Clemens was riding.[88]

The story underlines the way in which Sam Clemens's habit of comic abuse, magnified by the carnivalesque atmosphere of Virginia City and made public in

87. See Putnam, "Dan and Mark Twain," 3.
88. See Mack, *Nevada*, 195ff, 239.

print through the pen name "Mark Twain," necessitated rhetorical tightrope walking to remain within the social pale. Yet such efforts to remain respectable were doomed to failure. Clemens was bound to fall from the tightrope because the basic impulse behind the playful malice of teasing requires making others look foolish. The problem inevitably arises even though unwritten rules exist— for example, a gentleman excuses women as targets for raillery, and prudence dictates that strangers be left out as well. William Wright's story about his troubles after printing a joke about a man he did not know makes this point clear.[89] Similar customs apply to practical joking, which also has the goal of making another look foolish. Nevertheless, such customs guarantee nothing, not even with the best of friends like Clement Rice and Joe Goodman, who did not mind the ridicule Sam Clemens heaped on them, giving as good as they got (see ETS 1:267, 248).

In this context of mock aggression, the Mark Twain pen name, when it appeared in February 1863, should have signified not only a comic attitude and a play frame; "Mark Twain" also should have signified to contemporary readers a license alerting everyone that Sam Clemens was just kidding when he said things that were not true about William Wright or Joe Goodman or Clement Rice—or even about fashionable women. "Mark Twain" meant fun first, not accurate reporting. These meanings, however, were not clear to all readers. Even if Sam Clemens had published a notice declaring that anything signed "Mark Twain" implied a comic license, the tightrope walking would remain, because customs about teasing and raillery and practical joking can only function as unwritten rules. For example, people should accept these forms of comic behavior with the tolerance of good humor. Such behavior can also reveal the depth of friendships, for the unwritten rule of "tease friends instead of strangers" implies that teasing and practical jokes unleashed on friends may be far more severe than those perpetrated on mere acquaintances.

Friendships can even be founded on the give-and-take inherent in practical jokes or the witty repartee that sometimes informs teasing. A good example of this outcome involves William Stewart, a successful lawyer in the litigation surrounding mining claims and later one of Nevada's first U.S. senators. His tactics earned him the epithet "Bullyragging Bill," which Washoe Mark Twain employed for Stewart on at least two occasions (ETS 1:250–51; WG, 26). However, Stewart met his match in 1862 during his first case against Alexander W. "Sandy" Baldwin, from California. Baldwin had already won several objections to Stewart's tactics when the latter attempted a frontal assault. Goaded by a final objection won by the five-foot-eight, 135-pound Californian, Stewart turned his six-foot-two, 200-pound

89. Davis, *History of Nevada,* 461–62.

frame menacingly toward Baldwin: "You little shrimp, if you interrupt me again, I'll eat you!" Baldwin immediately delivered his riposte: "If you do, you'll have more brains in your belly than you have in your head."[90] Stewart admired the comeback so much that he asked Baldwin to be his law partner, and the two men had a very successful partnership for years.

Yet one more unwritten rule about the dynamic of teasing and raillery and practical joking needs to be disclosed, a corollary to the one dictating acceptance with a good humor. If revenge must be sought, it should only be paid out in kind. The men irate about the fun Washoe Mark Twain made of their wives in "The Lick House Ball" understood this rule. Of course, the rule means that teasing or raillery or practical joking could theoretically continue forever, as long as playfulness and imagination hold out on both sides. Nevertheless, a sequence of comic revenges does have the possible consequence that one party finally loses his or her good humor. Because an angry conclusion can happen with the best of friends, jokers must have a good sense of the limit of their friends' forbearance so that it is not crossed and the friendship lost. Clemens knew this consequence and thus, in his burlesque fashion items, notes that he does not want to meddle with strangers because they "never exercise any charity in matters of this kind" (ETS 1:311; see also 318). In all of these comic behaviors, no matter how well one understands the unwritten rules, the problem remains of how to recognize limits, which are inevitably fluid according to circumstances. Even if one has a sense of limits based on past experience, it will not help if a new topic is sensitive for those being comically abused. The absurdity of the descriptions in "The Lick House Ball" clearly indicate comic intent, and Mark Twain asks for indulgence beforehand, but even so, some ladies were not amused.

Clemens stood on firmer ground with his newspaper colleagues, at least among the other local reporters on rival papers—Clement Rice and Adair Wilson of the *Virginia City Union*, Charles Parker of the *Virginia City Evening Bulletin*, Charles Sumner of the *Gold Hill Daily News*, and of course William Wright of the *Enterprise*—because of the reporters' long-standing custom of ribbing each other. The initial success of Washoe Mark Twain originates with a clever manipulation of the custom. First Sam Clemens had conformed to the rules of the game, kidding Clement Rice about being an unreliable reporter; he then elaborated on the custom, making up outrageous peccadillos committed by Rice rather than merely ribbing him about actual mistakes in his column. By telling stretchers about the behavior of Rice the Unreliable, Washoe Mark Twain raised the stakes for which the mock feuds of reporters were usually played. Clemens did not invent the comic game of mock combats in print, but he beat everyone

90. Mack, *Nevada*, 191; see also Charles C. Goodwin, *As I Remember Them*, 140, 231.

else at it with his extravagant manner of playing. As the summer of 1863 progressed, Parker, nicknamed "the Obese," made fun of Mark Twain, and Clemens responded while also maintaining his mock aggression against both Rice and Adair of the *Union*.[91] When William Wright returned to Virginia City in August, he would be ready to join the comic fracas. So too would Charles Sumner in October. The boom along the Comstock was in full swing, spirits and bank accounts were high, and almost anything was allowed.

The strategy of extravagance made the Mark Twain pseudonym well-known within weeks of its appearance, especially with the connivance of Joe Goodman. The local columns of Parker in the *Virginia City Evening Bulletin* and Sumner in the *Gold Hill Daily News* during the summer and fall of 1863 suggest the notoriety of the pseudonym as well as the good-natured reception by Clemens's peers. These two papers were newer than the *Union* or *Enterprise*, and as soon as they commenced publication, Mark Twain became a target for humorous raillery. Parker, during the first month of the *Bulletin*'s publication in July 1863, mentions either Sam Clemens or Mark Twain in nineteen separate items, almost all of them in the familiar mock-feud style. Sumner takes less notice of Mark Twain at the outset of the *News*'s publication in October, mentioning him only three times in the week before the hoax "A Bloody Massacre near Carson" commands everyone's attention. Sumner made up for this relative inattention by losing no opportunity in the months that followed the hoax to make fun of Mark Twain by alluding to it. In addition to kidding Mark Twain (or sometimes Sam Clemens) about miscues as a reporter, Parker and Sumner claim that Mark Twain drinks too much, eats too much, and steals, among other faults that sound very much like what Mark Twain has been saying of the Unreliable. Some items illustrate the no-holds-barred tactics of Washoe raillery. When a local business displays a large tapeworm in its window, Sumner declares that Mark will use it as a fishing line during his next expedition to Lake Tahoe. When someone leaves large and evil-smelling boots on a stagecoach, another rival claims they are Mark's. Other items suggest Mark Twain's notoriety: his criticism of a play, a bon mot uttered that day, and a rumor that he has proposed marriage are all considered worthy of mention.[92]

The facetiousness of nearly all the raillery that Sam Clemens indulged in and the comradery behind it can more clearly be seen when compared with the

91. Basso, *Bulletin and News*, 27, 23–24.

92. Ibid., 29; see also 18–19, 19–20, 32–33. Charles Parker of the *Bulletin*, despite all the raillery, seemed to know and be genuinely fond of Clemens. Noting a speech made by Clemens, Parker's column says: "Perhaps the speech of the evening was made by Sam Clemens. Those not familiar with this young man, do not know the depths of grave tenderness in his nature. He almost brought the house to tears by his touching simple pathos" (ibid., 13–14).

blackguarding routinely exchanged among the editors and reporters on Nevada and California newspapers. An example of this more serious yet still personal editorializing occurred during the debate on the first proposed constitution for Nevada. When the *Virginia City Daily Union* abruptly switched to a negative position on the issue, the *Enterprise* referred to it as "the Weathercock" and as "the Virginia Daily Stultifier, bartered, abandoned, unprincipled and daily stultifying itself," while another newspaper was satisfied with "contemptible, word-eating, blackmail sheet." The *Union* responded to one attack by referring to the rival paper as "that venal purchasable smut-machine."[93] These venomous exchanges, which could have deadly consequences, highlight the playfulness of the mock-severe roughhouse raillery of Mark Twain and his compeers.

Sam Clemens had the reputation of enjoying jokes on people but not of reacting well to being the victim of jokes and teasing. William Wright recalled Sam's pique at being presented a fake meerschaum pipe, as well as his sulking reaction when Charles Farrar Browne (Artemus Ward) teased Sam at a party.[94] Arthur McEwen revealed how Sam preferred to relieve such pique with his talent for swearing, especially when the *Enterprise* printers pulled their favorite trick, stealing the shade from Clemens's lamp.[95] With practical jokes and teasing a way of life, one had to know the differences among fighting words, swearing words, and laughing words, but those differences were not always obvious. Even good-natured raillery can become venomous lampoon if the target is hostile. Moreover, as Clemens discovered, the line between the satiric sting of the lampoon and the plain insult of blackguarding may be only in the ears of the listener.

93. Quoted in Fatout, *Virginia City,* 142–43.
94. Wright, "Reporting," 175; William Wright, "Artemus Ward in Nevada," 405; see also Paine, *Biography,* 1:224–27.
95. McEwen, "Heroic Days," 15. See also Paine, *Biography,* 1:214–15.

## FRAMING THE HUMOR OF RAILLERY

THE *INTENTION* AND NOT THE *ACT* CONSTITUTES CRIME—IN OTHER
WORDS, CONSTITUTES THE *DEED*. IF YOU CALL YOUR BOSOM FRIEND A
FOOL, AND *INTEND* IT FOR AN INSULT, IT *IS* AN INSULT; BUT IF YOU DO
IT PLAYFULLY, AND MEANING NO INSULT, IT IS *NOT* AN INSULT.

————

MARK TWAIN, "ANSWERS TO CORRESPONDENTS,"
*CALIFORNIAN*, JUNE 3, 1865

Clemens based Mark Twain's humor of raillery upon what Plato called "play-ful malice," which captures precisely the two motives of comic laughter: play and aggression. Ethology, the study of animal behavior, demonstrates the complex relationship between play and aggression, which involves complicated actions called "agonistic" behaviors. Mock combat epitomizes such agonistic behavior. Mock combat is a sophisticated behavior that necessitates a "frame" enclosing it within the play domain so that the actions mimic a deadly encounter rather than actually becoming one. Ideally, participants in a mock combat clearly perceive this frame, but the reality may be much more ambiguous. When one participant believes the other has stepped beyond the frame, playful bites can become painfully earnest. At a minimum, the game of play fighting stops. When the frame that differentiates cannot be perceived or is somehow lost, playful aggression transforms into serious aggression.[96]

The necessity for a differentiating frame explains why joking behavior can often go awry, as Sam Clemens demonstrated by becoming involved in duels. Joking expresses the ambivalent nature of playful aggression. To an individual outside the play frame, such behavior looks the same as serious aggression. However, to one who recognizes the frame, merely an air of earnestness exists, altering the behavior and rendering it as pretense. When Sam Clemens reserved his more pungent railleries for other newspapermen he knew well, such as William Wright and Clement Rice, he relied on the surest guarantee for a play frame, a warm friendship. Joe Goodman recalled that when Clemens made fun of legislators, he chose "congenial" men.[97] And when Clemens burlesqued the fashions

96. Gregory Bateson, "A Theory of Play and Fantasy"; see also Richard Alford, "Humor Framing Conventions: Techniques and Effects"; and Don Handelman, "Play and Ritual: Complementary Frames of Meta-Communication."
97. Goodman, "Memories," 3.

of actual women at a gala ball, he chose "ladies whose tempers I think I can depend upon" (ETS 1:316).

Sigmund Freud recognized the problem of playful aggression's ambivalence becoming the ambiguity of joking utterances when he elaborated the playfully aggressive nature of jokes. Freud captures a joke's ambiguity in his descriptive metaphor of a joking "envelope" that contains a nub of serious thought. In Freud's analysis, this envelope functions as a bribe for or a distraction of the internal moral censor that would normally not allow the pleasure of play to be expressed.[98] The envelope metaphor suggests in another way how jokes can go astray even when a play frame is manifest: individuals in an audience for a joke may choose to discard the playful envelope and to retain only the serious thought. Because the best jokes are often about very serious matters, their ambivalent nature and ambiguous expression always allow someone to ignore the playfulness and take the utterance seriously. When Sam Clemens joked about the Sanitary Commission Fund, without question the women from Carson City as well as the staff of the *Virginia City Daily Union* discounted the routine playfulness of Washoe Mark Twain's raillery and decoded the joke as an imputation against their honesty and loyalty during wartime. Because teasing is largely a matter of performance—of tone and manner all too easily lost in print—the seriousness of the topic predominated for them, even though the pseudonym "Mark Twain" should have functioned as a play frame.

Like tickling, verbal teasing or printed raillery are basic forms of playfully aggressive behavior meant to cause comic laughter. Tickling simulates an attack on people's bodies; teasing and raillery simulate attacks on their characters. Teasing is spontaneous, exhibiting a broad range of tones, from relatively mild to absolutely scathing. Once two people engage in the repartee of mutual teasing, the dynamic of the mock combat begins. Teasing can be related to insults in the same way that mock combat relates to actual combat: as a form of play constrained by more or less understood rules beyond which true insult is meant— or can be taken as such. One might say that Clemens's printed railleries, signed "Mark Twain" and directed against his good friends, can be taken as playful versions of Sam's famous cursing performances, which were apparently genuine expressions of anger.[99]

Teasing thus walks a fine line between playful malice and actual malice. Moreover, playing with that boundary is integral to teasing, making it the pleasurable though dangerous activity that it is. Presumably the staged railleries of Sam Clemens and his *Enterprise* colleague William Wright created that pleasure for

98. Sigmund Freud, *Jokes and Their Relationship to the Unconscious*, 92–93.
99. McEwen, "Heroic Days," 15.

their readers, joking, for example, about stealing each other's shirts to wear or about actual accidents both men suffered.[100] How far one can strain against the frame of playfulness before it collapses into true insult—just exactly what the rules are—can never quite be spelled out, for in an important way those rules emerge from the very specific circumstances that help to frame the teasing (or any mock combat) as playful pretense. Moreover, teasing's playful malice can be organized formally in a variety of formats. When one "plays the dozens," for example, the game's more formal organization will allow for much more playful malice than the looser circumstance of simply teasing a good friend in the course of a conversation. Furthermore, a long-established friendship allows for more playful malice than does a relatively new relationship. Part of the pleasure of such play, then, resides in the artfulness with which one takes advantage of the organizing circumstances that enable the teasing. One also needs to be able to gauge any audience's reactions to the performance.

None of these distinctions would have helped Sam Clemens. As a public figure, Washoe Mark Twain behaved as though the community of readers perceived a play frame for his humor of raillery when in fact no such official communal sanction existed. Persisting as an unofficial carnival clown meant Washoe Mark Twain was playing with comic dynamite.

100. William Wright, "No Head nor Tail," 5. Recounting accidents, Clemens wrote "Frightful Accident to Dan De Quille" and "[Dan Reassembled]." Wright countered with "An Infamous Proceeding" and "Mark Twain Takes a Lesson in the Manly Art." The *Golden Era* reprinted Wright's sketches, with "Frightful Accident" on May 1, 1864, as "'Mark Twain' and 'Dan De Quille' *Hors de Combat.*" Paine reprinted the second Mark Twain piece, the title of which is conjecture. See ETS 1:364.

# SCENE TWO

PLAYING WITH COMIC DYNAMITE

## READING A REPORTER WHO MOCKS JOURNALISM

OUR FRIEND, MARK TWAIN, IS SUCH A JOKER THAT WE CANNOT TELL
WHEN HE IS REALLY IN EARNEST.

———

CARSON CITY INDEPENDENT, FEBRUARY 13, 1864

The danger for Washoe Mark Twain the inveterate teaser, the danger entailed in his humor of raillery, existed on both the social and professional levels. The professional danger for Clemens began even before inventing his literary alter ego. Henry Nash Smith has argued that the *Enterprise,* during the legislative session of 1862, made a distinction between Sam Clemens and Mark Twain, one providing straight political reporting, the other providing "personal journalism, mostly humorous" (MTEnt 9). The daily dispatches were signed "Sam Clemens" and the weekly letters, comically seasoned, prototyped Mark Twain. Smith's argument implies that assimilating the comic attributes of "the boys" to his ostensible reporter's role created problems for Sam Clemens. Signing materials with two names suggests potential uncertainty for contemporary readers trying to decide what "Mark Twain" signified and thus distinguish the man from the comic narrator, the reporter from the yarn spinner. Because Mark Twain appeared in a respected newspaper—reporting local items or the activities of the legislative session on a daily basis, or providing accounts of events in Carson City on a weekly basis—readers might expect good journalism from him, that is, accuracy, objectivity, and a sober tone. However, Smith's formulation—"personal journalism, mostly humorous"—implies Sam Clemens's comic impulse toward raillery and the fantastic, an impulse at cross-purposes with the conventions of standard journalism, and one evident as early as his substitute editorship on Orion's newspaper, the *Hannibal Journal.*

Thus, at the same time that Mark Twain in his Washoe phase was striking the funny bone of the Nevada community at large, an item from the *Enterprise* reprinted in the *Oroville (California) Butte Record* on February 28, 1863, with the following headnote, suggests that personal journalism's mixing of the facetious with the serious did not always sit well with some contemporaries in the newspaper community: "Local of the Virginia Enterprise, who is continually blundering in his items—making misstatements one day, correcting them the day following—gives one of his victims satisfaction after this style" (ETS 1:408). Though an assessment of Sam Clemens's accuracy as a reporter in comparison to his peers in Nevada and California is not possible because the *Enterprise* files are lost, most coworkers agreed with William Wright, who recalled that Clemens had little interest in compiling paragraphs of facts.[101] Wright usually covered the technicalities of mining while Clemens covered the more informal news of the town, social items and the sensational.[102] Another person who claimed to have worked with Clemens on the *Enterprise* for a short while said that the "freedom with which Sam Clemens sketched the 'news' in those days was such as to take away the breath from many a silver pilgrim who had previously been accustomed to think that sound and sensible things only, ought to be said in print."[103] I have been arguing that "Mark Twain" signifies a play frame, which created an ambiguity about when Clemens was joking, to which the epigraph from the *Carson City Independent* testifies. That frame licenses a deliberate playing in print even with the conventions of journalism. Nevertheless, when a contemporary comprehends a joke, he finds it "scandalizing to the reportorial profession and public journalism."[104] Similarly, the judgment of the *Butte Record* does not account for the comic intent shown in "Apologetic," in which an apology for the original misstatement of fact serves as pretext for a joking insult.

The tactics to which some newspapermen objected, as Clemens concocted a comic narrator and character, can also be found in "Silver Bars—How Assayed." The *Enterprise* published this half-sketch, half-report without the Mark Twain signature. On the whole, the piece conveys a good grasp of facts about the technical topic. After all, Clemens spent several months as a miner. Little doubt can exist, however, that a California newspaper reprinted the piece because the narrator recounting the assaying process already sounds like Washoe Mark Twain. Some readers along the Comstock might have wished for descriptive accuracy, but most could not have failed to appreciate the manner in which Clemens portrays his experience of the scale used to measure the amount of base metal in a silver bar. The scale was so delicate that "You might weigh a musquito [*sic*] here, and then pull one of his legs off, and weigh him again, and the scales would detect the difference. The smallest weight used . . . looks like an imperceptible atom clipped from the invisible corner of a piece of paper whittled down to an impossible degree of sharpness—as it were" (ETS 1:212).

Like the image of the giant nutmeg grater to describe covered wagons scarred by bullets, this description comically conveys an important aspect of the process. Moreover, the image conveys the point without compromising the report's general integrity. As part of a deliberately constructed comic narrator, however, such imagery may seem worse than facetious to those expecting the piece to be

101. Wright, "Reporting," 171.
102. Mack, *Nevada*, 243.
103. *San Francisco Illustrated Press*, "Mark Twain," 21.
104. "Meridian," " 'The Third House' and Other Burlesques," 2.

scrupulously accurate. Moreover, in the case of "Silver Bars—How Assayed," Clemens complicates the question of accuracy by making it a topic for fun. Mark Twain starts the piece by confessing a worry about the correctness of his memory and then later admits that his memory is bad because he drank too much beer before he was shown the assaying process. Apparently, the worst suspicions of the scrupulous are correct; Sam Clemens is a sloppy reporter because he drinks too much. Whatever the drinking habits of Clemens actually were, that assessment misses the comic effect of a narrator and character who mirrors the habits of a stereotypical miner. Moreover, a focus on accuracy misses the way Washoe Mark Twain's comic foibles split the compounded identity of Sam Clemens the reliable correspondent, which fuses the implied author with the narrator's master role of respectable reporter. Remarkably, Sam Clemens, from the beginning of his professional career, was willing to allow comic effects to displace capable reporting. "Silver Bars—How Assayed" provides an excellent example of how the narrator's second master role of unsanctified reporter, a humorously ineffectual Washoe Mark Twain, can subversively disrupt sober journalistic practice. A downside for such antics exists, however. When drinking creates a foolishly incompetent persona and manifests the role of unsanctified reporter, the implied author's reliability can be questioned because the journalistic competence assumed by the implied author is separated from the narrator's other master role of respectable reporter.

This danger might be implicit, as in the "report" Mark Twain makes about his participation in a party thrown by stockbrokers. With Mark Twain's virtual confession that he became drunk during this party, the facts reported might be regarded with a suspicious eye (ETS 1:240). As Clemens fashioned and refashioned Washoe Mark Twain in 1863, he explicitly joked about liquor causing him to forget the facts (ETS 1:213) or to lose his notebook (MTEnt 70). Even when the notebook remains safe, Mark Twain jokes about the "hieroglyphics" he finds there (MTEnt 80). Joking about his own unreliability also can be found when Clemens covers the 1863 territorial legislature: one report is "mighty shaky [due to] mysterious short-hand notes" he himself has supposedly taken (MTEnt 95). These displays of incompetence later transform into a clear self-deprecating humor when, in the midst of his first burlesque fashion item, Mark Twain worries that he "might unwittingly get something wrong, and give offense" (ETS 1:311). These instances represent variations on the narrator's master role of an unsanctified newspaper reporter surfacing in the midst of a news report and threatening to transform the genre into a comic sketch. This dynamic annoyed, even outraged, some readers as it confused others.

Such playfulness with reporting creates very different results, however, when apparently exhibited through the narrator's master role of respectable reporter who possibly employs wit but always projects competence. Reporting on a thwarted duel between newspaper editors Joe Goodman and Tom Fitch in "A Duel Prevented," Mark Twain spells out the "inexorable duty" of the reporter: "to keep the public mind in a healthy state of excitement" (ETS 1:266). While the drunken or forgetful Mark Twain provokes laughter at a character doing a poor job of reporting, the witticism about a reporter's duty invites ridicule at the integrity of reporters in general and at the expectation that they will be truthful. Mark Twain in the latter instance ridicules the expectation by blatantly admitting he will substitute emotion for facts. This comically cynical view declares that drama rather than truth constitutes the marrow of reporting. Laughter is even better. Along with the editor of the *Carson City Independent*, a reader might say that he or she cannot tell if Mark Twain is earnest in expounding this cynical view because the narrator's master role of respectable reporter shrouds its doppelgänger, the unsanctified newspaper reporter.

Clemens manages another intricate joke about a reporter's credibility when he again shuffles the two master roles for Mark Twain the narrator in a self-conscious comment: "As I have said, the fashion synopses heretofore written by myself, have been uncouth burlesques—extravagant paraphrases of the eloquence of female costume, as incomprehensible and as conflicting as Billy Birch's testimony in the case of the atrocious assassination of Erickson's bull by 'Jonesy,' with his infamous 'stuffed club.' But this time, since a lady requests it, I will . . . write a faithful description of the queenly dresses worn at the Lick House party by several ladies whose tempers I think I can depend upon" (ETS 1:316). The laugh here comes from the cleverness with which Mark Twain exploits the situation. Having been the author of an earlier mock fashion item whose mockery in part depended upon the earnest tone of the silly descriptions, Mark Twain now mocks his own silliness by comparing it to a minstrel sketch (see ETS 1:490). However, he gives the funny business another twist, admitting his earlier mock earnestness by just as earnestly saying that this time he will provide a "faithful description." Because Mark Twain has been inept in his reporting in the past, no reason exists to expect anything but a faithless description of the ladies' attire, and the phrase "ladies whose tempers I think I can depend upon" gives the game away. The joke plays with expectations about a serious reporter by pretending to do the job correctly (or at least of *wishing* to do the job correctly) but somehow failing.

Clemens aims to be funny with that failure. However, not all contemporary readers laughed humorously with such sophisticated playfulness about the "inexorable duty" of a reporter, as the complaint noted before by the *Oroville (California) Butte Record* indicates. One of Sam Clemens's colleagues, Rollin M. Daggett, recalled how some of the *Enterprise* staff patronized a beer saloon in the newspaper office's basement so often that they formed a drinking club. Clemens was "among the regular attendants."[105] How many readers, knowing Sam's habits, ignored the humor in his Washoe Mark Twain character and assumed that he really tried to present the facts correctly in a particular news report but failed, his memory clouded by foamy drink? An item from the *Gold Hill News* suggests that some contemporaries may have mistaken one possibility for the other: "Mark Twain, Jim Hardy, Judge Leconey, See-Yup, and a lot of other Chinamen at Virginia, are having a series of 'high old' drunks [with] the vile stuff that forms the staple food of those bummers."[106] And when Clemens jokingly implies that Washoe Mark Twain does not always pay his hotel bill on time, what should be inferred from this note, dated October 1863, San Francisco? "Mark Twain again afflicts us with his presence. Tell this to the landlord of the Lick House, who would doubtless like to 'see him.'"[107] Is this the good-natured raillery of the local column or the barbed raillery of the editorials?

Where does Washoe Mark Twain stop and Sam Clemens begin? When should one believe the news in an item signed "Mark Twain"? In 1862, during Clemens's first stint as *Enterprise* reporter of the territorial legislature, one member submitted a resolution asking that Sam Clemens "restrain his imagination and confine himself to the truth" when reporting what legislators said (ETS 1:26). Clemens's reporting during 1863 increasingly blurs into the fictionalization or dramatization of events, giving the questions some force. The problem can be found in the way Clemens fictionalized his summer vacation in San Francisco with Clement Rice (ETS 1:250–53) or his stagecoach rides to and from San Francisco and Virginia City (ETS 1:255–56, 293–295). In another "report," the news about a duel between Joe Goodman and Tom Fitch nearly becomes lost in Mark Twain's focus on waiting for the duel, his headlong ride out to witness it, and his planned revenge against Marshal Perry and his constables for stopping it (ETS 1:265–66). The comic misfocus illustrates how the impulse to create fiction invades and transforms factual description. Clemens often prefers to take literally the joke that a reporter has a duty to dramatize.

A reporter turning news into comic fodder has a number of precedents, but they did not occur until the market for newspapers changed. When overtly connected to the political issues of the day, comic writing in American newspapers had been mostly political satire. Once the urban penny newspapers of the 1830s reshaped the landscape of American journalism, however, something new appeared: comic material written about nonpolitical, quotidian news. Such comic writing was not a deliberate invention and does not appear as an easily

---

105. Daggett, "Recollections," 15. In this connection, see Paul Fatout's reprint of an *Enterprise* item about the "Lager Beer Club," which he attributes to Clemens (*Virginia City*, 47–48).

106. *Gold Hill News*, "Stars," October 26, 1863, 3.

107. Quoted in Fatout, *Virginia City*, 99.

identified comic genre at its inception, for reporting news with comic flourishes was only one possible technique in the service of the penny newspapers' general goal: to render news into entertainment. Moreover, the first individual who might be named in a genealogy of comic newspapermen (rather than political satirists), George Wisner, was not hired to be funny. Instead, Wisner was the *New York Sun*'s first full-time police reporter. Nevertheless, Wisner's police reports, appearing on page 3, remained in the *Sun* for years not because of their factual accuracy, but because Wisner mixed facts with good storytelling.[108] William Huntzicker explains that the penny press's circulation depended upon crime, humor, and humor about crime. While that formula may be as old as eighteenth-century English broadsides about notorious criminals, daily reports on urban crime, seasoned with levity, seem to have been a distinctly American invention. The success of the *New York Sun* spawned imitators in New York City, such as the *Daily Transcript* and *Herald,* papers that dramatically increased sensationalist coverage on crime. The *New Orleans Picayune* produced another reporter like Wisner. Denis Corcoran, during the late 1830s and into the 1840s, covered the police courts for the *Picayune,* and his humorous sketches of court scenes helped to build circulation.[109]

Undoubtedly, other reporters on many other newspapers acquired local reputations for their comic journalism. Two reporters for major newspapers, however, established national reputations and profitable careers in part by turning the newspaper report into a comic genre. Both represent significant precedents for Mark Twain. After the commercial success of the first collection of his Philander Doesticks comic sketches, Mortimer Thomson spent part of his day reporting on one of the New York City police courts for the *Tribune.* His one or two columns of "news" frequently became a venue for comic storytelling, complete with dialogue. These narratives, the veracity of which is doubtful, became part of a second compilation of comic items published with the Doesticks pen name.[110] Besides inserting Artemus Ward letters into his local column, Charles Farrar Browne often used other comic techniques to enliven his reports for the *Cleveland Plain Dealer* at the end of the 1850s. The column's name, "City Facts and Fancies," suggests the mixed genre produced by all comic newspaper reporters.

Those precedents, however, did not predict a significant way Clemens used Mark Twain: to burlesque the act of reporting and thus by extension newspapers

---

108. See Isabelle Lehuu, *Carnival on the Page: Popular Print Media in Antebellum America,* 50.
109. William E. Huntzicker, *The Popular Press, 1833–1865,* 13, 98.
110. The complete title of the book is *The History and Records of the Elephant Club.* The authors listed are "Knight Russ Ockside [Nitrous Oxide], M.D." and "Q. K. Philander Doesticks, P.B." The other pseudonym is that of Edward Fitch Underhill, who was also a reporter for the *Tribune* and was well-known as an excellent stenographer.

themselves and their claim to represent the truth. Dressing up the news with a comic presentation did not break the rules; George Wisner had been doing it since the early 1830s. Mark Twain, however, undermined his own claims to journalistic respectability with his comic indifference to the facts, his readiness to fabricate amusing news rather than report observed events, and his invitations to laugh at the dullness of local items on the one hand and the sensationalizing of news on the other.

Christopher Wienandt has recently taken Sam Clemens to task for violating "tenets of acceptable journalism, even in rough-and-tumble frontier Nevada."[111] Though Wienandt's analysis misses the implications of the wide-open style of Washoe journalism, which allowed for personal attitudes to be added to news stories and editorials, its examination of Clemens as journalist does raise a useful question. How many contemporary readers of Mark Twain thought the pseudonym signified a funnyman whose primary intent was to entertain, not inform? If those readers understood "Mark Twain" to denote a reporter, then clearly Clemens cannot have much credibility: from the beginning of his *Enterprise* career, too many items entertain more than they inform. However, if "Mark Twain" signified funny business and not plain business to his readers, holding Clemens to *any* journalistic standard of accuracy makes little sense. Using journalism as a metric for evaluating Washoe Mark Twain would necessarily fail to account for the more profound comic effects Clemens achieves with his playful approach to the commonsense distinction between fact and fiction. This basic tactic makes Clemens vulnerable to attacks for sacrificing accuracy to laughter, attacks his contemporaries made and Wienandt echoes. Sam Clemens in Nevada deliberately and consistently conflated fiction with fact so that Washoe Mark Twain confuses readers for laughs.

Despite his penchant for embroidering facts with comic devices, embroidery that at times became wholesale yarn spinning, the bulk of the writing Sam Clemens did for the *Enterprise* had no comic intent, even when he pairs Mark Twain with the Unreliable. For every reprinting of a feature-length, quasi-comic piece like "Silver Bars—How Assayed," several days' worth of local items have not been reprinted and thus cannot take their place in the record. Nevertheless, the initial pattern for Washoe Mark Twain had emerged early. The pseudonym "Mark Twain," when it appeared in February 1863, did not unleash a comic impulse in the writings of Sam Clemens. Rather, Mark Twain the character gathered together comic elements, present since Clemens's earliest extant local column, into a pen name that should have signified to readers to be wary—the

111. Christopher Wienandt, "Mark Twain, Nevada Frontier Journalism, and the *Territorial Enterprise:* Crisis in Credibility," 163.

smooth sailing of accurate reporting will founder on the shoals of comic foolishness and unsanctified behavior. The leadsman's warning cry of "mark
twain"—signifying water barely safe for a steamboat's passage—is apt. For
Clemens, the signature "Mark Twain" functioned as his claim to the license of
carnival, not only granting him a measure of freedom from the necessity of
merely reporting facts but also signifying his desire to make fun of that necessity, even to disrupt and subvert it.

By the end of February 1863, two roles for Mark Twain as narrator had emerged
in the work of Sam Clemens, narrative roles embodying the two fundamental
aspects of his comic journalism—the respectable and the unsanctified newspaper
reporters. The first generally denotes a competent, clever observer who nevertheless turns a comic phrase or employs tall-tale conventions to suggest just how
windy it was yesterday. This narrative role can be found, for example, in early feature pieces like "The Spanish Mine." Under the varying demands of being an entertaining as well as informative reporter, the respectable reporter might express a
comic viewpoint that can easily become acerbic (ETS 1:182), or even satiric, in a
conservative mode that supports status quo (ETS 1:401). The second master role
for the narrator, the unsanctified newspaper reporter, entails the clown and the
fool in Clemens's comic journalism. Thus at the textual level of narrator, Mark
Twain exhibits the contradiction of an oxymoron. Respectable yet unsanctified, he
demonstrates his literary debt to the Gentleman Roarer figure.

Various personae manifest both narrative roles: Mark Twain might be drunk
or forgetful to portray foolish ineptitude, as we have seen. These personae provide Clemens with a range of possibilities for either dimension of his Mark
Twain narrator as he experiments with comic perspectives. The role of
respectable newspaper reporter, witty and competent, was of course not original. Charles Farrar Browne, for example, created his first comic reputation with
such a column in the *Cleveland Plain Dealer*. What made Clemens different was
the boldness with which he stretched the role for comic purposes. Washoe Mark
Twain embodies the carnival spirit of Virginia City during the boom time of the
early 1860s. That embodiment meant that Mark Twain reflected the communal
values of the Comstock, such as a roughhouse, frontier equality expressed by
practical jokes and mock feuds. However, Washoe Mark Twain also upended
centric values by satirizing first families' pretensions, burlesquing literary genres, and spinning yarns about fellow reporters that moved well beyond the customary practice of mock feuding.

Clemens's experimentation with comic personae for his doubled Mark Twain
narrator resulted in the respectable author implied by the writings of the *Enterprise*'s local editor metamorphosing repeatedly into the foolishly, even wildly,
comic character Mark Twain. Those transformations caused laughable disrup-

tions that were persistent and multileveled. This comic narrator in its Nevada incarnation, "Washoe Mark Twain," signifies not just the disruption of well-mannered and genteel behavior, not just the disruption of the newspaper game of mock feuding, but also the disruption of journalistic conventions of reporting. Successful with his Washoe brand of Mark Twain, with its humor of raillery, Clemens must have believed he could afford to remain unsanctified and outside the pale.

---

## Lying to the Public for Laughs

For Heaven's sake give me at least the peace & quiet it will afford me to know that no stumping is to be done for the unlucky Sanitary Fund.

———

Letter to Orion Clemens, May 25, 1864

Reporting, reporting with a dramatic or comic flair, burlesquing reporting, fictionalizing events for comic purposes, making up stories to rail at your friends and annoy your enemies—once one arranges the writings of Sam Clemens in Nevada along this spectrum, only a short step remains to a final category: "reporting yarns," or hoaxes. Hoaxes are a radical variation of the informative but comic feature article; they disguise themselves as information but are meant to be wholly comic. Given the propensity by Washoe journalists to be comic as they report the news, a local reporter might reverse the emphasis and use apparent information as dressing for a joke. A hoax like "The Petrified Man" or "A Bloody Massacre near Carson" has the same comic impetus present in burlesques, lampoons, and practical jokes: all exhibit the comic abuse of raillery.

"Petrified Man" apparently had as its target not only the habit newspapers had of printing all sorts of stories about petrified objects being dug up but also a Humboldt county judge, a man named G. T. Sewall. Clemens must have felt that a sufficient number of petrified objects had been reported on recently so that a burlesque making fun of such stories would be appreciated. "Petrified Man" requires a foundation of plausibility in order to work, and the rash of news stories and tales about petrified objects provided the necessary background. Naming an actual person also camouflages the story as a local news item. Why Clemens decided to name Sewall in the tale and make him look foolish in his serious reaction to the nonexistent petrified specimen is not clear. If one knew they were the best of friends, as Clemens and Rice were, then one could say with assurance that the raillery was only good-natured fun between equals. In the absence of a friendship—indeed, with some evidence that they disliked one another[112]—the sketch transforms into a satiric lampoon meant to ridicule Sewall's officiousness, pomposity, or possibly his lack of humor (ETS 1:155–58).

Stopping here in the analysis, however, would miss the way that "Petrified Man" as hoax differs from its cousins, stretchers like "Unfortunate Blunder" (ETS 1:286–87) and "Mr. Billet Is Complimented by a Stranger" (ETS 1:295). Whereas a tall tale trips up readers who are greenhorns, the hoax targets all who are careless as they read the piece. If someone reading "Petrified Man" does not visualize the position of the petrified figure's hands as they are described, he or she will miss the basic joke, for the man is simultaneously winking and thumbing his nose at everyone—including the reader. Sewall looks foolish partly because he is much too serious about the corpse of a man whose basic posture says, "Who cares?" but if readers do not catch that posture, they will be just like Sewall—much too serious about the overdone coverage of discovering fossils. When one reads "Petrified Man" not as a lampoon of Sewall but as a burlesque of newspaper reporting, the "Who cares?" attitude becomes directed toward stories about fossils, an attitude a savvy reader adopts.

Published on October 4, 1862, "Petrified Man" appeared less than a month after Clemens had begun to work for the *Virginia City Territorial Enterprise* and four months before "Mark Twain" debuted in the paper. Though Sewall cannot have been pleased about the piece, other readers apparently were not displeased. At least, no record exists of a backlash. Readers along the Comstock had some experience with stretchers and hoaxes in the papers that they otherwise depended upon to give them accurate information.[113] "Petrified Man" was not the first western hoax about a fossilized human being (ETS 1:157). Moreover, given the atmosphere of joking that prevailed in Comstock mining towns, most readers fooled by "Petrified Man" probably reacted good-naturedly when they found out or figured out the truth. Nevertheless, when Clemens published another hoax about a year later, on October 28, 1863, not all were amused.

Clemens originally entitled this second hoax "A Bloody Massacre near Carson." The sketch pretends to recount how a man named Pete Hopkins lost his money because of phoney or "cooked" dividends. Driven mad by his financial ruin, Hopkins kills his wife and children with an axe, then slits his own throat and rides into Carson City, dying in front of a well-known saloon (ETS 1:324–

---

112. Arthur Pettit, *Mark Twain and the South,* 26. Clemens may have been taking revenge for a threat by Sewall to whip him "on sight" for his secessionist sympathies.

113. Fatout, *Virginia City,* 108.

26). By October 1863 Mark Twain was a well-known if not universally well-liked comic figure, and Clemens was well on his way toward creating his own extravagant brand of Washoe journalism. Many newspaper readers understood "Mark Twain" as a code name for Sam Clemens's comic disruptions of journalistic norms. Given that the *Enterprise* published "A Bloody Massacre near Carson" over this pseudonym that signified joking, only those readers who mistook Mark Twain for a standard reporter could have failed to see it as a clever joke among many he had perpetrated. However, instead of the laughs "Petrified Man" garnered, "A Bloody Massacre near Carson" unleashed a "howl from Siskiyou to San Diego" that included calls for Sam Clemens to resign, joking references for months afterward, and enough bitter emotion to ensure that allusions to the tale would be made for the rest of the decade. William Wright's version of the fallout has Sam Clemens so worried he cannot sleep. In Paine's account, Clemens offers his resignation to Joe Goodman.[114] When one pieces together what has been unearthed of the contemporary record, however, the resultant scene does not include these dramatic gestures. Moreover, Sam Clemens not only rolled on undeterred in his unsanctified humor of raillery, but the reputation of Mark Twain enlarged in the months remaining before Clemens left Virginia City.

As with the other hoaxes and stretchers he had written, Clemens constructed "A Bloody Massacre near Carson" as a plausible account nested among routine stories about fights and murders with which the Comstock abounded in 1863. The hoax also had as background a very specific and recent axe murder (ETS 1:321). As before, Clemens used the name of an actual person, in this case Abram Curry. However, Curry functioned not as the butt of the joke or as an incidental bystander. Rather, Curry supposedly told the tale of the massacre to Mark Twain. The tactic is daring. Abram Curry was a respected early settler of Carson City. He had laid out its street plan, erected the stone buildings in the town, and was probably instrumental in having the legislature meet in Carson City, offering his hotel for the first legislative session. He was a member of the territorial legislature in the second and third sessions.[115] For the *Gold Hill Daily News*, this use of a well-known citizen's name was crucial: this "respectable source" made the paper overcome its doubt about the veracity of the massacre and partially reprint the tale (ECM 199). Clemens had employed this same device earlier in the month, attributing a wild tale called "The Great Prize Fight" to another well-known and respected man of the community. At the conclusion of that piece, Mark Twain claimed that John B. Winters had told him the tale about the absurdly bloody fight between Governor Stanford of California and Frederick

114. Wright, "Reporting," 172; ECM 202; Paine, *Biography,* 1:231.
115. Bancroft, *History,* 86, 159; Elliott, *History of Nevada,* 71.

Low, the man who had just defeated him to become the governor-elect. Like Curry, Winters was a businessman and a member of the territorial legislature—and presumably Clemens felt he knew both men well enough to put their names into his wildly gory tales without incurring their wrath.

However, he could not escape the wrath of others. It did not matter that Clemens created a playful frame with several clues to indicate the story's fictional nature. It did not matter that more than one-fourth of the narrative discusses phoney dividends, pointing the reader to the true target of the hoax. The horror engendered by the grisly details of the axe murders drove out all attention to the tale's intent—for some contemporary readers. "A Bloody Massacre near Carson" had a different reception than anything else Clemens had written up to that time because the initial group of readers fooled by the hoax included other newspapermen, and they did not enjoy being misled—or "sold," in the slang of the day. Admitting that it had believed the tale, the *Grass Valley (California) National* (November 3, 1863) wrote, "The ass who originated the story doubtless thinks he is 'old smarty'—we don't."[116] Because the hoax satirized San Francisco newspapers that had warned about Nevada companies cooking dividends while overlooking the fact that California companies engaged in the same crooked schemes, those newspapers were especially unhappy about the story turning out to be a hoax. Their ire must have been doubled when Clemens the next day published a mock apology saying that such tales were the only way to get the facts into the San Francisco papers.[117] The *San Francisco Journal* declared that as long as the editors of the *Enterprise* "keep the author of that hoax in their employ we shall not trouble their columns for news matter."[118] Such threats of course provided convenient distraction from the accusations embedded in the hoax.

In addition to the chagrin of individual editors, the negative reaction to "A Bloody Massacre near Carson" entailed two serious claims to support labeling the hoax detrimental. The first claim involved the Nevada Territory's reputation. In their immediate reactions to the hoax, the *Gold Hill Daily News* and the *Virginia City Evening Bulletin* worried that the tale augmented the already infamous reputation the Nevada Territory had for violence. Outsiders will believe any and all wild narratives as a consequence of what Mark Twain had "reported." Clemens must have known that he would not have the San Francisco newspapers on his side in publishing what he later called his "sarcasm" on cooking dividends (MTEnt 160). He could not have known that Nevada papers, feeling the territory's honor was impugned by the fictitious murders, would also be against

116. Quoted in Fatout, *Virginia City,* 102.
117. Putnam, "Dan and Mark Twain," 3.
118. Quoted in Fatout, *Virginia City,* 103.

him. The outrage professed in the second charge united Nevadan and Californian newspapers, however: the hoax violated the duty of journalists to find the facts and tell the truth. Moreover, the *Enterprise* had abandoned its duty as a responsible newspaper by printing the tale. Over and over again, other papers castigated the *Enterprise* and, like the *San Francisco Journal,* threatened to abstain from reprinting anything else from its pages. As the days turned into weeks, the censure increased. A month after Joe Goodman had published "A Bloody Massacre near Carson," two California newspapers noted other recent stories in the *Enterprise* but refused to believe in them: "You can't play Mark Twain upon us folks in Watsonville," said one.[119]

The comment by the Watsonville paper suggests how much for some contemporary readers the narrator's master role of respectable reporter comprised *all* of Mark Twain. From the beginning, however, Sam Clemens, playing hell with Washoe Mark Twain, had included joking about the reliability of newspapers themselves as well as joking about his reliability as a reporter. With "Bloody Massacre near Carson," his playfulness was significantly lost on his peers. A *Virginia City Evening Bulletin* editor thought that playing at being a reporter precisely defined the problem with Sam Clemens, both before and after the hoax:

> The genius who hashes up the locals for the Enterprise, and who outraged the feelings of the whole community yesterday by publishing a really disgraceful sensation story, wholly without point, other than the giving expression to a sort of natural talent he possesses, this morning comes out in another article [a mock apology] on the same subject even worse than that published yesterday. We say worse, because the fact of the almost universal condemnation of the story, when it was discovered to be an unmitigated falsehood, compelling its author to swallow his own words, and his doing so publicly, is even more injurious, or should be, *to the reputation of an editor* than the first promulgation of the untruth. (ECM 200, emphasis added)

The *Evening Bulletin* may have had a particular reason to complain. Paine says that the hoax was meant to punish the *Bulletin* for constantly attacking Washoe mining frauds while always praising California's sound mining practices.[120] In any case, for its editors, Mark Twain's comic play only "hashes up" the truth of the local items and jeopardizes his reputation as a competent journalist, yet distance from the business of reporting the news had always been crucial to his humor: the most profound fun generated by Washoe Mark Twain came from his habit of prying himself loose from serious journalism. The criticisms multiplied nonetheless. Several newspapers questioned if there was any joke buried in the tale—only in the

119. Ibid., 104.
120. Paine, *Biography,* 1:229.

mind of the author, said one. Another wondered if the author even understood what a joke was. William Wright recalled Sam Clemens saying, "I am being burned alive on both sides of the mountains,"[121] meaning Nevada and California, but the remark also applies to the way contemporaries criticized Clemens about both roles for his comic narrator. To his critics, Mark Twain had failed to be either a competent funnyman or a competent straight man.

At first, Clemens did not take the fuss seriously. He *was* taking seriously the underlying issue of phoney dividends and their danger to small investors, however, and the next day he issued his mock apology, which actually spelled out the perfidy of the San Francisco press for failure in its journalistic duty to tell the truth of the matter. On the second day following the hoax, October 30, Mark Twain apparently maintained his sarcastic tone in a mock complaint, saying that when the *Gold Hill Daily News,* on the twenty-ninth, had published him as the author of a lie, the small caps used for "A LIE" were not big enough to suit him. Furthermore, he referred to the *News* editor as a "little parson" while he dubbed the *Evening Bulletin* editor an "oyster-brained idiot" (ECM 201). Washoe Mark Twain had raillery aplenty but no remorse. On October 31 or possibly November 1, Clemens left Virginia City for Carson City to begin reporting on the constitutional convention. He used part of his first weekly letter on the convention to explain that "Pete Hopkins and A. Curry have compromised with me, and there is no longer any animosity existing on either side. They were a little worried at first, you recollect, about that thing which appeared recently (I think it was in the Gold Hill News), concerning an occurrence which has happened in the great pine forest down there at Empire" (MTEnt 89). The implication was simple: if the two people named in the hoax had expended whatever pique they may have had, everyone else should relax. The letter reports the beginning of the convention, with only a comic phrase or two, and sounds an unabashed note of pride in the delegates and of patriotism for the territory of Nevada. Beyond making sure that Curry and Hopkins were not miffed, Clemens apparently cared little for the dissatisfaction of other journalists.[122]

Nevertheless, the dissatisfaction did not recede. At the very least, "A Bloody Massacre near Carson" remained a topic of discussion in Carson City and elsewhere, for Clemens, in his second letter on the convention, interrupts his report to joke about "ANOTHER BLOODY MASSACRE!" the details of which occupy the rest of the letter. The massacre turns out to be the biblical story of Samson slaying a thousand Philistines with the jawbone of an ass. The postscript reveals

121. Wright, "Reporting," 172.

122. Pete Hopkins was the proprietor of the Sarazac Saloon in Carson City, in front of which the fictional P. Hopkins dies. Wright thought that "A Bloody Massacre near Carson" was written to ridicule Hopkins for some slight (ibid., 173).

the joke's target as the editor of the *San Francisco Journal,* who, Mark Twain says, will not find the tale when he looks "carefully" through the newspaper exchanges and will therefore post Mark Twain as a hoaxer again before discovering how "the jaw-bone of one of his ancestors" was used.

The piece contains more than a clever way to call the editor an ass, however; it also shows Clemens aware, albeit comically, of the basic issue—a reporter's reliability: "I am sorry that it was necessary for me to furnish you with a narrative of this nature, because my efforts in this line have lately been received with some degree of suspicion; yet it is my inexorable duty to keep your readers posted, and I will not be recreant to the trust, even though the very people whom I try to serve, upbraid me" (MTEnt 91). As a strategy to blunt criticism, Clemens here makes light of the issue of reliability, but when the outrage of his fellow journalists did subside, Clemens capably presented the issue in a more serious fashion. On February 1, 1864, Sam's niece Mollie, aged ten, succumbed to the spotted fever that killed many during the winter. In a letter to the *Enterprise,* Mark Twain attacked the monopoly of the Carson City undertaker, which allowed him to charge exorbitant rates. The ire expressed on the topic obviously issued from the recent experience of the Clemens family. In the midst of the attack, Mark Twain wondered why the *Carson City Independent* had said nothing about the undertaker's price-gouging ("Concerning Undertakers," MTEnt 151).

The editors answered that they had said nothing because they had heard no complaints. This weak response ignited Mark Twain's sarcasm in another letter devoted entirely to satirizing the faults of the *Independent:*

> Any editor in the world will say it is *your* duty to ferret out these abuses, and *your* duty to correct them. What are you paid for? what use are you to the community? what are you fit for as a conductor of a newspaper, if you cannot do these things? Are you paid to know nothing, and keep on writing about it every day? How long do you suppose such a jack-legged newspaper as yours would be supported or tolerated in Carson, if you had a rival no larger than a foolscap sheet, but with something in it, and whose editor would know, or at least have energy enough to find out, whether a neighboring paper abused one of the citizens justly or unjustly? (MTEnt 160)

Despite the opinions of some newspaper editors, Clemens obviously knew the duty of a journalist to his community and the role a responsible newspaper plays in that community. What some of the editors failed to see, however, was how Mark Twain's Washoe humor of raillery, often done just to tease friends and annoy enemies, also served the community. Clearly, Clemens meant Mark Twain's abuse of the undertaker to stir up the citizens of Carson City, who would find out the facts in the process of defending the undertaker. Here the persona of a satiric defender of status quo values manifests the master role of respectable reporter. Clemens goes on to discuss "A Bloody Massacre near Carson" in terms that indicate he felt his hoax functioned in exactly the same way: a comic abuse meant to stir people into finding out the truth.

Despite his stated intention, the furor over the hoax persisted. Yet another effort at counterattack suggests the persistence, this salvo fired between November 15 and 20. Under the heading "Still Harping," Clemens copied items of censure and made reference to "picayune papers." He also published "Lives of the Liars; or, Joking Justified," a compilation of other hoaxes supposedly found in the exchanges, which begins by comparing "A Bloody Massacre near Carson" to the parables from the New Testament![123] A comment in the *Gold Hill Daily News* on November 21 indicates the list's intent: to demonstrate that truth was not a necessary ingredient for local news items and that the louder a newspaper squawked about being hoaxed, "the more applicable the epithet 'one horse.'" However, these latest efforts probably indicated frustration, not worry, on the part of Clemens. In any case, like the mock apology and complaint a month earlier, they are obviously not meant to placate.

The *Gold Hill Daily News* was particularly irked at the use of the parables in "Lives of the Liars; or, Joking Justified," which suggests the aptness of Clemens's earlier epithet of "little parson." Indeed, Clemens's epithets hint at a long-harbored negative attitude about some newspapermen, and "A Bloody Massacre near Carson" may have provided a chance for those peers to express a preexisting dislike for Sam Clemens and his Mark Twain alter ego. Paul Fatout refers to the following comment of the *Austin (Nevada) Reese River Reveille,* published November 7, as "contemptuous," and it does seem to justify the conclusion about chronic animosity: "Some of the papers are expressing astonishment that 'Mark Twain'... should perpetrate such a 'sell.'... They don't know him. We would not be surprised at ANYTHING done by that silly idiot." Because so much of Washoe Mark Twain's comic fun consisted of railing at individuals, Sam Clemens inevitably rubbed some readers the wrong way. As early as April 1863, an anecdote about one irate Comstocker found its way into print. When the angry citizen stormed into the *Enterprise* offices and threatened to boot the local reporter all over the territory, Sam Clemens, in his best Washoe Mark Twain manner, supposedly drawled, "Well, if you think you've got money enough to put me over all these toll-roads, just start in!" The next month, the senior editor for the *Enterprise,* Joe Goodman, acknowledged the basic humor of Washoe Mark Twain, describing him as reigning "by the Grace of Cheek."[124]

123. Original dates of publication are unknown. Both were reprinted in the *Reese River Reveille* on November 21, 1863. See ECM 202; Fatout, *Virginia City,* 103.

124. Fatout, *Virginia City,* 103, 45, 44.

Months after the hoax, the *Virginia City Evening Bulletin* responded to an April Fool's joke this way: "Mark Twain, who is notorious for constantly lying—under a mistake—made another mistake by perpetrating the following supposed-to-be sensational item as a 'goak,' but we can't for the life of us see where the laugh comes in. . . . We suppose our neighbor thinking because this is April Fool's Day, he had a greater license than usual. But we don't see it. He who is a fool all the rest of the year, has no special rights on this particular day."[125] Paul Fatout portrays a Mark Twain popular with those contemporary readers who enjoyed rough-and-tumble joking—which fits the implied audience of "the boys"—but disliked by the more conventionally minded reader who found Mark Twain flippant, impious, and scandalous in his lies.[126] In a letter to Orion and Mollie, Clemens had once portrayed the second sort of reader: one without a sense of humor (CL 1:307–8). "A Bloody Massacre near Carson" neatly highlights these opposing reactions to Sam Clemens's comic character.

While Fatout's judgment about the split in the contemporary audience for Clemens rings true, it masks a problem about Washoe Mark Twain's humor, that is, his chronic raillery at individuals: how can present-day readers tell when the raillery is good-natured and when it is not? Take, for example, the comment made by the *Reese River Reveille*. On the face of it, one has to agree with Fatout calling it "contemptuous"; it reads like the harshest of personal attacks on Sam Clemens during the uproar over "A Bloody Massacre near Carson." Nevertheless, the comment is anything but contemptuous because it almost certainly was written by a fellow Missourian and good friend, Adair Wilson, who had left his reporter's job at the *Virginia City Daily Union* the first week in October to assume the editorship of the *Reveille*. In several pieces written in the summer of 1863, Clemens clearly notes Wilson as a good friend, and of course the railer's way to indicate friendship is to call him names—as Wilson does when he asserts how well he knows Mark Twain (see CL 1:264). Faced with not being sure about the relationships Clemens has with individuals, one can easily read animosity into words exchanged about the hoax—more than may have been there originally.

Similarly, more has been made of the negative nature of the newspapers' reactions than is justified once one makes the distinction between editorialists and local columnists. The complaints about the hoax made by the *Virginia City Evening Bulletin,* for example, occur on October 28 and 30, but on October 31 the *Bulletin* printed an item headed "Poor Wretch, We Pity Him," which explicitly forgives Clemens and teases him about his various "sins." Almost certainly, the complaints were written by H. C. Bennet, a senior editor, while the comic forgiveness

125. Basso, *Bulletin and News,* 62, 64.
126. Fatout, *Virginia City,* 97.

comes from the pen of the local columnist, Charles Parker, who continues as before to rail at Clemens good-naturedly, and who would in the coming weeks add mocking references about the hoax to his comic arsenal.[127] The same pattern appears in the *Gold Hill News.* The *Bulletin*'s editorial on October 30 had (among other suggestions) called on the local reporter for the *Gold Hill News*, Charles Sumner, who was fooled so badly, to give Clemens a hard time in retribution. The *News* did print two complaints about the hoax,[128] probably written, however, by editor and publisher Philip Lynch or his editor-in-chief, Hiram R. Hawkins, yet within days Charles Sumner was *not* indulging in retribution. Instead, he also maintained the local columnists' habit of friendly joking. He even encouraged Clemens to joke again in an item entitled simply, "Mark Twain":

> This favorite writer is "immelancholy"; he has got the mulligrubs. . . . We haven't had a good square joke out of poor Mark these four or five days. He sits behind that historic pine table morose and melancholy, and drinking mean whiskey to drown his misery. Cheer up, friend Mark, the courier brings the welcome news that all is quiet at Dutch Nicks, the "har" on Mrs. Hopkins' head is coming out like a new "red" shoebrush, the murderer has had that gash in his throat caulked and pitched, and the blood in that pine forest is not ankle deep. Awake, Mark, arise and toot your horn if you don't sell a clam.[129]

Nevertheless, the editors and publishers of the *Bulletin* and *News* felt it necessary to castigate Sam Clemens about the reputation of Nevada and the ethics of responsible journalism, echoing complaints from the California papers while representing respectable folks along the Comstock. The reporters who wrote the local columns, Clemens's peers, quickly forgave Sam's "faults" as a journalist. They humored him and represented the not-so-respectable folks, the implied readership of "the boys." However, according to the customs of the mock feud, the other local reporters did not forget the hoax. The numerous allusions to it in the weeks and months that followed the initial storm of protest stemmed from the local columnists' friendly feuding, not the serious admonishments of the editorial writers. Even William Wright, Clemens's *Enterprise* colleague and erstwhile roommate, makes references to the hoax in two *Golden Era* pieces, both written in imitation of Charles Farrar Browne. Browne was visiting San Francisco and Virginia City late in 1863 as part of his West Coast tour, playing the famously funny showman Artemus Ward. In one sketch, Artemus Ward supposedly leaves San Francisco for Washoe by steamboat. When a ship is sighted and someone thinks it may be the

---

127. Basso, *Bulletin and News,* 39.
128. *Gold Hill News,* "That Sell"; "Still Harping On."
129. Basso, *Bulletin and News,* 40.

infamous Confederate raider the *Alabama,* a second character says that the ship is captained by "blud-thursty Ole Hopkins."[130]

Whatever may have been the intensity of the heat generated by the controversy over "A Bloody Massacre near Carson," and whatever one infers from Clemens's various counterattacks against the negative reactions of his peers, the demands of reporting the constitutional convention did not leave him with much time to fret. In a weekly letter to the *Enterprise,* Clemens claimed that the reporters were working eighteen-hour days (MTEnt 93). Henry Nash Smith calculates that however one imagines the process of collaboration that went on between Sam Clemens and Andrew Marsh, they averaged more than four thousand words a day for the thirty-two days of the convention. Moreover, Smith points out that the experience reporting the constitutional convention trained Clemens well enough to be an equal reporting partner with Clement Rice when the third territorial legislature convened in January 1864 (MTEnt 11). Ironically, as Sam Clemens was being castigated during November 1863 for his poor performance as a reporter due to "A Bloody Massacre near Carson," he was actually significantly improving his reportorial skills. His preeminent joke during the second territorial legislature, dubbing Clement Rice "Unreliable" and himself "Reliable," despite Clemens's rookie status as reporter, had lost its rationale.

Notably, the storm the hoax generated in the journalists' community did not affect Sam Clemens's standing in the political community. At the conclusion of both the constitutional convention (December 11, 1863) and the third territorial legislature (February 20, 1864), Clemens was elected president of the "Third House" and presided over its meetings. These gatherings were carnival inversions of the convention and the legislature, and Clemens's presiding suggests that many elected officials did not think his hoax had done significant damage to the Nevada Territory's reputation. These men understood that Mark Twain was not Sam Clemens, as a remark by Cornelius Brosnan, a convention delegate, indicates. Judge Brosnan corrects, in Washoe Mark Twain style, a detail in Clemens's account of a speech the judge gave during a Union party convention in December 1863. Clemens includes the statement in his editorial, "The Bolters in Convention":

> The gentleman who reported the proceedings of the Union mass meeting last evening for the ENTERPRISE, unintentionally misquotes. He says Mr. Brosnan slandered the defunct "Nestor." Not so—Mr. B——made no allusion to that hair-brained, crazy old fool, "Nestor," nor to his "wardrobe." But Mr. B——did mention *that* other jealous and wicked "cuss," Nessus, and his historical, villainous "shirt."

130. William Wright, "Onto the Deep"; "Amung the Seelestials."

Now, if that facetious sinner, blunderer, and *sage-brush painter,* "Mark Twain," had thus libelled me, I could forgive him; but to be thus misrepresented (though undesignedly) by the "intelligent" reporter of the Enterprise is, as Mrs. Partington would say, assolutely inseparable. (MTEnt 117–18, original emphasis)

Leading men of the territory were not only unconcerned about the facetious sins of Washoe Mark Twain but also actually enjoyed them. The attitude of the San Francisco literary community, represented by the *Golden Era,* remained equally friendly. Before "A Bloody Massacre near Carson," the *Golden Era* had reprinted Mark Twain items and published three pieces written expressly for that magazine. After the hoax, the *Golden Era* continued to reprint Mark Twain, and within one month of Clemens's moving to San Francisco in the spring of 1864, he was again writing for the magazine. Moreover, Clemens extended his literary reputation beyond San Francisco. One of the pieces the *Golden Era* reprinted, "'Ingomar' over the Mountains" (WG 58–60), was also reprinted in April 1864 by the New York comic periodical *Yankee Notions.* In February 1864, Mark Twain published two original pieces in another New York magazine, *Sunday Mercury* ("Doings in Nevada" and "Those Blasted Children"), a result of Charles Browne's influence exerted after his comic lecture in Virginia City in December 1863. When Fitzhugh Ludlow, former editor for the New York comic periodical *Vanity Fair,* visited San Francisco, he wrote these remarks for the *Golden Era* late in 1863: "In funny literature, that Irresistible Washoe Giant, Mark Twain, takes quite a unique position. He makes me laugh more than any Californian since poor Derby died. He imitates nobody. He is in a school by himself."[131] If Sam Clemens as Washoe Mark Twain was "burned alive on both sides of the mountain" over his gruesome hoax, the flames were short-lived and from such a distance no one saw the smoke.

Sam Clemens's use of Mark Twain in the *Enterprise* soon after the hoax also shows no sign of compromising his madcap, carnivalesque ways. The narrator continues to act as an unsanctified reporter, making fun of whomever and whatever comes his way, including what a journalist does and how he does it. In two of the four extant weekly letters to the *Enterprise* covering the constitutional convention, Washoe Mark Twain made jokes that validated Brosnan's comic epithet of "blunderer." In these, Washoe Mark Twain "forgets" that he has promised not to reveal financial problems of the Nevada Territory and provides a verbatim report of a speech made by a Mr. Sterns, which, because of Mark's "mysterious short-hand notes," only has the style of but not the substance of the speech (MTEnt 89, 95). These apparent errors are not the worst, however. In another of

131. Fitzhugh Ludlow, "A Good-Bye Article," 5.

these weekly letters, which has a whole section comically abusing William Stewart while making a point about the taxation clause in the proposed constitution, Mark Twain implies that he has been bribed by Stewart while serving on a jury (MTEnt 97). Moreover, when Clemens reports the third territorial legislature, he even expands his comic methods, continuing to experiment with ways to convey information yet entertain. Rather than keep his previous distinction between straight daily dispatches and the more comic weekly letters, as he had when reporting the second territorial legislature, in the daily dispatches Clemens writes on the third legislative session, he interpolates comic comments into redactions from notes of the proceedings. Clemens writes the redactions with his *Virginia City Daily Union* partner, Clement Rice, and Rice may have written some of the comic comments signed "rep.," which appear in both the *Union* and *Enterprise* accounts of the legislature. Clemens signs other comic comments "Mark" or "Mark Twain," which appear only in *Enterprise* accounts (MTEnt 139, 153).

These dispatches covering the third territorial legislature allow for experimenting with Washoe Mark Twain as satirist. Although he had made comic comments before with a satiric intent, Clemens, with his interpolated remarks, could now bring his quirky, unafraid-to-rail-at-anyone Washoe Mark Twain character to bear more directly on politics. Other examples from Sam Clemens's writings between October 1863, when he published "A Bloody Massacre near Carson," and May 1864, when he left Virginia City to live in San Francisco, indicate once again how little the furor over the hoax affected the elaboration of comic elements. Instead of retreating, Clemens more readily and ably dramatizes these elements. In addition to interpolating comic comments (MTEnt 139–40), he makes outrageous statements to excuse or to cover his mistakes (MTEnt 155), spins yarns (MTEnt 132–33), or invents a character who tells Mark Twain a story to make a point (MTEnt 127–28). With these tactics, Clemens shaped facts with dramatic technique, allowing his respectable reporter narrator to be more vivid in delivering the news. This comic vividness is especially evident in his report on a renegade meeting of the Union party, entitled "The Bolters in Convention." In these examples, Sam Clemens projects a brilliant reportorial narrator, one generally read as the cleverest of comic figures in the raucous world of Washoe journalism.

Insofar as Washoe Mark Twain merely indulged in mock feuds, as other local editors did, peers as well as readers at large recognized and enjoyed his humor of raillery, despite its inherent risk of relying on an unclear and unstable play frame. When Clemens made fun of journalism as a profession, he greatly increased that risk. Reactions to "Bloody Massacre" demonstrated it, revealing a deep hostility to Washoe Mark Twain in a segment of the contemporary audience that insisted on truth and accuracy above all from a journalist. Clemens preferred instead his comic methods, even when subversive. Critiquing journalistic practice with those methods, suggesting in laughable ways how respectable journalists failed to live up to their own professed ideals, was a service to the community Clemens could render best. Ludlow had awarded his accolade of "the Washoe Giant" after the negative reactions to "A Bloody Massacre near Carson." Sam Clemens as Washoe Mark Twain not only persisted in his unsanctified ways, but he was unrepentant, too.

Nevertheless, Clemens would soon prove the adage "the bigger they are, the harder they fall" when yet another hoax backfired. The subject this time was too serious for jesting. Moreover, no ground of plausibility existed for the accusation buried in the joke, a claim that funds raised for the Western Sanitary Commission were being diverted from their stated purpose. The implication that the society women who had raised the money were either duped or compliant in the diversion could not be laughed away. To compound the problem, Clemens also used the Sanitary Fund to joke his way into a quarrel with the *Enterprise*'s chief rival, the *Daily Union*. Violating boundaries in these matters tapped reservoirs of ill will too deep to be overcome with laughter.

In 1861, two private organizations were formed to raise money for the relief of the sick and wounded soldiers of the Civil War: the U.S. Sanitary Commission, based in New York; and the Western Sanitary Commission, based in St. Louis. These organizations inspired a host of smaller charity efforts. Monies raised for these smaller, local versions of the Sanitary Commission at the town and county levels were usually amassed by putting together a subscription list of contributors. In the larger cities, a popular method for raising money was staging a Sanitary Fair, "a huge bazaar accompanied by devices like auctions, lotteries, and raffles."[132] The Western Sanitary Commission staged such a fair in St. Louis, starting on May 17, 1864. The fair lasted nearly a month and collected almost six hundred thousand dollars (CL 1:284–85n4). Some weeks before its opening, news of the big event reached the Nevada Territory through the newspaper exchange, but probably also from relatives in Missouri, like Pamela Moffett, Sam Clemens's sister. Clemens wrote a letter to Pamela and his mother about the fund-raising efforts in Nevada that was published in a St. Louis newspaper sometime near the end of May while the fair was still open. The letter's version of events has Pamela asking Sam to do something in Virginia City for the St. Louis fair, and Sam contacting the president of the Storey County sanitary commission, who in turn rouses the women of Gold Hill to sponsor a benefit ball (CL 1:281–87).

Although sanitary commissions based in the counties of the Nevada Territory always used public events such as elections to appeal to people for contributions, apparently the news about the St. Louis fair inspired the respectable women who

132. Fatout, *Virginia City*, 187.

lived in Gold Hill to hold a ball on April 20 to raise money to "buy a silver brick that will cause the good people of St. Louis and the country round about to stare in astonishment."[133] Not to be outdone, prominent women from Carson City, including Sam's sister-in-law, Mollie, held their own fancy dress ball on May 5 for the Sanitary Commission. Virginia City initially contented itself with a meeting in Maguire's Opera House on May 1 to put together a subscription list. With so many events being planned, fund-raising for the soldiers must have been a major topic in Nevada during the spring of 1864 for all civic-minded individuals.

Thus when a mayoral election in Austin, Nevada, was held on April 19, the mania for raising funds for the Western Sanitary Commission precipitated one of the more colorful events from the palette of social life in Comstock mining towns during the 1860s. Reuel C. Gridley, a Missourian and schoolmate of Sam Clemens, ran as a Democrat and made a bet on the election's outcome with a Union party man, H. S. Herrick, who supported Gridley's opponent, Charles Holbrook. Gridley bet that if Holbrook won, he would carry a fifty-pound sack of flour to Clifton, a nearby town. If Gridley won, Herrick would make the trip. When Gridley lost, he decorated the sack with small American flags and with red, white, and blue ribbons, and walked the mile and a quarter carrying it, accompanied by the newly elected city officials, most of the town, and a band playing "John Brown's Body." Gridley delivered the sack to the Bank Exchange saloon in Clifton, where thirsts were quenched and speeches made. Everyone then paraded back to Austin and a second saloon for free drinks, where Gridley proposed that the sack be auctioned for the benefit of the sanitary commission. When the highest bidder purchased the sack for $350, he gave it back to be auctioned again. Gridley paid $305 for it the second time—and also gave it up for bidding. The sack was sold and resold all day long, to a wildly cheering crowd, and the process was repeated the next day. Other items, including property in Austin, were auctioned as well: total receipts were $5,335. The *Austin Reese River Reveille* published a long account of the affair, which gave it a great publicity in the West.[134]

In the much larger town of Virginia City, where the May 1 fund-raising effort netted only $1,800, a plan to take advantage of the publicity and to stir civic pride resulted in an invitation to Gridley to haul his sack to Virginia City for another mock auction. An initial round of bidding on Sunday, May 15, brought only an additional $580, apparently because Gridley had arrived in town unexpectedly. The next day, however, the results were quite different. In the morning, a noisy parade escorted Gridley and his sack to Gold Hill to give that town first chance to top Austin's contribution—and to build anticipation in Virginia City.

---

133. Quoted in Mack, *Nevada*, 307.
134. Details are taken from Fatout, *Virginia City*, chapter 8; Mack, *Nevada*, chapter 20.

The *Gold Hill Daily News* reported that "'Tone' was given to the procession by the presence of Gov. Twain and his staff of bibulous reporters, who came down in a free carriage, ostensibly for the purpose of taking notes, but in reality in pursuit of free whiskey."[135]

Clemens no doubt had his share of free drinks, but he also produced for the *Enterprise* two long news reports on the saga of the flour sack that Paul Fatout calls "far superior to those of any other papers in Nevada and California."[136] After hours of bidding in Gold Hill, the total monies collected amounted to $6,062. Austin had been beaten. The parade moved to Silver City through an afternoon rain for an additional $800 in pledges, then to Dayton for $1,835. Now the procession backtracked, destination Virginia City. However, such was the festive hilarity and aroused civic pride of Silver City and Gold Hill that second auctions had to be held as the parade counter-marched through them, adding over $600 and nearly $1,000 respectively to their contributions. By the time the carnivalesque parade, dubbed by Mark Twain in his *Enterprise* articles "The Army of the Lord," approached Virginia City, it covered several hundred yards. As it entered Virginia City, the level of excitement it generated, along with the firsthand reports of what other towns had pledged, guaranteed that its mock auction would verge on the hysterical. The citizens of the Queen of the Comstock were madly determined to outbid everyone else in the territory. With the aid of many large corporate bids, especially from mining companies, they triumphed. Mark Twain reported the sum for the evening as "a fraction less than thirteen thousand dollars," nearly doubling Gold Hill's cumulative bid.

Soon after the auction finished, Clemens returned to the *Enterprise* offices to write the first of the serious reports of the day's events. At the same time, Clemens also concocted the hoax about the Carson City ball for the Sanitary Fund, apparently based on remarks he had heard sometime during the general hilarity of the auction. This item also appeared on May 17, 1864. The *Enterprise* for that day does not survive, and no reprinting of the item exists from other papers. However, a description is extant, buried within a letter dated May 18 protesting the item. The letter is signed by the four Carson City women in charge of the ball:

> Editors of Enterprise: In your issue of yesterday, you state "that the reason the Flour Sack was not taken from Dayton to Carson, was because it was stated that the money raised at the Sanitary Fancy Dress Ball, recently held in Carson for the St. Louis Fair, had been diverted from its legitimate course, and was to be sent to aid a Miscegenation

---

135. *Gold Hill News,* "The Austin Flour Sack," 2.

136. The authorship of these two unsigned items is generally supposed to be Clemens. See Fatout, *Virginia City,* 188; see also RI 316–19. Neither of the original *Enterprise* articles are extant.

Society somewhere in the East; and it was feared the proceeds of the sack might be similarly disposed of." You apparently mollify the statement by saying "that it was a hoax, but not all a hoax, for an effort is being made to divert those funds from their proper course." (CL 1:289)

Because it is not clear how much of the original item this quotation represents, one cannot be sure what Clemens had in mind. Based on other remarks in the letter, one can surmise that the committee of women from Carson City in charge of the Sanitary Fund monies from their ball had had a debate about whether to send the money to the Western Sanitary Commission of St. Louis or the U.S. Sanitary Commission of New York. The debate arose because the circular for the Western Sanitary Commission's fair in St. Louis (probably sent to Mollie Clemens by her sister-in-law, Pamela Moffet) stated that a portion of the money raised by the fair would support the Freedman's Society, and some of the Carson City committee felt that all money raised for the Sanitary Commission should go only to that organization. Sam undoubtedly knew about the debate from Mollie or Orion. Possibly, he agreed that money raised for one purpose could not in good conscience be used for another purpose, however worthy might be its function. Using the joke about the miscegenation society may have been Clemens's inveterate comic way of "exposing" what he felt to be an improper suggestion for the use of Sanitary Fund money. By stating that the overheard remarks were only a hoax, yet also maintaining that "an effort is being made to divert those funds from their proper course," Clemens could attribute his outrageous joke to unknown persons in the auction crowd while alerting the public to the debate within the Carson City committee and his view of it.[137]

Had Clemens confined his joking about the Sanitary Fund to the crack about miscegenation, his impending troubles would have been limited to mollifying the women from Carson City, but he had more tricks in his bag of comic abuse. Sometime near midnight on the seventeenth, the day after the flour sack auction, Clemens, in the *Enterprise* offices, wrote a letter to his mother and sister recounting the previous day's wild events. At the close of the letter, Clemens relates that a competition between the *Virginia City Daily Union* and the *Virginia City*

---

137. The term *miscegenation* was coined for a pamphlet published in December 1863 in New York and entitled *Miscegenation: The Theory of the Blending of Races, Applied to the White Man and the Negro*. Written by Democrats, the pamphlet was a hoax, meant to arouse the hostility of voters toward Republicans by making it seem that they advocated intermarriage. By the time it showed up in western newspapers in the spring of 1864, the term had become a rhetorical club with which the Union party attacked the Southern sympathies of Democrats. Thus the hoax by Mark Twain alleges malfeasance of funds and implies that the women of Carson City were disloyal "Copperheads," the slang term for Northerners sympathetic to secession (Fatout, *Virginia City*, 197–98; MTEnt 196–97).

*Territorial Enterprise* existed during the auction for the flour sack to see which newspaper would bid the most. Clemens had strict instructions from "the proprietors always to 'go them a hundred better,'" and when he left to make up his report, the *Enterprise* held the lead. Then a representative from the *Union* had returned to bid another hundred dollars. "It was provoking.... But I guess we'll make them hunt their holes yet, before we are done with them" (CL 1:284). On the eighteenth, Clemens published a follow-up story on the improbable consequences of Reuel Gridley's bet, "Travels and Fortunes of the Great Austin Sack of Flour." As temporary editor-in-chief while Joe Goodman was away, he also published an unsigned editorial (May 18, 1864) about the Sanitary Fund, apparently one designed to make the *Union* folks "hunt their holes": "How Is It?— While we had no representative at the mass meeting on Monday evening, the UNION overbid us for the flour—or at least ex-Alderman Bolan bid for that paper, and said that he would be responsible for the extra hundred dollars. He may have an opportunity, as we are told that the UNION (or its employés, whichever it is,) has repudiated the bid. We would like to know about this matter, if we may make so free" (CL 1:287). The question seems mild enough by the standards of Washoe journalism, probably only half-serious, but like the miscegenation joke, it touched upon the honor and honesty of the people mentioned.

Whether joke or no, the "How Is It?" item ignited a serious quarrel with members of the *Union* staff. On May 19, the *Union* published an editorial in response to the question of "How Is It?" full of harsh diction and stating that Clemens dealt in "unmanly public journalism" (CL 1:290). Clemens responded the next day with an editorial, and the epithet "unmanly" and Clemens's response combined to move the quarrel within hailing distance of a duel. Clemens possibly also had words with James Laird, the editor of the *Union*, that led Clemens to believe that a formal challenge to a duel might be the only way to settle the matter. Just as the quarrel with the *Union* escalated, Clemens, on the twentieth, received a letter from the Carson City women. That timing explains why, in a letter written the same day to his sister-in-law, Mollie (CL 1:287–88), meant to explain and apologize for the miscegenation joke, Sam nevertheless talks about challenges and weapons to satisfy that quarrel. Moreover, the conjunction of an impending fight with Laird and the arrival of the Carson City letter explains why Clemens felt he could not respond to the letter publicly:

> My Dear Mollie:
>     I have had nothing but trouble & vexation since the Sanitary trip, & now this letter comes to aggravate me a thousand times worse. If it were from a man, I would answer it with a challenge, as the easiest way of getting out of a bad scrape, although I know I am in the wrong & would not be justified in doing such a thing. I wrote the squib the

ladies' letter refers to, & although I could give the names of the parties who made the offensive remarks I shall not do it, because they were said in drunken jest and no harm was meant by them. But for a misfortune of my own, they never would have seen the light. That misfortune was, that that item about the sack of flour slipped into the paper without either my consent or Dan's [William Wright]. We kept that Sanitary spree up for several days, & I wrote & laid that item before Dan when I was not sober (I shall not get drunk again, Mollie,)—and said he, "Is this a joke?" I told him "Yes." He said he would not like such a joke as that to be perpetrated upon him, & that it would wound the feelings of the ladies of Carson. He asked me if I wanted to do that, & I said, "No, of course not." While we were talking, the manuscript lay on the table, & we forgot it & left it there when we went to the theatre, & I never thought of it again until I received this letter tonight, for I have not read a copy of the Enterprise for a week. I suppose the foreman, prospecting for copy, found it, & seeing that it was in my handwriting, thought it was to be published, & carried it off.

Now Mollie, whatever blame there is, rests with me alone, for if I had not had just sense enough to submit the article to Dan's better judgment, it would have been published all the same, & not by any mistake, either. Since it has made the ladies angry, I am sorry the thing occurred, & that is all I can do, for you will see yourself that their communication is altogether unanswerable. I cannot publish that, & explain it by saying the affair was a silly joke, & that I & all concerned were drunk. No—I'll die first.

Therefore, do one of two things: Either satisfy those ladies that I dealt honorably by them when I consented to let Dan suppress that article upon his assertion that its publication would wound their feelings—or else make them appoint a man to avenge the wrong done them, with weapons in fair & open field.

They will understand at a glance that I cannot submit to the humiliation of publishing myself as a liar (according to the terms of their letter,) so long as I have the other alternative of either challenging or being challenged.

Mollie, the Sanitary expedition has been very disastrous to me. Aside from this trouble, (which I feel deepest,) I have two other quarrels on my hands, engendered on that day, & as yet I cannot tell how either of them is to end.

Mollie, I shall say nothing about this business until I hear from you. If they insist upon the publication of that letter, I shall still refuse, but Dr. Ross [husband of a woman who signed the letter] shall hear from me, for I suspect that he is at the bottom of the whole business.

> Your affectionate Brother,
> Sam

Clemens obviously hopes that his frank but private apology to Mollie, who was herself active in sponsoring the ball for the Sanitary Commission, will be transmitted to the other Carson City women and will be sufficient to keep the matter private. The women's communication is "unanswerable" publicly because their terms are so uncompromising: "the whole statement is a *tissue of falsehoods*, made for *malicious* purposes" (CL 1:289, original emphasis). Paul Fatout, speaking of Sam's letter to Mollie, wonders why Clemens should have been so upset by the Carson City letter: he had been called a liar before, and when he more or less retracted "A Bloody Massacre near Carson," he had admitted to "fancy lying."[138] While the mere epithet "liar" would not have bothered a veteran of Washoe journalism like Clemens, its context in the Carson City letter necessarily does. The letter's harshest accusation asserts that the lie was "made for *malicious* purposes," and the only way to avoid that charge is to admit to being the damned drunken fool that some people already think he is. The reputation of Washoe Mark Twain as a "facetious sinner, blunderer, and sagebrush painter" traps Sam Clemens.

Washoe Mark Twain's reputation also propelled Sam Clemens's deadly quarrel with James Laird, one of the owners and editors of the *Union*, which obviously caused more worry as the week started out than the complaint of the Carson City women. The joke about miscegenation became intertwined with the crack about the *Union* repudiating its Sanitary Fund pledges, exciting the animosity of that particular journalistic peer. This animosity for the brand of journalism Washoe Mark Twain represents evoked past furor over "A Bloody Massacre near Carson." In an editorial published May 21 and presumably written by Laird, the *Union* repeated its assertion that Clemens acted in "the most unmanly manner" and then went on to unleash—in the most personal of terms—whatever pent-up negative feelings existed about Sam Clemens as Washoe Mark Twain:

> Never before, in a long period of newspaper intercourse—never before in any contact with a cotemporary, however unprincipled he might have been, have we found an opponent in statement or in discussion, who had no gentlemanly sense of professional propriety, who conveyed in every word, and in every purpose of all his words, such a groveling disregard for truth, decency and courtesy, as to seem to court the distinction only of being understood as a vulgar liar. Meeting one who prefers falsehood; whose instincts are all toward falsehood; whose thought is falsification; whose aim is vilification through insincere professions of honesty; one whose only merit is thus described, and who evidently desires to be thus known, the obstacles presented are entirely insurmountable, and whoever would touch them fully, should expect to be abominably defiled. (CL 1:291)

That same afternoon Sam Clemens formally challenged Laird to a duel. For the next three days, Laird refused to accept the challenge despite an escalating rhetoric in subsequent challenges that began with "cowardly sneak" and "craven car-

---

138. Fatout, *Virginia City*, 200.

cass," then culminated in "unmitigated liar," "liar on general principles, and from natural instinct," "abject coward," and "fool." Evidently, both Clemens and Laird could match the scurrilities of the fictional editor of the *War-Whoop* in the sketch "Journalism in Tennessee."

On May 24, Clemens published all the notes of challenge and reply in the *Enterprise*. Even before Clemens publicly denounced Laird, he evidently felt that Laird would not fight him. In a letter dated May 23 to Mrs. Cutler, one of the signers of the Carson City letter, Clemens claimed that he could not originally acknowledge that letter because it "came at a moment when I was in the midst of what *ought* to have been a deadly quarrel with the publishers of the Union" (CL 1:296, emphasis added).[139] The same issue of the *Enterprise* that published the "Personal Correspondence" between Laird and Clemens also included "Miscegenation" (CL 1:297), which finally did acknowledge the Carson City letter and apologized for not doing so earlier as well as apologizing for the original insult in the hoax. Given Laird's unwillingness to fight and the public apology, Clemens, on Tuesday the twenty-fourth, must have felt that a week after smoke had first appeared, the fires were all but out. The next day, however, everything had changed again. His apology did not prevent someone, probably one of the husbands of the women who had signed the Carson City letter, from sending a letter to the *Virginia City Daily Union*, which published it in the form of a public notice on May 25—and on the twenty-sixth and twenty-seventh as well. In a letter to Orion and Mollie dated May 25, Clemens seems to equivocate between pursuing matters with Laird further or taking no notice. He is "quits" with the women from Carson City but is not sure about their husbands (CL 1:298). A letter to Orion on May 26 reveals the same equivocation. Sam has decided to leave the Nevada Territory with Steve Gillis, a good friend and another *Enterprise* staff member, and he did not want his departure to be held up by quarrels with "Laird or Carson men" because of the law against dueling. "However, if there is any chance of the husbands of those women challenging *me*, I don't want a straw put in the way of it. I'll wait for them a month, if necessary, & fight them with *any* weapon they choose" (CL 1:299). Apparently he did receive a challenge from William Cutler two days later, despite his wife's forgiveness, but somehow nothing came of it. The next day, May 29, 1864, Sam Clemens left Virginia City, no longer an employee of the *Territorial Enterprise*.

139. According to an observer, one who knew both Laird and Clemens well, Laird was "an arrant coward." Tom Fitch, who had fought a duel with Joe Goodman in September 1863 when he was an editor for the *Union*, claims that when Laird received the challenge from Clemens, he tried to sell his interest in the paper to Fitch, who was then practicing law, and that the terms included assuming the duel. He declined ("Fitch Recalls," 6F).

## PUNCHLINES THAT HURT

THEY HAVE SOME CURIOUS CUSTOMS [IN THE SANDWICH ISLANDS];
AMONG OTHERS, IF A MAN MAKES A BAD JOKE, THEY KILL HIM.

————

MARK TWAIN, "OUR FELLOW SAVAGES OF THE SANDWICH ISLANDS,"
1866–1867

One of the fashionable places for young men in Virginia City to be during daylight hours was M. Chauval's Fencing School and Gymnasium. While Sam Clemens and Joe Goodman and William Wright practiced fencing, some of the *Enterprise* staff preferred boxing, particularly Goodman's partner, Denis McCarthy, and an assistant editor named George Dawson. According to Wright, Dawson "prided himself upon being a hard hitter" and only McCarthy among the newspapermen dared to put on the gloves against him regularly. One day Clemens donned gloves in Dawson's presence and began to shadowbox.

> Dawson observed his antics with astonishment not unmixed with awe. He evidently considered that they were made for his special benefit and intimidation. . . . At all events, in view of Mark's movements of supposed warlike import, Dawson kept a wary eye on him, never once suspecting that the ex-Mississippi pilot was merely making a bid for his admiration.
>
> Presently Mark squared off directly in front of Dawson and began working his right like the piston of a steam engine, at the same time stretching out his neck and gyrating his curly pate in a very astonishing manner.
>
> Dawson took this to be a direct act of defiance—a challenge to a trial of skill that could not be ignored. Desperately, therefore—and probably not without a secret chill of fear at his heart—Dawson drew off and with full force planted a heavy blow squarely upon Mark's offered nose, the latter not making the least movement toward a guard. The force of the blow fairly lifted Mark off his feet and landed him across a settle that stood against the wall on one side of the hall. . . . His nose streamed blood.[140]

Sometimes the consequence of an audience failing to know the difference between battle and mock battle is literally painful. Within the humor of personal mock insult and raillery that flourished on the Comstock, everyone jabbed at each other in a game of perpetual kidding that was not always friendly. The game, however, had no rules, or rather, the boundary between what was friendly

---

140. Wright, "Salad Days," 14.

and what was not friendly was too fluid to prevent hard feelings or plain outrage. Sam Clemens had crossed that boundary, one demarcating the mock combats of local columns from the fiercely serious statements of editorials. Like George Dawson taking Sam's playful boxing seriously and giving him a bloody nose, some people in Carson City and Virginia City took Washoe Mark Twain's joking about donations to the Sanitary Commission Fund seriously and gave him a symbolic knockdown blow.

Nevertheless, Sam Clemens should be given the benefit of the doubt about the miscegenation joke. Whatever imp of mischief prompted him to write that item, as soon as William Wright pointed it out, he knew that implying the dishonesty of the Carson City women was out of bounds. He had been careful about merely making fun of how society women dressed in "All About the Fashions." Moreover, he had suffered the consequences of exceeding the limits of forbearance with "A Bloody Massacre near Carson." He did not need Wright to tell him twice that portraits of absurd dresses can be forgiven but sarcastic comments about mishandling charity monies could not. The miscegenation slur itself is another matter, but clearly Clemens repeating the slur was a misguided tactic for drawing attention to other issues. The attack on the *Union* staff presents a more difficult case to assess because editors routinely engaged in blackguarding one another on all manner of issues, and the "How Is It?" article does not stand out from the contemporary parade of printed insults. Moreover, the article straddles the line between humorous portraiture and satiric lampoon. Did Sam Clemens really think that the *Union* folks would renege on their pledges? Or did he just want to rile them up for amusement and thus revenge their having bested the *Enterprise* in the self-created competition over the flour sack?[141]

Whatever Sam Clemens's intent may have been, the behavior of Washoe Mark Twain the facetious sinner had unexpected consequences, mainly because he had created jokes that toyed with journalistic accuracy. Thus, for many of his critics, Sam Clemens was simply a liar. These critics tallied Washoe Mark Twain's comic misdeeds concerning accuracy in the same way that mistakes by Sam Clemens would be counted. They allowed no comic license, nor acknowledged a play frame in this accounting. Perhaps Clemens thought such bookkeeping merely a pinched-faced way to deny the use of jokes as part of the reporter's writing repertoire. Perhaps he thought that sour critics were inevitable yet surmountable. In any case, the furor over his jokes about the Sanitary Fund provided an exemplary lesson about the need to control his comic material so that

141. For a comparison in ad hominem argument, see *Gold Hill News,* "The Church Story," for an account of how one editor, Frank Lovejoy, perpetrated a hoax on another, John Church, claiming that he was arrested as a Copperhead while attending a political convention back east.

readers could not mistake the comic intent, the frame that signaled merely play-ful malice. What was the difference between "The Great Prize Fight" and "A Bloody Massacre near Carson"? One attributes a yarn about an outrageously violent prize fight to a prominent businessman named Winters. The second attributes a yarn about an outrageously violent murder to a prominent busi-nessman named Curry. Both contained absurdities meant to alert the readers not to take the tale seriously despite the attribution to well-known and well-respected citizens. No one is on record as being angry about "The Great Prize Fight," despite the prominent people given roles in that tale. "A Bloody Massacre near Carson," however, raised ire in enough readers to make the tale remem-bered on the Comstock for years afterward.

Sam Clemens in Nevada had created not only the master role of an unsanc-tified comic narrator to enliven his work as a local editor; he had also created a comic character whose quirky humors and misadventures were as much the stuff of fiction as they were exaggeration of fact. Moreover, the character pre-sents a complicated profile, with multiple comic personae. When the unsancti-fied reporter dons an uncouth persona, Washoe Mark Twain becomes one of "the boys," bantering via printed raillery the way one verbally teases friends. This uncouth persona can generate the criticizing laughter of satire when the comic character appears cloddish and dim-witted, caricaturing "the boys" and their manners. Washoe Mark Twain then demonstrates the classic counterexample function of comic material sanctioned by Plato and other theorists of the Comic. When Washoe Mark Twain's unsanctified antics caricature how not to behave, the implied author Sam Clemens assumes the satirist's conservative function, indirectly preserving the status quo for an implied reader who represents the respectable segment of the community. The other master role Clemens invents for his narrator, the respectable reporter, embodies that respectable faction of the Comstock mining community by directly offering a satiric perspective sup-porting the status quo. For example, in his attack on the *Carson City Independ-ent* in February 1864, Washoe Mark Twain castigates the newspaper for the failure to serve its community by investigating and publishing the facts of uneth-ical business practices. Mark Twain here champions centric values not by the counterexample of caricature but rather by the frontal assault of comic sarcasm.

Though Mark Twain can speak for a respectable community and its centric values, he does so with a comic attitude, which always harbors potential trans-gression. Washoe Mark Twain's characteristic humor of raillery inevitably dis-rupts social norms. Placed in the context of the antebellum comic tradition, such disruption evokes the Gentleman Roarer, but Washoe Mark Twain specifically reflects the wild frontier of the Comstock. Portraying miners' rough manners in an exaggerated fashion represented disruptive behavior in the eyes of the consciously respectable people along the Comstock, but especially in Carson City and Virginia City. More disruption issued from the willingness of Sam Clemens to create hoaxes and thereby test the boundaries of his frontier community's good-humored habit of indulging comic horseplay. At this level, the narrator's master role of competent reporter taps comic transgression in a way that ultimately does not support the status quo. Mounting satires via hoaxes, Sam Clemens does not simply target an absurdly inflated interest in fossils, or lambast California mining companies that "cook" their dividends, or even spotlight a debate about how to dispose properly of monies collected for the Sanitary Fund. As centric as the values are that lie behind the ridicule of those targets, the satiric hoaxes of Washoe Mark Twain disrupt more profoundly by obscuring the conceptual divide between fact and fiction. When yarns are reported as facts in a respectable newspaper, even for a worthy satiric purpose, a significant breach of trust in the credibility of newspapers occurs.

More disruptive still is the way that Washoe Mark Twain becomes a comic character whose quirky humors always threaten to displace the news narratives in which Clemens situated him. By creating this character, Clemens once again necessarily employed a strategy of manipulating the purpose of a newspaper and the function of its reporters. Clemens was aided and abetted in this comic design by a community of practical jokers and in particular by the practices of the subcommunity of Washoe journalists, with its habit of personalizing news and editorials. Washoe Mark Twain was the biggest of journalistic jokers, but Sam Clemens most obviously earned the epithet "unsanctified" because he used his comic character to ridicule and to undermine his own profession.

Washoe Mark Twain enacts the symbolic comic drama of a Citizen Clown through these multileveled disruptions. This "sin" of transgressing respectability calls attention either to what should be proper behavior, thus supporting the status quo, or to the way proper behavior has somehow gone amiss and needs to be corrected or possibly jettisoned for something new. The trouble for Washoe Mark Twain acting as Citizen Clown in Virginia City occurs because nothing formal existed in the community to sanction the comic drama. His symbolically transgressive behavior thus had inconsistent support: as unofficial carnival, Virginia City allowed the parodic aggression of mock feuds, but its normative values proscribed what looked like unbridled comic raillery.

The Mark Twain that first appeared in early 1863 in the Nevada Territory comically mirrored the mining community on the Comstock Lode and the way it lived: playful, extravagant, boisterous, uncouth. With this earliest Mark Twain, Clemens created the figure of an erstwhile local reporter who sometimes finds the facts to report the truth but who also vagabonds about to discover where the jokes lie. Once developed, Washoe Mark Twain displays a wisecracking personality whose humor for raillery produces comic insults and lampoons of individuals, burlesques of literary styles and narrative genres, satires of human behavior and institutions, and literary hoaxes. Though never lost, the competent reporter's role of Washoe Mark Twain often takes a backseat to his unsanctified aspect, allowing the clowning function of the pseudonym to predominate. Mark Twain in Nevada carries on like a cap-and-bells journalist in mining country, prospecting around people, personalities, and institutions not merely to report on them but also to discover whatever comic ore they possess in order to blow them up with explosive laughter. Such funny business made Sam Clemens his first reputation, one that almost immediately exceeded the boundaries of the Nevada Territory and reached into San Francisco. During his meteoric success on the Comstock with Mark Twain, however, Clemens learned that exceeding boundaries does not always signal success. Even in freewheeling mining camps and towns, where elastic boundaries provided great latitude for what kind of raillery can be taken good-humoredly as a good joke, a limit existed beyond which the madcap journalist harms himself.

# Act Three

MARK TWAIN IN SAN FRANCISCO

# SCENE ONE

"STRIKE UP HIGHER" IN THE PERIODICAL WORLD

## A National Campaign

ARTEMUS WARD SAID THAT . . . I OUGHT TO . . . LEAVE SAGE-BRUSH
OBSCURITY, & JOURNEY TO NEW YORK WITH HIM, AS HE WANTED ME
TO DO. BUT I PREFERRED NOT TO BURST UPON THE NEW YORK PUBLIC
TOO SUDDENLY & BRILLIANTLY, & SO I CONCLUDED TO REMAIN HERE.

———

LETTER TO JANE LAMPTON CLEMENS, JANUARY 2, 1864

Sam Clemens left the Comstock and Virginia City with mixed reviews. Frank Lovejoy of the *Virginia City Old Piute* expressed his genuine good wishes for "S. L. Clemens, Esq. alias 'Mark Twain.'"[1] Presumably Clemens's local column pals, Parker and Sumner, Rice and Wright, were sorry to see him go, as was his boss, Joe Goodman. An editorial from the *Gold Hill Daily News* on May 30, 1864, probably written by owner Philip Lynch, represented those who did not mind seeing the back of Mr. Clemens and his alias:

> Among the few immortal names of the departed—that is, those who departed yesterday per California stage—we notice that of Mark Twain. We don't wonder. Mark Twain's beard is full of dirt, and his face is black before the people of Washoe. Giving way to the idiosyncratic eccentricities of an erratic mind, Mark has indulged in the game infernal—in short, "played hell." Shifting the *locale* of his tales of fiction from the Forest of Dutch Nick's to Carson City; the *dramatis personae* thereof from the Hopkins family to the fair Ladies of the Sanitary Fair; and the plot thereof from murder to miscegenation—he slopped. The indignation aroused by his enormities has been too crushing to be borne by any living man, though sheathed with the brass and triple cheek of Mark Twain.[2]

Lynch's attitude of good-riddance, precipitated by the miscues with the Sanitary Fund, had its origins not in hoaxes per se but rather in Sam Clemens's unforgivable habit of conflating news narratives with fictional narratives, presented with the supremely blithe attitude—the "brass and triple cheek"—of his alter ego Mark Twain. Some simply could not forgive Clemens for being a newspaper reporter who seemed completely indifferent to telling the truth, "whose instincts are all toward falsehood," as the *Virginia City Daily Union* wrote on May 21, 1864.[3]

---

1. Quoted in Fatout, *Virginia City,* 212.
2. Ibid., 211.
3. Ibid., 202.

However, nothing connected with the Sanitary Fund jokes slowed down the career of Sam Clemens. He arrived in San Francisco on Monday, May 30. The following Monday, he began work as the new local reporter for the *San Francisco Morning Call,* for which Clemens had written a series of letters in the latter half of 1863.[4] One week later, on June 13, the *San Francisco Alta California* printed a speech Mark Twain had made on behalf of the city to Major Edward C. Perry, a marine engineer who had recently completed a salvage operation of the ship *Aquila.* The salvage was important to the city because the *Aquila* held the pieces of the ironclad *Camanche,* which was to be a major component of the harbor's defense against naval raids by the Confederacy. Selecting Sam Clemens to perform this function so soon after his arrival in San Francisco demonstrated that his Mark Twain funnyman personality appealed to city officials rather than repulsed them.

Working for the *San Francisco Morning Call,* however, proved to be a mixed blessing. Obviously, the editors of the *Call* thought Clemens could be reliable despite what his Comstock detractors had to say on the subject. The editors had clearly hired Sam Clemens the reporter rather than Mark Twain the comic character, for throughout the four months that Clemens labored for the *Call*—during which time some five thousand, four hundred local items were published—no comic sketches signed "Mark Twain" were printed in the newspaper.[5] The confidence in his reporting abilities apparently did not include a license to joke. Without the freedom Joe Goodman had granted him, Clemens cramped down hard on his Mark Twain style of writing. His job plain and simple was reporting local events. News-gathering focused on three areas—the Police Court, the District Court, and the theaters—but his efforts overall had to be wide-ranging to fill his daily quota of words. In 1906, Clemens remembered those full-time efforts: "After having been hard at work from nine or ten in the morning until eleven at night scraping material together, I took the pen and spread this muck out in words and phrases and made it cover as much acreage as I could. It was fearful drudgery, soulless drudgery, and almost destitute of interest."[6] Clemens goes on to say that his lack of interest became apparent to the senior editor, who one day politely fired him. George Barnes, the editor who did the firing, states that Clemens admitted his "reportorial shortcomings" and that the parting was friendly, occurring "when it was found necessary to make the

4. Edgar M. Branch, introduction to *Clemens of the "Call": Mark Twain in San Francisco,* 16. Information about Clemens's job with the *Call* is taken from Branch.

5. The list of items in the *Call* attributed to Clemens was compiled by Branch, in *Clemens of the "Call".*

6. MTA, dictation of June 13, 1906. See Samuel L. Clemens, *Clemens of the "Call": Mark Twain in San Francisco,* 282. Originally in Samuel L. Clemens, *Mark Twain in Eruption,* 255–56.

local department more efficient." Some forty years later, Rudyard Kipling would hear from members of the *Call* staff how Mark Twain was "a reporter delightfully incapable of reporting according to the needs of the day."[7]

While the stories told about Clemens to Kipling delighted in Mark Twain's being incapable of good reporting, that apparent incapability more than the inefficiency claimed by Barnes hints at the comic character established on the Comstock with inconsistent success. Sam Clemens the inept reporter was a studied comic persona, grounded in personal disposition, like his legendary drawl and laziness. Sam himself might have said that the comic attitude behind the persona oozed out of his soul, leaked from every joint despite his best efforts to caulk himself over with sober accuracy: Clemens used similar phrasing in the "Prefatory" to *Roughing It*. The persona and its unsanctified attitude had guaranteed that local items during his stint on the *Virginia City Territorial Enterprise* would be seasoned with comic phrasing to create a jaunty style, one the *San Francisco Morning Call* repressed.

The comic persona of the inept reporter embodies Clemens doing much more than creating an amusing reportorial style. Though masked as local news items, many Mark Twain comic squibs and sketches reached toward the outrageous in their imaginative impulse. That impulse had carried Clemens beyond merely reporting for a daily newspaper, and it ensured his being published in literary weeklies even before he joined the staff of the *Call*. During the fall of 1863, San Francisco's most prominent literary weekly, the *Golden Era*, had showed its first interest in Mark Twain by reprinting an item from the *Enterprise*. Within a month, another reprinting plus three original Mark Twain sketches had appeared in the *Golden Era*. That success intimated a promising writing career in the world of literary periodicals.

Publication in New York literary periodicals could strengthen the promise, and Clemens had already managed that feat, too. Well before the 1860s, no other city in the United States had as lively a scene for literary periodicals as New York. Mark Twain's first New York publications were the direct result of intervention by Charles Farrar Browne. Browne had obviously been impressed with Clemens's abilities during his visit as Artemus Ward to Virginia City in December 1863. He had not only encouraged Clemens to aim for a New York audience but had also promised to smooth the way by contacting colleagues from his days as an editor with *New York Vanity Fair*. In a letter to Clemens dated January 1, 1864, Browne says he will write "a powerfully convincing note to my friends of 'the Mercury.'"[8]

---

7. George E. Barnes, "Mark Twain as He Was Known during His Stay on the Pacific Slope," 1; Branch, introduction to *Clemens of the "Call*," 24.

8. Quoted in John J. Pullen, *Comic Relief: The Life and Laughter of Artemus Ward, 1834–1867*, 89.

The next month, the *New York Sunday Mercury* published two original pieces by Mark Twain, "Doings in Nevada" (MTEnt 122–25) and "Those Blasted Children" (ETS 1:351–56). In April 1864, *New York Yankee Notions* republished from the *Enterprise* a burlesque review of an opera (WG 58–60). The *Sunday Mercury*, with its circulation of 145,000 before the war,[9] was an excellent magazine in which a West Coast comic writer might first appear. Well-established, the *Mercury* had a stable of writers with a mixture of styles appealing mainly to the taste of lower- and middle-class readers.[10] Work by highbrow writers such as William Gilmore Simms and Bayard Taylor would occasionally appear next to routinely printed sensationalist thrillers by writers such as "Ned Buntline" as well as funny pieces from some of the most popular comic pseudonyms of the day: "Artemus Ward" (Charles Farrar Browne), "Orpheus C. Kerr" (Robert Newell), and "Miles O'Reilly" (Charles G. Halpine).[11] Browne's encouragement of and help for Clemens represented the judgment of a successful comic author: Mark Twain could compete with the best writers in the fiercest periodical market.

Despite this substantial East Coast recognition of Mark Twain, the "soulless drudgery" of being merely a newspaper reporter apparently came close to destroying Sam Clemens's comic invention altogether during the summer of 1864. Beset by a number of debts and faced with precipitous drops in the value of mining stocks held jointly with his brother Orion, Sam Clemens contemplated accepting an appointment to be a government pilot on the Mississippi River for three hundred dollars a month, more than twice his *Call* salary. When Sam told a friend who was an editor for the *Alta California*, John McComb, that he might abandon his newspaper career to return to piloting, McComb gave him this advice: "Sam, you are making the mistake of your life. There is a better place for you than a Mississippi steamboat. You have a style of writing that is fresh and original and is bound to be popular. If you don't like the treadmill work of a newspaper man, strike up higher; write sketches, write a book; you'll find a market for your stuff, and in time you'll be appreciated and get more money than you can standing alongside the wheel of a steamboat" (ETS 1:28).

The application to the U.S. government to return to piloting in the midst of the Civil War reveals how deeply the Sanitary Fund episode had affected Clemens, despite having his work printed and reprinted not only in San Fran-

---

9. Frank Luther Mott, *A History of American Magazines, Volume II, 1850–1865*, 37.

10. *New York Tribune*, [The Audience for *New York Sunday Mercury*], 1.

11. See Letter to Jane Lampton Clemens, January 2, 1864 (CL 1:267). Clemens originally planned to be a regular contributor to the *New York Sunday Mercury* (ETS 1:348). Mary Noel, *Villains Galore: The Heyday of the Popular Story Weekly* (51, 104–6), makes the point that before 1857 and the success of the *New York Ledger*, the *Sunday Mercury* did not use sensationalist "story paper" writers like "Ned Buntline."

cisco's premier literary periodical, the *Golden Era,* but also in the New York press during 1863 and early in 1864. Given his substantial Comstock success and praise from national writers like Fitzhugh Ludlow and Charles Browne, Sam Clemens should have moved to San Francisco ready to raise his literary ambition to their level. Instead, during his first weeks of residence in the city, Clemens had serious doubts about making a living with his pen and verged on a return to the steady employment he had known before venturing west. In *Roughing It,* Clemens paints a picture of himself slinking around San Francisco in 1864 because of debts (RI 428–429) and later claimed he had held a loaded pistol to his head about this time (CL 1:325n6). Though I find the suicide story implausible, the first few weeks of living in San Francisco and absorbing the fall from Comstock celebrity on the *Enterprise* to common reporter for the *Call* clearly is the nadir in the early career of Mark Twain. Without John McComb's encouragement, Clemens apparently agreed with Philip Lynch of the *Gold Hill Daily News:* "Mark Twain's beard is full of dirt, and his face is black." The next day, however, Clemens told McComb that he had thought about his advice and had decided to follow it.[12]

The remarkable part of Sam Clemens living and working in San Francisco was not that he almost left California and thus very nearly ended the career of Mark Twain before many outside the West Coast would notice it had existed. More important than merely staying was the decision to shift career focus from newspaper dailies to literary weeklies. Concentrating his best efforts on writing sketches for the world of literary weeklies committed Clemens not just to a professional writing career much more ambitious than newspaper reporting. Writing for the literary weeklies also committed Clemens to a readership different from that of newspapers, one whose aesthetic taste differed because its gender and economic status were typically different. The story of Sam Clemens in San Francisco, therefore, is the story of how he reworked Washoe Mark Twain to fit this more literary ambition. Aiming consistently for the middle-to-upper class and largely feminine audience that literary weeklies represented rather than "the boys" for whom the *Enterprise* staff wrote, Clemens took his cues from two writers who had demonstrated their literary abilities, who could already claim to be *feuilletonistes* rather than mere reporters: Francis Bret Harte and Charles Henry Webb.

This new orientation revised the master role of unsanctified newspaper reporter rather than transformed it. As a kaleidoscope contains all the colors it

12. The story about Sam Clemens almost returning to the river is cited in ETS 1:28. Henry Nash Smith says that McComb was the foreman of the *Alta*'s pressroom (MTCor 55), which might make his opinion on literary matters less forceful. Apparently, McComb moved from compositor to editor early in 1867 (CL 2:12n1).

requires to present new designs to the eye, the Mark Twain pseudonym in May 1864 implied all the guises and techniques necessary to meet Clemens's upgrade of his literary ambition. Nevertheless, having all the colors and finding the best pattern for them to accomplish the upgrade are two very different things. To achieve success in the bigger arena of literary weeklies, Clemens experimented throughout the stay in San Francisco, continually adjusting his comic kaleidoscope and creating different patterns by emphasizing different laughable elements. The inept reporter remains an important persona, but Mark Twain's inability to relate the correct story will less likely be the result of being drunk and more likely be the consequence of garrulous digression or of having his ostensibly naive nature imposed upon by others. Mark Twain the unsanctified reporter continues to make fun of newspaper reporting, but his burlesques will be aimed at more literary targets in a bid to assume the role of a comic critic of art and literature. This refocus affords an opportunity to expound an aesthetic instead of simply to attack personalities; lampoon and personal invective will often be redirected into the more sociably acceptable channel of cultural satire. However, despite Clemens more consistently rechanneling the wild energy of Washoe Mark Twain's comic raillery, the character retained an inevitably transgressive nature capable of overflowing any channel in dangerously disreputable ways. In the artistic environment Clemens encountered in San Francisco, this comic transgression—the "brass and triple cheek" of Washoe Mark Twain—often erupted as a Bohemian irreverence for staid social values and worn-out literary conventions. This Bohemian irreverence created a major shift in comic design, coloring new opportunities for Mark Twain performing as Citizen Clown.

Though the comic design shifted, the Mark Twain character retained its foundation in the news. Committing himself to becoming a *feuilletoniste*, Clemens still sought inspiration in actual events and people. No matter how sarcastic the sketches or wildly funny the tales, Clemens therefore maintained the other master role for his Mark Twain narrator, a capable reporter. This master role depended upon a habit of observing, a habit nurtured in his letters back home during various travels, long before signing on with the *Enterprise* or the *Call,* and strengthened from Sam's training as a pilot.[13] Keen observation remained the deepest root for Clemens as a professional writer. The habit of observation enabled his meteoric success on the *Enterprise*—an irony, given the *Gold Hill News* editor's point of view in the spring of 1864. In eighteen months, Sam Clemens had come to dominate the comic arena prominently on display in the

---

13. Both Benson (MTW) and Branch, *Literary Apprenticeship,* use early personal letters to narrate the development of Clemens as a writer. See also the *Keokuk Gate City* letters collected by Franklin Rogers (LG). These letters will be discussed in a later section.

newspapers of the Nevada Territory, a domination expressed in Fitzhugh Ludlow's nickname for Mark Twain, "the Washoe Giant." In San Francisco, Clemens planned to enlarge his success in what amounted to his first campaign for a national reputation.

## Periodicals and the Professional Comic Writer

The present age is emphatically the Age of Fun. Everybody deals in jokes, and all wisdom is inculcated in a paraphrase of humor.

*New York Knickerbocker*, August 1846

Had Sam Clemens's decision to become a comic *feuilletoniste*, that is, a professional comic writer for periodicals, come a generation earlier, it would have been a fool's errand. The 1840s had first demonstrated, with the phenomenal success of Nathaniel Parker Willis, that the marketplace in the United States for periodical writing of *any* kind had grown large enough to support a professional. Joseph C. Neal complained in 1842 that one could not make a living in the United States writing literature,[14] and only Washington Irving and James Fenimore Cooper provided exceptions to Neal's statement. If Neal had said that one could not make a living as a periodical writer, no exceptions existed before 1842. Without an international copyright, an American editor or publisher could easily reprint English writers free. The Harper brothers were making a fortune during the 1840s with such reprints, relegating novels by American writers to a second-rate status. Payment to even the best American writers for material in a periodical was therefore virtually nonexistent. The situation changed only when George R. Graham conducted his new magazine with a policy of generous payment for American writers. *Graham's Magazine,* born from an 1839 merger of two older magazines, quickly attained a great popularity for an upper-middle-class taste culture.[15]

Once Graham demonstrated that liberal payment to American writers could result in a profitable periodical, a second notable editor and publisher, Louis A.

14. Frank Luther Mott, *A History of American Magazines, Volume I, 1741–1850,* 495.
15. The term "upper-middle-class taste culture" is adapted from a hierarchy of "taste cultures" elaborated by Herbert J. Gans, *Popular Culture and High Culture: An Analysis and Evolution of Taste.* Details of the hierarchy will be in a subsequent section.

Godey, followed suit. In part, Graham and Godey could be generous because of their unprecedented move in 1845 to copyright their magazines' contents. *Graham's Magazine* set the standard for payments, though there could be quite a range, depending on the fame of the writer. A page in the magazine was about a thousand words, and the payment for a five-thousand-word article was between twenty and sixty dollars—nearly a living wage for the times. Nathaniel Parker Willis, whom Frank Luther Mott calls "the first great American magazinist," by 1842 was making fifteen hundred dollars a year from four magazines (the *Mirror* and *Ladies' Companion* as well as *Graham's Magazine* and *Godey's Lady's Book*) while touring Europe in comfort for about five hundred dollars.[16] Thomas Baker remarks on Willis's money problems prior to this time, as well as on an estimate by Henry W. Longfellow in 1840 that Willis was making ten thousand dollars a year. Most of that amount came in the wake of the enormous popularity of *Pencillings by the Way*, published in 1835.[17] In effect, George Graham and his editorial policies had introduced a new era into magazine publishing in the United States. "By the end of the 1840s, the magazine writer had become perhaps the most characteristic American literary figure, and the tastes of magazine readers were coming to determine the most characteristic modes of American literature."[18]

Though Willis throughout the 1840s proved the financial viability of a literary career as a periodical writer, it took some time longer for a writer to sustain him- or herself on the proceeds garnered from comic writing. The 1850s saw the rise of the professional comic writer only because periodicals had already become specialized enough and profitable enough to support such a writer. Several threads, however, had to be woven together before a comic Nathaniel Parker Willis could appear. First, successful magazines in which comic material appeared routinely had to exist. Moreover, that comic material had to strike a balance between buffoonery and vulgarity on one side and any earnest or sentimental use of laughter on the other. By the end of the 1830s, two magazines for such material existed: *New York Knickerbocker,* a monthly edited by Lewis Gaylord Clark, and the *New York Spirit of the Times,* a weekly edited by William T. Porter.

Porter published the *Spirit of the Times* from 1831 to 1861, its longevity demonstrating how a reputation for comic materials could be part of a formula for successfully marketing a periodical subtitled "A Gazette of the Literary, Fashionable, and Sporting World." During the 1840s, the *Spirit* became famous for publishing and reprinting some of the best original comic material from all over the United States, but in particular the *Spirit* became a home for comic frontier

16. Mott, *Magazines, Volume I,* 495, 506, 507.
17. Thomas N. Baker, *Sentiment and Celebrity: Nathaniel Parker Willis and the Trials of Literary Fame,* 68, 84, 88.
18. Michael Davitt Bell, *Culture, Genre, and Literary Vocation,* 138.

stories from the Old Southwest region. Charles F. M. Noland was first among comic writers Porter published in the late 1830s. Though both Porter and his counterpart at the *Knickerbocker,* Lewis Gaylord Clark, conceived of their ideal readership as the gentlemen of society, and though neither published an exclusively comic periodical, the *Spirit*'s emphasis on sporting events, especially horse racing, gave it an informal tone that led to the *Spirit*'s becoming the locus for much original comic writing in antebellum America.

In contrast, the *Knickerbocker* (1833–1865) under Clark always emphasized the literary over the comic, and its pages are more notable for including nearly all the famous American poets and dramatic fiction writers of the period than they are for including comic writers, though the periodical's name extends an obvious homage to the comic work of Washington Irving. Clark featured Irving during 1839–1841 with his series *Wolfert's Roost,* and he often favored Irving's good-humored, high-culture style when printing comic material from other writers. Examples of funny items in the *Knickerbocker* include parodies of famous authors and a burlesque of country newspapers, "The Bunkumville Chronicle." Characteristic, too, was the light verse of John G. Saxe and Oliver Wendell Holmes, though some comic versifiers in the *Knickerbocker* used dialects, establishing links with the more original comic American writers featured in the *Spirit.* Comic fiction came from well-known, high-culture writers. Frederic S. Cozzens wrote light-hearted serials, including *Sparrowgrass Papers* (1856) and *Acadia; or, A Month among the Blue Noses* (1859). Charles Godfrey Leland's *Meister Karl's Sketch Book* (1855) echoed Irving even at a later date.

Clark's own column, "The Editor's Table," with its clever mix of good-humored jests and serious commentary, became the periodical's most famous jocular feature. Perhaps owing something to the earlier tête-à-tête style of Nathaniel Parker Willis's "Editor's Table" in *American Monthly Magazine* (1829–1831), Clark's version of editorial chitchat was much imitated. By 1852 when Clark published selections entitled *Knick-Knacks from an Editor's Table,* his column occupied a third of the magazine's pages and, being in smaller type, constituted more than half of the total words. Clark's own genial editorial persona contributed greatly to the success of the *Knickerbocker* and carried the banner for the periodical's policy of featuring good-natured comic material.[19]

The *New York Knickerbocker* and *New York Spirit of the Times* both claimed a wide readership. Although their subscription lists may not have topped ten thousand, Porter once boasted he had forty thousand customers. Despite not being avowedly comic, both magazines routinely published comic material over such a long period—more than twenty-five years in both cases—that between

19. Benjamin Franklin Fisher, *"The Knickerbocker,"* 130–31; Mott, *Magazines, Volume I,* 608–10.

them nearly every antebellum comic writer can be found in their pages. Frank Luther Mott calls the *Knickerbocker* "the best comic periodical of the times,"[20] while later scholars have argued for the *Spirit* as the most important publication for promoting American comic writers.[21]

The *Spirit* and *Knickerbocker* as long-lived, partially comic periodicals created a first phase in the professionalization of comic writers by offering a reliable outlet for their work. The second enabling condition for this professionalization required successful magazines that were avowedly comic. The *Boston Yankee Blade,* a weekly published from 1842 to 1856, demonstrated early how a comic magazine could achieve a modest commercial success, even in the relatively staid environment of Boston: despite its longevity, its circulation was only several thousand. The *Yankee Blade* managed this feat by appealing to a less-refined audience for comic materials. In addition to reprinting jokes and comic anecdotes from other periodicals, the *Yankee Blade* routinely published original stories, mostly anonymously, often featuring the Yankee stereotype. These Yankee tales, which helped to give the periodical its distinctive New England flavor, were pirated by periodicals all over the country.[22]

The *Boston Carpet Bag,* begun in 1851 and edited by Benjamin P. Shillaber and Charles G. Halpine, has the distinction of being the first comic periodical aimed at a more refined audience. Perhaps the relative success of the *Yankee Blade* had influenced Shillaber to start another comic periodical in Boston. In any case, the *Boston Carpet Bag* initially promised to deliver grave as well as humorous material, but given the talents of its two editors, comic items dominated by the second year. Its attitude toward laughter and comic material imitated the *Knickerbocker*'s penchant for geniality and cheerfulness, making the *Carpet Bag* well suited to reach a high-culture audience. Because the original publishers also printed a profitable railway guide, Shillaber had a distribution system aimed at achieving a national readership to match his ambition of achieving a national reputation.[23] As Porter had done with the *Spirit,* Shillaber encouraged contributors throughout the United States. In addition, Shillaber was already well-known for his comic character Mrs. Partington, who continued in the *Carpet Bag*'s pages, adding to the periodical's broad appeal.

20. Lorne Fienberg, *"Spirit of the Times,"* 278; Mott, *Magazines, Volume I,* 607, 612, quotation on 424.

21. Norris Yates, *William T. Porter and the "Spirit of the Times": A Study of the Big Bear School of Humor;* Richard Boyd Hauck, "The Literary Content of the New York *Spirit of the Times,* 1831–1856."

22. Daniel Royot, *"Yankee Blade,"* 318.

23. Ronald J. Zboray, in *A Fictive People: Antebellum Economic Development and the American Reading Public,* 13, discusses how railroads in antebellum American became an important means of distributing cheap books and periodicals.

The *Carpet Bag*'s reputation as an excellent comic periodical came from its many comic styles and many funny contributors. The *Carpet Bag* published or reprinted all manner of comic material, from Yankee humor to comic tales with a western flavor, dialect stories featuring Irishmen, and a burlesque of the 1852 presidential campaign. However, its chief historical importance came from encouraging new writers. No other publication at midcentury provided an outlet for so much new comic talent, including Charles Farrar Browne ("Artemus Ward"), George Derby ("John Phoenix"), Matthew Whittier ("Ethan Spike"), and Sam Clemens—besides Shillaber himself and his coeditor Charles Halpine ("Miles O'Reilly") as well as a school of smaller fry. Publishing what Shillaber later called "an exclusively humorous paper" proved untenable in Boston during the early 1850s, possibly because he tried to make it all top quality: a national subscription list, a diversity of comic materials, a stable of comic talent that included new writers.[24] Nevertheless, the *Carpet Bag* set the bar for a high-quality comic periodical. Moreover, Shillaber's venture encouraged newspapers to feature comic writers, which created a favorable climate for beginners like Sara Willis Parton ("Fanny Fern") and Mortimer Thomson ("Q. K. Philander Doesticks, P.B."), who established their careers shortly after the demise of the magazine.

Two more significant but short-lived comic periodicals also exhibited elements that aimed for the better class of readers: the *New York Yankee Doodle* (1846–1847) and the *New York Pick* (1852–1854). *Yankee Doodle* was a lavishly illustrated weekly with an announced program of satire. One of its editors, Cornelius Mathews, was an accomplished satirist, and targets political, theatrical, and journalistic were all featured. Ostensibly national as well as local in its orientation, *Yankee Doodle* frequently imitated London's *Punch* with Cockney speakers. The magazine focused on urban life in New York City with a short series on "City Characters" and "The Philosophy of Omnibus Riding." The *New York Pick* also had a decidedly New York City orientation. Joseph Scoville's editorial persona, "Mr. Pick," was a cultivated commentator on the national as well as local scene not unlike Lewis Gaylord Clark, though more nationalistic in his satires and in his burlesques of foreigners.

Although *Yankee Doodle* and *Pick* along with Shillaber's Boston enterprise failed quickly,[25] antebellum comic periodicals could be profitable. The *Carpet Bag*'s failure suggested that a successful comic periodical must stake out the lower rather than the higher ground when it comes to taste. The *Boston Yankee*

24. Clyde G. Wade, *"The Carpet-Bag,"* 46, 49, 50.
25. Other notable but short-lived comic magazines were *Elephant, John Donkey, Brother Jonathan,* the *Satirist,* and *Judy.* See the list in David E. E. Sloane, ed., *American Humor Magazines and Comic Periodicals,* 565–66.

*Blade* had shown the wisdom of this strategy starting in the early 1840s. Three other long-lived publications—*New York Yankee Notions,* a monthly (1852–1875); *New York Nick Nax,* a monthly (1856–1875); and the most important in this group, *New York Picayune,* a weekly (1847–1860)—reinforce the point.

The success of the two monthly comic magazines, *Yankee Notions* and *Nick Nax,* indicates that an urban clientele provided the steadiest market for comic materials. *Yankee Notions* lasted nearly twenty-five years, longer in fact than any other strictly comic magazine begun during the antebellum period. Cameron Nickels calls it "a representative anthology of the best as well as the worst of the native wit, humor, and satire of nineteenth-century America in word and in picture." Every issue featured an original full-page cover illustration. The publisher, T. W. Strong, was an engraver, and much of his budget went to engravers for original illustrations. Every page of every issue was filled with comic material of all kinds, from Yankee to backwoods humor and Literary Comedians, but Strong borrowed nearly all of it, the editors reprinting every major comic writer except James Russell Lowell, including early pieces by Charles Farrar Browne and Sam Clemens. *Yankee Notions* routinely exposed the pretensions of the urban middle class—"its fashions, tastes, and romantic follies [using] consistently good humor."[26] With a circulation of at least thirty thousand in the late 1850s, *Yankee Notions* established the profitability of a judicious pirating of comic prose coupled with original illustrations. *Nick Nax* was published in New York for all of its sixteen-year existence. A monthly like *Yankee Notions, Nick Nax* was its chief competitor. *Nick Nax* could not boast original comic illustrations, but like *Yankee Notions,* it managed to fill its thirty pages (costing ten cents) with reprints of well-known comic authors. Most of the material featured humor about urban life and emphasized local color rather than politics.[27]

The oldest of the New York City trio of successful comic magazines, and the most important to the rise of the professional comic writer, was the weekly *New York Picayune.* Started in 1847, "the Pick" had a circulation of forty thousand by the middle of the 1850s, often issuing a second edition and adding a "Pictorial Picayune" for the holidays. "Sketches of city figures were mixed with digests of foreign and domestic news. Typical items were the 'Dashes about Town' series by 'The Doctor,' literary humor about New York middle class life. Julius Caesar Hannibal [a pen name of William Levison, an early editor] offered his series of burlesque scientific discourses in comic Black dialect."[28] When the *Picayune* shifted to an emphasis on social instead of political issues, it created a favorable

26. Cameron Nickels, *"Yankee Notions,"* 322, 324.
27. David E. E. Sloane, *"Nick Nax (For All Creation),"* 195.
28. David E. E. Sloane, *"The New York Picayune,"* 192.

environment for comic material more urbane and more oriented toward literary burlesques, which greatly aided the careers of Mortimer Thomson and Charles Farrar Browne. In late 1857, Thomson became editor along with the comic illustrator Frank Bellew, a post he held until the magazine folded in 1860. Low-priced at three cents and focused on the urban scene in all its aspects, the *Picayune* represented the ultimate popular comic periodical of the 1850s—its audience the less rather than the more refined.

In 1856, the *Boston Yankee Blade* ceased publication. Once *Nick Nax* started selling in the streets in 1856 alongside the *Picayune* and *Yankee Notions,* New York City boasted all three successful comic periodicals of the 1850s. The solid success of multiple comic magazines by the mid-1850s meant that catering to the urban market, especially New York City, marked the surest path to commercial success. The circulation of *Nick Nax* is unknown, but a very conservative estimate of ten thousand, a third that of *Yankee Notions,* would mean forty thousand customers a month purchasing a comic magazine, matching the *Picayune*'s weekly sales. Such persistent demand signified a market ripe for a comic periodical of high literary aspirations, one that would consistently tap the New York City scene for material.

*Vanity Fair* filled that niche, starting in 1859 and lasting until 1863 when uncertainties in the cost of paper and in editorial policies, both caused by the Civil War, ensured its demise. Henry Louis Stephens, a well-known cartoonist, was a principal founder and remained the art editor throughout the periodical's brief existence. Modeled on London's *Punch, Vanity Fair* was notable for its illustrations, especially for a full-page political cartoon by Stephens printed on the last page of every issue. David Sloane calls Stephens's work "significant pre-Nast political-comic art." The paper advertised itself in the preface to its first number as a "satirical paper," whose true mission is "not extermination but reformation." On the literary side, *Vanity Fair* carried out its mission with burlesques as well as with political and social commentary. Two of its editors, Charles Godfrey Leland and Charles Farrar Browne, were well-known for their comic writings, Leland especially for his "Hans Breitmann" sketches and Browne, of course, for his "Artemus Ward" letters. Their eye for comic material no doubt helped *Vanity Fair* to enlist some of the better writers of the day, but, as David Sloane points out, the paper from the first had a strong connection with New York City's literati, and *Vanity Fair*'s avowed mission to reform the status quo with laughter meshed especially well with the literati's irreverent and eccentric Bohemian perspective. The periodical boasted a formidable list of excellent contributors, including George Arnold (whose burlesque war correspondence as "McArone" was a mainstay), Ada Clare, Fitzhugh Ludlow, Henry Clapp, Matthew Whittier, Richard H. Stoddard, Edmund C. Stedman, Thomas Bailey Aldrich, Fitz-James

O'Brien, William Dean Howells, and John G. Saxe—as well as editors Leland, Browne, Frank Wood, and Charles Dawson Shanly. With its literary mix of superior comic writers, *Vanity Fair* was the *Boston Carpet Bag* taking up residence in New York City and adding superior illustrators to its staff. The paper was enormously popular in the exchanges. Its superior literary quality may be inferred by the fact that *Atlantic Monthly* purchased advertising space.[29]

Starting in the 1830s, Crockett almanacs had revealed a sizable market for American comic materials. The *Boston Yankee Blade* by the mid-1840s enjoyed modest success with a small but reliable market. After publishers during the 1840s and 1850s discovered that literary periodicals in a monthly "magazine" format or in a weekly newspaper format could be profitable, they also learned that printing book collections of comic fiction appearing originally in periodicals could make money. In 1844, the Philadelphia publishing house of T. B. Peterson printed a "greatly enlarged" second edition of William Tappan Thompson's *The Courtship of Major Jones* on the strength of its initial popularity. The success of William Porter of the *New York Spirit of the Times,* when he gathered together and edited comic pieces from the *Spirit* into *The Big Bear of Arkansas: Illustrative of Characters and Incidents in the Southwest* (1845), confirmed the trend. *The Big Bear of Arkansas* sold its first edition of four thousand almost immediately and had four reprints in the next ten years.[30] When Porter followed that success with a second profitable anthology, *A Quarter Race in Kentucky* (1846), he left no doubt that original American comic material had a wide appeal and that money could be made publishing it. In the same year, the publishing house Carey and Hart capitalized on that appeal by launching its popular series, "Library of Humorous American Works." The money-making capacity of "The Library of Humorous American Works" can be gauged by the fact that the original 1846 series of eighteen books was reprinted in 1849 by Carey and Hart's successor, A. Hart, with eleven new titles. When T. B. Peterson and Sons bought the plates in 1854, the company added new titles once more before reissuing the series a third time.[31] Most importantly for Sam Clemens deciding in 1864 to pursue a career as a comic *feuilletoniste,* these facts clearly demonstrate that by the mid-1850s producing comic writing for periodicals carried with it for the first time the possibility of earning substantial money and thus making a living.

The first example of a financially successful comic writer for periodicals was Sara Willis Parton, better known as "Fanny Fern." In 1856, Robert Bonner, the

29. David E. E. Sloane, *"Vanity Fair (1859–1863),"* 301, 302. Many of the writers listed are noted in a *Vanity Fair* advertisement in the *Cleveland Plain Dealer,* [Contributors to *Vanity Fair*], 6.

30. Fienberg, *"Spirit,"* 276.

31. Grady W. Ballenger, "Carey and Hart," 83.

editor of the *New York Ledger,* signed Parton to publish her latest novel serially at a hundred dollars a column, making Parton the highest paid periodicist in the United States. For nearly twenty years after that, Sara Parton wrote her weekly "Fanny Fern" column in the *Ledger* for twenty-five dollars. Parton reprinted these columns in book collections five times during her career, constituting her financial mainstay.[32] Bonner signing Parton to produce her column on a routine basis culminated the earlier successes for writers and editors of comic materials. Mortimer Thomson, who started writing for the *New York Tribune* in 1855, also made a good living with his comic writings. His first book, *Doesticks: What He Says,* apparently sold over eleven thousand copies within a week of publication. In 1855, publisher George Putnam claimed that sales of ten thousand copies of a book was the minimum for a "decided" hit.[33] As professional comic writers, Thomson and Parton had careers that would have been alien to the frontier humorists from the Old Southwest in the previous decade.

The more immediate professional influence felt by Sam Clemens came from Charles Farrar Browne. By 1862, at the outset of Sam Clemens's career as a newspaperman, Browne, in his guise as "Artemus Ward," had become America's most successful professional comic writer and burlesque lecturer, far more successful financially than either Mortimer Thomson or Sara Parton had been in the 1850s, at the top of a contemporary heap that also included George Arnold ("McArone Letters"), Joseph Barber ("A Disbanded Volunteer"), Charles Halpine ("Miles O' Reilly"), David Ross Locke ("Petroleum Vesuvius Nasby."), Fitzhugh Ludlow ("Primpenny Papers"), Robert Newell ("Orpheus C. Kerr"), and Henry Shaw ("Josh Billings"). Browne's status as a professional writer and comic performer is as important to Clemens and his elaboration of Mark Twain as any stylistic or thematic influence. Without the example of Charles Farrar Browne, Sam Clemens could not have even contemplated success for his decision to make a living writing comic sketches for literary periodicals. Along with Browne, Sara Willis Parton and Mortimer Thomson had demonstrated that a career could be established by compiling such sketches into a book. In 1864, Sam Clemens had turned down the pilot's commission with every intention of repeating their success.

32. Parton received a ten-cent royalty on *Fern Leaves from Fanny's Portfolio* (1853), the first book compilation of her witty and acerbic newspaper columns. One biographer says that the book sold almost a hundred thousand copies in the United States and Britain the first year (Nancy A. Walker, *Fanny Fern,* 17). Another says that the sales in those two countries totaled 125,000 and that the royalties for her first two books after two years were ten thousand dollars (Marion Marzolf, "Sara Payson Willis Parton [Fanny Fern]," 359).

33. *New York Tribune,* [11,300 copies sold of *Doesticks*], 1; Zboray, *Fictive People,* 4.

# Scene Two

SATIRE AND THE BOHEMIAN JOURNALIST

## THE SATIRIST REPORTING FOR THE *MORNING CALL*

SAN FRANCISCO IS A CITY OF STARTLING EVENTS. HAPPY IS THE MAN
WHOSE DESTINY IT IS TO GATHER THEM UP AND RECORD THEM IN A
DAILY NEWSPAPER!

———

MARK TWAIN, "SPIRIT OF THE LOCAL PRESS," *ENTERPRISE,*
DECEMBER 27, 1865

Edgar Branch's meticulously documented presentation of Clemens's work in
the *Call* demonstrates that the Washoe version of Mark Twain could not be
completely repressed, even under the strictures placed upon him as a member
of its staff. Sam Clemens in San Francisco did not rest content with his comic literary device. Instead, he began to develop a comic vision, not merely discovering
the laughable in individuals and everyday incidents, but also measuring the
foibles and vices of humanity as well as the shortcomings of social institutions.
The process allowed Mark Twain to claim the nickname "The Moral Phenomenon" to take its place alongside *Golden Era* monikers "The Wild Humorist of the
Land of Silver and Sagebrush" and the "Sagebrush Humorist from Silverland,"
bestowed apparently to contrast with its appellation for Artemus Ward, "The
Wild Humorist of the Plains." Paul Fatout indicates that in early January 1864,
the *Enterprise* called Mark Twain the "Moral Phenomenon" despite later referring to the figure as "the great demoralizer and notorious corrupter of Saints"
(ECM 198). No doubt both times Goodman was joking about Mark Twain's
well-established habit of irreverence. Clemens refers to himself as the "Moral
Phenomenon" in a *Call* piece (CofC 134).[34]

While in Nevada, Clemens apparently channeled his talent for comic phrasing and portraiture mainly into a humor of personal abuse rather than social
satire. Because the record of his writing from this period is incomplete, "apparently" must be stressed. Much of Mark Twain extant from the *Enterprise* consists
of reprints, which suggests the popularity of the Washoe humor of personal
abuse, with its extravaganzas and burlesques laced with invectives. This abuse
often displays a mock ridicule presented in friendly lampoons, aligning itself
with the spirit of practical joking prevalent in the mining towns. Such comic
abuse employs the levity of a joke, not the justified abuse found at the core of

34. *Golden Era,* "Brick Pomeroy's Cold" 6; *Golden Era,* [Editorial Headnote], 3; *Golden Era,*
"Artemus Ward, Wild Humorist of the Plains," 4; Fatout, *Virginia City,* 150 (see ETS 2:524).

social satire.[35] However, in numerous *Enterprise* items, signed "Mark Twain" or left unsigned, Clemens may also have attempted social satire. For Ivan Benson, Mark Twain's comic writing during the third territorial legislature (January to February 1864) "became more substantial . . . more thought-provoking, less ephemeral, and much less coarse" (MTW 101). His assertion implies a sharp division in Clemens's work—creating phases of "before" social satire and "after" social satire—that misleads in the face of the incomplete record. Bernard DeVoto notes that the *Enterprise* work had its share of social satire and that "A Bloody Massacre near Carson" featured social reproof "embedded in the native joke." Edgar Branch points out that social satire existed in Mark Twain's signed *San Francisco Morning Call* letters written in the summer of 1863.[36] The extant record, however, simply does not provide very much of the daily material that would allow for a better gauge of Clemens's efforts at satire while on the Comstock. Nevertheless, Benson correctly draws attention to the dispatches Clemens sent to the *Enterprise* while covering the legislative session: they are the first extant, sustained satiric effort signed "Mark Twain."

The material reprinted by Edgar Branch from the *San Francisco Morning Call* also provides a focal point to assess the early stages of Mark Twain the satirist. A substantial number of the *Call* items written by Clemens in 1864 illustrate how Mark Twain, already saturated by the humor of personal abuse, retools his ridicule to create satire. The legislative dispatches early in 1864 had shown Clemens experimenting with the brashness of Mark Twain in a political setting. That setting provided topics necessarily important enough to allow lampoon and witty ridicule to be harnessed in service to social satire. The *Call* material from the summer of 1864 adds something else, providing for the first time a body of material that also depicts the satirist's world of knaves and fools rather than merely the humorist's congregation of eccentric characters.[37]

This satirist's world is not a deliberate creation of a Dickensian order but rather emerged from the daily pressure of providing copy when Sam Clemens's regular beat included the courts and jails of San Francisco. The theaters, political gatherings, fairs, and events about town added variety to this daily review of court proceedings and complemented his rounds of news gathering. These news sources in San Francisco were not different from what Clemens covered in Virginia City, with the obvious exception of reporting the mines along the Comstock. Rather, compulsion versus freedom marked the difference: with the

35. Elliott, *Power of Satire,* 11, 77, 266, 273.
36. Bernard DeVoto, *Mark Twain's America,* 161, 155; Branch, *Literary Apprenticeship,* 79.
37. Branch compiled the *Call* pieces attributed to Clemens after reviewing the 5,400 local items for the pertinent time period (introduction to *Clemens of the "Call,"* 289–300). The list contains 471 items, less than 10 percent, and Branch reprints fewer than half.

*Enterprise,* Clemens apparently could choose which sources and when to visit them or perhaps alternate with William Wright; with the *Call,* the courts were a daily chore. The repetition of writing up the courts—especially the police court, with its cases of assault and battery, drunk and disorderly, swindling, larceny, and immorality—this compelled repetition provided the impulse for Sam Clemens's traversals past lampoons and buffoonery toward social satire. His sustained view in San Francisco of the damned human race and its flawed institutions developed Clemens into the "purposeful satirist."[38]

The foibles and vices that Clemens ridiculed include the vanity of folks dancing at a holiday fair, the naïveté of a young merchant swindled by con men, the drunken and sometimes violent behavior of both men and women, and the thoughtless thrill-seeking of young boys racing their wagons through public streets. All of these instances demonstrate foolishness, some stupidity, some knavish stupidity. Other news items report worse than knavish behavior, such as those chronicling rape, physical abuse, and calculated mayhem. Debased sexual morality appears infrequently, along with another potentially inflammatory topic, dubious religion. One instance of the latter, however, foreshadows the irreverent comic commentary that would help make *The Innocents Abroad* a best seller. The item contains a simple, seemingly offhand comment about an admission fee that closes a mostly factual description of "The Christian Fair," an event held to benefit the Sanitary Commission Fund: "It has occurred to us just at this moment, that if any of the bare-footed Disciples, travelling according to their custom 'without purpose or scrip,' should return to Earth, and happen into the Fair, they couldn't [enter], could they? Consequently, it is risky, charging.... isn't it? Manifestly" (CofC 103).

Another topic appearing later in Mark Twain's writings, one that starkly dramatizes the capacity of human beings for knavish behavior, is a crowd transforming itself to a mob. At the open house of a new hotel, Clemens estimates the crowd during the entire day at thirty thousand, a "vast assemblage of refined gentlemen, elegant ladies, and tender children [mixed with] a lot of thieves, ruffians, and vandals [who] stole everything they could get their hands on.... The masses, wedged together in the halls and on the staircases, grew hot and angry, and smashed each other over the head with canes, and punched each other in the face with their fists, and to stop the thieving and save loss to helpless visitors, and get rid of pickpockets, the gas had to be turned off in some parts of the house" (ETS 2:463). A year earlier, Mark Twain had reported on a riot in Virginia City developing during a major fire, when people feared for their lives. The main street seethed with men, "packed together closer than a box of matches." Hands

38. DeVoto, *Mark Twain's America,* 164.

gripping hammers and similar "weapons" were visible above heads, regularly appearing and disappearing as reckless individuals fleeing the fire clubbed others out of their way. Gratuitous violence then trumps this deplorable and desperate behavior. Mark Twain notes that some men among those looking down from windows and roofs "were cowardly enough to toss a brick into the midst of the struggling crowd below, occasionally" (MTCall no. 3). In both instances, vivid description enables justified outrage.

Clemens champions the working class in the *Call* material, creating yet another notable theme. He targets businesses refusing to pay a reasonable wage or the government effectively committing the same offense by paying its employees in debased paper money. He also frequently highlights the related topic of shady business practices that defraud workers. Rounding out the topics that were the targets for Mark Twain's satire are the manifest inefficiencies of bureaucracy, the manifold shortcomings of the judicial system, and the absurdity, venality, and corruption of politics.

The courts and especially politics had been ridiculed before by the comic character. The *Golden Era* reprinted (from a letter published November 19, 1863, in the *Enterprise*) a sarcastic comment on the blithe way the courts released murderers. As an *Enterprise* reporter, Clemens had at least twice invited public scrutiny of the Nevada Territory's constitutional convention in 1863 for ignoring the financial consequences of its proposals, most notably with a dubious wording about taxing mines (MTEnt 88–89, 97–98). These news articles exist on the fringe of satire, projecting the sense of violated principles that sanctions satirical abuse but with minimal comic technique to arouse a ridiculing laughter. The items from the *Call* by Clemens that report politics are also mostly straight reporting, but here and there they contain the easiest of satiric techniques, sarcasm. Political items focus on the Democratic party in California, which was rife with Southern sympathizers. During the election of 1864, Mark Twain seasons his descriptions of speakers at Democratic rallies and their ideas with scornful phrasing. Men present at one meeting amount to "a very short row of potatoes" (CofC 267), and they show up at another "for the purpose of effervescing a little" (CofC 270). He characterizes specific speakers as "feeble" or "troubled with Alcatraz on the brain," a reference to the occasional imprisonment of people judged to be so publicly disloyal to the war effort that their speech amounts to treason (CofC 277).

The modest comic phrasing in these political reports for the *Call* stands in contrast to what Clemens had achieved earlier in 1864 with Mark Twain's remarks interpolated into dispatches on the territorial legislature for the *Enterprise*. The contrast highlights the freedom Clemens had been given by the senior *Enterprise* editors. While Clemens often displayed the humors of Mark Twain in these interpolations, he also ridiculed with satiric intent, sometimes at length, on various issues: major legislative battles over minor procedural rules, legislators not being present to vote for important bills, a controversy about which city will be the capital for the state of Nevada, and a bill that effectively created a monopoly for telegraph service in the territory. On occasion, Clemens displays satire and Mark Twain's Washoe humor together. Complaining that the legislators had killed a "pet" bill of his when he was "absent a moment . . . on important business, taking a drink," Mark Twain reveals that the bill has been reinstated because he has promised to apologize for the past ridicule he had been slinging at the bill that established telegraph service: "in conformity with my promise above referred to, I hereby solemnly apologize for their rascally conduct in passing the infamous telegraph bill above mentioned" (MTEnt 156). Mark Twain then goes on to say that those who voted for the bill cannot be held responsible because they were influenced—by vicious Humboldt whiskey. The ridicule found in these political dispatches rates among the strongest examples from early extant Mark Twain with a claim to social satire, including the *Call* material.

The *Call* material in general is tamer. At times, comic phrasing remains at the level of personal abuse, as in this example, which uses a favorite comic technique of Clemens—describing someone in an inappropriate jargon: "The bigamy case [was] dismissed . . . inasmuch as the only two witnesses to be had were the two alleged wives of the defendant—or rather, only one . . . as the old original wife, the first location, or the discovery claim on the matrimonial lead, could not be compelled to testify. . . . The injured and deserted relocation now proposes to have Hingman arrested again" (CofC 184). The misappropriation of mining vocabulary conjures the crooked grin of the humorous local editor, Washoe Mark Twain, rather than the penetrating eye of the angry satirist.

The daily pressure of producing news copy, it should be stressed again, ran counter to taking much care to create social satire. Edgar Branch's account of how he chose the modest number of items to reprint makes clear the overwhelming percentage of factual reporting Clemens did for the *Call*. When Clemens began to add Mark Twain's inveterate comic phrasing to these reports, however, he can use even simple descriptions to project the outrage of a satirist—descriptions of boys racing wagons in the streets, a captain abusing one of his sailors, or a man transformed to a would-be suicide simply because he was fired after asking for a raise. In other instances, simple description gives way to a scornful analysis. The previously mentioned *Enterprise* letter about possible mining taxes in the proposed Nevada constitution provides an example of this satiric analysis. Another earlier example involves Mark Twain reporting bogus mining stocks in "A Gorgeous Swindle" (MTEnt 119–21). In the *Call* material,

Clemens performs similar analyses in "Looks Like Sharp Practice" (CofC 164) and "Intelligence Office Row" (CofC 232).

When Clemens does create satiric effects in his reporting for the *Call* by liberally sprinkling comic phrasing or comic commentary throughout a news item, he employs a variety of tones, such as the sarcasm noted in the reports on the Democratic party, or the bland understatement in "Extraordinary Enterprise." In the latter, Mark Twain wonders about quail served a mere six hours after the season for hunting them has opened and pretends to worry that the hunter will "wear himself out" with his enterprise (CofC 64). The description of Mary Kane, a habituée of the jail, strikes a harsher chord: "drunk as a loon, [this] accomplished old gin-barrel [again has] a full cargo aboard by this time [and] will probably clear for her native land in the County Jail to-day . . . , with her noble heart preserved in spirits, as usual" (CofC 146). Clemens ambiguously winds up his account of a swindle. The con man "deserves to be severely punished, but perhaps the merchant ought to be allowed to go free, as this was his first offence in being so criminally green" (CofC 162). Feigned astonishment accompanies his comment on a witness who said that "Providence provided her with invisible wings" when escaping an assailant: "Judging by the woman's appearance, and her known character and antecedents, this interference of Providence in her behalf was remarkable, to say the least, and must have been quite a surprise to her" (CofC 162, 161).

At times, comic phrasing can become a barrage of ridicule. This more sustained effort occurs in "What Goes with the Money?" (CofC 239–40), which vigorously attacks mining companies for consistently hiding the state of their financial soundness, to the detriment of stockholders, and calls for an honest company to step forward and voluntarily publish a monthly statement. Another clear example of a news item becoming deliberate satire is "A Small Piece of Spite," published September 6, 1864. This item attacks the coroner's office for refusing to maintain a regular means of providing reporters with information. The caricature of the coroner's assistant transforms the report into a comic sketch. The "slate" refers to the routine means of giving out basic information, a chalkboard, which has been withdrawn—apparently after someone added a false entry as a practical joke (MTW 115)—and thus inspired the following diatribe.

> You ask one of [the coroner's assistants] a dozen questions calculated to throw more light on a meager entry in the slate, and he invariably answers, *"Don't know"*—as if the grand aim of his poor existence was not to know anything, and to come as near accomplishing his mission as his opportunities would permit. . . . What do you suppose the people would ever know about how their interests were being attended to if the employees in all public offices were such unmitigated ignoramuses as these? One of the fellows

said to us yesterday, "We have taken away the slate; we are not going to give you any more information; the reporters have got too sharp—by George, they know more'n *we* do!" God help the reporter that don't! (CofC 236)

Clemens liked this item enough to brag about it in a letter home to Jane Clemens and Pamela Moffet as "the wickedest article . . . I ever wrote in my life" (CL 1:313).

Drudgery that it was, the experience with the *San Francisco Morning Call* nevertheless functioned as a workshop for Sam Clemens, providing him with the raw material for continuing to develop the weapons of a satirist that he had used effectively when reporting on the Nevada territorial legislature. The *Call* experience thus de-emphasized Washoe Mark Twain's humor of personal raillery. Comic invective would still be a large part of Clemens's stock in trade as Mark Twain, but its use in journalistic feuding, serious or playful, diminished substantially once Sam Clemens had left the Comstock. In this development, Clemens belatedly joined a paradigm shift in American journalism. Although invective among newspapermen had been the rhetorical tactic of choice in the personal style of partisan politics that had defined newspapers since the founding of the republic, by the middle of the nineteenth century a newer, information model of journalism was taking hold. Personal invective had once not only defined political boundaries but also provided entertainment, helping to sell newspapers during the 1830s and 1840s. As the information model of journalism developed in the 1850s, personal invective and its baggage, such as dueling, was criticized and even seemed superfluous.[39] The Washoe style of newspaper reporting and editorial writing during the 1860s may have been the last major exhibition of personal journalism in the United States.

Washoe Mark Twain's success had been meteoric. Clemens regained this spectacular momentum, starting in the fall of 1864, with a sustained appearance in a high-quality literary periodical, the *Californian,* despite nearly quitting his writing career and then being sidetracked by his stint as a reporter during the summer. Supported by the editorial freedom of the *Californian* and informed by Clemens's decision to become a professional comic writer, satiric purpose, partially revealed in his reporting for the *San Francisco Call,* reshaped his comic alter ego.

39. Huntzicker, *Popular Press,* chapters 2 and 3; Hazel Dicken-Garcia, *Journalistic Standards in Nineteenth-Century America,* 109; Mott, *Magazines, Volume I,* 165; Lambert A. Wilmer, *Our Press Gang; or, A Complete Exposition of the Corruptions and Crimes of the American Newspapers.*

SATIRIST AS LITERARY CRITIC: MARK TWAIN IN THE *CALIFORNIAN*

> NOW ISN'T IT INFAMOUS THAT A PROFESSED HUMORIST CAN NEVER
> ATTEMPT ANYTHING FINE, BUT PEOPLE WILL AT ONCE IMAGINE THERE
> IS A JOKE ABOUT IT SOMEWHERE, AND LAUGH ACCORDINGLY.

———

MARK TWAIN, "WEBB'S BENEFIT," *NAPA COUNTY REPORTER,*
DECEMBER 2, 1865

> REFINED SATIRE AND INGENIOUS BADINAGE ARE NOT AMERICAN, AND
> ARE APT TO SHARE THE COMMON FATE OF EXOTICS.

———

"AMERICAN HUMOR AND HUMORISTS," *NEW YORK ROUND TABLE,*
SEPTEMBER 9, 1865

Between October 1864 and April 1866, two dozen sketches signed "Mark Twain" appeared in the *Californian.* Most of these comic pieces came in two distinct time frames. The first ran from early October to early December 1864, the second from early May to early July 1865. Bret Harte solicited the first batch after he had recently taken over the editorship while Charles Webb vacationed.[40] When the dates for editorship and publication of Mark Twain sketches are compared, one finds that the overwhelming majority of them were printed when Harte rather than Webb was in the editor's chair. The opportunity to publish regularly in the *Californian* provided Clemens the freedom to experiment with Mark Twain as a comic character while continuing in new and more literary ways the satiric efforts associated with the *Call:* the humorous Washoe Mark Twain, local editor, becomes the acerbic Bohemian Mark Twain, literary critic. Clemens's satiric impulse in the *Californian* material accentuates cultural issues by overwhelmingly concerning himself with writing, literature, and aesthetics. Clemens treated these subjects with his favorite comic tactic, burlesquing the usual way that periodicals—newspapers as well as literary weeklies—covered them. Mark Twain makes fun of common features in periodicals such as "Answers to Correspondents" columns or invites laughter at specific fads, such as the craze for conundrums.

---

40. Margaret Duckett, *Mark Twain and Bret Harte,* 24.

This revision of unsanctified newspaper reporter into unconventional literary critic occurred because of the high-culture literary aspirations of the *Californian* and its two principals, Bret Harte and Charles Webb.[41] Clemens met Harte first and, despite later animosity, developed a much closer relationship with him while in San Francisco than with Webb. The offices of the *Call* were housed in three stories of the same building that held the San Francisco branch of the U.S. Mint, where Bret Harte worked as secretary to the superintendent. Shortly after Clemens started work for the newspaper, the editor, George Barnes, introduced the two men. In May 1864, Bret Harte was the best-known of a group of young writers in San Francisco who often congregated at his Mint office. Of the six writers besides Harte and Clemens that Franklin Walker identifies as producing "the best literature of the Far-Western frontier"—Ina Coolbrith, Prentice Mulford, Henry George, Charles Warren Stoddard, Ambrose Bierce, and Joaquin Miller— only George was not associated with the frequent gatherings in Harte's office. The *Californian's* first issue had come out two days before Clemens's arrival. During his stay in San Francisco, Clemens had frequent contact with Harte, no doubt often as part of his literary coterie.[42] A compelling topic for discussion among Harte and his friends throughout the summer of 1864 would very likely have been the progress of the *Californian,* especially when the circle included Webb. This artistic company provided Sam Clemens with social opportunities to participate in literary discussions in what amounted to a San Francisco–style salon atmosphere; those opportunities must have developed his ambition to write earnestly for literary weeklies. Whether Clemens already had that ambition when his friend John McComb told him to set his sights higher and write for literary journals rather than newspapers, or whether McComb's advice reinforced the perfect opportunity represented by the *Californian* to make that change is not clear. In any case, sketches signed "Mark Twain" begin to appear regularly in the *Californian* shortly after Clemens left his job with the *Call.*

The burlesque approach Clemens used to score satiric points against the bad writing so often found in popular literature comically expressed the *Californian's* high-culture literary aspirations. The emphasis in the *Californian* on literary topics linked the journal to specific East Coast publications. Making satiric attacks on inferior literature in a burlesque style had been fashionable in New York City at least since the early 1860s when Charles Farrar Browne had published burlesques of popular types of novels in *Vanity Fair,* sometimes signed

41. Joe Goodman's reaction to Webb and Harte's self-identity as professional writers was in some measure negative, once calling them "the little literary oligarchy of the *Californian*." Quoted in the *San Francisco Bulletin,* January 6, 1866 (Gary Scharnhorst, *Bret Harte,* 13).

42. Duckett, *Mark Twain and Bret Harte,* 22–23; see also Walker, *Literary Frontier,* 190–91.

"Artemus Ward" and sometimes not.[43] That New York comic periodical had been a fertile ground for burlesquing the serialization of novels that defined the story papers and routinely occupied significant space in so many literary weeklies like *Harper's Monthly* and the *Golden Era*. Browne's efforts were complemented during *Vanity Fair*'s brief existence with other burlesques by Fitzhugh Ludlow, George Arnold ("McArone"), and Robert Newell ("Orpheus C. Kerr").

This efflorescence of comic mockery was far from being an isolated phenomenon. The burlesquing impulse had been indulged on stage at the New York Olympic theater since the late 1830s, mostly at the expense of famous operas, and reached something of a climax during the 1850s at Burton's Chambers Street theater due to the writing and acting of John Brougham. Minstrel shows were built primarily on burlesque. The first famous comic writer in California, George Derby, had written numerous burlesques signed "John Phoenix," published in 1855 as *Phoenixiana; or, Sketches and Burlesques*. Though burlesquing popular novels in English was at least as old as Henry Fielding's *An Apology for the Life of Mrs. Shamela Andrews* (1741), American comic writers at midcentury were probably influenced by William Thackeray's *Catherine,* a burlesque of "Newgate novels" that romanticized crime. Published in serial form in 1839–1840, it was included in Thackeray's *Miscellanies* (1855–1857). Thus burlesque had been rife in antebellum popular culture, a ready tool for a writer who wished to deflate pretension, laugh at the latest sensation, or display familiarity with classic material. The irreverent attitude that underlies burlesque and parody as well as the application of those comic tactics to all manner of art—including dramatic, musical, and literary productions—are the identifying characteristics for many of the significant comic writers who followed the Old Southwest writers. Insofar as the category "Literary Comedian" signifies a recognizable group of comic writers, the tactics of burlesque and parody bind them together. Insofar as Sam Clemens favored burlesque and parody in his Mark Twain sketches for the *Californian*, he belongs to the category of "Literary Comedian."[44]

The most immediate models for Clemens to employ literary burlesque were the founders of the *Californian*, Francis Bret Harte and Charles Henry Webb.

43. Charles Farrar Browne, "Mossy the Sassy; or, The Disguised Duke"; "Marion: A French Romance"; "The Fair Inez; or, The Lone Lady of the Crimson Cliffs. A Tale of the Sea"; "Woshy-Boshy; or, The Prestidigitating Squaw of the Snakeheads." Browne in 1858 had also published three installments of "Our Novel," which burlesqued popular romance novels, in his column for the *Cleveland Plain Dealer,* "City Facts and Fancies."

44. For more on burlesques, see Walter Blair, "Burlesques in Nineteenth-Century American Humor"; George Kummer, "The Americanization of Burlesque, 1840–1860"; William J. Mahar, *Behind the Burnt Cork Mask: Early Blackface Minstrelsy and Antebellum American Culture,* chapter 3; and Franklin Rogers, *Mark Twain's Burlesque Patterns,* chapter 2.

Bret Harte would achieve his first national reputation publishing a book of condensed burlesque novels originally appearing in the *Californian* between July 1865 and June 1866. Even before he cofounded the *Californian,* he had shown his burlesque abilities. For example, in the *Golden Era* he had published a comic poem, "The Lost Beauty."[45] In rollicking meters, the poem tells how a young belle floats out a window during a ball, borne aloft by the gas her chemist boyfriend had used to inflate her skirt so that her ladylike glide would surpass any her peers might manage with their fashionable hoopskirts. Though Harte would often succumb to sentiment in his writings, in this poem he not only comments caustically on the sartorial pretensions of society women but also burlesques the standard pathos of a tale that ends with a lost love and a wistful lover who cannot help gazing in the distance for her though she is irretrievably gone.

Harte's counterpart on the *Californian,* Charles Webb, already had a reputation as a wit before he came to California, built initially on his work for the *New York Times.* Since arriving in California April 1863, that reputation had been augmented by several efforts: his weekly letter for the *Sacramento Union* as "John Paul," another column for the *San Francisco Evening Bulletin* signed "Inigo," and a series of comic columns called "Things," written for the *Golden Era* and also signed "Inigo." In addition, he had a dramatic hit called *Arrah-no-poke* (1865), a parody of Dion Boucicault's runaway stage success, *Arrah-na-pogue.* After leaving California, Webb would write parodies of two famous novels: *Liffith Lank* (Charles Reade's controversial *Griffith Gaunt*) and *St. Twel'mo* (Augusta Wilson's popular *St. Elmo*). Given his editors' indulgence in the vogue of burlesquing, Sam Clemens's work for the *Californian* as a comic critic shows the particular influence of Harte and Webb as well as the generalized influence of burlesque.

Clemens had displayed Mark Twain in a literary critic's guise before. The first Mark Twain piece reprinted in a New York City periodical (*Yankee Notions,* April 1864) burlesqued theater reviews. Printed originally in the *Enterprise,* it was entitled "Ingomar over the Mountains" (WG 58–60). A number of serious reviews of theater performances in the *Enterprise* undoubtedly had been written by Clemens during his Nevada tenure, perhaps along with other burlesques not reprinted. Clemens had also during his time with the *Call* shown his ability as a comic literary critic by turning two news items into burlesques of popular literature. The first, "Attempted Suicide," burlesques sentimental fiction despite its forbidding title. In writing up the local item, Clemens makes fun of the would-be suicide, Emanuel Lopus, mostly because serious doubt exists that he ever

---

45. Bret Harte, "John Jenkins; or, The Smoker Reformed, By T. S. A-th-r"; "The Ninety-Nine Guardsmen, By Al-x-d-e D-m-s"; "The Lost Beauty: A Philosophical Narrative."

made an attempt, but also because in the past a drunken Lopus had often, in sentimental and maudlin terms, threatened to kill himself. Clemens opens his caricature of Lopus with a clever sentence featuring reportorial objectivity, which gives way to the language of sentimental fiction appropriate to this maudlin habit. He then deflates its rhetoric by switching to legalistic phrasing at the end of the sentence, faintly echoing "Ye Sentimental Law Student": "Yesterday at eleven o'clock in the forenoon, Emanuel Lopus, barber, of room No. 23, Mead House, wrote to the idol of his soul that he loved her better than all else besides; that unto him the day was dark, the sun seemed swathed in shadows, when she was not by; that he was going to take the life that God had given him, and enclosed she would please find one lock of hair, the same being his." The article completes the ridicule with an irony characteristic of Mark Twain: "If we have succeeded—if we have caused one sympathetic tear to flow from the tender eye of pity, we desire no richer recompense" (CofC 151–52).

In a second item, "Original Novelette," Clemens explicitly employed the condensed novel format Browne had used at *Vanity Fair*. The piece reports the story of a woman living with a man who had come to California ahead of his wife. When his wife finally arrived, she chased the woman out of the house. Clemens divides the news report into very brief "chapters" and introduces them by saying that the "only drawback . . . to the following original novelette, is, that it contains nothing but truth, and must, therefore, be void of interest for readers of sensational fiction" (CofC 128).

While both news items show how Clemens even at the *Call* can make satiric points by recognizing how life imitates art, the second one also laughs at how people read the news for its sensationalism. When he writes for the *Californian*, Clemens again ridicules the public's appetite for sensationalized news with "The Killing of Julius Caesar, Localized." Part of the joke stems from simply treating such a famous event, immortalized by Shakespeare (whose play Clemens had obviously been reading), in the strident rhetoric of contemporary newspapers. However, the burlesque mainly satirizes the public's appetite for the inevitable sensationalizing of murders by the press, which gives ironic force to the clichéd comment about people reading "carefully and dispassionately before they render . . . judgment" (ETS 2:112).

Though both "Attempted Suicide" and "Original Novelette" ridicule the way newspapers sensationalize news, their satire also targets sentimental novels. Another *Californian* piece, "Lucretia Smith's Soldier," burlesques the same subject and again uses the condensed novel form. Clemens creates comic drama by juxtaposing contingent reality with the sentimental wishes of the vain and selfish heroine, Lucretia. He neatly captures this clash by mixing slang into a rhetoric of sentimentality. Lucretia's bookish ideas about the glory of war and the satisfaction of nursing her wounded lover are shattered by a mistaken identification (ETS 2:132). This wake-up-call effect will be used by Clemens against foolish sentiment throughout *The Innocents Abroad* and in "Old Times on the Mississippi." "Lucretia Smith's Soldier" was very popular on both coasts, reprinted in periodicals in New York and California, making it the first big hit signed "Mark Twain" in the literary weeklies.

In "Whereas," Clemens's ambition as a critic shows. Presenting a more complicated version of Mark Twain, he again takes aim at people whose attitudes about romance come straight out of sentimental and popular novels. The article has two sections. In the first, meant to serve as a preface to the theme of true love shown in the second half, Mark Twain talks like a sentimentalist when he misapprehends the sign "Love's Bakery" and falls into apostrophizing (and punning) about the kind of lovers' hearts being baked inside. This joke echoes a famous story told about George Derby, who stopped a wagon with the legend "Eagle Bakery" painted on it and asked to buy "three golden eagles, baked brown and crisp." Lewis Gaylord Clark had retailed the story and Franklin Walker retells it and notes Mark Twain's echo of it.[46] The second section introduces a letter from "Aurelia Maria," which states the problem she is having with her fiancé and asks for Mark Twain's help, evoking an advice-to-correspondents column. Her plight would "touch the heart of a statue" (ETS 2:91), says Mark Twain, and such overwrought language echoes his lyrical treatment of Love's Bakery. However, by the time the letter's contents are fully revealed, Mark Twain has changed his tone to pragmatic bordering on the callous. The young lady's fiancé, Caruthers, habitually falls sick or sustains injury, including having smallpox and erysipelas and losing both arms and a leg in accidents. He also manages to be scalped by "the Owens River Indians" (ETS 2:92). Aurelia Maria truly loves (what is left of) Caruthers and thus still wants to marry him, but parents and friends object. What should true love do in such a dilemma, she asks? Mark Twain answers that even though Caruthers did not have the sense to have "started with his neck and broken that first," none of the problems are his fault, and she should marry him. Besides, with his "infernal propensity for damaging himself every time he sees a good opportunity, his next experiment is bound to finish him" (ETS 2:93).

The heart of Clemens's efforts to give Mark Twain the voice of a satiric literary critic can be found in six *Californian* pieces, all with the title "Answers to Correspondents," which appeared from June 3 to July 8, 1865.[47] The series parodies its

---

46. Lewis Gaylord Clark, "Reminiscences of John Phoenix"; Walker, *Literary Frontier*, 45, 191.

47. The *Californian*, [Josh Billings], mentions "Josh Billings" (Henry Wheeler Shaw) conducting an "Advice to Correspondents'" column for the *New York Sunday Mercury*. Possibly the idea for the Mark Twain series was suggested to Clemens and/or Harte by his example.

main target, the column devoted to answering any sort of question from all manner of correspondents, mocking the genre it pretends to be. Because the *Golden Era* featured such a column, Mark Twain's "Answers to Correspondents" not only implicitly ridicules questionable taste in literary weeklies in general but also invites laughter at the *Californian's* rival. Carrying out this agenda allows Clemens to assume different roles by creating multiple items in each column. Mark Twain in one item can therefore be an acerbic literary editor, railing at bad writing, and in another a sarcastic metacritic, ridiculing bad theater criticism.

In this parodic advice column, Sam Clemens for the first time directly plays the role of the cultural critic. For example, Mark Twain discusses at length artwork for the Fourth of July festivities in San Francisco as well as what other periodicals have to say about it (ETS 2:221–29), or he dismisses a particular picture at the art gallery as a "petrified nightmare" (ETS 2:207; see also "The Portraits," MTCor 61–62). In other items, Mark Twain maneuvers to ridicule poets (e.g. "Literary Connoisseur," ETS 2:194–96). Other satirical attacks on similar targets include "Real Estate vs. Imaginary Possessions, Poetically Considered" (SofS 188–89) and "More Outcroppings" (MTCor 66–69). Twice Mark Twain the literary critic indirectly attacks the bad poetry persistently featured in contemporary periodicals, both times using fictitious letters. "Melton Mowbray, Dutch Flat" on one level makes fun of Byron's "The Destruction of Sennacherib" by creating a pretentious and dishonest miner named Melton Mowbray, who sends the poem to the *Californian* as though it were his. A second fictitious letter also attacks bad poetry, "Simon Wheeler—Sonora." Again a miner, this time named Simon Wheeler, supposedly sends in a poem, a eulogy for a poker-playing minister who lost all his money trying to turn two pair into a full house. "He Done His Level Best" parodies the verse regularly appearing in the poetry columns of literary papers and newspapers alike. Mark Twain as literary editor comments unambiguously: "the poet crop is unusually large and rank in California this year" (ETS 2:192).

To create his parody, Mark Twain maintains an unhelpful attitude at odds with the conventional answers-to-correspondents, advice-giving columnist. This unhelpful Mark Twain in the persona of a witty literary critic stands ready to excoriate, ridiculing the questions as often as he answers them or giving advice in a down-to-earth manner bordering on the rude and condescending. He mercilessly targets the correspondents, who are capable of asking about "the difference between Geometry and Conchology" (ETS 2:204). By dispensing sarcastic advice to young lovers about their romances or to a yahoo about how to behave in public places like the theater, Mark Twain openly proclaims their inanity so that his attempts to "help" promote proper behavior display a cranky Lord Chesterfield, an echo of Mark Twain's treatment of the Unreliable in Nevada. At the end of the series, in an item entitled "Student of Etiquette," Mark Twain explicitly names the biggest satiric target by wondering at the foolishness of editors "gravely" answering the seemingly endless stream of "foolish," "unnecessary," and "absurd" questions (ETS 2:229).

Over and over again, Clemens uses Mark Twain to attack the root of the ridiculous questions: people's foolish beliefs. In "St. Clair Higgins, Los Angeles," Mark Twain laughs at sentimental language and fiction to target the unrealistic attitudes supporting them:

> "My life is a failure; I have adored, wildly, madly, and she whom I love has turned coldly from me and shed her affections upon another; what would you advise me to do?" You should shed your affections on another, also—or on several, if there are enough to go around. Also, do everything you can to make your former flame unhappy. There is an absurd idea disseminated in novels, that the happier a girl is with another man, the happier it makes the old lover she has blighted. Don't you allow yourself to believe any such nonsense as that. The more cause that girl finds to regret that she did not marry you, the more comfortable you will feel over it. It isn't poetical, but it is mighty sound doctrine. (ETS 2:183–84)

In other examples where Clemens's talent for ridicule has shifted from the personal emphasis in his Washoe style to attacks on issues and attitudes, Mark Twain makes fun of conventional and genteel sentiments mindlessly and endlessly reiterated, such as praising small children ("Young Mother," ETS 2:204–6), or people's self-righteousness concerning morality and patriotism ("Moral Statistician," ETS 2:189–90; "True Son of the Union," ETS 2:200–202). Such pieces reveal a new depth to the satiric attacks of Mark Twain, delving into literary practices to reach the cultural values within them. Although Sam Clemens's work for the *Call* and for the *Californian* illustrates the sharp divide between reporting for a daily metropolitan paper and a weekly high-culture literary periodical, the material from both publications demonstrates a significant shift, moving Mark Twain away from relying on the Washoe tactic of personal raillery and toward articulating a comic vision.

## FITZ SMYTHE AND THE SANCTIFIED

IF YOU WOULD SEE AROUND YOU A PEOPLE WHO ARE FILLED WITH THE
KEENEST APPRECIATION OF PERFECTION IN MUSICAL EXECUTION AND
DRAMATIC DELINEATION, AND PAINFULLY SENSITIVE TO THE SLIGHT-
EST DEPARTURES FROM THE TRUE STANDARD OF ART IN THESE THINGS,
YOU MUST EMPLOY . . . YOUR NEWSPAPER CRITICS CAPABLE OF DIS-
CRIMINATING BETWEEN MERIT AND DEMERIT, AND ALIKE FEARLESS IN
PRAISING THE ONE AND CONDEMNING THE OTHER.

---

MARK TWAIN, "STILL FURTHER CONCERNING THAT CONUNDRUM,"
*CALIFORNIAN*, OCTOBER 15, 1864

WE OF BOHEMIA KEEP AWAY FROM CARLETON'S [NEW YORK PUBLISH-
ING HOUSE].

---

LETTER TO CHARLES W. STODDARD, APRIL 23, 1867

Writing for the *Californian* had transformed Clemens's alter ego into a self-consciously literary Mark Twain. Moreover, Clemens continued to put a large effort into attacking bad writing after he stopped regular contributions to the *Californian*. Following a hiatus in the Sierra Nevada, Clemens, by the middle of 1865, had become a regular correspondent for the *San Francisco Dramatic Chronicle* and the *Virginia City Territorial Enterprise*, though he would also occasionally contribute again to the *Californian*. In all of these publications and throughout the remainder of his residence in San Francisco, Clemens vigorously exhibited his talent for invective and insult in comic ambushes designed to criticize poor writing. He did not even shrink from abusing his friend and colleague William Wright, to ridicule conventionally sentimental writing ("Uncle Lige," ETS 2:378–79).

Poetry occupied Clemens's comic talents in the fall of 1865 because of a controversy surrounding Bret Harte's anthology of California poets, *Outcroppings*. Clemens defended the book in his review for the *Enterprise* ("Caustic," MTCor 19–22), though other writers for that paper—including Joe Goodman—had panned it. In *Californian* sketches published before the review, Clemens had employed mock poems to ridicule how not to pen verse, and he returned to the subject again during this time with a burlesque, "The Ballad Infliction" (MTW

194–95). The urge to ridicule bad poetry continued into 1866. In a letter to his mother and sister dated January 20, Clemens wrote that he and Bret Harte had plans to burlesque a new book of poems by California writers due out in the spring. "Then you'll hear these poetical asses here tear around worse than a pack of wildcats. . . . We shall only burlesque a few of the prominent ones, but we will introduce each burlesque poem with a blast of trumpets & some comments that will be eminently worth reading, no doubt. I am willing enough to go into this thing, because there will be *fun* in it" (CL 1:329, original emphasis). During the controversy over the choices in the *Outcroppings* anthology, Harte in the *Californian* had imagined in a mock review a burlesque book of poems called *Tailings: Rejections of California Verse*.[48] The piece targeted Joe Goodman, among others, and no doubt inspired the book Clemens mentions the next month in his letter. The fact that Sam was ready to participate in a project that surely would have parodied his former employer, who was well-known for his poetry and who was vehement in his attack on Harte's anthology, suggests how close to Harte Clemens had become and how much the "fun" of burlesque enlisted his talents.

A large target for Mark Twain the comic literary critic could be found in the writing for the local newspapers. One of his *Californian* contributions is a clever piece written with this subject in mind and entitled simply, "The Facts." According to the narrative, a friend of Mark Twain's, John Skae, shows up suddenly in the offices of the *Californian* and tearfully asks Mark Twain to print a manuscript about a distressing accident. Mark Twain stops the press to insert the item, "cherishing the hope that to print it would afford a melancholy satisfaction to [Mr. Skae's] sorrowing heart" (ETS 2:254). The item turns out to be incomprehensible—one long, introductory subordinate clause without sense, information, or main clause to end the thought—and Mark Twain admits that the editors of the *Californian* are very angry at him for printing the item without first reading it. He then suspects he has been hoaxed by Skae (who was a good friend of Clemens; see ETS 2:72–73). Mark Twain turns bitter, knowing that the "storm of abuse and ornamental blasphemy" unleashed on him by the editors comes from allowing Skae's "snuffling distress" to touch his feelings (ETS 2:256). So much for a sentimental heart. The sketch's tone suddenly shifts, however, after Mark Twain rereads the piece and declares that "I do not see that it is any more obscure than the general run of local items in the daily papers after all" (ETS 2:257) and proceeds to discuss all the San Francisco papers in terms of Skae's nonsense item: it is no worse than the jokes in the *Alta California,* the poetry in the *Flag,* the bad grammar in the *Call,* or the awkwardly written letters from country correspondents in the *Bulletin.*

48. Bret Harte, "A New California Book."

Clemens through much of the fall of 1865 constantly ridicules the way that other newspapermen write. He also does not exempt a well-known newspaper-woman. On two occasions Mark Twain makes fun of Lisle Lester's writing style, by turns overly wrought and obscure (ETS 2:483–84, 489). Other jabs target the trivial nature of local columns (ETS 2:417–18) and the inane comments about obvious topics made in editorials (ETS 2:341–42). Mark Twain scours the local writing corps for weeks without pause until he jokes that he has fixed all the problems and has nothing to do (ETS 2:504).

The biggest specific target for Mark Twain as a comic literary critic was Albert Evans, who wrote for the *Alta California,* sometimes under the comic pseudonym "Fitz Smythe." When he was with the *Call,* Clemens had railed at Evans, whom he sometimes called "Stiggers" in a deliberate confusion of the reporter with a comic creation of his, for inept reporting and for drinking up all the liquor at the dedication of the new Chinese temple (CofC 82–83, 84). The charges would sound familiar to longtime readers of Mark Twain, reminding them of his earlier tilts with the Unreliable. Clemens mounted a more sustained attack in the winter of 1865–1866, making caustic comments about the dubious character and bad politics of Evans as well as his poor writing ("Delightful Romance," ETS 2:510; "Facetious," ETS 2:338–39; "Gorgeous New Romance" and "Another Romance," MTCor 25–32; "Fitz Smythe's Horse," ETS 2:345–46; "Closed Out," ETS 2:348; "Take the Stand, Fitz Smythe," ETS 2:350–52; "Remarkable Dream," ETS 2:355–58). At first glance, the running battle with Evans, whom Clemens most often addressed as "Fitz Smythe," looks simply like a San Francisco version of Washoe Mark Twain's mock feuds with William Wright and Clement Rice. However, there was nothing companionable about Clemens's persistent efforts to ridicule Evans, because he represented exactly what the comic literary critic Mark Twain had been attacking: conventional thinking expressed in conventional writing. Clemens's attacks on Evans were also not as humorous and friendly as custom dictated, because Evans had defended the San Francisco police during the campaign Clemens waged against them in the winter of 1865–1866.[49]

The attitude about the aesthetics of writing that Mark Twain implied in the *Californian* sketches invited laughter at the usual genteel methods of composing poetry and fiction. The burlesque poems and satiric commentaries on peri-

---

49. The *Californian* had frequently ridiculed Evans in a regular feature called "The Lion's Mouth," designed to roar at humbugs. The feature presented extracts from other periodicals that were commented on, often with a superior tone, especially when questions of taste and belles lettres were the topics, and it contributed to the weekly's Bohemian iconoclasm. Evans was a target as late as April 6, 1867, when "The Unhappy Fitz Smythe" appeared, which called him "the imbecile humorist of the Pacific Coast" and a "born fool." The piece also recalled how often Mark Twain had ridiculed Evans.

odical writing show by negative example what constituted a literary standard for Sam Clemens during his stay in San Francisco. Mark Twain promotes a more direct and plainer way of phrasing than what popular writings often trumpeted, particularly in the blood-and-thunder adventure tales or romances that dominated popular story papers. Plainer phrasing became especially important for expressing strong emotion by promoting a vigorous style of writing neither inundated by bathos nor carried away by grandiloquence. The *Californian* exemplified good writing for Clemens. He made the judgment clear while working for the *Call*, characterizing the journal as a "sterling literary weekly [and] the best paper in its particular department ever issued on this coast" (CofC 63).

In mounting his attacks both during and after his regular contributions to the *Californian*, Clemens used Mark Twain not only to exercise his satiric abilities on the topic of aesthetics, but also to conduct that exercise from an unconventional perspective loosely defined in the 1850s and 1860s as "Bohemianism." Honoré de Balzac may have given the earliest definition of Bohemia as a condition of artistic potential rather than a geographic place of residence when he wrote in an 1840 story, "Bohemia . . . is made up of young people, all of whom are between twenty and thirty years of age, all men of genius in their own style, almost unknown, but who will make themselves known, and then they will be persons of real distinction."[50] However, another French *feuilletoniste,* Henri Murger, popularized the image of talented but struggling artists in his sketches "La Vie de Bohème" (*Corsaire Magazine,* 1844–1849). The sketches became a play in 1849 before he collected them into a book as *Scènes de la Bohème* in 1851. For Murger as for Balzac, Bohemia signified a stage in an artist's career, the preface to fame and fortune.

For nineteenth-century Americans writing in periodicals, the label "Bohemians" did not carry such a promising connotation. Certainly, attitudes toward those given the label varied. Definitions varied even more, and individuals applied the label inconsistently. Though painters and actors are frequently named as Bohemians, freelance journalists and writers for periodicals compose the largest single group within the tribe. Bohemians, according to George William Curtis, did not exist "until literature became a profession." For W. L. Alden, periodicals are a nexus for these professional writers. "Writers, who write to live from day to day, and not for fame or to influence their fellows; who regard literature as a trade, and who sell their brains to the highest bidder, are preeminently Bohemians." For an anonymous editor of the *Manufacturer and Builder,* "the term was properly applied to those writers and reporters who make

50. Honoré de Balzac, "Un Prince de la Bohème," 22, my translation.

a precarious living by enlisting their pens in the service of any periodical that will give them employment for the time being."[51]

Opinions varied about whether being poor was a necessary condition for being a Bohemian. Moreover, those who included poverty as an attribute could hold very different attitudes about that "fact." For Alden and Curtis, Bohemians were reckless about money and often in dire need of new clothes or unsure about their next meal, yet they both projected a romanticized nostalgia about the carefree state of the Bohemians they had known, their hardships, and their generosity toward one another. Bret Harte had the same attitude, writing that Bohemians were poor but not immoral, living by their wits to produce the literary "bouquets" they sold to the public.[52] The editor of the *Manufacturer and Builder* called them frauds, writing on any subject, whether they knew anything about it or not, simply to alleviate their chronic poverty.

Though commentators in American periodicals could not agree about the heft of the typical Bohemian purse, general agreement existed about Bohemians and social propriety. They were "Needy, and all seedy," "Whatever is not 'respectable,'" "men of indomitable irregularity and indolence," and men or women who lived "in disregard of or in opposition to the conventional proprieties of life." An anonymous *Galaxy* editor declared that "A family, a well-ordered household, a settled home, however humble, a decorous and steady life—with these Bohemianism is radically incompatible." Bohemians therefore are "the *demi-monde* of the literary and artistic world."[53] Although these judgments appear consistent with a charge of fraudulent writing, immoral behavior was not always implied. Like all groups of people, both moral and immoral Bohemians could be found. Immorality in any case was not the real issue. Rather, by signifying potential artistic ability, Bohemians were placed at odds with conventional aesthetics. Bohemians also signified a threatening potential for attitudes and behaviors different from the bourgeois or genteel norm—significantly different yet perhaps not inferior or wrong. George William Curtis spoke in contradictions to describe the conflict: "There are plenty of men among [the Bohemians] worthy of respect—but none who are technically respectable." "[Bohemia] is the lawlessness within law, the camp within the castle court." W. L. Alden called them "civilized vagabonds [who disregard] the established customs of 'respectability.'" One well-known denizen of Bohemia, Ada Clare, stated the proposition

51. George William Curtis, "Editor's Easy Chair: What Is a Bohemian?" 705; W. L. Alden, "The Four Nations," 703–4; *Manufacturer and Builder*, "Bohemianism," 248.

52. Bret Harte, "Town and Table Talk: The Bohemian at the Fair."

53. George William Curtis, "The Editor at Large" [Bohemians], 437; Curtis, "What Is a Bohemian?" 705; Alden, "Four Nations," 703; *Galaxy*, "Nebulae" [The Word "Bohemian"], 369.

more positively: "The Bohemian is not, like the creature of society, a victim of rules and customs; he steps over them all with an easy, graceful, joyous unconsciousness, guided by the principles of good taste and feeling."[54]

The American who managed best to step over rules and customs was Henry Clapp. An ardent believer in the socialism of the French thinker Charles Fourier and an equally strong proponent for the abolition of slavery, Clapp's circumvention of prevailing social thought was not a matter of joyous unconsciousness. He spent three years in Paris learning French and acquiring a French *mentalité*. By early 1856 he had returned to New York City, hoping to establish an artists' colony modeled on what he had experienced in the Latin Quarter. By 1858, that colony had found its omphalos in Pfaff's Cellar, New York City's answer to the Left Bank, with Clapp as the leading figure. William Winter, a habitué of Pfaff's at the time and later a theater critic for the *New York Tribune*, described Clapp as "intolerant of smug, ponderous, empty, obstructive respectability."[55] The literary weekly Clapp founded in 1858 and edited throughout its brief career, the *New York Saturday Press*, reflected this Bohemian attitude toward bourgeois values and aesthetics.

Even while in Nevada, Sam Clemens had been associated with a Bohemian point of view. The *Gold Hill News*, apologizing to its respectable readers for an irreverent item written the day before by its local reporter, Charles Sumner, calls him a "reprobate of the order of Mark Twain" and refers to "Mark Twain and that crowd of Bohemians 'lost to society, lost' who do items for the Washoe papers." Clemens himself understood the difference between his Bohemian pals and the respectable public. Writing from Carson City for the *Gold Hill News*, "China" reports that Mark Twain will speak at a fund-raiser for the new Presbyterian church. He goes on to say that he overhead Mark Twain asking the Unreliable to collect the money at the door and admonishing him to refuse entry to any "damn'd Bohemian" who will not pay.[56]

A better measure of how easily Sam Clemens fit a Bohemian profile can be found in his aesthetic. Two Mark Twain reviews of popular performers demonstrate how that aesthetic did not fit the conventional mold established by standard, high-culture ideas about artistic endeavor. "A Voice for Setchell" discusses Dan Setchell, a well-known stage comedian who had come to San Francisco in April 1865 and who had been playing to enthusiastic houses for weeks when

54. Curtis, "What Is a Bohemian?" 705; George William Curtis, "Editor's Easy Chair" [Palmer's Studio], 269; Alden, "Four Nations," 703; Ada Clare, "Thoughts and Things."
55. Quoted in Tice L. Miller, *Bohemians and Critics: American Theater Criticism in the Nineteenth Century*, 18.
56. *Gold Hill News*, "Irreverence"; "China," "Carson Correspondence."

Clemens wrote his short notice praising the actor's comic abilities. The second piece appeared in the *San Francisco Dramatic Chronicle* with the title "Enthusiastic Eloquence." In it, Mark Twain compares three different banjo players with the famous concert pianist Louis Gottschalk—and Gottschalk loses. To carry his message of Bohemian alignment against conventional aesthetics, Mark Twain presents comically exaggerated images of gentility: "The piano may do for lovesick girls who lace themselves to skeletons, and lunch on chalk, pickles, and slate pencils. But give me the banjo" (ETS 2:235). Genuine music like the banjo playing of Tommy Bree had the same effect as the comic performances of Dan Setchell, providing "more real pleasure" than all the operas and tragedies combined (ETS 2:172). Favorably comparing Setchell's "funny personations and extempore speeches" to operas and tragedies again signals a preference for what conventional society would call a low-culture taste over symbols of a high-culture taste, just as the comparison of banjo to piano did.

In both reviews, a perception of vitality elevates what is normally considered low. That vitality, however, threatens a standard social decorum. Mark Twain associates the piano with fainting girls and insubstantial food. Even Gottschalk's acclaimed ability does not escape comparison with such feeble parlor fare. In contrast, the "glory-beaming banjo" gives a listener goose bumps, and Mark Twain links it with hot whiskey punch, strychnine, and measles. The danger of this power becomes even more comically explicit in a suggestion to smash pianos in favor of banjos. Similarly, Mark Twain implicates Setchell's performance style in such metaphoric assaults on genteel aesthetics and decorum because the laughter he elicits happens "naturally and unconfinedly." Finally, Clemens through his Mark Twain alter ego completes his Bohemian stance on what constitutes good music and theater by endorsing Setchell's abilities despite the cavils of the prominent critics. He votes down the conventional taste of such critics because the audiences laugh "extravagantly." Though out of place in and even threatening to the gentility of parlor aesthetics, Clemens reads such natural and genuine laughter as a sign of excellence in comic literature. "That kind of criticism can always be relied upon as sound, and not only sound but honest" (ETS 2:173).

Sam Clemens's affinity with Bohemian aesthetics, then, comes in several forms. Mark Twain scoffing at the sentimental pretensions and melodramatic sensationalism of Albert Evans as Fitz Smythe represents Sam Clemens's sense of well-established newspapers' complacency and the small-mindedness of some reporters. The satiric inversion of the mock "Advice to Correspondents" column in the *Californian* resulted in a sarcastic and cranky Mark Twain dispensing refreshingly candid advice that ridiculed literary genres and their implied genteel social attitudes. Mark Twain's advocacy of a less-than-genteel aesthetic also testifies to a rebelliousness against standards social and literary.

Clemens's Bohemian willingness to shock the proprieties of conventional thinking may be best seen in his frequent and often violent jokes about children. As with the reviews of Gottschalk and Setchell, the comic violence expressed on this subject reveals how Clemens revises the cultural barbarity of Mark Twain's Gentleman Roarer heritage into a Bohemian assault on middle-class values as well as aesthetics. The joking had started with "Those Blasted Children," published in the *New York Sunday Mercury.* In the piece, Sam Clemens first displayed his considerable talent at rendering children's slangy dialogue. When children speak, they expose how much they imitate the bad manners and petty jealousies of their parents. The sketch closes with Mark Twain imagining comic ways to cure the children of diseases, cures that would ensure death or disfiguration. For example, brain fever should be cured by removing the brains and stuttering by removing the underjaw. Cramps are best remedied by parbroiling the patient (ETS 1:355–56).

The real target of "Those Blasted Children," the rhetoric and sentiment used by genteel society to idealize children, appears in the last two paragraphs, which are composed of exactly such overwrought rhetoric and overdone sentiment about memories of childhood. The comic violence surprised at least one writer associated with Bohemianism, who took the sketch as an attack on children. When Ada Clare arrived in San Francisco in the spring of 1864, she wrote several pieces for the *Golden Era* in a letter format that replaced Charles Webb's column, "Things," when he took that feature to his newly founded *Californian.* In one of her columns, she was clearly taken aback by "Those Blasted Children," saying, "I don't quite like Mark Twain's last article on children. He is funny, of course; but he is guilty of misunderstanding God's little people."[57]

Ada Clare's reaction to the violent comic tactics in the piece suggests how unusual was the melding of the backwoods comic tradition with a Bohemian point of view, something Clemens indulged again while working for the *Call,* when children get the funny business twice, in "Children at the Fair" and "More Children." The former merely notes that many adults need to be on hand when children visit the fair to prevent "Young America from getting ground up in the machinery" (CofC 113). The second notice drops any veneer of safety concerns. When he writes of seeing "the army of school children that swarmed into the Fair yesterday," Mark Twain adopts the viewpoint of King Herod, lamenting that he will have to "suffer the discomfort of knowing he could not slaughter them under our eccentric system of government without getting himself into trouble" (CofC 114). The outrageous fantasy threatens to overwhelm the one fact in the item, noted at the last, that nearly eight hundred children attended the fair.

---

57. Ada Clare, "Washoe Wanderings."

Conventional proprieties in the 1860s agreed with Ada Clare: children are God's little people, a phrase investing them with a degree of sacredness that should protect them from rough rhetorical treatment or outright ridicule, let alone the violent fantasies projected by Mark Twain, even if clearly meant to be comic. Franklin Walker suggests that sentimental writing about family and children garnered particularly strong favor in California at this time, with men greatly outnumbering women, prostitution flagrant, divorce common, and family life either nonexistent or "reduced to its minimum by residence in hotels." Carl Bode's study of antebellum popular culture makes it clear that the topic "children" licensed a rhetoric genteel and sentimental as well as a flood of narrative fiction similar in tone.[58] Such fiction either sought to teach children moral behavior or used children as exemplars of an instinctive morality, one meant to instruct adult readers while reflecting Wordsworth's famous line from "Ode: Intimations of Immortality" about children's heaven-sent nature: "trailing clouds of glory." California had by 1865 produced well-known writers of fiction and poetry for and about children, including Elizabeth Chamberlain Wright, who wrote under the pseudonym "Topsy-Turvey." The best-known perhaps was Mary Richardson Newman, who wrote three children's books as "May Wentworth" and who frequently contributed to the *Golden Era*.[59]

Bohemian irreverence often shattered the serenity of genteel conventions represented by such writers. Notably, Clemens had company in daring to use irreverence with the subject of children. Charles Webb provides examples equally bold. In "Stories for Good Little Boys and Girls," he creates several very short ironic tales, sarcastic in tone and without the expected sentimental moral as a conclusion. In his column for the *Californian,* "Things," Webb publishes a Thanksgiving story for children, one that extols the advantages of *not* being industrious. One of his "John Paul" letters to the *Sacramento Union* matches Clemens for violent fantasy. Discussing the Christmas season, Webb recalls groups of children annoying him by playing with the tin horns they had received as presents. The din has him wishing for each horn to be "well-loaded with a pound of powder, and provided with a percussion cap, which would explode on being blown upon." He then cheerfully imagines heads "sailing away."[60]

Not all sketches undermining conventional attitudes about children employed violence in their reversal of the topic's standard moralistic treatment. "Pleasant Games for California Children," signed "Wode" but probably Webb's,

---

58. Walker, *Literary Frontier,* 222; Carl Bode, *The Anatomy of American Popular Culture, 1840–1861.*

59. CL 1:330n7; Walker, *Literary Frontier,* 223.

60. Charles Webb, "Stories for Good Little Boys and Girls"; "Things" [November 26]; "Letter from San Francisco" [December 29].

consists of seven short paragraphs, each describing a game, and all of which encourage bad behavior, such as ringing doorbells and rigging ropes to trip people. Bret Harte's "Stories for Little Girls" offers a milder satire. The stories burlesque boys' adventure tales by imagining female heroines, which manages to twist conventional attitudes about gendered behavior without using violence. Another example found in the *Californian* also twists conventional attitudes about gendered behavior, though it does use violence and does not confine itself to children, despite its title. "Stories for Good Little Girls," signed "Ancient," provides a trio of tales about young women being disappointed in love and suggests as remedies either shooting lovers or chopping off their heads. These shockingly improper tales virulently ridicule the popular poetry and fiction that present as models of behavior young women who suffer modestly and in silence.[61]

In these pieces about children and young women, the satire targets conventional notions of what constitutes goodness and proper behavior as well as the myriad examples of stories, poems, advice columns, and etiquette books that served to inculcate those values. When Mark Twain pretends to offer helpful advice to young boys and girls in two short ironic pieces written for the *San Francisco Youths' Companion,* "Advice for Good Little Boys" and "Advice for Good Little Girls," they take their place amid the other sketches projecting Bohemia's fundamentally irreverent attitude toward conventional proprieties. The two mock advice sketches also employ the frontier tradition of comic violence. In them, Mark Twain ruthlessly parodies a clichéd genre symbolic of those proprieties, the moral literature of the Sunday school. In the brief lists of ironic advice in both *Youths' Companion* pieces, Mark Twain invites mordant laughter at the joyful piety informing moral literature for youth. Boys "ought never to knock your little sisters down with a club. It is better to use a cat, which is soft" (ETS 2:242). The girls receive a similarly helpful hint: "If at any time you find it necessary to correct your brother, do not correct him with mud—never on any account throw mud at him, because it will soil his clothes. It is better to scald him a little; for then you attain two desirable results—you secure his immediate attention to the lesson you are inculcating, and, at the same time, your hot water will have a tendency to remove impurities from his person—and possibly the skin also, in spots" (ETS 2:244). Mark Twain's irreverence, his "brass and triple cheek," is possibly never more in evidence than with these two brief items, for Clemens unleashes his madcap character not just to ridicule Sunday school literature but also to scald with satiric laughter the conventional, sweetly cheerful attitude of his readers toward family life, an attitude that promoted a syrupy, sentimental tone.

61. Charles Webb, "Pleasant Games for California Children. By 'Wode'"; Bret Harte, "Stories for Little Girls"; "Ancient," "Stories for Good Little Girls."

Clemens trumps those two shorter items with "The Christmas Fireside," using, as he did in "Those Blasted Children," a sarcastically ironic perspective to render how children actually behave. Subtitled "The Story of the Bad Little Boy That Bore a Charmed Life," the entire sketch is structured by irony. The main title evokes an image of the domestic hearth and the family gathered together, a harmonious picture reinforced by Mark Twain becoming "Grandfather Twain" to tell the tale. By taking on the guise of a wise patriarch, benevolently dispensing moralistic wisdom around the Christmas hearth, Clemens substantially raises the comic stakes as he takes aim at the same literary target as the pieces written for the *San Francisco Youths' Companion:* predictably and thus boringly moralistic Sunday school literature. In this tale "everything turned out differently with [the hero Jim] from the way it does to the bad Jameses in the books" (ETS 2:408). Familial love, even a mother's love, counts among the tale's many victims of comic inversion, a tactic that escalates in tall-tale fashion as the narrative proceeds. Nothing bad happens to Jim despite his many sins, and "he grew up, and married, and raised a large family, and brained them all with an axe one night, and got wealthy by all manner of cheating and rascality, and now he is the infernalest wickedest scoundrel in his native village, and is universally respected, and belongs to the Legislature" (ETS 2:410). A more sweeping condemnation of American life encompassed in one sentence would be difficult to accomplish. Mark Twain laughs at sentimental moral tales for children, which were especially popular at Christmastime, while also ridiculing Protestant morality, family life, political ethics, and social behavior.

The literary consciousness developed by Sam Clemens when he wrote for the *Californian* turned Mark Twain into a comic critic of culture. When added to Clemens's debt-ridden circumstances during his stay in San Francisco and his reporter's habit of cruising the city's nightlife, such eccentricity plus his new literary consciousness brought Clemens close to qualifying as a full-fledged Bohemian.[62] The use of comic violence by Clemens especially underscores the outside-the-pale attitude of his Bohemian aesthetic and Bohemian irreverence for social norms. Late in 1865 and early in 1866 this opposition to genteel norms led Clemens into his most conspicuously unconventional comic behavior, a satiric barrage directed mainly at the San Francisco police, though he included the *San Francisco Call* in the courageous campaign. Unfortunately, the printed record is incomplete, but this

62. An item in the *San Francisco Dramatic Chronicle* indicates other unconventional behavior: "It appears that a 'Hasheesh' mania has broken out among our Bohemians. Yesterday, Mark Twain and the 'Mouse-Trap' man [Tremenheere Lanyon Johns] were seen walking up Clay street under the influence of the drug, followed by a 'star,' who was evidently laboring under a misapprehension as to what was the matter with them. The 'experiences' of the twain may be looked for in the next number of the Californian" ("Hasheesh Eaters").

episode in Clemens's career began while he was working for the *Call* during the summer and fall of 1864. Clemens had apparently witnessed an attack on a Chinese man and had written up a local item full of outrage, satirizing the police's lack of efforts in the incident. The editors of the *Call* suppressed the piece. On December 12, 1865, more than a year after he quit the *Call*, Clemens had a similar occasion to be outraged, but this time he had an outlet that would print his scathing sarcasm, the newly established *San Francisco Dramatic Chronicle*:

OUR ACTIVE POLICE—The *Call* gives an account of an unoffending Chinese ragpicker being set upon by a gang of boys and nearly stoned to death. It concludes the paragraph thus: "He was carried to the City and County Hospital in an insensible condition, his head having been split open and his body badly bruised. The young ruffians scattered, and it is doubtful if any of them will be recognized and punished." If that unoffending man dies, and a murder has consequently been committed, it is doubtful whether his murderers will be recognized and punished, is it? And yet if a Chinaman steals a chicken he is sure to be recognized and punished, through the efforts of one of our active police force. If our active police force are not too busily engaged in putting a stop to petty thieving by Chinamen, and fraternizing with newspaper reporters, who hold up their wonderful deeds to the admiration of the community, let it be looked to that the boys who were guilty of this murderous assault on an industrious and unoffending man *are* recognized and punished. The *Call* says "some philanthropic gentlemen dispersed the miscreants"; these philanthropic gentlemen, if the police do their duty and arrest the culprits, can probably recognize them. (ETS 2:511)

Mark Twain ridicules the *Call*'s lack of interest in justice for the Chinese man in equal measure with the police department's indifference. When Clemens in May 1870 first recounted the *Call*'s suppression of his satire on the racism of the San Francisco police, he maintained that money was the motive: too many subscribers to the *Call* were Irish, and to defend the Chinese was to offend the Irish, who hated and feared them (CG 43). A week after the *Dramatic Chronicle* had printed "Our Active Police," it ran "How Dare You?" which once again accused the *Call* of worrying more about its bottom line than public safety and social justice. This time misdeeds of soldiers stationed at the Presidio provoke Mark Twain: "The secret of this persecution of 'the boys in blue' lies just here—they don't advertise in the little *Call*, and the little *Call* don't allow people to do as they 'darn please,' *unless they advertise in it*. Then it is all right. Don't you think now, little *Call*, that you had better sling away that subject and tackle a fresh one— 'The Blue Laws of Connecticut,' for instance, if you must 'chaw up' something blue?" (ETS 2:512). "Our Active Police" and "How Dare You?" stirred up Charles Webb. In a "John Paul" letter, he mentions ruffians beating up Chinese men and the police not only not preventing such attacks but setting the example for them.

In a second "John Paul" letter, Webb talks about the dreadful behavior of the Presidio soldiers. Webb's "Pleasant Games for California Children" suggests the chronic nature of the problem for the Chinese: the first pleasant game is called "Hunt the Chinaman," and the police protect the children who play it.[63]

Apparently, the attack on the San Francisco police formed part of a sustained satiric campaign conducted at least until early 1866 and waged mainly in Mark Twain's daily letters to the *Virginia City Territorial Enterprise* as its San Francisco correspondent. Probably on January 15, 1866, the *Enterprise* printed a letter that exemplified the campaign. The *Golden Era* reprinted a portion of the letter under the title, "What Have the Police Been Doing?" The occasion for this sarcastic diatribe came from the death of a man in police custody. The piece not only ridicules (once again) the police's indifference to the health of an individual, but its opening paragraph also catalogs a long list of police faults attended by a series of ironic questions. A major transgression that deserved a set of questions all its own was the laziness of police officers, who can often be found "back up against a lamp-post . . . smiling till they break plum down" (WG 97). One story about Clemens at this time has him playing a practical joke on an officer to ridicule his laziness. Finding the officer asleep on his beat, Clemens obtained a large cabbage-leaf and used it as a fan, collecting an amused crowd. In print he sharpened his ridicule, reporting instances of bungling, denouncing the practice of using informants, and accusing the chief of police, Martin Burke, of whitewashing any complaints against his cronies. The climax to Mark Twain's satiric exposé of the San Francisco police apparently occurred in an *Enterprise* letter no longer extant, in which Clemens penned a screed about corruption and immorality so withering that he doubted the fearless Joe Goodman would print it. The letter supposedly began, "The air is full of lechery, and rumors of lechery." The steady barrage of satiric ridicule incensed Police Chief Burke, who threatened a libel suit against Clemens and the *Enterprise*.[64] The power of

63. Charles Webb, "Letter from San Francisco" [December 15]; "Letter from San Francisco" [December 22]; "Pleasant Games." Edgar Branch speculates that the suppression by the *Call* of the 1864 item about police racism may have contributed to Clemens leaving the *Call*. His account also discusses newspaper coverage of an incident that may have been the occasion for the suppressed item. The difference in coverage between the *Call* and competitors makes the bias of the former clear (Branch, introduction to *Clemens of the "Call,"* 23–27). Notable for this topic is an 1864 newspaper item by William Brief that tells of Clemens walking arm-in-arm down a San Francisco street with an African American newspaperman, Peter Anderson (Branch, introduction to *Clemens of the "Call,"* 303n47).

64. The letter to the *Enterprise* is described in the January 23, 1866, editions of the *Gold Hill Daily News* and the *Virginia City Daily Union*. The story about the sleeping policeman is from Paine, *Biography* (1:258), as are the quote from the letter and the comments about Goodman and Burke (1:264). Henry Nash Smith (MTCor 10–12) catalogs Clemens's assaults in print, notes the threatened libel suit, and speculates on police efforts to discredit Clemens. Paine mistakenly places

Clemens's satiric attacks in late 1865 and early 1866 coincides with his growing reputation as a writer—and his growing confidence in his talent.[65]

The unconventional boldness of Clemens as a satirist in late 1865 and early 1866 can be appreciated by comparing his attacks on the police with an earlier comic piece about the criminal justice system. About three weeks after beginning his job with the *San Francisco Morning Call,* Clemens wrote a sketch for the city's literary weekly, the *Golden Era,* in which he dramatized something he had been reporting from the courts: witnesses swearing to contradictory versions of events. "The Evidence in the Case of Smith vs. Jones" uses dialogue, sprinkled with boxing jargon, to point out the absurdity of this cross-swearing (ETS 2:14–21). Clemens emphasizes a witty Mark Twain who makes jokes about two friends, about mining assessments, and about the wisdom and ability of people to discover truth. An amusing satiric commentary results, based on his experience as a reporter for the court of Judge Shepheard, whom he praises. Such commentary should cause a thinking person to ask questions about the fate of truth in a courtroom—when he or she has stopped laughing. The sketch demonstrates how Clemens, through a playwright's devices, can create effective satire about actual events. However, the satire on cross-swearing merely attacks disreputable individuals whose behavior tangles court proceedings. The satires on the San Francisco police department not only indict its entire operation, including the behavior of its chief, but also encompass that segment of the respectable population, represented by Fitz Smythe and the *Call,* who blindly supported and defended the department's incompetence and inhumanity in the name of law and order. While "Evidence" attacks an abuse of law, the various later pieces against the police and the *Call* underscore the way people can employ the principle of law to support abuse and corruption. In addition, they target the *Call's* bottom-line mentality that placed profit above justice.

By early 1866, Washoe Mark Twain's tendency to spoof the reporter's role had been redirected. Clemens consistently used his comic character to attack not only the usual ways of writing for and editing a newspaper, but also the usual ways to write literature or the usual ways that conventional writers treated certain literary topics—such as love always being linked with noble feelings or children always being entwined with sentimental morality. His comic treatment questions the sacredness of those subjects in the pantheon of middle-class

---

the attacks on police brutality and corruption in the fall of 1864 and makes Burke's counterattack a main cause for Clemens's sojourn with Steve Gillis at Toulomne from December 1864 to February 1865. Clemens did not start writing for the *Enterprise* as its San Francisco correspondent, however, until June 1865 (Edgar M. Branch, introduction to *Early Tales and Sketches, Volume I [1851–1864],* 30).

65. Branch, introduction to *Early Tales,* 30–35.

beliefs. Clemens had significantly enlarged in Mark Twain the capacity for satiric attack so that neither a morally flabby police force nor mindlessly sweet literary genres could escape. The enlarged satiric capacity of Mark Twain endowed the comic figure with a Bohemian attitude about centric norms, a significant risk in that the resulting satire could be read as scoffings at ideals of an orderly citizenry and its harmonious family life. The Fitz Smythes of the world, those who thought of themselves as the sanctified, were experiencing a Mark Twain who had developed new dimensions within an unsanctified nature.

---

## Readers and Aesthetics in the Marketplace of Literary Periodicals

THE GOLDEN ERA INCLUDES AMONG ITS CONTRIBUTORS ALL THE PROMINENT WRITERS OF LITERARY REPUTE IN CALIFORNIA AND ON THE PACIFIC COAST [AND] A HOST BESIDES OF POPULAR AND WELL APPROVED WRITERS, [WHO] FURNISH THEIR CHOICEST PRODUCTIONS TO ADORN THE LITERARY FEAST WHICH IS OFFERED WEEKLY.

———

*Golden Era*, January 17, 1864

I QUIT THE "ERA," LONG AGO. IT WASN'T HIGH-TONED ENOUGH. . . . THE "CALIFORNIAN" CIRCULATES AMONG THE HIGHEST CLASS OF THE COMMUNITY, & IS THE BEST LITERARY PAPER IN THE UNITED STATES.

———

LETTER TO JANE LAMPTON CLEMENS AND PAMELA A. MOFFETT, SEPTEMBER 25, 1864

Success for Sam Clemens as a *feuilletoniste* depended upon his comic style as Mark Twain finding its place within the differing aesthetic tastes of potential readers. As the satiric forays enabled by the style more and more showed an underlying Bohemian attitude, success entailed negotiation on two fronts: with belles lettres and with the marketplace. These two forces differentiated readers' tastes into strata. The kind of material printed by various competing periodicals implies the range of those tastes, while the circulation of a given periodical indicates the number of people within the marketplace of literary periodicals who might be classified by a specific segment within the range. This background of implied and historical readers explains why Clemens, during his stay in San Francisco, bragged about being published routinely in the newly established literary periodical: the *Californian* signified artistic aspiration, though sometimes in unconventional ways; being a regular contributor granted access to the most influential of periodical readers.

To name the various segments of aesthetic tastes that characterized periodical audiences, I have adapted Herbert Gans's hierarchy of "taste cultures." His divisions escape strict class distinctions and provide more range than the obvious high-, middle-, and lowbrow categories.[66] "High culture" begins the hierarchy, a category dominated by well-educated editors and critics as well as contemporary artists. These are the cultural elite, the students and creators of art and literature. Walt Whitman's "divine literatus," the leader of a democratic culture of enlightened individuals, fits into this segment of the taste-culture hierarchy. Next comes "upper-middle culture." Educated women and professional men who have sufficient leisure to cultivate an appreciation of both classical and contemporary art mostly compose this segment. The largest and most heterogenous group follows, the "lower-middle culture," characterized by individuals who often possess significant education; people who work in management positions; those who occupy lower-level jobs such as printing, clerking, and bookkeeping; or those who perhaps own small businesses. They may also be housewives or even Lowell mill girls.[67] Folks in this group consume most of popular literature's offerings, but they may also have significant contact with and interest in belles lettres and fine art. They form the backbone of Whitman's democratic culture because theoretically they can most easily be educated to appreciate new artists. The last segment is "low-culture" taste. Skilled and semiskilled mechanics and workers as well as laborers make up its majority. With little formal education, and with only inconsistent leisure time for art, they embody "mass culture." Combined, low-culture taste and lower-middle-culture taste often create the abstract "public" a publisher has in mind when calculating sales of popular writers, the group Clemens called "the Belly and the Members" of the reading audience.[68]

66. Beside Gans, *Popular Culture,* 100–120, the taste hierarchy is based on ideas taken from Walt Whitman, "Democratic Vistas"; Dwight MacDonald, "Masscult and Midcult I," and "Masscult and Midcult II"; and Van Wyck Brooks, "America's Coming of Age."

67. Lehuu, *Carnival,* 30. The town of Lowell, Massachusetts, was well-known for its mill factories, which maintained a largely young and female workforce.

68. Other useful discussions of popular culture versus high culture include Clement Greenberg, "Avant-Garde and Kitsch"; T. S. Eliot, *Notes toward a Definition of Culture;* and Theodor Adorno and Hans Horkheimer, *Dialectic of Enlightenment.* Clemens made the "Belly and Members" comment in a letter to English critic Andrew Lang in 1890 (Tom Quirk, ed., *The Portable Mark Twain,* 571).

Generalizations about historical antebellum readers complement this theo-retical hierarchy of implied readers. First, journalists in the period subscribed to the belief that gender marked reading as an activity and affected both content and format. Newspapers constituted a male domain, and thus they could con-tain elements ruled inappropriate for the genteel literature addressed to women. Other periodicals, especially weekly miscellanies and "family story papers," were a mixed lot, though in general they signified a female domain. Insofar as a par-ticular periodical had no political focus, its audience was sure to be overwhelm-ingly female. Although this gendered division within readers of antebellum periodicals is generally accurate, its boundary was porous. Thomas Leonard makes it clear that evidence from women's diaries, letters, and memoirs shows how often women read newspapers, especially as the century continued. In addi-tion, some newspapers made great efforts to provide family reading.[69]

Whatever the gender nuances of the antebellum reading public's demograph-ics were, the core of an audience for literary periodicals was clearly female. In large part, increasing leisure produced this female dominance. As a growing urban and industrial sector influenced society in the United States, a sharper distinction between work and leisure times could be discerned. Within the burgeoning mid-dle class, this distinction acquired a gendered inflection. Wealth to have more leisure time defined the rising middle class, and as wealth and leisure accumulated, women rather than men increasingly spent them. Certain commodities, such as novels and gift annuals, signified leisure, and because woman had more leisure time, those items—even reading itself—were increasingly associated with their gender. Thus categories of work and leisure, as well as gender, intertwine in under-standing the historical readers who consumed periodicals—daily and weekly newspapers, weekly miscellanies, story papers, and the monthly reviews.[70]

Using class to characterize antebellum readers first entails the point that the middle class, by midcentury, partly defined itself with its everyday casual read-ing. Thus middle-class individuals were distinguishable by their purchase and use of large numbers of guidebooks, manuals, handbooks, and books of refer-ence. This consumption of print by the middling classes first established the idea of a "reading audience."[71] The growth of this reading audience throughout the antebellum period resulted from a surge in literacy rates. As a market, this book-buying public grew also because of an increased production of printed materi-als. Some historians equate the increase in both production and consumption

69. Thomas C. Leonard, "News at the Hearth: A Drama of Reading in Nineteenth-Century America." See also Amy Thomas, "Literature in Newsprint: Antebellum Family Newspapers and the Uses of Reading."
70. David D. Hall, "Readers and Reading in America: Historical and Critical Perspectives," 357.
71. Burton J. Bledstein, "Storytellers to the Middle Class," 10.

of print with a spread of democracy.[72] However, significant evidence reveals an inevitable limit to the lower class's participation in the reading of books and periodicals: no matter how cheap books and periodicals became, many working-class folks were nevertheless unable to afford spending money on reading materials.[73] Another point about class and a historical readership involves those working-class readers who did purchase books and periodicals regularly. Despite the inevitable limit to an ability to buy, working-class consumers of printed materials did *not* routinely read only the most popular and cheapest items. Class and taste in what one read were not an absolute correlation. Just as middle-class readers might be part of the public consuming dime novels, working-class readers might be reading texts intended for a more educated public associated with upper levels on a socioeconomic scale.[74]

However one divides the antebellum reading audience with categories of class, gender, and taste, its growth was constant, even astonishing. Newspaper and magazine circulation throughout the nineteenth century far outpaced the growth in population. Their aggregate circulation already stood at more than seven times the population by 1840.[75] This appetite for reading could be fed because the means of producing printed materials improved dramatically during the 1830s and 1840s. All the major publishers in the large cities used steam-power presses, which meant that the 1850s saw an "ocean of print that flooded the market along with the wide array of other consumer goods."[76] The American reading public during the 1850s therefore consumed periodicals, including literary monthlies and weeklies, in unprecedented numbers, turning efforts to write and publish quality poetry, fiction, and nonfiction into profitable endeavors.[77]

A concentrated attention from readers and writers alike on periodicals with a literary focus started in the 1840s and continued into the 1850s. A desire for quality meant that literary taste for a widespread, more diverse, growing reading public formed and re-formed amid the market dynamics of editing and publishing periodicals. Since early in the nineteenth century, periodicals existed in the United States whose editors explicitly understood their publication to be formative of literary taste, such as the early and long-running *North American Review*, William Cullen Bryant's short-lived *New York Review and Atheneum*

72. Hall, "Readers," 343–44.

73. Zboray, *Fictive People*, 11–12.

74. Hall, "Readers," 355; Lehuu, *Carnival*, 29–31.

75. Leonard, "News at the Hearth," 384.

76. Ronald J. Zboray and Mary Saracino Zboray, "Books, Readings, and the World of Goods in Antebellum New England," 587; see also Bell, *Culture*, 70–74.

77. Susan Belasco Smith and Kenneth M. Price, "Periodical Literature in Social and Historical Context," 5–6.

*Magazine,* or the later *New York Round Table.* These high-culture publications had relatively small circulations. As the century advanced and a market mentality increasingly informed publication, editors with literary values inevitably experienced a tension between a view of literature emphasizing quality versus one stressing sales. The *Democratic Review* (1837–1859) provides a first example of how to run a periodical with high literary values yet not sacrifice accessibility, thus creating an upper-middle-culture taste. Though focused on political issues for most of its existence, the *Democratic Review* published original poetry and stories as well as informed criticism. Many of Nathaniel Hawthorne's best tales appeared first in its pages.

Two other periodicals launched in the 1850s also aspired to the belles lettres quality entailed in an upper-middle- or high-culture taste. One combined this goal with a serious review of political affairs. George Putnam began *Putnam's Monthly* in 1853 to showcase American literary talent and thus to contrast with *Harper's Monthly* being the venue for English literary talent. Associate editor Parke Godwin made *Putnam's* a voice for reform politics in the 1850s, especially for the newly created Republican party. Ably edited on the literary side by Charles Briggs and George William Curtis, *Putnam's* became a more accessible version of the *Democratic Review.* Before the financial panic of 1857 forced the magazine out of business, many leading American authors were published in its pages. Praised by William Thackeray as "better than Blackwood is or ever was,"[78] *Putnam's Monthly* became the best literary magazine in the United States, serious but not ponderous like the quarterly reviews.

When *Putnam's* folded, another high-quality literary magazine, the *Atlantic Monthly,* began. From the perspective of the twentieth century, Frank Luther Mott says that the *Atlantic Monthly* was the most important magazine in America for belles lettres. Moreover, for many contemporaries, whatever was printed in its pages constituted literature and high-culture taste.[79] Published in Boston, about two-thirds of the *Atlantic Monthly's* contributors were from New England for most of its first fifteen years, and it could count most writers important to the "American Renaissance" in its roster. James Russell Lowell was its first editor. He gave the magazine's nonfiction articles a more scholarly cast than *Putnam's,* but he also printed short stories more realistic than the usual romantic and sentimental sort. Oliver Wendell Holmes revived his Autocrat series expressly for the new magazine. The *Atlantic Monthly* was not at first successful financially, a sign that Lowell's editorship had moved it too close to the relative inaccessibility of the *North American Review.* When the Boston publishers Ticknor and

---

78. Quoted in Gordon Milne, *George William Curtis and the Genteel Tradition,* 66.
79. Mott, *Magazines, Volume II,* 33.

Fields bought the magazine in 1861, James Fields became the editor and adjusted its offerings to be more accessible. Even then, the *Atlantic Monthly,* as the epitome of high-culture taste, did not enjoy a large circulation, reaching only thirty-two thousand in 1863.

One other magazine belongs in the high-quality category, though it did not have a long publication life; the *Saturday Press* began in October 1858, stopped in December 1860, and began again in 1865. William Dean Howells rated it on a par with the *Atlantic.* Henry Clapp ("Figaro") and Edward Howland were the chief editors, with Thomas Bailey Aldrich and Fitz-James O'Brien as early staff members, plus George Arnold, Charles Stanley, Walt Whitman, Ada Clare, and William Winter as contributors. Not mainstream and likely to attack political and intellectual humbugs with a Bohemian irreverence, *Saturday Press* was called a "satire with no kindness in it." Social pretenses in New York City were dealt with "epigrammatically," and it was popular with younger literary talents.[80]

The *Atlantic Monthly* and *Saturday Press*—together with the *Democratic Review, Putnam's Monthly,* and the *North American Review*—represent a sustained cultural effort in the antebellum periodical world to encourage high standards for writing. These periodicals demonstrated reasonable success as business ventures while emphasizing the quality side of the inevitable balancing act between artistry and marketplace. However, a change in the antebellum reading audience presented a different problem for magazines like the *Democratic Review,* which saw itself as an exponent of a literary effort tied to particular politics. During the 1840s the reading audience interested in culture and literature became overwhelmingly female, and any magazine with aspirations to be a standard of literary quality *and* to build a strong circulation had to adjust.

Two journals successfully recognizing the new reality were the *New York Home Journal* (1846–1901), edited by Nathaniel Parker Willis and George P. Morris, and *Godey's Lady's Book* (1830–1898), edited by Louis Godey. Of thirty important magazines published between 1850 and 1865 with a female audience in mind, the *Home Journal* was the most sophisticated and clever.[81] The *Home Journal* aimed at a high-income, "upper-tendom" audience, presuming that wealth correlates with high cultural standards.[82] Nevertheless, antebellum high-culture writers who had serious literary aspirations probably did not think first of the *Home Journal* as the place for their work. Commensurate with its largely female audience, the *Home Journal* boasted fashion plates and features on clothes. It

80. J. Douglas Tarpley, "Thomas Bailey Aldrich," 29.
81. Mott, *Magazines, Volume II,* 56–57.
82. N. P. Willis invented the term "Upper Ten" for New York society (Baker, *Sentiment,* 101). Webb and Harte's vision of their audience for the *Californian,* as enunciated by Clemens in this section's epigraph, was the San Francisco analogue.

published a mix of writers, with some high-culture material that contrasted with popular sentimental fiction and inevitable articles on fashions aimed at upper-middle and lower-middle tastes. The main attraction, however, was Nathaniel Parker Willis. Willis's stories of the beau monde, and his articles on opera and culture and fashions, which appealed to the upper classes and ostensibly represented high-culture taste, typified the magazine. Willis had a talent for creating a tone that cloaked high-society attitudes in high-culture taste. Even in his wittiest moments, Willis did not employ burlesque or trenchant sarcasm to make his reform-minded points about social behaviors; he never forgot that his readership was overwhelmingly female. The *Home Journal* enjoyed commercial success, but not because it sought an exclusive readership in the sense of the privileged or highly educated few. Rather, it catered to a reading public whose members fancied a refined and therefore ostensibly exclusive aesthetic taste, even if their economic status registered as middle class. Though the middle class defined itself as distinct from the gilded gentility of the upper tendom—"industrious" and "useful" rather than idle and often dissolute—it also aspired to gentility.[83] The *Home Journal* took advantage of that desire.

*Godey's Lady's Book* maintained a less pretentious tone than the *Home Journal* in its appeal to a female reading audience. Its decided success starting in 1837 under the editorship of Sara Joseph Hale made it *the* popular place for female readers, editors, and writers in the 1840s within a lower-middle taste, with a subscription list of 70,000 by 1851 and 150,000 just before the Civil War.[84] *Godey's* published all the popular authors between 1837 and 1850, though writers such as Bayard Taylor and Edgar Allan Poe also appeared in its pages. Most importantly, the formula for the success of the *Home Journal* and of *Godey's Lady's Book* during the 1840s—cater to a largely female audience with hand-colored steel engravings; a few writers of a more original sort; and many imitative, popular writers—showed the way for the much larger commercial successes of the 1850s.[85]

These larger commercial successes would be claimed mostly by "story papers," such as *Leslie's Illustrated* and *Sunday Mercury,* which adjusted the formula of the *Home Journal* and *Godey's* to center on imitative writers. Sacrificing originality to cash in on the popularity of second-rate writers, the story papers became the breeding ground for mass popular culture. The biggest and most profitable story paper, the *New York Ledger,* tapped an enormous market starting in 1855, using formulaic writers as its foundation. Yet the *Ledger's* unprecedented commercial success had other elements, too. Its operation throughout the 1850s set new

83. Bledstein, "Storytellers," 5.
84. Smith and Price, "Periodical Literature," 5.
85. Lehuu, *Carnival,* chapter 5; Bell, *Culture,* chapter 5.

management standards because of its flamboyant editor and owner, Robert Bonner. Bonner's outlandish advertising campaigns made him famous and put him at the head of the newer breed of editors for whom publishing was first about markets. Modeled perhaps after the very popular and profitable *London Journal,* the *Ledger* appealed to the tastes of a literate working class above all other implied audiences and thus pitched itself between lower-middle- and a low-culture tastes. Blood-and-thunder serials anchored the periodical's success, but the *Ledger* featured sentimental stylists like Sylvanus Cobb and Mrs. South-worth, too. Bonner also routinely published an original writer, Sara Willis Par-ton. As "Fanny Fern," Parton wrote a reform-minded and satirical column exclusively for the *Ledger.* Innocuous romance, adventure, and sentiment com-posed the *Ledger*'s general editorial policy, but because Bonner paid his writers well, he also attracted literati (including Edward Everett, Henry W. Longfellow, William Cullen Byrant, Hubert Bancroft, and Harriet Beecher Stowe). With a circulation approaching four hundred thousand by 1860, Bonner's occasional mixing of high-culture articles with his routine printing of low-culture material meant that interested individuals within the middle and working classes could encounter authors writing for an upper-middle- or high-culture taste.[86]

Unlike Bonner, publishers and editors genuinely interested in artistic quality as well as commercial success had to find a middle ground that emphasized art without sacrificing accessibility. While the weeklies tended toward the lower end of the taste spectrum, the monthlies proved to be a better format for wedding popularity with quality. Perhaps the *New York Knickerbocker* first exemplified this middle ground, with its judicious mix of writing, running a gamut from sentimental fiction and poetry to light essays and verse, with some comic mate-rial, and on to more substantial contributions from top-notch authors. This strategy guaranteed an appeal to readers on strict literary merit without alto-gether denying broader and more popular grounds, and it held out a promise of commercial success.

*Graham's Magazine* (1841–1858) was an early literary periodical with a high-culture editorial policy that nevertheless approached the popular in its circula-tion. Largely written for women, *Graham's* favored light essays, eschewed politics, and featured excellent, exclusive illustrations. While *Graham's Maga-zine* did not scorn the sensational tales and sentimental poetry featured promi-nently in magazines like *Godey's* (and later the serialized novel made popular by *Harper's Monthly*), it nevertheless attracted many of the best antebellum writ-ers, giving it a higher literary quality than its nearest rivals in the 1840s, the

86. Noel, *Villains Galore,* chapters 8 and 9.

*Knickerbocker* or the *Home Journal.* Two facts produced this literary edge. First, George Graham decided to pay good money for original American work, which no magazine did before Graham started the practice. Second, Graham could count on a series of very capable coeditors—Charles J. Peterson, Edgar Allan Poe, Ann Stephens, Rufus Griswold, Bayard Taylor, and Charles G. Leland—who knew which writers were worth paying. With a circulation of forty thousand in 1842, *Graham's Magazine* demonstrated the sizeable demand for a periodical that neither pandered to the public nor tried to be its cultural arbiter. Furthermore, George Graham demonstrated that a publisher could be financially successful buying and selling quality. By the late 1840s, *Graham's* and *Knickerbocker* together embodied a first in American culture: a large market for relatively high-quality writing, implying an audience composed of both the upper- and lower-middle taste segments.

Profits from *Graham's* and *Knickerbocker* in the 1840s foreshadowed success in the even bigger market of the 1850s for a new monthly combining accessibility with quality. George Graham had shown how a publisher could make modest but steady sums of money with relatively high-quality literary work. Fletcher Harper showed how immense sums of money could routinely be made with such literary work. *Harper's Monthly* (1850 to present) in some respects followed the formula of *Graham's:* good editing and printing, a mix of more substantial writing with light and popular articles, an avoidance of politics, and very good illustrations. In other ways, *Harper's Monthly* broke new ground, soon printing far more illustrations per issue than any other magazine on far more pages—up to 50 lithographs on 144 pages instead of the usual 80 or 96 pages.

*Harper's Monthly* stood apart definitively from its competition, however, and became a money machine for the Harper's publishing firm, by featuring contemporary English fiction writers in a serialized format. The money flowed into the coffers of the Harper brothers because these English fiction writers were enormously popular with the American reading public—and because *Harper's Monthly* pirated their work, just as the Harper brothers had with hundreds of cheap reprints of English novels prior to 1850. Even when *Harper's* began paying for "advance sheets" in 1852, they acquired rights to book publication as well as serialization. With a circulation of fifty thousand within six months, reaching upward of two hundred thousand by 1861, *Harper's Monthly* proved immensely profitable, even though its literary quality remained high. The combination was unprecedented, making the magazine's publication an "epochal happening."[87] As much as any other single event in antebellum publishing

87. Mott, *Magazines, Volume II,* 391, 3.

history, the founding of *Harper's Monthly* defined the size and literary taste of the American reading public.

The rivalry of the *Golden Era* and the *Californian* in San Francisco during the mid-1860s reiterates the most important point from this story of the antebellum marketplace for publishing periodicals: the tension between art and commerce, between an editorial policy advocating quality and one insisting on quantity. The *Golden Era* had been San Francisco's undisputed literary weekly for over ten years before Charles H. Webb launched the *Californian* as the new contender for San Francisco's reading public on May 28, 1864.[88] Already well-known in New York literary circles, Webb had made a name for himself since coming to San Francisco in April 1863 as a columnist in the *Golden Era* and as the literary editor for the *San Francisco Evening Bulletin,* contributing to the *Sacramento Union* as well. Bret Harte, who also had been a notable writer for the *Golden Era,* was the chief contributor. Webb and Harte planned to make the *Californian* the best-written and best-printed literary weekly in the west. "The *Californian* was distinctly a metropolitan literary journal, planning to be to San Francisco what the *Round Table* was to New York."[89] Webb and Harte's vision for the *Californian* in 1864 would not only continue the tradition of cultural arbiter but also print original poetry and fiction.

The first several issues contained items from other members of San Francisco's Bohemian literary scene, besides Webb and Harte, all of whom had written for the *Golden Era:* Mark Twain, Charles W. Stoddard, Ina Coolbrith, W. A. Kendall, Ambrose Bierce, Emilie Lawson, and Henry George. One measure of Clemens's literary aspirations, represented by the *Californian,* is the fact that he did not submit "Jim Smiley and His Jumping Frog" for publication in 1865, even though he had been a regular contributor for more than a year. In contrast to the *Golden Era,* the *Californian* did not feature local color. Reprints rather than original matter dominated, and Webb signaled his high-toned approach by choosing a translated French novel to be the journal's first offering for serialized fiction. As Clemens's letter in this section's epigraph indicates, the *Californian* catered to the finest of tastes. Representing a "highest class," that historical read-

---

88. Some controversy exists about nomenclature for periodicals up to and after the Civil War. For example, Mott calls the *New York Sunday Mercury* a "story paper" (*Magazines, Volume II,* 11) while Noel excludes it from that category (*Villains Galore,* 51). Noel refers to the *Golden Era* of the 1850s as a "story paper," which by her definition meant light entertainment for a "decidedly unliterary public" (23), featuring sensationalized stories in serial form, no serious coverage of news or politics, no advertising, and payment for its original tales (32). Though the *Golden Era* of the 1860s comes close to that definition, it also routinely featured comic material, which "in a true-blue story paper . . . had no place whatever" (51).

89. Walker, *Literary Frontier,* 180.

ing public would ostensibly have had the most education and the most leisure to support such refinement.

Though western local color did not appear in its fictional pieces, the *Californian* did have much to say about people and places in San Francisco and California. The attitude in the new literary weekly toward local culture, however, was anything but reverent, beginning with the regular column of Webb's that he had transferred from the *Golden Era,* "Things." In his column, Webb made unflattering remarks about forty-niners, pioneer spirit, California's climate and scenery, and the community's literary tastes. Webb had come to San Francisco straight from the New York circle of Bohemians at Pfaff's cellar, not only working for the mainstream *New York Times* as a columnist and literary editor, but also contributing to some of New York's less conventional periodicals, such as *Saturday Press* and *Vanity Fair.* His penchant for burlesque, satire, puns, and sarcastic remarks, along with a well-developed literary taste, had initially made him a highly regarded writer on the West Coast: the *Golden Era* had paid him the largest salary ever for one of its regular contributors.[90] However, given free rein as owner and editor of the *Californian,* Webb's irreverent tongue ultimately did not make the literary weekly popular with its intended audience. By 1866, Webb had sold the *Californian* and returned to the East Coast, his experiment of promoting quality writing with unconventional Bohemian irreverence a failure. Two years later, the *Californian* ceased publication.

Unlike the *Californian,* The *Golden Era* above all promoted Pacific Coast writers. Founded by Rollin Daggett and J. MacDonough Foard in 1852, the *Golden Era* quickly became popular among the mining camps because of its shrewd mixture of local items with materials selected from other publications. In 1860 Daggett and Foard sold the journal to James Brooks and Joe Lawrence, Lawrence becoming the editor-in-chief. He kept the friendly tone of the "Correspondents' Column" and the other local departments, such as mining and agricultural intelligence, that had made the *Era* indispensable in the rural districts. To this foundation, Lawrence added enough literary tone to make the *Era* important in San Francisco, too—theater reviews, town gossip, and literary contributors and commentators. Establishing himself in San Francisco's best hotels—the Lick House and later the Occidental—Lawrence made sure that he met all writers and artists and performers who came to San Francisco. Lawrence also made sure that any writing talent he encountered appeared in the *Golden Era.* Bret Harte and William Wright were regular contributors by 1862, and Lawrence took early notice of a talent on the rise, Sam Clemens, by publishing original Mark Twain

90. Stanley J. Kunitz and Howard Haycroft, "Charles Henry Webb," 789; Walker, *Literary Frontier,* 133, 134.

material when the pseudonym was but a few months old. During 1863, a steady stream of East Coast talent took up residences of varying lengths in San Francisco: Fitzhugh Ludlow, Frances Fuller Fane, Robert Newell, Adah Menken, and Charles Farrar Browne, besides Webb. All contributed to the *Golden Era*. When Jane McIlherny, another famous East Coast "Bohemian" who signed herself "Ada Clare," came to San Francisco in the spring of 1864, she soon contributed regularly as well. Lawrence's genial nature and eye for talent transformed the *Golden Era* into the literary club of San Francisco in the early 1860s; he did more to develop Pacific Coast writers than any other periodical owner.[91]

In contrast to the *Californian*, which aimed for the highest class of metropolitan readers, one composed mainly of literati and society women, the *Golden Era* obviously wanted to appeal to a much broader historical reading public. Following the standard set by *Harper's* in the 1850s, the *Era* specialized in the serialized novel, featuring installments on page 1 with a lithograph. However, the *Era* was more diverse in its choices than *Harper's;* the novelists might be British (such as Bulwer Lytton) or American (such as Thomas S. Arthur). Often the style was romantic or sensational, but just as often authors wrote the stories specifically for the *Era,* for example, Bret Harte's "The Story of M'Liss: An Idyll of Red Mountain." In addition, local writers wrote many of the shorter fiction and nonfiction pieces featured in an issue's midsection. The poetry, too, was often locally produced, generally in the sentimental and effusive style of the day, but Lawrence also printed Adah Menken's free-form efforts as well as poems by Elizabeth Barrett Browning and Robert Browning. While a corps of local writers produced essays on local topics, selections from nationally known writers such as Bayard Taylor and Fitzhugh Ludlow were printed to accompany lighter pieces by the famous Benjamin P. Shillaber. Humorists included the nationally famous— "Artemus Ward," "Orpheus C. Kerr," and "Josh Billings"—complementing the regionally famous tandem of "Dan De Quille" and "Mark Twain."

This range of authors implies the middling taste of the *Era*'s readership, one solidly in the lower-middle range but reaching into both the upper-middle and lower taste segments. The *Golden Era*'s masculine slant can be found not only in its frequent willingness to print humorists, but also in its frequent sketches of mining-camp life that Frank Luther Mott characterizes as "racy," meaning they contained vernacular language or realistic details typically banned from the symbolic stronghold of female readers, the parlor.[92] The *Californian* aspired to exhibit the best in literary taste and thus to have the best readers, but the *Golden Era* had a more modest goal. While the *Era* also wished to have a readership with

91. Walker, *Literary Frontier,* 116–17, 122.
92. Mott, *Magazines, Volume II,* 117.

a taste for the best literature, the editors featured popular local writers and thus did not narrowly define what constituted "the best."

The *Golden Era*'s more catholic idea of "the best" stakes out a large zone of middling taste in American culture both before and after the Civil War. This taste lies between belles lettres as one boundary and mass popular literature as another, between deliberately equating literature with a particular aesthetic and mindlessly consuming writings thoroughly oriented toward the marketplace in their formulaic and ephemeral nature. In San Francisco, "Mark Twain" signified comic material with a Bohemian irreverence and sophistication, as Sam Clemens reached toward the upper-middle- and high-culture taste of the *Californian*'s implied reader. However, Clemens writing successfully for varied publications like the *New York Sunday Mercury,* the *Golden Era,* and the *Californian* underscores the hierarchical nature of the periodical market when he shifted his focus from newspapers to literary weeklies. Despite Clemens's pleasure at being associated with the lofty ambitions of the *Californian,* the broader editorial goals of the *Golden Era* denote Mark Twain's most consistent readership, one that straddles the lower- and upper-middle taste cultures but has some appreciation of high-culture writers, too. This reading public encompasses the middling classes economically, yet it likely includes working-class readers too, who certainly do not have a place in the audience Webb envisioned for the *Californian.* Mark Twain's appeal thus will continue to reach down into the lower-middle taste culture represented by men whose chief reading material was a newspaper, as in Nevada. Mark Twain spanned literary tastes. Broad appeal promised economic security yet demanded its own kind of literary decorum. How to woo and keep such a large audience despite his Bohemian, comic approach to brownstone respectability could never have been far from Sam Clemens's mind while living in San Francisco and striking up higher in the periodical world.

# SCENE THREE

AMERICAN *FLÂNEURS*

## Of *Flâneurs* and *Feuilletonistes:* The Example of Bret Harte

Errer est humain; flâner est parisien (To wander is human; to stroll is Parisian).

———

Victor Hugo, *Les Misérables*, 1862

In San Francisco, Sam Clemens worked to become what the French called a *feuilletoniste,* a freelance professional writer for literary periodicals. In the process, he developed the satirical possibilities of Mark Twain commenting on social values as well as a new persona for his alter ego: a Bohemian literary/cultural critic. Clemens also developed another similar persona, a comic version of the *flâneur,* a figure embodying a literary journalism that characterized the most sophisticated of periodical correspondents. The *flâneur* relied upon a reporter's habit of close observation, a skill Bret Harte employed to provide thick descriptions of San Francisco and its inhabitants. Today's reader knows Harte best as the local-colorist who wrote short stories like "The Luck of Roaring 'Camp" or "The Outcasts of Poker Flat," tales that romanticized and sentimentalized the early days of California, when frontier mining operations dominated the state's destiny. Readers in the early 1860s would have known Bret Harte the Bohemian *flâneur* from *"Feuilletons,"* a series of columns written for periodicals at the beginning of his literary career in California. These early writings of Harte suggest how the *flâneur*'s pose would have circulated among writers and been available for Clemens to adapt to his comic purposes.

The *flâneur* as a cultural figure emerged from the matrix of the modern capitalist and industrial city, with its huge consumer market and its unique publishing invention, the mass periodical. Established in post-Napoleonic Paris early in the nineteenth century, the *flâneur* was known for his strolls through the city's arcades, absorbing the spectacle that modern everyday urban life provides. The figure, however, represents more than a mere spectator, because the *flâneur propre* has a philosophical and artistic sensibility that equips him to probe beneath what is observed and to render the urban scene in vivid detail. The *flâneur* thus "reads" urban life and creates a representation that interprets and explains. His reading interprets details of everyday life—using contexts sociological, historical, or philosophical—and endows those details with a greater significance than possible when noted by an ordinary observer. Moreover, the ideal *flâneur* does not simply explain the greater significance of the quotidian display; he also describes vividly. In Charles Baudelaire's phrase, the *flâneur* is the "painter of the passing moment." In addition, the *flâneur* executes his descriptive canvases without a commercial interest. Because his artistic sensibility ostensibly exists without a desire to buy what is seen or to sell what is learned in his perambulations, the *flâneur* in its ideal conception occupies a place outside bourgeois society with its emphasis on the marketplace. Celebrated by the journalists of the day, the *flâneur* thus embodied the ultimate in high-culture taste, modernity's replacement for a civilized nobility.[93]

Despite this lofty conception of ability and motive, the *flâneur* historically appeared at the same time as did mass periodicals as well as a new and complex image for an author. The image projected a writer who embodied a tension created by modern capitalism: an artist writing with an aesthetic independent of marketplace melded into a journalist writing with deliberate intent to sell to the highest bidder. Such a writer's aesthetic perspective on art, literature, fashion, and manners may not be conventional in a bourgeois sense, but he certainly is not disinterested in commerce.[94] When *flânerie* translates into authorship, reductions of the urban show to a representative sketch were routinely consumed by the public via periodicals. Yet however much a *feuilletoniste* in a *flâneur* mode must cater to a market, he can also be an *artiste* with an unconventional attitude, one that came to be associated with the label *Bohemian*. *Bohemian* and *flâneur* both signified an artist during the 1840s, with Honoré de Balzac as the key to their dissemination.[95] Balzac also adumbrated and lived the new image for an author.[96]

Bret Harte was the first periodical writer in San Francisco to adopt the persona of a Bohemian *flâneur,* though Franklin Walker points out that Harte's temperament was not Bohemian.[97] Nevertheless, Harte wrote columns and sketches from June 1860 until June 1866 with a variety of titles for both the *Golden Era* and the *Californian* that provide the credentials for evaluating him as a *flâneur.* These *"Feuilletons"* present Harte doing what *flâneurs* do best, wandering about the city and interpreting what he observes with a refined sensibility that displays an

---

93. Richard D. E. Burton, *The Flâneur and His City: Patterns of Daily Life in Paris, 1815–1851,* stresses the intellectual side of the *flâneur,* his habit of reading city life as a text. Bruce Mazlish, "The Flâneur: From Spectator to Representation," discusses the *flâneur*'s spectatorship in terms of a history of representation. Priscilla Parkhurst Ferguson, "The *Flâneur* on and off the Streets of Paris," provides a historical perspective on the figure. Burton distinguishes the *flâneur* from the *badaud,* the latter merely a loafer on the streets, what an anonymous writer in *Vanity Fair* sarcastically called the "man about town" ("Natural History: The Man about Town," 45). Baudelaire's phrase is from "The Painter of Modern Life," (5), first published in 1859.

94. Mazlish, "Flâneur," 47.

95. Ferguson, *"Flâneur,"* 29.

96. Pierre Loubier, "Balzac et le Flâneur"; Albert Mechtild, "Désir, commerce, and la création, ou le dilemme de l'artiste Balzacien."

97. Walker, *Literary Frontier,* 132.

aesthetic Bohemian in its unconventionality. Harte had only recently joined the *Golden Era* as a compositor and occasional contributor when he wrote "Bohemian in San Francisco" for the June 17, 1860, issue. Though this first column reads more like a local editor's effort in a newspaper—items and events reported rather than topics discussed—Harte had hit a *flâneur*'s stride by his third column.[98]

The title captures the essence of these early writings, a miscellany of subjects about the urban scene discussed from a Bohemian viewpoint. Harte, in several columns over the years, explicitly defined this viewpoint as an artist's conscious opposition to a marketplace mentality and to the bourgeois values of utility, practicality, and efficiency. One might distill this opposition to Beauty versus Business, which Harte dramatizes by describing Bohemia as "a fairy land" where the inhabitants gathered flowers, arranged them into bouquets, and sold them to the people who did not live in Bohemia.[99] This devotion to aesthetics rather than commerce turns a person into an "impractical, roving, unprofitable gipsy," the exotic Bohemian who speaks elegant French in the face of American slang.[100] Harte returns to the roving gypsy metaphor to convey his Bohemian comportment, speaking of hotels as full of nomads and therefore a "natural resting place" for Bohemians, or invoking a "vagabond instinct" to account for the behavior of Bohemians.[101] Though their impractical love of beauty makes them materially poor and perhaps disreputable in appearance, Bohemians for Harte are seldom immoral and always intriguing.[102]

Having defined Bohemians, Harte adopts their perspective to color his reporting on special events about town, such as the Mechanics Fair, full-dress concerts, or balls, as well as reporting on particular places to go, such as the cheap theaters, Russ' Garden, clubs, or hotels. As journalism, Harte's *"Feuilletons"* sketch highly personalized accounts far beyond the mere recordings of a reporter-at-large free to mention anything. Because his narrator is more reflective and his analysis more complex, Harte evokes the artistic depth of the *flâneur* when he expounds on the Chinese in San Francisco, female gymnastics, and the

---

98. Bret Harte, "Town and Table Talk: A la Bohemian." At different times, the titles for the columns in the *Golden Era* are "Town and Table Talk," "Bohemian Feuilleton," and "Bohemian Papers." Many of the pieces that appear under the heading "Bohemian Papers" in Harte's collected works are from the *Californian*. Indeed, the majority of pieces selected for inclusion in "Bohemian Papers" are from the *Californian* despite no explicit identification with Bohemianism in the original publications. To avoid confusion with the pieces Harte collected under "Bohemian Papers," I will refer in the aggregate to the material analyzed here as *"Feuilletons."*

99. Bret Harte, "Town and Table Talk: The Bohemian Concerning."

100. Harte, "Bohemian at the Fair."

101. Bret Harte, "Bohemian Papers, No. 1: Melons"; "Bohemian Feuilleton: Hotel Life"; see also "Bohemian at the Fair"; and "A Boys' Dog."

102. Bret Harte, "Bohemian Concerning"; Bret Harte, "Bohemian Papers: On Restaurants."

prospect from his bachelor's window; dilates on the meaning of Thanksgiving, Christmas, and the New Year; or simply holds forth philosophically.[103]

A *flâneur*'s stroll structures the best of Harte's *"Feuilletons."* The stroll might be circumscribed by a focus on his own neighborhood, the fair, or the cheap theaters, or it might begin as a "purposeless ramble" that ends at the Mission Dolores. Perhaps Harte focuses on a simple Sunday stroll with a friend, in which well-dressed women whom he conceptualizes as "high art" form the chief delight,[104] but in each case the impact of an individual column comes from Harte's ability to present to the reader's imagination not just what is observed by the eye but rather what is apprehended by a sensibility. Fashionable women well-dressed thus become spontaneous *tableaux vivants,* the behavior in trolley cars transforms to a fable of manners, and the occupants of hotels are typed and ready to be understood as dramatis personae for the world as a stage. This sense of life and art interpenetrating, the drama inherent in the quotidian urban display, demonstrates how "reporting" by a *flâneur* qualitatively differs from other kinds of journalism. Painting the passing moment, the *flâneur* composes his vivid descriptions with a keen sense of the larger meanings of what he observes.

On one occasion, Harte the Bohemian *flâneur* sets out deliberately to gather larger meanings both philosophic and aesthetic.[105] Harte plans his stroll through San Francisco to gather a Bohemian's impressions of how well the city has spent tax money to make civic improvements. The plan directly responds to a letter in one of the daily newspapers, signed "Taxpayer," who argued that more money has already been spent for such improvements than will ever recompense the taxpayers. The "impractical" Bohemian decides to look about to assess the validity of the argument. He pays a visit to the Plaza and to Washington Square, but both are so dismal looking that Harte has difficulty noticing that *any* tax money has been spent to improve them. A third public square, examined but unnamed, fares no better. The first part of the argument by "Taxpayer" is in doubt. Sitting on a bench, the Bohemian has a vision that challenges the second part. The vision pictures a thoroughly improved civic square, with a well-maintained and inviting landscape that makes the point about what kind of recompense is important in this ad hoc debate. The square bustles with citizens and their children, who are recompensed by nothing more than their own leisure, for which the square functions as an enabling space. No practical payment returns to "Taxpayer" for such civic improvement. As an inviting, aesthetically pleasing spot in the urban environment,

103. Bret Harte, "Town and Table Talk: The Bohemian Grows Reflective and Discursive."
104. Bret Harte, "San Francisco on Sunday."
105. Bret Harte, "Bohemian Papers: City Improvements."

the imagined square dramatizes the narrowness of the practical mind that sees all actions as business transactions evaluated by the bottom line.

Bret Harte manages very well the *flâneur*'s art of seizing details and wresting meaning from them. For example, Harte has an epiphany when he suddenly ducks into a Catholic church during its Easter service on a dawn ramble near his lodgings.[106] Details of the service inside the church contrast with the sights and sounds outside on the street, accumulating as proof of the enfeebling and passé nature of Catholicism. Inside one notes a hushed, dead, incensed air; the drowsy voice of the priest speaking in a "long-buried tongue"; the submissive feet of the worshippers shuffling on the polished floor; the threadbare drapery on the altar; the "rouge on [the] sallow cheek" of the Virgin's statue. Outside, Harte the *flâneur* experiences the quick and pleasant air, the warm flood of morning light, cheery voices, and rapid footsteps. These contrasts "symbolized a faith," or more precisely a modern American Protestant's comparison of two versions of a faith, the conclusion that names one as superior dramatized by the arrangement of the details.

In another instance, the details and the meanings they yield do not result in the focused enlightenment of an epiphany but, rather, provide a set of insights persistently gathered from a routine walk. Harte makes a virtue of necessity by using a walk from home to work (and back) to catalog "a few of the speculations which have engaged [his] mind during these daily perambulations."[107] The most ordinary of events, the random encounters with friends and the observation of strangers, become fertile occasions to discern manners and character traits in simple behavior. The preoccupation of the typical Californian with business can be seen in his inability to lounge. Properly speaking, Californians lie in wait rather than lounge, and a gentleman can be discovered when one observes correct lounging. Similarly, a gentleman can be discovered by the way he meets one's gaze with calm eyes, not seeking observation (the prig or snob) nor evading it (the bashful or mean). The manner in which a man "appropriates his part of the sidewalk" also reveals character. For example, the awkward man, "who gets in your way, and throws you back upon the man behind you, and so manages to derange the harmonious procession of an entire block, is very apt to do the same thing in political and social economy." Harte also evaluates the bad manners of fashionable young men and the coquetry of fashionable young women. He prefaces the entire piece with an observation from a Bohemian perspective: too many people insist on every moment being useful and deny themselves the idle pleasure of leisurely observing the spectacle before them.

106. Bret Harte, "Bohemian Feuilleton: An Easter Morning Walk."
107. Bret Harte, "Sidewalkings."

Bret Harte, in his *"Feuilletons,"* represents American journalism incorporating the idea of the *flâneur*.[108] A series of strolls about a modern city allows for a collection of observations on a variety of topics—literally whatever may be presented to the eye. Filtered through a philosophic and aesthetic consciousness, these observations are re-presented in writings that are part memoir, part essay, part sketch. The tone strikes the reader as both familiar, befitting a letter from a friend, and particularly informative, as though the friend were an expert on reported topics. The author designs such writings for consumption by periodical readers, who in effect can stroll about the city with the writer. Periodical readers thus become voyeurs learning about a city far away or about an unexpected aspect of the city in which they live. Cousin to the travel letter, such journalism records the urban stroll.

## COMIC *FLÂNEUR:* CHARLES WEBB

IF I WERE NOT INIGO, I THINK I'D RATHER BE A SACRAMENTO RIVER STEAMER THAN ANYTHING ELSE IN LIFE! FOR RUNNING PEOPLE DOWN IS MY STRONG SUIT.

————

CHARLES H. WEBB, "THINGS," *CALIFORNIAN,* JULY 9, 1864

Though Bret Harte modeled the serious *flâneur* with the figure's artistic sensibility, Charles Webb undoubtedly provided the best model of a comic writer in a *flâneur* mode with whom Sam Clemens would have been familiar. Webb wrote a series for the *Golden Era* called "Things" that ran from late July 1863 until May 1864, when he transferred the column to the pages of his literary weekly, the *Californian.* The format for the series crossed a correspondent's letter with the genre of the local column. For the *Golden Era* group, Webb began most of the columns addressing himself to various individuals. A majority address two well-known men in the San Francisco community, General Wright, commander of Pacific forces, and Ingraham Kip, Episcopal bishop. Some hail other prominent citizens, including Lewis Leland, owner of the Occidental Hotel; "Florence Fane," the alias of Mrs. Frances Fuller Victor and another regular contributor to the *Golden Era;* Mr. Grosch, owner of the "Grosch and Silver Mining Company"; John G. Downey, a governor of California; and Admiral Popoff, who commanded Russia's Pacific

108. Though Nathaniel P. Willis, when he focuses on New York City, could be nominated as an earlier instance, one might also add Edgar Allan Poe, with his "Doings of Gotham," detailing his strolls about New York City to a Philadelphia journal, *Columbia Spy.*

fleet. One installment addresses Webb's friends in general, another the American people. These addressees furnish a link to the lead subject, the main thing, discussed in "Things." However, the latter portions of the column usually function as a local column in a newspaper, as Webb routinely reviews plays and operas while taking note of particular events of the past week or providing advance notice for next week's events.

Despite its "local items" appearance and a comic tone that includes a prodigious number of puns, "Things" consistently presents a wealth of thoughtful commentary on the urban scene. Moreover, Webb's manner as he makes his comments is such that one could never mistake "Things" for a local items column in a newspaper. Like Harte, Webb fits the *flâneur* mold because he has the ability to explicate what he observes and thus to provide the expected sociological, psychological, or moralistic depth to social events and people's behavior. Unlike Harte, Webb projects his *flânerie* through a humorous persona, "Inigo."

Inigo's perambulations around San Francisco convey the sense of a gentleman's leisurely stroll. Outside of his theater and opera reviews, most of the specific events that Webb discusses would be classified as society affairs. He attends all of the season's major balls as well as important benefits, such as a fair sponsored by the Episcopalian church. One week he devotes considerable space to narrating a gentlemen's boating excursion on the bay. "Things" focuses on society and art above all other possible topics to discuss, and Webb critiques the arts as well as the respectable society that considers itself to be the chief support of such civilized endeavors. Webb does not report what he observes as a reporter provides the day's news. Rather, he comically renders what he observes, as a *flâneur* dispenses his analytic snapshots of contemporary life.

Webb usually confines his discussions of art to performances of plays and operas recently attended. He admires the famous and controversial Adah Menken for the genius of her acting, the "wild poetry in her every pose,"[109] but when he discusses a favorite actress, Mrs. George Jordan, Webb reveals what style of theater trumps Menken's old school of histrionic gestures by praising Jordan above all for her "naturalness." Moreover, Webb faults the play Jordan stars in for portraying unrealistically the manners of a corporal in the presence of his general and his general's wife.[110] The same emphasis on realistic portrayal occurs in Webb's lavish praise of Albert Bierstadt's paintings of the Yosemite Valley, a critical approach that anticipates Clemens's later review of Dan Setchell's comic acting ability.[111]

---

109. Charles Webb, "Things" [Adah Menken as Mazeppa].
110. Charles Webb, "Things: The Spanish Ball, A Bunch of Fives, Mrs. George Jordan and Her Engagement."
111. Charles Webb, "Things: [Hotel Living], Bierstadt's Sketches."

The strength of Charles Webb's column, however, lies in the studied sardonic manner in which he elaborates the significance of the week's events and of people's behavior. Though sardonic, Webb also lightens his wit with frothy puns and unexpectedly funny phrasing. He is not above mixing slang with French phrases. As a comic *flâneur,* Charles Webb provides commentary with a satiric quality, and though his criticisms at times are very direct, the tone of "Things" never strikes a peevish or querulous note. When he extols a good opera and cannot understand why people do not attend, he produces a characteristically mixed tone of admonition and light-heartedness, sarcastic yet cheerful, flippant and even silly.[112] Though Webb's Inigo is sardonic and as ready to run people down as completely as a Sacramento River steamer would, he also at times presents a self-deprecating quality not unlike Mark Twain, attributing foibles and faults to himself. In one installment of "Things," Inigo behaves just like Washoe Mark Twain, becoming drunk at a wedding and talking to a door as he struggles to retire to his room.[113]

The fearless manner in which Charles Webb dispenses his satire is the most remarkable aspect of "Things." In the middle of the Civil War, he criticizes loudly proclaimed patriotism more than once. He notes the way in which perfectly respectable but unremarkable men who have been commissioned officers become annoying with their condescension—and boring in their ostensible knowledge of military strategies. Twice he spends considerable time criticizing the way Bishop Kip has conducted the Episcopalian fair. Complaining about the diluted brandy punch and lack of patriotic music at the event, Webb insinuates that both faults can be traced to the bishop being more concerned about the money for "a mortgage on [God's] house" than allowing people a good time. He follows this charge with one worse, using a barrage of puns to level the bishop to his essential dullness:

> It isn't very clear to my mind that an Ecclesiastical Brigade would not be a good thing in the present war. Canons of the church are not easy things to take. Sermons, too, you know, are not unfrequently rifled—from various sources—and that the bore is sometimes immense, very few will dispute.
>
> Colonel Drumm tells me that he intends to mount some cannons, 10 inch bores, on Rincon Hill.
>
> It suddenly occurs to me that perhaps he intends to mount you there, Bishop.
>
> I suppose the battery on the Hill will be called a wind-battery, in contradistinction to the water-battery below.[114]

112. Charles Webb, "Things" [August 6].
113. Charles Webb, "Things: Caviare for the General; An Apple Pairing."
114. Charles Webb, "Things: Discursive, Hippophagous, Theatrical."

Webb also stands ready to ridicule public opinion. In the better part of one entire column, addressed to the American people, Webb lists several prominent events, both recent and remote in time, in which public opinion loudly came down on the wrong side of important issues. With sarcastic irony, the column begins with Inigo saying how happy he is to be an American and how he cannot understand why everyone is not immigrating to enjoy the liberties guaranteed by the Constitution. The comic pivot comes when he notes he is happy to be an American because it is so pleasant to contemplate the consistently poor foreign policy of the United States. Apparently, the Constitution protects the freedom to be short-sighted and hypocritical in foreign affairs.[115]

Webb's ready and waspish tongue spares little. For someone who attends balls regularly and presumably faces those elements of society who mount such affairs, Webb is anything but the society columnist. He once says that all such balls are boring. In another column, he declares that women's party dresses cannot be pleasing because they symbolize artificiality. His reporting on "the Russian Ball" creates an antidote to all the routine write-ups of big social events that inevitably praise everything, for he comically retails all the problems of the evening, ending with the claim that his hat and overcoat were stolen.[116] Nothing sets Webb off, however, as much as pious respectability and a propensity for gossip. In a section of one column called "Concerning California," Webb ridicules the habit of bragging about the wonderful climate and then complains that no society in San Francisco can exist because talk of business crowds out discussions of art and literature.[117] He finishes making fun of Californians by noting how much they indulge in gossip about scandals and about the affairs of others. Only a hypocritical concern for propriety could be greater than a genuine love for gossip, which explains why so many people came to see Adah Menken in her scandalous version of "Mazeppa": "It had been privately whispered around that the play was an excessively improper one, and consequently every one went to see it."[118]

Webb's treatment of sexuality also indicates his staunch Bohemian manner. Rather than pretend otherwise, as respectably polite society would demand, Inigo asserts that "one of the greatest pleasures which this miserable and transitory world affords to the well regulated mind is looking at pretty women."[119] In another column, Inigo states that he would not mind a stay at Alcatraz if officials also lock up female prisoners.[120] When he defends the staging of "Mazeppa," in

115. Charles Webb, "Things: [Foreign Affairs], Lighter Things."
116. Charles Webb, "Things: The Russian Ball, The Bohemians in Court, The Hegira."
117. Charles Webb, "Things: The Young Man Bret, Concerning California, Those That Tattle."
118. Webb, "Things" [Adah Menken].
119. Webb, "Things: Spanish Ball."
120. Charles Webb, "Things" [July 30].

which Adah Menken as Mazeppa is stripped of clothes down to tights to simulate nudity, Webb states that no difference exists between men and women in tights exhibiting themselves in public. Webb has in mind a recent set of male *tableaux vivants,* about which women in particular were interested. When he talks about pretty young women taking part in high-culture *tableaux vivants* as part of the Episcopalian fair, he not only discusses individual *tableaux,* but he also underscores the physical beauty of the women and jokes about one of them winking at him. Perhaps such comments were the reason the *Boston Saturday Evening Gazette* referred to "Things" as "racy" and "snappy.[121]

Circumspect about sexuality, genteel propriety also entails respect for religion. Early in November 1863, Webb imagines an alternative to the *Golden Era,* to be called the *Ishmaelite,* as part of his raillery against the incompetencies of the *Era* editors.[122] The next week, Webb's column begins with a complaint about the editors censoring his interpretation of the biblical story of Hagar and Ishmael.[123] A printing of the excised passage follows. In that passage, Webb criticizes Abraham for exiling Hagar and Ishmael and then goes on to criticize Jacob's underhanded treatment of Esau as well as Peter's cowardly denial of Jesus. The *Era* editors had suppressed the passage as profane and offensive to their readers. After asserting that the criticism of these biblical figures is his, not the *Era*'s, Webb defends himself in a thoroughly Bohemian manner: he writes for his own amusement, not to affect someone's morals for good or for ill. Moreover, Webb implies that he has his own morality and thus cannot be "too profane for the columns of a Sunday newspaper."

Though the treatment of Abraham, Jacob, and Peter obviously concerned the *Era* because many readers would construe it as disrespectful of Christianity, the editors' censorship also indicated worry about Webb's broader attack on respectable society. A specific comment about Abraham creates the worry: "No doubt he did tell [Hagar] his conscience compelled him to do as he did, for according to all accounts he was a conscientious man, a pillar of the primitive church, and an ornament to the society of that early day."[124] Like Webb's criticisms of Bishop Kip, this judgment about Abraham ultimately goes against the dubious ways "good" society maintains its respectability. "You must not think that I wish to be captious, Bishop," says Inigo, "nor do I intend to be irreverent at all. But I am nothing if not critical. A great many people are nothing if not hypocritical."[125]

121. *Californian,* [Charles Webb's "Things"].
122. Charles Webb, "Things" ["The Ishmaelite"].
123. Charles Webb, "Things: High Moral Ground, The Ishmaelite! Good Works, The Opera, Artemus and His Babies, The Jordan."
124. Ibid.
125. Webb, "Things: Discursive."

The willingness to risk appearing irreverent, to risk seeming immoral when treating sexuality, to challenge the rightness of public opinion, and to ridicule favored people and favored behavior—all define a Bohemian aesthetic. Webb elaborates the principles underlying his aesthetic when he talks about his imagined literary weekly the *Ishmaelite*. The title itself suggests the Bohemian standing outside the circle of respectable society. This stance against fossilized respectability includes a challenge to the predominately weak intellectual tone of "good" society, especially because of its embodiment in the old dandies and silly young girls who form a majority for such society. The *Ishmaelite* will be the literary opposite of the *New York Ledger*, Webb declares, without sensational serial novels, without regular reports from the courts such as the "staid, steady-going, stupid, and respectable daily papers" always have. The *Ishmaelite* will not be pious in its premises, nor will it think that "it is a sin to laugh and be jolly."[126] If the proposed journal must preach, its chief doctrine will be to encourage all to place "a charitable construction" on neighbors' words and actions—if judgments must be made. Minding one's business, however, is better. Very likely it was Webb's joke about starting the *Ishmaelite* with Harte that provided the seed of inspiration for their joint venture with the *Californian* the next spring: the list of qualities for the imagined periodical aptly describes the actual one.

Charles Webb's persona in "Things," Inigo, embodies much of what might constitute a comic *flâneur*: witty and satiric, whimsical and possessed of a self-deprecating humor, intelligent in his attempts to explicate the urban scene, adept in his discussions of affairs aesthetic, and judicious in his criticisms of affairs social. Webb's very style, mixing puns and slang with French phrasing, suggests the comic balance he achieves when assessing people's behavior. Reading "Things," one garners exactly what the comic writer as *flâneur* promises, an in-depth and amusing rendition of urban life, in this case, of mid-1860s society in San Francisco. Van Wyck Brooks felt that however much Sam Clemens as Mark Twain owed to Charles Farrar Browne as Artemus Ward, he owed more to Bret Harte.[127] No doubt Harte as editor and as artistic model impressed Sam Clemens as he moved past his newspaper origins as a professional writer. However, his debt to Charles Webb was greater still, because Webb's Inigo showed Clemens how to wed his Washoe humor of raillery to a literary, Bohemian sensibility.[128]

126. Webb, "Things" ["Ishmaelite"].
127. Van Wyck Brooks, *The Times of Melville and Whitman*, 284–85.
128. See Rogers, *Burlesque Patterns*, 20.

# SCENE FOUR

*FLÂNERIE* THAT SUBVERTS THE NEWS

## Mark Twain's Comic *Flânerie*

I HAVE ALWAYS HEARD THAT THE ONLY TIME IN THE DAY THAT A TRIP
TO THE CLIFF HOUSE COULD BE THOROUGHLY ENJOYED, WAS EARLY IN
THE MORNING. . . . I TRIED IT THE OTHER MORNING WITH HARRY, THE
STOCK BROKER, RISING AT 4 A.M.

————

MARK TWAIN, "EARLY RISING, AS REGARDS EXCURSIONS TO THE CLIFF
HOUSE," *GOLDEN ERA*, JULY 3, 1864

For Sam Clemens, developing into a freelance writer for literary periodicals implied that the satiric possibilities he found as a *Call* reporter would be given Mark Twain's peculiar comic treatment. Moreover, freelancing not only meant the freedom to be satiric *à la Bohème*. Mark Twain could also operate as a comic *flâneur* when the character reports on the city scene. Although Charles Webb would have been riveting for this project with his sarcastic presentation of the so-called respectable social world, Clemens did not simply adapt Mark Twain to the specifications of Webb's Inigo. Mark Twain also parodies the *flâneur*.

Clemens manufactures his parodic *flânerie* by overturning the priority of the spectator's gaze, the keen observation, that informs the serious *flâneur*. Rather than maintaining a journalist's distance from the object of his gaze, Mark Twain as a *flâneur* somehow becomes laughably entangled in what he was merely to observe and then explicate. Clemens was infamous in the Nevada Territory for creating a comic figure embodied within the represented scene who neverthe-less functioned as alter ego, which lead to charges about chronic lying. Mark Twain the unsanctified newspaper reporter was, for his detractors, too much in the scene. After Clemens finished his stint as a reporter with the *Call* and began his association with the *Californian,* he presents Mark Twain trying to render the scene as would that most sophisticated reporter, a *flâneur.* Unable to fulfill the role, Mark Twain embodies instead a humorously inept parody.

On a small scale, Mark Twain as a comic *flâneur* can be found even in items Clemens wrote for the *Call,* as he narrates what one might come across in the midst of a stroll through town. Consider, for example, how he tells his readers about houses being moved through the streets on giant rollers. Several times Clemens inserted fanciful items on the topic in his *Morning Call* column that turned the houses into morally questionable females who are wandering about at all hours on their own. No profound reading of the moment is forthcoming, no creation of an analogy between demoralized-looking houses and the sorts of people who inhabit them, as the serious *flâneur* might do. Instead, attributing human emotions to the houses merely creates a memorable snapshot. Mark Twain also etches the contours of the image by presenting his emotional reaction to the pathetic fallacy. In "Disgusted and Gone," Clemens embellishes the reaction: "That melancholy old frame house that has been loafing around Commercial street for the past week, got disgusted at the notice we gave her in the last issue of the *Call,* and drifted off into some other part of the city yesterday. It is pleasing to our vanity to imagine that if it had not been for our sagacity in divining her hellish designs, and our fearless exposure of them, she would have been down on Montgomery street to-day, playing herself for a hotel" (CofC 47). The item features a familiar Mark Twain, with his mock modesty, as much as it presents the so-called news about the house, a standard strategy of Clemens in Virginia City. The interpretation of the house's supposedly true intention obscures any news or presentation of "fact." The melodramatic hint about "divining her hellish designs" sounds whimsical yet burlesques sensationalist news, and the phrase "our fearless exposure" of those designs pokes fun at the stereotype of an uncompromisingly accurate reporter. In two sentences Mark Twain presents for broad laughs the absurdity of a house depicted as a woman of questionable morals who acts grand ("playing herself for a hotel"), complete with satiric jabs at newspapers and newspapermen.

This whimsical yet edgy, burlesquing humor flashed on other occasions when Clemens worked for the *Call.* A favorite topic for it was earthquakes. Mark Twain describes the tremors as "regular semi-monthly" affairs that come straight from below, possibly with "urgent messages from . . . departed friends." When Clemens experiences an earthquake while on the third story of a building, he has Mark Twain report in "Boss Earthquake" that "the sensation . . . was as if we had been sent for and were mighty anxious to go" (CofC 41). In another instance, Clemens uses the topic of earthquakes to suggest, in a rare display of the risqué, the life of a bachelor:

NO EARTHQUAKE: In consequence of the warm, close atmosphere which smothered the city at two o'clock yesterday afternoon, everybody expected to be shaken out of their boots by an earthquake before night, but up to the hour of our going to press the supernatural boot-jack had not arrived yet. That is just what makes it so unhealthy—the earthquakes are getting so irregular. When a community get used to a thing, they suffer when they have to go without it. However, the trouble cannot be remedied; we know of nothing that will answer as a substitute for one of those convulsions—for an unmarried man. (CofC 41)

A *flâneur* observing women's fashion should be expected to comment as a critic might on a piece of art—and the ideal *flâneur* provides penetrating comment about the significance of hoops, hairstyles, and the cost of certain fabrics. When Mark Twain examines fashion, he displays a critic's artistic sensibility, but with a humorous coloring, similar to Mark Twain's "reports" on moving houses and earthquakes. The humor becomes obvious, for example, when Mark Twain discusses a new bonnet made to accommodate a new hairstyle for women, the "waterfall." Clemens's startling descriptions clearly depict both fashions as worse than ugly. Women in the square and tightly fitted bonnet look "as distressed in it as a cat with her head fast in a tea-cup." The hairstyle creates a "great fat, oblong ball, like a kidney covered with a net . . . [that] vividly reminds you of those nauseating garden spiders . . . dragging a pulpy, grayish bag-full of young spiders slung to them behind" (ETS 2:318, 319). Clemens reserves his greatest ire, however, for the slavish manner in which American women copy the toilette and dress of the Empress Eugénie, the originator of these new fashions.

When Mark Twain reports on the Pioneers' Ball for the *Enterprise,* he again combines his more biting comments with whimsical, even absurd humor. Like his earlier, famous mock fashion articles written for the *Golden Era* in 1863, this piece invites laughter at women's fashions by describing in absurd ways how individuals supposedly dressed. The difference in 1865 is the extent to which Clemens shifts attention from clothes to the bodies of the fictional women: one has false teeth, another a glass eye, a third has enameled her nose—which she blows "with easy grace," and the last victim not only wears the dreaded waterfall hairstyle but also has "decayed teeth" and a "dismal pug nose" and is so artificially constructed "scrap by scrap" that pulling out her "key-pin" would cause her to "go to pieces like a Chinese puzzle" (ETS 2:370). The focus on female bodies even includes a daring though disguised representation of nudity: "Mrs. C. N. was superbly arrayed in white kid gloves. Her modest and engaging manner accorded well with the unpretending simplicity of her costume, and caused her to be regarded with absorbing interest by every one" (ETS 2:369).

Mark Twain's Bohemian disregard for the impropriety of representing female nudity was not without recent precedent. In one instance of Charles Webb's "Things," Inigo jokes about women in *tableaux vivants* appearing in "classical costume," pretending that the costume was "invented by Eve" and therefore would reveal "not only feet but also a multitude of other things." As he notes that the San Francisco climate is too cold for such a fashion, Inigo invokes an infamous example of a nude, a statue called *The Greek Slave.* Despite the cold, Inigo pleads, "do not expose me to the torrid effects of a Greek Slave, wearing only a pair of ear-rings, and handcuffs." Finally, as though the image were not strong enough, Webb's next sentence exhorts the reader: "Think of it—a Greek Slave with only ear-rings and bracelets on!"[129] As does Clemens, Webb invites his male readers to imagine the unmentionable.

---

129. Charles Webb, "Things: Sad, Theological, Operatic, and Other Things."

Mark Twain repeats once more this Bohemian flouting of the bourgeois circumspection with which writers were supposed to treat women's bodies in what survives of Clemens's early writings, this time as part of a column for the *Golden Era*. Once again, the topic is fashions. Mark Twain laments "that it was hard to tell what was good orthodox fashion, and what heretical and vulgar." The wearing of hoops only appears to sort the vulgar from the respectable: "Little 'high-flyer' schoolgirls of bad associations, and a good many women of full growth, wear no hoops at all [and] we suspect these. . . . Some who I know to be ladies, wear the ordinary moderate-sized hoop, and some who I also know to be ladies, wear the new hoop of the 'spread-eagle' pattern—and some wear the latter who are not elegant and virtuous ladies" (WG 43). Mark Twain then abandons equating "orthodox" fashions with proper behavior. However, having raised the issue of clothes as a sign of respectability and discarded it, he next tramples on respectable sensibilities by noting that the new "spread-eagle" hoops will furnish the observant with a free show of ankles, legs, and garters if one stands at the bottom of a steep street and looks up: "It reminds me of how I used to peep under circus tents when I was a boy and see a lot of mysterious legs tripping about with no visible bodies attached to them" (WG 44). Invoking boyhood and the circus and the surreptitious pleasure of peeking under the tent does not quite soften the shock against propriety that Mark Twain creates not by simply imagining what is under women's skirts but also by advising his readers on how to obtain an actual view.

Noted for his Victorian attitude about sexual matters, Clemens exhibited a less-than-restrained approach in San Francisco, probably inspired by Webb. Certainly Clemens, in these examples, was no more unrestrained than Webb when, in a column addressed to Bishop Kip, he discussed a particular *tableau vivant* entitled "The Game of Life," which portrayed an angel watching a man play a game of chess with the devil. Noting the attractiveness of the woman who was impersonating the angel, Inigo says, "Had she been a Pawn, and had I been the Bishop in that game, I think I'd have taken her."[130] Other double entendres and allusions and sly remarks about women could be added, but Webb also does more than shock when discussing sexuality. For example, in his very first "Things" column, he jokes about the lowbrow Melodeon Theater drawing respectable customers with its undressed performers and then ends on a moral note about the degradation of females.[131] And in the very next column, he admits cruising the red-light portion of the Chinese section of town but uses the occasion not for levity but to provoke compassion for the prostitutes.[132]

130. Charles Webb, "Things: Illuminative, Picturesque, Festive, Critical."
131. Charles Webb, "Things: Military, Festive, Dramatic, Musical, and Other Things."
132. Webb, "Things: Sad."

While the Bohemian attitude of Charles Webb as the most prominent and able comic model for Sam Clemens no doubt enlarged the latter's sense of journalistic freedom, Mark Twain does not consistently display as much overt moralizing as did Inigo. Webb almost always used Inigo as a mouthpiece; Clemens often used Mark Twain not just to make his satiric points but to dramatize them. These performances of Mark Twain as a character within the narration create his most obvious comic *flânerie*. When the performances dramatize an ironic outcome, Mark Twain parodies the *flâneur*. For example, in "Early Rising, as Regards Excursions to the Cliff House," Mark Twain and a companion arrange a dawn departure in an open buggy for the Cliff House, a well-known restaurant and hotel overlooking the Pacific Ocean. The plan includes a road "unencumbered by carriages, and free from wind and dust; a bracing atmosphere; the gorgeous spectacle of the sun in the dawn of his glory; the fresh perfume of flowers still damp with dew; a solitary drive on the beach while its smoothness was yet unmarred by wheel or hoof, and a vision of white sails glinting in the morning light far out at sea" (ETS 2:26).

The excursion should be pleasurable. In addition, the account of the trip should refresh the reader vicariously, possibly even inspire him or her to undertake the trip. However, with the exception of a road unencumbered by carriages, nothing happens as planned by Mark Twain and his companion. The road beckons, free of other carriages, because nothing has arisen yet, including the sun. The air slaps the travelers more than braces them, with the very cold wind blowing hard from an ocean that Mark Twain imagines dotted with icebergs. The fresh perfume of flowers cannot compete with the smell of the horse-blankets required to keep warm. The wind blows dust onto Mark Twain and his companion, and Mark Twain feels especially favored in this regard, receiving a "three-cornered" bit of gravel in the eye. So much for an exhilarating ride at dawn.

When they arrive at the Cliff House, no picturesque view enchants them. Rather, Mark Twain speaks of a "ghastly picture of fog, and damp, and frosty surf, and dreary solitude." The charming and sportive seals on the rocks have a "discordant [bark], writhing and squirming like exaggerated maggots" (ETS 2:28). So foul is Mark Twain's mood that the cheerful demeanor of the barkeep at the Cliff House causes the excursionists to leave immediately for the Ocean House. When a cold fireplace greets them upon arrival, Mark Twain "sought surcease of sorrow in soothing blasphemy" (ETS 2:29). Only "red-hot" coffee and the gloom of the man who brings it can thaw them out and brighten the mood. The irony of feeling better because a bad mood engulfs someone else epitomizes the comic results of the excursion. As an exercise in acquiring romanticized sentiments about the healthfulness of drives into the country and the beauty of the natural world, the excursion turns out to be a laughable disaster. Two epigraphs to frame the experience adorn the sketch. One is Franklin's famous saying from Poor Richard's Almanac: "Early to bed, and early to rise, / Makes a man healthy, wealthy, and wise." Mark Twain in the end may be able to endorse a ride to the Cliff House, but his narrative shows that doing it at the crack of dawn displays manifest foolishness. The whole piece therefore confirms the second epigraph, attributed to George Washington: "I don't see it." Putting the refutation of Franklin's wisdom into poker slang and into the mouth of George Washington encapsulates the comic strategy of narrating the excursion: a vulgar practicality trumps not just a romantic sentimentality about interaction with the natural world, but also the respectable practicality of the ultimate bourgeois role model, Ben Franklin.

In other excursions, Mark Twain does not simply encounter difficulties or unpleasant circumstances that diminish the intended pleasure of the trip. Rather, Mark Twain either fails completely to arrive at the intended destination, or, having arrived successfully at the proper venue, he nevertheless fails to witness the event that has brought him out on the excursion. In "How I Went to the Great Race between Lodi and Norfolk," published in the *Californian*, Mark Twain the would-be *flâneur* again plans an excursion, one that ultimately misfires. The essay's opening lines signal the parody: "There can be no use in my writing any account whatever of the great race, because that matter has already been attended to in the daily papers. Therefore, I will simply describe to you *how* I went to the race" (ETS 2:165). The first sentence announces the *flâneur*'s raison d'être. Though the daily papers provided immediate accounts of the race with descriptions and results, a weekly like the *Californian* will provide an in-depth report. The second sentence, however, undercuts that assumption, promising not a *flâneur*'s richer account of the event but instead an account of a trivial topic: how Mark Twain went to the race.

Eager to see a much-publicized horse race, Mark Twain in his "report" first dramatizes the impossibility of hiring a vehicle to see the race. The most promising means of conveyance would be renting for nineteen dollars the neck of a horse carrying six other passengers. In despair, Mark Twain meets his friend Benjamin Homestead, who apparently solves the problem by declaring he is going to the race and saying, "I've a vacancy and want company" (ETS 2:167). However, when Mark Twain arrives at the prescribed time and place, he encounters 150 other men, all apparently going with Homestead. When Homestead appears and declares himself ready to depart, one of the men asks how he is going. The reply, "I'm GOING TO WALK," delivers the story's punchline. (The actual racecourse was seven miles from the rendezvous at the hotel.) Homestead stating he had a vacancy when he invites Mark Twain to accompany him implied a vehicle without specifying one. The crowd of victims symbolizes the magnificence of the joke as it gives the narrative a tall-tale quality. Sam Clemens's joke, however, lies elsewhere. When Mark Twain reveals the ambiguous phrasing, it explains the essay's peculiar beginning with its abandonment of telling about the race. Mark Twain not only does not tell the reader about the race, but he does not even tell the reader about the trivial topic of how he went to the race, as promised, for the simple reason that he never arrived. For both the reporter as well as the would-be *flâneur,* nothing happens.

"'Mark Twain' on the Launch of the Steamer 'Capital'" unfolds in much the same way. Once again the event to be explicated has stirred the community. Several thousand spectators were on hand to witness the actual launch of the new steamboat the *Capital* on November 4. As he plans to present the event, Mark Twain does not merely imply the *flâneur*'s role of moving significantly beyond the reporting of events, as he did when he acknowledges he will not report the race between Lodi and Norfolk: "the papers would teem with the inevitable old platitudinal trash which this sort of people have compelled to do duty on every occasion like this since Noah launched his ark—but I aspired to higher things. I wanted to write a report which should astonish and delight the whole intellectual world—which should dissect, analyze, and utterly exhaust the subject—which would serve for a model in this species of literature for all time to come" (ETS 2:362). Mark Twain elaborates the difference between the plodding reporter of events and the poetic, philosophic explicator of events, and makes an explicit declaration of his intention to fulfill the exalted role of the *flâneur.* To accomplish this end, Mark Twain has secured the services of an expert on steamer launchings, Mr. Muff Nickerson. Mark Twain manages to arrive at the scene, on board another steamer in the bay, with a good view of the *Capital* in its launching scaffold. He has not been victimized by unreliable transportation. However, when someone notes the existence of a bar belowdecks and invites Mark Twain and Muff Nickerson to take a drink, they agree. A series of yarns follows that culminates in Nickerson's tale, told in his vernacular style, about a pianist working for a traveling panoramist who constantly plays music inappropriate to the spiritual pictures. As the story concludes, someone comes into the bar declaring the launch a splendid success. Mark Twain has missed the event again, despite being there. Ready to be the *flâneur extraordinaire,* instead he can not even match the level of the lowly reporter.

Leisure is the premise of the *flâneur.* Only a man with leisure time can stroll about the city. The *flâneur* therefore explicitly contrasts with the businessman who must keep appointments in a schedule. Ironically, the *flâneur*'s portrait being predicated upon leisure results from his writing for periodicals, a modern form of publishing that embodied the fast pace of urban life by keeping its reading materials brief. Periodicals created the light essay as well as the short story; they are deeply implicated in the business world as "the first date-stamped commodity."[133]

Clemens in San Francisco uses Mark Twain at times like a *flâneur* in the mold of Charles Webb's Inigo: a satirist of culture and society who also projects a quirky and humorous personality while explicating observations from travels about town. Mark Twain explicates what he observes, with an intention of providing a greater significance to the scene. Moreover, the characteristic comic phrasing of Mark Twain renders the scene vividly, and the resulting perspective elicits laughter. In all this, "comic *flâneur*" aptly describes an important persona for Mark Twain that Clemens has developed since leaving the Nevada Territory, one that further elaborates his satiric impulse.

"Comic *flâneur*" for Clemens, however, also signifies a parody of the *flâneur* when Mark Twain fails to explicate, even in comic terms, the significance of his excursions. By definition, an excursion is a bounded event with a specific itinerary. An excursion frames what is seen through its itinerary or the singular event that marks the trip's destination. In contrast, an urban stroll has no planned route, relying instead upon the randomness of what is presented. Nevertheless, like the *flâneur* strolling in the Parisian arcades and stopping at a café to watch *promeneurs,* the reporter as excursionist expects not only to observe the passing scene but also to interpret it, to wring a meaning from it. The meaning rounds off the experience, giving it a shape and linking it to other similar experiences.

For Mark Twain as comic *flâneur,* however, the experience of an excursion has a different shape. Excursions invite Mark Twain to participate in the event: he once again becomes a comic character within the narration. The humor of his parodic *flânerie* occurs with Mark Twain's surrender to the pure fun of the moment. In this humor, Mark Twain negates the *flâneur*'s interpretive role. Thus the biggest laugh Mark Twain garners from his comic *flâneur* persona comes from his thwarted intention to provide greater significance for the quotidian scene or the special event. By being unable to provide the explication expected of the *flâneur,* by being unable to attend the special event or by failing to pay attention to the event once present, Mark Twain embodies the idea that no larger significance exists for either daily events or the special occasions punctuating their routine—other than taking pleasure in them. The pleasure of simply being present, the pleasure of simply narrating, may be the comic "message" of the stories that do not happen, such as "'Mark Twain' and the Launch of the Steamer 'Capital.'" In those instances, Mark Twain descends to being a mechanical recorder of the passing scene. When the event does not happen, Mark Twain nevertheless tells his readers all about it.

133. Margaret Beetham, "Towards a Theory of the Periodical as a Publishing Genre," 21.

Mark Twain as journalist and excursionist does not stroll about town to observe and explicate. As an unsanctified newspaper reporter, Mark Twain exhibits more purpose in his urban travels than a stroll suggests. He prowls the city for noteworthy items. The need for copy must curtail the leisure of *flânerie,* whether the demand is daily for the *Call* or weekly for the *Californian* or *Enterprise.* Yet Mark Twain escapes the demand. Apparently locked into his reporter's duty to provide copy, Mark Twain the would-be *flâneur* instead comically symbolizes an individual most liberated from the strictures of business schedules, liberated even from the moral imperative of satire. In his failures to find meaning in the urban scene and explicate it, Mark Twain the comic *flâneur* escapes the need for meaning by adhering only to the desire for the fun of travel and talk. Not even a Bohemian morality, but pleasure only, defines this Mark Twain persona. The comic *flâneur* may be the ultimate expression of the Citizen Clown, for his foolishness calls into question the wisdom of his fellow citizens being constantly serious.

## THE POSE OF NAIVE INNOCENCE

I FEEL THE IMPORTANCE OF CAREFULLY-DIGESTED NEWSPAPER CRITI-
CISM IN MATTERS OF THIS KIND—FOR I AM AWARE THAT BY IT THE
DRAMATIC AND MUSICAL TASTES OF A COMMUNITY ARE MOULDED,
CULTIVATED AND IRREVOCABLY FIXED—THAT BY IT THESE TASTES ARE
VITIATED AND DEBASED, OR ELEVATED AND ENNOBLED, ACCORDING TO
THE REFINEMENT OR VULGARITY, AND THE COMPETENCY OR INCOM-
PETENCY OF THE WRITERS TO WHOM THIS DEPARTMENT OF THE PUB-
LIC TRAINING IS ENTRUSTED.

MARK TWAIN, "STILL FURTHER CONCERNING THAT CONUNDRUM,"
*CALIFORNIAN,* OCTOBER 15, 1864

One challenge for Clemens as a developing writer of comic sketches was how to find ways to present Mark Twain simultaneously as a consciously satiric commentator on the human scene before him and as an unconsciously humorous character participating in that scene. Notable in this regard is the way in which Mark Twain's humor of ineptness evolves into a persona, the naive innocent. Clemens employs an especially notable version of the laughable innocent with a good Samaritan whose charity is misplaced, thus doing harm rather than good. This misplaced charity can manifest itself as the helpful friend who dispenses advice, though sometimes it becomes the helpful critic who dispenses opinions. Clemens had experimented with this ironically helpful pose earlier, for example in "All About the Fashions," "The Lick House Ball," and "Those Blasted Children." The persona of the naive innocent has the potential to elicit a complex range of laughter. Moreover, this distinctive guise can easily function as disguise, a deadpan obscuring readers' understanding and making them wonder whether Mark Twain is ironic or foolish in a given utterance. The disguise allows Clemens in his best comic moments to camouflage satire with burlesque and fanciful humor by combining in one sketch the humor of Mark Twain the inept comic *flâneur* with the satire of Mark Twain the literary critic.

Clemens develops the persona of the naive innocent in several *Californian* sketches. In some instances, the pose merely flashes at moments within the narrative. In both "The Killing of Julius Caesar, Localized" and "Lucretia Smith's Soldier," Clemens gives Mark Twain the voice of a literary critic ready to satirize popular forms of writing, but in "Julius Caesar" he also has Mark Twain flirt with a foolish and inept persona before ultimately projecting the witty and competent critic needed to carry out a satiric design. In "Julius Caesar," Clemens leavens his alter ego's comic character with touches of vanity and sententiousness, inviting laughter at Mark Twain, who embodies in some measure the reporter eager to paint gory details yet moralize about them. In "Lucretia Smith's Soldier," Clemens prefaced the burlesque novel with a parodic statement of acknowledgments in which Mark Twain proclaimed himself "an ardent admirer of those nice, sickly war stories in *Harper's Weekly*" and gave thanks to the New York Brewery for its "excellent" beer, which provided the inspiration "to soar so happily into the realms of sentiment and soft emotion" (ETS 2:128). Mark Twain the literary critic in these instances is transparently sarcastic and ironic, establishing an obvious distance between him and the earnest writers—and readers—of such stories. No one laughs at Mark Twain in these examples.

"Whereas" reveals Clemens experimenting with the poles of Mark Twain's comic character and trying to combine the inept/humorous and the competent/witty to elicit both tolerant and scornful laughter. Unlike "Lucretia Smith's Soldier," Mark Twain in the first section of "Whereas" provokes scornful laughter at himself because he identifies with the overblown rhetoric brandished by sentimental fiction. His misapprehension of the sign "Love's Bakery," imagining the types of hearts being baked, sounds an extravagantly silly note, and the sketch's first section exposes the silliness by exaggerating it. In the second section, however, Mark Twain provokes scornful laughter at sentimental fiction but not at himself. His own sarcastic remarks about the young man Caruthers open a conspicuous distance between him and the cliché of true love. Sentimental fiction remains in the crosshairs of satire, but Mark Twain does not.

By turns ironically sentimental and mordantly comic, "Whereas" reads as a piece divided against itself because the narrator embodies opposing functions, demonstrating a problem encountered when Clemens tries to have Mark Twain be both dramatized vehicle and spokesman for the satire. When he reprints this piece later in *The Celebrated Jumping Frog of Calaveras County and Other Sketches* (1867), the problem has been solved by Charles Webb, who eliminates the first section and retitles the piece "Aurelia's Unfortunate Man." As Clemens in San Francisco continued to experiment with comic personae and attempted to direct laughter at literary offenses, he also tried to fashion a comic character who would behave in laughable ways while pointing out to his readers the problems dramatized by the behavior.

The problem Clemens has in "Whereas" becomes a question for a reader: how can one understand the satire of Sam Clemens when Mark Twain can be read as donning two very different personae at once? "Melton Mowbray, Dutch Flat," part of "Answers to Correspondents" (June 10, 1865), on one level makes fun of Byron's "The Destruction of Sennacherib" by creating a pretentious and dishonest miner named Melton Mowbray, who sends the poem to the *Californian* as though it were his. When Mark Twain reviews the poem, he calls it "blubbery" verse (ETS 2:186). Because Mark Twain seems to accept the poetry as Mowbray's, he also seems pretentious, dismissing the poem with a few snide remarks, no doubt dramatizing the chronically ridiculing attitude of many editors of literary periodicals. One can also read the item as a hoax sent by miners to the *Californian*. Inept and unaware of the hoax, Mark Twain looks foolish as well as pretentious. However, if Mark Twain is a competent literary critic, then he has recognized the hoax and is playing along, which allows him to ridicule the poem without attacking Byron directly. In any case, Clemens himself in a later issue of the *Californian* made it clear that however one reads Mark Twain's competence as a literary critic, *he* knew the poem was Byron's, despite a claim from the *Gold Hill News,* which said Mark Twain had showed an earnest ignorance. Clemens replied that only an intellect "so dense that it would take the auger of common sense longer to bore into it than it would to bore through Mont Blanc with a boiled carrot" could claim that such a "glaring burlesque" should not be read as a joke (ETS 2:193, 194).[134] Nevertheless, the

---

134. This exchange with another newspaper writer, probably Philip Lynch, who had attacked Clemens in print when he left Nevada, echoes the controversy over the "Empire City Massacre." The comment that Mark Twain did not recognize the poem as Byron's, in conjunction with Clemens's reply, also illustrates how early in his career Clemens aids and abets readers in conflating him with his literary alter ego. Though he says Mark Twain, the *Gold Hill News* editor means Sam Clemens is ignorant of Byron, and Clemens answers as Mark Twain. The question about Mark Twain's apprehension of Melton Mowbray's hoax also echoes scholars' discussion of Simon Wheeler in "Jim Smiley and His Jumping Frog": is Wheeler earnestly recounting Smiley's amazing deeds, or simply deadpanning? See Paul Schmidt, "The Deadpan on Simon Wheeler."

exchange with the *Gold Hill News,* as well as the failure of "Whereas" to fuse together the inept and competent elements of Mark Twain the newspaper reporter, illustrates the difficulty Clemens had in developing comic complexity in his character, a complexity capable of dramatizing morality in laughable ways and thus enabling a Mark Twain who functions as a Citizen Clown. In the examples that follow, Clemens achieved a much more satisfactory level of success.

Clemens's literary targets in the *Californian* material included the inept art criticism published in newspapers and literary papers. In "Young Actor," an item in the "Answers to Correspondents" column of July 1, 1865, Clemens invented a letter from a young actor who attempts with disastrous results to follow the bad advice given him in the theater reviews by inept critics. Mark Twain as competent literary critic instead provides the sound advice of listening to audiences' reactions. Earlier, however, in "Still further Concerning That Conundrum" and "An Unbiased Criticism," Mark Twain had embodied the inept critic. In the first piece, Clemens ridicules incompetent critics when a pompous Mark Twain delivers an opera review that focuses solely on the "performance" of a stagehand (ETS 2:81–85). The effect resembles his inept comic *flâneur:* Mark Twain unable to deliver the promised story. The introduction to the foolish review thus creates a delusional as well as a pompous Mark Twain. However, the introduction also manages to be a relevant comment about the proper relationship between good art criticism in periodicals and good public taste (reproduced in the epigraph for this section). The burlesque review dramatizes the critics' habit of fastening upon trivialities in their comments by having Mark Twain embody the habit. In the second piece, Clemens takes the critics' habit of discussing the trivial to its ultimate conclusion, for Mark Twain becomes lost in his own digressive introduction and never discusses the pictures on exhibit at the California Art Union, his ostensible assignment (ETS 2:137–43). His tangled digression again evokes the non-story of the comic *flâneur:* Mark Twain apparently thumbs his nose at meaningful narration. In these two would-be art criticisms, Mark Twain provides variants of the inept literary critic. The boastful version who cannot deliver a proper review strikes an unsympathetic note and comes closest to embodying fully the satiric target of actual pretentious critics. As a victim of his own humorously garrulous nature, the non-boastful version has a more endearing tint to his ineptness. An implied reader's laughter would be mostly scornful in the first and more tolerant in the second.

The humor of ineptness, as old as Sam Clemens's ironically calling himself "The Reliable" in the midst of his mistakes while reporting the 1862 Nevada Territorial legislative session, takes on a much greater comic depth in two other *Californian* pieces. In them, Mark Twain plays the role of the Good Samaritan whose good deeds ironically garner just deserts. This pose varies an earlier, similar one found in "How to Cure a Cold," in which Mark Twain heeds advice that makes things worse for his ailment. In "Important Correspondence" and "Further of Mr. Mark Twain's Important Correspondence," Clemens uses the Good-Samaritan-gone-wrong scenario to greater effect by having Mark Twain offer advice that makes things worse for himself as well as for someone else. By combining Washoe elements of his comic character with the guise of a naive innocent, Clemens can dramatize a satiric point about religious hypocrisy in an indirect and amusing way.

The jokes for these two items garner plausibility from naming actual people, well-known through events recently reported in the news. When Reverend Ingraham Kip resigned from the Episcopalian Grace Cathedral, the church attempted to fill the position with a famous eastern minister. Three different men were offered the job, but all declined. Mark Twain ostensibly writes to one of these men, Reverend Hawks, to encourage him to reconsider. The first article prints the supposed exchange of letters between Mark Twain and Reverend Hawks, along with introductory and closing remarks by Mark Twain. The second article prints telegrams supposedly from the other two ministers offered the Grace Cathedral position, Reverends Brooks and Cummings, sent when they heard that Mark Twain intended publishing their replies to his request to them to reconsider their refusals. Also included is a fictitious letter with commentary by Mark Twain from a California minister who applies for the job. Both sketches reveal the ministers as more interested in this material world than the spiritual one to come. Hawks admits that his refusal was actually meant as a negotiating gambit, that he now has a better position in a new city with a bigger salary than ever (which was actually true), and that his financial investments also prevented him from accepting the Grace Cathedral position. Cummings and Brooks are supposed to be so horrified that their letters to Mark Twain will be published—presumably because they too will not sound pious—that they telegraph Mark Twain with what amount to bribes so that he will suppress the letters. When the supposedly real telegrams are printed instead, the result is the same.

The Mark Twain in these two articles displays characteristics associated with the character from the early days in Virginia City, the insouciant slang style in which his letter is written being the most obvious. Mark Twain also offers to share his wardrobe and his friends with Mr. Hawks. The friends can be depended upon, Mark Twain assures him. "If you were to point out a man and say you did not like him, they would carve him in a minute" (ETS 2:152). The contrast Mark Twain's vulgar manner and language makes with an educated man of the cloth creates comic texture for the sketch, while foreshadowing Scotty Briggs and the minister in *Roughing It*. The greatest satiric dividends, however, come with the guise of innocence that Mark Twain maintains because it allows him in his letter to assume that money constitutes the most important part of the "job" at the church—an assumption that Hawks's letter proves to be true and the telegrams from Cummings and Brooks reinforce. That innocent's guise also allows Clemens to ridicule multiple targets of respectability during Mark Twain's ramblings, as he tries to convince Hawks how easy the job will be:

> You would like this berth. It has a greater number of attractive features than any I know of. It is such a magnificent field, for one thing,—why, sinners are so thick that you can't throw out your line without hooking several of them; you'd be surprised—the flattest old sermon a man can grind out is bound to corral half a dozen. You see, you can do such a land-office business on such a small capital. Why, I wrote the most rambling, incomprehensible harangue of a sermon you ever heard in your life for one of the Episcopalian ministers here, and he landed seventeen with it at the first dash; then I trimmed it up to suit Methodist doctrine, and the Rev. Mr. Thomas got eleven more. (ETS 2:150)

This marvelously effective sermon also serves all the other denominations, salvaging 118 reprobates before it wears out.

Mark Twain analyzes Hawks's letter in his closing remarks, and Clemens makes his character complex enough to wonder about the ironies and sarcasms in the letter without being sure. This brief emergence of the Bohemian critic of culture also allows Clemens to fire off one more round against religious hypocrisy. When Hawks ends his letter by saying he will pray for him, Mark Twain says that, in the hierarchy of those for whom a congregation prays, he would probably "come in under the head of 'sinners at large,'" but he does not mind. When he reveals, however, that the category comes absolutely last in the order—after everyone in North America, Europe, "the inhabitants of Norway, Sweden, and Timbuctoo; and those of Saturn, Jupiter, and New Jersey," followed by the Chinese, Hindoos, and Turks (ETS 2:155)—and sometimes sinners at large are even forgotten altogether, clearly he does mind. Moreover, when at the end he makes a suggestion about how to change the practice to something more fair, Clemens suddenly discards the innocent guise for the Bohemian critic directly expressing a satiric view: "How would it answer to adopt the simplicity and the beauty and the brevity and the comprehensiveness of the Lord's prayer as a model? But perhaps I am wandering out of my jurisdiction" (ETS 2:156).

The mix of innocent and knowing poses in the first article sets up the trouble Mark Twain has in the second article and his reaction to it. Though the highbrow ministers will not accept the post in San Francisco, Mark Twain receives forty-eight applications from others, "a swarm of low-priced, back-country preachers" (ETS 2:160). He prints one application letter as a sample, then reveals that the swarm has accepted his offer to stay at his house. Mark Twain had started out like a Good Samaritan, doing a good deed in "a spirit of enlarged charity and good feeling, [with only] the approval of my own conscience" as a reward (ETS 2:150), but the consequence of his actions has shattered this serenity. He wonders, "Why in thunder do they [the back-country preachers] come harassing *me?* What have *I* got to do with the matter?" (ETS 2:161). He ends with this worry: given the tradition on the Mississippi River that having two ministers on a steamboat invites disaster, the dozen boarding with him will produce an earthquake. Like the ministers' piety and the congregation's prayers for sinners, Mark Twain's charity proves to be naught but a show.

The Good Samaritan pose is one of Clemens's most sophisticated roles for Mark Twain to date. The pose has its roots in the humor of the inept and unsanctified reporter, but Clemens has refined it by establishing that good intentions cause the ineptness. Invested with good intentions, Mark Twain generates a laughter of humorous tolerance: his mistakes are mere foibles. In the two pieces concerning that "important correspondence," the shift to satiric attack is not abrupt, as it is with "Whereas." A more complex Mark Twain results: the Citizen Clown who embodies the very behavior being satirized, a figure whom the reader can therefore laugh at and laugh with when considering the plague of country ministers.

"An Unbiased Criticism" also displays this more complex Mark Twain. A humor of garrulousness, displayed by a vernacular narrator, Ben Coon, as well as by Mark Twain, transforms the burlesque art review into comic fiction. More humorous than satiric, Mark Twain in this instance cuts an endearingly inept figure. His comic failure to cover the assignment comes not from drinking beer or scribbling down unreadable notes as it did in Nevada, or from failing to get to an assigned event, as in other San Francisco items, but from telling the wrong story. The joke is not rooted in the pretense of a reporter handing in a muddled rendition of the facts or even of a comic *flâneur* who misses his assignment while in a bar. Rather, Clemens directs laughter at a garrulous literary critic who apparently is unable to discuss any of the relevant facts simply because other things interest him more. The comic emphasis does not fall on twisting for laughs a factual version of a real event. The inept critic instead becomes a narrator who talks about completely different events, who tells his own story rather than delivering the review. In this instance, Mark Twain does not simply subvert the role of the reporter recounting the news; he replaces the news altogether with himself. Becoming the news culminates the logic of the unsanctified newspaper reporter's playfulness.

Similarly, the three columns on conundrums that were the first pieces written for the *Californian* (October 1, 8, 15, 1864) had also collectively featured a reporter sidetracked from the assignment and unable to finish what he had started. In addition, "A Touching Story of George Washington's Boyhood" also approximates "An Unbiased Criticism" in its construction around a narrator who begins to tell one story but ends up telling another because he loses himself in the garrulousness of his introductions (ETS 2:95–99). The two pieces together are especially significant because they precede and follow Clemens's sojourn in the Sierra Nevada between December 1864 and February 1865, during which time he heard Ben Coon tell a yarn, the inspiration for "Jim Smiley and His Jumping Frog." Written and published in March 1865, "An Unbiased Criticism" also imagines Angel's Camp and its inhabitants (ETS 2:262–72). Despite the pretense of being factual, "A Touching Story" and "An Unbiased Criticism" operate as fiction and read very much like their more famous narrative counterpart, demonstrating how much Clemens could manipulate the art/theater review format and the role of the serious critic. Like "Jim Smiley and His Jumping Frog," "A Touching Story" and "An Unbiased Criticism" achieve their comic impact by using a narrator whose humor of digressive storytelling blocks the true tale from being told. Satiric jabs at sentimental, moralistic tales are overshadowed in the one case, raillery at the pettiness of art critics or political electioneering in the other.

---

## Spinning Yarns out of Facts

To me, the spectacle of a man drifting serenely along through such a queer yarn without ever smiling was exquisitely absurd.

---

"Jim Smiley and His Jumping Frog," *New York Saturday Press*,
November 18, 1865

The digressive storyteller provides another variant of the inept reporter Mark Twain. The character type who mindlessly chatters without malice has a long lineage, back to the garrulous slaves and nurses of Greek New Comedy, but Clemens retooled it for his own purposes. The emergence of compulsive storytelling as a comic technique signals an important development during the San Francisco phase of Sam Clemens's career. The Mark Twain signature had always implied yarn spinning, but a local editor, even one endowed with the humorous traits of Washoe Mark Twain, allows actual events to tell the news story. Mark Twain in his *Californian* sketches, however, becomes a character among many telling a comic story, one just as garrulous as Simon Wheeler in "Jim Smiley and His Jumping Frog." Under the guise of a news story, comic fiction emerges. Yarn spinning supplants reporting.

When writing pieces signed "Mark Twain" for the *Enterprise*, Clemens had looked for ways to dramatize his raw observations and hence enliven his reporting. Telling stories signifies a desire to dramatize; telling yarns signifies a desire to dramatize comically. These desires made Clemens chafe under the restraints of routine reporting and its stock phrases. This dissatisfaction with merely relating facts laid him open to the charge of giving such straight reporting "a lick and a promise," as William Wright phrased it. Yet the impulse to yarn—or just twist a description with comic phrasing or sarcastic comment—names an essential part of Mark Twain the unsanctified newspaper reporter. The sort of reader represented by Philip Lynch of the *Gold Hill News* might complain about the results of this impulse to yarn, but it fueled the stories Rudyard Kipling heard about Clemens the *Call* reporter. While on the *Call,* Clemens had occasionally been able to construct comic scenes from his tireless comic phrasing in a manner reminiscent of his *Enterprise* work. The format of the *Californian* allowed yarning, that is, dramatizing comically—the a priori condition for an unsanctified Mark Twain divorced from the straight reporter's role. The success of the *Californian* allowed the Mark Twain signature to make a big impact in the East Coast world of periodicals. Whatever the tone taken by his inveterate comic phrasing, when Mark Twain related his perambulations, he seasoned them with laughs as Clemens showed his readers the madcap or silly or absurd in everyday events. And because Clemens always looked for ways to dramatize comically, his efforts, whether humorous or satiric, often veered toward pure yarn spinning.

Stretching the facts into a fiction begins with a talent for weaving bare facts into a compelling narrative. Because Sam Clemens the historical reporter entangles himself with Mark Twain the narrator and comic character, the man and his occupation cocooned by the fictional figure, specific news items can fascinate a reader with their illusion of comic singularity. In some pieces, the alter ego barely disturbs the reporter; in others, the reporter with his news intrudes into a comic letter. As Clemens became more sophisticated in his presentation of Mark Twain, however, one reads a few narratives and wonders, Should these merely be acknowledged as "fictionalizing events" or suspiciously labeled as "reporting yarns"?

Two excellent examples of Clemens's ability to blend fact with fictional technique are "Original Novelette," written for the *Call,* and "More Romance," part of a letter to the *Enterprise.* The titles are ironically sarcastic, for the stories are neither original nor romantic but instead recount the sordid details of men and women cheating on each other. The circumstances may differ, but Clemens casts both sets of facts into an implicit contrast between the real world, which contains degraded individuals and ugly consequences, and the melodramatically ideal world of sentimental fiction, which depicts the noble behavior of handsome heroes and beautiful heroines. The contrast helps Clemens plot his would-be tales while the comic phrasing of Mark Twain provides the satiric perspective.

In "Original Novelette," an adulterous affair ends with the sudden arrival of the man's wife, and Clemens shapes the implied reader's attitude by repeated ironic references to sentimental fiction, such as "the fallen heroine of this history" and "the noble maiden." Clemens also alludes to a specific and immensely popular example of such fiction, Susan Warner's *The Wide, Wide World* (1850). In case one is not sure who to blame for the adultery, the reader learns that the "noble maiden," now "adrift upon the wide, wide world, without a rudder, . . . doesn't mind . . . because she has never been used to it" (CofC 128). Ironic use of clichés from popular fiction also structures "More Romance." Concerned with attempted murder, the story features a beer lager girl who favored a miner until he ran out of money. She was possessed of "well seasoned charms [including] garlicky sighs" and a face that would "have to be scraped before one could tell the color of [its] complexion." The miner, when "she told him she would not marry him . . . very properly tried to blow her brains out. But he was awkward, and only wounded her dangerously. He killed himself, though, effectually, and let us hope that it was the wisest thing he could have done, and that he is better off now, poor fellow" (ETS 2:397, 398). The narrative resulting from presenting facts structured as fictions creates a burlesque effect, inviting the reader to see how life imitates art.

Two other examples, these from his Nevada days with the *Enterprise,* illustrate Clemens's ability to create narratives whose factual status seems overtaken by fictional technique. "Unfortunate Blunder" tells about a drunken Irish miner bursting into a First Presbyterian Church service. The Irishman in slurred dialect berates the parishioners with his problems in the mines for a few minutes before being told by someone he recognizes in the congregation, Colonel Collins, that he was not addressing his club, the Union League (ETS 1:287). The plausibility in the wild story comes from the fact that the First Presbyterian Church in Virginia City did for a time hold its service in the same room where the Union League had its meetings on weekday evenings. The joke turns on the stereotypically drunk and thick-headed Irishman, but can any one be so drunk and thick-headed as not to know the difference between Sunday morning and Wednesday night? Maybe.

The other apparent stretcher, "Mr. Billet Is Complimented by a Stranger," has a similar structure. After a stagecoach ride that turns his face "the meanest possible shade of black," a certain Mr. Billet steps into a railroad depot to write a note, thereby gathering a group of Pike County Missourians who are astonished that an African American can write. The tale's plausibility comes from so much dust accumulating on a fellow who "isn't particularly white, anyhow, even under the most favorable circumstances" that he looks like a black man (ETS 1:295). The joke turns on the proverbially dim-witted Piker, but would even one of them be so dim-witted? Maybe.

Both of these items are from letters published in September 1863, one in the *San Francisco Morning Call,* the other in the *Virginia City Territorial Enterprise.* Both letters contain a variety of news items, the way the local column in a newspaper does, which also serves to mask the yarns as the news. Both letters are signed "Mark Twain," so the knowledgeable historical reader should expect an entertaining mix of information and fiction. However, "Unfortunate Blunder" and "Mr. Billet Is Complimented by a Stranger" are such good entertainment that one wonders if an emphasis on telling a story well has not managed to squeeze out whatever information once existed. Does it help one believe in the stories to know that Colonel Collins and Mr. Billet were real people—Collins is also mentioned in another *Enterprise* letter (MTEnt 88)—or should that fact lead one to suspect yarn spinning at their expense? If the narratives are yarns rather than news stories, are the jokes part of a humorous portrait hatched from friendly raillery or are they barbed lampoons?

In these four examples, local news items become virtual comic sketches by the addition of comic phrasing to a backbone of apparent facts. These relatively simple attempts to dramatize comically do not have Mark Twain within the represented scene, but they do exhibit a narrator who intrudes upon what purports to be the news. The next step occurs when Mark Twain becomes the news, when the comic *flâneur* rather than the scene is placed before the reader's mental eyes, as earlier examples have shown. The logical conclusion to the humor of Mark Twain the unsanctified reporter who becomes as important as the news he supposedly reports is Mark Twain the storyteller completely subverting the news. Consider these two 1864 *Call* items:

> MAN RUN OVER: A man fell off his own dray—or rather it was a large truck-wagon—in Davis street, yesterday, and the fore wheels passed over his body. A bystander stopped the horses and they backed the wheels over the man's body a second time; after which he crawled out, jumped on the wagon, muttered something about being "tired of sich d—d foolishness," and drove off before a surgeon could arrive to amputate him! (CofC 45)
>
> HAD A FIT: A lad of some twelve years was seized with convulsions, while sitting in a buggy at the corner of Sacramento and Montgomery streets, yesterday afternoon. Restoratives were speedily brought into play, and in a short time the youth went on his way, viewing with astonishment the multitude that had collected, which was variously estimated at from one thousand to four thousand eight hundred and eighty. One kind-hearted person, whose condition bordered on the "salubrious," had his place close to the convulsed boy, and puffed smoke from a villainous cigar into his eyes with seeming industry, until gently remonstrated with by a Policeman, on whom he turned furiously, insisting upon tobacco smoke as an infallible remedy for fits, and that he would give the officer fits if he interfered further. However, during this sanitary dispute, the subject had come to and gone off; and the opportunity for determining fully the efficacy of burnt tobacco and whiskey fumes in cases of fits, was unfortunately lost for the present. (CofC 53)

A comic presentation dominates these two examples so that they read suspiciously like yarns. When the *Unionville Humboldt Register* reprinted "Man Run

Over," the heading it added was "One of Mark Twain's Whoppers" (CofC 307n114). Like the best yarns, both stories stretch whatever facts and truth might be at their foundation without falling into implausibility (see "What a Skyrocket Did," CofC 130–32). Once a reader suspects that the narrative should be categorized as a yarn rather than a news story, Mark Twain has taken over completely. On the other hand, a reader might conclude that people are stupid and rude enough to make the narratives perfectly true. Sam Clemens as Mark Twain in these tall-tale-style narratives, as he had done while working on the *Enterprise*, balances between obvious fictionalizing and mere reporting, suggesting not only that truth is stranger than fiction but also that readers prefer the dramatic, the sensational, and the outrageous story over relating simple facts.

A final item from the *Call* material is noteworthy here as a tour-de-force comic character sketch. The apparently accurate and minute description blurs into the literary effect of the yarn. The prose effortlessly renders John Smith; the comic catalog is wonderfully zany:

THE "COMING MAN" HAS ARRIVED—and he fetched his things with him.—John Smith was brought into the city prison last night, by Officers Conway and Minson, so limbered up with whiskey that you might have hung him on a fence like a wet shirt. His battered slouch-hat was jammed down over his eyes like an extinguisher; his shirt-bosom (which was not clean, at all,) was spread open, displaying his hair trunk beneath; his coat was old, and short-waisted, and fringed at the edges, and exploded at the elbows like a blooming cotton-boll, and its collar was turned up, so that one could see by the darker color it exposed, that the garment had known better days, when it was not so yellow, and sunburnt, and freckled with grease-spots, as it was now; it might have hung about its owner symmetrically and gracefully too, in those days, but now it had a general hitch upward, in the back, as if it were climbing him; his pantaloons were of coarse duck, very much soiled, and as full of wrinkles as if they had been made of pickled tripe; his boots were not blacked, and they probably never had been; the subject's face was that of a man of forty, with the sun of an invincible good nature shining dimly through the cloud of dirt that enveloped it. The officers held John up in a warped and tangled attitude, like a pair of tongs struck by lightning, and searched him, and the result was as follows: Two slabs of old cheese; a double handful of various kinds of crackers; seven peaches; a box of lip-salve, bearing marks of great age; an onion; two dollars and sixty five cents, in two purses, (the odd money being considered as circumstantial evidence that the defendant had been drinking at a five-cent house;) a soiled handkerchief; a fine-toothed comb; also one of coarser pattern; a cucumber pickle, in an imperfect state of preservation; a leather string; an eye-glass, such as prospectors use; one buckskin glove; a printed ballad, "Call me pet names"; an apple; part of a dried herring; a copy of the Boston Weekly Journal, and copies of several San Francisco papers; and in each and every pocket he had two or three chunks of tobacco, and also one in his mouth of such remarkable size as to render his articulation confused and uncertain. We have purposely given this prisoner a fictitious name, out of the consideration we feel for him as a man of noble literary instincts, suffering under temporary misfortune. He said he always read the papers before he got drunk; go thou and do likewise. Our literary friend gathered up his grocery store and staggered contentedly into a cell; but if there is any virtue in the boasted power of the press, he shall stagger out again to-day, a free man. (CofC 147–48)

The complex comic presentation, with sarcastic title and copious details rendering the degraded state of John Smith, at first lead one to hang Mr. Smith in the caricature gallery along with other portraits of friends and enemies Clemens created while reporting. On that level, "The 'Coming Man' Has Arrived" reads like a particular image of the damned human race so much in evidence in the San Francisco courts and jails. The title, however, in its ironic reference to a successful man, also points toward the sympathy for John Smith, his essential humanity despite appearances, found in the sentence, "the subject's face was that of a man of forty, with the sun of an invincible good nature shining dimly through the cloud of dirt that enveloped it." Suddenly, the ridicule of caricature that the details of his clothes engender is leavened with the notion that appearances can be deceiving, that John Smith's drunkenness and slovenliness do not sully a basic goodness. In this reading, some of the degrading details of his clothes and possessions become positive, reinforcing a sympathetic view. His coat thus functions as metaphor for the idea of basic goodness: like the man, it had seen better days; like the man, it once was graceful. The one buckskin glove and the eyeglass, "such as prospectors use," complete the sympathetic portrait. John Smith is simply a miner down on his luck, maybe rich once, now "suffering under temporary misfortune." Smith is just one of "the boys" from the Comstock, probably at the end of a spree. Perhaps Sam even knows him, which explains the last sentence: the "boasted power of the press" in the hands of Clemens shall make Smith a free man today. One may still smile at John Smith's appearance and condition, but many historical readers have been there too—or perhaps have a sense of how close everyone is to misfortune.

Examining the piece yet again, one might conclude that this "sympathetic portrait" reading is too sentimental, though not without some power to blunt the ridicule of the "caricature portrait" reading. In addition, the extravagance of the comic list of items taken from Smith's pocket strongly undercuts the factuality of Clemens perhaps knowing the unfortunate miner. By the time the reader gets past the *Boston Weekly Journal,* the "several San Francisco papers" *and* the two or three chunks of tobacco "in each and every pocket," he or she may have begun to suspect a tall tale. How could one man carry all that stuff? Moreover, the phrase "the consideration we feel for him as a man of noble literary instincts" reeks of irony and sarcasm, which greatly diminishes, or perhaps just carefully hedges, the sentiment informing the sympathetic portrait reading. Finally, what should one make of the biblical phrasing that endorses Smith's habit of reading newspapers before he gets drunk? The joke's implications ricochet at several odd angles. Drinking and newspaper reading should be understood as similar activities? The Bible sanctions these activities? These activities represent rituals from a miner's true religion? The news can only depress a reader, what rational person would not get drunk afterward? In short, this piece is as complex as anything Mark Twain will produce in *The Innocents Abroad.*

Discovering the madcap in the mundane provided Clemens with the raw materials and a sense of comic structure to fashion items like "The 'Coming Man,'" "Man Run Over," and "Had a Fit." Moreover, once he grasps (and no doubt embellishes) the comic structures within actual incidents, Clemens can proceed from the other end, creating wild fictions with a veneer of plausibility such as "An Unbiased Criticism" or "Jim Smiley and His Jumping Frog." Both of these stories show Clemens experimenting with adding comic garrulousness to Mark Twain during late 1864 and early 1865. Indeed, in an earlier version of "Jim Smiley and His Jumping Frog," Mark Twain rather than Simon Wheeler narrates. In that discarded version, Mark Twain digresses so much that he never tells the story of the jumping frog, giving the sketch a structure and an ending just like "An Unbiased Criticism."

The garrulous and yarn-spinning Mark Twain takes his place with related personae that Clemens created for his comic character, the naive innocent as well as the comic *flâneur.* These personae have their basis in the humor of the inept reporter. The garrulous narrator in "Jumping Frog" does not create parodic *flânerie,* digressing so much that the assignment is lost. Instead, Simon Wheeler's garrulity produces the marvelously humorous and exquisitely absurd spectacle of a man drifting serenely through his "queer yarn without ever smiling." The quirkiness of Jim Smiley, always ready to bet, matches the quirkiness of Simon Wheeler, always ready, like a jack-in-the-box, to pop up and retail Smiley's dubious exploits in minute detail. The mechanical quality of Wheeler's memory echoes the mechanical quality of the comic *flâneur,* who records the scene without assigning significance.[135] Whether or not Wheeler's serene narrating of the tall-tale absurdities in the sketch should be read as a raconteur's deadpan that consciously masks the lies is secondary to the fun itself.[136] Similarly, one could simply enjoy the stage performance of Browne's Artemus Ward or consider how Browne constructs his show of serenely drifting into absurdity. Simon Wheeler has his wonderful ability to drift serenely from fact to fiction because no distinction between fact and fiction existed for him. The stretchers of Mark Twain the unsanctified newspaper reporter have the same genesis.

135. See James E. Caron, "Mark Twain's Comic *Bildungsroman.*"
136. See Schmidt, "Deadpan."

# Scene Five

---

"FOREMOST OF THE MERRY GENTLEMEN OF THE
CALIFORNIA PRESS"

## THAT CELEBRATED JUMPING FROG

A LITTLE BOOK FULL OF . . . HUMOR GENIAL AND INEXHAUSTIBLE.

———

REVIEW OF *THE CELEBRATED JUMPING FROG OF CALAVERAS COUNTY*, *NEW YORK HERALD*, MAY 12, 1867

[MARK TWAIN] IS AT TIMES A LITTLE MORE COARSE THAN ONE COULD WISH, BUT HE IS NEVER WICKED.

———

REVIEW OF *THE CELEBRATED JUMPING FROG OF CALAVERAS COUNTY*, *SAN FRANCISCO EVENING BULLETIN*, JUNE 1, 1867

Literary critics since the 1950s have made the publication of "Jim Smiley and His Jumping Frog" a pivotal moment in an influential interpretation of Sam Clemens's career, one that highlights his relationship to the writers of the Old Southwest school of the American comic tradition and that builds on Albert Bigelow Paine's calling the tale "the initial block of a towering fame." Walter Blair, Edgar Branch, Pascal Covici, Kenneth Lynn, Paul Schmidt, and Henry Nash Smith, for example, have all commented on the tale's frontier heritage. Gladys Bellamy considers the story notable for its "native portraiture unalloyed by the tincture of social reproof."[137] However, one might ask this question: if "Jim Smiley and His Jumping Frog" was crucial to his career, why did Sam Clemens call it "a villainous backwoods sketch"? Discussing both the sketch and Mark Twain's first book, *The Celebrated Jumping Frog of Calaveras County, and Other Sketches,* in the context of contemporary periodicals and popular culture provides an answer to that question. My alternative interpretation ignores the regional clash of vernacular West and genteel East as well as class dynamics implied by conceptualizing Mark Twain as *the* culmination of the Old Southwest school. Instead, the separation of a well-spoken narrator from a dialect-speaking character tallies with Clemens's efforts in San Francisco to transform Mark Twain into a comic *feuilletoniste,* a magazinist for high-culture literary periodicals. Far

---

137. Paine, *Biography,* 1:280; Gladys Carmen Bellamy, *Mark Twain as a Literary Artist,* 153. See also Blair, *Native American Humor,* 156; Branch, *Literary Apprenticeship,* 122–28; Covici, *Mark Twain's Humor,* 48–52; Lynn, *Southwestern Humor,* 145–47; Schmidt, "Deadpan"; Henry Nash Smith, *Mark Twain: The Development of a Writer,* 11.

from the vernacular frontier tradition of the Old Southwest, the role of the comic *feuilletoniste,* with its Bohemian overtones, also excludes Mark Twain from representing the genteel East.

The scholarly narrative linking Mark Twain with the Old Southwest writers transforms "Jumping Frog" into the epitome of the frame-story device said to characterize the school. Clemens in this view used the frame device because it separated Mark Twain from the backwoods dialect of Simon Wheeler, apparently replicating the regional or class dynamics of the frame story. However, the tale's form depends more upon Charles Farrar Browne than the comic writers of the Old Southwest.[138] Clemens had seen Browne deliver his famous Artemus Ward lecture "The Babes in the Woods" at the end of 1863 in Virginia City. Browne's principal comic stage technique was a rambling narrative style, a pretense of saying funny things unconsciously, as Simon Wheeler does: "the spectacle of a man drifting serenely along . . . without ever smiling." Moreover, such an unconsciously garrulous narrator was not the property of the Old Southwest school. The figure had long been connected with a Yankee tradition of humor before the New Englander Browne employed it in the 1860s. Digressive and garrulous comic figures had appeared on stage two generations earlier as Yankees, starting with Charles Mathews's one-man show,[139] and continued by another comic actor, James Hackett. Hackett abandoned his version of the garrulous Yankee after 1830, not because it was losing its popularity, but because another actor, George "Yankee" Hill, was performing it better.[140]

These facts seriously weaken any reading of "Jim Smiley and His Jumping Frog" that renders the tale symbolic of a significant trace of Old Southwest influence on Sam Clemens as he fashioned Mark Twain in the 1860s. Nor did Clemens consciously view the tale in the Old Southwest tradition. Instead, believing that the sketch would be part of Browne's second Artemus Ward book, and having seen Browne's platform style, Clemens probably would have made the decision to frame Simon Wheeler's yarn about Smiley and his frog with Mark Twain's more educated voice even if Clemens had not met a real-life version of the comically garrulous narrator in Ben Coon during his Tuolomne sojourn.[141] However, having met Ben Coon and—more importantly—having already experimented with garrulous narrators before he began writing the tale, Clemens most likely employed the frame device to continue those experiments,

138. Paul C. Rodgers Jr., "Artemus Ward and Mark Twain's 'Jumping Frog.'"
139. Charles Mathews, *The London Mathews, Containing an Account of This Celebrated Comedian's Trip to America.*
140. Francis Hodge, *Yankee Theater: The Image of America on the Stage, 1825–1850.*
141. Rodgers, "Mark Twain's 'Jumping Frog,'" 280.

to echo Browne's platform style, to echo the epistolary format of Browne's previous Artemus Ward work, and to maintain Mark Twain's occasionally slangy but nevertheless nondialect and nonvernacular voice.

A second argument for the paramount importance of "Jim Smiley and His Jumping Frog" to the literary career of Sam Clemens also ignores the regional link to the Old Southwest while emphasizing success in New York City. When the *Californian*'s new partner, Richard Ogden, reported from Gotham on the city's enthusiasm for "Jumping Frog," he wondered: "cannot the *Californian* afford to keep Mark all to itself?"[142] This complaint to the journal's editors, Webb and Harte, about missing the opportunity to print the sketch implies its major role in the advancement of Clemens as a periodical writer: reaction to the tale had convinced one contemporary that Clemens had become a writer too large for the West Coast to contain. In addition, having a sketch printed in Henry Clapp's *New York Saturday Press* was itself a coup. Though considered by some as merely a Bohemian literary weekly, the *Saturday Press*, for William Dean Howells, was one step below the *Atlantic Monthly* in quality.[143] Nevertheless, Clemens's sizeable reputation had been apparent well before "Jim Smiley and His Jumping Frog" found its way into print. To say that the popularity of the tale demonstrates Sam Clemens's East Coast success oversimplifies the historical record. Because the figure of Simon Wheeler, the garrulous yarn spinner, takes his place among a set of inept personae with which Clemens had been experimenting in 1865, "Jim Smiley and His Jumping Frog" played a more modest role than scholars usually claim: the sketch dramatizes but one vernacular instance of the garrulous yarn spinner, and its marvelous execution reflects Clemens's growing confidence in creating comic fiction.

While this modest role obviates the regional argument for the tale's paramount importance, a history of the growing reputation of Mark Twain clarifies the marketplace argument, predicated upon success in New York City. The history begins with the fact that the first round of contributions to the *Californian* during the fall of 1864 had immediately propelled that reputation to a new level. Next, the pseudonym "Mark Twain" had already reached an East Coast audience with some frequency by early 1865. The *Californian* had been routinely raided by the New York papers from its inception, especially for work by Bret Harte. In a letter to his mother and sister dated September 28, 1864, Clemens noted that the *Californian* had already been liberally copied in the east, and he explicitly stated the fact as a chief reason for his satisfaction at becoming a regular contributor. By the end of February 1865, the habit of liberal copying has Charles

142. Richard Ogden, "Letter from New York," 1.
143. Mott, *Magazines, Volume II*, 40.

Webb complaining that his *Californian* authors, including Mark Twain, are being frequently reprinted in New York periodicals such as the *Mercury, Leader,* and *Atlas* without credit to his journal. The East Coast weeklies' focus on the *Californian* in general and on Mark Twain and Bret Harte in particular resulted in Clemens's first national hit signed "Mark Twain." After the *Californian* published "Lucretia Smith's Soldier" in December 1864, nearly a year before "Jumping Frog," periodicals on both coasts reprinted the sketch. Concentrating on writing for the *Californian* had obviously paid significant dividends for Clemens in a relatively short time, but there was more to come.

To the extent that the *Californian* continued to be reprinted in the east during 1865, Mark Twain remained before the reading public on both coasts simultaneously, which gave the pseudonym exposure in the biggest market in the country, New York City. Henry Clapp's editorial note when he printed "Jim Smiley and His Jumping Frog" confirms this preexisting, widespread popularity: articles signed "Mark Twain" "have been so extensively copied as to make him nearly as well known as Artemus Ward" (ETS 2:271). Even if one allows for the hyperbole of an editor publicizing an original sketch in his periodical, Clapp's estimation of Mark Twain's fame in November 1865 reinforces what Webb's complaint earlier in the year had implied: Clemens's work in the *Californian* had firmly established the pen name "Mark Twain" in the collective mind of East Coast periodical readers well before the appearance of "Jim Smiley and His Jumping Frog." When he published the tale, Henry Clapp bragged that Mark Twain "will shortly become a regular contributor to our columns" (ETS 2:270). A seasoned editor and longtime participant in the New York City literary scene, Clapp was obviously happy to have a Mark Twain sketch appear in the *Saturday Press* without even knowing if "Jumping Frog" would be a particularly big success, and he planned to have him appear again. Mark Twain was already a well-known draw. No wonder Richard Ogden, who had recently become part-owner of the *Californian,* worried about losing the writer whose reputation the journal had so obviously boosted when he commented on Gotham's reaction to "Jumping Frog."

A second round of contributions to the *Californian,* from March to July 1865, elicited the first important critical accolade for Mark Twain from the eastern press, published in the *New York Round Table* in September 1865 and probably written by editor Charles Dawson Shanly. Shanly hailed Mark Twain as the "foremost among the merry gentleman of the California press. . . . He may one day take rank among the brightest of our wits."[144] The East Coast critical attention represented by the *Round Table*'s comments foreshadowed the public acclaim

---

144. Charles Dawson Shanly, "American Humor and Humorists," 2.

represented by the popularity of "Jim Smiley and His Jumping Frog" two months later. The acknowledgment of Mark Twain in an article printed in a New York literary periodical that names preeminent comic writers past and present was predicated upon the regular appearance of Mark Twain in the *Californian,* the most elegant and literary of San Francisco's periodicals. The attention on Mark Twain created by "Jim Smiley and His Jumping Frog" in the periodical world, then, represents a high-water mark early in the literary career of Sam Clemens only because it crested above an entire year of previous successes. In October 1865, after the *San Francisco Dramatic Chronicle* had reprinted the article from the *Round Table* praising him, yet before Mark Twain appeared in the *Saturday Press,* Sam made explicit in a letter to his brother Orion the literary ambition that he had been pursuing since moving to San Francisco and that he had so forcefully demonstrated in the last year: "I *have* had a 'call' to literature, of a low order—*i.e.* humorous. It is nothing to be proud of, but it is my strongest suit.... *You* see in me a talent for humorous writing, & urge me to cultivate it. But I always regarded it as brotherly partiality on your part, & attached no value to it. It is only now, when editors of standard literary papers in the distant east give me high praise, & who do not know me & cannot of course be blinded by the glamour of partiality, that I really begin to believe there must be something in it" (CL 1:322–23).

Clemens called "Jim Smiley and His Jumping Frog" "a villainous backwoods sketch" because he had worked hard to make his comic writing acceptable to the standard literary papers in San Francisco and New York City. Written mainly in dialect, "Jim Smiley and His Jumping Frog" was not an obvious candidate for periodicals with high-culture taste. Despite Richard Ogden's complaint about the *Californian* missing the chance to publish the tale, Harte and Webb might have declined the opportunity if Clemens had not written it for Charles Farrar Browne but had offered it to them first. Unlike the *Golden Era,* which routinely featured local color sketches, the *Californian's* fictional offerings were often not regional but national or even international in flavor. In any case, when the *San Francisco Dramatic Chronicle* reprinted the *Round Table's* praise for Mark Twain, Bret Harte and Charles Webb reacted by saying, in effect, that the East Coast finally had discovered what they had known for a long time: how good Sam Clemens was at creating laughter.[145]

Trimmed to fit an interpretation by twentieth-century scholars about regional influence and misunderstood within the context of the contemporary periodical world, "Jim Smiley and His Jumping Frog" has assumed a significance

---

145. Bret Harte, "Home Culture"; Charles Webb, "Letter from San Francisco" ["John Paul": Critical Accolade for Mark Twain]; see also Charles Webb, "Inigoings."

out of proportion to the facts. Moreover, these misapprehensions have obscured the Mark Twain Clemens created in San Francisco, one representing neither the vernacular West nor the genteel East but rather the Bohemia of a literary avant-garde. The same Mark Twain appears in *The Celebrated Jumping Frog of Calaveras County and Other Sketches,* which features literary burlesques instead of vernacular dialects. Collecting the best of Mark Twain's sketches and yarns into a book gave Clemens a chance to solidify his reputation as a first-rate comic writer with those already familiar with his work, as well as to introduce himself in a commanding fashion to the book-buying public who did not as yet know Mark Twain. Published in the spring of 1867 in New York City, the book featuring the frog was more important to the literary career of Sam Clemens than the sketch. Certainly, its publication had more impact on his pocketbook, for the publicity about publication amplified the publicity entailed with his simultaneous efforts on the lecture platform, where sums of money larger than book sales were more assured. A mid-April letter to his mother suggests that once the publication date for the book was set, Clemens coordinated his lecture on Hawai'i in New York City to take advantage of the notices and reviews (CL 2:23).

Though the lectures in New York and Brooklyn were successful, book sales were disappointing: not even four thousand copies by 1870.[146] Just before he sailed for Europe on the *Quaker City,* Sam, in another letter to Jane Clemens, claimed that he never expected to make money from the book, and that he "published it simply to advertise myself" (CL 2:57). Possibly, he expected a much better return from his planned book on "the Sandwich Islands." He tried sometime during his stay in New York City to sell the manuscript to the firm of Dick and Fitzgerald, probably hoping that his impending publication of *The Celebrated Jumping Frog of Calaveras County and Other Sketches* would persuade them to take a chance, but without success (CL 2:48, 57). Because the disappointing nature of the book's sales would not be known until after he returned from the *Quaker City* voyage, Sam Clemens in May 1867 must have been more than a little satisfied with the progress of his career. Seeing the book in print clearly vindicated his decision to heed the call to literature of a humorous and low order by striking up higher in the world of periodicals.

*The Celebrated Jumping Frog of Calaveras County and Other Sketches* nicely represents Mark Twain the comic character and Sam Clemens's efforts through 1865 as an unsanctified reporter making literature, with one exception. Mark Twain as a comic *flâneur,* prowling about San Francisco or New York City with humorous intent, does not appear in the book. Webb's treatment of "Mark

---

146. CL 2:40–44. However, Webb apparently never paid Clemens any royalties. Pirated editions in England had sold forty-three thousand copies by 1873 (CL 2:58n1).

Twain on the Launch of the Steamer 'Capital'" demonstrates his indifference to this burgeoning aspect of Mark Twain. Webb omits the section from the original introduction that shows a Mark Twain desirous of writing the ultimate *flâneur* piece on steamboat launching.

The Mark Twain Webb creates in *The Celebrated Jumping Frog* instead is the slangy, cranky, ironic and sarcastic, irreverent and sometimes silly burlesquer of all manner of writing genres, from biographies to love tales and sensationalized news items. Over half of the twenty-seven items in the collection burlesque other kinds of writing. One of the selections, "Answers to Correspondents," is actually a small collection of fifteen different answers, ten of which are themselves literary burlesques. Webb also exhibits a natural bias toward material from his own journal, the *Californian.* Ten pieces were originally published in the *Californian,* and seven more were reprinted in that periodical, Webb using titles given to the reprints. Another clear bias in Webb's editing is his selection of pieces originally published in New York City periodicals. The emphasis on New York periodicals becomes obvious when one notes which excerpts from the Hawai'i travel letters appear in the book. Of all the material originally in the *Sacramento Union,* only sections reprinted in the *New York Weekly Review* are chosen by Webb. Material from the *Territorial Enterprise* forms a third emphasis: seven items are reprinted. However, the preponderance of material from the *Californian* and New York periodicals suggests that Webb consciously aimed at the New York market. He had fashioned a book featuring a specific Mark Twain, one with a burlesque spirit and a Bohemian irreverence apropos to the New York literary scene from which Webb had come when he moved to California and to which he had returned. *The Celebrated Jumping Frog* portrays a Mark Twain whose aesthetic was especially recognizable to the avant-garde segment of New York City writers and editors.

Recognizable to New York City writers and editors, Mark Twain in *The Celebrated Jumping Frog* nevertheless occasionally exhibits a West Coast quality. Though Webb carefully edited topical allusions or local references that might confuse the East Coast reader, the sagebrush flavor of the Comstock mining country can be discerned. The title sketch places Simon Wheeler's vernacular speech front and center, and Webb includes two other sketches that feature similar characters. However, these are the only instances where Mark Twain's voice does not dominate. Notably, Webb's scissors creates one of the instances by extracting a vernacular speech originally buried within a larger narrative ("Literature in the Dry Diggins"). In short, beyond the title sketch, Webb has to work hard to call attention to vernacular voices.

The twin emphases in the book of burlesques and local color sketches frames a Mark Twain who thus fits into what the contemporary East Coast reader would have perceived as a gallery of "California" writers, a gallery that would certainly feature Bret Harte as the latest star, with perhaps George Derby and Alonzo Delano as earlier western representatives of the burlesque and the local color sketch. Vernacular characters and a slangy Mark Twain, as well as the perceived "low" or "western" humor of the sketches in general, all presented the danger of drifting into areas deemed coarse by gentility and polite literature. To be sure, Webb did not mind allowing the avant-garde, Bohemian aspect of Mark Twain to figure prominently in the collection, and the Bohemian iconoclasm behind the literary burlesques obviously ran counter to the literary establishment. The combination of slangy "western" humor and Bohemian aesthetics had given the early Mark Twain a fresh and original quality separating him from other comic writers. That comic edge is what Webb and Harte had appreciated in Clemens when the *Californian* flourished, and it dominates *The Celebrated Jumping Frog*.

In his preface to the book, Webb makes the point that Mark Twain does not depend upon tricks of spelling to create laughter, a reference to the fashionable cracked orthography begun by Charles Farrar Browne with his semiliterate character Artemus Ward. Though Browne had only recently died that spring, two popular heirs to the tradition of comic misspelling were current, David Ross Locke ("Petroleum Vesuvius Nasby") and Henry Wheeler Shaw ("Josh Billings"). The *San Francisco Bulletin* in particular picks up on the point, saying that Mark Twain is "worth a hundred" Nasbys and Billingses. The *New York Round Table* and the *Sacramento Union* argue that Mark Twain is either as good as or better than Artemus Ward, the *Round Table* saying that Mark Twain approaches Artemus Ward both as lecturer and humorist.[147] This last comment pays quite a tribute, for the Artemus Ward letters had made Browne a national figure just before the Civil War broke out, and the lecture tours he undertook during the war made him the most popular and best-known professional funnyman in the United States.

In addition, two California newspapers, the *Sacramento Union* and the *San Francisco Alta California,* compare Mark Twain favorably to John Phoenix, the comic pseudonym of George Derby.[148] Lieutenant Derby was a legend in California in the 1850s where he was stationed with the Army Corps of Engineers. He published comic sketches in newspapers and periodicals on both coasts, was praised by the editor of the *New York Knickerbocker,* Lewis Gaylord Clark, and had two book collections published, *Phoenixiana; or, Sketches and Burlesques* (1855) and *The Squibob Papers* (1865), the latter posthumously. By reprinting familiar material, Charles Webb no doubt intended that *The Celebrated Jumping Frog of*

---

147. *San Francisco Bulletin,* "Mark Twain's New Book," 1; *New York Round Table,* "Literary Table," 332; *Sacramento Union,* review of *Jumping Frog,* 1.

148. *San Francisco Union,* review of *Jumping Frog; San Francisco Alta California,* "New Publications," 2.

*Calaveras County and Other Sketches* would remind its East Coast audience how much they already knew Mark Twain. For its West Coast audience, the book may have presented Mark Twain as more than simply suggestive of George Derby's narrator, John Phoenix, as though Webb were anointing Mark Twain heir to the king of the California humorists. Whatever speculations might be made about editors' intentions and reviewers' comparisons, *The Celebrated Jumping Frog of Calaveras County and Other Sketches,* apprehended in the context of its contemporary popular culture, presents a Mark Twain whose persistent display of the impishly irreverent spirit of literary burlesque places him at a far remove from the villainous backwoods sketches of the Old Southwest writers.

## A Taste for Comic Material

The mass of the community has a coarse digestion. It likes strong condiments, and consequently swallows the Dime Novels. It likes horse laughs, and consequently finds "Nick Nax" amusing.

*North American Review,* April 1866

I *have* had a "call" to literature, of a low order—*i.e.* humorous.

Letter to Orion Clemens, October 19, 1865

The *Saturday Press*'s publication of "Jim Smiley and His Jumping Frog" illustrates the inroads achieved by Sam Clemens within high-culture periodicals since moving to San Francisco and starting work with the *Call.* The tale's flash of success with the public's taste complemented the *Round Table*'s critical accolade and fueled an ambition to become a literary *feuilletoniste* and professional comic writer. Tracking the appearance of Mark Twain in the *New York Weekly Review* after the publication of "Jim Smiley and His Jumping Frog" provides another way to measure how far Clemens had come toward achieving his ambition as well as an entrée to evaluate his comic style as Mark Twain.

Published and edited by Theodore Hagen, the *Weekly Review* in 1866 focused on music. Readers could peruse regular features, for example "Music Abroad" as well as "Music at Home," and immerse themselves in essays such as "Bach, Handel, and the Ecclesiastical Modes," a two-part analysis by F. L. Ritter. Literature received an equally serious treatment, with "Book Notices" and "Literary Notes," plus articles such as "Thorvaldsen and His English Critics," reprinted from the British periodical *Fortnightly Review*. Poems in the *Weekly Review* might be originals from the pens of William Winter, George Arnold, and Charles Warren Stoddard, or they might be reprints of Ralph Waldo Emerson, Algernon Charles Swinburne, and Christina Rossetti. Far from a "story paper" like the *Ledger*, the *Weekly Review* nevertheless occasionally printed an original tale, though more often it would reprint from elsewhere. Short pieces by Bret Harte appeared throughout 1866. More likely to appear in the pages of the *Weekly Review* than fiction are critiques of writers. Charles Halpine, for example, attacked popular fiction in "Miss Braddon, Mrs. Southworth, and Their Literary Trash." A regular column on drama along with correspondents from Boston, Philadelphia, Washington, D.C., and St. Louis rounded out the periodical. These elements gave the *Weekly Review* a high-culture aesthetic as well as a national scope.

For most of 1865, Henry Clapp had written the drama column for the *Weekly Review* under his "Figaro" pseudonym, and he probably first drew Hagen's attention to Mark Twain (ETS 2:300–301). The immediate result was the publication of "The Great Earthquake in San Francisco" on November 25, 1865, one week after "Jim Smiley and His Jumping Frog" appeared. During 1866, Mark Twain sketches turn up in the pages of the *Weekly Review* on seven more occasions. The first 1866 appearance occurred on February 3, when "The Christmas Fireside for Good Little Boys and Girls by Grandfather Twain" was reprinted from the *Californian*. Reprints of other Mark Twain sketches included one from the *Territorial Enterprise* and excerpts from the *Sacramento Union*'s Hawai'i travel letters. The *Enterprise* sketch appeared as "A New Biography of Washington" (May 5), and the *Sacramento Union* letters from Hawai'i appeared as "'Mark Twain,' at Sea: The Old Nor'west Swell" (June 2) and "Two Views of Honolulu" and "The Steed Oahu" (June 9). The items in the June 9 issue were from two separate Hawai'i letters. Original Mark Twain sketches appeared in the *Weekly Review* on three more occasions: "An Open Letter to the American People," "How, for Instance?" and "Depart, Ye Accursed!" These sketches all appear on page 1, column 1, immediately after the customary short poem. A reprint of a Charles Dickens tale appears on the same page as "Depart, Ye Accursed!" By the end of 1866, then, Mark Twain could be found in very good literary company indeed, being published with some regularity in a New York periodical cultivating a high-culture taste.[149]

149. On January 20, 1866, Clemens was writing to his family to say that he had quit the *Californian* and would only write for the *Weekly Review* and the *Saturday Press*, perhaps a joking way of conveying a wish to surpass his achievement with the *Californian* by having a regular job with New York City periodicals known for their high-culture taste (CL 1:328).

The publication of *The Celebrated Jumping Frog of Calaveras County* in the spring of 1867 marked a plateau of success in the most lucrative market for comic material, New York City, and set the stage for creating a national reputation. The positive reviews of the book provide more tangible evidence that Sam Clemens had reached the goal set by his friend John McComb in the summer of 1864. As swift as Mark Twain's success in Nevada had been, a success that had made Sam Clemens famous and infamous on the West Coast, the speed with which the pen name became well-known on the East Coast was no less remarkable. More remarkable still is the paradoxical nature of Clemens's success as assessed by periodical editors: Mark Twain's comic style fits comfortably into the standard highbrow view of comic material yet retains the fresh and original quality Fitzhugh Ludlow had recognized when he called Mark Twain "the Washoe Giant." Standard yet original, the comic style of Mark Twain by early 1867 had propelled Sam Clemens well beyond his Washoe colleagues and given him a reputation in the same league as Charles Webb or Bret Harte.

The professional comic writer was not likely to be published in periodicals such as the *Weekly Review* unless he fit into the standard aesthetic for comic writing. The standard and "correct" aesthetic for comic writing—for any writing— can be glimpsed in the hierarchy from high to low cultures of literary taste delineated earlier in "Readers and Aesthetics in the Marketplace for Literary Periodicals." That hierarchy of American periodicals symbolizes a mid-nineteenth-century cultural process encouraging readers to seek the best, that is, the most refined writers. Moreover, the hierarchy could function as a beginner's curriculum for anyone wishing to become an educated consumer of literature. Advanced curriculum would mean reading what informed critics claimed as the best literature produced in all cultures and using those acknowledged classics as Matthew Arnold had suggested—as touchstones to judge contemporary authors.[150] This educating process creates a refined and sophisticated taste, which enables one to employ the classics as specialized critical tools whose aesthetic superiority generates a magnetic field that will identify new literary work as excellent by drawing one to the other. The downside to this advanced education of taste is its tendency to impair an individual's ability to judge innovation effectively. The classics then become not instruments for assessing the contemporary best but a mystical means for dismissing what remains unmoved by their proclaimed excellence. This stifling outcome characterizes the genteel tradition, with its characteristic nostalgia, inevitably glancing back to take its bearings.[151]

---

150. Matthew Arnold, "The Study of Poetry," 13.
151. See George Santayana, "Genteel American Poetry."

The import of educating one's literary taste resonated in arenas beyond aesthetics. For the increasingly dominant middle class, reading the best literature in the 1850s was also a practice they used to define themselves against the lower classes, part of a burgeoning sense of social responsibility.[152] Using acknowledged classics as touchstones to judge the best of contemporary authors (and thus asking the question, "What qualities define 'best'?") therefore had to bear social and civic freight, too. For Americans in the 1860s, obvious morality and readily available sentiment became paramount in answering this question because these qualities mapped onto normative ideas of proper social and civic behavior. Having good manners, for example, epitomized proper behavior and implied good taste, in literature as well as in all kinds of art, because an understood sense of decorum structured all arenas. Aesthetic excellence, the "best" in literature, should reflect the morality and sentiment that served a societal perception of what is properly decorous and thus respectable. Josiah Holland's "Timothy Titcomb" letters epitomize this linkage of manners with morality. Holland was himself emblematic of the middle class's cultural aspirations.[153]

Comic literature in the period leading up to the Civil War and to the appearance of Mark Twain in 1863 demonstrated the same hierarchy of taste cultures and therefore the same norming process for educating one's sensibility found in all forms of writing. Problematic for distinguishing levels of taste within comic material, however, is Matthew Arnold's dismissal of Geoffrey Chaucer from the category of aesthetic excellence because he lacks a moral quality, "high seriousness."[154] If one followed Arnold faithfully in his theory of how to create an educated literary taste, as many in America did,[155] comic literature would simply be forbidden in any curriculum featuring the best. Despite Arnold's removal of Chaucer from criticism's sack of aesthetic touchstones, proper and correct comic material existed in the United States throughout the antebellum period because two acknowledged touchstones were employed: Washington Irving and Charles Dickens, writers whose genial humor created a high-culture norm. A genial humor established the norm because it fit polite society's educated sense of propriety and respectability, allowing for levity while maintaining the decorum of obvious morality and readily available sentiment.[156] This formula guaranteed an appeal to the largest segment of the publishing market, the middle class with

---

152. Stuart M. Blumin, *The Emergence of the Middle Class: Social Experience in the American City, 1760–1900,* 1–3; Bledstein, "Storytellers," 7.

153. Robert J. Scholnick, "J. G. Holland and the 'Religion of Civilization' in Mid-Nineteenth Century America," 62–63, 77.

154. Arnold, "Study of Poetry," 26.

155. Douglas W. Sterner, *Priests of Culture: A Study of Matthew Arnold and Henry James,* 14–15.

156. See Bode, *Anatomy,* especially chapters 10 and 13.

its upper-middle and lower-middle taste cultures. Comic writers therefore garnered praise again and again from nineteenth-century critics in terms that echo and elaborate these qualities. Their "light" literature is acceptable for having "a point and moral," for having an "earnest aim," for "never [having] descended to trashiness," or for eschewing the "broadest and rudest" kind of comic writing, that is, the "humor of low purpose." "Low," "broad," "coarse," and "vulgar" comic material elicit the "horse-laugh," indicative of a subhuman quality at worst or—in what is a clear echo of Lord Chesterfield's advice to his godson about any kind of laughter—a lack of restraint in manners at best.[157] Thus the man who laughs loudest is stigmatized as an "incontinent" fellow.[158]

Within the domain of comic literature, humor fits the genteel norm of propriety better than wit because "humor is wit and love"; "Wit is more the offspring of the brain, while humor comes from the whole soul." Humor thus encompasses the emotional as well as the moral realm. Even for an avowed Bohemian like Ada Clare, laughter and sentiment are strongly linked: "I not only think that where humor is found there is often pathos, but I think the former can hardly exist without the latter." Another writer makes humor and sentiment nearly synonymous. "True humor . . . is closely allied to pathos—indeed, they may be said to have twinned at birth." The humorist becomes someone who can "move the emotions of the reader at will either in the direction of mirth or tears," someone who "unites the exuberance of fun [with] simple pathos . . . and quick sympathy and perception." The best stories and sketches and novels and essays from comic writers are those that are "graceful, humane, and genial."[159] These qualities and their complements are conspicuously present in writers whose comic work consistently finds favor with high-culture taste. Tom Hood, for example, receives praise as "one so genial, so kind, so charitable, so sparkling, so humorous," while J. Ross Browne's humor is "generally tinged with sentiment or pathos."[160] Accolades for Frederick Cozzens flow from his "delicate and gentle humor" and "sweet sarcasm," and Charles Leland becomes the "genial" author of the Meister Karl sketches.[161] Lewis Gaylord Clark, editor of the *New York Knickerbocker,* gave the highest praise of this standard view of humor in a

157. Philip Dormer Stanhope, "Letter to His Godson, December 12, 1765."

158. *Vanity Fair,* "Natural History," 45.

159. William Thackeray, "Charity and Humour," 270; *Democratic Review,* "Wit, Humor, and Fun," 78; Ada Clare, "The Question of Humor," 3; Oliver Bell Bunce, "Table Talk," 582 [1870]; *Golden Era,* "Humorists, Past and Present," 1; and *Putnam's Monthly,* "*The Sparrowgrass Papers* by Frederic Cozzens," 99.

160. *Californian,* "Hood's Humor," 2; Richard Ogden, "Literary Gleanings and Gossip: Ross Browne's New Book," 4.

161. *Democratic Review,* review of *The Sparrowgrass Papers,* 519; *Putnam's,* "Sparrowgrass," 99; *New York Tribune,* review of *Meister Karl's Sketchbook,* 7.

reminiscence about George Derby: "The great beauty of the humor of 'John Phoenix' was that there was not a particle of ill-nature about it."[162] The issue of the character of the humorist—his ill nature or good nature as he doles out his gibes and quips about society—had been an issue in English letters in the eighteenth century with the essays of Addison and Steele and went back at least to Ben Jonson. An editor of the *Brooklyn Standard* assessing American humor listed pathos, delicacy, and grace as part of "true humor . . . and all that comes of high culture. It is precisely in culture that most of our humorists are conspicuously deficient." Undoubtedly, Edmund Stedman had this deficient majority in mind when he asserted in a letter to Bayard Taylor, dated September 16, 1873, that comic writers were at fault for promoting a degeneracy in taste.[163]

The high-culture norm of genial humor must be factored into Sam Clemens's assessment that his "call" to literature is of a "low order," for it exposes the hierarchy of taste dividing comic material: a low rank exists within a domain that belles lettres already designates as low. Moreover, the high-culture norm of genial humor meant that if writers employed certain comic elements, they risked finding themselves outside the pale inevitably erected by the centric values of the norm. Comic writers who wished for careers within the respectable norm had to steer between the Scylla of "low" comic style—which includes slapstick, dialect, and coarse topics—and the Charybdis of stringent satire, which includes biting wit, irony, and not-so-sweet sarcasm. Even though William Tappan Thompson in the 1840s had shown with his Major Jones character that slapstick presentation, dialect use, and an occasional depiction of coarseness did not necessarily mean a sacrifice of respectability, such stylistic elements subvert the maintenance of a genteel decorum and the sense of refinement it entailed. A genteel decorum hedging comic material demanded that anything said to be "coarse" automatically signified a lowered standard and implied a laughter more suited to the less-educated, less-refined, and stereotypically less-conscious lower classes. Clemens therefore would have been pleased to read the *London Saturday Review*'s assessment of *The Celebrated Jumping Frog*. The reviewer called the book good and funny—and readable "by the most fastidious mother to a family circle."[164]

Genial humor as a high-culture norm implied that too much biting wit in the service of a satiric presentation risked a negative judgment, while the use of scathing sarcasm or mordant irony would also call forth complaints of stridency and genteel requests to tone it down—and probably result in fewer sales. When

162. Clark, "John Phoenix," 7.
163. *Californian*, "American Humor," 10; Edmund Clarence Stedman, *The Life and Letters of Edmund Clarence Stedman*, 1:477.
164. *Californian*, review of *Jumping Frog*, 8 [June 1].

Richard Ogden commented on the satire of J. Ross Browne, he mentions its "kindly and catholic . . . spirit, never picturing a foible as a crime, or a folly as a sin." Similar restraint can be found in the first issue of *Vanity Fair*. The publisher notes that he has engaged "writers and artists of the highest order of talent to combine in producing the *most refined,* witty, *sarcastic—if need be—*and altogether readable WEEKLY JOURNAL OF HUMOR ever published in this country" (emphasis added). Few Americans in the 1860s apparently had a stomach for the more strenuous forms of satire, a chief reason why William Thackeray never achieved the popularity of Charles Dickens. Charles Farrar Browne articulated this judgment when he declared his preference for Dickens over Thackeray because the former "laughs heartily at the foibles of humanity" while the latter "grins malignantly at them."[165]

Genial humor, then, requires the avoidance of the stronger aspects of comic technique. Such avoidance necessarily works to contain the inevitably transgressive quality of comic energy and thus privileges a counterforce of centric, conventional values. The disruptive quality of comic artifacts and the comic laughter they induce has been recognized since ancient times, and much effort has been spent to contain potential transgressiveness, beginning with Plato and Aristotle. Freud's conception of *witz* and Bakhtin's of carnival are both predicated upon lawlessness. Sacred clowns in traditional societies function as ritual embodiments of antisocial behavior. Containment, then, results in easily predictable patterns of laughter, at best. Without sufficient eccentricity, an ostensibly laughable work becomes diminished and enfeebled, or perhaps transformed into sentimentality by too much pathos and delicacy. Clemens in 1865 had expressed a different aesthetic, one expressing the transgressive and dangerous potential of comic energy, when he compared the piano to the banjo. The piano he associates with fainting girls and insubstantial food—"chalk, pickles, and slate pencils" (ETS 2:235), the "glory-beaming banjo" with hot whiskey punch, strychnine, and measles.

In contrast, editorial praise for Bret Harte makes him representative of the norm, genial humor. The *New York Weekly Review* made the point explicitly when it compared Harte to Charles Lamb and called the former the most "talented, cultivated, and refined" writer yet to appear in California. An editor for the *Californian* after Harte had left the periodical claimed Harte has "genuine humor [that] is delicate, with just a tinge of sentiment held in severe restraint lest it should verge on sentimentality, and a dash of subtle satire." A review of Harte's *Condensed Novels* summed up these judgments: his humor has "delicacy and

165. Ogden, "Ross Browne's New Book," 4; *Vanity Fair,* "Preface," iv; Charles Farrar Browne, "City Facts and Fancies: [Thackeray vs. Dickens]," 5.

good taste."[166] Harte thus was categorized as a literary descendent of high-culture writers who had produced genial comic material in the midcentury literary periodicals: Frederick Cozzens, John G. Saxe, Oliver Wendell Holmes, Charles Godfrey Leland, James Russell Lowell, and George William Curtis. The comic styles of these authors generally curbed rather than flaunted the lawless energy of laughter.

In polite American society before and during the Civil War, with its genteel notions of morality and sentiment that practically equate with the best in literary taste, comic literature always proceeded with a shackle on one foot because certain comic elements were proscribed a priori. When someone wrote for comic periodicals like *Nick Nax*, which had the mass of the community as its intended audience, such proscriptions carried less force, if the multitudes signify an appetite for the coarse. Publication in newspapers, the periodicals assumed to be for the less-refined masculine taste, also allowed an author to ignore genteel proscriptions up to a point. The relative freedom of the newspaper domain from the strictures of gentility during the antebellum period meant that writers for that segment of the periodical market could often give free rein to their comic technique. Whether comic writers came from the frontier regions of the Old Southwest or whether comic writers had an urban address in the eastern cities, they were most likely to appear first in newspapers. Artemus Ward and Mark Twain both appeared first in newspapers and then invaded the domain of the literary and/or comic weekly. Having accomplished that invasion, however, a comic writer who wished to move up the taste hierarchy from that segment of the marketplace represented by *Nick Nax* must necessarily feel more strongly the power of the taste hierarchy that associates the "best" with conventional hedges against comic literature. The comic writer who aspires above *Nick Nax*, who wishes to appear in the *Weekly Review*, for example, cannot ignore those conventional hedges.

Sam Clemens in San Francisco was determined to "strike up higher" in the periodical world, to aim toward the high culture represented by the *Weekly Review*. As bold as he had been in Virginia City with his Washoe style of journalism, and as successful as his Mark Twain figure had been in approximately eighteen months, Clemens was no less bold in aiming for a more refined reader. With the accolades for *The Celebrated Jumping Frog of Calaveras County* and his publications in the *Weekly Review*, Clemens had reached high-culture readers in very nearly the same time frame. His association with the *Californian* provided the indispensable condition for success in this second phase of his professional writing career. The key individuals in helping Mark Twain gain a measurable

166. *New York Weekly Review*, [Editor's Note: Bret Harte], 1; *Californian*, [Bret Harte's Humor], 4; *Californian*, "Mr. Harte's New Book" [*Condensed Novels*], 8.

notice within the high-culture end of the periodical world were Bret Harte and Charles Webb. Both contemporaries were crucial to Clemens's aspirations in two ways. First, as the editors of the *Californian, the* West Coast literary periodical for the East Coast literary periodicals, they were willing to print sketches signed "Mark Twain." Second, Harte and Webb became the most immediate literary models for Clemens to study as he contemplated how to accomplish his goal.

The reprintings on the East Coast of sketches from the *Californian* signed "Mark Twain" and "Bret Harte" demonstrate how national success for Clemens began not only with the influence of the *Californian* but also with the popularity of Bret Harte as a comic writer. Together, the reputations of Harte and of the *Californian* formed a wedge for the pen name "Mark Twain," allowing Clemens access to East Coast readers with high-culture taste. Bret Harte's comic style represents high culture because it generally embodies the first essential trait, geniality. Harte's comic style also employs sophisticated syntax, elevated diction, and classical allusions. Harte occasionally runs the risk of allowing in his voice the tone of acerbic satire, for example in "From a Balcony," when serenaders interrupt the poetic reverie of the narrator, who not only hurls invective at them and their progenitors but also throws a decaying orange and an old boot. The *Golden Era* had noted this tone when it compared Mark Twain and Bret Harte as comic writers, saying that both used sarcasm and irony.[167] With Harte, however, the superior position of a satirist to his subject much more often comes wrapped in a genial, even sentimental though humorous perspective, reminiscent of Washington Irving's narrator in *Sketch Book.* Harte's usually mild comic voice presents genially humorous images of San Francisco, when they are not sentimental or nostalgic.

Though Bret Harte today is not recognized as a comic writer, his self-designated "Bohemian" sketches of urban life as well as his Irvingesque stories about California legends, his comic poetry, and his burlesque condensed novels were more than enough for contemporary reviewers and essayists in periodicals, who put his name in lists of comic pseudonyms,[168] or who referred to him as the "latest star" of American comic writers.[169] Samuel Bowles of the *Springfield Republican* declared Harte "the best of the California humorists." Bowles also compared Bret Harte to Mark Twain, judging the former superior because his satire was "delicate and innocent."[170] Bowles's judgment represents a quintessential high-culture standard. Satire from that viewpoint should not be a scourge

---

167. Bret Harte, "From a Balcony," 8; *Golden Era,* [Satire: Mark Twain's vs. Bret Harte's], 2.
168. *North American Review,* review of *Artemus Ward: His Travels.*
169. Oliver Bell Bunce, "Table Talk" [1871].
170. Samuel Bowles, [Bret Harte as California's Best Humorist], 1; [Bret Harte and Mark Twain Compared], 4.

or a lash against human folly and social evils. Rather, satire should somehow, like Harte's, exhibit polite society's virtue par excellence, geniality, with its hints of delicateness. The *Golden Era*'s distinction between Harte and Clemens implicitly echoes this judgment: the latter, as Mark Twain, uses slang and extravagance and "western" humor while the former does not.[171]

For a representative of the genteel tradition like Samuel Bowles, slang and extravagance and "western" humor excluded Mark Twain from the highest levels of taste in comic writing. However, for critics Bohemian and not-so-genteel such as Charles Webb, these qualities created the freshness and originality of Sam Clemens's comic style. Critics accused Clemens of coarseness at every stage of his early writing career, though the charge was effectively a minority report, and the reviews of *The Celebrated Jumping Frog* reflect the pattern. The charge appears in the otherwise positive review from the *San Francisco Bulletin*, but only the *New York Post* gives the condemnation a general cast, judging the whole book to be "a mistake—not suitable to the East Coast." The *London Saturday Review* more than offsets this comment by stating the book contains no sketch that could not be read by mothers to their family circles. When the *Californian* reprints this remark, the editors add that they are pleased the *Saturday Review* does not agree with those who charge Mark Twain with coarseness.[172]

Civilized respectability clearly demanded that vulgar comic tactics be severely constrained. And though obvious moral purpose was necessary too, geniality with a tinge of sentiment was the other side of civilized respectability, even when delivering satire. Being tasteful and artistic with comic material demanded attention to these parameters. Yet Sam Clemens and the writers he most resembles all managed to create comic styles often distinctively more exuberant—banjo instead of piano—than self-consciously highbrow competitors. The trick to having commercial success without losing an artistic edge involved creating a style that liberated comic exuberance without merely pandering to the coarse digestion of the masses who eagerly swallow *Nick Nax*.

Charles Farrar Browne and the comic techniques employed to create his character Artemus Ward illustrate how popularity can indicate a chasm from a high-culture taste and also imply a readership limited to lower-middle or even low taste culture. Browne's chief comic device was a fractured orthography, meant to suggest dialect speech but also to depict the showman's ignorance of spelling and therefore his low social status. A reviewer for *Continental Monthly*, probably Charles Godfrey Leland, notes this link between the "broad eccentric humor"

171. *Golden Era*, [Satire], 2.
172. *San Francisco Bulletin*, "Mark Twain's New Book," 1; *New York Post*, "Gossip about Publishers and Books," 28; *Californian*, review of *Jumping Frog*, 8 [June 1].

of Browne and his character's low social status when he calls Artemus Ward a "truthful conception of one of the multitude."[173] Insofar as the showman parodied the multitude, Browne's material would appeal mainly to the middle class, whether their taste culture was upper middle or lower middle, because they could easily laugh at the obvious inferiority of Artemus Ward. When Browne manifests the Gentleman Roarer to depict the pugnacity of the showman or his fondness for drink, he risks losing individuals with an upper-middle literary taste. His style illustrates the perils of a more unrestrained presentation of comic material, which invited charges of coarseness and virtually guaranteed a masculine audience that probably did not reach higher than the lower-middle level on the taste-culture spectrum. Appealing to the lower-middle-level taste and below may be sufficient to be popular and successful commercially, as Browne proved, but it necessarily linked the comic writer to dime novels and *Nick Nax,* as the *North American Review* writer puts it in one of this section's epigraphs.

David Sloane has made a good argument for the way in which Artemus Ward at times speaks for middle-class values, a position with which one anonymous contemporary reviewer in the *New York Sunday Times* agreed when he called the showman "not merely a man of unfailing humor, but a philosopher and a patriot."[174] Insofar as Browne's contemporary middle-class audience recognized the showman as a spokesman, their laughter at him for his ignorant, money-grasping ways—their malignant grin à la Thackeray—would switch to the hearty and implicitly sympathetic laughter with him that Browne saw as characteristic of Dickens. However foolish and silly his methods, when Artemus Ward chases away office seekers from President Lincoln, speaks man-to-man with Prince Edward of England, or denounces the excesses of so-called reformists—and then delivers his commonsense speech on the issue at hand—Browne garners his biggest audience, encompassing not just the lower-middle taste culture but also easily reaching the upper-middle- and possibly even the high-culture taste. In this respect, Browne's use of fractured orthography is not incompatible with the way Seba Smith, James Russell Lowell, and George Washington Harris had previously employed vernacular dialect: to create the figure of a wise fool whose rustic or uneducated appearance masks his common-man common sense.

This occasional comic depth, however, may be more apparent now than in the 1860s, for Charles Browne's style also illustrates the perils of allowing his love for the absurd, what one anonymous reviewer called his "dry whimsicality" and another his "buffoonery," to overwhelm the serious intent of satire. During the

173. Charles Godfrey Leland, review of *Artemus Ward: His Book,* 107.
174. *Golden Era,* "Our Humorous Satirists," 5.

1860s, some highbrow commentators expressed incredulity at Browne's popularity, and even the anonymous admirer in the *North American Review* has faint praise for Browne's "humor of low purpose." The same reviewer gives even less for Browne's satire, which does not attack "the idols which society sets up and holds in honor, but simply uses as its butt the laughing-stock that society already ridicules." Bret Harte, in a review of Browne's comic lecture in San Francisco that defends him from detractors, nevertheless admits that Browne's humor is "not exactly the highest nor the most ennobling type [nor one of a] more artistic standard." Browne as Artemus Ward offers "fun without application," said Harte, an observation echoed by the *North American Review,* which says Browne has "no object but laughter."[175] Without the obvious morality of a clear satiric purpose, such as Harte notes for Robert Newell's "Orpheus C. Kerr" series of comic letters, Browne cannot lay claim to the highest levels in the hierarchy of taste cultures, in which a writer yokes obvious moral purpose to a geniality of comic technique.

For the New York correspondent to the *Californian,* "Artemus Ward is merely funny and absurd."[176] Ironically, much of what remains appealing today in Browne's style rests upon the sheer silliness of his absurd and whimsical turns of phrase, a style that anticipates the zaniness of the Marx Brothers. On stage as a parodist of lyceum lecturers, Browne made the absurd and the whimsical, along with the buffoonery of malfunctioning stage props, the mainstays of his burlesque performance technique.[177] Given what contemporaries have said about his jocular nature,[178] Browne, when performing Artemus Ward on stage, was probably closer to his usual self, with more a pretense of puzzled innocence on display than the ignorance of the showman. This stage persona, which Clemens adapted for his platform style, was enormously popular and probably created demand for Browne's books rather than the other way around. Undoubtedly, that stage presence rather than the showman character expressed the truest aspect of Browne's comic genius. Today's reader, who cannot experience the stage presence, thus finds it difficult to fathom Browne's unparalleled popularity in the early 1860s simply by reading the sketches, with their predictable comic effects and distant satiric targets. Browne's comic style, then, demonstrates the limits of "low" elements.

175. *Galaxy,* "Nebulae" [*Artemus Ward*], 222; *North American Review,* review of "*Artemus Ward,*" 587; Bret Harte, "Artemus Ward," 1; *North American Review,* review of "*Artemus Ward,*" 588.
176. *Californian,* "Our New York Letter" [Artemus Ward], 9.
177. John Q. Reed, "Artemus Ward as a Comic Lecturer."
178. Enoch Knight, "The Real Artemus Ward"; C. C. Ruthrauff, "Artemus Ward at Cleveland"; James F. Ryder, "Artemus Ward"; Archer H. Shaw, "Artemus Ward"; Wright, "Artemus Ward in Nevada."

William Dean Howells implies the risk from the other end of the taste spectrum with his comment on a comic writer from California, George Derby, which echoes Lewis Gaylord Clark's earlier appraisal: "Before 'John Phoenix' [Derby's most famous pseudonym], there was scarcely any American humorist—not of the distinctly literary sort—with whom one could smile and keep one's self-respect."[179] George Derby enjoyed a notoriety gained from burlesques of science and technology in which he employed an educated voice to create genial humor as well as scientific hoaxes. This tactic did nothing to endanger George Derby's place within the standard high-culture view of comic material expressed by Howells. William Wright also used the figure of an earnest pedant insistently dispensing (apparent) information with educated diction and syntax to create his most famous hoaxes, "Solar Armor" and "The Traveling Stones of Pahrahagat." The danger for William Wright as well as George Derby was not that they might be misunderstood as being merely vulgar and with no object other than laughter, as was the case with Charles Farrar Browne. Rather, the danger was that they might be too tame, that they might merely be what Howells calls humorists "of the distinctly literary sort," that is, comic writers confined by the strictures of high-culture taste. Derby's sense of whimsy and wordplay approaches Browne's, and this feature perhaps more than any other contributes to a sense of genial humor as well as to a sense of restrained satire that defined the genteel norm for comic material. Wright's habit of letting the delicate innocence of geniality descend into sentimentality created the same sense of restraint. Yet his gentlemanly prose style can also become a comic deadpan for hoaxes. His "Solar Armor" may be without peer in this regard.

Charles Farrar Browne and William Wright demonstrate how a comic writer can construct a style less refined than that of the distinctly literary sort, like Bret Harte. Their styles in varying degrees incorporate elements considered "low," what cultural arbiters of taste such as Samuel Bowles disparagingly called "western" humor. "Low" might also be translated as "wild," "coarse," "vernacular," or "vulgar," but each shade of meaning in these variations signals a popularity with the masses. Wright's more extravagant comic sketches contain slapstick, comic violence, and tall-tale grotesquerie, complete with disreputable behavior. Browne also embraces the laughable chaos of slapstick situations. Their love of slapstick matches Clemens's comic style. Clemens and Wright, however, clearly outpace Browne in their ability with the tall tale and the hoax, those staples of frontier regions. The frontier tradition of the extravagant, the disreputable, and the vulgar contributes whatever is "low" in the comic styles of these writers. The Gentleman Roarer provides a template for the comic characters of Artemus

179. William Dean Howells, "Mark Twain," 781.

Ward, Dan De Quille, and Mark Twain. The contradiction of being the eccentric buffoon who nevertheless speaks for centric values provides a basic enabling structure that allows comic exuberance to challenge yet apparently fit the genteel norm. Each writer, however, must decide how to acceptably package the potential subversiveness of that comic exuberance.

Sam Clemens proved to be more daring in his packaging. Although Artemus Ward exhibits enough wild and disreputable behavior to add the figure to the list of Gentleman Roarers, Charles Farrar Browne's comic style in the Artemus Ward letters projects as much light-hearted whimsy in his character as wildly comic behavior. In contrast, comic anger must be counted as an important humor of Mark Twain, one which gives the character a sharp edge to be used darkly or irreverently, qualities that do not distinguish Artemus Ward. Notably, such comic anger does appear with Dan De Quille, but Wright chooses not to make it a leading trait of his comic alter ego. Despite Clemens in his early periodical work giving Mark Twain a fanciful and whimsical tone at times, the figure more frequently displays an acerbic, sarcastic, or just plain cranky humor. Despite some comic anger in certain Artemus Ward letters, Browne shows much more restraint than Clemens, largely because Artemus Ward's anger occurs in staged fictional scenarios, whereas Mark Twain's comic anger is also directed at actual people.

Reviews of *The Celebrated Jumping Frog* indicate the success Clemens had in his packaging of Mark Twain's comic energy. Despite the dangers of slang and burlesque marking the book as "low," reviewers were not just generally positive; more importantly, they often cast the book's comic qualities into terms that matched polite society's sense of propriety. Thus the humor is "healthy good humor" *(New York Evening Express),* "quaint" *(New York Times),* and "genial" *(London Fun, New York Herald).*[180] Given the Bohemian attitude in the book toward staples of polite literature such as sentimental tales of love, these judgments about the book's comic quality portend the significant prospect of reaching a readership high on the scale of taste. Much of the positive reaction came from the critics' sense that Mark Twain possessed the other requisite for polite society's acceptance of comic writing besides "genial and genuine" humor, namely, a moral seriousness that directs laughter. Whatever geniality and proper decorum of humor appropriate for the entire family that reviewers could discover in Mark Twain, the moral seriousness they found had more long-term consequences for the subversive power of Sam Clemens's comic style than low elements did. The *San Francisco Bulletin* clearly expresses this underlying purpose: "Beneath the surface of his pleasantry lies a rich vein of serious thought. He

---

180. Unless otherwise noted, quotes from reviews can be found in Louis J. Budd, ed., *Mark Twain: The Contemporary Reviews,* 25–31.

instructs as well as amuses and even his broadest jokes have a moral more or less obvious."[181] Other reviewers imply this aspect when they speak of "keen satire" (*Brooklyn Eagle*), "pithy wisdom" (*New York Times*), and "satirical power."[182] Some reviewers praise the serious, underlying purpose of Mark Twain's jokes in terms that highlight the reportorial skills at the foundation of Sam Clemens's comic talent. Thus the *Boston Transcript* notes the "sagacity of observation [and] keen perception of character," while the *Sacramento Union* speaks of "keen observation [and] a quick perception of oddity in everyday life." For the reviewer in the *Californian*, Mark Twain shows "shrewd observation [and] keen perception of the foibles of character [which suggests] a certain value and significance quite independent [of laughter]." Richard Ogden had noted before *The Celebrated Jumping Frog*'s publication that Mark Twain was a "thoughtful and discriminating observer—a quality which underlies his love of fun and humor, and gives it a peculiar force." Bret Harte had also praised Mark Twain for his high-culture moral purpose: he is "an original and broadly humorous writer [who] has a shrewdness and a certain hearty abhorrence of shams which will make his faculty serviceable to mankind."[183] Here is the ennobling quality that Harte did not find in the work of Charles Farrar Browne as Artemus Ward.

Clemens, then, does not merely indulge the lawless quality of comic energy, for that would cast Mark Twain as the Backwoods Roarer Redux. The more subversive transgression of genteel norms by Clemens does not occur at the vulgar end of the Scylla and Charybdis dilemma—as much as he may have enjoyed employing those elements. Rather, the more dangerous transgression contradicted the rule against stringent satire. Sam Clemens's irreverence with centric norms initially focused on burlesquing literary genres, but that attitude often extended to the ideas and customs that informed those genres. Charles Webb stands as the model for Clemens in this regard, presenting an authentic Bohemian version of culture in contrast with Bret Harte's ultimate embrace of centric geniality. Webb's Bohemian view of what should be praised as the best in culture was important for Sam Clemens's development as a comic writer because it showed him a way to aspire to the higher reaches of culture, as it was represented in literary periodicals, without losing the fiercer aspects of Mark Twain's humors. Rather than emphasizing a genial humor that displays no ill-natured behavior but instead features kindliness, delicacy, and charity, Charles Webb, especially through his pseudonym "Inigo," created a comic style in which acerbic satire, witty comments, and outrageous

181. *San Francisco Bulletin*, "Mark Twain's New Book," 1.

182. *Sacramento Union*, review of *Jumping Frog*, 1.

183. Ibid., 1; *Californian*, review of *Jumping Frog*, 9 [June 1]; Richard Ogden, [Ed. comment for "Mark Twain at Honolulu"], 5; Bret Harte, "From California: A New Lecturer in the Field," 1.

puns mixed with humorous anger and an occasional moment of slapstick. Webb routinely embodied the edgy comic *feuilletoniste* in a way that Harte's Bohemian pose rarely achieved. Only Webb can match Clemens, for instance, in the vehemence of his comic attacks on children. Only Webb approaches Clemens in his moments of Juvenalian fury at an ostensibly respectable society. Clemens most resembles Webb of all his early contemporaries, not only due to the intensity of their comic energy, but also due to its volume, that is, their consistent willingness to use all manner of comic devices—witty satire, elaborate puns, double entendre, sexual allusions, impious jokes, disreputable behavior, and mere slapstick—in order to challenge and disrupt centric patterns of thought and behavior.

An equal measure of questioning respectable society, however, comes not from the frontal assaults on the tired clichés of accepted literary standards nor from the ridicule heaped on the self-elected, the sanctified such as Fitz Smythe, but rather from the power of Sam Clemens's comic playfulness, which casts Mark Twain as an agent of the pleasure principle. In this role Mark Twain resembles Sut Lovingood. Just as Sut enjoys yarning for its own sake, Mark Twain at times assumes the persona of the garrulous narrator who fails to tell the promised story and talks instead about whatever interests him at the moment. Uniquely Mark Twain is his role of parodic *flâneur,* the comic man-about-town who bungles the *flâneur*'s duty to explicate and instead embodies the pure pleasure of merely talking about vagabond wanderings. Donning this persona, Sam Clemens expresses the ultimate Bohemian mentality, traveling without apparent limit, and indulges in the ultimate Bohemian assignment, reporting on whatever aspects of that travel fit the observer's mood. Sam Clemens's success by early 1866 in aiming for the most respectable of audiences in the periodical world ironically allowed him to write two sets of travel letters in which he continued to develop a subversively comic questioning of respectability. As Mark Twain travels to Hawai'i and then back to New York City via Central America, the profounder questions that gave Sam Clemens his clear moral purpose and his "call" to literature of a low order—what constitutes respectability, what values and behaviors create the difference between the sanctified and the unsanctified, the civilized and the savage—remain to be more deeply delved into, talked about, and laughed over.

# Act Four

## CORRESPONDENT ON ASSIGNMENT

# SCENE ONE

WORK AND LEISURE IN TWO CULTURES

## Sam Clemens in Hawai'i

I HAVE JUST GOT BACK FROM A SEA VOYAGE—FROM THE BEAUTIFUL
ISLAND OF MAUI. . . . IT HAS BEEN A PERFECT JUBILEE TO ME IN THE
WAY OF PLEASURE. I HAVE NOT WRITTEN A SINGLE LINE, & HAVE NOT
ONCE THOUGHT OF BUSINESS, OR CARE, OR HUMAN TOIL OR TROUBLE
OR SORROW OR WEARINESS.

LETTER TO MOLLIE CLEMENS, MAY 22, 1866

I GENERALLY GET UP AT ELEVEN O'CLOCK, BECAUSE I AM NATURALLY
LAZY, AS YOU WELL KNOW.

LETTER TO WILL BOWEN, AUGUST 25, 1866

Hawai'i today is a premier travel destination, a place celebrated not just for its scenery and climate but also for signifying "vacation," a psychic landscape where no work takes place. By the 1860s, the Hawai'ian Islands had already begun to acquire the image of a travel destination to escape the routine of the workaday world. The California Steam Navigation Company, which owned the steamship *Ajax,* in which Clemens would reach Hawai'i, advertised its new route to the islands by calling it "a most favorable opportunity for invalids and pleasure seekers to enjoy the salubrious climate of the Hawaiian Group."[1]

Clemens implied his own wish to escape to the fabled repose of Hawai'i as early as March 1864 when he wrote in a letter to his sister that "Joe Goodman is gone to the Sandwich Islands" and that he had wanted to go with him (CL 1:275). In another letter, this one sent to William Wright after Clemens had moved to San Francisco, he noted a mutual acquaintance's departure for "the Sandwich Islands," which again stimulated his desire to escape from routine. Thinking about traveling to Hawai'i has given him "the 'Gypsy' only in a mild form" (CL 1:304). When the *Ajax* in January 1866 had steamed from San Francisco on its first trip to Honolulu, Sam wrote his mother and sister shortly after, mentioning the event and the fact that the fifty-two passengers were "the cream of the town." "I got an invitation,

1. *San Francisco Alta California,* [Hawai'i and the *Ajax*], 4.

but I could not accept it, because there would be no one to write my correspondence while I was gone. But I am so sorry now. If the Ajax were back I would go—quick!—and throw up the correspondence. Where could a man catch such another crowd together?" (CL 1:329–30). Giving up his regular *Enterprise* correspondence to join a crowd of pleasure seekers would have been a golden opportunity to indulge in a thoroughgoing holiday from the constant pressure of writing for periodicals to make a living. Given his association of Hawai'i with holiday for the past two years, the same period in which Clemens had worked so hard to create a solid reputation for his Mark Twain pseudonym, no wonder he laments not accepting the invitation to be part of "the cream" of San Francisco society when the *Ajax* first arrived in Honolulu on January 27, 1866.

Besides mentioning Hawai'i, Sam's January letter to his mother and sister retails plans for books; his ambitions were growing with his reputation. Nevertheless, he soon writes again to say that he is leaving for "the Sandwich Islands," not to report that he has accomplished significant progress on his book plans. The change suggests that Clemens cannot decide about how to execute a desire to move beyond periodicals to authoring a book. A Nevada newspaper article about this time also reflects the indecision with its report of his plan to travel into the interior of the United States and down the Mississippi River after the Hawai'i trip (CL 1:331n8). In any case, Clemens could now afford to give up his regular correspondence for the *Enterprise*. Joe Goodman was evidently not prepared to pay for letters from Hawai'i, but the *Sacramento Union* was, at a rate equal to what Clemens was receiving from Goodman. Clemens probably had expressed his sense of lost opportunity to Charles Webb, who then arranged for Clemens to become a special correspondent to the California newspaper. Webb had written his "John Paul" letters for the *Union* almost since he had arrived in San Francisco in 1863 and therefore knew the editors and owners well.[2]

In 1866, the *Sacramento Union* was "the greatest and most powerful journal in the West."[3] The *Union* owners must have seen the suggestion by Webb to hire Clemens as a confluence of good fortune. After the favorable notices in the eastern press and the particular success of "Jim Smiley and His Jumping Frog" late in 1865, the Mark Twain pseudonym clearly had a sufficient audience to be a worthwhile investment. Moreover, the mere existence of a regular steamship route between San Francisco and Honolulu guaranteed that Hawai'i, and more specifically trade with Hawai'i, would be a topic of interest. Congress had already

2. The rate of pay for the letters is mentioned in a letter to his mother and sister dated March 5, 1866. The evidence for Webb as the probable link to the *Sacramento Union* can be found in a 1900 letter from Webb to Edmund Clarence Stedman (CL 1:333–34n1).

3. Ezra Dane, introduction to *Letters from the Sandwich Islands, Written for the "Sacramento Union" by Mark Twain*, viii–ix.

voted monies to establish a mail steamer service between the United States and China by way of Honolulu and Japan.[4] Those monies had encouraged interest in Hawai'i from the business community, spurring the California Steam Navigation Company to inaugurate a regular steamship run to the islands out of San Francisco. Hiring Clemens to write travel letters on Hawai'i signed with the popular Mark Twain pseudonym must have seemed to the *Union* editors like a double surety for attracting interested readers on a major topic of public concern.

Interest in the Kingdom of Hawai'i had for some time prior to 1866 been especially strong on the West Coast, but also persistent throughout the United States. Agricultural imports from Hawai'i to California had been routine before the Civil War, and the war created an even bigger market for Hawai'i's growers. Trade in horses and in sea otter fur had also established a link to California.[5] The *San Francisco Bulletin* had correspondents from Honolulu as early as 1860. The well-established system of newspaper exchanges insured that during the 1850s routine paragraphs of news about the island kingdom appeared not only in influential East Coast papers such as Horace Greeley's *New York Tribune* but also in important Midwest papers such as the *Cleveland Plain Dealer,* where Charles Browne had started his Artemus Ward letters. A letter in the *Plain Dealer* written by "Clevelander" recounts the rhythm of business dictated by the whaling ships and gives details about wages and the cost of living.[6] During the 1840s, American whalers had begun to stop routinely in Honolulu or Lahaina for outfitting. For pious Christians in the United States, the Hawai'ian Islands had been a topic of interest since the 1820s, when the American Missionary Board had sent its first companies to begin the work of converting the Hawai'ians. A comic column called "Ollopodrida" suggests how familiar people in California might have been with Hawai'i and its history. In a section called "His Royal Highness," which describes a local San Francisco character known as "Emperor" Norton, the writer characterizes the would-be emperor with a variety of comparisons to well-known rulers, a list that includes saying Norton has "the quiet deportment of Kamehameha," the first king of Hawai'i.[7]

For Clemens personally, Hawai'i would have taken visible shape in the Hawai'ians he could see in Virginia City. "The sidewalks [of Virginia City] were thronged with persons of every color and nationality—negroes, Sandwich Islanders, Chinamen and Indians, mingling promiscuously with those wearing

4. Ralph S. Kuykendall, *Twenty Critical Years, 1854–1874,* 169ff.

5. Edward D. Beechert, *Honolulu: The Crossroads of the Pacific,* 46.

6. *Cleveland Plain Dealer,* "Affairs in Honolulu"; "From the Sandwich Islands" [April 16]; "From the Sandwich Islands" [June 1]; "Clevelander," "From the Sandwich Islands."

7. *Golden Era,* "Ollopodrida," 5.

whiter skins."[8] Undoubtedly, San Francisco presented the same human spectacle. After 1860, Honolulu had become a primary source of sailors for all manner of ships traveling from the islands. In 1868, five thousand to six thousand Hawai'ians were estimated to be living and working on the Pacific Coast as well as in the interior.[9] The scattered presence in the west of those mostly young Hawai'ian men implied their adventurous spirit, but it also signified the hardworking life of sailors, a counterimage to the tourist view of Hawai'i as a land of eternal repose.

Clemens's behavior during his stay in the Hawai'ian Islands consisted of a startling combination of apparent indolence and very hard work. Coming in the middle of his perambulations around the Hawai'ian Islands, the letter from Sam to sister-in-law Mollie quoted in the epigraph demonstrates that his visit to Mau'i to investigate the sugar industry had transformed into a complete holiday—a jubilee. He apparently had planned to visit the islands of Kaua'i, Mau'i, and Hawai'i as well as the main island of O'ahu, but his initial leisurely pace caused him to change his itinerary. Because in the first part of his visit he had spent five weeks on Mau'i and had not written "a single line," he subsequently rushed through a horseback excursion of the Big Island, Hawai'i, in three weeks. His haste resulted in saddle boils and left him with neither the time nor the inclination to rush to Kaua'i after he had recovered. He spent his last month in the Kingdom of Hawai'i on O'ahu instead. Part of that month included interviewing the survivors of the *Hornet* disaster, despite the effects of the saddle boils, and writing the first newspaper account for the United States of their ordeal. In addition, Clemens attended and wrote about the mourning ceremonies and funeral for Princess Victoria Kamāmalu, the heir to the Hawai'ian throne. However, Clemens also spent half of that last month at the ranch of a prominent American family—again, not writing a single line. The rhythm of the trip to the Kingdom of Hawai'i therefore reveals a schizophrenic quality, a frenetic work schedule colliding with a very leisurely vacation pace. Clemens from the outset probably thought of the *Sacramento Union* assignment to write up Hawai'i in his inimitable Mark Twain style as a working vacation.[10]

Work interrupting leisure fits a comic self-image Sam Clemens liked to project. Even though he had supported himself since he was a teenager, Clemens had

8. *Gold Hill News*, "On a Saturday," 3.

9. Beechert, *Honolulu*, 70; see also Harold Whitman Bradley, *American Frontier in Hawai'i: The Pioneers, 1789–1843*, 228.

10. In his May 22, 1866, letter to Mollie from Honolulu on O'ahu, Sam stated his intention to visit the islands of Hawai'i and Kaua'i after returning from Mau'i. Presumably, he had intended from the outset to visit all four islands, which held the majority of the population. The itinerary for Clemens: leave San Francisco, March 7, 1866; arrive in Honolulu, March 18; leave for Mau'i around April 15 or 16; return to Honolulu, May 22; leave for Hawai'i, May 26; return to Honolulu, June 16; leave for San Francisco, July 19; arrive in San Francisco, August 13.

a habit of presenting himself as "naturally a lazy, idle, good for nothing vagabond" (CL 1:264) or as "the Genius of Indolence" (CL 1:329). His legendary drawl could become exaggerated at times as a theatrical accompaniment to this impersonation of "natural" laziness. The impersonation made an impression, judging from a remembrance by an acquaintance of the time out west, Carrie Pixley, who called Sam "a big hearted, restless, lazy, good natured chap, that every one loved" (CL 1:216n8). Other contemporaries confirmed the image: "Clemens was sloth-like in movement, had an intolerable drawl, and punished those who offended him by long-drawn sneering speech"; "Mark Twain was abnormally lazy and made Dan [William Wright], who was almost his peer in humor, do nearly all the work"; "Sam was kind of lazy or slow in his movements"; "Mr. Clemens was not liked much in Virginia [City] by his office associates, partly from his laziness and shiftlessness."[11] Even after his West Coast days, Clemens projected an image of extraordinary laziness for public consumption: "I am naturally lazy"; "I am . . . phenomenally lazy, lazy in every way you can possibly imagine"; "I *have* seen slower people than I am—and more deliberate people than I am—and even quieter and more listless, and lazier than I am. But they were dead."[12] Annie Moffett Webster remembers a comic song sung by Clemens about his own laziness (MTBM 39–40).

"Leisure versus work," then, usefully organizes an examination of Mark Twain's travel letters from the Kingdom of Hawai'i because the assignment to report on the islands as well as Clemens's attitude toward the assignment were clearly bifurcated by the opposition. The letters partially record a tourist's holiday, full of jokes and other signs of pleasure, meant, as far as the *Sacramento Union* editors were concerned, to convey to their readers an exotic place in Mark Twain's breezy style. The travel letters from Hawai'i also partially record a veteran reporter's awareness that the *Ajax* represents a potential step forward in further binding the Hawai'ian and United States economies, a process well established by 1866 because of the long-standing whaling trade and the burgeoning sugar industry. The opposition also provides a way to understand the Americans living in the Kingdom of Hawai'i in 1866, especially to comprehend the influence of the American missionaries on all things Hawai'ian. Moreover, mapping "leisure versus work" reveals how Mark Twain in Hawai'i becomes a vehicle for Sam Clemens to describe his own culture as much as a means to describe an exotic society. Because American culture becomes an important topic in the letters, Mark Twain

11. McEwen, "Heroic Days," 15; Daggett, "Recollections," 15; Goodman, "Memories," 3; *San Francisco Illustrated Press,* "Mark Twain," 22.

12. *New York Sun,* "Not Quite an Editor: The Story of Mark Twain's Connection to the *Hartford Courant,*" 47; *Melbourne Argus,* "Mark Twain in Sydney: A Further Interview," 112; CG 108.

for the first time explores a cultural comparison, one that examines the hybrid society that had been created in the Kingdom of Hawai'i, but one that also includes satiric critiques of assumptions underlying Sam Clemens's own culture.

This de facto investigation of two cultures in the "Letters from the Kingdom of Hawai'i" takes place within Clemens's basic strategy of elaborating both master roles for Mark Twain as narrator.[13] The unsanctified newspaper reporter employs several tones for his comic voice, depending on how Clemens uses Mark Twain's new comic sidekick, Mr. Brown. This tonal variety allows Mark Twain to be satiric as well as to indulge in low humor, the character behaving in pompously centric or subversively eccentric ways. To contrast with the fun generated by a pair of comic characters, Clemens also prominently displays Mark Twain the respectable and reliable reporter. The competent local editor transforms into an out-of-town correspondent to discuss everyday commerce in the islands as well as detail extraordinary events, such as the *Hornet* disaster. Clemens had made this change in duties when he worked for the *Enterprise* and reported on the Nevada legislature and the territory's constitutional convention. Because the correspondence in this case originated from an exotic locale, reporting becomes writing travel letters, and Mark Twain often sounds like the narrator of a standard travel book. In effect, Clemens assumes without parody the *flâneur*'s role found in the *Californian* sketches.

The disappearance of the subversive comic *flâneur* in the *Union* letters demonstrates how the demands of serious reporting made on Mark Twain the narrator results in a noticeable curtailing of eccentricity in Mark Twain the character. Despite all the subversive possibilities of adding an unsanctified comic attitude to the narration of travel letters, Clemens segregated the pleasure of laughter in the Hawai'i correspondence. Covering the commerce and industry of the islands, complete with dry statistics, tends to encase Mark Twain's voice in an earnest monotone. Thus the narrator often projects the normative values of gentility, for example, when he provides the fine "word-painting" prose expected of travel books with literary aspirations. With Americans as his main informants and American culture perceived by those informants to be struggling against a deleterious British influence on Hawai'i's king, Clemens, in a significant portion of the correspondence, virtually buries Mark Twain's recently constructed Bohemian aspect so that his literary alter ego often sounds anything but unsanctified.[14]

---

13. The correspondence from Hawai'i was not given any title when it originally ran in the *Union,* and Clemens never republished the letters. I will refer to them collectively as "Letters from the Kingdom of Hawai'i." I have examined the original letters in the *Union* as well as A. Grove Day's reprintings.

14. See Smith, *Mark Twain: Development,* 13.

## AMERICAN MISSIONARIES AND HAWAI'IAN CULTURE:
### INDUSTRY AS SALVATION

RAISED 30,000 LBS LAST YEAR [OF SEA ISLAND COTTON] WILL RAISE
50,000 THIS. ALL THAT IS NEEDED IS LABOR—INDUSTRY—NATIVES
WON'T PICK IT EVERY DAY—LAZY & SHIFTLESS.

WHALERS LIKE KANAKAS BETTER THAN ANY OTHER SAILORS—TEM-
PERATE, STRONG, FAITHFUL, PEACEABLE & ORDERLY.

———

NOTEBOOK ENTRIES DURING HAWAI'I TRIP, 1866

THE HAWAI'IANS WERE IN OLD DAYS A STRONG AND HARD-WORKING
PEOPLE SKILLED IN CRAFTS AND POSSESSED OF MUCH LEARNING. . . .
CULTIVATION OF THE LAND WAS THEIR MAIN INDUSTRY.

———

S. N. KAMAKAU, "HAWAI'I BEFORE FOREIGN INNOVATIONS,"
KA NUPEPA KU'OKO'A, DECEMBER 7, 1867

"The Letters from the Kingdom of Hawai'i" record Clemens's four-month island experience; they also record what Clemens learned from various informants. Clemens's interrogation of knowledgeable individuals began even before arrival. Coming over to Hawai'i with him on the *Ajax* were not only three whaling captains who provided their views on the whaling industry and on the prospects of a routine steamship route between San Francisco and Honolulu, but also Americans born and raised in the islands. These individuals were sons and daughters of the missionaries who had begun arriving in Hawai'i in 1820. Reverend Thomas Thurston was returning to Hawai'i after eight years of training for the ministry at Yale University and at Union Seminary in New York City. With him was his married sister, Mary Thurston Hayden, and her three children. Their parents were Asa and Lucy Thurston, who had been part of the first company of missionaries. Also on board was William Henry Dimond, son of Henry Dimond, who was part of the seventh company of missionaries. Dimond was a captain in the Union army.[15]

15. The passenger list in the *Honolulu Friend* ([*Ajax* Passenger List], 32) has "Rev G T Thurston," "Mrs Mary T Hayden and three children," and "Capt W H Dimond and lady, Misses Dimond."

Understanding the public writing-up of Hawai'i in the letters to the *Union* is complicated by the fact that Clemens also writes up Hawai'i in two private places: letters to family and friends as well as notebook entries to himself. Clemens's notebooks used during his stay in Hawai'i indicate that en route he was having a variety of conversations with passengers who are telling him what they know and think about native Hawai'ians, their government and politics, missionary influence in politics, superstitions, population, religious factions, agriculture, the struggle Americans are having against English influences, and the blue laws in Honolulu, among other topics. The majority of notebook entries made before arrival indicate that the three whaling captains were probably the most accessible initial informants for Clemens. Comments on the American missionary community's struggle against English influences on the royal family were most likely from the Thurstons and/or Dimond. Business as a topic implies that some potential informants on board who called Hawai'i home were neither whalers nor the children of missionaries.

Throughout his stay in the islands, Clemens used Americans as his chief means of information. The method was obvious. Whatever letters of introduction he had were from Americans either in California or Nevada to the American community in Hawai'i. Franklin Austin's reminiscence has Sam Clemens pulling out a batch of letters and selecting one to use to introduce himself to Franklin's father, Judge Austin. Clemens's traveling companion during this part of his journey around the Big Island Hawai'i was an Englishman named Edward Howard. Austin reports that Howard said he came with Clemens from the Volcano House to Hilo because he showed him the batch of letters, suggesting that he would be well received, including one to Captain Thomas Spencer.[16] People like Captain Spencer would naturally be of interest to the American audience back home; they would want to know about the condition of the American community in Hawai'i, both as an end in itself and as part of reporting on business prospects. Because Americans constituted most of the business community in the islands, discussing their habits and views necessarily moved from business topics to cultural and political issues. The predictable results of this method in the letters is a habitual reinforcement of American views. At times, Clemens even acts as a mouthpiece for the American community in Hawai'i.

Take, for instance, the issue of whether Hawai'ians are typically hardworking or whether they are inherently lazy. The comments from the notebooks used as epigraphs for this section, one obviously recorded on shipboard and one written

16. Franklin H. Austin, "Mark Twain Incognito—A Reminiscence," 250; see also 201, 253. Austin's memory is not always accurate. He places Sam Clemens's visit in 1871 and recounts a conversation between his mother and Clemens about the authorship of *The Celebrated Jumping Frog of Calavaras County and Other Stories,* a copy of which they supposedly owned at the time.

down after Clemens had been on Oʻahu for a time, suggest that the American perception on the matter was inconsistent as a whole. There can be no doubt, however, what the American missionaries' view was and had been. From their perspective, the leisurely and apparently carefree way of life found in Hawaiʻi does not just demonstrate literal laziness but signifies moral sloth, too.[17] The Reverend John Emerson, an early missionary, wrote to his brother, "I cannot go on preaching to a lot of people sitting on their haunches with no purpose in life."[18] A report written in 1830 by Asa Thurston and Artemus Bishop, prominent members of the first company of missionaries, claims that "the mass of inhabitants [live life as] a round of indolence, with barely sufficient labor to keep them from starvation. . . . They must be taught how to work [because they have] idle and sluggish habits."[19] In order to attain salvation, Hawaiʻians clearly needed to be converted not just to a belief in Christ but also to a faith in the Protestant work ethic.

The contradictory nature of American perceptions about the capacity of Hawaiʻians to work results from a combination of myths and realities, providing a good example of how one culture can misunderstand another. To begin with, there is the Western expectation, derived from the myth of Polynesia as a paradise, that no work takes place in Hawaiʻi. Notwithstanding this myth of paradise, plenty of hard work was obviously required to build the infrastructure for living in traditional Hawaiʻian society. James Cook and George Vancouver had been impressed by the amount of work required for the construction of irrigated taro plantations, for instance. Moreover, the habit of hard work in traditional Hawaiʻi survived at least the initial years of postcontact: Archibald Menzies, who visited Kauaʻi in 1792–1793, said that the efforts to cultivate and irrigate the land "surpassed anything of the kind we had ever seen before"; Archibald Campbell, who lived in Honolulu from 1809 to 1810, thought Hawaiʻians worked harder than any other people he had seen.[20]

Despite these opinions, the mythic expectation of no work appears to be confirmed by the experience of others, like Thurston and Bishop. In a subsistence economy such as existed in precontact Hawaiʻi, a strict rhythm of hard work and holiday would have been the norm for the commoner, and much of that work would be maintaining the basics: fishing, tending taro fields, repairing fishponds and houses, making clothes, and cooking meals. However, by definition, no surpluses exist in a subsistence economy—and thus no markets. Because Hawaiʻians divided their calendar into the domains of the gods Ku and Lono, which translated into strict periods of work and leisure; because the reciprocal relationship between

17. Gavin Daws, *Shoal of Time: A History of the Hawaiʻian Islands,* 65, 178.
18. Quoted in Noel Jacob Kent, *Hawaiʻi: Islands under the Influence,* 28.
19. Quoted in Bradley, *Frontier,* 362–63.
20. Archibald Menzies, *Hawaiʻi Nei 128 Years Ago,* 105; Daws, *Shoal,* 49.

commoner *(makaʻainana)* and high chief *(aliʻi nui)* meant that the former supports the latter in exchange for administrative organization and military protection; and because the concept of *ʻohana* (extended family) guaranteed that any chance surplus was shared, work in the modern Western sense, that is, within a market economy to accumulate wealth, could appear to Americans to be virtually nonexistent. Lilikala Kameʻeleihiwa argues that the hallmark of civilized behavior for precontact Hawaiʻian society was generosity, a willingness to share wealth *(waiwai)*, the opposite of capitalism's assumption that work exists to accumulate wealth. A proper high chief would therefore redistribute any forms of accumulated wealth (except land, which no one owned).[21]

Americans understood the contrasting economies within their own cultural perspective, but this inevitable viewpoint often gave Americans (and Westerners in general) the idea that Hawaiʻians were incapable of sustained work, especially if their experience of Hawaiʻian culture had been framed by the cultural prejudice inherent in the myth of a Polynesian paradise. Despite Clemens's efforts to comprehend Hawaiʻi through his reading and his powers of observation, misinterpretations were all too easy for him to make or repeat. His own cultural perspective, reinforced and elaborated by his informants in the American community in Hawaiʻi, not only effectively deprived him of crucial facts but more importantly also created a misleading framework for understanding what he saw and heard. Thus Mark Twain will wonder how a road or a stone edifice can possibly be built by any Hawaiʻian society, either an ancient version or the one he is experiencing (MTLH 252, 254). In fact, the irrigation systems, terracing, and fishpond complexes Clemens would have seen were all clear evidence of the engineering skills and intensive work of precontact Hawaiʻian society.[22]

Clemens's confusion is partially understandable. The society described by Cook, Vancouver, Menzies, and Campbell had existed because earlier the old ways were still largely intact. By the mid-1850s, well before Clemens arrived in the islands, that society had radically changed, mostly because of the American whaling fleet.[23] Significant traditional cultural practices nevertheless remained,

21. Lilikala Kameʻeleihiwa, *Native Land and Foreign Desires: "Pehea La E Pono Ai?"* 11. For the concept of the *ʻohana*, see E. S. Craighill Handy and Mary K. Pukui, *The Polynesian Family System in Kaʻu, Hawaiʻi*, 2–3; E. S. Craighill Handy and Elizabeth G. Handy, *Native Planters in Old Hawaiʻi: Their Life, Lore, and Environment*, 287–88; and Irving Goldman, *Ancient Polynesian Society*, 235–37. E. S. Craighill Handy (*Cultural Revolution in Hawaiʻi*, 18–20) quotes many early Western visitors about the industry of Hawaiʻians, especially for agricultural practices that included extensive irrigation systems.

22. Handy and Handy, *Native Planters*, 25–26.

23. Ralph S. Kuykendall, *Foundation and Transformation, 1778–1854*, 305–13; Daws, *Shoal*, 169–72; see also Handy, *Cultural Revolution*.

giving Hawai'ian society a distinctively hybrid quality. The *Mahele* in 1848 illustrates the radical change ascendent Western ways had on Hawai'ian society as well as the fact that traditional ways could still regulate behavior. *Mahele* (division) promulgated a set of new laws replacing the traditional land system of the Hawai'ians with a Western capitalist system. Theoretically, this change could have benefited common Hawai'ians, who were awarded under the reform portions of land to claim or to buy that were separate from lands set aside for the chiefs. Some Americans certainly felt that way. In practice, however, the *Mahele* spawned disastrous results for the common Hawai'ian, who often did not understand a concept like "deed," and who therefore became easy prey for the unscrupulous or who were effectively disenfranchised by Westerners, including missionary families, who understood how the new system worked.[24] Many Hawai'ians simply elected to continue to live outside the new schema of property rights as well as the wage system of capitalism. For the missionaries among the American community, Hawai'ians who made that choice were thought to be idle and unproductive.[25]

Though many Hawai'ians chose not to work in the Western sense, there were also some who were quite ready to labor for wages. When the gold rush in California created an enormous demand for produce of all kinds, especially potatoes, the Kula district on Mau'i, already known as one of the best areas for growing potatoes, was expanded by giving small lots to enterprising Hawai'ians who were eager to cash in on the new market.[26] The perspective of planters noted in one of the epigraphs indicates that many Hawai'ians were still able and willing in 1866 to perform work in a manner understood as normal by Americans. Given that traditional Hawai'i comprised the section of the Polynesian triangle that had distinguished itself through its extensive and elaborate agriculture, their ability and perhaps even their willingness should not surprise.[27] "The economy with which these people laid out and managed their ground and the neatness with which they cultivated their little fields made the whole valley appear more like a rich garden than a plantation."[28] More gardeners than farmers, Hawai'ians kept their livelihood "centered in the cultivation of the soil." Agriculture was far more important than fishing, and the "continuous organized enterprise . . . essential to systematic gardening operations" in Hawai'i had no comparison in other Polynesian societies. Moreover, the extent to which arable land was under

---

24. Daws, *Shoal,* 124–28; Kame'eleihiwa, *Native Land,* especially chapter 10.
25. Daws, *Shoal,* 178.
26. Kuykendall, *Foundation,* 321.
27. Samuel M. Kamakau, *Ruling Chiefs of Hawai'i,* 237ff.
28. Menzies, *Hawai'i Nei,* 185.

cultivation and the variety of plants cultivated indicated an intensive pursuit of agriculture unmatched elsewhere in the Pacific.[29]

While the epigraph taken from Samuel Kamakau's history underscores the Hawai'ians' strong agricultural tradition, it was at sea, not on land, that Hawai'ians flourished under the wage system of capitalism. As early as 1800, Westerners discovered Hawai'ians were excellent sailors, and when the American whaling fleet became the commercial lifeblood of the islands beginning in the 1840s, Hawai'ians maintained their reputation. So many able young men were leaving the islands to work on ships during the period 1845–1847 that discussion ensued about the wisdom of continuing to allow so many to leave and potentially never return.[30] Edward Beechert estimates that several thousand Hawai'ian men were living outside the kingdom, all along the western coast of North America, by the time Clemens visited Hawai'i.[31] Given the notebook entry that quotes one of the whaling captains on board the *Ajax* about the positive work habits of Hawai'ians, it is no wonder that so many were hired as sailors.

Some of this discrepancy among opinions on the Hawai'ian capacity for work can be attributed to where one was looking. Some industrious Hawai'ians were at work in rural districts while even more able Hawai'ians could not be found in the islands because they were at sea most of the time or living and working elsewhere. Making judgments about Hawai'ian work habits based on the native population in the port towns of Honolulu and Laihaina could not provide an accurate account. Honolulu and Laihaina, in the context of whaling, acted as powerful incubators for all manner of indolence and pleasure. Nu'uanu Street, a main thoroughfare in Honolulu, was known as Fid Street (a "fid" is sailors' slang for a drink) because of its barrooms and brothels.[32] Though the more raucous days in the town were over by 1866 because of the decline in the whaling fleet, Honolulu nevertheless still functioned as the principal port for the kingdom, and much of Nu'uanu Street as well as the area near the docks and wharves remained less than respectable when Clemens walked through them.

Some of the discrepancy also occurs due to a difference in cultural attitude about the nature and meaning of work. Hiram Bingham, the leader of the first missionary company, had noted that the Hawai'ians could not be made to work consistently throughout the day but were quite willing to practice *hula* by danc-

---

29. Handy and Handy, *Native Planters*, v–vii, 21, 71. See also Patrick Vinton Kirch, *The Wet and the Dry: Irrigation and Agricultural Intensification in Polynesia*, 252; and Goldman, *Ancient Polynesian Society*, 201–2.

30. Bradley, *Frontier*, 33, 227; Kuykendall, *Foundation*, 312–13.

31. Beechert, *Honolulu*, 70.

32. Daws, *Shoal*, 164ff; see also Richard A. Greer, "Grog Shops and Hotels: Bending the Elbow in Honolulu."

ing for hours in the hot sun.[33] The perceived backwardness of the Hawai'ians on such a fundamental aspect of behavior brought forth a chronic lamentation from the American missionaries. The Puritan strain in Christianity elevated even simple work to the status of virtual prayer, promoted an identity that entwined work and worship, and conceptualized material wealth as a sign of God's grace, thereby transforming industry into a means of salvation. Traditional Hawai'ian religion, the system of *kapu* (taboo) that regulated worship of the gods and dictated social behavior, did not treat work in a similar fashion. "Idle hands are the devil's workshop" would make no sense in Hawai'ian culture. *Kanaka'aina* (commoners) were responsible for producing the food that not only fed themselves but also maintained their *ali'i* (chiefs). Though *mo'i* (paramount chief or king) and *ali'i nui* (high chiefs) approached the status of gods, working hard for them did not operate as a means of salvation in an afterlife. Commoners were also free to abandon a specific *ali'i* who had abused them and to move onto lands controlled by another. Ordinary work was therefore linked primarily to the political district of the *ali'i* and to his individual behavior as a leader who could protect people from the depredations of other *ali'i*.[34] One missionary had noted that "few [Hawai'ians] of either sex devote more than four or five hours of the twenty-four to work."[35] *Kanaka'aina*, however, had no cultural rationale to work more than was strictly necessary. Accumulated wealth was not a sign of the gods' grace. In traditional Hawai'i, any goods owned by *kanaka'aina* could be seized by *ali'i* at any time and for any purpose. "Saving for a rainy day" by accumulating surplus therefore made no sense.

In his *Union* letters from Hawai'i, Clemens supported the American missionaries' perception of Hawai'ians, including their puritanical view on work. This general approbation can be found in letter 16, wherein Mark Twain represents the missionaries as "great men—men who would be great in wider and broader spheres . . . , [as] drilled and hardy veterans" (MTLH 172). The military phrasing turns romantically patriotic when Mark Twain also calls them "devoted old Puritan knights," but that last phrase comes in the middle of a description more notable for the sense of Yankee hardheadedness it conveys. Thus the missionaries are "tenacious, unyielding, tireless, industrious, devoted old Puritan knights who have seen forty years of missionary service; whose time was never fooled away in theorizing, but whose lightest acts always meant business" (MTLH 171). Mark Twain offers the core of a positive representation of the missionaries: worthy descendants of the Puritans and Pilgrims; hardworking, practical Americans

33. Hiram Bingham, *Residence of Twenty-one Years in the Sandwich Islands*, 123.
34. Kamakau, *Ruling Chiefs*, 230.
35. Charles S. Stewart, *A Residence in the Sandwich Islands*, 151.

who are earnest in everything they do. At this point in the letter, Clemens has launched an attack on Bishop Staley, the somewhat unorthodox Anglican bishop of Honolulu, and so the Puritan heritage of the missionaries is invoked as a chauvinistic tactic designed to ridicule the Englishness of Staley. Clemens could be ambivalent about the missionaries until the English butted in—then American pride takes over (NB 1:135n80).

Because praise for the missionaries in Hawai'i defines them in terms that emphasize their tireless industry, they are also praised for their results. Once again, Mark Twain invokes the Americanness of the missionaries, this time by noting that their efforts are imbued with "the spirit of democracy and the religious enthusiasm" underpinning America's "whole religious fabric today" (MTLH 172). In this encomium, the missionaries become not simply God's agents but God's American agents, and conversion to Christianity entails a larger, apparently benevolent conversion to American ideas about politics and human behavior:

> The missionaries have clothed [the natives], educated them, broken up the tyrannous authority of their chiefs, and given them freedom and the right to enjoy whatever the labor of their hands and brains produces, with equal laws for all and punishment for all alike who transgress them. The contrast is so strong—the wonderful benefit conferred upon this people by the missionaries is so prominent, so palpable, and so unquestionable, that the frankest compliment I can pay them, and the best, is simply to point to the conditions of the Sandwich Islanders of Captain Cook's time, and their condition today. Their work speaks for itself. (MTLH 54–55)

Presenting the work of the missionaries as a benevolent influence prima facie of course replicates the standard attitude of Westerners toward indigenous peoples in the Americas as well as Oceania. For Americans, the enterprise of conversion was understood as high-minded on both the political and religious levels, with no question about the disinterested nature of the missionaries' efforts. The proof of their selflessness lies in the fact that they were merely reproducing in Hawai'i the positive transformation of America that had created the United States: the "Puritan spirit which subdued America ... [has] subdued these islanders" (MTLH 172).

Kekuanaoa, the president of the Hawai'ian Assembly and father of King Kamehameha V, embodies the contrast between precontact Hawai'i and the Hawai'i of 1866. He is a paragon of the American missionaries' successful efforts to bring civilization to a benighted people. Dignified and well-dressed as he carries out his legislative duties, Kekuanaoa nevertheless is old enough to have fought with club and spear for Kamehameha the Great in the old days of clan warfare (MTLH 108–9), an image Mark Twain summons in order to heighten the claim of obvious improvement.

The climax of Mark Twain's presentation of the missionaries as disseminators of the benefits of American civilization comes with his repetition of what could be called the myth of origin for the American missionaries in Hawai'i. As with all myth, the story articulates a cultural raison d'être. The mythic quality of the story turns upon the timing of the first missionaries' arrival in Hawai'i. When Kamehameha the Great died in 1819, his son Liholiho became king. However, Kamehameha's favorite wife, Ka'ahumanu, an ambitious and high-spirited queen dowager (but not Liholiho's mother), effectively ruled the kingdom. As a female, though, Ka'ahumanu was restricted in certain ways by Hawai'ian customs and *kapu*. She and Liholiho's mother, Keopuolani, encouraged Liholiho to violate the fundamental *kapu* against men and women eating together in order to symbolize her freedom from such laws.[36] They performed the transgression publicly, and it resulted in a general weakening of belief in the Hawai'ian religion, evidenced by the ensuing destruction of the statues of Hawai'ian gods. The sequence of these events is not disputed, but its import as a mythic narrative lies in the way Clemens links the events in order to provide a foundation for the identity of the missionaries. "The missionary ship arrived in safety shortly afterward, timed by providential exactness to meet the emergency, and the gospel was planted in a virgin soil" (MTLH 247). Told this way, the story implies that the deity always directs the actions of the missionaries, a claim that defines righteousness.

However, righteousness exists only a small step away from self-righteousness. Clemens's perception of the American missionaries' self-righteousness, their sense that they can do no wrong, makes his alignment with them inconsistent. In one notebook used during his stay in the islands, Clemens links the missionaries with self-righteousness by noting the "missionary—I should say *preacher* feature of insincerity & hypocrisy, [that] marks the social atmosphere of the place" (NB 1:133). In another entry, Clemens notes that there are about one hundred preachers in the islands and concludes that there is "more gospel here in proportion to population than any other place in the wide world" (NB 1:135). Although this entry can be read with a variety of tones, ranging from sarcasm to admiring astonishment, when linked with the previous quote, it suggests the smothering nature of the missionary presence in Hawai'i.

In his favorable representation of the missionaries as "Puritan knights" quoted above, Mark Twain says that they have a grip on the Hawai'ians and that they will not let go until they choose to do so (MTLH 172). However, that grip was not just confined to Hawai'ians. Clemens himself clearly felt it when he recorded in another notebook entry the missionaries' negative view of him: they accuse him of murder and arson, he says jokingly (NB 1:133). The essential problem is evident

36. Kamakau, *Ruling Chiefs*, 222–28.

in yet another notebook entry—this one dated July 30, when Clemens was on the voyage back to California—that discusses how the earnestness of the missionaries and their children caused problems for him, who jokes by nature and by profession. Clemens says that missionary children are so distressed by jokes that they cry, and when he talks about negative reactions to his joking, he quotes from the journal of a missionary girl (NB 1:152–53). Thus the missionary community made him feel like John Phoenix in Boston when he (Clemens) "perpetrated the diabolism of a joke" in their presence. The earnestness of the missionaries, so praiseworthy in Clemens's eyes at other times, now works against them.

Not surprisingly, when the *Sacramento Union* letters are read by the missionaries, they are "outraged by [their] levity . . . , & have so expressed themselves—but in sorrow, not in anger" (NB 1:153). In another notebook entry, Clemens returns to the topic of reactions in Honolulu to his letters with a reference to "Whitney about the cats." Henry Whitney, owner and editor of the *Pacific Commercial Advertiser,* had reprinted only part of letter 4, describing Honolulu as having hundreds of cats, despite being on relatively good terms with Clemens according to a printer who worked for Whitney, William Brash.[37] The headnote to the 1866 reprinting of the letter has Whitney saying he wishes that Mark Twain were more "accurate." Clemens apparently has remembered this comment—and perhaps others like it delivered in person when he was in the *Advertiser*'s offices—in the remainder of the entry: "I'll tell you what's the matter with *you*—you have no conception of a joke—of anything but awful long-facedness & petrified facts. You have got *this* spirit on you" (NB 1:154). Maybe this spirit—this lack of a sense of humor on Whitney's part—explains why only part of one letter was reprinted, even though in many places in the letters Mark Twain echoes Whitney's values and political views. For example, Whitney had supported a property qualification to vote during the revision of the constitution in 1864,[38] a change which stayed in the new constitution and which Mark Twain endorsed (MTHL 106). In almost the last entry in his notebook on Hawai'i, Sam Clemens recounts the ambivalent reception he received from American missionary families, and he sums up the ambivalence he felt about them in return (NB 1:165–66). Whitney's recollection of Clemens also seems ambivalent: he says that jokes and stories made Clemens's visits "very welcome," but he also notes that the visits meant "at least one box of cigars disappeared every week on average," suggesting not only that Sam was free with Henry's supply of smokes but also that Sam spent a lot of free time in the office of the *Advertiser*.[39] Also rel-

---

37. *Pacific Commercial Advertiser,* "Hawaii Schools Ready to Observe Mark Twain Day," 9.
38. Henry M. Whitney, "Notes of the Week: The Election"; "Property Qualifications."
39. Henry M. Whitney, "Better Fifty Years in Hawaii Than a Cycle of Cathay," 6.

evant here is Mark Twain pretending in a later sketch that Whitney is a cannibal whose good taste can distinguish among the best families (CG 108). Notably, none of the private comments on missionaries is harsher than ones published in the "Letters from the Kingdom of Hawai'i." However, before examining further how Clemens expresses antipathy to the missionaries, the fullest extent to which Sam Clemens aligns himself in Hawai'i with the missionary point of view will be discussed—when Mark Twain reports on the *hula*.

---

## How *Hula Hula* Turned Mark Twain into a Missionary

THE LASCIVIOUS HULA-HULA . . . WAS PERFORMED BY A CIRCLE OF GIRLS WITH NO RAIMENT ON THEM TO SPEAK OF.

———

"HONOLULU (S.I.) APRIL 1866 [NO. 8]," *SACRAMENTO UNION*, MAY 21, 1866

Clemens in the travel letters from Hawai'i used his literary alter ego to express the doubts he had been recording in his notebook concerning the way in which the American missionaries' puritanical outlook impacted the islands' culture. These doubts indicated a profound ambivalence about both cultures. Though Clemens understood the hypocrisy of the missionaries' self-righteousness, he also allowed Mark Twain to sing their praises. Moreover, when Hawai'ian cultural issues become entwined with a political struggle pitting British against American interests, Clemens strongly backed the United States. The way Clemens, through Mark Twain, represented the performances of *hula* that he saw most obviously represents this centric position.

When Sam Clemens arrived in the Hawai'ian Islands in March 1866 for his four-month whirlwind visit, the kingdom and its society were in transition, especially economically. The islands were shifting from a dependence on whaling, a trade that was dying out, to a dependence on raising sugarcane, a commodity that would soon dominate the islands' economy. The kingdom was also in the middle of a prolonged transition from a traditional oral culture based on allegiances to *ali'i* (chiefs), who ultimately derived their authority from the gods, to a Christian monarchy, one that modeled itself on Britain. Despite Hawai'ian royalty's emulation of the British court, their conversion to Christianity had originated with the American missionaries and their descendants. The hybrid society encountered by Clemens was in significant measure shaped by the struggle between the Congregationalist and republican Americans who dominated the islands' business community and the Anglican and monarchist English who influenced Hawai'i's kings. The king who ruled in 1866 embodied this struggle. Educated at the American missionary school for the children of *ali'i*, Lot Kapuaiwa, as Kamehameha V, turned his back on his upbringing, becoming an uncompromising advocate for Hawai'ian culture who also admired the British monarchy.[40]

In the midst of its transition to a new identity, one very important aspect of Hawai'ian society remained discernibly Polynesian after nearly fifty years of efforts to convert the populace to Western ways: the dances known collectively as *hula*. These dances epitomize Hawai'ian culture, now as well as then. That fact alone renders what Mark Twain has to say about *hula* important to gauge Clemens's reaction to Hawai'ian culture, but he also was lucky to witness an old-style performance of chanting and dancing. This display of Hawai'ian culture in a relatively pure form honored Princess Victoria Kamāmalu, the twenty-seven-year-old sister of King Kamehameha V and presumptive heir to the throne, who died during Clemens's stay in the islands.

What Mark Twain says about *hula* replicates what the American missionaries had been saying for a long time about its morality and aesthetics. Moreover, the background provided by Clemens to the unusual display of nearly unadulterated Hawai'ian culture represented by the funeral ceremonies for the princess echoes the American side in the ongoing struggle against British influence in Hawai'i. In particular, Clemens supported the missionaries' attacks on the Church of England and its bishop, Thomas Staley. This solidarity all but guaranteed that Clemens would fail to appreciate the aesthetic of *hula* and would implicitly condemn it on moral grounds; it also meant that he would misunderstand the *hula*'s political dimension.

Mark Twain mentions *hula* briefly in letters 8 and 14 to the *Union*, but in letter 16 he reports on the *hulas* he witnessed in honor of Princess Victoria Kamāmalu. On June 29, the night before the princess was buried, Clemens stood on a balcony of the Hawai'ian minister of the interior, an Englishman named Ferdinand W. Hutchinson. From there, Clemens had a view down into the grounds of I'olani Palace, where hundreds of Hawai'ians were watching performers dance *hula* and listening to them chant *mele*, the poems to which any *hula* is danced.

In the course of the sixteenth letter, Mark Twain describes six separate instances of dancing, chanting, or both. One performance featured Christian hymns sung in Hawai'ian. The others were, in the sequence reported: women dancing with arms locked together and with much violent swaying; boys dancing in a way similar to the women; men dancing very vigorously; men chanting

40. Daws, *Shoal*, 160–62.

while sitting and beating on gourds that they often raised into the air; and women dancing again, starting slowly and increasing to a vigorous tempo. Only the last performance is called *hula-hula* by Mark Twain, but in fact all of them, even the one with men sitting, are *hula*. The sitting *hula* is easy to identify as *hula pa ipu; pa ipu* is Hawai'ian for the gourd used. *Hula pa ipu* was and is one of the most popular *hula*, though just one of twenty-eight different kinds.[41] Sam Clemens can be easily forgiven for not knowing the elaborate articulation of *hula* in the Hawai'ian culture, but a question remains: why does his comic alter ego Mark Twain identify only the last performance as *hula?*

The way Mark Twain refers to *hula* provides the first clue. He characterizes *hula* as "lascivious" (MTLH 70, 168, 170), but it is "demoralizing" and called a "barbarism," too (MTLH 71, 170). Mark Twain makes these judgments both before and after he reports any dancing. After the women dance the second time to finish the sequence of performances, Mark Twain makes his most notable comment: "After the drumming came the famous hula-hula we had heard so much about and so longed to see—the lascivious dance that was wont to set the passions of men ablaze in the old heathen days, a century ago" (MTLH 168). For Clemens, *hula* was associated with sex.

Investigating Mark Twain's appeal to historical precedent for always calling *hula* lascivious uncovers more clues. Written descriptions of *hula* begin with Captain James Cook's voyages of 1778 and 1779. A description of *hula* witnessed in 1779 by Cook's men tells of a dance like the one Mark Twain calls *hula-hula* in his sixteenth letter: performed by women only, who start very slowly and then dance faster and faster. Vancouver, in 1794, also witnessed such a dance. The descriptions of *hula* by early voyagers often appreciate the aesthetics of the dancing. Chamisso's description (1816) is the most favorable, and Barrot (1836) has obviously paid close attention to the dancing he has seen, noting how much the art form has changed. Some Westerners found the chanting monotonous at times. Clemens obviously disliked the chanting, calling it "howling" (MTLH 164), "unmusical" (MTLH 165), and "unearthly caterwauling" (MTLH 168). Early Western accounts, however, mainly objected to *hula* and *mele* with sexual themes, such as the *hula ma'i,* mentioned in a description by Vancouver. Thus early explorers recognized that *hula* is not always connected with sexuality.[42]

41. Nathaniel B. Emerson, *Unwritten Literature of Hawai'i: The Sacred Songs of the Hula.*
42. Western reactions to *hula* in Dorothy B. Barrère, "The Hula in Retrospect," 18, 20–21, 23, 38. David Samwell, surgeon of *Discovery* on Cook's third voyage, wrote down translations of two songs with sexual themes from a performance of *hula* on February 27, 1779, at Waimea Bay, O'ahu (ibid., 15, 17). Kanalu G. Terry Young (*Rethinking the Native Hawai'ian Past,* chapter 2) discusses the centrality of *mele* to Hawai'ian culture.

How is it that Clemens comes to have a different view—one that always makes the connection—and to state it so unequivocally? Subsequent to initial Western contacts, the *mele* and *hula* with sexual themes were likely to be the most memorable performances, the type so famous to sailors in the early days of contact with Hawai'i and so infamous to missionaries after their arrival. Certainly, Mark Twain calling *hula* "lascivious" as though that were its defining characteristic fits the conjecture that for many Westerners, the *hula ma'i*, with its sexual themes, had come to represent *all hula* because those were the dances that had from the beginning received the most attention: "the famous hula-hula we had heard so much about and so longed to see," as Mark Twain puts it. The perception by foreigners that *hula* always entails a sexual display must have been complicated by a characteristic dance step called *'ami*, which appears in different types of *hula*. The step involves a rotation of the hips, which can be executed in a number of ways and with varying degrees of meaning, most not vulgar.[43] Clemens identifying only the final dance as *hula* therefore fits what was by 1866 the stereotypical view. However, the probability is high that Clemens also correctly picked out the *hula* meant to have a sexual theme: the dance Mark Twain calls *hula-hula* was almost certainly a *hula ma'i*, because his account has it as the last dance performed in the set given by the various *halau* (dance troupes). *Hula ma'i*, with its theme of the sexual prowess of a specific chief, was the "traditional conclusion of a formal presentation of dances honoring [a] chief."[44] The chanting of *any mele* clearly had no aesthetic appeal for Clemens. He only has praise for Hawai'ians singing Western style. In addition, only one type of *hula* interests him, not so much for any intrinsic aspect, but rather for what it had come to symbolize to Westerners, saints and sinners alike: the legendary sexual freedom of Polynesia.

Sam Clemens's inability or unwillingness to understand *hula* and *mele* as art forms with their own aesthetic, taken together with the moral disapproval entailed in the repeated epithet "lascivious," sounds remarkably like judgments made by a group of missionaries who, in 1858, had petitioned the legislature to ban *hula*. Among the signatories was Samuel Damon, whose house and library Clemens visited and browsed on more than one occasion, and William P. Alexander, at whose house on Mau'i Clemens dined several times.[45] Hiram Bing-

43. Mary Kawena Pukui and Samuel H. Elbert, *Hawai'ian Dictionary*, 23.

44. Barrère, "Hula," 21.

45. See Noenoe K. Silva, "*He Kanawai E Ho'opau I Na Hula Kuolo Hawai'i*: The Political Economy of Banning the Hula," 40, for the 1858 petition. Several entries in Clemens's notebooks testify to the time spent with the Reverend Samuel Damon (NB 1:199, 200, 215). Moreover, an entry in one of the Hawai'i notebooks in someone else's hand may be Damon's. The entry lists some of the newspapers in the kingdom. An earlier entry that also lists newspapers is recorded amid others referring to Reverend Damon, suggesting that he had supplied the first list and wrote down the second (NB 1:201, 204).

ham, the leader of the first group of American missionaries during the reign of Kamehameha II, made the case against *hula* this way:

> much of the person is uncovered; and the decent covering of a foreign dress was not then permitted to the public dancers. . . . The musicians who sung without dancing, played on various unharmonious instruments, the drum, the long gourd-shell, or double-calabash [which,] standing upright on the ground, is beaten and often raised by the hands of the musician, sitting on his heels. . . . Melody and harmony are scarcely known to them, with all their skill and art. The whole arrangement and process of their old *hulas* were designed to promote lasciviousness.[46]

Labeling the performances for Princess Victoria Kamāmalu "barbarisms" (MTLH 170) because of a common Western prejudice, Clemens ignores most of the dances he sees and condemns as immoral the specific *hula* he had "so longed to see." This ambivalent attitude is reminiscent of how Mark Twain does not watch the cancan in Paris: the hands "covering" his eyes actually provide ample space between the splayed fingers for a good look (IA 136). However, the comic ambiguity in that image about viewing a provocative dance like the cancan is absent from the longest presentation of *hula*, in letter 16, even though a joking dimension exists due to an exchange with Mr. Brown about the festivities. In a letter written after he returned to California, Clemens joked that he had "gone into the Missionary business" (CL 1:364). Insofar as *hula* and *mele* were concerned, Clemens had indeed adopted the missionary attitude.

Mark Twain's background commentary on the ceremonies for the princess also indicates solidarity with American missionaries; in addition, it reflects his thoroughly American sources. Mark Twain lays the blame for the outburst of heathenism on Thomas Staley, bishop of the Reformed Catholic Church of Hawai'i, the name given to the Hawai'ian version of the Church of England. In his attack on Staley, Clemens almost certainly repeats what he has heard either from American clergy like William Alexander and Samuel Damon or from other Americans like newspaper editor Henry Whitney, the son of a missionary. Bishop Staley had been a focal point for American fear and loathing of the Hawai'ian monarchy's English sympathies since his arrival in 1862: he had quickly baptized most of the important members of the royal family and court.[47] However, in his focus on Staley, Clemens failed to register how King Kamehameha V used traditional Hawai'ian culture for political ends. To understand this dimension, the evolution of *hula*'s function for Hawai'ian rulers must be comprehended.

46. Bingham, *Residence,* 123–25.
47. Kuykendall, *Critical Years,* 93–99.

Traditionally, *hula* accompanied chants or *mele*. These *mele* were always more important than *hula* dancing, for they were the repositories of Hawai'ian mythologies as well as the chiefs' genealogies, the most important kinds of information in the Hawai'ians' precontact oral culture. Because of its link to *mele* within the traditional Hawai'ian culture, *hula* formed a primary reservoir of social knowledge and history. The "content, form, and production" of *hula* and chant therefore "were integral to the reproduction of the hierarchical social structure."[48] As symbolic forms of action, *hula* and *mele* marked the ideological center of traditional Hawai'ian culture. Given this cultural importance, *hula* and *mele* inevitably were intertwined with political power.

The link between *hula* and chiefly prerogative is crucial for understanding the role of dance in the half-Polynesian, half-Western Hawai'ian society of 1866. For the period just before Western contact, two accounts by Hawai'ian historians, Samuel Kamakau and John Ii, exist about *hula* performances for a specific chief. Kamakau mentions one for Liholiho when he is king and another for the birth of Kuakini to the *ali'i nui* Namahana and Ke'eaumoku. John Ii mentions *hula* in connection with Liholiho.[49] These accounts indicate that *hula* in ancient Hawai'i was popular everywhere as entertainment for the common people but was also performed at the behest of *ali'i* or chiefs, especially as part of important celebrations of and by a chief. Any important chief in ancient Hawai'i probably would have had retainers on call to perform *hula;* this practice certainly could be seen in postcontact Hawai'i. When George Vancouver visited in 1794, Kamehameha the Great and his queen Ka'ahumanu staged *hula* on the Big Island Hawai'i. Kamehameha II (1819–1824), who was very fond of *hula,* promoted it as part of the yearly commemorations of his father. By the time of Kamehameha III's reign (1824–1854), these ad hoc uses of *hula* had become much more formalized; *hula* had become court entertainment as well as functioning to entertain important visitors.[50]

The embedding of *hula* in the royal Hawai'ian court occurred despite the best efforts of the missionaries, who always saw *hula* as a major obstacle to conversion and who enjoyed some success very early in a long-term campaign to eradicate the practice. In January 1824, a missionary named Charles Stewart could report that "For a year past . . . we have scarce heard the sounds of the native songs and dances [in Lahaina, Mau'i]." This statement misleads, however, if one imagines its particular claim as a condition of the entire kingdom. Some *ali'i* had

48. Barrère, "Hula," 22; Elizabeth Buck, *Paradise Remade: The Politics of Culture and History in Hawai'i,* 109, quote from 102.

49. Kamakau, *Ruling Chiefs,* 250; John Papa Ii, *Fragments of Hawai'ian History,* 137.

50. Barrère, "Hula," 19, 20, 35.

embraced Christianity and were actively suppressing *hula*. The most notable in this group was Kaʻahumanu the Queen Mother, baptized in 1825. Thus in areas near the mission stations or within the control of Christian chiefs, *hula* disappeared. In areas away from missions or in the control of chiefs not baptized, however, the old ways continued.[51]

This dichotomy remained even in 1830, when Kaʻahumanu, practically a coruler with the young king, Kamehameha III, forbade the performance of *hula* in public. After her death in 1832, chiefs and commoners alike blatantly ignored her edict, especially in 1833 when Kamehameha III revived precontact customs. Even after he re-embraced a practice of Christianity, *hula* remained visible *and* grew in importance, achieving the state function noted before—as formal entertainment for important visitors. Throughout the 1840s under the reign of Kamehameha III, *hula* continued to be taught and performed, especially in the country districts where its existence was never in doubt.[52] Nathaniel Emerson records *hula* performed for Kamehameha III in Waimanalo (1846), Waimea (1847), and Kahuku (1849)—villages all on Oʻahu but far from Honolulu. However, when dancers performed *hula* for the king at official functions, the traditional *hula maʻi* may have been left out—as policy. For instance, *hula (hula ka ekeʻeke)* was performed in 1850 at the royal palace without mention of *hula maʻi*.[53] *Hula* performed to *mele* with sexual content was nevertheless always popular in the countryside and with commoners.[54]

In postcontact Hawaiʻi, these kinds of *hula* most probably dominated any public performance charging money, such as ones to which Mark Twain refers in letter 8 when he notes that the only way to see *hula* is behind closed doors for a fee of ten dollars (MTLH 71). The dubious moral status of such commercial performances of *hula* is indicated by attempts to control them with laws first published in 1851. Places of performance were restricted, and performers needed a license. The law provided for fines and the imprisonment of transgressors. These latter elements of the law were reduced in 1864 and 1870. Such laws never stopped the performance of *hula* within the Hawaiʻian community, however, whatever effect it may have had on performances available to *haole* (outsiders or foreigners) like Clemens. The later reduction in the amount of fines and the time of imprisonment for those who broke the law of 1851 indicates how throughout the 1850s and 1860s an open indulgence in *hula* by kings and chiefs occurred that was imitated by the common folk. During the same time period, ample evidence

51. Ibid., 33 (quotation), 34.
52. Ibid., 40; Buck, *Paradise,* 108.
53. Barrère, "Hula," 40.
54. George Washington Bates, *Sandwich Island Notes. By a Haole,* 284–85.

exists in the form of letters to Hawai'ian-language newspapers that many Hawai'ians had adopted the Western, Christian attitude toward *hula*.[55] One letter even includes negative comments on *hula* performed during the mourning ceremonies for Princess Victoria that Clemens witnessed in 1866.

Not surprisingly, the most pronounced emphasis on *hula* connected with sexual display began when dancers performed for sailors during whaling fleet visits.[56] The places where Clemens boarded while in Honolulu were only a short walk from the area where performances of ten-dollar *hula* would have been found. No mention of visiting such an establishment is made in his notebooks, but if he sampled any of the demimonde entertainments available in Honolulu, such a stop would be likely. The articulation of *hula* from an art form patronized by chiefs and practiced communally by the folk into commercial performances for foreign audiences symbolizes the changes occurring in Hawai'ian culture in the first half of the nineteenth century.[57] As early as the 1840s, public displays of *hula* were most likely either of the more dignified variety featured at royal entertainments or the "lascivious" variety featured at commercial displays for *haole*. This stark difference in how *hula* could be experienced suggests why the old-style performances in memory of Princess Victoria Kamāmalu, complete with *hula ma'i*, scandalized Americans: because such evocation of ancient Hawai'i was almost unknown in their polite Honolulu social circles in 1866, they would have associated it with the degraded commercial version.

Thus the *hula* experienced by Sam Clemens had a mixed and complicated status. Very soon after the missionaries arrived in 1820, *hula* had become a publicly contested cultural practice—a situation that lasted until the overthrow of the monarchy in 1893. For the missionaries, *hula* immediately epitomized the heathen ways of the Hawai'ians, and they made every effort to suppress it. For the Hawai'ian chiefs who were not baptized, *hula* just as quickly became a way to assert their own power against the influence of the American missionaries. The importance of that assertion only escalated as the monarchy became institutionalized, especially when Alexander Liholiho became Kamehameha IV in 1854. Apparently, the *hula* in the first years of his reign enjoyed a resurgence, prompting Henry Whitney to complain in his newspaper that *hula* performances "have been slowly reviving around this city, until they are now to be met with in every village on this island." In October of the same year, Whitney, through the *Advertiser*, bluntly assigned blame for the change: "It was only on the accession to power of his majesty and his present Ministry, that the revival of

55. Barrère, "Hula," 41, 43–46.
56. Ibid., 41.
57. Buck, *Paradise,* 106.

hulas was permitted, and it is said that they have been ever since specially patronized by Chiefs high in authority." For Henry Whitney, the remedy was passage of
new laws to ban *hula* completely. The king and his brother, Lot Kapuaiwa,
actively opposed such efforts.[58] Prince Lot, at the time both the minister of the
interior and a member of the house of nobles, played a key role in ensuring that
the proposed legislative ban did not happen. As Kamehameha V (1864–1872),
Lot undoubtedly used Hawai'ian culture, especially *hula,* as a public vehicle for
asserting his own independence and Hawai'ian sovereignty during the mourning ceremonies when his brother died in 1864, elevating him to the throne.[59]
Lot, who rejected his missionary upbringing and who feared the economic and
political dominance of Americans, repeated the gesture of cultural (and thus
political) sovereignty with the display of *hula* during the 1866 mourning ceremonies for his sister, Princess Victoria Kamāmalu. By then, *hula* had long been
a symbol of royal prerogative. Thus when Mark Twain singles out Bishop Staley
as the one person responsible for the "revival" of *hula* (MTLH 169–70), he
greatly oversimplifies.

Mark Twain makes this charge as part of a sustained attack on the bishop and
his Hawai'ian Reformed Catholic Church. The diatribe against Staley, triggered
by the ancient form of the mourning ceremonies for the princess, represents the
clearest example of Mark Twain functioning as a mouthpiece for the American
missionaries. Anglican English and Congregationalist Americans had been
locked in a struggle for influence with the Hawai'ian community even before
Staley arrived in the islands in October 1862. The struggle revealed political contours as much as religious ones, a fact echoed in what Mark Twain has to say
about Staley and his actions. The funeral for the princess becomes the occasion
for Clemens to hear from his American sources all about the perfidious behavior, past and present, of the bishop. In addition, Mark Twain's claim that one
more Hawai'ian generation without *hula* would guarantee its permanent demise
was never likely because its premise was wrong: there had not yet been a generation without *hula.* The opposite happened when a great resurgence of interest
in *hula* occurred in 1875 under King David Kalakaua, who also saw *hula* as a
symbol of the Hawai'ianness of his kingship. The reaction of Sam Clemens to
*hula,* stereotypically linked to sexual display, demonstrates how much Mark
Twain could at times talk like a respectable missionary to the islands. Mark
Twain's presentation of *hula* also suggests how far from indigenous sources Sam
Clemens remained during his tour of Hawai'i.

58. Henry M. Whitney, *"Hulahula,"* 2; quoted in Silva, "Banning," 36, see also 34–42.
59. See Buck, *Paradise,* 155.

# SCENE TWO

MARK TWAIN'S COMIC RAID
ON THE KINGDOM OF HAWAI'I

## Scenes in Honolulu

I start to the Sandwich Islands day after to-morrow . . . in the steamer "Ajax." We shall arrive there in about 12 days [and] I am to remain . . . a month & ransack the islands, the great cataracts & the volcano completely.

Letter to Jane Clemens and Pamela Moffet, March 5, 1866

Examining the serious aspects of the letters from Hawai'i delineates the links to normative views about work and leisure, while also exposing Mark Twain's alignment with the most respectable of American groups in Hawai'i, the missionaries and their descendants. Necessary as these aspects are to understand the variety of purpose in composing the letters, their comic quality gives them whatever immediate appeal they might have for readers today.

The comic aspect of the "Letters from the Kingdom of Hawai'i" can be conceptualized as a loosely knit narrative recounting the misadventures of Mark Twain and his sidekick, Mr. Brown. This narrative has three phases, coinciding with the probable time of the letters' composition. While in Hawai'i, Sam Clemens preferred to write and send his letters in batches, presumably so that the *Sacramento Union* editors could publish them at clear intervals, thus building an audience that would anticipate the series. This strategy is suggested by the first group of letters, which totaled seven, the largest number dispatched at one time. Reading this initial group as a whole, one quickly understands that Clemens meant to give the *Union* enough variegated material—travel book descriptions, business information, and funny sketches—to insure that the series would start strong and continue to command attention in a market where travel letters were routine fare and all too often routinely written. In addition, Clemens obviously meant to "spread himself" in order to guarantee that the letters would make his readers laugh. The first phase of the Hawai'ian misadventures of Mark Twain and Mr. Brown are therefore lively, even lighthearted, and often feature low humor and slapstick.

Even in the more informative sections of the letters, Clemens displays his comic forte, a seemingly effortless ability with funny phrasing. His large blocks of paraphrasing from James J. Jarves's history of the islands, used to provide background, also emphasize by contrast a general tone of levity.[60] Most importantly,

---

60. Jarves's history was published in 1843. Frear says (MTH 157) that the Jarves account was long the standard nonmissionary view. Clemens found the history in Reverend Samuel Damon's

Clemens resurrects Mark Twain's comic sidekick from his *Enterprise* days, the Unreliable—although he calls him Mr. Brown.[61] The presence of Mr. Brown brought Clemens back to a comic space that allowed room to unleash the more antic and less refined elements of Mark Twain to romp amid any other, milder comic poses and thus to recall for Clemens's West Coast readers the rough-and-tumble Comstock origins of his alter ego. This range of comic behaviors by Mark Twain dominates the first group of letters from Hawai'i.

After sending off the group of seven letters based on his first sojourn in Honolulu, Clemens wrote ten more letters while in Hawai'i. These ten letters together constitute a middle phase of the Hawai'ian misadventures of Mark Twain and Mr. Brown and are characterized by a sporadic effort to create comic effects. That inconsistency apparently resulted from the pressure of circumstances, which forced Clemens at times to hurry his composition. After letters 8 through 11 were dispatched as a group, probably between April 9 and 15, Clemens wrote the remaining correspondence in the middle phase between trips to Mau'i and the Big Island Hawai'i as well as during a second long stay on O'ahu. Thus Clemens wrote letters 12, 13, and 14 in the midst of a hectic itinerary, as much to keep the series going as to report specific unusual events or to elaborate comic ideas. Letter 14 begins with Mark Twain saying that he is too tired from his Big Island trip to report on it: "I only want to write a few lines at present by the *Live Yankee,* merely to keep my communications open, as the soldiers say" (MTLH 123). Circumstances simply crowded out the narrative of Mark Twain and Mr. Brown's comic misadventures because they provided two other compelling stories, ones that were particularly dramatic and serious: the death, prolonged mourning ceremonies, and funeral of Princess Victoria Kamāmalu; the arrival of survivors from the burned clipper ship *Hornet,* who had endured forty-three days at sea in an open boat before landing near the town of Hilo. The entangle-

---

library in Honolulu: this was the volume that Clemens apologized to Damon for taking with him and that the press teased Mark Twain for stealing. Clemens brought with him two books, Lorrin Andrews, *A Dictionary of the Hawaiian Language,* which had just been published the year before, and *Hawaiian Phrase Book* by Artemas Bishop (1854). In his notebook, Clemens refers to "155 books on Hawaii—86 scientific papers—27 newspapers and periodicals," probably a reference to Damon's extensive library (NB 1:159).

61. One of the *Ajax* passengers was a W. H. Brown. The editors of the Hawai'i notebooks refer to him as "an American merchant" (NB 1:182n6) and assert that it is not possible to say how he might have influenced the creation of Mark Twain's comic sidekick. Nevertheless, the numerous references to "Brown" offer some clues through their variety. Two suggest that scenes with the fictional Brown had a basis in actual incidents involving the historical Mr. Brown: being seasick and waiters refilling a water glass (NB 1:190, 191). Other entries indicate a personality that could have inspired the comic character of Brown: a joke about his spiritless horse; his ire at a pointless story; his drinking (NB 1:119, 138, 139). Still other entries suggest that "Brown" became a convenient hook upon which to hang ideas for sketches or drafts of sketches (NB 1:118, 131–32, 154, 158).

ment of Sam Clemens in the politics of the kingdom also contributed to the decrease in comic content. This entanglement encouraged him to change the narrative's knockabout frontier tone by emphasizing satiric lampoons. In this middle phase, Mark Twain thus reads less like an eccentric, humorous character not unworthy of a pairing with Mr. Brown and more like the acerbic satirist found in the pages of the *Californian*. Clemens even enlists Mr. Brown, "the impetuous child of nature" (MTLH 121), in the enterprise.

In the third and final phase of the Hawai'ian misadventures of Mark Twain and Mr. Brown, the broader comic tone from phase one returns. That echo is probably no accident. These last eight letters were all written after Clemens left Hawai'i, almost certainly after he had arrived in San Francisco, and probably after he had reviewed what he had written at the outset of the series and had gathered renewed inspiration from it. Obvious parallels can be found in both the first and third groups. Mark Twain begins both with a comic scene involving an overabundance of unwanted island fauna, especially insects, and then moves on to a scene involving seasick passengers (1 and 18). Clemens also reuses, in letter 19, the comic trick first seen in letter 4: Mr. Brown reading over Mark Twain's shoulder and commenting on what he finds. The Washoe humor of raillery so noticeable in the first set of letters also regains prominence in the third set. Finally, the ghoulish souvenir bone hunters in letter 7 become the outlandish and persistent souvenir hunting of Mr. Brown in letters 19, 20, and 21.

The likelihood of Clemens repackaging and elaborating earlier comic ideas increases when one notices that the first four letters in the last group (numbers 18–21 in the series), which contain these parallels, were all published in weekly installments beginning on August 18, a few days after he arrived back in San Francisco. Read as a unit, these letters feature the comically irreverent voice of Mark Twain, to which is added comic scenes with the incorrigible Mr. Brown. As with the first group of letters, laughter takes center stage, despite other important elements: the occasional spots of word painting for picturesque scenes, long historical excerpts on Captain Cook or the Hawai'ian god Lono, bits of history and legend, and the quick recountings of moments at specific places like the City of Refuge. This same mixture organizes letters 22 and 24. The wisecracking irreverence from Mark Twain and Mr. Brown about everyone and everything encountered is only interrupted in the final group of letters by the summary of the sugar trade in the islands (the only use Clemens made in the original letters of his Mau'i trip) and by the elaborate description of the volcano Kilauea, which is nearly devoid of any comic aspect.

These last-mentioned letters represent efforts different from attempts to produce laughter, and they in fact have as much to do with current events in San Francisco as they do with past events in Hawai'i. The letter on the sugar industry epitomizes the master role of Mark Twain the reliable reporter, which Clemens uses to provide information to the San Francisco business community. The final letter, which recounts the visit to the Kilauea volcano, exemplifies Clemens's attempt to orient his writing abilities toward the more refined species of travel narratives that featured detailed word paintings. This aspect of Mark Twain not only grew out of his efforts with literary periodicals like the *Californian,* the *Weekly Review,* and the *Saturday Press;* it also was connected to a more immediate concern: the current shaping of his lecture on the Sandwich Islands, which featured a bold combination of jokes, information, and word painting. The description of the volcano became a lecture set piece, celebrated especially by those reviewers who looked for something in the lectures to talk about other than the comic foolery.

Comic foolery, however, defines Mark Twain, and the majority of the letters in the series demonstrates that Clemens remained ready to display his literary alter ego in all of its comic complexity: Mark Twain's capability for teasing all and sundry, including ridiculing topics to create a prodigious streak of irreverence; his flair for comic irascibility, which entails a humor of raillery and a habit of lampooning; his potential for foolishness, sometimes dramatized in the role of a comic victim, sometimes of a slapstick clown; in short, his capacity to be laughably disreputable.

---

## MARK TWAIN AND MR. BROWN RANSACK THE ISLANDS

I HAD RATHER SMELL HONOLULU AT SUNSET THAN THE OLD POLICE COURTROOM IN SAN FRANCISCO.

———

"SCENES IN HONOLULU, NO. 4," *SACRAMENTO UNION,* APRIL 19, 1866

Clemens employs Mark Twain's basic comic tactic, entertaining phrasing, everywhere in the Hawai'i letters. The tone can often be playful rather than scathing, as when Mark Twain refers to men aboard the *Ajax* sliding on chairs because of a rough sea as those who "sail away . . . on the ebb" (MTLH 6), or whimsical when glasses sliding off a table in the same rough sea are said to be "prospecting for the deck" (MTLH 6), or ironic when he describes Brown's teasing of seasick passengers as "kind and thoughtful" (MTLH 6), or sarcastic when he says that the men play cards for amusement while the women are seasick for amusement (MTLH 15) and when he calls coconut trees "ragged parasols"

(MTLH 52). Clemens also uses Mark Twain to indulge in obvious puns: the swells of the oceans are like a Broadway swell (MTLH 9), and his "latter end" is both a thought about death and a backside sore from riding a horse (MTLH 44).

Throughout all these comic tonalities Mark Twain manifests the equal-opportunity effort by Sam Clemens to make fun of anything and anyone within his ken. This ecumenical ridicule occasionally has Mr. Brown's help. Brown, for instance, refers to his bunk in an interisland schooner as a "coffin" (MTLH 196), and within a few sentences, Mark Twain repeats the sarcastic comment. Mr. Brown has a knack for irreverent renaming, calling poorly baked bread "ballast" (MTLH 205). Topics that deserve Mark Twain's or Mr. Brown's ridicule include romantic, youthful tales about the calm Pacific Ocean (MTLH 10); romantic, youthful ideas about becoming a fireman on a steamer (MTLH 19); the King of Hawai'i, Kamehameha V (MTLH 27–28); the American missionaries in the islands, who appear as an item in a comic list of bothersome insects (MTLH 32); the dreadful nuisance of a popular song endlessly sung by all and sundry, even by Hawai'ians "at the very outpost and fag-end of the world" (MTLH 65); *kanakas* (people) made "blithe" by eating sour poi (MTLH 68);[62] *kanakas* sociable with vermin (MTLH 69, 196); native judicial sagacity (MTLH 129); a constantly crowing rooster (MTLH 196); and an endless supply of stewed chicken (MTLH 204), a diatribe reminiscent of a story by William Wright in which he tells of being served the dish by everyone when he returns home to Iowa to visit.[63] Mark Twain's tone might express comic exasperation. Often, his ridicule has an irreverent edge, for example, when he uses the slang phrase "'bust' the Hawaiian exchequer" and claims it is a popular missionary term (MTLH 233–34).

Irreverence seems inevitable when Mark Twain comments on religious belief. Specific reasons for ridicule vary. The missionaries' insistence on constant hard work, which ruins Hawai'i as a paradise, provides one occasion (MTLH 53). In other cases, Mark Twain aims his barbs at the missionaries because they are excessive in their morality (MTLH 60, 127ff), or because they are hypocritical about their interest in making money (MTLH 212). He is equally prepared to mock a Hawai'ian temple to the rain god, saying that its location well up the mountainside guaranteed rain: "You would seldom get to your Amen before you

---

62. Despite the joke about sour poi, Clemens, according to his erstwhile traveling companion Howard, liked the dish, traditionally eaten in various states of fermentation—hence somewhat sour. "Here we got something to eat and the native . . . fed us on roast pig and boiled taro and some nasty paste he called 'poi' which Sam seemed to relish" (Austin, "Incognito," 253). In his notebook, Clemens wrote "poi not bad food" (NB 1:137). Franklin Austin's memory of Clemens approaching his father's plantation on the Big Island pictures him with some items of local dress: a "native lauhala straw hat" and sheepskin leggings (250). He also made efforts to learn the Hawai'ian language (NB 1:234–35). To some extent, then, Clemens felt comfortable within the local scene.
63. William Wright, "Petrified! or, The Stewed Chicken Monster."

would have to hoist your umbrella" (MTLH 239). Most notably, Mark Twain mercilessly derides the "charming Sunday School" story about Obookia,[64] the Hawai'ian said to have precipitated the mission to the islands when he sat on a church step in New England and wept because his people did not have the Bible. Pretending that Obookia's uncle runs a temple he visits, Mark Twain imagines, not the pious Christian, but the onetime pagan: "Here that gentle spirit worshiped; here he sought the better life, after his rude fashion; on this stone, perchance, he sat down with his sacred lasso, to wait for a chance to rope in some neighbor for the holy sacrifice; on this altar, possibly, he broiled his venerable grandfather, and presented the rare offering before the high priest, who may have said, 'Well done, good and faithful servant.' It filled me with emotion" (MTLH 237–38).

Very little escapes such comic abuse. Mark Twain does not hesitate to blame Captain Cook for his own death (MTLH 221), and he clearly thinks Paulet and Charlton are arrogant and greedy when retelling that famous incident in Hawai'ian history (MTLH 231ff). He destroys a legend that claims a hole in a tree was made by a cannonball fired by Cook's men the day the legendary explorer died, simply by commenting, "It is a very good hole" (MTLH 237). He flouts the genteel literary convention of "the gentle reader" by saying that he does not care if the gentle reader will pardon his digressions or not (MTLH 164). Clemens does portray a limit, however, to this typical care-for-nothing spirit of irreverence. Early in the letters, on a horseback ride around Diamond Head crater, Mark Twain and his companions come across an area covered with human bones, in what appears to be the remnants of a battlefield. Some of the party decide to take home souvenirs, which leads to ghoulish conversation. Mark Twain acknowledges remorse but blames the missionaries, saying it is their fault for not making the Hawai'ians clear away the boneyard (MTLH 60).[65]

Early on, Clemens apparently had understood the secret nature of the ceremony that surrounds the burial of *ali'i nui* in Hawai'ian culture but not the sacred aspect of securing the bones from discovery and defilement. Because *ali'i nui* were manifestations of gods, their remains had specific rituals for disposal, which included hiding bones.[66] Only in the last batch of letters, written in San Francisco and recounting his time on the Big Island, does respect for this sacred

64. The Hawai'ian spelling is *Opukahaia*.

65. The bones on Oʻahu could be from a battle or possibly from the 1804 epidemic of cholera or typhoid that swept through the islands as Kamehameha was about to invade Kauaʻi. He had assembled an enormous fleet and army for the purpose that never left leeward Oʻahu near where Clemens and company find the bones (Daws, *Shoal,* 42–43).

66. Goldman, *Ancient Polynesian Society,* 218; Douglas Oliver, *Polynesia in Early Historic Times,* 176.

dimension find expression. Mark Twain and Mr. Brown prospect some caves in a cliff side and accidentally disturb a burial site. "I climbed in [to the cave] and put the relic back into the canoe, with its fellows, and I trust the spirit of the deceased, if it was hovering near, was satisfied with this mute apology for our unintentional sacrilege" (MTLH 278). While still in Hawai'i, Clemens had written another tale about human bones, "A Strange Dream," which appeared June 2, 1866, in the *New York Saturday Press*. Though he devoted his talent while in Hawai'i to writing for the *Union*, this story was the exception, Clemens keeping open his lines of communication to the East Coast literary press with the offering. In the tale, Mark Twain dreams he has discovered the burial site of Kamehameha the Great. "Dream" clearly burlesques the thrilling and endless cheap tales featured in lowbrow story papers like the *New York Ledger*, for the comic ending debunks the magic and mystery of finding the burial chamber in a corner of the immense crater of Kilauea volcano.

Along with inevitable irreverence, the irascible humor of raillery, so evident in Washoe Mark Twain, appears throughout the Hawai'i letters. At one point, Mark Twain claims that there are times when it is "a sanitary necessity to snarl at something or perish" (MTLH 203). Clemens had always used Mark Twain to vent his spleen. Mark Twain first strikes this vein of humor while in Hawai'i by denouncing Balboa as a "shameless old foreign humbug" (MTLH 8) and "infatuated old ass" because he misnamed the Pacific Ocean, "thus uttering a lie" (MTLH 10). Growling to obtain relief from a bad humor also occurs when Mark Twain pronounces a "fervent curse upon the man who invented the American saddle" (MTLH 47), or when he imagines the pleasure he would have attending the funeral of a man who has been tormenting him by endlessly playing one tune on a flute, badly (MTLH 112–13). Mark Twain has epithets for Hawai'i's legislators, calling them "woodenheads" (MTLH 111) and "clacking geese" (MTLH 112). Legislative assemblies in any case make easy targets for robust ridicule, always full of one-horse-village lawyers and solemn asses from the cow or taro patch counties. Mark Twain sees the Hawai'ian legislature as a shade better mannered than the early Nevada legislature he had covered in 1861 and 1862 (MTLH 120), which is not much of a compliment and creates a good comic instance of damning with faint praise (see MTEnt 39–41). Most members knew "just about enough to come in when it rained, and that was all," spending their time dispensing buncombe with feet on the desk, eating, smoking, or simply falling asleep (MTLH 109, 110, 120).

Government ministers must also be tongue-lashed. Mark Twain merely warms up with Mr. Hutchinson, who has sandy hair and complexion—"is altogether one of the sandiest men I ever saw, so to speak" (MTLH 119), and M. de Varigny, a Frenchman, who pronounces English so badly that if he were morally as bad as he speaks that language, "nothing but a special intervention of Providence could save him from perdition hereafter" (MTLH 119). Mark Twain reserves the true satiric whippings for the minister of finance, Charles Harris. An attack on Harris dominates much of letter 13, in which Harris by turns is "that blasted Harris" (MTLH 163) and "unworthy of the name of American" (MTLH 117), a man who is "the soul and spirit of obsequiousness" (MTLH 164), yet assumes an air of importance equal to a Richelieu (MTLH 165). When the ever-voluble and pompous Harris tries to be funny, however, Mark Twain indulges his choleric tendency: "If I had had a double-barreled shot-gun, I would have blown him into a million fragments" (MTLH 118).

The antipathy for Harris that Clemens conveys reflects the view of the American missionary party and has its roots in the political struggle over the revision of the constitution in 1864. When Harris was named to the cabinet of Kamehameha V, the Americans thought they had an ally. When Harris supported the king's proposal to change the constitution in a way that strengthened monarchical power, the Americans felt betrayed.[67] In their eyes, Harris had sold his Americanness to Hawai'ian loyalty. That charge is why Mark Twain accuses Harris of being *hoopilimea'ai,* which he translates as "obsequious."[68] Clemens almost surely heard this manner of describing Harris from James McBride, the American minister. McBride had sent a letter to Secretary of State Seward, dated January 15, 1866, saying that Harris had sold his American birthright for a mess of pottage.[69] Clemens had dinner with McBride at least once, and his notebook has a section of entries that are probably jottings from a conversation with him (CL 1:334; NB 1:121–22, 123–24).

Not everyone agreed with these assessments of the lawyer from New Hampshire. Charles de Varigny, who served for years in the king's cabinet with Harris, was obviously no friend but nevertheless called him "a man of action, resourceful, persevering even to an excessive degree, combining the merits along with the failings of the American lawyer."[70] The American minister after McBride, Edward McCook, was even more favorable, saying in a letter to President Grant that Harris was the most adroit and able of Hawai'i's public men and could be counted on during any problems that a possible annexation might bring.[71] Clemens's fervent belief in the McBride position on Harris blazes fiercely in a notebook entry written on the return trip to San Francisco. The topic is "THE

67. See Charles de Varigny, *Fourteen Years at the Sandwich Islands,* 186.
68. Pukui and Elbert, in the *Hawai'ian Dictionary,* translate it as "to fawn."
69. Kuykendall, *Critical Years,* 207.
70. Varigny, *Fourteen Years,* 130.
71. Phillip H. Harris, "Charles Coffin Harris: An Uncommon Life in the Law," 169.

KING," and it begins: "It riles me to hear an American (that [—]cking Harris) stand up & pay titular adulation" (NB 1:149).

Also favored with an overflow of waspish venom is the head of the Royal Hawai'ian Church, Bishop Thomas Staley. As noted before, Staley deserved special attention because he condoned the traditional mourning rites for Princess Kamāmalu. Among his other sins of liberality, Staley attended a performance of *hula*, "with his holy head tricked out in the flower and evergreen trumpery worn by the hula girls" (MTLH 170). Mark Twain calls Staley a "weak, trivial minded–man" (MTLH 170), who was "built into a lord by the English Bishop of Oxford" (MTLH 130), but who commands a limited sphere: a "little cathedral [with] thirty pews of ten individual capacity each" (MTLH 173).

Playful, irreverent, irascible—the comic phrasing and description, raillery and lampooning that Clemens employs throughout the "Letters from the Kingdom of Hawai'i" spotlights the sharp-tongued aspect of Mark Twain. However, the comic scenes Clemens invents for Mark Twain and Mr. Brown contribute the most to enlivening the letters and to creating a reading experience markedly different from standard travel letters. Immediately setting a quick pace for broad laughter, Clemens begins the letters with slapstick scenes. The first has Mark Twain in his underwear, killing millions of mosquitos by sitting on them (MTLH 3). The second features Mark Twain's attempts to walk on the deck of the *Ajax* during high seas: after colliding with the mainmast, he decides to stay seated, and then returns belowdecks, "discouraged" (MTLH 5). Later in the series, when recounting his trip on the Big Island Hawai'i, Clemens adds other slapstick scenes with Mr. Brown. In one, Brown and Mark Twain sit in an outrigger canoe with a native paddler, and Brown's clumsiness dumps them all into the ocean. In another, Mr. Brown and Mark Twain explore caves they spot high in a bluff as they are approaching Honaunau, the City of Refuge. Mark Twain orders Brown to mount his shoulders and to enter and investigate one. After several moments of waiting for a report, Mark Twain becomes drowsy in the heat: "about this time, the investigator backed suddenly out of the hole and crushed me to the earth. We rolled down the slight declivity and brought up in a sitting posture face to face" (MTLH 277).

Mark Twain also looks foolish when he plays cards with whaling captains on board the *Ajax*. His inept play dooms himself and his partner. The partner then entertains all with his extravagant expression of anger. The scene also allows Clemens to elaborate a favorite comic trick, bringing slang or jargon into an inappropriate context. Mark Twain's partner, who is one of the whaling captains, calls unimportant cards "blubber" and elaborately compares the disastrous manner in which they lost the game to a shipwreck (MTLH 16; see also NB 1:191). Another scene that dramatizes various encounters with critters on board an interisland schooner, notably with rats and cockroaches "as large as peach leaves," puts Mark Twain into the role of comic victim. When a "procession" of cockroaches camps in his hair while a "party" of fleas turns double somersaults, he begins to feel "really annoyed," gives up trying to sleep, and goes on deck (MTLH 197).

One section of the "Letters from the Kingdom of Hawai'i" recounts the troubles Mark Twain has with his "steed Oahu" (MTLH 46–47, 63–64), mostly showing Mark Twain again in the role of a foolish victim. His bony horse stops at the gate of every house, trying to climb most of them as well as a stone wall encountered on the way out of town. Oahu tops his perfidies by falling asleep. The riding scenes culminate with a twist, when Mark Twain attempts to impress a young lady with his horsemanship. Rather than being a comic victim, Mark Twain in this scene deserves to be ridiculed for his vanity as he tries to catch her attention by parading before her on Oahu. His metaphoric fall comes when he discovers from Mr. Brown that the young lady's interest in him is far from flattering. She believes that his slouchy riding and slow drawl indicate a drunken state, and she fears he will hurt himself. Mark Twain can only manage a "hollow, sepulchral laugh" (MTLH 64) when he finally understands why she pays him so much attention. The comic scenes featuring Mark Twain's horse Oahu formed one of the most popular topics from the initial group of letters. Some of the scenes were frequently reprinted, and Clemens also included parts in *The Celebrated Jumping Frog of Calavaras County*.[72]

In one of the longest single comic scenes in the series, Mr. Brown and Mark Twain wait for their schooner to overcome contrary winds and pick them up after a day of sightseeing on the Kona coast of the Big Island. Their intricate comic interplay makes the scene memorable. The fun begins with Mark Twain repeatedly thwarting Mr. Brown's mania for souvenirs: Brown wants to hijack anything said to have been touched by Captain Cook, including a large piece of a temple. In the conflict, Clemens casts Mark Twain as the civilized gentleman who must constantly admonish the selfish and ill-mannered Brown. This dynamic of genteel and boorish behaviors sets the stage as the two men must wait several hours for the ship. After passing "an hour of sentimental meditation," the refined Mark Twain decides to sing "There Is No Place Like Home" and thus soothe himself and Mr. Brown in their plight. This pretentious conclusion to his sentimental thoughts, however, has the opposite effect on Brown, who says that he "ain't going to be put upon and aggravated when I'm so miserable [with]

---

72. Frear catalogs newspaper reprintings (MTH 257–60) but does not include the *Weekly Review*'s June 2 and 6, 1866, reprintings of parts of letters 2, 4, and 6; nor the *Hawaiian Herald*'s September 14 and October 6, 1866, partial reprints of letters 19 and 9.

any more yowling" (MTLH 225). Mark Twain does stop, immediately, since Mr. Brown has a "dangerous calm in his voice," but he also says to himself that Brown is a "vulgar creature . . . his soul is dead to the heavenly charm of music" (MTLH 225–26). The clash of refined and vulgar tastes results in a comic standoff. The joke turns on the inability of Mark Twain to sing well, which allows the implied reader to sympathize with Brown's complaint and laugh at Mark Twain. Nevertheless, the refined view that Mark Twain represents, which claims that those with vulgar taste are incapable of responding to music, remains intact. The cultured Mark Twain, who has laudably prevented the depredations of Brown the souvenir hunter and responded fashionably to the melancholy of their situation with a pathetic ballad, may look foolish when he actually sings, but the justice in Brown's complaint about the singing does not diminish his basic vulgarity.

As the waiting continues and as the sun sets, both men become hungry. The suave Mark Twain gains the upper hand in their conflict, not so much because of the virtues of expressing (even awkwardly) a correct aesthetic for the situation, but rather because he supplements his good taste with a manipulating shrewdness. Mark Twain reveals his shrewd side when Brown interrupts the gloomy and hungry silence by noting just-out-of-reach coconuts, whereupon Mark Twain says, "What an idiot you are not to have thought of it before" (MTLH 226). Within minutes, Mark Twain has Brown wearing himself out throwing stones at the coconuts, having divided the labor of getting their food into two parts: Brown knocks the nuts down, and Mark Twain will retrieve them. When the stone-throwing strategy fails, Mark Twain convinces Brown to climb the tree, an experiment that garners no coconuts but does result in Brown destroying "the transom to [his] trousers" (MTLH 228). Only the accident of a Hawai'ian boy passing by saves them; for a few coins, the boy easily harvests enough coconuts to satisfy both men until the ship can pick them up. The boy also prepares the nuts by tearing off the husks with his teeth, something Mark Twain doubts either he or Brown could have done. "I would have kept Brown trying, however, as long as he had any teeth" (MTLH 230).

Brown is not unaware of Mark Twain manipulating the situation to his favor. In the midst of their futile exertions for the coconuts, Brown says that he will not rest until Mark Twain does. "But it's singular to me how you always happen to divide up the work about the same way. I'm to knock 'em down, and you're to pick 'em up. I'm of the opinion that you're going to wear yourself down to just nothing but skin and bones on this trip, if you ain't more careful" (MTLH 227–28). Mark Twain characterizes such complaints as "mutiny," and Mr. Brown throughout the scene remains in the subordinate role such language implies, consenting to the comic divisions of labor Mark Twain proposes, such as "if he would climb the tree, I would hold his hat" (MTLH 228). Brown does have the last word, however. In a final moment that recapitulates the clash of genteel and vulgar tastes over polite singing, Mark Twain spins out a picturesque description of a majestic palm tree, marvelously framed in the last sunlight. For a refined taste, the word painting approximates singing an appropriately sad song. However, when nature's painting moves Mark Twain to exclaim "fervently" about the beauty of the coco palm, Brown objects. People who write about the tropics, he says, "always shove one of those ragged things into the foreground [even though] it looks like a feather duster struck by lightning" (MTLH 229). Glancing at Brown's ragged pants, Mark Twain decides not to answer. Slapstick in its tone, this elaborate scenario features both Mr. Brown and Mark Twain as multifaceted comic characters, by turns foolish, vulgar, refined, manipulative, malleable, rebellious, independent, pompous, and angry.

Clemens in the "Letters from the Kingdom of Hawai'i" exhibits Mark Twain in all phases of his comic moods, but the scene with Mr. Brown and the coconuts demonstrates a shrewdness in Mark Twain that points toward his more disreputable qualities, which include laziness. On occasion, Mark Twain acknowledges this laziness (MTLH 41) or lets others suggest it (MTLH 43). Other disreputable elements are suggested by jokes about being right at home in prison (MTLH 72, 76) or about not being respectable enough to use the front entrance to the legislative chamber (MTLH 107). Sometimes the irascible temper of Mark Twain exceeds cultivated boundaries, breaking out into cursing (MTLH 46). Once, he intensifies such undignified behavior by striking his recalcitrant horse, Oahu (MTLH 63). However, in two conspicuous scenes, which do not include Mr. Brown, Clemens luxuriates in a comic mood of nonconformity to reveal an especially disreputable Mark Twain.

In the first scene of remarkably disreputable behavior, Mark Twain is a petty thief. After a few days in Honolulu, Mark Twain meets a "solemn stranger," who greets him as a preacher. When Mark Twain says he is not a preacher, the stranger asks his pardon and addresses him as "captain." When this salutation fails, he assumes Mark Twain to be a government official. Disabused of this final notion, the stranger succumbs to disbelief: "Here his feelings became too much for him, and he swooned away. I pitied the poor creature from the bottom of my heart. I was deeply moved. I shed a few tears on him and kissed him for his mother. I then took what small change he had and 'shoved'" (MTLH 43). Clemens dramatizes his point that all of the Americans one meets in Honolulu seem to be either preachers, whalers, or government officials (NB 1:225). However, his little drama invokes all the mock-feud jokes in Virginia City in which newspapermen claim their colleagues lie and steal and drink to excess—as though Mark Twain in Hawai'i has merged into the Unreliable or suddenly is admitting to the truth of those earlier jokes. The "boys" in the newsrooms along the Comstock must have laughed uproariously at Mark Twain's overdone sentiment, followed by his rifling of the stranger's pockets.

In a second scene, Mark Twain again reveals his affinity with "the boys" by garnishing a risqué parody of flirtation with slang from the mines:

> At noon I observed a bevy of nude native young ladies bathing in the sea, and went down to look at them. But with a prudery which seems to be characteristic of that sex everywhere, they all plunged in with a lying scream, and when they rose to the surface, they only just poked their heads out and showed no disposition to proceed any further in the same direction. I was naturally irritated by such conduct, and therefore I piled their clothes up on a boulder in the edge of the sea and sat down on them and kept the wenches in the water until they were pretty well used up. I had them in the door, as the missionaries say. I was comfortable, and I just let them beg. I thought I could freeze them out, maybe, but it was impracticable. I finally gave it up and went away, hoping that the rebuke I had given them would not be lost upon them. I went and undressed and went in myself. And then they went out. I never saw such singular perversity. (MTLH 240; see also NB 1:219)

The remarkable willingness to joke about sex recalls the Bohemian attitude sometimes seen during Sam Clemens's earlier days in San Francisco. That influence was in fact right at hand: Clemens again resided in San Francisco when he wrote the letter containing this scene. Such conduct justifies Mark Twain's self-assessment when he stands at the rim of the volcano Kilauea: "The smell of sulphur is strong, but not unpleasant to a sinner" (MTLH 297; see also 130).

The comic elements in these letters establish Mark Twain as a character curiously inconsistent as any version of the Gentleman Roarer figure one might encounter through previous comic writers. However, Mr. Brown most fully represents the heritage of the frontier comic figure. Brown does not have the legendary pugnacity of the Roarer, but we hear first about his drunkenness, and Mark Twain's phrasing plays with the traditional frontier habit of tall-tale stretchers: "Brown had had a couple of peanuts for lunch, and therefore one could not say he was full of whiskey, solely, without shamefully transcending the limits of truth" (MTLH 4). And if there was any doubt about Brown's uncivilized nature, Mark Twain dispels it with a gift of soap: "[Brown] bit into it, and then shook his head and said that 'as a general thing, he liked to prospect curious foreign dishes and find out what they were like, but he couldn't go that'—and threw it overboard" (MTLH 4). Brown's low position on a scale of social manners and his degraded aesthetic taste, implied in his biting the soap and throwing it away, evoke the comic frontier of antebellum writers, and his habit of using slang also confirms his indebtedness to their comically inferior figures: "ornery"; "clean you out like a jug" (MTLH 6); "go to blazes" (MTLH 7); "snatch him bald-headed"

(MTLH 13); "it ain't any odds" (MTLH 32); "chawed up"; "truck"; "plum through" (MTLH 33). In addition, Brown associates himself with yarning, a talent traditionally a part of the Backwoods Roarer's verbal repertoire. Brown not only discounts ("coppered," MTLH 41) a tale told by a whaler because he suspects it is a yarn, but hints at his own ability to "stretch the blanket" when he says he is so full that he couldn't eat "a sirloin steak off'm a sand fly" (MTLH 7). At one point, Mark Twain explicitly notes Brown's capacity to lie: "[Brown] has a generous heart and fervent imagination, and a capacity for creating impossible facts and then implicitly believing them himself, which is perfectly marvelous" (MTLH 15). Mr. Brown's raucous character is completed when Mark Twain refers to his "spirit of irreverence" (MTLH 196) and his bitter opposition to sentiment (MTLH 199). With Mr. Brown as a robust component of his comic strategy, Sam Clemens in effect had brought along a member of his original newspaper audience, "the boys."

Because Mr. Brown represents "the boys," Clemens in the Hawai'i letters apparently employs the sidekick to sanitize Mark Twain. With this buffoon to kick around, Clemens has a complete palette of comic tints available to him yet can still emphasize the more highbrow, literary-periodical version of Mark Twain that he had worked so hard to create while living in San Francisco. However, the several examples discussed so far suggest that Clemens did not worry about maintaining a consistent and obvious separation between Mark Twain and Mr. Brown. Clear differences do exist, of course. The lowest of low behaviors are reserved for Mr. Brown, for example, when he bites into the soap cake because he is so ignorant and primitive as to mistake it for food. Nevertheless, Mark Twain rifling through a stranger's pockets or undressing to bathe with young Hawai'ian girls hardly presents a well-bred figure, and the quote about smells that is the epigraph to this section is Mark Twain's, not Brown's, demonstrating how indelicate Clemens allows his literary alter ego to be. Mr. Brown is not the only embodiment of an important Nevada audience, "the boys"; the comic Mark Twain Sam Clemens employs in the "Letters from the Kingdom of Hawai'i" also forcefully recalls the wildest Washoe version of the character. Mr. Brown may descend from one of Clemens's best-known early comic creations, the Unreliable, but Mark Twain can match him for boorish behavior. More importantly, their comic interaction enables the most elaborate fictions that Clemens had created to date.

Mr. Brown and Mark Twain in the "Letters from the Kingdom of Hawai'i" represent in large measure a return to "the triple brass and cheek" that characterized Sam Clemens's comic style for the *Territorial Enterprise* at the very outset of his professional writing career. However, at the same time that Clemens works diligently to gather together his most appreciative implied readership, he remains mindful of the connection his trip to Hawai'i has with commerce, illustrated by the *Ajax*'s second voyage. When this aspect of his assignment from the *Sacramento Union* amalgamates with the islands' politics, the nationalist in Sam Clemens is awakened. In such circumstances, even the lout Mr. Brown can be enlisted in the cause.

## Mr. Brown Defends a Centric Vision of Hawai'i

[Bishop Staley] miscalculated the force, the confidence, the determination of that Puritan spirit which subdued America and underlies her whole religious fabric today—which has subdued these islanders, and whose influence over them can never be unseated.

———

"Scenes in Honolulu [No. 16]," *Sacramento Union*, July 30, 1866

When Mark Twain describes his arrival on a Sunday into Honolulu harbor, he pauses to offer this meditation:

> We steamed through the narrow channel to the music of six different church bells, which sent their mellow tones far and wide, over hills and valleys, which were peopled by naked, savage, thundering barbarians only fifty years ago! Six Christian churches within five miles of the ruins of a pagan temple, where human sacrifices were daily offered up to hideous idols in the last century! We were in pistol shot of one of a group of islands whose ferocious inhabitants closed in upon the doomed and helpless Captain Cook and murdered him, eighty-seven years ago; and lo! their descendants were at church! Behold what the missionaries have wrought! (MTLH 26; see also NB 1:202–3)

This romanticized and melodramatic narrative ranging the forces of civilization against the forces of barbarity exhibits stylistic flourishes typical of a blood-and-thunder tale, the sort found in the *New York Ledger* and other story papers that had dominated American popular culture since midcentury. Ferocious barbarians, hideous idols, and human sacrifice are exotic narrative elements to hold their own with anything George Lippard or "Ned Buntline" could conjure. The series of exclamation points Clemens adds to his sentences underscores the heightened emotions such fare was meant to produce at the lower end of the American reading audience. The only thing that could better suit the taste of that audience than a gory tale is a gory tale told to portray the triumph of good over evil, and the version of Hawai'i's history Mark Twain suggests in his meditation contains the ultimate such triumph: American Christian missionaries converting heathens.

The biblical phrasing of "lo" and "behold" invokes the sacred quality of the transformation that Mark Twain invites his readers to contemplate. Mark Twain intimates the divinely sanctioned nature of the missionary work signified by the tolling church bells, an implication made explicit in a subsequent letter, by retelling an important segment of Hawai'ian history: when Liholiho, the second King Kamehameha, broke the *kapu* against men eating with women and then defeated an army led by an *ali'i nui* (high chief) who had championed the old ways:

> when the day was done, the rebels were flying in every direction in hopeless panic, and idolatry and the tabu were dead in the land!
>
> The royalists marched gaily home to Kailua glorifying the new dispensation. "There is no power in the gods," said they; "they are a vanity and a lie. The army with idols was weak; the army without idols was strong and victorious!"
>
> The nation was without a religion.
>
> The missionary ship arrived in safety shortly afterward, timed by providential exactness to meet the emergency, and the gospel was planted in virgin soil. (MTLH 247)

This passage reveals the true power of the melodramatic narrative of civilization versus barbarity invoked by the tolling of church bells as Mark Twain enters Honolulu harbor: the events of this thrilling tale form a pattern within the cosmic design. Added together, these two moments in the letters from Hawai'i do much more than romanticize the missionaries by casting them into a blood-and-thunder tale, a genre every literate American in 1866 could understand; they establish a myth of providential design and divinely sanctioned success. This tale compels faith as well as imagination.

The consequences of understanding Hawai'ian history within this mythic narrative are far-reaching. For example, the challenge by Liholiho to the *kapu* system and his military victory that justifies the challenge are rescripted as an "emergency" answered by the arrival of the missionaries. Although the fight for the throne that the challenge to the *kapu* system had touched off obviously precipitated a crisis within Hawai'ian society, Liholiho's perspective could not have interpreted the arrival of the missionaries as answering an emergency. His forces had won. He was still the *mo'i* (king). Where is the emergency? The rhetoric speaking of emergency only makes sense within the mythic narrative woven about the missionaries, itself part of the Christian melodrama of cosmic good versus cosmic evil. When a periodical writer like Clemens adds the gory wrapping of the blood-and-thunder tale to that ultimate melodrama, he produces a hybrid story guaranteed to sell, a blood-and-thunder mythic narrative. Its combination of gore and virtue is irresistible.

With that irresistible quality, the hybrid narrative inscribes itself everywhere—onto history, the landscape, and the people. In that narrative, the native Hawai'ians have a certain childlike (MTLH 246) and superstitious (MTLH 277) character, which indicates a fundamental primitivism. Such people are therefore often depicted with bestial qualities, naked (MTLH 69, 70, 104, 112) and unclean (MTLH 67, 196, 250). In addition to a problem with physical hygiene, Hawai'ians are also perceived as morally tainted with a licentiousness that seems inborn (MTLH 282), as the habit of young girls bathing nude suggests (MTLH 279), and the ineradicable custom of *hula* apparently confirms (MTLH 70–71). At their worst, native Hawai'ians cast within the mythic narrative can easily be depicted as always about to resort to their former savagery. That potential relapse is one implication of Mark Twain marveling over the figure of Mataio Kekuanaoa, father of the last two kings and legislative leader, who is old enough to have worshiped hideous idols and witnessed human sacrifice but now is "a man practiced in holding the reins of an enlightened government" (MTLH 108). The fear of relapse is more a feature of the thrilling blood-and-thunder story than the myth of providential design. Mark Twain demonstrates as much when he finishes his rumination about Kekuanaoa by saying that "the experiences of this old man's strange, eventful life must shame the cheap inventions of romance" (MTLH 109). However, fear serves both aspects of Mark Twain's melodramatic narrative of good against evil, providing an emotional thrill on the one hand and a spiritual resolve on the other. Moreover, the hybrid narrative's impact can be understood in other ways. Even if no one believes that men like Kekuanaoa will revert to ancient and "savage" ways, the blood-and-thunder story authorizes reprintings of the wildest customs from precontact times that Clemens came across in his reading about Hawai'i (MTLH 53, 125, 131).

Choosing to reprint descriptions of these customs signifies how the thrills of a blood-and-thunder narrative rationalize not only specific textual excerpts from his reading but also filter what Clemens recalls from his sightseeing and then records. Yet employing his hybrid of Christian myth and gory tale to frame and explain what he sees can fail, too. How, for example, could such simple people have had a culture sophisticated enough to invent on their own the concept of the City of Refuge (MTLH 251)? How could their knowledge of science and engineering have been enough to create massive temple walls (MTLH 252) or to move large stones (MTLH 253)? When a road looks exactly like the Roman roads "one sees in pictures," Mark Twain cannot attribute its existence to what he calls "an untaught and degraded race" (MTLH 254). Rather, he designates these items encountered on his tour of the Kona coast of the Big Island as mysteries.

The blood-and-thunder mythic narrative does its best job of explanation when its argument for providential design comes to the forefront to speak of the conversion of the native Hawai'ians. In that design, the missionaries become God's holy instrument to transform the natives into something better—something less superstitious, for example (MTLH 131, 170). Moreover, political and economic subplots that function as supports to the mythic narrative are also transforming Hawai'i and Hawai'ians into something better—a superior form of government with a capitalistic work ethic. Henry Whitney, son of missionary parents and owner of the *Pacific Commercial Advertiser,* said that Hawai'ians were "destined to be laborers in developing the capital of the country."[73] These conversions will save the islands and their people, will meet the "emergency." To the extent that Clemens writes up Hawai'i and Hawai'ians using the mythic narrative framework of providential design, Mark Twain's "Letters from the Kingdom of Hawai'i" defend an imperialistic (if not simply racist) sense of manifest destiny, a thoroughly centric vision about certain social values as far from a rebellious, counterculture, San Francisco Bohemian attitude as one could imagine.[74]

Much of this centric viewpoint's elaboration occurs in the first and middle phases of the letters. When Mark Twain talks about commerce and urges support of the *Ajax* venture, when he takes pains to construct an argument for San Francisco superseding Honolulu as the home port for the American whaling fleet, the narrator details the subplots to the blood-and-thunder mythic narrative. These serious reportorial efforts run counter to the pleasure of laughter, an effect especially notable in the letters' middle phase. Comic scenes involving Mark Twain in that phase dwindle considerably. Letter 9 is an exception, providing a comic tour de force when a whaling captain's wife describes a shopping trip in sailors' slang. However much hilarity that scene generates, it nevertheless relegates Mark Twain to the background. Moreover, as a prelude to a serious discussion of the whaling trade, the episode of the whaling captain's wife also partially bolsters the serious discussion of commerce. Clemens thus segregates the comic tour de force from the misadventures of Mark Twain and Mr. Brown. That isolation highlights the way in which the middle phase of the letters focuses on people encountered and sights seen at the expense of developing the fictional eccentricities of the main comic figures.

---

73. Quoted in Silva, "Banning," 45.

74. To what extent the charge of racism makes sense is debatable, but as a Southerner, Clemens was particularly aware of shades of skin color. In several places he characterizes these shades (see NB 1:152), but once in the letters, his epithets of "dark-skinned" and "barbarous" (MTLH 65) link racism and imperialism. In his notebooks, Clemens also showed his prejudice (NB 1:157). Once he calls Hawai'ians "niggers" (NB 1:135), the king a "heathen blackamoor" (NB 1:149).

Moreover, when Mr. Brown appears in the middle phase of the letters, Clemens tones him down considerably. For example, Brown talks neither foolishly nor vulgarly but makes sense in his two appearances in letter 8 (MTLH 67, 75). And despite Brown being called an "impetuous child of nature" (MTLH 121) in letter 13, Clemens highlights Brown's sensible side in other appearances. Any remaining comic energy manifests itself either as satire against the Hawai'ian legislature (and all legislatures) or as lampoon darts hurled at Bishop Thomas Staley and Minister Charles Harris. Even Mr. Brown conforms to this centric posture, for his function in the middle section is to help Clemens make the case against Bishop Staley and defend the missionaries.

Reading the middle phase of the letters (numbers 8–17) as a unit emphasizes how the sparseness of the comic elements aids an earnest trumpeting of a centric and respectable vision of Hawai'i, how a very funny comic device, Mr. Brown, can be fitted into the ultimate earnestness of the blood-and-thunder mythic narrative. The earnest quality also has reinforcement from the two news stories that dominate this phase of the letters' composition: the drama of Princess Victoria Kamāmalu's death and the saga of the *Hornet* survivors. Both stories simply have too serious a tone to be amenable to comic descriptions and too strong a narrative to attempt inserting fictitious comic scenes into them. Nevertheless, the animus against Bishop Thomas Staley, bound up in the story of the mourning ceremonies for the princess, was fierce enough to employ all available weapons, even if it meant giving Brown a new role and intruding his comic presence into the politics surrounding those ceremonies.

Clemens chronicles the death, mourning ceremonies, and funeral of Princess Victoria Kamāmalu in three different letters, all written after his return from his Big Island trip. These three letters, along with another recounting the ordeal of the *Hornet* survivors, are the last ones Clemens wrote while in the islands. The princess had been dead for nearly three weeks, her body lying in state at 'Iolani Palace, when Clemens returned to O'ahu on June 16. Her story, as well as related news, dominated his final Hawai'i correspondence. Clemens paid a nighttime visit to the palace, either on the twenty-first or twenty-second, and reported on the singing of the *ali'i* (chiefs) in the funeral chamber and the chanting of the *maka'āinana* (commoners) on the grounds. Foreigners were not allowed onto the palace grounds to see the mourning rites. Admitting that he did not witness these rites, Clemens has Mark Twain nevertheless speak of their "old-time barbarous character." Mark Twain also refers to the similar mourning rites that had occurred three years earlier when King Kamehameha IV had died, noting that "while the missionaries were in power [these performances] were considerably toned down." The blame for the backsliding falls on the "more liberal regime of the new Reformed Catholic dispensation" (MTLH 127), that is, Bishop Thomas

Staley. The American missionaries had made progress against these "barbarous" customs, but Staley's liberality countenanced them and the results are disastrous. Thomas Staley was indeed liberal by mid-nineteenth-century standards, enlightened by present standards, in his views on social policy in general and on Hawaiʻian culture in particular. So long as Hawaiʻian cultural practices did not conflict with Christian morality, he championed the indigenous culture, attacking the Congregationalists' puritanical view of Hawaiʻians as ignoble savages.[75]

Robert Semes designates Clemens's friend, the Reverend Franklin S. Rising, as the probable source of the attack on Staley, but the chief informants for all this background more likely were inhabitants of the islands.[76] Candidates on Mauʻi would include the Reverend William Alexander as well as the family of missionaries Richard and Clarissa Armstrong, at whose home Clemens boarded. On Oʻahu, two of Clemens's most consistent informants would have been Henry Whitney, owner and editor of the *Pacific Commercial Advertiser,* son of first company missionaries, and Henry MacFarlane, a writer for the *Advertiser* and son of a prominent Honolulu businessman. Clemens had made the *Advertiser*'s offices a routine stop during his first stay on Oʻahu, and he had visited the MacFarlane house at least once in that period. His equestrian expedition on his steed Oahu had been arranged by MacFarlane. Clemens copied into letter 16 part of an article on Charles Harris that MacFarlane had written for the *Advertiser,* and when Clemens made a reference to "scribblers like myself" (MTLH 127) who had written against Staley allowing barbarous customs to prevail again, he was almost certainly referring to MacFarlane and Whitney.[77]

On June 29, the final day of the official mourning period for the princess, Clemens and a few other foreigners were allowed to witness the last ceremonies to be conducted on the grounds of ʻIolani Palace. He arrived about eight in the evening at the home of the minister of the interior, next door to the palace, to view the rites from a second-story balcony. He left shortly after midnight. This experience confirmed for Clemens all that had been and might be said against Bishop Staley, resulting in the diatribe against the bishop that dominates letter 16 and echoes whatever Whitney and others of the missionary party already had said about the mourning rites not only for the princess but also for her brother the king three years before.

---

75. Robert Louis Semes, "Hawaiʻi's Holy War: English Bishop Staley, American Congregationalists, and the Hawaiʻian Monarchs, 1860–1870," 123–25.

76. Ibid., 127.

77. For Clemens and William P. Alexander's relationship, see Mary Charlotte Alexander, *William Patterson Alexander in Kentucky, the Marquesas, Hawaiʻi,* 448. Clemens would have known the Armstrongs from his tour of the sugar plantations. For Clemens in the *Advertiser* office, see Whitney, "Better Fifty Years"; and *Advertiser,* "Mark Twain Day."

When Clemens writes up what he has seen of the Hawai'ians mourning their princess, he decides to employ Mr. Brown to help Mark Twain deride the bishop. Clemens builds his derision through a series of exchanges between Mr. Brown and Mark Twain, ostensibly made as they watch the mourning rites unfold before them. The tactic has the virtue of providing an illusion of immediacy, as though the reader, too, stood on a balcony of a house next door to the palace, looking down into the grounds. The exchanges cast Mark Twain into the role of the refined gentleman while Mr. Brown plays his inevitably lowbrow self. However, the cosmopolitan language with which Mark Twain defends the bishop does not help his cause, just as the slang Mr. Brown uses to criticize the mourning rites does not injure his position. Mark Twain's elegant language and the forces of civilization that it ostensibly represents ultimately function ironically, as does his praise of the "good and wise" bishop (MTLH 165). The same ironic strategy encompasses Mark Twain's reference to scripture and the image of Jesus weeping for Lazarus. The refined Mark Twain calculates the reference as the ultimate answer to Brown's impertinent persistence about the mistake Staley has made in allowing the old-style mourning. Brown, however, refuses to be silenced. He instead turns the allusion back on Mark Twain merely by repeating "Jesus wept" until the latter admits his error in defending Staley: the tears of Jesus for his friend Lazarus cannot be analogous to the Hawai'ians mourning for their princess. Brown triumphs. The mourning for the princess was "rather overdone" (MTLH 166): "I could not disguise from myself that the gentle grief of the Savior was but poorly imitated here—that the heathen orgies resurrected by the Lord Bishop of Honolulu were not warranted by the teachings of the master whom he professes to serve" (MTLH 168–69). This acquiescence by the refined Mark Twain to the vulgarian Mr. Brown happens despite the scorn heaped upon Brown, whose "conduct is shameful" (MTLH 167), and whose "ignorance is his misfortune—not his crime" (MTLH 166). Mark Twain's superior position in a cultural hierarchy sanctions the scorn: "it ill beseems *such as you* to speak irreverently" (MTLH 165, emphasis added). Mr. Brown, who can do no right, whose gaffes provide a major source of laughter elsewhere in the letters, strikes a blow here for the missionaries and for reverent behavior.

## Eccentric yet Civilized(?) Mark Twain and Mr. Brown

Brown call[s] the Missionaries the Serious Family.
The mish's are outraged by the levity of my letters, & have so
expressed themselves.

———

Notebooks entries during Hawai'i trip, 1866

Reading the "Letters from the Kingdom of Hawai'i" with one eye on their comic aspect and the other on their history of composition in three phases immediately highlights their periodicity, that is, the need for Clemens to produce copy for a big urban daily newspaper. The tactic also points to the reporter's dependence on both the randomness of unusually important events and the painstaking recording of everyday observances in his notebook. Though the twenty-five letters from Hawai'i were the single largest series Clemens had written to date and contained his biggest effort yet to write comic scenes and to elaborate Mark Twain as a comic character, they were written for a daily newspaper and without a comic design. "Inform" was their first imperative: inform especially about the commerce and industry of the islands, given the new enterprise that the *Ajax* represented. After that, the quirkiness of Mark Twain—aided by the outrageousness of Mr. Brown—provided the comic glue to hold the correspondence together. Obviously, the *Union* counted on those comic features from the pseudonym "Mark Twain"; they had been so conspicuous in the growing fame of Sam Clemens prior to the assignment. Only the blood-and-thunder mythic narrative that organizes much of the serious elements in the letters compares as a major unifying device.

However, reading these letters with one eye on their comic aspect and the other on a romantic and melodramatic narrative pitting civilization against barbarity uncovers a comic subversiveness surprisingly coherent in the face of the scouting assignment for California capitalists. Clemens in his Hawai'i letters thus wrote himself into two competing attitudes about the island kingdom. As previous sections have demonstrated, one attitude was thoroughly centric, even chauvinistic in its view of the United States of America. When Mark Twain endorses this centric vision, he manifests the master narrative role of respectable correspondent and projects a social, political, and literary figure with bourgeois attitudes. Mark Twain confirms the status quo by playing the role of the refined gentleman of good taste, well-mannered socially, mainstream in his support of political manifest destiny. Nevertheless, to the extent that Clemens allows Mr.

Brown to undermine directly this persona of Mark Twain, Clemens can create a subversive counterflow of laughter. This laughable subversion of centric American values can be plainly glimpsed through the comic interplay of Mr. Brown and Mark Twain.

As part of the scene with Mr. Brown and the coconuts, a genteel Mark Twain attempts to sing a conventionally pathetic ballad to express the loneliness of their situation. Brown threatens Mark Twain with being pushed overboard if he continues (MTLH 225). In this and in other parallel instances, Mark Twain represents a normative taste for art forms. Brown is clearly the vulgarian, yet the former never wins in the scenes that dramatize their clash of correct and incorrect aesthetics. The contest may end in a draw, as it does in the coconut scene, but more often the conventionally correct aesthetic wilts under ridicule. Clemens twice fashions this ridicule in an extreme manner. Nineteenth-century American society held to the long-standing tradition that poetry marked the summit of literary endeavors. In the Hawai'i letters, Clemens mercilessly parodies poetry's stature as the highest expression of noble sentiments by transforming it into a physical purgative. With Brown seasick, Mark Twain tries pathetic narratives, eloquent declamation, and humorous anecdotes to help. Only the recitation of a poem he had been writing, a rhyming paraphrase of Polonius's advice to his son, provides relief. "As I finished, Brown's stomach cast up its contents, and in a minute or two he felt entirely relieved and comfortable" (MTLH 201). His contemporary audience apparently found the scene so funny that Clemens felt compelled to repeat it (MTLH 283–84).

Another vehicle for the expression of fine sentiment, picturesque descriptions of natural scenery, suffers the same comic fate. Typically, these picturesque descriptions grace the narratives of gentlemen travelers recounting their trips. The direct disparagement of one instance by Brown in the coconut scene has already been noted: Mark Twain pens a fine paragraph about the beauty of the coco palm etched in silhouette against a setting sun, and Brown scorns the tree as a feather duster struck by lightning (MTLH 229). Brown has also debunked Mark Twain's elaborately elevated description of Honolulu by insisting on adding to it the frightful reality of its insect population (MTLH 32). In another example, the comically down-to-earth quality of Brown's aesthetic is underscored when Clemens uses the horse Oahu to deflate the high-blown literary rhetoric of Mark Twain (MTLH 63). Brown's aesthetic possesses more than common sense; it has horse sense, too.

Brown also disparages gentlemen's travel narratives, what he calls the "mush-and-milk preacher travels [that are] shoemakered up by them pious bushwackers from America" (MTLH 210). In these books, the problem with the descriptions of natural scenery is not that they become so concerned with the correct literary style that they gild over and therefore obscure the actual object or view. Rather, when these writers come to "any heavy sort of scenery, and it is too much bother to describe it, they shovel in another lot of Scripture, and wind up with 'Lo! what God hath wrought!'" Brown finishes his literary review by saying, "Confound their lazy melts" (MTLH 211). Mark Twain, the gentleman newspaper correspondent who has brought Mr. Brown along as a companion to "travel in some degree of state, and so command the respect of strangers," feels obliged to issue a reprimand. However, Mark Twain not only remains silent about the specifics of this instance of Brown's ridicule of a standard aesthetic but also loses what respect he might command by finishing his reprimand with an order to Brown to "proceed to the nearest depot and replenish the correspondent['s] fountain of inspiration," fancy talk for a jug of beer. When Brown notes that Mark Twain seems to need inspiration every time he, Brown, "chances an opinion," the respectable correspondent cuts him off with, "Good afternoon, Brown" (MTLH 211). Clemens, then, uses Brown to induce laughter against multiple targets: Mark Twain's fine-grained literary rhetoric, the way preachers write travel books, travel books in general, and poetry and fine literary style in general.

Enlisted in defense of the missionaries, Brown also proves useful in conducting a guerrilla war against American civilization's self-image. Refined and genteel notions about music and literature contribute to that image for a society. With Brown looking over Mark Twain's shoulder, however, the image seems little more than pretense, as bathing dresses are "an affectation of modesty born of . . . high civilization" (MTLH 279). Worse, civilized society's projection of its moral self might be hypocritical, as when Mark Twain's pompous superiority gives way to a request for more beer, or when he says that whiskey has been a civilizing factor in Hawai'i (MTLH 246).

As pivotal as Brown is to this guerrilla war, however, he is not necessary for Clemens to dramatize the flaws in civilized society's view of its moral superiority. During his trip to the Big Island, Mark Twain has an experience from which he draws a stark conclusion that impugns civilization. As the schooner he is aboard sails down the Kona coast at night, a storm begins, and the ship is "tossed about like a cork" (MTLH 280). When he spots a light flashing in and out of the waves, Mark Twain knows that a canoe is making its way toward the schooner, and he wonders what "desperate extremity" could drive a person out onto such a sea. When it turns out to be a Hawai'ian who wishes to make a present of food to the ship, Mark Twain cannot believe it. "'He has got an axe to grind.' I spoke in that uncharitable spirit of the civilized world which suspects all men's motives—which cannot conceive of an unselfish thought wrought into an unselfish deed by any man whatsoever, be he pagan or Christian" (MTLH 281). Affected, hypocritical, cynical—these qualities seem to be the legacy of the civilizèd man as much as any positive ones that might be adduced. Such a counter-view of the benefits of a civilized society echoes an ideology of primitivism that extols traditional societies as it points out the flaws in Western civilization. This Rousseauistic primitivism values the traditional behavior of Hawai'ians, not that of mainstream America with its Protestant work ethic. Within that ideological framework, the natural man stands superior to the refined man; Brown, "the impetuous child of nature" (MTLH 121) and obvious heir to the legacy of the Backwoods Roarer, rates above the genteel Mark Twain.

Such an ideology of primitivism circulates a narrative, one potentially as pow-erful an explanation of events and behaviors as the hybrid, blood-and-thunder tale of providential design. Rescripted within the narrative of primitivism, the naturally unselfish Hawai'ian trumps even the missionary. The eccentric can become the norm. The comic aspect of the Hawai'i letters, but Mr. Brown in particular, opens a space that not only undermines Mark Twain in his centric phase but also links his disreputable side to a set of values within an alternative narrative that reinvents what is meant by "respectable." The Protestant work ethic epitomizes values that define respectable in the centric narrative, but a list of the values from the alternative narrative of primitivism might begin with an acknowledgment that repose and tranquillity are as precious as industry and commerce. And yet the Protestant work ethic declares folks in repose to be lazy. The disreputable aspects of Mark Twain include his confessed laziness, as seen in the coconut episode in letter 20, and even his pride in it, for example, when Mark Twain watches the sailors going about their tasks on the *Ajax*. "I sat down on a bench, and for an hour I took a tranquil delight in that kind of labor which is such a luxury to the enlightened Christian—to wit, the labor of other people" (MTLH 5). Mark Twain enunciates a wonderfully subversive idea. The superior Christian, the enlightened Christian, is the person who can imagine a value other than understanding work as a constant hymn to God and who therefore con-ceptually ignores the Protestant work ethic.

This comic maneuver is important because the inability to think past their own values and acknowledge the possibilities of other value systems exposes the American missionaries to the harshest criticisms that issue from the mouth of Mark Twain. In one such criticism early in the series of travel letters, Clemens begins in a comic fashion to describe the ancient Hawai'ian custom of human sacrifice, but the tone and the target of comic ridicule changes radically as he continues describing the time,

> long, long before the missionaries braved a thousand privations to come and make [the Hawai'ians] permanently miserable by telling them how beautiful and blissful a place heaven is, and how nearly impossible it is to get there; and showed the poor native how

dreary a place perdition is and what unnecessarily liberal facilities there are for going to it; showed him how, in his ignorance, he had gone and fooled away his kinfolks to no purpose; showed him what rapture it is to work all day long for fifty cents to buy food for next day with, as compared with fishing for pastime and lolling in the shade through eternal summer, and eating of the bounty that nobody labored to provide but nature. (MTLH 53)

Though the rhetorical flourishes such as "eternal summer" and the image of no one working in ancient Hawai'i obviously constructs Polynesia as a paradise, this excerpt is more remarkable for its tacit recognition that the Hawai'ians have lost something culturally important because of the missionaries' work ethic. The Edenic motif evoked—people eating by simply picking the fruits of nature that are all around them—becomes a satiric counter to the biblical injunction that man must live by the sweat of his brow as well as a satiric comment against the missionaries' enforcement of the injunction in a place where God himself seems to have given a dispensation. In a neat piece of comic foolery by Mark Twain, Clemens thereby manages to convey the alien nature of Western ways in Hawai'i with a diction choice—"rapture"—that at the same time connotes the spiritual fervor of evangelical Christianity.

In another letter, Clemens again notes the passing of the old Hawai'ian ways and links the change to the Protestant tradition that defines work as a form of worship—and thus dismisses recreation and "lolling in the shade through eternal summer" as morally wrong: "This weekly stampede of the natives [during gala Saturdays] interfered too much with labor and the interests of the white folks, and by sticking in a law here, and preaching a sermon there, and by various other means, they gradually broke it up" (MTLH 71). Mark Twain implies that white folks are spoilsports, like Malvolio, apparently thinking that because they are righteous there shall be no more cakes and ale—or *poi* and *'awa*.

The racial element in the phrase "the interests of the white folks" ricochets in different directions, but one trajectory links it to the need in 1866 to find plenty of cheap labor for the islands' plantations, an important topic in letter 23, on sugar, which interrupts the narrative of the Big Island trip that comprises the last set of eight letters. Cheap and plentiful labor interests the white folks who own the plantations because the Hawai'ian population has been decimated by diseases introduced through Western contact and because Chinese laborers have been imported for more than a decade before Clemens visits.[78] These "coolies"

78. Silva, "Banning," discusses cheap labor in the context of attempts in the 1850s and 1860s to ban *hula* (see Kuykendall, *Foundation*, 328–31; and *Critical Years*, chapter 6). The scale of decimation depends on the size of the precontact population. Lieutenant James King, who took over Cook's expedition when he was killed in 1779, estimated the population of the islands to be

are expected to do all manner of work, even that which is exhausting drudgery, "drudgery which all white men abhor and are glad to escape from" (MTLH 272). In his comments about "white folks" (the missionaries) breaking up the festive Saturday markets, Clemens implicitly accuses them of pious hypocrisy, yet his comment about Chinese laborers endorses a "natural" division of labor along racial lines.

Part of Mark Twain's attack on the missionary community of 1866 assumes that they are self-righteous, and plenty of historical examples existed to support the assumption. The classic instance of missionary self-righteousness occurred with Hiram Bingham, one of the first two ministers set aside for Hawai'i by the American Board of Commissioners for Foreign Missions. Though the board expected the missionaries to effect a social revolution, converting savages and sinners to civilized Christians, they were not to interfere politically. Nevertheless, once in Hawai'i and put to the test of whether or not to participate in politics, Bingham and "most of the missionaries discovered in themselves a contempt for caution" and rather readily insisted on taking a hand in all aspects of island life. For a man like Bingham, the justification was the divinely sanctioned nature of the task of conversion. For Bingham, Hawai'i was not a paradise without the necessity of work, but instead a place where the people were filled with "unrighteousness, fornication, wickedness, murder, debate, deceit, malignity," a place where people were "whisperers, backbiters, haters of God, despiteful, proud, boasters, inventors of evil things, disobedient to parents, without natural affection, implacable, unmerciful."[79] The myth of providential design, which scripts Hawai'ians as savages, was never more forcefully expressed.

Dr. Gerrit Judd, who came to the islands in the early 1840s as a medical missionary, embodied the logical extension of Bingham's initial willingness to be a part of Hawai'i's politics. During the 1840s, under Kauikeaouli (Kamehameha III), Judd was minister of finance and, as someone who saw no point in confining his good judgment to one department, unofficial minister of foreign affairs. As a condition of employment, Judd and others who worked in the Hawai'ian government signed an oath of allegiance to the king, an act that did not sit well with Americans in the islands. The animus his oath raised foreshadowed the attack on Charles Harris twenty years later that Clemens witnessed and in which he participated. In control of the kingdom's purse strings and often in command

---

between 400,000 and 500,000. Robert C. Schmitt ("New Estimates of the Pre-Censal Population of Hawai'i") estimates 200,000 to 250,000. David Stannard (*Before the Horror: The Population of Hawai'i on the Eve of Western Contact*) makes the case for a much larger population: 800,000 to 1,000,000. Missionaries in 1832 estimated the Hawai'ian population to be about 130,000.

79. Daws, *Shoal*, 63, quotation on 64.

of decisions concerning foreigners, Judd was a formidable presence in the Hawai'ian government until he was ousted in 1854 by his enemies. If Gerrit Judd epitomized the missionaries' willingness to be power brokers in Hawai'i's politics, other examples—such as Samuel N. Castle (one of the founders of the present-day corporation Castle and Cooke) and Sanford Dole (who owned the island of Lana'i and amassed a fortune growing pineapples)—suggest how able and willing the children of missionaries were to be economic forces. The ultimate instance of the consequence of missionaries becoming more interested in politics than religion was the Hawai'ian League. First formed in January 1887 and marking the beginning of the organized opposition to the monarchy that would culminate in its overthrow in 1893, the league was headed by descendants of Protestant missionaries.[80]

Missionaries past and present, then, could be praised by Mark Twain because their "lightest acts always meant business" (MTLH 171), but claiming that they are all business forges a two-edged sword suggestive of how spiritual work and material industry had become fused together. This fusion had a long historical basis even by 1866. Certainly, it was evident when Samuel Castle advocated establishing new sugar plantations to benefit idle Hawai'ians: "As it is true that indolence begets vice, so it is true that industry promotes virtue. All successful efforts taken to produce industry by proper means tend to promote virtue and must be beneficial to that people on whom they are bestowed."[81] Promotion of such industry, however, obviously provided different benefits to different groups of people. Clemens could use Mark Twain to promote a centric, normative view of what the American missionaries had accomplished, but a passage from the fourteenth letter from Hawai'i also shows that Clemens understood the ambiguity of their work:

> the Sandwich Island missionaries are pious; hard-working; hard-praying, self-sacrificing; hospitable; devoted to the well-being of this people and the interests of Protestantism; bigoted; puritanical; slow; ignorant of all white human nature and natural ways of men, except the remnant of these things that are left in their own class or profession; old fogy—fifty years behind the age; uncharitable toward the weaknesses of the flesh; considering all shortcomings, faults, and failings in the light of crimes, and having no mercy and no forgiveness for such. (MTLH 129)

In developing this eccentric and subversive perception of the missionaries' work, Clemens takes advantage of the ambiguity, "they are all business," to expose precisely the entanglement of spiritual work and material industry, to expose not

---

80. Ibid., 143, 243, 292, 294; Kent, *Hawai'i*, 73.
81. Quoted in Kent, *Hawai'i*, 28.

just how the missionaries and their descendants go about God's work in the islands, but how they are also typical entrepreneurial Americans who are going about their own business, too. Mark Twain could thus be sarcastic about speculation (MTLH 211–12) and offer opinions that do not flatter the missionaries (NB 1:135, 152–53, 165–66, 211, 213).

A comment from Sam Clemens glosses the topic of how a disreputably lazy Mark Twain enables a critique of nineteenth-century American society's view of itself: "I like kanakas . . . because they're not ashamed to acknowledge that they're lazy. White men are. Though we are all intrinsically disinclined to hard labor, we all work more or less and make a bluff to be thought mighty industrious."[82] The thought fits well with the excerpts from the letters criticizing the missionaries for brazenly assuming that their way must be the divinely sanctioned way for people to behave, for making their Christian morality serve their own monetary interests, and for making other racial groups labor at jobs their own work ethic rates as drudgery. Apparently assuming a negative stereotype propagated by a missionary perspective, Clemens maneuvers to strike his satiric blow. First, he suggests that the positive image of hard work associated with Americans is a mere show. He then transcends all ethnic or national groups to assert that everyone is really lazy, thus negating the stereotypical premises of the first statement. Any supposed admission by *kānaka maoli* (native Hawai'ians) Clemens had met that they are lazy—in other words, that by the standards of the missionaries they are lazy—is as liberating as the wildest comic scene Clemens devises in the letters from Hawai'i: Brown's rapacious souvenir hunting for Cook's monument or Mark Twain's sudden disrobing and ecstatic participation in surf-bathing with "native young ladies." In all these cases, the comic effect occurs because the usual silence about the unconscious wish to transgress at fundamental levels is broken. The resulting laughter comically questions what it means to claim to be civilized.

By asking this question, the comic aspect of the "Letters from the Kingdom of Hawai'i" contributes to a narrative that runs counter to and subverts the myth of providential design. While the myth authorizes the Protestant mission to convert Hawai'i and Hawai'ians into an island image of America and Americans, the counternarrative champions a comic primitivism in which the misadventures of Mark Twain and Mr. Brown ironically signal a truly enlightened civilization.

---

82. This remark is attributed to Clemens by a Mr. Armstrong, who says that he met Sam in Virginia City and that Sam "boarded at our house" in Wailuku, Mau'i (E. S. Goodhue, "Mark Twain's Hawai'ian Home," 180). This stay would have been during his visits to the three Wailuku Sugar Company plantations (CL 1:335–41). Goodhue's Armstrong is said to be in his old age and a "clerk of the court" (179). Frear (MTH 50) speaks of a G. Armstrong as clerk of the Mau'i circuit court.

# SCENE THREE

WRITING TRAVEL LETTERS

## THE OUT-OF-TOWN CORRESPONDENT

BUT I DON'T WANT TO GO TO ASIA, OR SOMEWHERE—OH NO, I GUESS
NOT. I HAVE GOT THE "GYPSY" ONLY IN A MILD FORM. IT WILL KILL ME
YET, THOUGH.

————

LETTER TO WILLIAM WRIGHT, JULY 15, 1864

THE MOST USEFUL AND INTERESTING LETTERS WE GET HERE FROM
HOME ARE FROM CHILDREN SEVEN OR EIGHT YEARS OLD. THIS IS PET-
RIFIED TRUTH. . . . THEY WRITE SIMPLY AND NATURALLY, AND WITH-
OUT STRAINING FOR EFFECT.

————

"AN OPEN LETTER TO THE AMERICAN PEOPLE,"
*NEW YORK WEEKLY REVIEW,* FEBRUARY 17, 1866

With the success of the letters from Hawai'i, Sam Clemens had discovered how to indulge his wanderlust and make it pay, demonstrating that his travel letters would be a valuable addition to the columns of any newspaper. The Hawai'i correspondence provided a large canvas for Clemens to display his considerable talents for clear reporting and vivid description, rendered through a quirky personality. The travel letter had already been an auspicious format. The more routine newspaper version of that genre, a letter from an out-of-town correspondent, first featured the Mark Twain signature in the *Territorial Enterprise* of February 1863. Moreover, the first original item by Sam Clemens for a New York City periodical, "Doings in Nevada" (MTEnt, 122–25), featured the same genre. Similar efforts include "Washoe—Information Wanted" (ETS 1:367–71) and "The Great Earthquake" (ETS 2:303–10). Though such correspondence entails careful descriptions of scene or detailed reports on people and their behavior, Clemens blended these reportorial elements with clever phrasing and comic wit to create the signature insouciant tone of Mark Twain. Even unsigned pieces for the *Enterprise* exhibit this blend of the objective and the comic, for example, his reports on the events surrounding money-raising efforts for the Sanitary Fund, two of which were reprinted in the *San Francisco Bulletin,* while a third, "The History of Gold and Silver Bars," appeared in an unknown St. Louis newspaper, possibly before the end of May (MTEnt 186–89).

Mark Twain's quirky comic personality dominates the Hawai'i correspondence, whether its facets are the satirist's sharp tongue or the humorist's merry and peculiar turn of phrase. Moreover, Clemens does not rest content with merely sketching the shenanigans of Mark Twain; he provides double the fun with Mr. Brown. With their comic dynamic always at the ready, Clemens reinvents the travel letter by merging the antebellum comic tradition of mock travel letters, exemplified by Seba Smith's Major Jack Downing, with the highbrow style of travel writing represented by Bayard Taylor. The new kind of travel letter accommodated a mixture of the necessary reportage and expected literary description with comic misadventures as likely to be fictional as not. Readable because of Mark Twain's comic personality, the "Letters from the Kingdom of Hawai'i" are the most original travel correspondence printed in the United States since N. P. Willis's *Pencillings by the Way,* which appeared in the 1835, and the most successful at interpolating comic elements into the narration since J. Ross Browne's letters from Europe and the Middle East, which became *Yusef; or, The Journey of the Frangi* in 1853.

The mock letter was an important genre for American comic writers in the nineteenth century. Newspapers in the antebellum period were especially fond of printing parodies of their semiliterate correspondence from frontier areas. Because newspapers provided an obvious site for all manner of issues to be aired in a democratic society, such correspondence together with its parodic counterpart formed an apt symbol of that airing's contested nature. The mock travel letter proved to be even more useful in this regard. By writing parodies of travel letters to periodicals, writers could satirically explore any number of topics while maintaining before the reader's imaginative eye a fresh variety of scenes. The parody of travel letters also developed a variety of comic personae and allowed for the installation of comic sketches within the letter format. Famous examples in antebellum America of how manipulating letter writing for comic purposes led to developing comic personae and creating comic sketches for them, besides Smith's Major Downing, would include Charles Noland's Colonel Pete Whetstone, William T. Thompson's Major Joseph Jones, Mortimer Thomson's Philander Doesticks, and Charles F. Browne's Artemus Ward. During the Civil War, Robert Newell could be added to the list with his Orpheus C. Kerr letters, David R. Locke his Petroleum Vesuvius Nasby letters, and Charles Smith his Bill Arp letters. This rich background guaranteed a public long accustomed to fictitious comic letters when Sam Clemens began writing up his trip to Hawai'i from the comic perspective of Mark Twain.

The widespread and long-standing habit of parodying correspondence, both private and public, suggests how pervasive letter writing was in nineteenth-century America. In William Decker's view, letter writing was "a discursive practice to which people of nearly every class and level of literacy had recourse."[83] The importance of personal letter writing can be attributed to the restless mobility of the population as it spread across the continent. By the 1860s—after the rush to the Oregon territory, the California goldfields, and the Comstock silver mines—separation from friends and family and the consequent necessity for letters to stay in touch and report on the new territories could easily be sentimentalized as well as parodied. "There is a vacant chair in nearly every household in the Union, from Maine to Louisiana, from Wisconsin to Florida; and the forms that should fill them are scattered far and wide among the mines and ranches of California, Nevada, Oregon, Mexico, Utah, Idaho, Montana, Colorado—everywhere that gold lures, or adventure invites."[84] The habit of writing letters for publication in various periodicals, and thus for public use, underscores how newspapers functioned as digests of information from many correspondents. Editors built that commercial habit upon a primary need found in the personal letter—to report on the new territories to the folks back home. Just as personal correspondence functioned to maintain family ties, public correspondence in newspapers functioned to maintain a sense of union among the states, by 1866 spread from sea to shining sea.

Private correspondence is "a communication that figures successfully in an interpersonal relationship."[85] Such familiar letters, with their inevitably subjective qualities, are nevertheless constructed with a broadly realistic intent that makes the genre a basis for any journalistic reporting in published newspaper correspondence. Newspaper editors and reporters by the 1860s had recognized the value of simply recording an event and omitting the personal and the subjective. Nevertheless, newspaper correspondence, a particular subgenre of reporting, when well done, necessarily shares characteristics with private and personal correspondence. Writers of both genres wish to be engaging as well as informative. Moreover, the writer of especially good newspaper correspondence will successfully mimic a sense of intimacy that occurs naturally in the private letter. Mark Twain praises exactly these qualities in "An Open Letter to the American People" (JF 26–33), a comic lesson in how not to write a personal letter. The mock essay ridicules letter writers who cannot create the necessary texture of accurate detail on subjects that will interest a reader. After displaying poor examples, Mark Twain reveals his idea of a model letter, written by a child who tells all she sees with vividness and intimacy.

83. William Merrill Decker, *Epistolary Practices: Letter Writing in America before Telecommunications*, 4.
84. *New York Weekly Review*, [Headnote for "An Open Letter to the American People"], 1.
85. Decker, *Epistolary Practices*, 19.

The same qualities of vividness, intimacy, and accurate detail on subjects that will interest a reader also create successful travel letters, which wed good reportorial skills to a familiar relationship with the reader. Correspondence about traveling, however, differs markedly from mere newspaper correspondence in the literary quality of its descriptions of people and places, that is, in its self-consciously created aesthetic. This distinction does not mean that literary set pieces cannot appear in newspaper correspondence or even in private letters. Certainly, brief passages of brilliant phrasing may not be uncommon to particular writers, whatever the genre, but such overt literary qualities came to be expected for nineteenth-century travel letters targeting the highbrow American market:

> The author must begin with the excitements of the ocean voyage itself and devote at least a portion of a chapter to the thrill, so long anticipated, of setting foot on foreign soil. From this point on he should mix architecture and scenery with comment on philanthropies, skillfully work in a little history cribbed from Murray's guides, taking care to add a touch of sentiment or eloquence when the occasion permitted. If the essay or book required a little padding, it was always possible to retell an old legend or slip in an account of dangers surmounted in crossing the Alps.[86]

Given his propensity to talk and yarn, Sam Clemens seems to have always had a facility for these genres with their conversational tone and manner. Moreover, Clemens's best work, whether he signs it "Mark Twain" or not, always involves creating the illusion of conversation. One of his tricks for creating that illusion was interrupting himself, a device that appeared, for example, in his correspondence with the *San Francisco Call* on July 15 (MTCall no. 1) and August 20, 1863 (MTCall no. 3).

Like so many Americans who had traveled thousands of miles from home to seek fortune, Sam Clemens regularly wrote to the family and friends he had left behind to recount his travels and to report on the new territory he inhabited. Unlike many of his fellow Americans, Sam Clemens showed a highly developed literary manipulation of the letter to folks back home—well before he invented Mark Twain. Local newspapers published several letters to his family, three of them in the *Keokuk Gate City,* but apparently Jane Clemens also had a habit of showing Sam's letters to folks (CL 1:245, 307, 308, 347). His style even in those earlier letters has enough effervescent personality to enliven its journalistic reporting of facts and to lift them above the routine. The paradigm for the argument that reading Clemens's personal letters makes one aware of his professional potential as a comic correspondent are the ones published in the *Keokuk Gate*

86. Quoted in Paul Wermuth, *Bayard Taylor,* 32.

*City* between November 1861 and May 1862. As Franklin Rogers demonstrates, the letters appearing in the *Gate City* are the products of skillful literary invention and, in one case, deliberate revision. Clemens consciously used the intimacy of private correspondence to create letters ready for newspaper publication, complete with a comically fictitious mother as addressee and a persona, "Sam," as author.

In the first letter, "Sam" promises his mother that he will comment on the country of Nevada and "let nonsense alone" (LGC 22), but he immediately violates his promise with a comic catalog of the Nevada Territory's "produce." The long list includes various minerals and then mixes the reputable and the disreputable promiscuously, naming ladies, children, Chinese immigrants, murderers, Christians, thieves, sharpers, poets, and "jackass-rabbits" among other things. "Sam" jokes about the vast desert by commenting, "birds that fly over the land carry their provisions with them" (LGC 23), yet he also gives vivid descriptions of sagebrush, of the mountains around Carson City, and of typical living quarters. He waxes ironic about the dust and tarantulas and scorpions. The second letter recounts a mining trip Clemens took, which features the antics of a horse and a dog. A comic tirade against romantic images of Indians that "mother" supposedly holds dominates the third letter. "Sam" ridicules these images because they masquerade as factual description of the Paiutes and Shoshones who lived near Carson City. The burlesque tactic used to attack a sentimental literary cliché foreshadows articles to be written for the *Californian*. The letters' blend of conversational intimacy, reportorial detail, and comic attitude makes them superior to routine newspaper correspondence.

The *Keokuk Gate City* letters suggest the facility with writing out-of-town correspondence Clemens brought with him to the *Enterprise*. The Hawai'i letters suggest how inventive Clemens had become in manipulating the travel letter to accommodate his elaboration of Mark Twain as a comic character. Reprinted on both coasts, the "Letters from the Kingdom of Hawai'i" were well received because Mark Twain's humor made them so much more readable than most of the great mass of travel correspondence that newspapers printed from various locales as a standard feature. Comic technique invading consistently and successfully the domain of travel writing was unusual. Briefly comparing Mark Twain's Hawai'i correspondence to a set of letters from Hawai'i written for another California newspaper at the same time puts the accomplishment into perspective.

Beginning at least five months before Clemens arrived in Honolulu in March 1866, the *San Francisco Bulletin* had been publishing "Letters from Honolulu: From Our Own Correspondent." Of various lengths and appearing nearly anywhere in a given edition of the *Bulletin,* from front page to buried near the back on page 5, these anonymous "Letters from Honolulu" typify the correspondence from foreign cities that had been routinely appearing in important newspapers for decades. Carefully devoid of personality, comic or otherwise, such correspondence does not concern itself with entertainment in any form but, rather, insists on practical information, which means few vivid descriptions, while effective comic touches are fewer still. During 1866, the *Bulletin*'s correspondent assiduously notes business conditions, including the coming and going of particular ships, and provides details about political and legislative affairs. The inevitable topic of weather inevitably intrudes, and the staple events of newspapers—accidents, violent deaths, and scandal—are chronicled. Opinion on issues may provide glimpses of the writer's personality, but rarely does the column provide memorable description or even phrasing. Moreover, when the writer records extraordinary events, such as the *Hornet* disaster and the death of Princess Victoria, a journeyman's attitude about facts and straightforward description dominate.[87] This attitude carries its own virtue. "The best reporter is he whose sole object is to relate his event exactly as it occurred, and describe his scene just as it appeared; and this kind of excellence is attainable by an honest plodder and by a man of great and well controlled talent."[88] Innovative excellence, such as found in Clemens's Hawai'i correspondence, of course requires more.

The comparison with the *Bulletin*'s Honolulu correspondent may be too easy: after all, no evidence exists that he had literary talent or ambition. A better one would be an *Enterprise* colleague with manifest talent if not clear ambition, William Wright. Clemens's skills as an accurate reporter more than his growing reputation as a comic writer had landed him a job in the summer of 1863 with the *San Francisco Call* as its Washoe correspondent. This newspaper correspondence can be compared with near-contemporaneous letters by Wright, penned for the *San Francisco Golden Era* during the late summer and fall of 1863, after he had returned from his visit home to Iowa.

These two brief series of Washoe correspondence display remarkable similarities. Both writers provide ample journalistic detail about the main topics of the day, namely, the summer's new mining discoveries and the consequent building boom in Virginia City. Both men carefully maintain accuracy about these most important of topics for their readers, refusing to write anything specific about

---

87. *San Francisco Bulletin*, "Letter from Honolulu," [January 29, February 23, April 13]. Letters discussed were published from January 5 to July 17, 1866. Correspondence from Honolulu to the *Bulletin* had been running for years before that time period. The letters I discuss here were unsigned. The editors of Clemens's notebooks say that an H. D. Dunn wrote a series of travel letters for the *Bulletin* from January until April (NB 1:229n121), but I could find only one letter signed "H. D. D."

88. *Sacramento Union*, [Best Reporters], 3.

particular mines until they have made their own inspections. Mark Twain also reports in straightforward fashion on Fourth of July ceremonies, a dispute about the legitimacy of two judges, the consequences of a fire, theatricals and Maguire's new opera house, the constitutional convention, and political meetings (ETS 1:255–58). Besides mines and new buildings, Wright recounts his journey from San Francisco to Virginia City and reports on theatricals and Maguire's new opera house, the negative moral influence of hurdy-gurdy houses, new gaslights, the recent stampede to the Reese River mining district, and how surface mining is disappearing due to a need for bigger machines and more capital to reach productive ore. His letter is a masterpiece of vivid first-person reporting, summarizing his impressions of the growth of Virginia City during his absence.[89]

Wright once recalled Clemens's reputation for giving "'cast-iron' items . . . 'a lick and a promise,'" and characterized Sam as a reporter who "hated to have to do with figures, measurements and solid facts."[90] Neither Clemens nor Wright merely treat the subjects in their Washoe correspondence with "a lick and a promise," but they both do not shy away from making a point with a dramatic scene nor from mixing in comic elements or projecting a comic personality. Mark Twain makes typical frontier jokes about men causing famines with their appetites or about his habit of borrowing clothes or about his willingness to fight another reporter who "has taken umbrage at something I said in my last letter" (MTCall nos. 1, 3). As he approaches the Comstock district, Dan De Quille imagines he has become rich because the mining boom has no doubt made his own (fictitious) Pewtertinctum mine valuable, thus exemplifying the feverish excitement of the times. Instead, he is greeted with an assessment.[91] Mark Twain concocts a scene in a stagecoach featuring a sociable "sot" to make the point that the mining boom has collected many foolish speculators (ETS 1:256). Dan De Quille composes a scene in which his attempts to write his newspaper correspondence are continually interrupted by meetings to incorporate mines, no matter where he goes, to make the point that the mining boom has engendered a plethora of new mine incorporations. Millions are ready to be invested in these new mines, says Dan De Quille, and the nineteen-mile figure to express the entire sum would break teeth when speaking it.[92] This tall-tale pronouncement has a counterpart when Mark Twain comments on the heat: "The thermometer stands at a thousand, in the shade, today" (MTCall nos. 1, 2). Both writers insert comic anecdotes into their reporting, sometimes ostensibly involving themselves. The best

89. Wright, "Letter from Dan De Quille, " 8 [September 27].

90. Wright, "Reporting," 171.

91. William Wright, "Our Washoe Correspondence: Letter from Dan De Quille," 1 [September 20].

92. William Wright, "Our Washoe Correspondence: Letter from Dan De Quille," 8 [October 4].

of these anecdotes from Mark Twain is the hoax played on Attorney-General Bunker, who was asked to rule on a fictitious case involving one ranch sliding on top of another during an avalanche, a yarn reworked for *Roughing It* (ETS 1:280–81). Besides the tale of his disappointing Pewtertinctum mine, Dan De Quille recounts a hoax played on a disappointed lover.[93]

Though similarities are apparent when one compares William Wright's and Sam Clemens's out-of-town correspondence for periodicals other than the *Territorial Enterprise* home base, differences do come to the forefront. When given the chance to write an extended series of travel letters for the *Golden Era* on a newly discovered mining district, Wright fails to elevate Dan De Quille to the comic heights of Mark Twain and Mr. Brown. Rather than unleashing his comic powers, as Clemens did with the letters from Hawai'i, Wright instead noticeably curbs his comic abilities. The twelve installments in the *Golden Era*, entitled "Washoe Rambles," without doubt solidified the literary reputation of William Wright. These travel letters won Wright his position on the *Territorial Enterprise* a few months after their publication.[94]

"Washoe Rambles" demonstrates Wright's serious approach to the subject of a silver strike east of the Comstock, even though he knew that his audience enjoyed a comic sketch well told, under any circumstance. Wright in the past certainly had boldly indulged himself with comic elements. The serious account of his journey into a new mining district possibly represents his more natural approach to such subjects as well as a calculated decision about how to handle a big opportunity, his first chance to write a series of letters for a leading periodical. Years later, Wright felt Clemens's early work revealed a basic antipathy toward the necessary factuality of reporting, and "Washoe Rambles" reveals a basic temperament, too. However one assesses the motivation for its style, "Washoe Rambles" reads as an excellent journalistic portrait of the Nevada Territory in the early days of its first big mining boom, rendered in straightforward prose, the very plainness of which creates a clear picture. William Wright's facility for unadorned but compelling narrative, so well displayed in the recounting of his impressions of the growth of Virginia City, remains the source of his travel letters' still-considerable value.

Nothing in "Washoe Rambles" approaches the lavish description of Kilauea that closes Mark Twain's letters from Hawai'i. Self-consciously literary set pieces, or prose pictures, mark a clear difference from Wright's travel letters. The ultimate difference, however, turns upon Clemens's decision to insinuate a forceful

---

93. William Wright, "Our Washoe Correspondence: Letter from Dan De Quille," 8 [October 11].

94. Richard E. Lingenfelter, introduction to *Washoe Rambles*, 11–12. For more information on William Wright and his work, see Lawrence I. Berkove, ed., *The Fighting Horse of the Stanislaus: Stories and Essays by Dan De Quille*; and Dwyer and Lingenfelter, *Dan De Quille*.

comic alter ego throughout a travel narrative. Before as well as after Sam Clemens joined the *Enterprise,* William Wright was probably doing everything in his work that Clemens had done before and after inventing Mark Twain— more even, if one counts the sentimental material that Wright produced but Clemens apparently did not. However, the lack of *Enterprise* files makes a complete assessment impossible. Though Wright could be as outrageously comic as Clemens, he did not consistently develop Dan De Quille as a comic character, nor was he as consistently taken with the impish spirit of burlesque. A burlesque spirit allowed Mark Twain to play the role of the literary critic, comment on oratory, and focus on political affairs, aspects not found in Dan De Quille. Mark Twain also more consistently displayed a choleric humor.

Both Clemens and Wright had regional stages for their writings. The *Golden Era* and the *Sacramento Union* were looked upon as "institutions" by their audience of miners, merchants, and farmers in the mother lode territory.[95] How is it that "Washoe Rambles" landed Wright a job at the *Territorial Enterprise* with an attentive but merely regional audience while the "Letters from the Kingdom of Hawai'i" proved to be the literary vehicle that allowed Clemens to reach a New York City as well as a national audience? One answer might be that Wright never exorcised the fiend that always lured miners to the "big thing," so he stayed on the Comstock for thirty years because he never let go of the idea that the mines would make him rich. Another answer could be timing. Wright had exhibited the necessary literary talent long before Clemens did and had even written examples of comic sketches masquerading as travel letters, but the circumstances of Hawai'i as a compelling topic may have made the occasion more ripe for Clemens to achieve a bigger success. Finally, and not incidentally, Clemens capitalized on the Hawai'i letters by turning them into a lucrative platform lecture. Performing his literary fusion of comic sketch and travel letter earned Clemens the money necessary to leave California and to be in New York City when the opportunity to join the *Quaker City* cruise presented itself. The success of those performances drew upon the force of Mark Twain's comic personality, most prominently displayed in the Hawai'i correspondence. Moreover, the dynamic of Mark Twain and Mr. Brown in their misadventures guaranteed that only the sequels in the American Travel letters and the Quaker City letters could match the comic appeal of "Letters from the Kingdom of Hawai'i."

The hilarious dynamic of Mark Twain and Mr. Brown resembles that of Charles Noland's Pete Whetstone and his pseudonym "N." As "N" did for Noland, Mark Twain could be used by Clemens to express his most sophisticated, enlightened, and cultured thoughts. At this end of the spectrum, one finds

95. Walker, *Literary Frontier,* 120.

those aspects of Mark Twain that practically ignore the comic: his straight repor-torial voice as well as his cultured travel-book voice, with its lofty rhetoric and fine word paintings. However, a *cordon sanitaire* between Mark Twain and Mr. Brown does not exist the way it does between "N" and Pete Whetstone. Mark Twain in places acts the role of the high-toned gentleman with Mr. Brown, but usually that act functions as a setup to support Brown's vulgar point of view. Mark Twain plays the role straight, and the *cordon sanitaire* obtains in one instance, when Mr. Brown makes fun of a fellow passenger's seasickness by call-ing the bullock after him (Captain Gordon) because both lay down so much (MTLH 14). Because Captain Gordon is a thinly disguised version of Captain William Henry Dimond of the Union army, son of a missionary, Henry Dimond, and because being seasick does not rise even to the level of a laughable foible, the joke is in dubious taste. Clemens can get away with such ridicule by attributing it to Mr. Brown and by having Mark Twain reprimand him for his "inconsider-ate levity" (MTLH 14).

The maneuver to depict Mark Twain as the proper gentleman in contrast with Mr. Brown's barbarous manners usually entails the deflation of burlesque. Pos-sibly the most famous instance of this outcome in all twenty-five letters from Hawai'i occurs when Mark Twain pens a long description of Honolulu. The description showcases Clemens's ability to create a stylistic middle ground in his travel letters, one slangy and comic at times but also vivid in its observed detail. The description of Honolulu also demonstrates how Clemens was becoming adept at shifting from a middle style to the higher-toned literary descriptions characterizing the standard travel books of writers like Bayard Tay-lor. After a comic catalog of cats, the description becomes painterly, elevated, and ornate—with Latinate or archaic diction choices, alliteration, and a carefully constructed rhythm: "I saw on the one side a framework of tall, precipitous mountains close at hand, clad in refreshing green, and cleft by deep, cool, chasm-like valleys—and in front the grand sweep of the ocean; a brilliant, transparent green near the shore, bound and bordered by a long white line of foamy spray dashing against the reef, and further out the dead blue water of the deep sea, flecked with 'white caps,' and in the far horizon a single, lonely sail—" (MTLH 31). Once the pathetic fallacy of the "lonely sail" shows up, so does Mr. Brown, who proceeds not only to deride such fine writing as "that sort of truck" and "slop" (MTLH 33), but also to catalog the negative aspects of the islands, the heat and insect life especially, and finish his diatribe with a set of tall tales about people being bit by all manner of creatures.

Uncouth and irreverent in a classic tradition of American democratic humor, Mr. Brown also functions as the eccentric innocent who speaks the truth uncon-ventionally. In such instances, Mark Twain appears as merely conventional and centric, but he also can become pompous in his indignation. At other times, the dynamic shifts so that Mr. Brown exceeds the humorous foibles of an eccentric innocent, behaving instead with barbarous manners and a loutish behavior that carries him beyond the pale. Mark Twain then comes across as moderate, even refined, by contrast. Clemens can create this variegated comic interplay between his two characters because he presents Mark Twain in multiple guises and poses—an entire set of personae—as though the educated "N" and several versions of the rustic Pete Whetstone had been combined into one figure. Mark Twain could therefore rewrite Simon Suggs's famous claim, "It's good to be shifty in a new country," into his own maxim, "It's laughably good to be shifty with many comic personae in any country."

Although Mark Twain's presentation in the Hawai'i correspondence can recall the character's Washoe phase and its Gentleman Roarer heritage, Mr. Brown as the eccentric innocent or ignorant lout with barbarous manners especially invokes the civilized savagery or backwoods and uncouth civility embodied by the Gentleman Roarer. The comic antics of Mark Twain and Mr. Brown pose a large question. What is meant by a claim to be civilized? The theme of what defines truly civilized behavior proved to be so comically rich and rewarding that the "Letters from the Kingdom of Hawai'i" were but a rehearsal for clowning performances in subsequent travel letters.

# Act Five

## CORRESPONDENT AT LARGE

# SCENE ONE

AMERICAN TRAVEL LETTERS

## THE IRONIC RETURN OF WASHOE MARK TWAIN

BROWN ALWAYS SPOKE REVERENTLY OF SLIMMENS AS "THE CORRE-
SPONDENT"—BUT IT WAS SMALL DISTINCTION, BECAUSE HE ALWAYS
SPOKE OF ME IN THE SAME WAY, AND THE SAME WAY OF THE MONKEY.

[AMERICAN LETTERS, No. VI], *ALTA CALIFORNIA*, MARCH 17, 1867

After his return to California from the Kingdom of Hawai'i in August 1866, Sam Clemens continued writing letters about the islands for the *Sacramento Union*, composing nearly a third of the series. He also wrote pieces for the *Californian*, the *San Francisco Alta California*, the *San Francisco Evening Bulletin*, the *New York Weekly Review*, and the *Hawai'ian Herald*. In addition, he ventured into the business of platform lecturing, giving some dozen performances of "Our Fellow Savages of the Sandwich Islands" during the fall of 1866. The quasi-comic lecture proved to be popular entertainment, and the money it earned allowed Sam to plan a return to family and home. Before he left, however, Clemens arranged to write letters about the trip for the *Alta California*. The twenty-six letters that Clemens wrote for the *Alta* covered his voyage to the isthmus of Panama, his passage across the isthmus, voyage to New York City, his wanderings in Gotham, and his long railroad journey to St. Louis to see friends and family. This series of "American Letters" constitutes the most important writing that Clemens published between the "Letters from the Kingdom of Hawai'i" and the series of letters covering the *Quaker City* cruise to Europe and the Holy Land that he would revise into his 1869 best seller, *The Innocents Abroad*.[1]

The broad scope of the *Alta California* assignment meant that the "American Letters" would be different from those Clemens had just produced for the *Union*. Rather than writing with a focus on a single place, Hawai'i, everything seen in all segments of his journeys could be grist to the journalistic mill. Moreover, Clemens in Hawai'i had been caught up in the local political scene and had obviously felt compelled to support American culture and the American enterprise he found in the islands. Unencumbered by such particulars, Sam Clemens, in the "American Letters," has his first roving correspondent's assignment. The *Alta*

---

1. "American Letters" is the designation Walker and Dane give to the series in their 1940 reprinting of them. Quotes will refer to their collection as MTTB. The original letters in the *Alta California* were also examined. Walter Blair's essay "Mark Twain, New York Correspondent," which summarizes without analysis, is the only scholarly notice of these letters.

editors contracting with Sam Clemens for the freewheeling assignment testifies to the strength of his reputation. The fact that the *Alta* published each letter on its front page testifies to the marketability of his Mark Twain pseudonym.

Like the one from Hawai'i, this new series of travel letters was not as journalistic as the usual fare from eastern cities or foreign capitals, and Clemens did not compose it in the consciously literary mode exemplified by Bayard Taylor in the 1840s and 1850s, starting with *Views A-Foot.*[2] Sketching Mark Twain's quirky character by this time demanded a variety of humors, from the savagely sarcastic to the foolishly whimsical. The multiple personae of his literary alter ego bind together the journalistic and literary elements. The freedom to comment on everything for the *Alta* during his peregrinations allowed Clemens to employ whatever tonalities seemed appropriate for the voices of Mark Twain's personae. The broad palette of comic tones with which Clemens had experimented for nearly four years could now superbly render in laughable ways the ever-changing scenes he would encounter for the next eleven months: shipboard, Nicaragua, New York City, St. Louis and Hannibal, Paris, Rome and Genoa, and the Middle East.

As Clemens wrote up these varied scenes, he developed a comic rhetoric of sanctified saints and unsanctified sinners implicitly begun in his erstwhile defense of the American missionaries in the Hawai'i letters. Playing with an opposition of civilized behavior versus primitive barbarity had organized his representation of the islands. At times, Clemens scaled down this opposition and transformed it into a comic exploration of respectability, the ostensible culture of Mark Twain contrasting with the clear vulgarity of Mr. Brown. In the "American Letters," Mark Twain can be just as disreputable as Mr. Brown when the two appear together. Both claim membership in an incorrigible pack of men whose high-spirited antics earn them the Washoe epithet "the boys." The image of Mark Twain behaving as one of the high-spirited boys—clowning, joking, drinking, and swapping lies as though he were back on the Comstock—matches, even overwhelms, an image of Mark Twain the gentleman contrasting with Mr. Brown the vulgarian. Thus the behavior of Mark Twain and Mr. Brown again dramatizes the theme of sanctified versus unsanctified. However, Clemens now emphasizes an ironic perspective by examining what constitutes respectability through the eyes of a clearly disreputable Mark Twain. Clemens creates his irony by nearly eliminating the difference between Mark Twain and the vulgar Mr. Brown, yet having Mark Twain nevertheless claim to be a missionary. Mark Twain uses this comic pose of the unsanctified missionary to question normative values as he carries out his roving correspondent assignment.

2. Wermuth, *Bayard Taylor.*

Mark Twain the correspondent at large has a serious as well as a comic side. When not acting in concert with his merry traveling companions, when, in other words, Mark Twain deliberately gathers to himself a semblance of respectability, he acts the role of a *flâneur* in the "American Letters." As *flâneur,* Mark Twain becomes the tasteful man-about-town traveling the world, more educated and literate than the ordinary newspaperman, yet not to be mistaken for a man of letters à la Bayard Taylor. Clemens segregates whatever respectable and refined image Mark Twain has as *flâneur* from the scenes involving Brown. This segregation of Brown from commentary about art and aesthetics sharply distinguishes the two master roles for Mark Twain the narrator, one respectable and one unsanctified, even though the *flâneur*'s comments are themselves not always normative.

Exploiting the interest in aesthetics connected to this *flâneur* pose during the trip from San Francisco to New York City would be good preparation for satirizing the culture of Europe on the subsequent *Quaker City* voyage. Moreover, the unsanctified missionary pose initiated in the "American Letters" would reappear as a sophisticated comic critique of the "pilgrims" on that voyage. Thus in many ways the "American Letters" function as a developmental bridge between the Hawai'i letters and the *Quaker City* letters. This triad of travel letters established Mark Twain as a most extraordinary newspaper correspondent, an American *flâneur* whose freewheeling vernacular-and-slang comic spin on the scenes before him often gives voice to a perspective decidedly outside the boundaries of the dominant cultural values of the 1860s.

With the slapstick opening scene of the first letter, Clemens signals that a comic vision will predominate whenever possible. This initial scene manages to dramatize a world of foolishness, selfishness, and savagery as well as to exhibit Mark Twain's ambivalent attitude toward that world. People display foolishness in the repeated good-byes, issued with formulaic sincerity, by Mark Twain's friends as his ship prepares to leave San Francisco. Despite three rounds of good-byes, his friends attempt a fourth as the call "All ashore that's going!" sounds out. The crowd bodily sweeps the friends away just as Jones reaches out for yet another handshake, the press so great that "his eyes were well nigh bursting from his red-hot face" (MTTB 13). The comic details of the bulging eyes and red face reinforce the sense that the friends behave foolishly, and the picture stands complete when they are once more seen saying good-bye (no doubt repeatedly) to each other on the dock. More foolish behavior, indicative of selfishness, can be discerned in the comic catalog of items other friends ask Mark Twain and Mr. Brown to take with them and deliver: a box of fruit and a case of wine to Washington, D.C.; a keg of quartz specimens to New York City; and a glass jar stuffed with "fine tarantulas and scorpions" (MTTB 12) to Brooklyn. An air of mindless violence pervades the whole departure scene as Mark Twain constantly dodges apples and oranges hurled at the passengers by the crowd on the dock—when he is not trying to avoid the many peddlers repeatedly confronting him with their various wares.

Mark Twain's attitude augments the scene's comic quality. He remains marvelously calm and matter-of-fact about the crazy, even dangerous, behavior of the crowd and about the comic perversity of his automaton friends. Thus he tranquilly reports that the ship "backed out through a pitiless storm of apples and oranges" (MTTB 13) while he glimpses his friends still mouthing good-byes. Nevertheless, he does betray a ferocious side when he characterizes one peddler as possessing an "evil countenance" (MTTB 11) and another as a "cutthroat" (MTTB 12). The generally calm and understated quality of the description and this undercurrent of anger collide in a moment of irony, when Mark Twain refuses to buy outrageously priced cigars from a third peddler. "I was grieved to see a good-bye apple from the shore cave in the side of his head as he turned away" (MTTB 12).

The staged quality of his "grief" for the cigar peddler, indeed, the staged quality of the peddler's injury (for who would believe the tall-tale detail about an apple caving in a skull?) illustrates the penchant of Mark Twain to adopt comic poses. As soon as the ship moves away from the dock, he strikes another. "Then I stood apart and soliloquized: 'Green be my memories of thee as are thy hills this bright December day, O Mistress of the Occident! May no—'" (MTTB 13). At this point, Brown interrupts with, "Oh, dang the Occident!" and follows with a torrent of slang recounting the elopement of two young passengers. The apostrophe to San Francisco as "Mistress of the Occident" deliberately parodies his own farewell speech after his last comic lecture on December 10, 1866 (MTW 211–13). Clemens obviously expected his readers to remember the speech, which was printed in the *Alta California* on December 15, 1866, and appreciate his self-deprecating humor about its grandeur.

The tactic of Mark Twain the pompous gentleman being undercut by the straight-talking albeit ungrammatical and rude Mr. Brown is familiar from the Hawai'i correspondence, but it would rarely be repeated in the "American Letters." Though Mark Twain continues to play the gentleman as he admonishes Brown for his "vulgar metaphor" (MTTB 14) and then proceeds to investigate the story, by the end of the elopement tale the pose has switched again—to innocent comic victim. Hearing some passengers countenance the assertion by the young couple that they see nothing wrong with their liaison because they will eventually be married in Brooklyn, Mark Twain cries out, "God help me! I am an orphan and many and many a league at sea—with such a crowd as this!" (MTTB 18). The first letter dramatizes a satirist's comic world of knaves and fools, and it also suggests that Mark Twain's performance of various roles, assumed the way an actor dons a succession of costumes, deploys a necessary strategy within that world. Though "Mark Twain" all along has signified a collection of personae, that predilection to pose and adopt a guise now creates an aura of theatricality: "performance" has come front and center as a controlling metaphor, no doubt as a result of Clemens's recent platform success.

Within this comic world, Mr. Brown once again represents the uncouth—and often the foolish, too. His unremitting slang conveys his uncouth status, as for instance when he uses poker terms to start his story of the eloping couple (MTTB 13–14; see also 23, 26–27, 41). In contrast, Mark Twain rarely uses slang, though he occasionally quotes Brown when it suits him (see MTTB 115), and he frequently quotes other characters, such as Captain Waxman, and reproduces their slang speeches at length (MTTB 23–25; 30–33; 37–38). Employing others to speak in lowbrow fashion allows Clemens the luxury of enlivening his Mark Twain letters with colorful speech that contrasts with the correct English of a good newspaperman, while keeping his literary alter ego removed from easy accusations of vulgarity. Brown's vulgarity, however, goes beyond mere slang. In one instance, in which the reader has a peek into his journal, Brown unconsciously parodies the clichéd sentiments of courtship, but the entry clearly lies beyond the bounds of good taste: his girl, sighing and pensive in her usual place on deck as she reads poetry, is "picking her nose with a fork" (MTTB 79). Another time, Brown's slang hints at other uncleanliness. When Mark Twain extols the beauty of Nicaraguan peasant women, Brown cuts him off with, "But you just prospect one of them heifers with a fine-tooth—" (MTTB 41). In yet another scene, dubious language and slapstick come together to portray Brown's character. When the ship lurches just as Mark Twain opens the door to allow Brown to enter their room, he plunges in "head-foremost [and] stove in the middle berth and started his scalp." Mark Twain does not record the ensuing "chapter of blasphemy" (MTTB 22).

Though Brown's language marks him as a sinner and as one of the vulgar, he is much more the fool than the knave. He assumes outlandish identities in New York City (MTTB 98) and allows his clothes to become tatters because everyone there tells him not to buy new ones until he arrives in Paris, where they will be cheaper (MTTB 180–82). He slanders women in general as natural gossips (MTTB 26), wakes Mark Twain in the middle of the night to tell him a newly minted pun (MTTB 60), and is comically confused when he meets someone in New York City who says he is *not* joining the summer exodus to the Paris exposition (MTTB 194). Though Brown's thoughtless nature can encompass joking about cholera and smallpox while on the isthmus, a comment that results in a quarantine of steerage passengers for twenty-four hours and breeds talk among them about hanging him (MTTB 54–55), he can also be a sympathetic victim. During the isthmus crossing,

Brown acts as protector for a widow, three children, and a servant girl. The noble gesture, however, does little for his dignity. Tying all their mules together during the trek proves to be a mistake when his lead animal wants to race with other passengers' animals and it cannot be held back, with predictable results. "Occasionally Brown's mule stopped and fell to bucking, and then his other animals closed up and got tangled together in a helpless snarl" (MTTB 44).

Though Mark Twain early in the "American Letters" appears as the literate and polite gentleman who corrects Brown's language (MTTB 14) and amends his rudeness about Miss Slimmens (MTTB 26), the gentility seems little more than veneer by the end of letter 2, when Brown has finished his portrait of Miss Slimmens as queen of the sharp-tongued gossips aboard ship. Brown's revelations about Miss Slimmens include her declaration that Mark Twain was drunk rather than sick last night. Though he had admonished Brown to be "more respectful" of Miss Slimmens, and though he also states that Brown is "a man of no tact," Mark Twain, after hearing what Miss Slimmens says about him, calls her "that venomous old hag" (MTTB 26–27). A similar pattern can be detected in the middle of the series when Mark Twain tries to "compose a poem for a young lady's album" while traveling on a train to St. Louis. This genteel and literate image is undercut when a peddler distracts Mark Twain. "I gave up my poem and devoted all my energies to driving him away and trying to say things that would make him unhappy" (MTTB 154–55). Mark Twain apparently easily forgets the gentle part of "gentleman."

This forgetfulness heralds a return. As the "American Letters" unfold their comic scenes, Mark Twain less and less plays the role of gentleman, behaving instead more like his old, unsanctified Washoe self. For example, he is ready before they sail to borrow shirts and other gear from his prospective cabinmate on board the *Quaker City* (MTTB 247–48) and is ever ready to take a drink (MTTB 104). A reputation for thievery, based on the published incident of commandeering a book from Reverend Damon in Honolulu, has all hotels on guard against his stealing spoons, thwarting all attempts thus far (MTTB 213). This joke about light-fingered behavior fits neatly with another joke hinting that his creditors worry about his payment of bills (MTTB 274). Mark Twain can also joke about having lice (MTTB 104) and telling lies (MTTB 126), and he apparently does not mind the purser calling him a "Short card sharp [and] South Sea Islander" (MTTB 80) when filling out the customhouse statement for New York City.

Mark Twain understands that he rests more comfortably with the sinners than the saints. In one candid moment, he virtually admits an ignorance of moral culture (MTTB 135). Attending an Episcopal church in Key West, he says, "they gauged me at a glance and gave me a back seat, as usual" (MTTB 72). When he stays in St. Louis, he writes about a club that holds parties just for men. The moral advantage shines in its clear outline. "There are no ladies present, and so you haven't got to be kept under the tiresome restraints of proper conduct all the time" (MTTB 130). Though women signify propriety and restraint, in several other places in the letters they can also represent a desire to escape inhibition. While in New York City, Mark Twain says that seeing "a lovely girl of seventeen [in the new fashions] is enough to set a man wild. I must drop this subject—I can't stand it" (MTTB 88). Another time he proclaims a readiness to "fall down and worship" (MTTB 95) a pretty girl in her charming costume, a revealing turn of phrase, given that he is attending a church service at the time. Mark Twain repeats his comic confounding of sexual desire and religious devotion when he visits the Bible House, which prints and binds Bibles in all styles and in nearly all languages, and the pretty girls doing the work result in a confused description of the manufacturing process (MTTB 206–7). When he visits Harry Hill's, "one of the worst dens in all New York" (MTTB 274), the entire episode casts Mark Twain into a mock-innocent role, and thus a comedy of apparent misunderstanding cloaks his encounter with a streetwalker inside the tavern. However, when Mark Twain spots beautiful peasant girls in Nicaragua, his description of their charms includes a knowing comment about their probable lack of virtue, along with a notice of the "precious little drapery about them!" (MTTB 41).

These last examples place Mark Twain low on the gentility scale and next to Mr. Brown, yet Mr. Brown also stands higher than a first glance warrants. He is not simply a fellow to laugh at. As in the Hawai'i letters, Clemens occasionally presents Brown as an eironic figure, more sensible and worthy than he first appears. For example, Brown's insinuation about the perils of becoming intimate with the Nicaraguan beauties has a certain commonsense sound to it (MTTB 41), and he can express "fine irony" (MTTB 124) when he jokes about the slow speed of a train as well as when he delivers a sarcasm against a self-important conductor (MTTB 125). Moreover, on at least two occasions Brown employs that favored comic weapon of the frontier, the deadpan. His deadpan joke against using stamps as money underscores the absurdity of receiving postage as change (MTTB 73). His deadpan attack on a fellow passenger nicknamed "the Bore," explaining at length that an alligator could not climb a tree, signifies poetic justice rendered against a person who has plagued others with constant nonsense, and Mark Twain "never enjoyed anything better" (MTTB 57).

When one subjects the behavior of Mark Twain and Mr. Brown in the "American Letters" series to close scrutiny, the characters are more similar than dissimilar. Their behavior on shipboard symbolizes this similarity. Because so many passengers, particularly women and children, are seasick, ship's lanterns are in great demand: only the sick may have these large lanterns and burn them as long as they want. In order to procure a lantern so that they and their friends can play cards all night, Mark Twain and Mr. Brown devise a strategy of taking turns pretending to be sick (MTTB 61–62, 79). Mark Twain may be dismissive of Brown at times, but they are friends and partners in crime. Certainly, Mark Twain does not dismiss Brown's "harmless tropical drink [the] 'west-sou-wester'" (MTTB 61), consumed by the boys every day before dinner and during their card parties.

Brown's status as an eironic figure, despite frequent buffoonery, also links him to Mark Twain. Sinner though Mark Twain is, his pose as a missionary—ostensibly good and respectable despite all the obviously unsanctified behavior—creates a useful comic strategy for Clemens in the "American Letters." Clearly, Mark Twain expects no one to take the claim to be a missionary seriously. He behaves far from the pious ideal associated with missionaries and everyone knows it, which is why Mark Twain himself cannot completely stifle his laughter when he and a friend pretend to be signing up the Reverend Mark Twain as a passenger on the *Quaker City* (MTTB 113–15). "Missionary" in the "American Letters" functions as code for Mark Twain's satiric view and humorous behavior, and it names an ironic pose encapsulating the contradictory and the absurd that Clemens found in people's beliefs and behaviors.

---

## UNSANCTIFIED MISSIONARY

I HAD SOME NOTION OF JOINING THE MISSION, BUT THEN I THOUGHT I HAD BETTER CONTINUE TO HOLD ON TO MY POSITION AS A SANDWICH ISLAND MISSIONARY AND LET THESE PEOPLE WORRY ALONG THE BEST WAY THEY CAN.

———

[AMERICAN LETTERS, NO. XVI], *ALTA CALIFORNIA*, JUNE 10, 1867

THERE IS A GOOD DEAL OF HUMAN NATURE IN PEOPLE.

———

[AMERICAN LETTERS, NO. XVIII], *ALTA CALIFORNIA*, JUNE 23, 1867

The central joke of the "American Letters" series is Mark Twain posing as a Sandwich Island missionary. Clemens had first promulgated the conceit shortly after his return from Hawai'i in the *Californian*. Mark Twain pretends to apply for a vacant editorship with the journal, and he advertises himself as a good candidate because he can provide moral tone.

I am peculiarly fitted for such a position. I have been a missionary to the Sandwich Islands, and I have got the hang of all that sort of thing down to a fraction. I gave such excellent satisfaction in Hawaii nei that they let me off when my time was up. I was justly considered to be the high chief of that Serious Family down there. I mention here—and I mention it modestly—I mention it with that fatal modesty which has always kept me down—that the missionaries always spoke of me as the Moral Phenomenon when I was down there. They were amazed to behold to what a dizzy altitude human morality may be hoisted up, as exemplified in me. I am honestly proud of the title they have conferred upon me, and shall always wear it in remembrance of my brief but gratifying missionary labors in the Islands.[3]

Given the bachelor and Bohemian habits of Sam Clemens as well as the past comic antics of his alter ego and print personae, the joke obviously had a lot of mileage in it for any faithful reader of Mark Twain. Certainly, the joke had mileage for Clemens and his friends. The *Californian,* in a notice of Queen Emma of Hawai'i arriving in San Francisco, suggests that Mark Twain and "other Sandwich Island missionaries" be on hand to greet her. Clemens at times referred to his lectures as preaching and to his lecture tour that fall as "a missionary trip."[4] As it works through the "American Letters," the Sandwich Island missionary pose presents a richly ironic perspective. Clemens seems determined to appeal strongly to his core audience, "the boys," by emphasizing the Washoe side of Mark Twain. Threading the missionary pose through the letters functions not as a counterweight to Washoe Mark Twain but as a guise that enwraps and complicates the character, enabling Clemens to sound like a moralist when the need arises without sacrificing the quirky and disreputable humors that give Mark Twain his comic strength and flexibility.

The complicated nature of this comic strategy appears in several places. For example, *The Black Crook* may be "the wickedest show you can think of" (MTTB 84), and talking about the dozens of young and beautiful women in the show dressed in tights may touch the "missionary sensibilities" (MTTB 85) of Mark Twain, yet this straightforward moral outrage triggered by the claim of having missionary sensibilities can also be slyly undercut when invoked elsewhere. The New York City mission that Mark Twain thinks about joining in the first epigraph to this section is called the "Midnight Mission," which has the intent of reclaiming

---

3. "The Moral Phenomenon" (SofS 210–11). The phrase *Hawaii nei* literally means "this Hawai'i" but can be translated to indicate an affection for the land as "this beloved Hawai'i" (Pukui and Elbert, *Hawai'ian Dictionary,* 264).

4. Mark Twain called a missionary: *Californian,* "Her Majesty at Hand!"; *San Francisco Alta California,* "Amusements: Mark Twain's Lecture"; *San Francisco News Letter,* [Mark Twain's Lecture]. Mark Twain calling himself a missionary: Samuel L. Clemens, "Mark Twain's Interior Notes" (MTW 201–4); Samuel L. Clemens, "'Mark Twain' Explains the Mexican Correspondence."

prostitutes. "Their main depot is next door to one of the largest houses of ill-fame in the city, and so you can see they mean business" (MTTB 163). The traffic with prostitutes that this mission promises lures Mark Twain into thinking of giving up his supposed calling to the Sandwich Islands, the only time such a temptation arises. Mark Twain the missionary apparently is less than sincere in his moral zeal, an implication that may rebound against the commentary on flaunted sexuality in *The Black Crook*. Mark Twain cheerfully acknowledges the implication in St. Louis, where his comic lectures become "preaching." Though the missionary pose enables that comic transformation, the dubiousness of moral instruction in comic tales and jokes as well as the tenuousness of his claim to be a missionary are both admitted when Mark Twain addresses a Sunday school. Despite his supposed experience instructing the young, the remarks at "the altar" turn out to be a recounting of "Jim Smiley's Jumping Frog":

> I honestly intended to draw an instructive moral from that story, but when I got to the end of it I couldn't discover that there was any particular moral sticking out around it anywhere, and so I just let it slide. However, it don't matter. I suppose those children will cipher a moral out of it somehow, because they are so used to that sort of thing. I gained my main point, anyhow, which was to make myself respected in California, because you know you cannot help but respect a man who makes speeches to Sunday Schools, and devotes his time to instructing youth. (MTTB 135)

The laudable purpose of missionary work, providing moral instruction to the young and unenlightened, becomes a means to another end, gaining respect. This anecdote comes just after Mark Twain has been complaining about the need to behave properly because all his relatives are nearby. "I have kept up my lick so far, as the missionaries say, but I don't think I can stand it much longer. I never could bear to be respectable long at a stretch" (MTTB 135).

Traversing in and out of the realm of respectability describes the chief comic consequence of Mark Twain's missionary pose. He condemns *The Black Crook* for its scandalous display of women, but he has several moments of expressed sexual desire due to less provocation than the play provides. He can note the salutary effects of laws against selling liquor in New York City after midnight or all day on Sundays, can say "it suits me [because it has made] an orderly place out of this once rowdy, noisy, immoral town" (MTTB 183), yet create comic dividends out of his own drinking habit. He can visit the Bible House, claim that he reports on all the missionary societies in New York City because thousands of West Coast Christians will be interested, and say, "I don't write for the sinful altogether" (MTTB 209). He can finally return Reverend Damon's book, thus "growing more worthy everyday" (MTTB 213), and then crown all this respectability by remarking, "I haven't had such a moral siege for a year. I will now go out and blackguard somebody till I begin to feel natural again" (MTTB 213).

Clemens designs the claim to missionary credentials, then, not to convince any readers but to convulse them with laughter because of Mark Twain's well-known unsanctified behavior. The pose of the Sandwich Island missionary, however, also allows for easy references to proper behavior when Mark Twain on his travels encounters the everyday vulgar, foolish, and hypocritical. In some cases, such encounters with what Sut Lovingood calls "ornery" human nature deserve mild ridicule. In other instances, such encounters can produce commentary that approaches the tongue-lashings of an old-fashioned sermon. For example, the passengers on the voyage from San Francisco to the isthmus are clearly bored and thus liable to gossip (MTTB 26), while bored passengers from Nicaragua to New York engage in other dubious amusements, such as getting a monkey drunk (MTTB 62). Such behaviors, though deplorable, are small-bore, on a par with the pretty women in New York City who repeatedly cross a busy street on the arm of handsome policemen (MTTB 91); or similar to the pretentious young woman who claims to be cultured because she has traveled in Europe but knows nothing about the western United States (MTTB 265); or nearly the same as the females on the trip through the isthmus who mindlessly indulge in sentimental transports over any infant, no matter how squalid (MTTB 40). Other transgressions loom larger. The sexual desire implied with the pretty women and the handsome policemen is far more circumspect than the behavior of some men on omnibuses toward respectable women (MTTB 198). The pretension of the supposedly traveled young woman pales in comparison to members of Congress who embody a biblical verse about fools who carry themselves as though they were prudent men (MTTB 254). And the unthinking response to sentimental clichés about babies shown by women is minuscule compared to the way the public at large uncritically allows newspapers to shape opinion on political policy and fine art (MTTB 168, 173–74).

Hypocrisy provides a special target for Mark Twain's missionary ridicule. Going to church to criticize the fashions of everyone's clothes (MTTB 91) or gossiping in a sewing circle convened for the charitable purpose of making clothes for heathens in distant lands (MTTB 128) represent milder hypocrisies than folks getting drunk at a temperance picnic (MTTB 267–68)—and ones not as foolishly obvious. Worse are people who attack someone they previously admired when the individual falls on hard times (MTTB 36, 230). Mark Twain notes the worship of money above all else in Key West, where income from the tourists trumps health and safety concerns (MTTB 70). New York City presents a variation on the theme of money as the root of all evil: a rich individual losing status in that city is supposedly a more calamitous event than any poor individual losing his or her life (MTTB 107).

These numerous examples of Mark Twain's comic sermonizing suggest that Clemens wants his readers to see his comic character as superior to what he surveys. In some places, explicit superiority, with more than a little snobbishness, can be found. Thus the natives on the isthmus are harshly represented as inferior "barefooted scoundrels" (MTTB 39), the steerage passengers also are portrayed as inferior (MTTB 42, 64, 65), and "the negroes" at Key West are ridiculed for their odor (MTTB 71). However, such biased and snobby remarks can be matched with attacks on snobbishness, as when Mark Twain remarks that "fat" respectable people do not get cholera (MTTB 236), or when he mentions the "unspeakably respectable . . . Century Club" (MTTB 88). Setting such instances side by side illustrates how Mark Twain remains a creature of newspaper deadlines, Clemens creating his satire on the fly.

Contradictory perspectives also recall the very different stories Mark Twain hears about the elopement in the first letter (MTTB 14–15). Contradiction is symptomatic of human behavior, and so Mark Twain's contradictory behavior displays a nature no better than anyone else's. For example, when Mark Twain cannot execute his plan to be escorted through the demimonde of New York City, he does the next best thing: goes to inspect the Bible House instead (MTTB 202). This imp-of-the-perverse attitude also surfaces when Mark Twain discusses a new bridge in New York that spans a busy street. He notes that a washerwoman carrying an immense amount of clothing climbs the stairs to the bridge despite a comparatively quiet moment on the street: she wanted to exercise the privilege of walking across a new public bridge despite its obvious inconvenience. Mark Twain then admits to his own imp of the perverse. He had wanted to use the bridge for a month before it was complete, and he had abused the workmen for going slowly, but now that the bridge stands ready for all pedestrian traffic, he has become indifferent (MTTB 186). A similar logic has Mark Twain declare that ignorance of art constitutes bliss because he can therefore enjoy artwork (MTTB 238). A somewhat darker side of human nature emerges when Mark Twain finds himself ensconced in a hotel, cozy inside and happily looking out at those in the rain (MTTB 201). Darker still is Mark Twain's meanness to Mr. Brown on the trip to St. Louis, when he monopolizes a sleeping berth and makes Brown sit up all night "so that he could come and tell me in case the train ran off the track" (MTTB 125). The absurdity of having to announce such a calamity though he would be in its midst does not merely launch a joke about sleeping soundly: like the rest of the incidents cataloged, it suggests that there is indeed much human nature in people.

People everywhere, including Mark Twain, behave badly, a thought that crystalizes when Mark Twain recounts his stay in "the Station House" (MTTB 187–91). The incident epitomizes the way in which Mark Twain the self-proclaimed Sandwich Island missionary admits to his own faults even as he notes those of everyone else. He does not mind mentioning the incarceration because it happened when he and his companion tried to break up a fight. Being told that "nobody would ever know I had been in the Station House unless I told it myself" (MTTB 190–91) obviously does not stop him from writing about it to satirize human nature. Even a self-proclaimed missionary in the custody of the police presents a laughably inappropriate situation, though Clemens treats the episode seriously for the most part. At one point, Mark Twain talks to "a bloated old hag . . . with a wholesome black eye [and] a drunken leer in the sound one" (MTTB 188) who makes up one of the company awaiting a hearing. This conversation turns his humiliating experience into a lesson about the relative value of being respectable. "They were pretty good people, anyhow, though a little under the weather as to respectability. But even the worst in the lot [the drunken old hag] freely offered to divide her gin with me. It isn't everybody without a cent that would do so much" (MTTB 191). Other virtues exist, such as generosity, besides what passes for respectability. The incident also suggests ideas implied in many of the previous examples of human frailty: acknowledging one's common humanity is morally invaluable and should supersede maintaining one's supposed respectability.

Recognizing and admitting to his own "ornery" humanity does not stop the missionary impulse in Mark Twain. The impulse can even engender out-of-control, Juvenalian tongue-lashings when Mark Twain encounters particularly bad behavior. Ironically, encountering particularly bad behavior unleashes bad behavior in Mark Twain. The choleric Mark Twain reveals an all-too-human aspect, but the over-the-top satiric attitude also enables him to speak the frustrations of an ideal audience. Mark Twain vents his comic spleen in varied levels of annoyance against a range of targets. For example, the dullness of his fellow passengers on the Nicaragua trip calls forth a simple insult: they are "dry old sticks" (MTTB 41). The unending advice from people in New York City about how to travel in Europe elicits a greater ire and is therefore consigned to "Perdition" (MTTB 182). Mark Twain subjects the hypochondriac who imagines he might have cholera to an even greater contempt. The man of course shows no symptoms of the disease, yet he worries about being buried at sea, an emotional indulgence ruthlessly dismissed—"as if his dead carcase would be more comfortable being eaten by grub-worms than sharks" (MTTB 67). The confusion and endless bustle of New York City in general deserves "flights of sublimity in the matter of profanity" (MTTB 261), while the city's worthless barbers and villainous bartenders fare little better (MTTB 109–10). Other matters provoke a seething ire. The wretched singing of impromptu shipboard choirs has Mark Twain ready to scuttle vessels to stop the torment (MTTB 28–29; see also 59). He judges Barnum's museum to be such a sorry fraud that he hopes "some philanthropist" will burn it down again (MTTB 117). An equally dire wish comes from Mark Twain's experience riding the railroads from New York City to St. Louis:

he hopes that the train's board of directors will shortly need to be buried yet have no money for the deed (MTTB 124).

When Mr. Brown and Mark Twain visit Bishop Southgate's church, Brown notes the fancy windows reserved for and ready to be dedicated to rich members who die worthy of such an honor. He says that if he "had a grudge against one of them saints, and he was to die before I got even with him, I'd break his window the first thing" (MTTB 96). Imagining breaking church windows is nothing compared to the darkest fantasies of Mark Twain, who more than once wishes people dead. The individual might be one who sells an item that has become a popular mania (MTTB 255), an impolite "contraband" on an omnibus (MTTB 227), or even Brown (MTTB 99). Peddlers on trains deserve to have the train run over them (MTTB 155). These ominous wishes recall the comic insults prominently featured in Mark Twain's Washoe humor of raillery when Clemens was first creating his character in the *Territorial Enterprise*. In all instances, laughter comes from an outrageous flouting of decorum that expresses a desire to be free from it. A profound laughter results from such transgressions of proper behavior when both the speaker and audience recognize their own human nature in having such improper wishes.

One notable exception exists to this explanation for why Mark Twain's fervent wishes that someone would die can generate laughter. When Mark Twain, during his station house sojourn, encounters two "flash girls of sixteen and seventeen" arrested for propositioning men on the street, his grim wish carries a satiric weight but expresses a very different tone: "it was a pity that the merciful snow had not frozen them into a peaceful rest and forgetfulness of life and its weary troubles, too" (MTTB 189). Religious sentiment and satirical practicality collude in this instance of Mark Twain the unsanctified missionary to produce an unusually harsh comment on the bleak future for the two young women. Such Juvenalian satire elicits no laughter.

Though Clemens could vent his deepest ire with a Juvenalian perspective on human nature when needed, the most obvious scene in which Mark Twain strikes his missionary pose features a much more lighthearted mood. The scene also self-consciously draws attention to the habit of posing that inaugurates the "American Letters." Intending to be a part of the *Quaker City* excursion to Europe and the Holy Land, Mark Twain goes to the booking office to make inquiries. He is accompanied by a friend he identifies as working for the *New York Tribune*, whom he calls Smith. As they approach the office, they encounter another friend, who tells them that anyone booked on the cruise must have his or her "character and standing" examined and verified by a committee, a procedure Mark Twain calls "an appalling state of affairs" (MTTB 113, 114). Mark Twain's anxiety dissipates, however, when Smith introduces him to the booking agent as "the Rev. Mark Twain, who is a clergyman of some distinction, lately arrived from San Francisco [and] a missionary to the Sandwich Islands during a part of the last year" (MTTB 114). More accurately, Mark Twain's anxiety transforms into giddy mirth, for the rest of the scene depicts Smith trying to prevent Mark Twain from exposing the ruse because of his slang expressions and because of his tendency to laugh at Smith's efforts to fool the agent. "I sat [and] listened to instructive remarks about my missionary services and my Baptist congregation in San Francisco till the misery of trying to keep from laughing was unbearable, and we left" (MTTB 115).

Remarkably, this scene of explicit posing as a missionary casts Mark Twain into the role of the vulgarian who cannot help but speak in slang and who cannot refrain from unseemly laughter. Mark Twain has become Mr. Brown. Smith can maintain a gentleman's composure, but despite his best efforts, he cannot stop Mark Twain from continually jeopardizing the missionary pose with his merry reaction to Smith's performance. Though portraying Mark Twain as unable to speak without slang runs counter to the image of the character created nearly everywhere else in the "American Letters," the scene in all other ways depicts a familiar Mark Twain, ready to go along with a joke initiated by one of his compatriots, ready to laugh and have a good time, ready to strike a pose. The laughter at his missionary pose suggests a self-conscious awareness of the necessity and simultaneous absurdity of posing in a world full of poseurs.

Another part of the scene's joke centers on the request for the passengers to prove their respectability. Mark Twain laughs in part because he and Smith effectively perform rather than prove his respectability, a performance that seems to be working except for the moments when Mark Twain opens his mouth and either slang phrasing or laughter comes out. The performance works because of Mr. Smith's deadpan persistence. So adept is the performance that it cancels the initial negative reaction of the agent who, when he sees Mr. Smith and Mark Twain, acts with "that distant politeness proper toward men who travel muddy streets on foot, go unshaven, and carry countenances like—like ours, for instance" (MTTB 114). Mark Twain does not begrudge this reaction based solely on appearances. Rather, the scene proceeds to display the tenuous nature of appearances and the power of a good pose stoutly maintained to revise them. Similar to newspapers shaping and altering public opinions, Smith weaves a yarn able to override the judgment of the agent based on what he sees. Dramatic illusion trumps appearances.

In the end, the muddy boots and unshaven face of Mark Twain do not signify the true nature of his "character and standing" any more than does the adroit performance of his friend, Mr. Smith. The sequel to the scene of missionary posing in the booking office reinforces that message. Mark Twain returns to disclose his true status as roving correspondent and to offer references. However, all the references for his "high moral character" (MTTB 115) are comically ironic. For the main reference, Mark Twain names the Rev. Mr. Damon of Honolulu, though the book stolen from him remains unreturned. The rest are "men of bad character, [chosen] in order that my mild virtues might shine luminously by contrast with their depravity" (MTTB 116). This joke boomerangs on multiple levels. First, it insults all the friends he might name as references even though it admits that his own virtues are "mild." More importantly, the joke implies that moral character is merely relative at best and probably illusory when truly examined, founded on the mere say-so of other people, people not necessarily more reliable than Mr. Smith. Such moral references in a world of performers and poseurs result in a spotless character as reliable as they are. Barnum-like, Mark Twain says that if the committee can create a spotless character for him, he will copy it and have it framed (MTTB 115), as though the act of having it framed and therefore suitable for display constitutes authenticity.

Creating character out of the whole cloth spun from yarns, as Smith does for the Reverend Mark Twain, is what Sam Clemens has been doing as he writes Mark Twain into his various travel letters. In another example, Mark Twain again undergoes an identity transformation through mere words. Staying at the Heming Hotel in Keokuk, Iowa, Mark Twain asks for plenty of light so that he can read an hour or two before retiring. The parsimonious clerk gives him "two inches of sallow, sorrowful, consumptive tallow candle, that turned blue, and sputtered, and got discouraged, and went out" (MTTB 151). The porter promises to find him a lamp. When the clerk catches him with the lamp and asks what he is doing with it, the porter replies that he is taking it to room fifteen because the patron wants to read. The clerk objects until the porter declares that number fifteen says, "he'll burn the d—d old house down if he don't get a lamp!" (MTTB 151). The clerk relents. The same routine happens when the porter next tries to carry books to Mark Twain's room, and the clerk says he cannot have them. The porter, however, defeats the clerk's objection by raising the ante on his tall-tale game of portraying Mark Twain as a Backwoods Roarer: "But he says that he's mor'ly bound to have 'em; he says he'll just go a-rairin' and a-chargin' through this house and raise more——well, there's no tellin' what he won't do if he don't get 'em; because he's drunk and crazy and desperate, and nothing'll soothe him down but them cussed books" (MTTB 153).

Mark Twain says that the "genius of that porter was something wonderful." Like Mr. Smith, the porter's genius consisted of an unassailable deadpan that convinced his audience by disbursing an aura of credibility around his performance. Mark Twain spins yarns that transform, too. A favorite tactic places him into the role of the comic victim, for example, when he visits a Russian bath (MTTB 101–4) or the infamous Harry Hill's (MTTB 270–74). At other moments, other people clearly have an ability to transform themselves by performance, as when Mark Twain visits Henry Ward Beecher's church. Obtaining a seat in the church resembles finding a seat to see a sold-out play because the church service and Beecher's sermon resemble a play's performance (MTTB 93).

When Mark Twain turns his attention explicitly to the performances of others, he moves toward the role of the art critic, an aspect of the *flâneur*. One example of such critiquing has been noticed before, the singing in the shipboard choirs. Such bad performances may drive Mark Twain to consider destroying the ship as the one sure way to prevent more singing (MTTB 29, 59), but at least their amateur status excuses them. When Mark Twain considers the popular drama in New York City, however, no such remedy can be had, and he expresses annoyance in his comically savage fashion: he is ready to shoot entire tribes of bad actors (MTTB 87, 155). Occasionally, Mark Twain explicitly comments on other aspects of popular art as well, for example, the damnable quality of whatever is the new rage of the moment (MTTB 173–74, 255). He parodies the chronic popular taste for sensational stories in the tale of the old woman who felt cheated of a gory spectacle of victims when a burning ship at sea turns out to be merely a whaler with fires for "trying" whale blubber (MTTB 38). The implicit judgment against such popular literature reoccurs later when Mark Twain brutally dismisses the atrocious woodcuts of women on the covers of dime novels. Within the clichéd narratives of such tales, these women are sympathetic victims and deserve to be rescued. However, the woodcuts render them so ugly that they deserve instead a violent death (MTTB 155). In these instances, the choleric Mark Twain comically colors the *flâneur*.

When Mark Twain turns from popular drama and literature to painting and architecture, he portrays a calmer version of the *flâneur*. In these comments, Sam Clemens clearly displays his own aesthetic. This aesthetic piques attention for its rejection of both vulgar popularity and canonized high culture. Given the quirky, even irascible, nature of the Mark Twain character, which leads to an outspokenness about nearly every topic and person, his past aesthetic pronouncements have demonstrated an independence tinged with Bohemian rebellion. However, the middle course ultimately taken, what might be called a productive confusion of popular material with high-culture artistry, tempers the rebellious edge of such pronouncements. Recall, for example, the acting of Dan Setchell and the banjo playing of Tommy Bree that Clemens had discussed when writing for the *Californian* and the *Dramatic Chronicle*. Mark Twain's comments on those instances make it clear that being popular in itself does not deserve disparagement, a position implied in his brief review of George Washington Harris's comic stories about Sut Lovingood (MTTB 221). However, worthy examples of an art form must rise above unimaginative formulae and careless execution, evidenced in the woodcuts for popular novels and the stories they signify. Such worthy examples must also evoke genuine feeling, one that stands against not only any false sentimentality but the snobbishness of high-culture claims as well. Merely having the status of an "old master" does not guarantee praise in Mark Twain's aesthetic, not when the artist paints "a naked infant that was not built like any infant that ever I saw, nor colored like it, either." This failure to render nature properly deserves another comic outburst of choler: "I am glad the old masters are all dead, and I only wish they had died sooner" (MTTB 239). The willingness of Clemens to describe popular art forms in terms reserved for more respected kinds of art complements his willingness to look askance at the normative demand for automatic deference to the high-culture art represented by the "old masters." These two elements create the curiously unconventional aesthetic of Mark Twain the *flâneur*.

The aesthetic of Mark Twain the *flâneur* also includes another primary element, one that is very American: a privileging of what is "natural," based upon a perceived beauty in the natural world. The "Letters from the Kingdom of Hawai'i" especially made evident an appreciation of the natural world's beauty, culminating in the gorgeous word painting of the Kilauea volcano. That description marks Sam Clemens's first successful attempt at conveying a sense of sublimity. The elaborate description of Kilauea and other portions of the Hawai'ian landscape disclose his deep enjoyment of natural vistas. Crossing the isthmus, Mark Twain again reveals this sentiment, which borders on the religious, when he abuses advertisers, "who invade all sacred places with their rascally signs, and mar every landscape one might gaze upon in worship" (MTTB 40). Sam Clemens's love of landscapes stands out when Mark Twain visits an exhibition at the New York Academy of Design. Out of approximately three hundred paintings, "to me, only about thirty or forty were very beautiful. I liked all the sea views, and the mountain views, and the quiet woodland scenes, with shadow-tinted lakes in the foreground, and I just revelled in the storms" (MTTB 239). A paragraph detailing the beauties of a "dreamy tropical scene" follows, one that fits the literary style of the Kilauea description. Finally, an elaborate critique of an Albert Bierstadt landscape, probably "The Valley of the Yosemite" (MTTB 295), again signals Sam Clemens's love of landscapes as well as his preference for realistic portrayals of the natural world. Though Mark Twain has much praise for elements in the picture, he faults the sky and atmospheric effects because "nothing like it was ever seen in California" (MTTB 250). In summing up his critique of the painting, Mark Twain says, "As a picture, this work must please, but as a portrait I do not think it will answer. Portraits should be accurate. We ... do not want this glorified atmosphere smuggled into a portrait of the Yosemite, where it surely does not belong" (MTTB 251).

Mark Twain's complaint about Bierstadt's landscape involves a question of proper composition as well as a privileging of accuracy: the "glorified atmosphere" was out of place. Mark Twain levels a similar complaint against two examples of architecture. One is the marble residence of businessman Alexander Stewart. Contrasted with the "more graceful, more elegant" (MTTB 246) brownstone or the "rich, cream-colored Portland stone" (MTTB 247) used to face other stylish residences, the marble on the Stewart mansion makes it look like a mausoleum, and "it will never look entirely natural without a hearse in front of it" (MTTB 246). Another is the building that houses the New York Academy of Design, "defiled from top to bottom, with infamous flummery and filagreed gingerbread" (MTTB 241). Mark Twain declares that its Moorish style is an "architectural nightmare," and that the very idea of a Moorish style in America is laughable, "as if the atmosphere of antiquity and romance, that cast a charm around that style in its ancient home beyond the seas, could be reproduced here in the midst of railroads and steamboats, and business rush and clamor, and acres of brownstone fronts—and as if it could be anything but clownish and repulsive without that atmosphere!" (MTTB 242).

The rhetoric of the sanctified versus the unsanctified knits together both the "Letters from the Kingdom of Hawai'i" and the "American Letters." In reporting the hybrid culture he found in Hawai'i, Sam Clemens discovered that he could satirically present aspects of his own mid-nineteenth-century American culture. By finding incidents and behaviors that allowed him to comment on vulgar manners and proper taste, respectability and hypocrisy, self-righteousness, and what constitutes true civilization and decent humanity, Clemens through his Mark Twain alter ego in these two sets of travel letters had extended and deepened the thematic dramatized by the Gentleman Roarer: how to define civilization and savagery. Reminiscent of the Gentleman Roarer, Mark Twain maintains an attitude and a behavior that cannot be wholly on one side or the other of the debate. The multiple poses constituting that liminal status complicate Mark Twain in ways beyond the Gentleman Roarer figures of the earlier comic writers. The complication comes not just from the fact that Clemens uses Mark Twain in settings much more variegated than others, but also because Clemens had more consistently poured his own raw experience into those poses. A narrator who is also represented within the text as a comic character, a literary conduit who expressed sundry thoughts and emotions in a myriad of comic tones, Mark Twain by late 1866 had become for Sam Clemens even more. Mark Twain had become the means by which Sam Clemens could perform whatever comic role he might imagine, strike whatever comic pose he might fancy—as though he were a one-man *tableau vivant*.

# SCENE TWO

COMIC PERFORMANCE

## HAWAI'I'S QUEEN EMMA CONVINCES MARK TWAIN TO BECOME A COMIC LECTURER

THE PRESENCE OF QUEEN EMMA AND THE OPENING OF STEAM COM-
MUNICATION WITH THE SANDWICH ISLANDS MAKES THAT SECTION OF
THE PACIFIC ARCHIPELAGO OF MORE THAN ORDINARY INTEREST TO
SAN FRANCISCANS. MARK TWAIN . . . [WHO] RECENTLY VISITED THE
HAWAIIAN KINGDOM, ANNOUNCES A LECTURE THEREON. . . . IT CAN-
NOT FAIL TO PROVE ATTRACTIVE.

———

"CITY ITEMS," *SAN FRANCISCO ALTA CALIFORNIA,* SEPTEMBER 30, 1866

In *Roughing It,* Mark Twain recounts his debut as a comic lecturer in San Francisco on October 2, 1866, in Maguire's Academy of Music Hall with a tale full
of fear and trembling. That narrative of Sam Clemens performing Mark Twain
for the first time on stage has two fanciful elements in it: Clemens delivered the
lecture without much preparation; he feared an empty house and so had a panic
attack beforehand. Like any good tall tale, this narrative has just enough ground-
ing in actual events to seem plausible while stretching what really happened to
tell a good story. George Barnes of the *Morning Call* remembers Clemens coming into the newspaper's office with a sheaf of scribbled manuscript, looking for
advice about the wisdom of lecturing.[5] The story suggests haste and doubt in the
enterprise. Also, the day of the lecture, the *San Francisco Dramatic Chronicle*
printed a comic story that Mark Twain was so struck with stage fright that he
tried to leave the city and had to be "secured" by officers. Only a dozen bottles of
"Mrs. Winslow's soothing syrup" had calmed him. Perhaps this raillery provided
the germ of Clemens's own story of nerves. Given the fact that Clemens is known
to have been writing anonymous squibs for the *Dramatic Chronicle* at this time,
he may have written the initial story himself.[6] The phrase "Mrs. Winslow's soothing syrup" also appears in the transcript compiled by Fred Lorch and Paul Fatout
of the 1869 lecture. Regardless of the origins for the *Roughing It* narrative, the
contrast between the sense of impending failure for an impromptu enterprise
and the resounding success of the first lecture heightens the drama of the event,

5. Barnes, "Pacific Slope," 1.
6. *San Francisco Dramatic Chronicle,* "Sensational Rumor." For Clemens's connection to the
*Dramatic Chronicle,* see John R. Bruce, *Gaudy Century: The Story of San Francisco's 100 Years of
Robust Journalism;* and John P. Young, *Journalism in California.*

but the facts are otherwise. Clemens carefully planned everything. The *Rough-ing It* narrative should be understood as the last act in an orchestrated perfor-mance to insure the success of Mark Twain the comic lecturer, an effort that started well before Clemens stepped on the stage at the Academy of Music.

Though the first lecture by Mark Twain was not impromptu, a notable event in San Francisco precipitated its timing: the impending arrival of Hawai'i's Queen Emma. Weeks before the queen set foot in San Francisco on Monday, September 24, the city's newspapers had been carrying stories about her visits to New York City and Washington, D.C. Once Queen Emma left New York City and her arrival in San Francisco was calculated, the *San Francisco Alta Califor-nia* began a series of lengthy front-page articles on the Hawai'ian Islands, dis-cussing their history, natural resources, and finances as well as noting commercial links with San Francisco. In effect, the articles recapitulated the seri-ous sections of the Mark Twain letters from Hawai'i already published in the *Sacramento Union.* New letters in the *Union* series appeared during this time period, including Mark Twain's evaluation of the sugar industry. Hawai'i and its queen were creating what would now be called a media buzz. The huge crowd at the dock to greet Queen Emma provided good copy, and during her three-week stay in San Francisco, the city's papers continued to devote considerable space to the queen's activities, reporting on her efforts to raise funds for the new Epis-copal church in Honolulu, her attendance at Grace Cathedral, her visits to schools and the woolen mills, and her tour of the harbor fortifications. The queen was newsworthy not only because a royal person is by definition a spec-tacle, but also because people were genuinely impressed with Emma, "a pleasant-looking, lady-like woman with dark eyes," and her demeanor, "modest and unassuming, thus truly gracing a rank she appears well entitled to."[7]

Queen Emma's visit also occasioned jokes in the press about proper manners when calling on her and ignited a debate about Americans fawning over royalty. The *San Francisco Sunday Mercury,* an illustrated weekly, devoted virtually its entire issue of September 30 to Queen Emma, featuring a "splendid" portrait, a full account of her travels and parentage, and a comic story in which Caliban calls on the queen and introduces Topsy-Turvy to her majesty. Clearly, Sam Clemens was not the only one ready to exploit the queen's celebrity for commercial purposes.

The newspapers' attention on the queen and Hawai'i must have invigorated Sam Clemens's focus on the islands. Hawai'i had claimed a large portion of his literary effort since he had returned from the islands in mid-August. Without a regular correspondent's job, Clemens necessarily mined his Hawai'i experience

7. *San Francisco Dramatic Chronicle,* "A Disgraceful Imposition," 2; *San Francisco Alta Califor-nia,* "City Items: Arrival of Queen Emma," 1.

for all its saleable ore. Not only had he been writing up the Big Island portion of his trip and seeing the letters printed in the *Sacramento Union,* but also he rewrote his letter on the *Hornet* disaster for *Harper's* and apparently began to rework all of the Hawai'i material into a book format or possibly into a series of articles for publication in the eastern press.[8] In the reviews of the first "Sandwich Islands" lecture in the *Bulletin* and the *Dramatic Chronicle,* both San Francisco papers report Clemens's final words to the audience, when its applause called him back to the stage at the close of the performance: he had "inflicted" the lecture upon them to garner funds to publish a book on Hawai'i.

Having funds insufficient to do much of anything was occupying Sam Clemens's attention during this period.[9] Given his preexisting focus on Hawai'i, lecturing on the subject must have seemed like a perfect solution to his money woes once the papers began to fill their columns with material on Queen Emma's impending arrival and on Hawai'i in general. The sad state of Sam Clemens's finances at this time explains why he was so angry about the fake robbery after his lecture in Virginia City—in his straitened circumstances, the loss of several hundred dollars and a favorite watch must have been particularly painful.[10] His sad financial state also explains why Clemens suddenly did not depart from San Francisco after the second lecture there in mid-November: the proceeds from that lecture were apparently attached by a sheriff to pay for debts in Nevada, hence the hasty addition of lectures in Petaluma, San Jose, and Oakland.[11] Michael de Young of the *Dramatic Chronicle* remembers Clemens as a "good Bohemian . . . he ran up bills and owed money right and left." When the box office receipts were seized, de Young claimed that "Sam rushed to me and I told him to lecture under my auspices—and then he couldn't be attached . . . and it was officially announced in the *Chronicle* that way."[12]

Newspaper ads for the first lecture started running on Thursday the twenty-seventh, three days after the Queen's arrival.[13] If Barnes's story about the manuscript for the lecture is essentially correct, the meeting in the *Call's* offices probably took place early in the week, perhaps the Monday the queen arrived. When John McComb declared that the endeavor would work, despite what more literary friends had already said, Clemens the next day would have engaged the

8. Paine, *Biography,* 1:291.

9. Ibid., 1:292; see also Fred W. Lorch, *The Trouble Begins at Eight: Mark Twain's Lecture Tours,* 25.

10. See Doten, "Journalism, Part II."

11. Lorch, *Trouble,* 46.

12. Bruce, *Gaudy Century,* 127. I did not find such an announcement in the paper of this time period.

13. See, for example, *San Francisco Alta California,* "City Items: The Sandwich Islands."

Academy of Music and arranged for the newspaper ads. However, the decision to try lecturing had most likely been made the week before, when Queen Emma's imminent arrival had been announced and the *Alta* had begun its series of articles on Hawai'i. The manuscript Barnes and McComb saw was probably not a hastily scribbled effort but rather the product of a few intense days of choosing from the already-written Hawai'i material and rewriting it for an oral performance. The objections of the literary friends to whom Clemens had shown the manuscript was not that it was rough in the sense of being unpolished but that it was rough in the sense of being unable to pass muster by the standards of genteel taste.[14] In any case, Clemens had about a week to continue revising and to begin memorizing the lecture after the meeting with his newspaper friends.

Bret Harte's review of the first lecture substantiates the linkage of Queen Emma's visit and Sam Clemens's decision to lecture on Hawai'i that the *Alta California* implies in the epigraph to this section. Harte's review appears in the *Springfield (Mass.) Republican,* for which he had been writing a regular column on California. Harte notes that "Samuel Clemens, better known as 'Mark Twain,' the Honolulu correspondent of the *Sacramento Union,* took advantage of the interest attending the queen's visit to deliver a most entertaining lecture upon the Sandwich Islands."[15] George Barnes explicitly mentions Harte in the anecdote about the lecture manuscript as one of the literati who warn Clemens about the damage the lecture could do to his career. Given that Harte talked to Clemens about the wisdom of lecturing, the comment linking the queen with the lecture in Harte's review confirms that Queen Emma's visit convinced Clemens that the time was right to try lecturing, an idea he had been nurturing perhaps since his return to San Francisco. The free advertising the queen generated in the papers effectively fulfilled the last condition necessary to induce Clemens to take the gamble.

This sequence of events and decisions argues for the fictional nature of the picture Clemens paints in *Roughing It* of his intense fear that the lecture would fail. The image dramatizes the high stakes involved, but in reality Clemens had been hard at work preparing to insure success. Not only was he well prepared, but also the notices of the impending lecture often contained predictions of success and a full house. The *Dramatic Chronicle* warned people to get a ticket early. As Fred Lorch notes, an entrepreneur like Clemens would have monitored all preshow indications of success or failure carefully.[16] He would have known about the ticket sales and the papers' predictions. No reason existed to be fearful of the utter failure imagined in the *Roughing It* account. A letter to his mother dated

14. Barnes, "Pacific Slope," 1.
15. Harte, "From California," 1.
16. *San Francisco Dramatic Chronicle,* [Tickets to Mark Twain's Lecture], 2; Lorch, *Trouble,* 29.

November 2, 1866, confirms the meticulous nature of Clemens's preparations. In addition, the letter reveals the bold scope of his plan to enter the lecturing field: when he set out to tour the mining camps in California and Nevada, he had also scheduled a reprise in San Francisco, maximizing exposure and profits before a planned departure for New York City (CL 1:365). Once Sam Clemens had decided to perform his Mark Twain character on the lecture platform, the record shows none of the timidity or stage fright imagined in *Roughing It*. The variance between the evidence and the narrative only highlights how much more invested Clemens was becoming in performing Mark Twain.

## A FELLOW SAVAGE ON THE LECTURE PLATFORM

IN OCTOBER, 1866, I BROKE OUT AS A LECTURER, AND FROM THAT DAY TO THIS I HAVE ALWAYS BEEN ABLE TO GAIN MY LIVING WITHOUT DOING ANY WORK.

MARK TWAIN IN ERUPTION, 304–5

One newspaper editor said in a notice for the Mark Twain lecture on Hawai'i that he hoped Queen Emma would be in San Francisco on the date of the lecture, implying that she ought to be on hand to hear what Sam Clemens had to say about the island kingdom and its people. The record makes it clear that the queen did not attend, but it is worthwhile asking, as one way to evaluate the lecture, how she might have reacted if she had bought a ticket. The extant reviews were nearly unanimous in their praise, and their commentary displays persistent patterns. First, the so-called word paintings in the lecture, the descriptions of natural scenery—in particular the description of the volcano Kilauea—were noted for their surprising rhetorical effectiveness and sublimity. Next, reviewers enjoyed the manner of presentation, Mark Twain's comic style, for its inimitable humor. The enjoyment of the style led to a third pattern: more than one reviewer declared Mark Twain as a lecturer was superior to Artemus Ward. Finally, some reviewers remarked that the lecture was "preeminently humorous [with] much information" or encouraged people to attend by saying, "His lecture will be not only amusing but instructive."[17]

17. *San Francisco Alta California,* [Mark Twain's First Lecture], 1; *San Francisco Bulletin,* "Mark Twain's Lecture," 5.

The claim that the lecture contained much useful information has more to do with a highbrow desire to find information in a comic lecture rather than take it on its own laughable terms. The *Bulletin*'s recommendation obviously echoes Horace's *dulce et utile* dictum for literature. A careful listener to Mark Twain, however, would understand that the lecture is not literary and that his intent has little to do with instruction: nearly all the self-deprecating remarks made by Mark Twain are about his difficulty telling the truth. In the 1869 version of the lecture complied from several newspaper sources by Fred Lorch, Mark Twain made an explicit comment about his indifference to the truth: "I shall tell the truth as nearly as I can and quite as nearly as *any* newspaperman can. The non- sense with which I shall embellish it will not detract from its truthfulness; that will be but as the barnacle to the oyster. I don't know—*sotto voce*—whether the barnacle does stick to the oyster or the oyster to the barnacle" (FS 1867).[18] He does not know if nonsensical embellishments affect the truth, but he does not care because nonsensical embellishments constitute his stock and trade. How- ever, satire also has a favored place in Mark Twain's comic inventory, and though Clemens often exaggerates a fact in nonsensical ways, at other moments an exag- geration can produce the hardheaded and even grim truth of satire. Sliding along the boundary between fact and fiction has been a fundamental comic tactic for Clemens. Imagining Queen Emma's viewpoint can usefully trace that move- ment: how would an intelligent and well-educated Hawai'ian react to the "infor- mation" in the lecture? Ferreting out the bits of fact used in the lecture will show how Clemens manipulates them for comic purposes.

One piece of information that Queen Emma would say was misinformation can be found in the 1867 version, when Mark Twain claims that Hawai'i has no constitution. Mark Twain adds that the monarchy is an empty name, and that "Americans . . . are the kings of the Sandwich Islands" (FS 1869, Fatout)—appar- ently because they "own all the money, control all the commerce, and own all the ships" (FS 1867). However, Hawai'i not only had a functioning constitution, but it was of such recent vintage, being promulgated in 1864, that the fallout from the changes to the previous constitution had lingered during Clemens's visit to the islands. The twelfth letter from Hawai'i makes reference both to the new con- stitution and to the fallout. Moreover, a major difference in the 1864 constitu- tion concerned a property qualification for voting, a change King Kamehameha V insisted upon and Clemens agreed was needed (MTLH 106). The king's insis-

18. Originally in *St. Louis Missouri Democrat* (March 28, 1867). There are three other versions I have examined for this analysis: one compiled by Paul Fatout of the 1869 lecture (MTS 4–15), one compiled by Lorch (*Trouble*, 271–84), also of the 1869 lecture, and one compiled by Walter Frear of the 1873 lecture (MTH 431–36). All texts are available as part of Stephen Railton's Web site, "Mark Twain in His Times." Quotes are from the Web site texts.

tence on the change highlights the major consequence of the 1864 constitution: more power accruing to the king. The king had in fact dissolved the constitutional assembly of 1864 when it deadlocked on the issue of property qualification and proclaimed the new constitution without a vote.[19] The bitterness in the American community about the king's de facto coup was part of the fallout that Clemens heard about firsthand, certainly from Henry Whitney, who led the opposition. In the face of King Kamehameha V's triumph in the recent power struggle, Mark Twain's comment that the monarchy is an "empty name" is either wishful thinking to flatter the Americans living in Hawai'i or comic amnesia.

The misinformation and amnesia, especially in regard to Americans being the real kings because of their economic power, point to the emotional investment Clemens had made in the struggle between the monarchy and American business interests, a partisanship easily found in the "Letters from the Kingdom of Hawai'i" when Mark Twain discusses Bishop Staley or Minister Harris. The fact that these two men take their place as specific topics in the lecture, mentioned in advertisements and reviews, demonstrates how Clemens's natural sympathy with the Americans in Hawai'i as well as a pragmatic need to tailor material for his audience shaped both the lecture and the Hawai'i correspondence.

This same sympathy and pragmatism also colors Mark Twain's eloquent (to his Californian audience) tribute to the missionaries who have changed the pre-contact culture of *kapu* that organized social behavior in Hawai'i and that at times gave high chiefs and/or priests the power of life and death. However, the basic facts in the tribute are wrong. Mark Twain creates a litany of oppression starting with the king and moving on down through the ranks until the lowest level, the common man and woman, are depicted as "abject slaves." However, there was no slavery in precontact Hawai'i, while the concept of *mo'i* or paramount chief was only a recent reality when the missionaries arrived. The feudal analogy used is wrong, but that is immaterial, for it allows Mark Twain to praise the American missionaries for having "broke off the shackles" of the people. Because the pyramid of oppression has at the very bottom the common woman who is forbidden to eat with her husband or to eat "choice fruit," Mark Twain can also insert a joke about Eve and the fruit forbidden to her (FS 1867).

The tailoring of material for the better class of people that heard the lecture in San Francisco and Sacramento and Virginia City, as well as for the largely male and working-class audiences in the smaller mining towns and camps was done, however, not to instruct or to inform them but to induce their laughter. Queen Emma, then, would not only be forced to protest the political bias in the lecture

---

19. Kuykendall, *Critical Years,* 131–33; Jonathan Kay Kamakawiwo'ole Osorio, *Dismembering Lahui: A History of the Hawai'ian Nation to 1887,* 125–27.

but also to deplore the cultural superiority shown toward the habits and customs of Hawai'ians as they become the butt of many jokes in the lectures. As a piece of jokework, "Our Fellow Savages of the Sandwich Islands" mostly employs the structure of any ethnic joke. The point of view is that of the joke teller conspiring with the audience while the ridicule and comic disparagement is heaped upon the absent other. These jokes constitute the main portion of the lecture, and they proceed by bits of facts being held up as laughably exotic or by exaggerating the bits of facts until their strangeness becomes comical. For example, the Hawai'ian concept of *'ohana* or extended family and the practice of adoption called *hanai* form the basis for a joke about the Hawai'ian who was fired from his job by a *haole* boss from California because he kept asking for time off to bury all his mothers.

Though Clemens as Mark Twain uses Hawai'ian culture as the main butt of laughter in his lecture, he also inverts the assumed inferiority of the island culture in order to score points against American culture. A long litany of how the Hawai'ians "do everything wrong end first" becomes not just a comment against annexing the islands to the United States but also a satiric swipe at the commercial and political corruption Clemens will more prominently attack later in *The Gilded Age*: "Now you see what kind of voters you will have if you take these islands away from these people as we are pretty sure to do some day. They will do everything wrong end first. They will make a deal of trouble here too. Instead of fostering and encouraging a judicious system of railroad speculation, and all that sort of thing, they will elect the most incorruptible men to Congress. Yes, they will turn everything upside down" (FS 1869, Fatout). The final triumph of the comic inversion is the way that the Hawai'ians become morally superior to the Americans as voters in a democracy.

Given that Clemens constructs the bulk of the lecture as an ethnic joke, an apparent scruple in introducing comic tales about cannibalism is also noteworthy. Mark Twain says that there used to be cannibals in Hawai'i, "but they are almost played out" (FS 1867), and goes on to tell a tale about a cannibal dying because he could not digest an old missionary. In the 1866 tour of the lecture through California and Nevada, this tale became the occasion for Mark Twain to offer to demonstrate cannibalism if a mother would kindly lend him her child. To complete this outrageous joke, Mark Twain would pause and wait in silence for a few moments, as though expecting a child to be produced. Western audiences apparently found this very dark humor hilarious.[20] In some versions, Clemens elaborates the comic tale about ultimate indigestion, but the setup has changed: either it explicitly discounts the charge that Hawai'ians practiced can-

20. Lorch, *Trouble*, 47.

nibalism—"they were never cannibals" (FS 1873)—or becomes a defense: "It used to be said that the Kanakas were cannibals, but that was a slander" (FS 1869, Fatout). In later versions, the cannibal in the tale is a foreigner. Usually, he becomes tired of eating Hawai'ians and decides to see "how a white man would go with onions," eats a tough old whaling captain rather than a missionary, and dies "with the crime on his conscience [and] the whaler on his stomach" (FS 1869, Lorch). The 1873 version has Mark Twain repeating his offer to demonstrate cannibalism, again placing him in a most uncivilized category, from which he nevertheless protects the Hawai'ians.

Self-disparagement forms part of Mark Twain's humor of course. The title of the Hawai'i lecture most often used—"Our Fellow Savages of the Sandwich Islands"—underscores this tactic, one by which Mark Twain removes the superior position given to his American audience in the ethnic joke portion of the show and makes a satiric point. Moreover, the lecture title highlights Mark Twain adopting the Citizen Clown role, the laughable teller of truths about his own culture. More than a little willing to make fun of Hawai'i and the Hawai'ian Kingdom, its culture, history, and people, Mark Twain was also an equal-opportunity purveyor of ridicule, ready to induce laughter at the United States and its culture and social practices. Clemens always stood ready to risk being shunned by the respectable due to the presentation of his comic character. The phrase "Fellow Savages" questions his American audience's complacent respectability while it insists on a common humanity.

This ecumenical ridicule at times makes the Americans living in Hawai'i the butts of jokes—and by implication the audience, too. In one of the lecture's sections, Mark Twain portrays Honolulu as a comically innocent town. The place is so dull and free of nightlife that the gas company went broke because no one was awake after dark to use their gas lamps, a habit that Mark Twain suggests has nothing to do with customs in San Francisco. When he shifts the subject to drinking, Mark Twain first draws a contrast between Honoluluans and his present lecture audience—the "blessed ignorance" that keeps Americans in Honolulu from drinking should be "imported into California." He also suggests that the lecture audience behaves like the blessedly innocent Honoluluans, who "drink anything that is liquid—kerosene, turpentine, hair oil [and] a barrel of Mrs. Winslow's soothing syrup" (FS 1869, Fatout), as though they were miners out on a monstrous spree. Mark Twain satirizes the morals of the San Franciscans in either perspective.

This grouping of jokes makes Honolulu sound enough like San Francisco to imply that people everywhere are all the same, yet the ridicule is lenient compared to what Mark Twain says about the enterprise of the American missionaries in Hawai'i. Clemens's profound ambivalence about efforts to transform

Hawai'i's Polynesian society into a tropical version of the United States caused him to alternate between high praise and harsh criticism. In the lecture, however, the two poles are more stark in their contrast. Missionaries are called "sinless," and Mark Twain acknowledges their moral force in a way that implies its miraculous nature. Nevertheless, the missionaries were a target, too. A routine gibe in the lecture claimed that the missionaries could not understand Mark Twain's jokes because they had no sense of humor, a mild beginning. The most scorching satiric comment involves the price Hawai'ians have paid to be emancipated and educated by the missionaries. Mark Twain makes it by linking civilization and death in all of the extant versions of the lecture.

> Eighty or ninety years ago they had a native population of full 400,000 souls, and they were comfortable, prosperous, and happy. But then the white people came, and brought trade, and commerce, and education, and complicated diseases, and civilization, and all sorts of calamities, and the consequence was the poor natives began to die off with wonderful rapidity, so that forty or fifty years ago the 400,000 had become reduced to 200,000. Then the white people doubled the educational facilities; and it was just the same as turning the small pox loose in a community that hadn't been vaccinated at all! If they start but a few more seminaries of learning there, it will surely finish them. (Laughter.) The nation is doomed. It will be extinct within fifty years, without a doubt. Some people in the house may live to hear of the death of the last of the "Kanakas." (FS 1873)

The association of learning with genocide strikes satirically at the foundation of the missionaries' work with the destructive energy of a lightning bolt. One wonders what sort of laughter happened during the moment the transcript indicates—and what mood the audience was in when Mark Twain invites them to contemplate the extinction of the entire indigenous population after they have laughed.

In other versions, Mark Twain also attacks Americans' imperialistic desires by saying that when the process of extinction is complete, "we will take possession as lawful heirs" (FS 1869, Fatout).[21] The sarcastic irony of "lawful" echoes the rhetoric in which seminaries of learning figure as engines of destruction rather than dispensers of benevolence. At these moments in the lecture, Clemens has returned to an attitude in the *Sacramento Union* letters that joked about and questioned the good intentions of the missionaries. Education figures as a disease and Western

---

21. Clemens later expressed a similar ironic opposition to annexation at the close of two long articles written for the *New York Daily Tribune*: "The Sandwich Islands: Views of Mark Twain" (January 6, 1873), and "The Sandwich Islands: Concluding Views of Mark Twain" (January 9, 1873). Reprinted in MTH, 489–500.

civilization as a calamity for the Hawai'ians. By providing dry statistics and conjuring the decimation of the indigenous population, Clemens in his most performed Mark Twain lecture explicitly lays the holocaust proportion of the
population decline on the doorstep of the Americans. Queen Emma, who in 1859
was instrumental in establishing the first hospital in Honolulu exclusively for
Hawai'ians, would have understood this part of the lecture all too clearly. Information on the subject has been provided, but the uncompromising nature of Mark
Twain's satiric conclusion is the truly remarkable moment in the lecture.

The other most forceful parts of the lecture were the so-called word paintings,
literary set pieces routinely praised in the newspaper reviews. Apparently,
Clemens would vary the subjects of such ornate descriptions by including the
magnificent natural scenery in general or a particular Hawai'ian flower, but
describing the eruption of the volcano Kilauea became the mainstay for this part
of the show, a version of which had ended the Hawai'i correspondence for the
*Sacramento Union.* After the first lecture tour, the emphasis in the reviews on the
"word paintings" occurred because the audience was apparently unprepared for
the lavish details of the event, "described in a manner which brought the scene
vividly before the imagination."[22] Conjuring Kilauea in a word painting became
a highlight of the lecture. The immense success of this calculated belles lettres
moment provided Clemens with an opportunity for laughter, too. By the time
of the second lecture in San Francisco, Mark Twain deliberately undercut its sublimity and the spellbinding effect it had on the audience: he would interrupt
himself by pretending to forget a word. For variation in this debunking of the
lecture's most highbrow moment, he would also end the description with a clap
of his hands both to break the spell and to induce general applause (FS 1867), or
he would signal the finish by saying, "There—I'm glad I've got that volcano off
my mind" (FS 1869, Fatout). Nevertheless, reviewers continued to highlight the
descriptions, emphasizing their highbrow aesthetic. The *Bulletin* advertised the
third and final San Francisco lecture by claiming that the "description of the
great volcano alone is worth twice the price of admission," and the *Alta California,* in reviewing the second lecture in San Francisco, said that if Mark Twain
would publish the "passage of description of the scene from the peak overlooking the crater, his reputation as a 'fine writer' would jostle his eminent renown
as a humorist."[23]

22. *San Francisco Bulletin,* "'Mark Twain's' Lecture on the Sandwich Islands," 5; *San Francisco Dramatic Chronicle,* "Academy of Music," 3.

23. *San Francisco Bulletin,* "Mark Twain To-night," 5; *San Francisco Alta California,* "Amuse-ments," 1. The *Alta*'s comment suggests either that the description is considerably different from what had just been published the day before in the *Sacramento Union* as the twenty-fifth letter from Hawai'i or that the reviewer had not yet read the last installment in the series.

The unstinting praise for the literary description of Kilauea documents the contemporary recognition that Mark Twain had highbrow elements in his repertoire, though not enough to satisfy Bret Harte when Clemens showed him an early draft of the lecture. Possibly there was no Kilauea description in that draft. Certainly, the description finally published as part of the last Hawai'i letter would have been a polished iteration of the version given in the first lecture more than a month earlier. Though the "American Letters," written after the first lecture tour, show only a sporadic attempt to capitalize on this favorable notice from the highbrow portion of the audience, the more obvious examples of fine writing about scenery in *The Innocents Abroad* and *Roughing It* can be traced back to the success of the description of Kilauea in the Sandwich Islands lecture.

The word paintings in the lecture provided the most satisfactory moments for those in the audience who could not conceive of lectures as otherwise than edifying, but the ethnic joke structure organizes the lectures as a whole into an experience well below a highbrow taste. Nevertheless, the lectures were not characterized as "low." The elegant audiences the newspapers in Sacramento and San Francisco note for the lectures indicate that the better sort of people were happy to attend. This patronage was evident even in the third and final San Francisco lecture, despite some complaints about the questionable taste of portions of the earlier lectures. The *San Francisco Examiner* said that Mark Twain "verges . . . occasionally upon coarseness." The *Dramatic Chronicle,* usually so favorable to Clemens, judged that Mark Twain's second San Francisco lecture was too much in the mining-camp style and not fit for San Francisco, with jokes "so nearly improper—not to say coarse—that they could not be heartily laughed at by ladies." Descriptions about the natural world, literary in their composition, and jokes about Hawai'ians and missionaries, dubious in their taste—the Sandwich Islands lecture encompassed a range of effects, "this mixture of the sublime and the ridiculous," as Prentice Mulford noted for the *Golden Era,* and as Alf Doten implied when he praised both the "drollest humor" and the "lofty flights of descriptive eloquence" in his review for the *Virginia City Territorial Enterprise.*[24] This mix of high and low elements indicates both the remarkable range of emotional effects Clemens could create with his Mark Twain alter ego as well as the various segments of his historical audiences. The lectures nevertheless find coherence in their theatricality: the variable aesthetic elements constitute Mark Twain the comic character, performed on stage.

---

24. *San Francisco Examiner,* [Mark Twain's Lecture], 2; *San Francisco Dramatic Chronicle,* "Mark Twain's Lecture," 3; Prentice Mulford, review of "Our Fellow Savages of the Sandwich Islands," 3; Alf Doten, review of "Our Fellow Savages of the Sandwich Islands," 3; see also CL 1:366n1; and Lorch, *Trouble,* 40.

Clemens performed Mark Twain as a humorist who mocked the lyceum lecture system by burlesquing its protocols and its serious intent of conveying information to the audience. For this fundamental comic strategy, Clemens owed a debt to Charles Farrar Browne's performances of Artemus Ward. Browne's West Coast lecture that Clemens saw was called "The Babes in the Woods," but titles were irrelevant because whatever the announced topic, Browne constantly deferred it until the end and then dropped it altogether. As Browne himself put it, "The great merit of this lecture ... is that it contains so many things that do not have anything to do with it."[25] In later mock lectures, Browne parodied talks by travelers, using a panorama deliberately ill-designed so that it constantly malfunctioned.

Various commentaries written by editors in literary periodicals before and after Clemens took to the lecture platform illustrate the originally serious purpose of the lyceum lecture and its highbrow cultural standing. In a section of the "Editor's Easy Chair" written by George William Curtis in an 1865 issue of *Harper's Monthly,* he notes the recent success of Artemus Ward delivering "a special form of the Lyceum," but he asserts that the lecturing business will not disappear. However, the reason Curtis gives for his prediction that the lyceum will continue to flourish, even in New York City with its myriad forms of entertainment, is not the success of figures like Artemus Ward, but rather because the lyceum's business was "moving, controlling, inspiring the human mind." In 1872, Josiah Holland echoed this nobility of purpose. In the midst of a lament that the lyceum had been corrupted by buffoons and "triflers on the platform," Holland enumerates what used to give the lyceum lectures their true purpose: "Grave discussions of important topics; social, political, and literary essays; instructive addresses and spirited appeals." George William Curtis, in another edition of the "Editor's Easy Chair," picked up Holland's view that comic lecturers have debased the lyceum system. Attributing the rapid rise and growth of the comic lecture to the "masters," Artemus Ward and Mark Twain, Curtis remained more sanguine about the survival of the true lyceum lecture than Holland, perhaps because of his own extensive experience. Though the lecture platform "has gradually changed from an agency of instruction to one of amusement ... there are now the signs of a natural and healthy reaction," which is to be welcomed.[26]

The strong cultural emphasis upon instruction and even inspiration in the lyceum lecture motivated Clemens to include consistently in his lectures on Hawai'i prose-poem descriptions of natural beauty representing a fine-writing

25. Quoted in Edgar M. Branch, "'The Babes in the Woods': Artemus Ward's 'Double Health' to Mark Twain," 955.
26. George William Curtis, "Editor's Easy Chair [The Lyceum]," 263; Josiah Holland, "Triflers on the Platform," 489; George William Curtis, "Editor's Easy Chair [The Lyceum Endures]," 615.

tradition. This ingrained cultural attitude also motivated the reviewers of the Mark Twain lectures on Hawai'i to emphasize the prose-poem element, though it makes up a relatively small proportion compared to jokes and comic scenes. Despite this bias represented by the reviewers' praise of "word paintings," and despite Clemens clearly exploiting his historical audience's desire for such high-brow aesthetic moments to satisfy an earnest wish to be informed and educated, an underlying playful intent imbues his performances of Mark Twain. That intent is obvious in Clemens's persistent comic flourishes that undercut the perceived sublimity of his descriptions of the Kilauea volcano. Moreover, the deliberate, laughable dissipations of the sublime mood induced in the audience by the descriptions underscore Mark Twain's comic status as a cultural savage. Insisting upon Mark Twain's playfulness, however, does not mean that Clemens was not serious in his own way about using the lyceum format. Rather, Holland's standard, genteel view of the lyceum misses Clemens's method of edifying an audience because it cannot comprehend Mark Twain functioning as the laughable yet truth-telling Citizen Clown.

The lyceum lecture format for Clemens became de facto comic ritual—theater performed as though it were ceremony, within which Mark Twain's clowning could remind the social body, represented by the audience, how to behave and think. Clowning in Nevada as Washoe Mark Twain had caused Clemens trouble in part because American culture in the 1860s had no clearly defined secular ritual spaces for the playful satire with which he was experimenting through hoaxes and combative comic raillery. Without a clear play frame, Washoe Mark Twain necessarily had an ambiguous relationship with his readers. Some historical readers of Mark Twain sketches and hoaxes in Nevada did not even understand themselves to be an implied audience for playful satire and laughable truth-telling.

A comic lecture, however, has definitive time and space boundaries, providing a much better opportunity to establish a play frame. In addition, a comic lecture automatically gathered together an audience for the theater of the Citizen Clown. Moreover, members of the lecture audience effectively acknowledged they were ready for fun by entering the special space of the lecture hall; they would not forget that they had read Mark Twain sketches or heard of Clemens's funnyman reputation. And yet, the newspaper reviews of the lectures in California show how much built-in resistance existed in the dominant genteel culture to understanding "Our Fellow Savages of the Sandwich Islands" as a *comic performance*. Clemens understood the depth of that resistance. That instinctual understanding caused him to burlesque his well-polished sublime description of Kilauea volcano; it is also why he persisted in making mock introductions of himself.

these introductions [by others] were so grossly flattering that they made me ashamed, and so I began my talk at a heavy disadvantage. It was a stupid custom. . . . The introducer was almost always an ass, and his prepared speech a jumble of vulgar compliments and dreary effort to be funny; therefore after the first season I always introduced myself—using, of course, a burlesque of the time-worn introduction. . . .

My introduction . . . had to be carefully and painstakingly worded, and very earnestly spoken, in order that all strangers present might be deceived into the supposition that I was only the introducer and not the lecturer; also that the flow of overdone compliments might sicken those strangers; then, when the end was reached and the remark casually dropped that I was the lecturer and had been talking about myself, the effect was very satisfactory. (MTA 1:160–61)

Parodic introductions not only allowed Clemens to skip the tediousness of poor introductions by local dignitaries and thus to ridicule the protocols of the lyceum circuit. Mock introductions also pointed emphatically to the play frame for what was to follow, showing the historical audience that expectations of being educated and morally uplifted would not be met in the usual, ponderous fashion.

By the spring of 1867, "Mark Twain" signified two professional faces for the public. One was the author of *The Celebrated Jumping Frog of Calaveras County*. Charles Webb's editorial choices emphasize the mocking voice of a Mark Twain who often relied on burlesque to score his satiric points. The Bohemian aesthetic projected by this Mark Twain aptly fit into the New York City literary scene from which Webb had come. This congruence overpowers the "Western" flavor derived from the book's topical references and the slang in Mark Twain's diction. The other professional public face was the successful lecturer, which had a more immediate impact on contemporary popular culture, for Sam Clemens's stage performance of Mark Twain had no precedent. Mark Twain was not the lyceum lecturer but the mock lecturer, so the serious purpose of the lectures that began in the antebellum period bore little resemblance to the burlesque represented by the figure. Mark Twain on stage was also certainly not like the Jacksonian era's one-man comic shows of Charles Mathews or James Hackett, actors who featured multiple comic characters and dialects. Moreover, though contemporaries like George Curtis named Mark Twain and Artemus Ward the masters of the comic lecture, and though many reviewers of the Hawai'i lecture immediately compared Mark Twain favorably to Artemus Ward or even saw him as superior, Clemens and Browne had a clear and important difference. Satire complemented the quirky humors of the Mark Twain comic character while Artemus Ward merely displayed whimsy and absurdity. Thus the slangy and irreverent Mark Twain pretended to dispense information when he was actually interested instead in garnering laughter from shrewd observations of human behavior. Josiah Holland had asserted that "the stupidest man in the world is one who surrenders himself to the single purpose of making men laugh." Mark Twain, performed on stage, became Sam Clemens's best vehicle not just for the single purpose of making men laugh, but for the more complicated purpose of using laughter to make them think. Mark Twain, performed on stage, presents the purest form of the Citizen Clown's symbolic action, lashing the body politic with laughter to make it behave better than it normally does. In this second public face, Mark Twain has as descendants all the best stand-up comics of the twentieth and twenty-first centuries.

## THEATER AND ILLUSION

MARK TWAIN . . . SEEMED ALWAYS SOMEHOW TO MASK [CLEMENS]
FROM MY PERSONAL SENSE.

————

*MY MARK TWAIN,* WILLIAM DEAN HOWELLS, 1910

The newspaper praise for the Kilauea set piece in the Sandwich Island lectures underscored the oratorical skills of Sam Clemens. The *San Francisco Examiner* had feared that Mark Twain would not be able to speak as well as he wrote, yet the reviews clearly indicate just how good, how skillfully dramatic, Clemens was at public speaking. As a practiced storyteller, Sam Clemens already had ample opportunity to prepare for the lecture platform. Calvin Higby, Clemens's mining partner in Aurora, Nevada, recalled how Sam charmed him with yarns by the hour and could spend an entire morning in a country store single-handedly entertaining an audience.[27] By early 1867, Clemens was a seasoned platform performer, a fact that more than any other served to blur Mark Twain and Sam Clemens and to create the theatrical illusion of comic singularity.

Apparently, Clemens himself began to experience the power of that illusion, if a change in the way he signed letters is any indication. The record of published letters shows that Clemens first began to sign letters "Mark Twain" with a short note to the editors of the *Sacramento Union* upon his return from Hawai'i, understandable given his business relation with the paper. A week later, on August 25, 1866, Clemens wrote one of his oldest boyhood friends, Will Bowen, and signed himself "Mark." Perhaps more revealing, he signed the postscript "Sam," which is crossed out, and then "Mark" appears. Nearly all of the surviving correspondence for the fall of 1866, from the time of Clemens's return from

27. Phillips, "Reminiscences," 70.

Hawai'i in August until his departure for New York City in December, is signed with some version of "Mark Twain." This period coincides with his first comic lectures performing Mark Twain. On December 4, Clemens even sent a letter to his mother signed "Mark," though the last letter before he left California, dated December 14, 1866, is also addressed to his family and is signed "Sam." When Clemens sent a copy of *The Celebrated Jumping Frog of Calaveras County* the next year to his mother, he signed it "Mark Twain" (CL 2:39n2).

Signing a letter or an inscription to one's mother with a pseudonym obviously indicates a complex sense of identity. Sam Clemens was becoming Mark Twain, a process that the public appearances in the lecture tour during October and November 1866 had accelerated. Performing Mark Twain would become such a part of Sam Clemens that an instance of it occurring elsewhere than on the lecture platform is the very first anecdote William Dean Howells gives readers in his fond memoir, *My Mark Twain:*

> At the time of our first meeting, which must have been well toward the winter [of 1869] Clemens (as I must call him instead of Mark Twain, which seemed always somehow to mask him from my personal sense) was wearing a sealskin coat, with the fur out, in the satisfaction of a caprice, or the love of strong effect which he was apt to indulge through life. . . . With his crest of dense red hair, and the wide sweep of his flaming mustache, Clemens was not discordantly clothed in that sealskin coat, which afterward, in spite of his own warmth in it, sent the cold chills through me when I once accompanied it down Broadway, and shared the immense publicity it won him. He had always a relish for personal effect, which expressed itself in the white suit of complete serge which he wore in his last years, and in the Oxford gown which he put on for every possible occasion, and said he would like to wear all the time. That was not vanity in him, but a keen feeling for costume which the severity of our modern tailoring forbids men, though it flatters women to every excess in it; yet he also enjoyed the shock, the offence, the pang which it gave the sensibilities of others.[28]

The theatricality of Mark Twain confronts the reader everywhere in this passage. The very name masks the man, but Howells also emphasizes the way clothes functioned as costume for Clemens. The essential theater of Mark Twain is comically packaged in Howells's joke about accompanying down Broadway, not Sam Clemens, but the sealskin coat. However striking Howells's anecdote is for rendering the theater of Mark Twain, the story is also remarkable for Howells claiming that Clemens contrived the theater of Mark Twain in large measure for the pleasure of shocking staid sensibilities. Even the famous drawl could be employed to such shocking effect. Two years after Howells took his stroll with the

28. William Dean Howells, *My Mark Twain: Reminiscences and Criticisms,* 6.

MARK TWAIN AND THE SEALSKIN COAT.

PHOTO COURTESY THE MARK TWAIN HOUSE & MUSEUM, HARTFORD, CONNECTICUT.

sealskin coat, it appeared in the parlor of Mrs. Thomas Bailey Aldrich, courtesy of an invitation from Mr. Aldrich. By 1871, Clemens had enjoyed the success of his best-selling *The Innocents Abroad,* had met Howells and Aldrich, editors of the highbrow *Atlantic Monthly,* and had dined at the literary cynosure of Boston, the Saturday Club. Nevertheless, all Mrs. Aldrich saw was a sealskin hat and coat—fur out—trousers and socks yellowish-brown, coat and waistcoat gray, ensemble highlighted with a violet bow tie. What she heard was an exaggerated drawl. She actually did not know who her husband's friend was until afterward, but the costume and the drawl convinced her not just that this stranger was incapable of dressing like other men, but that he was drunk. When the time for dinner came and went, Clemens caught the hint and left.[29] Mrs. Aldrich and her staid sensibilities were clearly not the audience likely to enjoy the full-course performance of Mark Twain.

These two incidents suggest how much being Mark Twain meant performance and theater to Sam Clemens. After 1866, the lecture platform was providing a quasi-ritual space for performing Mark Twain during its bounded time frame and thus creating the best opportunities for Clemens to dramatize his comic style and satiric vision. However, the singularity of Sam Clemens and Mark Twain, being Mark Twain for the public, also meant exploiting the potential theatricality of everyday life whenever possible, regardless of purpose (for a personal effect or for the public effect of a well-constructed satire), and regardless of whether observers knew they were being treated as an audience. By the end of the 1860s, Clemens acted as though all the world were a lecture platform.

As Howells was shrewd enough to realize, the story he tells reveals a Sam Clemens who enjoys both on a personal as well as on a public level the theater his behavior generates. Clemens was not just extroverted; even in 1869 he apparently understood the value of publicity for nurturing celebrity, the ultimate ephemeral commodity.[30] Shocking genteel sensibilities was the modern way to nurture celebrity—and to mount a Bohemian attack on calcified aesthetics. Mrs. Aldrich's reaction to Sam Clemens's performance on that afternoon in 1871, however, illustrates the problem of performing Mark Twain, of joking about and playing with social norms and conventions, without a clear play frame such as the lecture format provided.

Howells's reaction in some ways sounds a more ominous note against a habit of performing Mark Twain. Mrs. Aldrich does not even know she has become an audience, and so her sense of offended propriety is virtually an unthinking reaction. Howells realizes that he is both audience and supporting actor in the

29. Justin Kaplan, *Mr. Clemens and Mark Twain: A Biography,* 145.
30. See Louis J. Budd, *Our Mark Twain: The Making of His Public Personality.*

dramatic parade of the sealskin coat down Broadway, but his meditated reaction is not laughter but rather "cold chills." Clemens repeatedly found himself in trouble during his Nevada days because many in the reading public were like Mrs. Aldrich: they did not realize that "Mark Twain" signified performance. Clemens's becoming a better comic writer since leaving Nevada in part meant conveying more clearly that sense of playful performance, the fictional drama, that is the first necessary condition for being Mark Twain. Howells's reaction to the sealskin coat scene represents members of a reading public who understand the performative aspect of "Mark Twain" but are not sure, after some consideration, that they like it. The reactions of both Mr. Howells and Mrs. Aldrich to their private performances of Mark Twain underscore a fundamental difficulty Clemens had during all of his career in making headway against the normative current of taste. Mark Twain as Citizen Clown, symbolically enacting cultural misbehavior as a satiric tactic, often sent cold chills through a reading public that preferred comic figures dressed with warm sentiment instead of animal fur, complete with its connotations of savagery.

# Afterword: The Clown and the Satirist

To my thinking, Shakspeare [*sic*] had no more idea that he was writing for posterity than Mark Twain has at the present time, and it sometimes amuses me to think how future Mark Twain scholars will puzzle over that gentleman's present hieroglyphics and occasionally eccentric expressions.

Charles Henry Webb, *Sacramento Union*, November 3, 1865

If you praise him among persons of Culture, they cannot believe that you are serious. They call him a Barbarian. . . . I do not mean to assert that Mark Twain is "an impeccable artist," but he is just as far from being a mere coarse buffoon.

Andrew Lang, "The Art of Mark Twain,"
*Illustrated London News,* 1891

When Charles Webb finds amusement from imagining chronically puzzled Mark Twain scholars, he displays features characteristic of his cheeky persona, Inigo. The superior literary judgment that accurately predicts the existence of "future Mark Twain scholars" complements Webb's comic distance from their bewilderment. When he links Shakespeare with Mark Twain, Webb underscores the audaciousness of his Bohemian judgment. The detachment of Webb's amused superiority enabled an insight that no one else realized in November 1865: Mark Twain will endure as a literary figure. Americans at the beginning of the twenty-first century proudly claim Mark Twain as a world-famous exemplar of their culture, confirming the insight. Moreover, one can extend Webb's prediction: the

393

writings signed "Mark Twain" will continue to be claimed by America's posterity for its literary heritage. Yet Andrew Lang's defense of Mark Twain against "persons of Culture" signals the aesthetic of a genteel literary tradition that judged Clemens to be merely a barbarian and a coarse buffoon, unworthy of Webb's accolades.[1] Somehow, the significance of Mark Twain for persons of culture has shifted from expressing a cultural barbarity deserving historical oblivion to being the cultural icon implied in Webb's statement, a status realized in the establishment of the Kennedy Center's "Mark Twain Prize for American Humor."

The obsolescence of the nineteenth century's genteel standards of taste in the twenty-first century is predictable because a society's culture—the system of shared knowledge upon which its way of life is based and through which its way of life is transmitted from generation to generation—inevitably changes. The very contours of culture change when social and historical circumstances change, a process that requires retoolings of what Kenneth Burke calls "the mental equipment (meanings, attitudes, character) by which one handles the significant factors of his time."[2] Burke's metaphor describes the way culture as a system of shared knowledge operates for an individual, providing the means to interact successfully with his or her world; it also suggests how literary taste can be formed and re-formed. Literature conceptualized as a repository of necessary "mental equipment" expresses why individuals within a cultural group produce literature, as well as other forms of art, and how they judge them. Those productions in effect register the individualized variations of meanings, attitudes, and character available within cultural parameters.

"Mark Twain" names the aggregate mental equipment devised by Sam Clemens interacting with his world. However, the evaluations from Charles Webb and Andrew Lang together indicate the contested significance of Mark Twain for American culture during Sam Clemens's lifetime, suggesting that the pseudonym can also function as a heuristic device to reveal assumptions buried in the evaluations. A particular instance of literature theoretically offers a site of analysis rich in potential for understanding the deep values of a cultural group because its architecture encodes detailed blueprints. A text can thus be analyzed for the way it manifests or expresses underpinning cultural codes as well as for the ways in which it manifests an individual's mental equipment. When Webb imagines "how future Mark Twain scholars will puzzle over that gentleman's

1. The dates of George Santayana's essay on the genteel tradition ("The Genteel Tradition in American Philosophy," 1911) and Malcolm Cowley's essay detailing rebellion against it ("The Revolt against Gentility," 1937) suggest its longevity as a cultural force.

2. Kenneth Burke, *Attitudes toward History*, 34. The formulation defining culture was made by anthropologists Kroeber and Kluckhohn in 1963 after surveying definitions in their field. Marcel Danesi and Paul Perron, *Analyzing Cultures*, 22–23.

present hieroglyphics," he suggests the complexity of reading the work of Sam Clemens to discern cultural values as well as mental equipment. "Mark Twain" thus denotes a node within the system of meanings, scripts itself as a cultural ideogram. "Mark Twain" can bear such conceptual freight because the pseudonym did not just indicate a rising star within the literary world, but also signified a self-reflexive comic process of Sam Clemens operating at multiple levels within the culture of the United States during the 1860s. Webb draws attention to the comic process when he mentions Mark Twain's "eccentric expressions." The ideogram "Mark Twain" carries its full charge of meanings because it draws upon the social nature of comic laughter, which stresses community, actual and symbolic, and the deep play inherent in comic art, which has the potential to subvert the social status quo.[3]

"Citizen Clown" names the more profound aspect of the ideogram's comic power, but that power issues from an ambiguous, in-between identity, what folklorist Arnold van Gennep called "liminality," a status manifested in Mark Twain's persistent maneuvering back and forth between being respectable and being unsanctified.[4] Moreover, as a textual figure, a comic character represented within comic narratives, Mark Twain exhibits a habit of posing. That habit spawns personae, including the inept newspaperman, the inept cultural critic, the irascible editor dispensing advice, the naïf, the put-upon good Samaritan, the wily yarn spinner who hoaxes, the serene yarn spinner who digresses, the snobbish defender of centric cultural values, the ironic missionary, the outraged satirist, and the laughable choleric. These personae disguise the primary narrative role of respectable and trustworthy reporter, as though Mark Twain were playing the cunning slave in a comedy by Plautus, donning a variety of masks in order to carry out his funny plot machinations. Adopting multiple disguises for an already ambiguous identity, Mark Twain garners a trickster's power to entertain and to satirize.

Clemens used his trickster alter ego to dramatize his comic perspective in a way that Victor Turner would recognize as exploiting the theatricality of everyday life. William Dean Howells's anecdote about accompanying Sam's sealskin coat down Broadway suggests how much Clemens relished this exploitation. A focus for Turner's research has been analyzing what he calls "social dramas," that is, the emergence of a sustained public action that has the processual form of "breach-crisis-redress-outcome." These social dramas, rooted in everyday life, are rudimentary cultural performances, ones that can be ritualized in a format

---

3. See Caron, "Ethology to Aesthetics," 272–74.
4. Victor Turner, "Liminality and the Performative Genres," 21; see also Victor Turner, "Liminal to Liminoid in Play, Flow, Ritual: An Essay in Comparative Symbology."

like carnival. Moreover, they provide a basis for the aesthetic mode of theater.[5] Social dramas are thus a prototheater that stages the quotidian conflicts and resolutions of a community.

Grounded in the everyday 1860s reality of publishing periodicals in the Nevada Territory, the mock combats among Comstock newspapermen exemplify this prototheater. The raillery of the mock combats were a quasi-ritualization of the spontaneous teasing that occurred everyday in the frontier communities along the Comstock. The art of Mark Twain in the first instance draws upon the social drama inherent in these communities to contribute to a comic literary form peculiar to newspaper publishing. The theater of the mock combat in print played out as a potentially never-ending process of comic give-and-take that replicated the culture of personal raillery to be found in the streets of a municipality like Virginia City. Once the personal raillery of printed mock attacks changes to an earnest ridiculing of a fault, satire meant to reform for the good of a community takes over. In just this way, Washoe Mark Twain became a satiric vehicle for Sam Clemens. The most sophisticated version of that vehicle is the Mark Twain who camouflages his satiric thrusts with a show of foolishness that necessarily includes him among those needing reform, the Mark Twain who knows that Sut Lovingood's epithet "a nat'ral born durn'd fool" describes him, too.

The everyday prototheater of the mock combat provides the foundation for the drama of the Citizen Clown, in which Mark Twain acts foolishly with the intent of reforming his community. This symbolic theater features a public liminality similar to collective rites of passage in traditional societies, such as those featuring sacred clowns. In ceremonies with a public orientation, liminality occurs in communal spaces like village greens or squares, which are ritually transformed using two basic forms. In one version, public liminality provides

> the scene and time for the emergence of a society's deepest values in the form of sacred dramas and objects—sometimes the reenactment periodically of cosmogonic narratives or deeds of saintly, godly, or heroic establishers of morality, basic institutions, or ways of approaching transcendent beings or powers. But it may also be the venue and occasion for the most radical skepticism—always relative, of course, to the given culture's repertoire of areas of skepticism—about cherished values and rules. Ambiguity reigns: people and public policies may be judged skeptically in relation to deep values; the vices, follies, stupidities, and abuses of contemporary holders of high political, economic, or religious status may be satirized, ridiculed, or condemned in terms of axiomatic values, or these personages may be rebuked for gross failures in common sense. In general, life-crisis rites stress the deep values, which are often exhibited to ini-

5. Turner, "Performative Genres," 19–20, 24.

tiands as sacred objects, while the commentary on society and its leading representatives is assigned to cyclical feasts and their public liminality. As dramatic genre, tragedy departs from the former, comedy from the latter.[6]

Mark Twain is Sam Clemens behaving as though he were the principal clown within the privileged time of a cyclical feast, like carnival, enabled by its public liminality to express a radical skepticism in relation to his society's deep values and to comment on leading people and public policies. As satiric vehicle, Mark Twain clowns in his own one-man drama, shape-shifting as he chooses which personae to employ. Mark Twain resembles a sacred clown because both dramatize transgressive behavior so that individuals within their cultural group are faced with a symbolic disruption of cultural mythos, a communal spectacle of how not to behave. "Citizen Clown" expresses Clemens's dramatic method of developing his satire, his engagement in a symbolic theater of comic antics.

Performative genres that feature public liminality, such as carnival or festival theater, are synecdoches for their culture: their performances symbolically reiterate the culture that enables them. The audiences that gather for such performances—a sacred clown ceremony or a drama staged during the Greek festival to honor Dionysus, for example—thus symbolize the body politic as it witnesses a reenactment of its culture. In the United States, Fourth of July parades and speeches, as well as the inauguration of a president, focus the deep values of democracy into a single formal event that performs the culture. Informally, Super Bowl Sunday and its attendant "ceremonies" stage a singular event that recapitulates American culture. Though the audience attending a presidential inauguration may consciously symbolize the body politic, while the audience for a Super Bowl unconsciously symbolizes the body popular culture, formal and sanctioned reenactments of American culture are scarce.[7] In its episodic and informal fashion, the periodical work of Sam Clemens responds to that scarcity with the art of Mark Twain. The symbolic drama of the Citizen Clown scripts Mark Twain's liminal status both as a member of the community being satirized and as a figure set apart. Being the satirist's mouthpiece as well as the object of satire, Mark Twain represents yet subverts with comic laughter the various communities in which he participates. Each community symbolizes the body politic as would an audience for a performance of public liminality.

6. Ibid., 22.
7. Silent-screen comics like Charlie Chaplin may deliberately create the body popular culture (James E. Caron, "Silent Slapstick Film as Ritualized Clowning: The Example of Charlie Chaplin"), but there seems to have been no counterpart to watching movies or sporting events for nineteenth-century Americans that could invoke a symbolic popular culture community.

The earliest version of Clemens's alter ego, Washoe Mark Twain, denotes a Comstock community of miners and journalists: "the boys." Although the historical audience for Washoe Mark Twain had several facets, mostly it was the thousands of miners and stampmill operators and teamsters who were the backbone of the economy in the Nevada Territory. Relatively young, mostly single, often with some education, this audience did not worry much about respectability and refinement when it wanted to read laughable material in periodicals. Members of this audience possessed solidly lower-middle tastes in Herbert Gans's aesthetic spectrum. Newspaper reporters and printers and editors composed an important subset of the historical audience. They had more education than most and could in some instances harbor stuffy pretensions to respectability, but they often enjoyed the rough-and-tumble of mock feuds. In addition, the ethic of frontier humor and practical joking meant that men of substance— mine owners, lawyers, physicians, and politicians—also enjoyed the broad humor Washoe Mark Twain embodied.

The humor of raillery that characterizes Mark Twain the unsanctified newspaper reporter in Nevada evokes the rough-and-tumble rhetoric of the day, especially in regard to political matters. Because joking behavior encodes cultural values in its playfulness, Washoe Mark Twain gathers into its identity the egalitarianism and commonsense virtue of the plain folk who made up the bulk of the Comstock's population. Moreover, by presenting a bantering columnist who can outmaneuver his mock-combat rivals with consummate raillery and artful, hoaxing lies, Clemens, as Mark Twain, played hell within the precincts of Nevada journalism. In a group of facetious "sinners," he was "the bully boy with the glass eye," the ultimate jokester amid a male-centered community that admired the practical joke, the witty comeback, and the tall tale. As a literary image, Washoe Mark Twain distorts historical reality because he represents only certain segments of the actual population, much as the Backwoods Roarer was said by easterners during the antebellum period to typify people in frontier communities. Nevertheless, Mark Twain, in his very first form, emblemizes the Nevada Territory in its madcap moods, its carnivalesque frontier democracy.

However, once the definition of community in the Nevada Territory expands to include not just miners and journalists and the demimonde but also families and schools and congregations, Washoe Mark Twain as comic champion of "the boys" takes on a more complex role. Judged by parlor standards, Mark Twain exhibits behavior and manners that are irreverent and foolish, facetious and boisterous. Indeed, Mark Twain's transgressions are not just social; they might be moral as well. The figure is thus potentially subversive to the sober values of the respectable community. Seen from this chamber-of-commerce perspective, Washoe Mark Twain's egregious behavior caricatures "the boys" and parodies their indecorous ways. Thus, Clemens at times can use Mark Twain to deploy a classic satire that ridicules in order to bring social misfits back to the centric values of home and hearth. For Clemens's first important implied audience and readership, "the boys," Washoe Mark Twain both mirrored their qualities and served as a fun-house mirror, satirically distorting them.

When Clemens moved to San Francisco, the specific, male-centered historical community that defined the implied audience for Washoe Mark Twain transformed into a coast-to-coast confederation of editors and critics and readers of literary periodicals. The majority of this community was committed to the tradition of belles lettres. As Clemens very consciously used Mark Twain to move beyond newspaper reporting and into the market for literary periodicals, Washoe Mark Twain metamorphosed, becoming, in the words of an East Coast editor, "the merriest gentleman of the California press." The title carries its own ambiguity, conjuring a Mark Twain who apparently will give up hoaxes and practical jokes to write for an upscale audience. In San Francisco, Mark Twain nevertheless continued to yarn slyly and mischievously, still ready, like Sut Lovingood, to expose his own faults as well as the faults of everyone else. Like Sut, Mark Twain resented in fiercely comic ways people like Fitz Smythe or Police Chief Burke, who cannot see or will not acknowledge their own foolishness.

While in San Francisco, as a "gentleman of the California press," Mark Twain represented his community of literate readers and editors in the role of a budding cultural critic. As the "merriest" gentleman, unsanctified Mark Twain invested written genres as well as the lecture platform with his comic attitude. Once freed from the constrictions of daily reporting for a newspaper, Clemens discovered that he could refashion Washoe Mark Twain into a comic version of the urbane man-about-town, a highbrow figure straight out of the world of French periodicals: the *flâneur*. Sam Clemens may not have consciously chosen this transformation. However, the concept of a comic *flâneur* explains how he reshaped in crucial ways what was already familiar to him. By transforming the routine round of reporting into the leisured stroll of observing, the *flâneur* embodied Clemens's goal of writing for literary periodicals. Moreover, the unsanctified portion of Mark Twain, which in Nevada had moved the figure far enough outside the centric norm of genteel culture to be comically distinctive, could be recast into a mold of Bohemian aesthetics germane to matters literary and cultural. As a freelance journalist, Clemens for a time certainly lived life *à la Bohême*. Most important for his development as a writer, he had literary models at hand in Bret Harte and especially in Charles Webb. Their attitude about the genteel norm of periodical writing was congruent with the *flâneur*'s ostensible position that the bourgeois marketplace should not dictate what qualified as genuine art. Moreover, their aesthetic opposition to the genteel literary norm, whether invoked by the figure of the Bohemian artist or the *flâneur,* provided a space within which unsanctified Mark Twain could wield his brand of opposition—a comic depiction of the world's shortcomings.

Functioning as a comic *flâneur,* Mark Twain roamed San Francisco and read what others said about the city, its inhabitants, and its institutions and then proceeded to burlesque, parody, and otherwise ridicule what had been observed and what had been written. These forays and the resultant comic writings show Sam Clemens learning how a humor of raillery can become the temperament of a satirist. At his best, however, Sam Clemens learned how to employ several humors associated with Mark Twain to serve satiric purposes. The incompetent Washoe Mark Twain, apparently incapacitated by drink, appears reborn as the reporter who comically fails to be a *flâneur.* The comic *flâneur* completely inverts the bourgeois world of business, with its insistence that "time is money," by observing all events and being unable to find their proportion, and by failing to complete the reporter's assignment. Ultimately, Mark Twain as a *flâneur,* comically failing to depict what is supposed to be central to the observed scene, represents nothing but the pleasure of the stroll itself, regardless of what happens and how any story is told. Like Washoe Mark Twain, who subverts the ethic of reporters with his hoaxes, Mark Twain the comic *flâneur* subverts the practice of *flânerie* with his digressive narratives. Instead, yarn spinning becomes the goal. The sheer pleasure of narrating, apparently without proportion, runs counter to the rationalized, centric norms of the bourgeois world, subverting them by suggesting a radically alternative way of behaving.

On assignment in Hawai'i, Clemens relied heavily on both master roles for his Mark Twain narrator. As a competent journalist, Mark Twain effectively represents the San Francisco business community interested in greater commerce with the Kingdom of Hawai'i. Clemens had always been a competent reporter, even in his wildest Nevada days, though it was most obvious in unsigned editorials and in articles such as his reporting on the Sanitary Fund processional auction, articles retailing facts, not fun. Several letters from Hawai'i were written within the strict confines of this competent-reporter master role. This emphasis resulted from the need to report on commerce with the islands, but it also resulted from Sam Clemens's genuine, though intermittent, admiration for the accomplishments of the American missionaries. Also, the use of Mr. Brown as a comic sidekick allows for a segregation of broad comic elements. Thus Mark Twain in both the Hawai'i correspondence and in subsequent travel letters more clearly than in previous incarnations represents respectable society, a tilt best illustrated by the rhetorical set piece on the eruption of Kilauea that highbrow critics called a "word painting." Nevertheless, in the aggregate these travel letters are comic, and though Mark Twain more often than before implies a centric and respectable audience, Mr. Brown's presence licenses low comic elements, and that presence enables scenes depicting the return of Washoe Mark Twain. At those moments, in both the Hawai'i and American travel letters, Mark Twain can easily satirize the centric community he ostensibly represents in other places. In the "American Letters," Mark Twain's eccentric claim to be a missionary expresses this liminality. Refusing to be respectable or to remain merely unsanctified, Mark Twain evokes the sacred clown, who is "neither wise nor foolish, being both, but never being wholly one or the other."[8]

Victor Turner's scheme of publicly liminal dramas features two forms of communal rites of passages: life-crisis rites affirming the group's deep values, "which are often exhibited to initiands as sacred objects," and cyclical feasts (such as carnival), which license skeptical commentary on a society and its leading representatives. The former reinforces the status quo; the latter enables criticism. The comic genius of Sam Clemens allows Mark Twain to work both sides of this communal street, representing yet potentially subverting the communities to which he belongs. In the Nevada Territory, Mark Twain behaves as one of "the boys," symbolic of a certain wildness and of the more wide-open social freedoms of the frontier. And yet Mark Twain satirizes their behavior by caricaturing it, suggesting its excess and thus representing the view of the conservative populace who would laugh with superiority at the uncouth segment of society. As an unsanctified reporter, Mark Twain claims membership in the Washoe community of journalists, an example of a newspaper's local-items editor, yet he often subverts the news he reports. When Mark Twain the reporter in Nevada becomes Mark Twain the critic of bad writing in San Francisco, the figure is both earnest in its critiques of the Fitz Smythes of the periodical world and mock-earnest about its critical function in sketches that portray an inept critic. When Mark Twain assumes the more ambitious and literary reporting of the *flâneur,* he comically dramatizes the limits of the role; he even subverts its basic interpretive function by replacing it with nothing more than the pleasure of the stroll itself. Mark Twain thus symbolizes his communities in complicated, even contradictory ways.

Mark Twain—standing as a typical member of a community, yet standing ready to subvert its values with laughter—defines the unsanctified newspaper reporter's mode of operation, with its trickster potential for transgressive behavior. The figure's humor of raillery, prominent while Clemens worked in Nevada, exudes comic transgressiveness, for raillery inevitably violates the boundary between true malice and playful malice. Exchanging the mock insults of raillery initiates a game of comic rudeness deliberately opposed to the politeness of everyday manners. The aggressiveness inherent in the game can trigger a mock combat. Once

8. Handelman, "Ritual Clown," 330.

Clemens no longer lived within the community of Washoe journalists that enabled these mock combats, he rarely engaged in them. However, their comic results encouraged him to feature a choleric humor for Mark Twain, exhibited in ways genuinely shocking to a normative sensibility, imagining mayhem for children or violent deaths for people who are annoying pests. Such comic imaginings transgress at a deep level, inviting a mass return of what is usually repressed.

This willingness to violate accepted social proprieties characterized the comic efforts of Sam Clemens even before he invented Mark Twain: the hoax of "The Petrified Man," for example. That will to transgress created in Clemens the beyond-the-pale attitude of his self-styled epithet "unsanctified newspaper reporter." This attitude translated into a repeated willingness to subvert the rules of journalism and thereby undermine conventional trust in the news. Mark Twain accomplishes his questioning of journalism both with dramatizations of inept reporting and with presentations of sharply critical commentary. The biggest joke executed by Washoe Mark Twain was to ridicule the requirements of his own job as a respectable newspaper reporter. Mark Twain therefore was journalist and mock journalist, an able correspondent to the *Enterprise* for the territorial legislature and constitutional convention as well as a reporter "whose instincts were all toward falsehood." Ultimately, Clemens wanted to raise laughter in order to reveal shortcomings, either in the pretensions of the journalists themselves, or in the venality of an audience that valued sensationalism over truth. The subversion of journalism's fundamental duty to report what has happened begins when Mark Twain's behavior or perceptions supplant reportage on a given event. Mark Twain becomes the news. This comic substitution happens most memorably when, like Tristram Shandy, a humor of digression grips Mark Twain, allowing almost anything to interfere with reporting the event. Nothing expected is told, and in the ensuing comic usurpation, everything might be mentioned before the narrative is completed. When the *flâneur*'s mission of elevating reporting to a high aesthetic plane provides the context for such laughable sketches, the increased distance between the actual results and the ideal intent only intensifies the resulting comic laughter.

These examples of deep play *(paidia)* feature a significant potential for satirically subverting community, a potential inherent in performances of public liminality such as a sacred clown and a Citizen Clown provide. Within traditional communities, this potential subversion clearly radiates danger. Zuni sacred clowns inspire fear, but also reverence: they cannot be touched nor can they be denied anything.[9] Deep play provides the wellspring for the awesome

---

9. Jacob Levine, "Regression in Primitive Clowning," 169; Handelman, "Ritual Clown," 345.

power of sacred clowns: presupposing formlessness,[10] they have a "constant potential for the elicitation of nonorder."[11] Their deep play thus represents "as near as cultural thought comes to conceptualizing a total, or near total, absence of order."[12] The major difference between the traditional sacred clown and Mark Twain as Citizen Clown is the former's ritual circumspection of this potential and the latter's routine exploitation of it.[13] Mark Twain repeatedly questions and undermines status quo values. The repetitive questioning of normative social values within the symbolic theater of the Citizen Clown manifests Clemens's willingness to indulge in the potential chaos of deep play more than would be allowed for a ritual clown in a traditional society.

For Mark Twain, deep play shows most fully in his habit of subsuming or dissolving the boundary between fact and fiction. The propensity to indulge in yarn spinning despite the implied author being a respectable and trustworthy reporter constitutes Mark Twain's fundamental comic transgression. Sam Clemens's habits as a writer were to observe what was funny in the scene before him and to embellish the observation as he rendered it into words. Recounting fictional narratives that use historical people and actual events as raw material deliberately confuses the usual distinctions between fact and fiction. This tactic was infamous in the Nevada hoaxes, but San Francisco friends like John Skae were used, and Clemens's notebooks for the Hawai'i assignment show that the extent to which Mr. Brown is fact or fiction must remain an open question. Yarn spinning and reporting—these two modes of narrating, or rather the apparent confusion of these two modes of narrating—form the marrow of Sam Clemens's comic art in the 1860s. The hoaxes of Washoe Mark Twain conflate yarn spinning and reporting, and the failures of Mark Twain the comic *flâneur* happen for the same reason—reporting becomes yarn spinning. Within a pragmatic Yankee culture whose Puritan heritage drew a sharp distinction between factual and fictional narratives, apparently ignoring that distinction would elicit a sense of nonorder, the cultural chaos of deep play. Whatever iconoclastic power contemporaries adduced to Mark Twain stemmed from the comic confusion or dissolution of the conceptual boundary between narratives of memory and tales of imagination.

10. Louis A. Hieb, "Meaning and Mismeaning: Toward an Understanding of the Ritual Clown," 174.

11. Arden R. King, "North American Indian Clowns and Creativity," 147.

12. Handelman, "Precariousness," 63.

13. Victor Turner states his position on subversion this way: "I have . . . stressed the potentially subversive character of liminality in tribal initiations . . . but this potentiality never did have any hope of realization outside a ritual sphere hedged by strong taboo." Quoted in Handelman, "Precariousness," 66. Hereniko (*Woven Gods*) agrees with Turner, while Robert Brightman ("Traditions of Subversion and the Subversion of Tradition: Cultural Criticism in Maidu Clown Performances") suggests a third way to think about the issue of subversion or conservation of the social status quo.

As symbolic gestures, all these comic transgressions by Mark Twain are analogous to the antics authorized by the public liminality of carnival theater or sacred clown ceremony. However, the drama of the Citizen Clown has no official demarcation of ritual space and time within American culture that provides the communal auspices and sanctioned gathering of the symbolic body politic enjoyed by carnival actors or sacred ritual clowns. Thus the Citizen Clown necessarily runs the risk of constantly appearing to mock and caper and cause laughter with no deeper purpose than laughter itself. Without an explicit myth, such as structures the dramatic conflict within which sacred clowns play their role, the Citizen Clown must first discover the cultural narratives that function as *mythoi*—that is, the narratives organizing a society's attitudes and values— and then perform his own comic drama of revealing their inadequacies. For Sam Clemens, the most compelling cultural narrative in the 1860s was the mythos of genteel respectability. Mark Twain routinely behaved in ways that erased the boundary set up by the mythos between propriety and impropriety. The running joke of being an unsanctified missionary that Clemens developed after returning from the Kingdom of Hawai'i in August 1866 illustrates this laughable obfuscation. Mark Twain as satirist claims a respectability and a moral purpose equal to a missionary, yet his humorous behavior undercuts the authority of his claim. As Sut Lovingood does in his comic preacher role, Mark Twain delivers the tongue-lashings of comic sermons by playing hell with genteel notions of propriety.

The cultural tale of genteel respectability organized American society into the sanctified and the unsanctified, but it also contained a starker division by separating humanity into the civilized and the savage. Within American culture, this starker division appears in the relationship between Mark Twain and the antebellum comic tradition, which reveals an amusing tale about democracy, twice told. At its core, the story in its first version asks a question: Can democracy create a civilized society and nurture an estimable culture? Antebellum writers answered equivocally. The Backwoods Roarer represents a particular antebellum experience of what some claimed to be American culture. Within the European-based definition that dominated the eastern seaboard communities, the frontier had no culture worth mentioning, a conclusion both horrific and funny to contemplate by those segments of society who considered themselves to be literate, educated, polite, well-mannered, respectable, moral—in short, those who claimed to be civilized. The Backwoods Roarer thus embodies a negative response to the tale's question. However, some antebellum writers answered with an unequivocal "maybe" by constructing comic figures who displayed a backwoods civility and whose assembled stories stitched together a crazy-quilt theme of comic barbarity. An oxymoron, the Gentleman Roarer, figured the theme.

Thus the first version of the story uses the Gentleman Roarer to dramatize a *dēmos* whose comic barbarity ambiguously proves the fundamental premise of democracy, that is, common folk can successfully rule themselves.

The tale's first version also presents the possibility of a new value as it weaves a comic metanarrative about democracy shaping an emergent culture: the unexpected respectability of a Gentleman Roarer, for example, Nimrod Wildfire. As a laughable expression of *dēmos,* the generic figure comically dramatizes the failings of plain folk without denying their positive qualities. Whatever negative effects on behavior the frontier experience might create and the Backwoods Roarer embody, the alternative perspective represented by the Gentleman Roarer implied a capacity for improvement. Colonel Pete Whetstone and Major Joseph Jones personify that potential. The Colonel and the Major had shown that ordinary people on the frontier could learn proper manners and conduct themselves in a respectable though unrefined fashion. These transformed characters project the image of a trans-Appalachian, American "gentleman," different from the individual of aristocratic birth found in Europe or from the figure of high society living on the Atlantic seaboard. This newest American is polite but not stuffy, serious when need be but also fun-loving. Probably not a drawing-room figure nor high on the social scale, he is more likely instead to be a man of affairs, a man on the make as well as on the move (even if he stumbles and bumbles), thus evoking and satirizing the commercial emphasis and restless tendency of the expanding nation. Colonel Pete Whetstone and Major Joseph Jones were prime comic evidence in this counterargument to the dominant culture's claim that "frontier" only signified savagery.

When the comic tale is retold with the specific character Mark Twain succeeding the generalized figure of the Gentleman Roarer as the comic protagonist, the question becomes: What does "civilized" and "cultured" mean in a democratic society? Mark Twain as a competent newspaper reporter provided stronger evidence for the tale's counterargument because his professional literacy manifestly demonstrated education and cultural progress. As a character within the tradition of American comic writing, Mark Twain climaxes the potential of *dēmos* for improvement. Whereas Pete Whetstone and Joseph Jones exhibited their country-folk literacy as the authors of letters to the editor, Mark Twain epitomizes the editors to whom such letters would be addressed. Perched on the bottom rung of professional writing, Mark Twain as reporter and editor is different in kind from Pete Whetstone and Joseph Jones, for he has access to the elite world of belles lettres. Mark Twain may be an avatar of the Gentleman Roarer, but he possesses more culture and more potential for culture than ever thought possible for the comic type. His literate but certainly not genteel reporting of the encountered world therefore represents, albeit comically, the middling status of the burgeoning middle class and its aspirations to acquire culture, a status and aspiration first prominent in the 1850s and 1860s.

Although the competent reporter's role emphasizes a desire for and attainment of respectability, Mark Twain's self-proclaimed unsanctified status (endorsed by the self-righteous in the community) becomes a comic strategy to revisit the antebellum question of what constitutes civilization and thus how one defines savagery. This strategy enables an incipient cultural critique of genteel respectability. The conflict within the twice-told comic tale was not the same for Mark Twain as for the Gentleman Roarer, whose antics suggest an incomplete (but laughable) ability of common folks to rule themselves. Mark Twain's antics suggest this lack, too, but in addition his Citizen Clown theater recasts the behavior of the saints/sanctified/respectable into a comic incompleteness, for the respectable are not necessarily moral or humane. Exposing the inconsistencies of the mythos of genteel respectability became his satiric theme. In San Francisco, the sanctified were represented by the venality of the *Call,* the smugness of Fitz Smythe, and the corruption of Police Chief Burke, the unsanctified by those who displayed a Bohemian attitude and aesthetic. In Hawai'i, the sanctified were represented by the American missionaries, undeniably selfless but selfish, too, the unsanctified by an indigenous and "savage" culture with its own worthy values, a culture capable of exhibiting a morality superior to that of the missionaries. When he traveled from San Francisco back to New York City and St. Louis in late 1866 and early 1867, Sam Clemens continued to encounter the cultural mythos of genteel respectability in a variety of forms and continued to use Mark Twain to question its operational truth.

Mark Twain, in the twice-told tale, represents an emergent culture, one whose characteristic aesthetic does not fit the usual categories. As George Santayana remarked, Mark Twain and his comic style embody a fresh iteration of American culture, but here I want to add that it has no discernible pedigree. Instead, the Mark Twain version resembles the "composite" dog in a story Sam Clemens liked to tell, "made up of all the valuable qualities that's in the dog breed—kind of a syndicate" (MTS 291). This emergent culture is different from what Henry Nash Smith delineates by opposing "vernacular" to "genteel." A Boston correspondent to the *Sacramento Union* seemed to perceive this composite style when he claimed that Mark Twain would fit into a new literary periodical that has positioned itself between "the heaviness and hyper-refinement of the *Atlantic* and the namby-pambyness of the *Ledger* family of literature."[14]

14. Santayana, "Genteel Tradition," 52; Smith, *Mark Twain: Development;* "Roland," "Letter from Boston: A New Literary Enterprise," 3.

Certainly, the composite culture Mark Twain represents is not the genteel sort that ruled American society in the 1860s. However, in his early manifestations, Mark Twain also does not represent a vernacular culture, though in some ways he retains the comic barbarity of the frontier, because his affinity for Bohemian values creates a much more sophisticated perspective. In San Francisco, this affinity meant using comic techniques, especially burlesque, to shatter conventional views about literary and cultural topics. Though burlesque might simply be the low blows minstrelsy directed against highbrow cultural forms, some writers also used it to attack drama and literature calcified by cloying sentiment and stifling morality. The most prominent offstage attacks were parodies known as "condensed novels." The writers who wrote such parodies and other burlesques ridiculing accepted styles of literature offered an aesthetic that provided an alternative to the genteel standard. Once Clemens rechanneled Mark Twain's humor of raillery into comic commentary on bad writing, whether journalistic or literary, his subversive and unsanctified attitude manifested itself in burlesques that aligned him with other writers looking for ways to alter the aesthetics of the literary landscape, men like Bret Harte, Charles Webb, and Henry Clapp. Influencing public taste by debating literary standards, these men had enough of an avant-garde thrust to their aesthetic, enough of what more mainstream editors like William Dean Howells or George Curtis would have called "Bohemianism," to allow them to appreciate the clownish satire of Sam Clemens as fresh, vigorous, and two cuts above the 1860s craze of fractured orthography put in motion by the enormous popularity of Charles Farrar Browne ("Artemus Ward") and continued by writers such as David Ross Locke ("Petroleum Vesuvius Nasby") and Henry Wheeler Shaw ("Josh Billings"). The relatively sophisticated use of burlesque to mock assumptions often found in genteel high culture moves Mark Twain well beyond the category "vernacular."

Nor does "masculine" aptly name the new culture and its aesthetic, despite Mark Twain's clear opposition to the sentimental and pious, genteel, and feminized norm found in much popular culture writing. Clemens called that kind of writing "gruel and nonsense." For him, the healthy and sensible aesthetic diet is not gruel for weak stomachs but instead something hearty and simple. Clemens makes this plain yet more vigorous aesthetic explicit with his reviews on the acting of Dan Setchell, the music of Louis Gottschalk, and the painting of Albert Bierstadt. Randall Knoper and Joseph Coulombe associate it with a masculine working class, particularly appropriate when Clemens was in Nevada.[15] However,

---

15. Randall Knoper, *Acting Naturally: Mark Twain in the Culture of Performance;* Joseph Coulombe, *Mark Twain and the American West.*

to the extent that American culture had associated the domain of fine arts with feminine activities and marked it by an antithesis to the masculine aggressiveness of marketplace economics, a Mark Twain aesthetic could be listed on either side of gendered metaphors dividing artistic and economic endeavors. Using "feminine" or "masculine" to describe Mark Twain's aesthetic mistakenly simplifies his composite comic style, and it remains as dissatisfying as invoking regionalism by calling it "Western," or invoking the frontier by calling it "vernacular."

Mark Twain's composite style employs popular elements yet demonstrates from a comic perspective a Bohemian awareness of the belletristic tradition; it exhibits the traditional opposition of belles lettres to marketplace judgments about fine art but also burlesques genteel timidity and stricture. Slangy in its tone and Bohemian in its outlook, the composite comic style allows for sentiment, high-culture rhetoric, and sophisticated comic techniques to be blended with low-comic elements like slapstick. Mark Twain thus represents an emergent culture whose aesthetic dictates an opposition to a standard, genteel taste; implies the priority of craft over marketplace economics, yet acknowledges the necessity of matching a wide band on the spectrum of audience tastes to achieve success; and stresses the way Clemens used his alter ego to release the deep play (*paidia*) of comic elements, with their potential for the creativity of improvisation and the destruction of tumult. Moreover, throughout the 1860s Mark Twain's composite comic style—the mental equipment of an unsanctified newspaper reporter—expressed Clemens's subversion of, or at least skepticism about, cultural norms, especially the genteel definition of respectability. The unsanctified epithet can be traced to the frontier legacy of the Gentleman Roarer. The legacy contributed to Mark Twain's comic power, which not only caused nervous laughter and polite horror in certain segments of the reading population in the 1860s but also, according to Andrew Lang, continued to perturb "persons of Culture" during the 1890s.[16]

In the twice-told comic tale about democracy, Mark Twain does not just embody the American dream, rising out of the rough-and-tumble frontier mining communities of the Nevada Territory, a literate improvement on country folk, content to join the respectable middle class. Unsanctified Mark Twain also presents a way to see through the pretensions of self-proclaimed respectability. Mark Twain is not "the coming man" who has arrived; he is the Gentleman Roarer going farther than expected by projecting through the symbolic theater of the Citizen Clown a sharply etched comic attitude calculated to burst like a flash of lightning upon timid sensibilities. His comic insights dazzle in their facility to provide dramatic perspective and momentary comic guidance, the

16. See Smith, "Mark Twain, Ritual Clown," 251.

way the "lightning pilot" in "Old Times on the Mississippi"—a man so good he could navigate a very difficult part of the river in his sleep—stuns his audience. My book has analyzed the early writings of Sam Clemens to understand how his comic technique operated within the contemporary culture. Its examination offers ways to discriminate among the individual efforts, but here at the close I retrieve examples of Mark Twain's comic skepticism that stun with the brilliant skill of the lightning pilot.

The first occurred during Clemens's residence in Virginia City. When early Nevada settlers organized themselves into a pioneer association called the "Pah-Utes" to designate their first-family status as the people who settled in the territory before the mining rush of May 1860, Mark Twain wrote a mock encomium. The skepticism of his lightning-pilot remark happens when Mark Twain refers to the members of this exclusive club as "happy, and lousy, and contented" (ETS 1:170). Because the association used the name for the indigenous people of the region, Mark Twain can pretend that Pah-Utes are really Paiutes and can attribute a stereotypical view of Native American hygiene to the white settlers, deflating the pride of place implied in their club's existence. The irony is particularly just, for the erasure of the name "Paiutes" by the name "Pah-Utes" symbolizes the appropriation of land by white settlers, an act that points to their *second-family* status and the racist denial of the true first-family status for the indigenous folks. Mark Twain's mock encomium pretends to take the claim to be first in Nevada as total and absolute by making a joke about lice and the Pah-Utes, erasing the difference between whites and Native Americans entailed in the stereotype about hygiene as well as erasing the perceived superiority of the Pah-Utes to all other white settlers. Mark Twain clowns by calling himself a "poor but honest half-breed," but his foolishness satirizes the false pride of the settlers.

During his time with the *Morning Call* in San Francisco, Clemens again demonstrates dazzling satire in a few deft sentences, in this instance questioning the motives and values of people who stake a claim on the moral high ground of a society. During the summer of 1864, Mark Twain reported on the Christian Fair in more than one brief item for the *Call*. In the midst of his description of the fair, Mark Twain becomes concerned about the entrance fee. Charging an entrance fee would prevent the indigent Jesus and his apostles from entering, should they show up—wouldn't it? (CofC 103). The fanciful idea skewers those Christians who loudly profess their piety at every turn, implying that the Christian Fair does not emulate Jesus in its overriding concern for making money. Indeed, is not any concern for money dangerous for the souls of pious Christians? Piety was an important value for most Americans in the 1860s, one that controlled and organized much social behavior. This satiric remark about money trumping piety points out that religious virtues are routinely ignored.

A second example during Sam Clemens's stay in San Francisco provides another scorching comic perspective on standard values. In "The Christmas Fireside: The Story of the Bad Little Boy That Bore a Charmed Life," which appeared in the *Californian*, Clemens targets a literary genre—moralistic Sunday school literature—but familial love, even a mother's love, also falls victim to the narrative's many comic inversions. In Mark Twain's burlesque moral tale, "everything turned out differently with [the hero Jim] from the way it does to the bad Jameses in the books" (ETS 2:408). Nothing bad happens to Jim despite his many sins, and "he grew up, and married, and raised a large family, and brained them all with an axe one night, and got wealthy by all manner of cheating and rascality, and now he is the infernalest wickedest scoundrel in his native village, and is universally respected, and belongs to the Legislature" (ETS 2:410). The sketch not only ridicules sentimental moral tales for children, which were especially popular at Christmastime, but also mocks Protestant morality, family life, and political ethics.

In yet a third instance from his time in San Francisco, Clemens again hurls a bolt at religiosity. In this example, Mark Twain makes fun of efforts to reclaim sinners; he also ridicules religious denominations. Speaking to a minister considering a move to San Francisco to be the head of Grace Cathedral, Mark Twain extols the new position by noting that "sinners are so thick that you can't throw out your line without hooking several of them," proving the claim by bragging that he "wrote the most rambling, incomprehensible harangue of a sermon you ever heard in your life for one of the Episcopalian ministers here, and he landed seventeen [sinners] with it at the first dash." Mark Twain then goes on to say that he "trimmed it up to suit Methodist doctrine, and the Rev. Mr. Thomas got eleven more." This marvelously effective sermon also serves all the other denominations, salvaging 118 reprobates before it wears out (ETS 2:150–51). The miracle sermon makes fun of the often fierce doctrinal battles among the myriad Protestant churches to differentiate themselves by suggesting that such theological differences are so inconsequential that one sermon with a bit of tinkering can effectively serve all denominations. Moreover, Mark Twain accomplishes the burlesque deflation of the serious business of saving souls by turning such efforts into a fishing trip, a mocking echo of Jesus recruiting the apostles Peter and Andrew: "Come, follow me . . . and I will make you fishers of men" (Matthew 4:18–19). Such tactics would surely shock the sensibilities of Mrs. Aldrich. One wonders what Mr. Howells might make of them.

A final example occurs in one of the letters from Hawai'i, when Mark Twain details cultural values that differentiate human behavior. On an interisland schooner off the coast at night and during a storm, Mark Twain, in the midst of the pitching and yawing of the ship, spots a Hawai'ian paddling his canoe away from shore. Watching the man steadily make his way through the waves, Mark Twain cannot believe that anyone sensible would paddle out to the ship in such conditions. When he asks himself what would motivate this behavior, the only answer he can find is profit—the man must think he is somehow going to make money. For an American who has been reporting on the commerce between California and the Hawai'ian kingdom, such risk as the canoeist takes could only be entrepreneurial in nature. No other explanation comes to a Yankee's mind. When it turns out that the man not only is bringing food to give to the passengers on the boat but also refuses to take money for it, Mark Twain is stunned— and then ashamed that his own sensibility could not move beyond the profit motive (MTLH 281). Here, the cultural blinders that characterized the pioneers in Nevada are worn by Mark Twain. In each of these instances, Clemens scrutinizes deep values of American culture. In some cases, he finds the values themselves to be ridiculous; in others, Mark Twain ridicules people for the ways that they do not live up to the values.

Written without capital letters, "mark twain" refers to a habit Sam Clemens had of ordering two drinks at once and telling the bartender to score his bill accordingly. Such is the yarn spun by Clemens's newspaper colleague Alf Doten.[17] If one invokes instead Sam Clemens's days as a steamboat pilot, "mark twain" refers to a shout by the leadsman indicating "two fathoms," a depth barely safe enough for a steamboat. These meanings, rooted in personal experience and historical circumstance, indicate the nature of Samuel Langhorne Clemens's literary alter ego. Doten's tale suggests yarn spinning, Clemens's comic playfulness with the narrative conventions of journalism as well as the travel letter genre, with their assumption of truth and accuracy. The leadsman's cry of "mark twain," which encodes transition from one state (the safety of sufficiently deep water) to another (the danger of insufficiently deep water), suggests a comic liminality rife with subversive danger. "Mark Twain" thus signifies the performance of comic narratives structured by a dangerous play with truth and accuracy.

Sam Clemens performing Mark Twain enacts a dramatic illusion, but one very different from that of an actor on stage. The actor subordinates self to the fiction of his role in order to create the illusion that he is the character. Clemens aggrandizes self with fiction, embellishes and alters it with fiction, to create the illusion that he is the character Mark Twain. By performing his comic character, Sam Clemens manifests the Citizen Clown role. In that role, Mark Twain makes fictions—tells tales, spins yarns, fabricates lies—for the necessary fun of chastising and teasing, ridiculing and entertaining, his fellow citizens. This performance results in the comic singularity called "Mark Twain."

17. Goodman, "Memories," 3.

For Wolfgang Iser, the fictionality of literature distinguishes it from other kinds of writing, marks its relationship to the real, and reveals its function of expressing "the imaginary," an inchoate realm below consciousness that is "the generative matrix of the text."[18] Mark Twain is Sam Clemens's chief fiction for expressing his imaginary realm, his means to play with the given social and cultural world and overstep its limits, his way to build a necessary mental equipment for dealing with the circumstances of his time. For Iser, all fictions playfully transgress a given world. However, Sam Clemens amplified this transgressive power through the structural multiplicity of his implied author and personae, his inveterate burlesque tactics, and his deep play with normative ideas about achieving objectivity in journalistic narratives, especially in news reports and travel letters. These kinds of narratives have pragmatic goals: rendering clear and accurate representations of the world. In pursuit of these goals, they conceal fictionality within themselves. Often, Sam Clemens used Mark Twain to exploit the way fictions pervade supposedly objective and "true" stories. Mark Twain's trickster habit of confusing fact and fiction for his brand of satiric literature may even threaten Iser's theoretical distinction between literature and other kinds of writing.

Charles Webb was correct when he predicted Mark Twain would endure and implied his status as a cultural icon, because Sam Clemens's alter ego has the capacity to comically manhandle his—and our—culture's deep values. Mark Twain at his lightning-pilot best forces the reader to reexamine a value or sentiment or thought usually taken for granted by providing an unexpectedly funny angle. This laughable alternative view of the familiar creates an opportunity for insight into cultural norms or social mores once the reader moves past the comic laughter to consider why he or she was amused. Mark Twain performs his satiric critique as would a sacred clown, disrupting social values to instruct his community. The performance employs all the fictional layers of Mark Twain, through which the clown routinely speaks like a satirist, and the satirist acts like a clown. Thus Sam Clemens was correct, too, when he said, "I am the king of the buffoons; I am a dangerous person."[19]

---

18. Wolfgang Iser, *The Fictive and the Imaginary: Charting Literary Anthropology*, 21.
19. Quoted in Budd, "Talent for Posturing," 94.

# WORKS CITED

## PRIMARY WORKS

Baldwin, Joseph Glover. *Flush Times in Alabama and Mississippi.* Gloucester, Mass.: Peter Smith, 1974.

Browne, Charles Farrar. "Another Letter from Artemus Ward." *Cleveland Plain Dealer,* February 8, 1858.

———. "Artemus Ward." *Cleveland Plain Dealer,* May 29, 1858.

———. *Artemus Ward: His Book.* In *Complete Works of Charles F. Browne,* 37–168. London: Chatto and Windus, 1887.

———. "Artemus Ward among the 'Spirits.'" *Cleveland Plain Dealer,* December 13, 1858.

———. "Artemus Ward Encounters the Octoroon." *Cleveland Plain Dealer,* April 21, 1860.

———. "Artemus Ward in the South: His Trials and Adventures." *Vanity Fair,* May 25, 1861.

———. "Artemus Ward on Forts." *Vanity Fair,* November 17, 1860.

———. "Artemus Ward on His Travels." *Vanity Fair,* January 12, 1861.

———. "Artemus Ward on His Visit to Abe Lincoln." *Vanity Fair,* December 8, 1860.

———. "Artemus Ward on the Shakers." *Vanity Fair,* February 23, 1861.

———. "Artemus Ward Sees the Prince of Wales." *Cleveland Plain Dealer,* September 17, 1860.

———. "City Facts and Fancies: Bad End." *Cleveland Plain Dealer,* February 11, 1858.

———. "City Facts and Fancies: Berlin Heights." *Cleveland Plain Dealer,* June 18, 1858.

———. "City Facts and Fancies: Dear Local." *Cleveland Plain Dealer,* January 28, 1858.

———. "City Facts and Fancies: Hyena Loose in Paulding County." *Cleveland Plain Dealer,* February 6, 1858.

———. "City Facts and Fancies: Remarkable Incident." *Cleveland Plain Dealer,* January 26, 1858.

———. "City Facts and Fancies: Our Novel." *Cleveland Plain Dealer,* March 16, 1858.

———. "City Facts and Fancies: Our Novel." *Cleveland Plain Dealer,* March 22, 1858.

———. "City Facts and Fancies: Our Novel." *Cleveland Plain Dealer,* March 29, 1858.

———. "City Facts and Fancies: Swill Milk in the Country." *Cleveland Plain Dealer,* June 14, 1858.

———. "City Facts and Fancies: [Thackeray vs. Dickens]." *Cleveland Plain Dealer,* June 8, 1858.

———. "City Facts and Fancies: The Hyena." *Cleveland Plain Dealer,* March 2, 1858.

———. "City Facts and Fancies: The Hyena—A Correction." *Cleveland Plain Dealer,* February 9, 1858.

———. "City Facts and Fancies: The Masquerade." *Cleveland Plain Dealer,* March 19, 1858.

———. "The Fair Inez; or, The Lone Lady of the Crimson Cliffs. A Tale of the Sea." *Vanity Fair,* July 27, August 3, August 10, August 17, August 24, 1861.

———. "Fourth of July Oration Delivered at Weathersfield, Connecticut." *Cleveland Plain Dealer,* July 16, 1859.

———. "Joy in the House of Ward." *Cleveland Plain Dealer,* November 12, 1859.

———. "Letter from Artemus Ward." *Cleveland Plain Dealer,* February 15, 1858.

———. "Letter from Artemus Ward." *Cleveland Plain Dealer,* February 27, 1858.

———. "Letter from Artemus Ward." *Cleveland Plain Dealer,* April 17, 1858.

———. "Letter from Artemus Ward." *Cleveland Plain Dealer,* July 10, 1858.

———. "Letter from Artemus Ward: He Visits Berlin Heights and Encounters the Free Lovers." *Cleveland Plain Dealer,* October 11, 1858.

———. "Letter from a Side Showman." *Cleveland Plain Dealer,* January 30, 1858.

———. "Marion: A French Romance." *Vanity Fair,* July 13, 1861.

———. "Mossy the Sassy; or, The Disguised Duke." *Vanity Fair,* June 15, 1861.

———. "Our Local Heard From." *Cleveland Plain Dealer,* February 2, 1859.

———. "Our Ward Correspondence." *Cleveland Plain Dealer,* March 20, 1858.

———. "Woshy-Boshy; or, The Prestidigitating Squaw of the Snakeheads." *Vanity Fair,* November 2, November 9, November 16, November 23, 1861.

Browne, J. Ross. *Yusef; or, The Journey of the Frangi.* New York: Harper and Brothers, 1853.

Clark, Lewis Gaylord. *Knick-Knacks from an Editor's Table.* New York: Appleton, 1852.

———. "Reminiscences of John Phoenix." *Californian,* May 28, 1864.

Clemens, Samuel Langhorne. [Bidding on Flour Sack for Sanitary Fund]. *Virginia City Territorial Enterprise,* May 17, 1864. Reprint, *San Francisco Bulletin,* May 19, 1864, as "Grand Austin Sanitary Flour-Sack Progress through Storey and Lyon Counties."

———. *The Celebrated Jumping Frog of Calaveras County and Other Sketches.* New York: Oxford University Press, 1996.

———. *Clemens of the "Call": Mark Twain in San Francisco.* Ed. Edgar M. Branch. Berkeley and Los Angeles: University of California Press, 1969.

———. *Contributions to the "Galaxy," 1868–1871.* Ed. Bruce R. McElderry Jr. Gainesville, Fla.: Scholars' Facsimiles and Reprints, 1961.

———. *Early Tales and Sketches, Volume 1 (1851–1864).* Vol. 15 of *The Works of Mark Twain.* Ed. Edgar M. Branch and Robert H. Hirst. Berkeley and Los Angeles: University of California Press, 1979.

———. *Early Tales and Sketches, Volume 2 (1864–1865).* Vol. 15 of *The Works of Mark Twain.* Ed. Edgar M. Branch and Robert H. Hirst. Berkeley and Los Angeles: University of California Press, 1981.

———. [Energetic Officers]. *Virginia City Territorial Enterprise,* December 1 [?], 1863. Reprint, *Gold Hill News,* December 2, 1863, as "Sarcastical."

———. "How, for Instance?" *New York Weekly Review,* September 29, 1866.

———. "How I Escaped Being Killed in a Duel." In *Tom Hood's Comic Annual for 1873,* 90–91. London: Fun Office, 1872.

———. *The Innocents Abroad.* New York: Oxford University Press, 1996.

———. "Lives of the Liars; or, Joking Justified." *Virginia City Territorial Enterprise,* November 21 [?], 1863. Reprint, *Gold Hill News,* November 21, 1863.

———. *Mark Twain: Business Man.* Ed. Samuel Charles Webster. Boston: Little, Brown, 1946.

———. *Mark Twain, San Francisco Correspondent: Selections from His Letters to the "Territorial Enterprise," 1865–1866.* Ed. Henry Nash Smith and Frederick Anderson. San Francisco: Book Club of San Francisco, 1957.

———. "'Mark Twain' Explains the Mexican Correspondence." *San Francisco Alta California,* December 10, 1866.

———. *Mark Twain in Eruption.* Ed. Bernard DeVoto. New York: Harper and Brothers, 1940.

———. *Mark Twain of the "Enterprise": Newspaper Articles and Other Documents, 1862–1864.* Ed. Henry Nash Smith. Berkeley and Los Angeles: University of California Press, 1957.

———. *Mark Twain's Autobiography.* Introduction by Albert Bigelow Paine. New York: Harper and Brothers Publishers, 1924.

———. *Mark Twain's Letters, Volume 1 (1853–1866).* Ed. Edgar M. Branch, Michael B. Frank, and Kenneth M. Sanderson. Berkeley and Los Angeles: University of California Press, 1988.

———. *Mark Twain's Letters, Volume 2 (1867–1868).* Ed. Harriet Elinor Smith, Richard Bucci, and Lin Salamo. Berkeley and Los Angeles: University of California Press, 1990.

———. *Mark Twain's Letters from Hawai'i.* Ed. A. Grove Day. Honolulu: University of Hawai'i Press, 1975.

———. "Mark Twain's Letters to the *Gate City.*" In *The Pattern for "Roughing It": Letters from Nevada by Samuel and Orion Clemens, 1861–1862,* ed. Franklin R. Rogers, 22–45. Berkeley and Los Angeles: University of California Press, 1961.

———. "Mark Twain's Letters to the *San Francisco Call* from Virginia City, Nevada Territory, July 9th to November 19th, 1863." Ed. Austin E. Hutcheson. *Twainian* 11, nos. 1–3 (January/February, March/April, May/June 1952), 1–4 in each number.

———. *Mark Twain's Notebooks and Journals, Volume 1 (1855–1873).* Ed. Frederick Anderson, Michael B. Frank, and Kenneth M. Anderson. Berkeley and Los Angeles: University of California Press, 1975.

———. *Mark Twain Speaking.* Ed. Paul Fatout. Iowa City: University of Iowa Press, 1976.

———. *Mark Twain's Travels with Mr. Brown.* Ed. Franklin Walker and G. Ezra Dane. New York: Alfred A. Knopf, 1940.

———. "Our Fellow Savages of the Sandwich Islands." Various texts available online at "Mark Twain in His Times," ed. Stephen Railton, University of Virginia, http://etext.lib.virginia.edu/railton/onstage/savagehp.html (accessed November 28, 2007).

———. *Roughing It.* New York: Oxford University Press, 1996.

———. [San Francisco Letter: Police Corruption.] *Virginia City Territorial Enterprise,* January 22 [?], 1866. Not extant; described in *Gold Hill Daily News* and *Virginia City Daily Union,* January 23, 1866.

———. *Sketches New and Old.* New York: Oxford University Press, 1996.

———. "Still Harping." *Virginia City Territorial Enterprise,* November 20 [?], 1863. Reprint, *Reese River Reveille,* November 21, 1863.

———. [That Flour Sack Again]. *Virginia City Territorial Enterprise,* May 18, 1864. Reprint, *San Francisco Bulletin,* May 20, 1864, as "Travels and Fortunes of the Great Austin Sack of Flour."

———. *The Washoe Giant in San Francisco.* Ed. Franklin Walker. San Francisco: George Fields, 1938.

Clemens, Samuel Langhorne, and Bret Harte. *Sketches of the Sixties.* Ed. John Howell. 2d ed. San Francisco: John Howell, 1927.

Cozzens, Frederic S. *Acadia; or, A Month with the Blue Noses.* New York: Derby and Jackson, 1859.

———. *The Sparrowgrass Papers; or, Living in the Country.* New York: Derby and Jackson, 1856.

Crockett, David. *A Narrative of the Life of Colonel David Crockett.* Facsimile ed. Introduced and annotated by James A. Shackford and Stanley J. Folmsbee. Knoxville: University of Tennessee Press, 1973.

Derby, George Horatio. *Phoenixiana; or, Sketches and Burlesques.* New York: D. Appleton, 1855.

Harris, George Washington. *"Sut Lovingood. Yarns": A Facsimile of the 1867 Dick and Fitzgerald Edition.* Ed. M. Thomas Inge. Memphis: Saint Luke's Press, 1987.

Harte, Bret. "Artemus Ward." *Golden Era,* December 27, 1863.

———. "The Bohemian at the Fair." *Golden Era,* September 9, 1860.

———. "Bohemian Feuilleton: An Easter Morning Walk." *Golden Era,* April 7, 1861.

———. "Bohemian Feuilleton: Hotel Life." *Golden Era,* April 21, 1861.

———. "Bohemian in San Francisco." *Golden Era,* June 17, 1860.

———. "Bohemian Papers." In *Works of Bret Harte,* 4:187–331. Boston: Houghton Mifflin, 1921.

———. "Bohemian Papers: City Improvements." *Golden Era,* February 15, 1863.

———. "Bohemian Papers: On Restaurants." *Golden Era,* February 1, 1863.

———. "Bohemian Papers, No. 1: Melons." *Golden Era,* October 5, 1862.

———. "A Boys' Dog." *Californian,* July 30, 1864.

———. "From a Balcony." *Californian,* September 16, 1865.

———. "From California: A New Lecturer in the Field." *Springfield (Mass.) Republican,* November 10, 1866.

———. "Home Culture" [Mark Twain's Success]. *Californian,* November 11, 1865.

———. "John Jenkins; or, The Smoker Reformed, By T. S. A-th-r." *Californian,* July 1, 1865.

———. "The Lost Beauty: A Philosophical Narrative." *Golden Era,* December 28, 1862.

———. "A New California Book" [mock review of *Outcroppings*]. *Californian,* December 23, 1865.

———. "The Ninety-Nine Guardsmen, By Al-x-d-e D-m-s." *Californian,* July 29, 1865.

———. "San Francisco on Sunday." *Golden Era,* July 29, 1860.

————. "Sidewalkings." *Californian,* June 24, 1865.

————. "Stories for Little Girls." *Californian,* May 20, 1865.

————. "The Story of M'Liss: An Idyll of Red Mountain." *Golden Era,* September 20, September 27, October 4, October 11, October 18, November 1, November 8, November 15, December 13, December 20, 1863.

————. "Town and Table Talk: A la Bohemian." *Golden Era,* August 12, 1860.

————. "Town and Table Talk: The Bohemian at the Fair." *Golden Era,* September 23, 1860.

————. "Town and Table Talk: The Bohemian Concerning." *Golden Era,* November 11, 1860.

————. "Town and Table Talk: The Bohemian Grows Reflective and Discursive." *Golden Era,* December 9, 1860.

Irving, Washington. *A History of New York from the Beginning of the World to the End of the Dutch Dynasty by Diedrich Knickerbocker.* New York: Putnam's Sons, 1880.

————. *Wolfert's Roost, and Other Papers.* New York: G. P. Putnam, 1855.

Leland, Charles Godfrey. *Meister Karl's Sketch Book.* Philadelphia: Parry and McMillan, 1855.

————. Review of *Artemus Ward: His Book. Continental Monthly,* July 2, 1862.

Longstreet, Augustus Baldwin. *Georgia Scenes.* Facsimile ed. Atlanta: Cherokee Publishing Company, 1971.

Mathews, Charles. *The London Mathews, Containing an Account of This Celebrated Comedian's Trip to America.* Philadelphia: Morgan and Yeager, 1824.

Noland, Charles F. M. *Cavorting on the Devil's Fork: The Pete Whetstone Letters.* Ed. Leonard Williams. Memphis: Memphis State University Press, 1979.

Parson, Sara Willis. *Fern Leaves from Fanny's Portfolio.* Auburn, N.Y.: Derby and Miller, 1853.

Paulding, James K. *Letters from the South, Written during an Excursion in the Summer of 1816.* New York: James Eastburn, 1817.

————. *The Lion of the West.* 1831. Reprint, *The Kentuckian; or, A Visit to New York.* Ed. James N. Tidwell. Stanford: Stanford University Press, 1954.

Poe, Edgar Allan. *Doings of Gotham: Poe's Contributions to The "Columbia Spy."* Folcroft, Pa.: Folcroft Library Editions, 1974.

Porter, William T., ed. *The Big Bear of Arkansas.* Facsimile ed. New York: AMS Press, 1973.

————. *A Quarter Race in Kentucky.* Facsimile ed. New York: AMS Press, 1973.

Thompson, William Tappan. *Major Jones's Courtship.* 2d ed., greatly enlarged. Philadelphia: Carey and Hart, 1844.

Thomson, Mortimer. *Doesticks' Letters: And What He Says.* Philadelphia: T. B. Peterson and Brothers, 1855.

———. *The History and Records of the Elephant Club.* New York: Livermore and Rudd, 1856.

Webb, Charles Henry. "Inigoings" [Success of "Jumping Frog" sketch]. *Californian,* January 13, 1866.

———. "Letter from San Francisco" ["John Paul": Critical Accolade for Mark Twain]. *Sacramento Union,* November 3, 1865.

———. "Letter from San Francisco" ["John Paul"]. *Sacramento Union,* December 15, 1865.

———. "Letter from San Francisco" ["John Paul"]. *Sacramento Union,* December 22, 1865.

———. "Letter from San Francisco" ["John Paul"]. *Sacramento Union,* December 29, 1865.

———. *Liffith Lank; or, Lunacy.* New York: Carleton, 1866.

———. "Pleasant Games for California Children. By 'Wode.'" *Californian,* September 9, 1865.

———. "Stories for Good Little Boys and Girls." *Californian,* June 4, 1864.

———. *St. Twel'mo; or, The Cuneiform Cyclopedist of Chattanooga.* New York: C. H. Webb, 1867.

———. "Things." *Californian,* July 30, 1864.

———. "Things." *Californian,* August 6, 1864.

———. "Things." *Californian,* November 26, 1864.

———. "Things" [Adah Menken as Mazeppa]. *Golden Era,* August 30, 1863.

———. "Things: Caviare for the General; An Apple Pairing." *Californian,* July 16, 1864.

———. "Things: Discursive, Hippophagous, Theatrical." *Golden Era,* August 16, 1863.

———. "Things: [Foreign Affairs], Lighter Things." *Golden Era,* September 13, 1863.

———. "Things: High Moral Ground, The Ishmaelite! Good Works, The Opera, Artemus and His Babies, The Jordan." *Golden Era,* November 15, 1863.

———. "Things: [Hotel Living], Bierstadt's Sketches." *Golden Era,* September 27, 1863.

———. "Things: Illuminative, Picturesque, Festive, Critical." *Golden Era,* August 9, 1863.

———. "Things" ["The Ishmaelite"]. *Golden Era,* November 8, 1863.

———. "Things: Military, Festive, Dramatic, Musical, and Other Things." *Golden Era,* July 26, 1863.

———. "Things: Sad, Theological, Operatic, and Other Things." *Golden Era,* August 2, 1863.

———. "Things: The Russian Ball, The Bohemians in Court, The Hegira." *Golden Era,* November 22, 1863.

———. "Things: The Spanish Ball, A Bunch of Fives, Mrs. George Jordan and Her Engagement." *Golden Era,* October 18, 1863.

———. "Things: The Young Man Bret, Concerning California, Those That Tattle." *Golden Era,* November 29, 1863.

Willis, Nathaniel Parker. *Pencillings by the Way.* London: John Macrone, 1835.

Wright, William. "Amung the Seelestials." *Golden Era,* January 17, 1864.

———. "Artemus Ward in Nevada." *Californian,* 4 (August 1893): 403–6.

———. *The Big Bonanza.* New York: Apollo Editions, 1969.

———. "An Infamous Proceeding." *Virginia City Territorial Enterprise.* Reprint, *Golden Era,* May 1, 1864.

———. "Mark Twain Takes a Lesson in the Manly Art." *Virginia City Territorial Enterprise.* [April 24, 1864.] Reprint, *Golden Era,* May 1, 1864.

———. "No Head nor Tail." *Golden Era,* December 6, 1863.

———. "Onto the Deep." *Golden Era,* December 13, 1863.

———. "Our Washoe Correspondence." *Golden Era,* February 24, 1861.

———. "Our Washoe Correspondence: Letter from Dan De Quille." *Golden Era,* September 20, 1863.

———. "Our Washoe Correspondence: Letter from Dan De Quille." *Golden Era,* September 27, 1863.

———. "Our Washoe Correspondence: Letter from Dan De Quille." *Golden Era,* October 4, 1863.

———. "Our Washoe Correspondence: Letter from Dan De Quille." *Golden Era,* October 11, 1863.

———. "Petrified! or, The Stewed Chicken Monster." *Golden Era,* August 30, 1863.

———. "Reminiscences of the Comstock." *San Francisco Examiner,* January 22, 1893.

———. "Reporting with Mark Twain." *California Illustrated* 4 (July 1893): 170–78.

———. "Salad Days of Mark Twain." *San Francisco Examiner,* March 19, 1893.

———. "Utah Correspondence." *Cedar Falls (Iowa) Gazette,* February 8, 1861.

———. "Washoe Pictures: Another Strike." *Golden Era,* March 24, 1861.

———. "Washoe Rambles: A Trip among the Mountains, Lakes, and Deserts to the Eastward." *Golden Era,* July 28–December 1, 1863. Reprint, *Washoe Rambles,* ed. Richard E. Lingenfelter. Los Angeles: Westernlore Press, 1963.

———. "The Wealth of Washoe: A Day in the Silver Mines." *Golden Era,* March 31, 1861.

SECONDARY WORKS

I. Contemporary Background

Alden, W. L. "The Four Nations." *Galaxy* 6 (November 1868): 702–8.

"Ancient." "Stories for Good Little Girls." *Californian,* September 2, 1865.

Angel, Myron, ed. *History of Nevada with Illustrations and Biographical Sketches.* Oakland, Calif.: Thompson and West, 1881.

Arnold, Matthew. "The Study of Poetry." In *Works of Matthew Arnold,* 4:1–41. London: Macmillan, 1903.

Austin, Franklin H. "Mark Twain Incognito—A Reminiscence." *Friend* 96 (1926): no. 9 (September): 201–4; no. 10 (October): 224–29; and no. 11 (November): 248–54.

Balzac, Honoré de. "Un Prince de la Bohème." In *Scènes de la Vie Parisienne,* 21–54. Vol. 11 of *Oeuvres Complètes de H. de Balzac.* Paris: Michel Lévy Frères, 1879.

Barnes, George E. "Mark Twain as He Was Known during His Stay on the Pacific Slope." *San Francisco Daily Morning Call,* April 17, 1887.

Bartlett, John Russell. *A Dictionary of Americanisms.* New York: Bartlett and Welford, 1848.

Basso, Dave, ed. *Mark Twain in the "Virginia Evening Bulletin" and "Gold Hill News."* Sparks, Nev.: Falcon Hill Press, 1981.

Baudelaire, Charles. "The Painter of Modern Life." In *The Painter of Modern Life and Other Essays,* trans. Jonathan Mayne, 1–40. London: Phaidon Press, 1995.

Bowles, Samuel. [Bret Harte and Mark Twain Compared.] *Springfield (Mass.) Republican,* January 16, 1867.

———. [Bret Harte as California's Best Humorist.] *Springfield (Mass.) Republican,* May 22, 1867.

Brooks, Ida L. "Did Mark Twain's Laziness Cost Him a Fortune? Calvin H. Higbie, to Whom *Roughing It* Is Dedicated, Tells the Other Side of 'When We Were Millionaires for Ten Days.'" *San Francisco Chronicle,* March 25, 1906.

Bunce, Oliver Bell. "Table Talk." *Appleton's Journal of Popular Literature, Science, and Art,* May 21, 1870, 582–83.

———. "Table Talk." *Appleton's Journal of Popular Literature, Science, and Art,* February 11, 1871, 174–75.

*Californian.* "American Humor." September 23, 1865. Reprint from *Brooklyn Standard.*

———. [Bret Harte's Humor]. April 13, 1867.

———. [Charles Webb's "Things"]. August 6, 1864. Reprint from *Boston Saturday Evening Gazette*.

———. "Her Majesty at Hand!" [Mark Twain as Missionary]. September 22, 1866.

———. "Hood's Humor." August 27, 1864.

———. [Josh Billings]. February 25, 1865.

———. "Mr. Harte's New Book" [*Condensed Novels*]. Reprint, [unnamed New York periodical]. November 16, 1867.

———. "Our New York Letter" [Artemus Ward]. December 31, 1864.

———. Review of *Jumping Frog*. June 1, 1867.

———. Review of *Jumping Frog*. October 5, 1867. Reprint from *London Saturday Review*.

———. "The Unhappy Fitz Smythe." April 6, 1867.

Chapman, John Gadsby. "Reminiscences of Colonel David Crockett in 1834." Introduced by Curtis Carroll Davis. *Proceedings of the American Antiquarian Society* 69 (October 1959): 165–73.

"China." "Carson Correspondence" [Mark Twain Speaks at Church Fundraiser]. *Gold Hill News*, January 25, 1864.

Clare, Ada. "The Question of Humor." *Golden Era*, April 17, 1864.

———. "Thoughts and Things." *New York Saturday Press*, February 11, 1860.

———. "Washoe Wanderings." *Golden Era*, April 3, 1864.

"Clevelander." "From the Sandwich Islands." *Cleveland Plain Dealer*, March 22, 1858.

*Cleveland Plain Dealer.* "Affairs in Honolulu." March 19, 1858.

———. [Contributors to *Vanity Fair*]. November 6, 1860.

———. "From the Sandwich Islands." April 16, 1858.

———. "From the Sandwich Islands." June 1, 1858.

———. "Mrs. Cunningham." May 5, 1858.

———. "A Polite Invitation Declined." November 6, 1860.

Curtis, George William. "The Editor at Large" [Bohemians]. *Putnam's Monthly Magazine of American Literature, Science, and Art* 4 (October 1854): 435–37.

———. "Editor's Easy Chair: What Is a Bohemian?" *Harper's Monthly* 19 (October 1859): 705–6.

———. "Editor's Easy Chair" [The Lyceum]. *Harper's Monthly* 30 (January 1865): 262–63.

———. "Editor's Easy Chair" [The Lyceum Endures]. *Harper's Monthly* 52 (March 1876): 614–16.

———. "Editor's Easy Chair" [Palmer's Studio]. *Harper's Monthly* 22 (January 1861): 269–70.

Daggett, Rollin M. "Daggett's Recollections." *San Francisco Examiner,* January 22, 1893.

*Democratic Review.* Review of *The Sparrowgrass Papers.* 37 (June 1856): 519.

———. "Wit, Humor, and Fun." 41 (January 1858): 77–83.

Davis, Sam P., ed. *The History of Nevada.* Reno, Nev.: Elms Publishing Company, 1913.

De Crevecoeur, Hector St. John. "What Is an American?" In *Letters from an American Farmer,* 39–86. London: J. M. Dent and Sons, 1945.

Doten, Alf. "Early Journalism in Nevada, Part I." *Nevada Magazine* 1 (September 1899): 45–58.

———. "Early Journalism in Nevada, Part II." *Nevada Magazine* 1 (October 1899): 181–89.

———. Review of "Our Fellow Savages of the Sandwich Islands." *Virginia City Territorial Enterprise,* November 1, 1866.

Dunn, H. D. "Letter from Honolulu." *San Francisco Bulletin,* February 16, 1866.

Fitch, Thomas. "Fitch Recalls Mark Twain in Bonanza Times." *San Francisco Chronicle,* March 30, 1919.

*Galaxy.* "Nebulae" [*Artemus Ward*]. January 3, 1867.

———. "Nebulae" [The Word "Bohemian"]. June 15, 1866.

*Golden Era.* "Artemus Ward, Wild Humorist of the Plains." January 17, 1864.

———. "Brick Pomeroy's Cold" [Mark Twain, "Wild Humorist of the Land of Silver and Sagebrush"]. June 5, 1864.

———. [Editorial headnote to "Mark Twain in the Metropolis" calling Mark Twain the "Sagebrush Humorist from Silverland"]. June 26, 1864.

———. "The Golden Era" [Our Contributors]. January 17, 1864.

———. "Humorists, Past and Present." December 6, 1863.

———. "Ollopodrida." October 2, 1864.

———. "Our Humorous Satirists." October 2, 1864. Reprint from *New York Sunday Times.*

———. [Satire: Mark Twain's vs. Bret Harte's]. April 19, 1863.

*Gold Hill News.* "Another 'Feet' Story." November 3, 1863.

———. "The Austin Flour Sack." May 17, 1864.

———. "The Church Story." June 13, 1864.

———. "Freeze Out." October 29, 1863.

———. "Irreverence." June 16, 1864.

———. "Ludicrous." October 27, 1863.

———. "More Complaining." October 30, 1863. Reprint from *Aurora Times.*

———. "The Old Thing." November 6, 1863.

———. "On a Saturday [in Virginia City]." April 23, 1864.

———. "Popular Discontent." October 30, 1863.

———. "Rumored Murder and Robbery." December 3, 1863. Reprint from *Virginia City Territorial Enterprise*.

———. "Salting." October 24, 1863.

———. "Social Improvement." November 17, 1863. Reprint from *Virginia City Territorial Enterprise*.

———. "Stars." October 26, 1863.

———. "Still Harping On." October 30, 1863.

———. "A Sure Indication." November 2, 1863.

———. "That Sell." October 29, 1863.

Goodman, Joseph T. "Artemus Ward: His Visit to the Comstock." *San Francisco Chronicle*, January 10, 1892.

———. "Joseph Goodman's Memories of [Mark Twain the] Humorist's Early Days." *San Francisco Examiner*, April 22, 1910.

———. "Mark Twain." *Virginia City Territorial Enterprise*, May 3, 1863. Reprint, *Early Tales and Sketches, Volume 1 (1851–1864)*, 248.

Goodwin, Charles C. *As I Remember Them*. Salt Lake City: Salt Lake Commercial Club, 1913.

Halpine, Charles. "Miss Braddon, Mrs. Southworth, and Their Literary Trash." *New York Weekly Review*, February 24, 1866.

Holland, Josiah. "Triflers on the Platform." *Scribner's Monthly* 3 (February 1872): 489.

*Honolulu Friend*. [*Ajax* Passenger List]. April 2, 1866.

Howells, William Dean. "Mark Twain." *Century* 24 (September 1882): 780–83.

———. *My Mark Twain: Reminiscences and Criticisms*. 1910. Reprint, Baton Rouge: Louisiana State University Press, 1967.

Hundley, Daniel H. *Social Relations in Our Southern States*. New York: Arno Press, 1973.

James, George Wharton. "Mark Twain and the Pacific Coast." *Pacific Monthly* 24 (August 1910): 115–32.

Knight, Enoch. "The Real Artemus Ward." *Overland Monthly* 18 (1891): 54–60.

Lang, Andrew. "The Art of Mark Twain." In *Critical Essays on Mark Twain, 1867–1910*, ed. Louis Budd, 87–90. Boston: G. K. Hall, 1982.

Ludlow, Fitzhugh. "A Good-Bye Article." *Golden Era*, November 22, 1863.

*Manufacturer and Builder*. "Bohemianism." 1 (1869): 248.

McEwen, Arthur. "In the Heroic Days." *San Francisco Examiner*, January 22, 1893.

*Melbourne Argus*. "Mark Twain in Sydney: A Further Interview." In *Critical Essays on Mark Twain, 1867–1910*, ed. Louis Budd, 112–14. Boston: G. K. Hall, 1982.

"Meridian." "'The Third House' and Other Burlesques." *Virginia City Daily Union*, January 30, 1864.

Mulford, Prentice. Review of "Our Fellow Savages of the Sandwich Islands." *Golden Era*, October 7, 1866.

Murger, Henri. *Scènes de la Vie de Bohème.* Paris: Librairie Garnier, 1851.

*New York Post.* "Gossip about Publishers and Books" [review of *Jumping Frog*]. In *Critical Essays on Mark Twain, 1867–1910,* ed. Louis Budd, 28. Boston: G. K. Hall, 1982.

*New York Round Table.* "Literary Table" [review of *Jumping Frog*]. May 25, 1867.

*New York Sun.* "Not Quite an Editor: The Story of Mark Twain's Connection to the *Hartford Courant.*" In *Critical Essays on Mark Twain, 1867–1910,* ed. Louis Budd, 46–48. Boston: G. K. Hall, 1982.

*New York Tribune.* [11,300 Copies Sold of *Doesticks*]. July 11, 1855.

———. [The Audience for *New York Sunday Mercury*]. May 26, 1855.

———. Review of *Meister Karl's Sketchbook.* December 25, 1855.

*New York Weekly Review.* [Editor's Note: Bret Harte.] January 27, 1866.

———. [Headnote for "An Open Letter to the American People"]. February 17, 1866.

*North American Review.* Review of *Artemus Ward: His Travels.* 102 (April 1866): 586–92.

Ogden, Richard ["Podgers"]. [Ed. comment for "Mark Twain at Honolulu"]. *Californian,* August 4, 1866.

———. "Letter from New York" [Mark Twain's "Jumping Frog" story]. *San Francisco Alta California,* January 10, 1866.

———. "Literary Gleanings and Gossip: Ross Browne's New Book." *Californian,* December 8, 1866.

———. [Mark Twain Superior to Artemus Ward]. *Californian,* May 12, 1866.

Olmsted, Frederick Law. *The Cotton Kingdom: A Traveller's Observations on Cotton and Slavery in the American Slave States.* 1861. Reprint, New York: Alfred A. Knopf, 1966.

*Pacific Commercial Advertiser (Honolulu).* "Hawaii Schools Ready to Observe Mark Twain Day." November 30, 1915.

Phillips, Michael J. "Reminiscences of Mark Twain by His Partner, Calvin Higbie." *Saturday Evening Post* 11 (September 1920): 22–23, 69–70, 73–74.

Putnam, Charles A. V. "Dan De Quille [William Wright] and Mark Twain." *Salt Lake City Daily Tribune,* April 25, 1898.

*Putnam's Monthly.* "*The Sparrowgrass Papers* by Frederic Cozzens." 8 (July 1856): 99.

"Roland." "Letter from Boston: A New Literary Enterprise." *Sacramento Union,* October 16, 1866.

Ruthrauff, C. C. "Artemus Ward at Cleveland." *Scribner's Monthly* 16 (October 1878): 785–91.

Ryder, James F. "Artemus Ward." In *Voigtlander and I in Pursuit of Shadow Catching: A Story of Fifty-Two Years' Companionship with a Camera,* 174–207. Cleveland: Cleveland Printing and Publishing Company, 1902.

*Sacramento Union.* [Best Reporters]. May 30, 1866. Reprint from *North American Review.*

———. Review of *Jumping Frog.* June 6, 1867.

*San Francisco Alta California.* "Amusements: Mark Twain's Lecture." November 17, 1866.

———. "City Items: Arrival of Queen Emma." September 25, 1866.

———. "City Items: The Sandwich Islands" [Mark Twain's Lecture]. September 30, 1866.

———. [Hawai'i and the *Ajax*]. January 5, 1866.

———. [Mark Twain's First Lecture]. October 3, 1866.

———. "'Mark Twain's' Lecture." December 11, 1866.

———. "New Publications" [review of *Jumping Frog*]. June 9, 1867.

*San Francisco Bulletin.* "Letter from Honolulu." January 29, 1866.

———. "Letter from Honolulu." February 23, 1866.

———. "Letter from Honolulu." April 13, 1866.

———. "Mark Twain's Lecture." November 16, 1866.

———. "'Mark Twain's' Lecture on the Sandwich Islands." October 3, 1866.

———. "Mark Twain's New Book." June 1, 1867.

———. "Mark Twain To-night." December 10, 1866.

*San Francisco Dramatic Chronicle.* "Academy of Music." October 3, 1866.

———. "A Disgraceful Imposition." September 25, 1866.

———. "Hasheesh Eaters." September 18, 1865.

———. "Mark Twain's Lecture." November 17, 1866.

———. "Sensational Rumor." October 2, 1866.

———. [Tickets to Mark Twain's Lecture]. October 1, 1866.

*San Francisco Examiner.* [Mark Twain's Lecture]. October 5, 1866. Reprint, *Sacramento Union.*

*San Francisco Illustrated Press.* "Mark Twain." 1 (February 1873): 21–22.

*San Francisco News Letter.* [Mark Twain's Lecture]. October 6, 1866.

Seabrook, E. B. "The Poor Whites of the South." *New York Galaxy* 6 (October 1867): 681–90.

Shanly, Charles Dawson. "American Humor and Humorists." *New York Round Table* 9 (September 1865): 2–3.

Stedman, Edmund Clarence. *The Life and Letters of Edmund Clarence Stedman.* Ed. Laura Stedman and G. M. Gould. New York: Moffat, Yard, 1910.

Sumner, Charles. "What a Worm." *Gold Hill Daily News,* October 22, 1863.

Thackeray, William M. *Catherine: A Story.* London: Smith, Elder, 1869.

———. "Charity and Humour." In *The English Humourists, Charity and Humour, The Four Georges,* 267–86. London: Dent and Sons, 1968.

———. "The English Humourists of the Eighteenth Century." In *The English Humourists, Charity and Humour, The Four Georges,* 3–263. London: Dent and Sons, 1968.

*Vanity Fair.* [List of *Vanity Fair* writers.] November 6, 1860.

———. "Natural History: The Man about Town." July 21, 1860.

———. "Preface." December 31, 1859.

Whitman, Walt. "Democratic Vistas." In *The Works of Walt Whitman.* Vol. 2, *The Collected Prose,* ed. Malcolm Cowley, 208–63. New York: Funk and Wagnalls, 1968.

Whitney, Henry M. "Better Fifty Years in Hawaii Than a Cycle of Cathay." *Pacific Commercial Advertiser (Honolulu),* January 1, 1900.

———. "*Hulahula*." *Pacific Commercial Advertiser (Honolulu),* July 2, 1857.

———. "Notes of the Week: The Election." *Pacific Commercial Advertiser (Honolulu),* April 23, 1864.

———. "Property Qualifications." *Pacific Commercial Advertiser (Honolulu),* May 7, 1864.

Wilmer, Lambert A. *Our Press Gang; or, A Complete Exposition of the Corruptions and Crimes of the American Newspapers.* Philadelphia: J. Lloyd, 1859.

## II. Mark Twain and the American Comic Tradition

Albanese, Catherine. "Davy Crockett and the Wild Man; or, The Metaphysics of the *Longue Durée*." In *Davy Crockett: The Man, the Legend, the Legacy, 1786–1986,* ed. Michael Lofaro, 80–101. Knoxville: University of Tennessee Press, 1985.

———. "King Crockett: Nature and Civility on the American Frontier." *Proceedings of the American Antiquarian Society* 88 (1978): 225–49.

Anderson, John Q. "Scholarship in Southwestern Humor—Past and Present." *Mississippi Quarterly* 17 (1963): 67–86.

Arpad, Joseph J. "The Fight Story: Quotation and Originality in Native American Humor." *Journal of the Folklore Institute* 10 (1973): 141–72.

———. Introduction to *A Narrative of the Life of Colonel David Crockett.* New Haven, Conn.: College and University Press, 1972.

Bellamy, Gladys Carmen. *Mark Twain as a Literary Artist.* Norman: University of Oklahoma Press, 1950.

Benson, Ivan. *Mark Twain's Western Years.* Stanford: Stanford University Press, 1938.

Berkove, Lawrence I., ed. *The Fighting Horse of the Stanislaus: Stories and Essays by Dan De Quille.* Iowa City: University of Iowa Press, 1990.

Bier, Jesse. "Literary Comedians: The Civil War and Reconstruction." In *The Rise and Fall of American Humor,* 77–116. New York: Holt, Rinehart, and Winston, 1968.

Blair, Walter. "Burlesques in Nineteenth-Century American Humor." *American Literature* 2 (1930): 236–47.

———. Introduction to *The Mirth of a Nation: America's Great Dialect Humor,* ed. Walter Blair and Raven I. McDavid Jr. Minneapolis: University of Minnesota Press, 1983.

———. "Mark Twain, New York Correspondent." In *Essays in American Humor: Blair through the Ages,* ed. Hamlin Hill, 143–53. Madison: University of Wisconsin Press, 1993.

———. *Native American Humor.* 1937. Reprint, with new material, New York: Harper and Row, 1960.

———. "Traditions in Southern Humor." *American Quarterly* 5 (1953): 132–42.

Blair, Walter, and Hamlin Hill. *America's Humor: From Poor Richard to Doonesbury.* Oxford: Oxford University Press, 1978.

Blair, Walter, and Franklin J. Meine. "Mike Fink in History, Legend, and Story." In *Half Horse, Half Alligator: The Growth of the Mike Fink Legend,* 3–40. Chicago: University of Chicago Press, 1956.

Boatwright, Mody. *Folk Laughter on the American Frontier.* Gloucester, Mass.: Peter Smith, 1971.

Branch, Edgar M. "'The Babes in the Woods': Artemus Ward's 'Double Health' to Mark Twain." *PMLA* 93 (1978): 955–72.

———. Introduction to *Clemens of the "Call": Mark Twain in San Francisco.* Berkeley and Los Angeles: University of California Press, 1969.

———. Introduction to *Early Tales and Sketches, Volume I (1851- 1864).* Volume 15 of *The Works of Mark Twain,* ed. Edgar M. Branch and Robert H. Hirst. Berkeley and Los Angeles: University of California Press, 1979.

———. *The Literary Apprenticeship of Mark Twain.* Urbana: University of Illinois Press, 1950.

Budd, Louis J. "Mark Twain and the Magazine World." *University of Mississippi Studies in English,* n.s. no. 2 (1981): 35–42.

———. *Our Mark Twain: The Making of His Public Personality.* Philadelphia: University of Pennsylvania Press, 1983.

———. "A 'Talent for Posturing': The Achievement of Mark Twain's Public Personality." In *The Mythologizing of Mark Twain,* ed. Sara de Saussure Davis and Philip D. Beidler, 77–98. Tuscaloosa: University of Alabama Press, 1984.

Budd, Louis J., ed. *Mark Twain: The Contemporary Reviews.* Cambridge: Cambridge University Press, 1999.

Caron, James E. "Backwoods Civility; or, How the Ring-Tailed Roarer Became a Gentle Man for David Crockett, Charles F. M. Noland, and William Tappan Thompson." In *The Humor of the Old South,* ed. M. Thomas Inge and Ed Piacentino, 161–86. Lexington: University Press of Kentucky, 2001.

———. "Laughter, Politics, and the Yankee Doodle Legacy in America's Comic Tradition." *Thalia* 10 (1988): 3–13.

———. "Mark Twain's Comic *Bildungsroman.*" *Modern Language Quarterly* 50 (1989): 145–72.

———. "Playin' Hell: Sut Lovingood as Durn'd Fool Preacher." In *Sut Lovingood's Nat'ral Born Yarnspinner: Essays on George Washington Harris,* ed. James E. Caron and M. Thomas Inge, 272–98. Tuscaloosa: University of Alabama Press, 1996.

———. "Silent Slapstick Film as Ritualized Clowning: The Example of Charlie Chaplin." *Studies in American Humor,* n.s. 3, no. 14 (2006): 5–22.

———. "Washoe Mark Twain." *Nevada Historical Society Quarterly* 46 (2003): 77–88.

Cohen, Hennig, and William B. Dillingham. Introduction to *Humor of the Old Southwest.* 3d ed. Athens: University of Georgia Press, 1994.

Cook, Sylvia Jenkins. "The Development of the Poor White Tradition." In *From Tobacco Road to Route 66: The Southern Poor White in Fiction,* 3–17. Chapel Hill: University of North Carolina Press, 1976.

Coulombe, Joseph L. *Mark Twain and the American West.* Columbia: University of Missouri Press, 2003.

Covici, Pascal, Jr. *Mark Twain's Humor: The Image of a World.* Dallas: Southern Methodist University Press, 1962.

Cox, James. "Humor of the Old Southwest." In *The Comic Imagination in American Literature,* ed. Louis D. Rubin Jr., 101–12. New Brunswick, N.J.: Rutgers University Press, 1973.

Dane, G. Ezra. Introduction to *Letters from the Sandwich Islands, Written for the "Sacramento Union" by Mark Twain.* Palo Alto, Calif.: Stanford University Press, 1938.

Davis, Curtis Carroll. "A Legend at Full-Length: Mr. Chapman Paints Colonel Crockett—and Tells about It." *Proceedings of the American Antiquarian Society* 69 (1959): 155–65.

DeVoto, Bernard. *Mark Twain's America.* Boston: Houghton Mifflin Company, 1967.

Duckett, Margaret. *Mark Twain and Bret Harte.* Norman: University of Oklahoma Press, 1964.

Dwyer, Richard A., and Richard E. Lingenfelter. *Dan De Quille, the Washoe Giant: A Biography and Anthology.* Reno: University of Nevada Press, 1990.

Eaton, Clement. "The Humor of the Southern Yeoman." *Sewanee Review* 49 (1941): 173–83.

———. "The Southern Yeoman: The Humorist's View and the Reality." In *The Mind of the South,* rev. ed., 13–151. Baton Rouge: Louisiana State University Press, 1967.

Emerson, Everett. *The Authentic Mark Twain: A Literary Biography of Samuel L. Clemens.* Philadelphia: University of Pennsylvania Press, 1984.

Estes, David C. "Sut Lovingood at the Camp Meeting: A Practical Joker among the Backwoods Believers." *Southern Quarterly* 25 (1987): 53–65.

Fatout, Paul. *Mark Twain in Virginia City.* Bloomington: Indiana University Press, 1964.

Fellman, Michael. "Alligator Men and Cardsharpers: Deadly Southwestern Humor." *Huntington Library Quarterly* 49 (1986): 307–23.

Fienberg, Lorne. "Laughter as a Strategy of Containment in Southwestern Humor." *Studies in American Humor,* n.s. 2, no. 3 (1984): 107–22.

———. "*Spirit of the Times.*" In *American Humor Magazines and Comic Periodicals,* ed. David E. E. Sloane, 271–78. Westport, Conn.: Greenwood Press, 1987.

Fisher, Benjamin Franklin, IV. "*The Knickerbocker.*" In *American Humor Magazines and Comic Periodicals,* ed. David E. E. Sloane, 128–33. Westport, Conn.: Greenwood Press, 1987.

Florence, Don. *Persona and Humor in Mark Twain's Early Writings.* Columbia: University of Missouri Press, 1995.

Frear, Walter Francis. *Mark Twain and Hawai'i.* Chicago: Lakeside Press, 1947.

Gernes, Sonia. "Artists of Community: The Role of Storytellers in the Tales of the Southwest Humorists." *Journal of Popular Culture* 15 (1982): 114–28.

Hauck, Richard Boyd. "The Literary Content of the New York *Spirit of the Times,* 1831–1856." Ph.D. diss., University of Illinois, 1965.

———. "Making It All Up: Davy Crockett in the Theater." In *Davy Crockett: The Man, the Legend, the Legacy, 1786–1986,* ed. Michael Lofaro, 102–23. Knoxville: University of Tennessee Press, 1985.

———. "The Man in the Buckskin Hunting Shirt: Fact and Fiction in the Crockett Story." In *Davy Crockett: The Man, the Legend, the Legacy, 1786–1986,* ed. Michael Lofaro, 3–20. Knoxville: University of Tennessee Press, 1985.

Hyde, Stuart W. "Ring-Tailed Roarer in American Drama." *Southern Folklore Quarterly* 19 (1955): 171–78.

Inge, M. Thomas. Introduction to *The Frontier Humorists: Critical Views.* Hamden, Conn.: Archon Press, 1975.

————. "Sut Lovingood: An Examination of the Nature of a 'Nat'ral Born Durn'd Fool.'" *Tennessee Historical Quarterly* 19 (1960): 231–51.

Jacobs, Robert D. "*Tobacco Road:* Lowlife and the Comic Tradition." In *The American South: Portrait of a Culture,* ed. Louis D. Rubin Jr., 206–26. Baton Rouge: Louisiana State University Press, 1980.

Justus, James. *Fetching the Old Southwest: Humorous Writing from Longstreet to Twain.* Columbia: University of Missouri Press, 2004.

Kaplan, Justin. *Mr. Clemens and Mark Twain: A Biography.* New York: Simon and Schuster, 1966.

Kesterson, David. "The Literary Comedians: A Review of Modern Scholarship." *American Studies* 30 (1985): 167–75.

————. "Those Literary Comedians." In *Critical Essays on American Humor,* ed. William Bedford Clark and W. Craig Turner, 167–83. Boston: G. K. Hall, 1984.

Knoper, Randall. *Acting Naturally: Mark Twain in the Culture of Performance.* Berkeley and Los Angeles: University of California Press, 1995.

Krauth, Leland. "Mark Twain Fights Samuel Langhorne Clemens's Duel." *Mississippi Quarterly* 33 (spring 1980): 141–53.

————. *Proper Mark Twain.* Athens: University of Georgia Press, 1999.

Kummer, George. "The Americanization of Burlesque, 1840–1860." In *Popular Literature in America: A Symposium in Honor of Lyon N. Richardson,* ed. James C. Austin and Donald A. Koch, 146–54. Bowling Green: Bowling Green University Press, 1972.

Kunitz, Stanley J., and Howard Haycroft. "Charles Henry Webb." In *American Authors, 1600–1900: A Biographical Dictionary of American Literature,* 789. New York: H. W. Wilson, 1938.

Lemay, J. A. Leo. "The Frontiersman from Lout to Hero." *Proceedings of the American Antiquarian Society* 88 (1978): 187–223.

————. "Origins of the Humor of the Old South." *Southern Literary Journal* 23 (1991): 3–13.

Lillard, Richard G. "Contemporary Reaction to 'The Empire City Massacre.'" *American Literature* 16 (November 1944): 198–203.

Lingenfelter, Richard E. Introduction to *Washoe Rambles.* Los Angeles: Westernlore Press, 1963.

Lofaro, Michael. "From Boone to Crockett: The Beginnings of Frontier Humor." *Mississippi Folklore Register* 14 (1980): 57–74.

Lorch, Fred W. *The Trouble Begins at Eight: Mark Twain's Lecture Tours.* Ames: Iowa State University Press, 1968.

Lukens, Henry Clay. "American Literary Comedians." *Harper's Monthly* 80 (1890): 783–97.

Lynn, Kenneth S. *Mark Twain and Southwestern Humor.* Westport, Conn.: Greenwood Press, 1972.

Mack, Effie Mona. *Mark Twain in Nevada.* New York: Charles Scribner's Sons, 1947.

Marzolf, Marion. "Sara Payson Willis Parton (Fanny Fern)." In *Dictionary of Literary Biography.* Vol. 43, *American Newspaper Journalists, 1690–1872,* 358–62. Detroit: Gale Research, 1985.

McHaney, Thomas. "The Tradition of Southern Humor." *Chiba Review* 7 (1985): 51–72.

Michelson, Bruce. *Mark Twain on the Loose: A Comic Writer and the American Self.* Amherst: University of Massachusetts Press, 1995.

Miller, Henry Prentice. "The Background and Significance of *Major Jones's Courtship.*" *Georgia Historical Quarterly* 30 (1946): 267–96.

Mott, Frank Luther. "The Beginnings of Artemus Ward." *Journalism Quarterly* 18 (1941): 146–52.

Nickels, Cameron C. "Yankee Notions." In *American Humor Magazines and Comic Periodicals,* ed. David E. E. Sloane, 322–25. Westport, Conn.: Greenwood Press, 1987.

Orwell, George. "Mark Twain—Licensed Jester." In *Collected Essays, Journalism, and Letters of George Orwell.* Vol. 2, *My Country Right or Left, 1940–1943,* ed. Sonia Orwell and Ian Angus, 325–29. London: Secker and Warburg, 1968.

Osthaus, Carl R. "From the Old South to the New South: The Editorial Career of William Tappan Thompson of the *Savannah Morning News.*" *Southern Quarterly* 14 (1976): 237–60.

Paine, Albert Bigelow. *Mark Twain: A Biography.* Author's National Edition. New York: Harper and Brothers, 1912.

Pattee, Fred Lewis. "The Laughter of the West." In *A History of American Literature since 1870,* 25–44. New York: Century Company, 1917.

Pearson, Michael. "Pig Eaters, Whores, and Cowophiles: The Comic Image in Southern Literature." *Studies in Popular Culture* 9 (1986): 1–10.

Pettit, Arthur G. *Mark Twain and the South.* Lexington: University of Kentucky Press, 1974.

Polk, Noel. "The Blind Bull, Human Nature: Sut Lovingood and the Damned Human Race." In *Sut Lovingood's Nat'ral Born Yarnspinner: Essays on George Washington Harris,* ed. James E. Caron and M. Thomas Inge, 148–75. Tuscaloosa: University of Alabama Press, 1996.

Pullen, John J. *Comic Relief: The Life and Laughter of Artemus Ward, 1834–1867.* Hamden, Conn.: Archon Books, 1983.

Quirk, Tom, ed. *The Portable Mark Twain.* New York: Penguin Group, 2004.

Reed, John Q. "Artemus Ward as a Comic Lecturer." *Educational Leader* 20 (1956): 3–12.

Rickels, Milton. *George Washington Harris.* New York: Twayne Publishers, 1965.

Rodgers, Paul C., Jr. "Artemus Ward and Mark Twain's 'Jumping Frog,'" *Nineteenth-Century Fiction* 28 (1973): 273–86.

Rogers, Franklin R. *Mark Twain's Burlesque Patterns.* Dallas: Southern Methodist University Press, 1960.

Rourke, Constance. *American Humor: A Study of the National Character.* 1931. Reprint, New York: Doubleday, 1953.

Royot, Daniel. "*Yankee Blade.*" In *American Humor Magazines and Comic Periodicals,* ed. David E. E. Sloane, 317–19. Westport, Conn.: Greenwood Press, 1987.

Scharnhorst, Gary. *Bret Harte.* New York: Twayne Publishers, 1992.

Schmidt, Paul. "The Deadpan on Simon Wheeler." *Southwest Review* 41 (1956): 270–77.

Seelye, John. "A Well-Wrought Crockett; or, How the Fakelorists Passed through the Credibility Gap and Discovered Kentucky." In *Davy Crockett: The Man, the Legend, the Legacy, 1786–1986,* ed. Michael Lofaro, 21–45. Knoxville: University of Tennessee Press, 1985.

Shackford, James A., and Stanley J. Folmsbee. Introduction to *A Narrative of the Life of David Crockett.* Facsimile ed. Knoxville: University of Tennessee Press, 1973.

Shaw, Archer H. "Artemus Ward." In *The Plain Dealer: One Hundred Years in Cleveland,* 62–72. New York: A. Knopf, 1942.

Skaggs, Merrill Maguire. "The Beginning: Southwest Humor." In *The Folk of Southern Fiction,* 25–35. Athens: University of Georgia Press, 1972.

Sloane, David E. E. *Mark Twain as a Literary Comedian.* Baton Rouge: Louisiana State University, 1979.

———. "*The New York Picayune.*" In *American Humor Magazines and Comic Periodicals,* 191–93. Westport, Conn.: Greenwood Press, 1987.

———. "*Nick Nax (For All Creation).*" In *American Humor Magazines and Comic Periodicals,* 195. Westport, Conn.: Greenwood Press, 1987.

———. "*Vanity Fair (1859–1863).*" In *American Humor Magazines and Comic Periodicals,* 299–303. Westport, Conn.: Greenwood Press, 1987.

Sloane, David E. E., ed. *American Humor Magazines and Comic Periodicals.* Westport, Conn.: Greenwood Press, 1987.

———. *The Literary Humor of the Urban Northeast, 1830–1890.* Baton Rouge: Louisiana State University, 1983.

Smith, Henry Nash. *Mark Twain: The Development of a Writer.* Cambridge: Harvard University Press, 1962.

———. "Mark Twain, Ritual Clown." In *American Literature, Culture, and Ideology: Essays in Honor of Henry Nash Smith,* ed. Beverly R. Voloshin, 235–54. New York: Peter Lang, 1990.

Spengemann, William C. *Mark Twain and the Backwoods Angel: The Matter of Innocence in the Works of Samuel L. Clemens.* Kent, Ohio: Kent State University Press, 1966.

Tandy, Jennette. *Crackerbox Philosophers in American Humor and Satire.* 1925. Reprint, New York: Kennikat Press, 1964.

Thorp, Willard. *American Humorists.* Minneapolis: University of Minnesota Press, 1964.

Trent, William P. "A Retrospect of American Humor." In *Critical Essays on American Humor,* ed. William Bedford Clark and W. Craig Turner, 32–46. Boston: G. K. Hall, 1984.

Wade, Clyde G. *"The Carpet-Bag."* In *American Humor Magazines and Comic Periodicals,* ed. David E. E. Sloane, 44–51. Westport, Conn.: Greenwood Press, 1987.

Walker, Nancy A. *Fanny Fern.* New York: Twayne Publishers, 1993.

Watson, Richie Devon, Jr. "Southwest Humor, Plantation Fiction, and the Generic *Cordon Sanitaire.*" In *Yeoman versus Cavalier: The Old Southwest's Fictional Road to Rebellion,* 56–69. Baton Rouge: Louisiana State University Press, 1993.

Weber, Brom. "The Misspellers." In *The Comic Imagination in American Literature,* ed. Louis D. Rubin Jr., 127–38. New Brunswick, N.J.: Rutgers University Press, 1973.

Wenke, John. *"Sut Lovingood's Yarns* [sic] and the Politics of Performance." *Studies in American Fiction* 15 (1987): 199–210.

Wienandt, Christopher. "Mark Twain, Nevada Frontier Journalism, and the *Territorial Enterprise:* Crisis in Credibility." Ph.D. diss., University of North Texas, 1995.

Williams, Leonard. "C. F. M. Noland and the Roots of Southwest Humor." In *Cavorting on the Devil's Fork: The Pete Whetstone Letters of C. F. M. Noland,* 1–54. Memphis: Memphis State University Press, 1979.

Yates, Norris. *William T. Porter and the "Spirit of the Times": A Study of the Big Bear School of Humor.* Baton Rouge: Louisiana State University, 1957.

Zanger, Jules. "The Frontiersman in Popular Fiction, 1820–1860." In *The Frontier Re-examined,* ed. John F. McDermott, 141–53. Urbana: University of Illinois Press, 1967.

## III. BACKGROUNDS

Addison, Joseph, and Richard Steele. *The Spectator.* Ed. Donald F. Bond. Oxford: Clarendon Press, 1965.

————. *The Tatler.* Ed. George A. Aitken. Facsimile ed. Hildesheim, Germany: Georg Olms Verlag, 1970.

Adelman, Jeremy, and Stephen Aron. "From Borderlands to Borders: Empires, Nation-States, and the Peoples in between in North American History." *American Historical Review* 104 (1999): 814–41.

Adorno, Theodor, and Hans Horkheimer. *Dialectic of Enlightenment.* Trans. John Cumming. New York: Continuum, 1972.

Aldis, Owen. *Play Fighting.* New York: Academic Press, 1975.

Alexander, Mary Charlotte. *William Patterson Alexander in Kentucky, the Marquesas, Hawai'i.* Honolulu: privately printed, 1934.

Alford, Richard. "Humor Framing Conventions: Techniques and Effects." In *Play as Context,* ed. Alyce Taylor Cheska, 268–79. New York: Leisure Press, 1979.

Ambrose, Stephen E. *Undaunted Courage: Meriwether Lewis, Thomas Jefferson, and the Opening of the American West.* New York: Simon and Schuster, 1996.

Andrews, Lorrin. *A Dictionary of the Hawaiian Language.* Honolulu: H. M. Whitney, 1865.

Arden, Heather. *Fool Plays: A Study of Satire in the "Sottie."* Cambridge: Cambridge University Press, 1980.

Aristotle. "Poetics." In *The Complete Works of Aristotle,* revised Oxford Translation, vol. 2, ed. Jonathan Barnes, 2316–40. Princeton: Princeton University Press, 1984.

Babcock, Barbara A. "Arrange Me into Disorder: Fragments and Reflections on Ritual Clowning." In *Rite, Drama, Festival, Spectacle: Rehearsals toward a Theory of Cultural Performance,* ed. John J. MacAloon, 102–28. Philadelphia: Institute for the Study of Human Issues, 1984.

Babcock, Barbara A., ed. *The Reversible World: Symbolic Inversion in Art and Society.* Ithaca: Cornell University Press, 1972.

Baker, Thomas N. *Sentiment and Celebrity: Nathaniel Parker Willis and the Trials of Literary Fame.* New York: Oxford University Press, 1999.

Bakhtin, Mikhail. *Rabelais and His World.* Trans. Helene Iswolsky. Bloomington: Indiana University Press, 1984.

Baldasty, Gerald J. *The Commercialization of News in the Nineteenth Century.* Madison: University of Wisconsin Press, 1992.

Ballenger, Grady W. "Carey and Hart." In *Dictionary of Literary Biography.* Vol. 49, pt. 1, *American Literary Publishing Houses, 1638–1899,* 80–83. Detroit: Gale Research, 1986.

Bancroft, Hubert Howe. *History of Nevada, Colorado, and Wyoming.* Vol. 25 of *The Works of Hubert Howe Bancroft.* San Francisco: History Publishers, 1890.

Barrère, Dorothy B. "The Hula in Retrospect." *Hula: Historical Perspectives.* Pacific Anthropological Records, no. 30 (1980): 1–68.

Bates, George Washington. *Sandwich Island Notes. By a Haole.* New York: Harper and Brothers, 1854.

Bateson, Gregory. "A Theory of Play and Fantasy." In *Steps to an Ecology of the Mind,* 177–93. New York: Ballantine Books, 1972.

Beechert, Edward D. *Honolulu: The Crossroads of the Pacific.* Columbia: University of South Carolina Press, 1991.

Beetham, Margaret. "Towards a Theory of the Periodical as a Publishing Genre." In *Investigating Victorian Journalism,* ed. Laurel Blake, Aled Jones, and Lionel Madden, 19–32. New York: St. Martin's Press, 1990.

Bell, Michael Davitt. *Culture, Genre, and Literary Vocation.* Chicago: University of Chicago Press, 2001.

Billington, Sandra. *A Social History of the Fool.* New York: St. Martin's Press, 1984.

Bingham, Hiram. *Residence of Twenty-one Years in the Sandwich Islands.* Rutland, Vt.: Charles E. Tuttle, 1881.

Bishop, Artemas. *Hawaiian Phrase Book.* 3d ed., rev. Honolulu: H. M. Whitney, 1878.

Blake, William. *The Marriage of Heaven and Hell.* Ed. Harold Bloom. New York: Chelsea House, 1987.

Bledstein, Burton J. "Storytellers to the Middle Class." In *The Middling Sorts: Explorations in the History of the American Middle Class,* ed. Burton J. Bledstein and Robert D. Johnston, 1–25. New York: Routledge, 2001.

Blumin, Stuart M. *The Emergence of the Middle Class: Social Experience in the American City, 1760–1900.* Cambridge: Cambridge University Press, 1989.

Bode, Carl. *The Anatomy of American Popular Culture, 1840–1861.* Berkeley and Los Angeles: University of California Press, 1960.

Boles, John B. "Evangelical Protestantism in the Old South: From Religious Dissent to Cultural Dominance." In *Religion of the Old South,* ed. Charles R. Wilson, 13–34. Jackson: University of Mississippi Press, 1985.

Booth, Wayne C. *The Rhetoric of Fiction.* 2d ed. Chicago: University of Chicago Press, 1983.

Bradley, Harold Whitman. *American Frontier in Hawai'i: The Pioneers, 1789–1843.* Gloucester, Mass.: Peter Smith, 1968.

Brightman, Robert. "Traditions of Subversion and the Subversion of Tradition: Cultural Criticism in Maidu Clown Performances." *American Anthropologist* 101 (1999): 272–87.

Brooks, Van Wyck. "America's Coming of Age." In *Three Essays on America,* 15–112. New York: E. P. Dutton, 1934.

———. *The Times of Melville and Whitman.* New York: E. P. Dutton, 1947.

Bruce, Dickson D., Jr. *Violence and Culture in the Antebellum South*. Austin: University of Texas Press, 1979.

Bruce, John R. *Gaudy Century: The Story of San Francisco's 100 Years of Robust Journalism*. New York: Random House, 1948.

Bruner, Edward M. "Experience and Its Expressions." In *The Anthropology of Experience,* ed. Victor W. Turner and Edward M. Bruner, 3–30. Urbana: University of Illinois Press, 1986.

Bucer, Martin. "De Honestis Ludis." In *Early English Stages, 1300–1600,* vol. 2, pt. 1, ed. Glynne Wickham, 329–31. New York: Columbia University Press, 1963.

Buck, Elizabeth. *Paradise Remade: The Politics of Culture and History in Hawai'i*. Philadelphia: Temple University Press, 1993.

Burke, Kenneth. *Attitudes toward History*. 2d ed. Los Altos, Calif.: Hermes Publications, 1959.

Burton, Richard D. E. *The Flâneur and His City: Patterns of Daily Life in Paris, 1815–1851*. Durham, England: University of Durham Press, 1994.

Caillois, Roger. *Man, Play, and Games*. Trans. Meyer Barash. New York: Schocken Books, 1979.

Campbell, Randolph B. "Planters and Plain Folks: The Social Structure of the Antebellum South." In *Interpreting Southern History: Historiographical Essays in Honor of Sanford Higginbotham,* ed. John B. Boles and Evelyn Thomas Nolen, 48–77. Baton Rouge: Louisiana State University Press, 1987.

Caron, James E. "From Ethology to Aesthetics: Evolution as a Theoretical Paradigm for Research on Laughter, Humor, and Other Comic Phenomena." *Humor: An International Journal for Humor Research* 15, no. 3 (2002): 245–81.

Cashin, Joan E. *A Family Venture: Men and Women on the Southern Frontier*. Oxford: Oxford University Press, 1991.

Christen, Kimberly A., ed. *Clowns and Tricksters: An Encyclopedia of Tradition and Culture*. Denver: ABC-Clio, 1998.

Cicero. *De Oratore*. Trans. E. W. Sutton. Cambridge: Harvard University Press, 1948.

Cowley, Malcolm. "The Revolt against Gentility." In *After the Genteel Tradition: American Writers, 1910–1930,* rev. ed., 3–20. Carbondale: Southern Illinois University Press, 1964.

Crane, R. S. "Suggestions toward a Genealogy of the 'Man of Feeling.'" In *Backgrounds to Eighteenth-Century Literature,* ed. Kathleen Williams, 322–49. Scranton, Pa.: Chandler Publishing Company, 1971.

Crumrine, N. Ross. "Capakoba, the Mayo Easter Ceremonial Impersonator: Explanations of Ritual Clowning." *Journal for the Scientific Study of Religion* 8, no. 1 (1969): 1–22.

Danesi, Marcel, and Paul Perron. *Analyzing Cultures.* Bloomington: Indiana University Press, 1999.

Davis, Chester L. "Goodman's Assistance on the Biography." *Twainian* 15 (1956): 2–4.

Daws, Gavin. *Shoal of Time: A History of the Hawai'ian Islands.* Honolulu: University of Hawai'i Press, 1974.

Decker, William Merrill. *Epistolary Practices: Letter Writing in America before Telecommunications.* Chapel Hill: University of North Carolina Press, 1998.

Dicken-Garcia, Hazel. *Journalistic Standards in Nineteenth-Century America.* Madison: University of Wisconsin Press, 1989.

Dirks, Robert. *The Black Saturnalia: Conflict and Its Ritual Expression on British West Indian Slave Plantations.* Gainesville: University of Florida Press, 1987.

Donatus. "A Fragment on Comedy and Tragedy." In *Theories of Comedy,* ed. Paul Lauter, 27–32. New York: Doubleday, 1964.

Eliot, T. S. *Notes toward a Definition of Culture.* New York: Faber and Faber, 1948.

Elliott, Robert C. *The Power of Satire: Magic, Ritual, Art.* Princeton: Princeton University Press, 1960.

Elliott, Russell R. *History of Nevada.* Lincoln: University of Nebraska Press, 1973.

Elyot, Thomas. *The Book Named the Governor.* Ed. S. E. Lehmberg. London: J. M. Dent and Sons, 1962.

Emerson, Nathaniel B. *Unwritten Literature of Hawai'i: The Sacred Songs of the Hula.* Rutland, Vt.: Charles E. Tuttle, 1965.

Ferguson, Priscilla Parkhurst. "The *Flâneur* on and off the Streets of Paris." In *The "Flâneur,"* ed. Keith Tester, 22–42. London: Routledge, 1994.

Fielding, Henry. *An Apology for the Life of Shamela Andrews.* Dublin: Oli Nelson, 1741.

Ford, Lacy K. "Popular Ideology of the Old South's Plain Folk: The Limits of Egalitarianism in a Slaveholding Society." In *Plain Folk of the South Revisited,* ed. Samuel C. Hyde Jr., 205–27. Baton Rouge: Louisiana State University, 1997.

Fox, Stephen. *The Mirror Makers: A History of American Advertising and Its Creators.* New York: William Morrow, 1984.

Freud, Sigmund. *Jokes and Their Relationship to the Unconscious.* Trans. James Strachey. New York: W. W. Norton, 1960.

Gans, Herbert J. *Popular Culture and High Culture: An Analysis and Evolution of Taste.* Rev. ed. New York: Basic Books, 1999.

Goldman, Irving. *Ancient Polynesian Society.* Chicago: University of Chicago Press, 1970.

Goodhue, E. S. "Mark Twain's Hawai'ian Home." *Mid-Pacific Magazine* 12 (1916): 177–81.

Gorn, Elliott J. "'Gouge and Bite, Pull Hair and Scratch': The Social Significance of Fighting in the Southern Backcountry." *American Historical Review* 90 (1985): 18–43.

Greenberg, Clement. "Avant-Garde and Kitsch." *Partisan Review* 6 (1939): 34–49.

Greer, Richard A. "Grog Shops and Hotels: Bending the Elbow in Honolulu." *Hawai'ian Journal of History* 28 (1994): 35–67.

Hall, David D. "Readers and Reading in America: Historical and Critical Perspectives." *Proceedings of the American Antiquarian Society* 103 (1994): 337–57.

Handelman, Don. "Play and Ritual: Complementary Frames of Meta-Communication." In *It's a Funny Thing, Humor,* ed. Anthony Chapman and Hugh Foot, 185–92. London: Pergamon Press, 1977.

———. "Precariousness in Play." In *Models and Mirrors: Towards an Anthropology of Public Events,* 63–81. Cambridge: Cambridge University Press, 1990.

———. "The Ritual Clown: Attributes and Affinities." *Anthropos* 76, nos. 2–3 (1981): 321–70.

Handy, E. S. Craighill. *Cultural Revolution in Hawai'i.* New York: American Council, Institute of Pacific Relations, 1931.

Handy, E. S. Craighill, and Elizabeth G. Handy. *Native Planters in Old Hawai'i: Their Life, Lore, and Environment.* Honolulu: Bishop Museum Press, 1972.

Handy, E. S. Craighill, and Mary K. Pukui. *The Polynesian Family System in Ka'u, Hawai'i.* Wellington, New Zealand: Polynesian Society, 1958.

Harrell, David Edwin, Jr. "The Evolution of Plain-Folk Religion in the South, 1835–1920." In *Varieties of Southern Religious Experience,* ed. Samuel S. Hill, 24–51. Baton Rouge: Louisiana State University Press, 1988.

Harris, Phillip H. "Charles Coffin Harris: An Uncommon Life in the Law." *Hawai'ian Journal of History* 28 (1993): 151–71.

Hereniko, Vilsoni. *Woven Gods: Female Clowns and Power in Rotuma.* Honolulu: University of Hawai'i Press, 1995.

Hieb, Louis A. "Meaning and Mismeaning: Toward an Understanding of the Ritual Clown." In *New Perspectives on the Pueblos,* ed. Alfonso Ortiz, 163–95. Albuquerque: University of New Mexico Press, 1972.

Hodge, Francis. *Yankee Theater: The Image of America on the Stage, 1825–1850.* Austin: University of Texas Press, 1964.

Huntzicker, William E. *The Popular Press, 1833–1865.* Westport, Conn.: Greenwood Press, 1999.

Ii, John Papa. *Fragments of Hawai'ian History.* Trans. Mary K. Pukui. Honolulu: Bishop Museum Press, 1959.

Immelmann, Klaus. *Introduction to Ethology.* New York: Plenum Press, 1980.

Iser, Wolfgang. *The Fictive and the Imaginary: Charting Literary Anthropology.* Baltimore: Johns Hopkins University Press, 1993.

———. *The Implied Reader: Patterns of Communication in Prose Fiction from Bunyan to Beckett.* Baltimore: Johns Hopkins University Press, 1974.

———. "Toward a Literary Anthropology." In *Prospecting: From Reader Response to Literary Anthropology,* 262–84. Baltimore: Johns Hopkins University Press, 1989.

Jarves, James J. *History of the Hawai'ian or Sandwich Islands.* Boston: J. Munroe, 1843.

Kamakau, Samuel M. *Ruling Chiefs of Hawai'i.* Rev. ed. Honolulu: Kamehameha Schools Press, 1992.

Kame'eleihiwa, Lilikala. *Native Land and Foreign Desires: "Pehea La E Pono Ai?"* Honolulu: Bishop Museum Press, 1992.

Kennedy, John G. "Bonds of Laughter among the Tarahumara Indians: Towards a Rethinking of Joking Relationship Theory." In *The Social Anthropology of Latin America: Essays in Honor of Ralph Leon Beals,* ed. Walter Goldschmidt and Harry Hoijer, 36–68. Berkeley and Los Angeles: University of California Press, 1970.

Kent, Noel Jacob. *Hawai'i: Islands under the Influence.* New York: Monthly Review Press, 1983.

King, Arden R. "North American Indian Clowns and Creativity." In *Forms of Play of Native North Americans,* ed. Edward Norbeck and Claire R. Farrer, 143–51. St. Paul: West Publishing Company, 1979.

Kirch, Patrick Vinton. *The Wet and the Dry: Irrigation and Agricultural Intensification in Polynesia.* Chicago: University of Chicago Press, 1994.

Kuykendall, Ralph S. *Foundation and Transformation, 1778–1854.* Vol. 1 of *The Hawai'ian Kingdom.* Honolulu: University of Hawai'i Press, 1938.

———. *Twenty Critical Years, 1854–1874.* Vol. 2 of *The Hawai'ian Kingdom.* Honolulu: University of Hawai'i Press, 1953.

Ladurie, Emmanuel Le Roy. *Carnival in Romans.* New York: Penguin, 1981.

Laird, Pamela Walker. *Advertising Progress: American Business and the Rise of Consumer Marketing.* Baltimore: Johns Hopkins University Press, 1998.

Lauter, Paul, ed. *Theories of Comedy.* New York: Doubleday, 1964.

Lehuu, Isabelle. *Carnival on the Page: Popular Print Media in Antebellum America.* Chapel Hill: University of North Carolina Press, 2000.

Leonard, Thomas C. "News at the Hearth: A Drama of Reading in Nineteenth-Century America." *Proceedings of the American Antiquarian Society* 102 (1992): 379–401.

Levine, Jacob. "Regression in Primitive Clowning." In *Motivation in Humor,* 167–78. New York: Atherton Press, 1969.

Lillard, Richard G. *Desert Challenge: An Interpretation of Nevada.* New York: A. A. Knopf, 1942.

———. "Studies in Washoe Journalism and Humor." Ph.D. diss., Iowa State University, 1942.

Lingenfelter, Richard E., and Karen Rix Gash. *The Newspapers of Nevada: A History and Bibliography, 1854–1979.* Reno: University of Nevada Press, 1984.

Loubier, Pierre. "Balzac et le Flâneur." *L'Année Balzacienne* 2 (2001): 141–66.

Lyman, George D. *The Saga of the Comstock Lode: Boom Days in Virginia City.* New York: Charles Scribner's Sons, 1934.

MacDonald, Dwight. "Masscult and Midcult I." *Partisan Review* 27 (1960): 203–33.

———. "Masscult and Midcult II." *Partisan Review* 27 (1960): 589–631.

Mahar, William J. *Behind the Burnt Cork Mask: Early Blackface Minstrelsy and Antebellum American Culture.* Urbana: University of Illinois Press, 1999.

Mathews, Donald G. *Religion in the Old South.* Chicago: University of Chicago Press, 1977.

Mazlish, Bruce. "The Flâneur: From Spectator to Representation." In *The "Flâneur,"* ed. Keith Tester, 43–60. London: Routledge, 1994.

Mechtild, Albert. "Désir, commerce, and la création, ou le dilemme de l'artiste balzacien." *L'Année Balzacienne* 4 (1984): 215–25.

Menzies, Archibald. *Hawai'i Nei 128 Years Ago.* Honolulu: W. F. Wilson, 1920.

Miller, Tice L. *Bohemians and Critics: American Theater Criticism in the Nineteenth Century.* Metuchen, N.J.: Scarecrow Press, 1981.

Milne, Gordon. *George William Curtis and the Genteel Tradition.* Bloomington: Indiana University Press, 1956.

Mitchell, William E. "Introduction: Mother Folly in the Islands." In *Clowning as Critical Practice: Performance Humor in the South Pacific,* 3–57. Pittsburgh: University of Pittsburgh Press, 1992.

Mott, Frank Luther. *A History of American Magazines, Volume I, 1741–1850.* Cambridge: Harvard University Press, 1930.

———. *A History of American Magazines, Volume II, 1850–1865.* Cambridge: Harvard University Press, 1938.

Nell, William. "Historical and Implied Authors and Readers." *Comparative Literature* 45 (1993): 22–46.

Noel, Mary. *Villains Galore: The Heyday of the Popular Story Weekly.* New York: MacMillan, 1954.

Oliver, Douglas. *Polynesia in Early Historic Times.* Honolulu: Bess Press, 2002.

Osorio, Jonathan Kay Kamakawiwoʻole. *Dismembering Lahui: A History of the Hawaiʻian Nation to 1887.* Honolulu: University of Hawaiʻi Press, 2002.

Owsley, Frank. *Plain Folk of the Old South.* Baton Rouge: Louisiana State University, 1949.

Passet, Joanne E. *Sex Radicals and the Quest for Women's Equality.* Urbana: University of Illinois Press, 2003.

Plato. "Laws: Book VIII, Book XI." Trans. Trevor J. Saunders. In *Complete Works,* ed. John M. Cooper, 1318–1616. Indianapolis: Hackett Publishing Company, 1997.

———. "Philebus." Trans. Dorothea Frede. In *Complete Works,* ed. John M. Cooper, 398–456. Indianapolis: Hackett Publishing Company, 1997.

Pukui, Mary Kawena, and Samuel H. Elbert. *Hawaiʻian Dictionary.* Rev. ed. Honolulu: University of Hawaiʻi Press, 1986.

Quintilian. [Laughter, Wit, and Humor]. In *Institutio Oratoria,* trans. H. E. Butler, 2:439–501. New York: G. P. Putnam's Sons, 1921.

Rabinowitz, Peter. *Before Reading: Narrative Conventions and the Politics of Interpretation.* Ithaca: Cornell University Press, 1987.

Radcliffe-Brown, Arthur R. "On Joking Relationships." In *Structure and Function in Primitive Society,* 90–104. London: Cohen and West, 1952.

Reckford, Kenneth J. *Aristophanes' Old-and-New Comedy.* Chapel Hill: University of North Carolina Press, 1987.

Ridgely, J. V. "The Southern Way of Life: The 1830s and '40s." In *Nineteenth Century Southern Literature,* 50–61. Lexington: University Press of Kentucky, 1980.

Riggan, William. *Picaros, Madmen, Naifs, and Clowns: The Unreliable First-Person Narrator.* Norman: University of Oklahoma Press, 1981.

Rogers, Tommy W. "D. R. Hundley: A Middle-Class Thesis of Social Stratifications in the Antebellum South." *Mississippi Quarterly* 23 (1970): 135–54.

Roof, Wade Clark. "Religious Change in the American South: The Case of the Unchurched." In *Varieties of Southern Religious Experience,* ed. Samuel S. Hill, 192–210. Baton Rouge: Louisiana State University Press, 1988.

Santayana, George. "Genteel American Poetry." In *The Genteel Tradition: Nine Essays by George Santayana,* ed. Douglas L. Wilson, 72–76. Cambridge: Harvard University Press, 1967.

———. "The Genteel Tradition in American Philosophy." In *The Genteel Tradition: Nine Essays by George Santayana,* ed. Douglas L. Wilson, 37–64. Cambridge: Harvard University Press, 1967.

Schmitt, Robert C. "New Estimates of the Pre-Censal Population of Hawaiʻi." *Journal of the Polynesian Society* 80 (1971): 237–43.

Scholnick, Robert J. "J. G. Holland and the 'Religion of Civilization' in Mid-Nineteenth Century America." *American Studies* 27, no. 1 (1986): 55–79.

Semes, Robert Louis. "Hawai'i's Holy War: English Bishop Staley, American Congregationalists, and the Hawai'ian Monarchs, 1860–1870." *Hawai'ian Journal of History* 34 (2000): 113–38.

Silva, Noenoe K. "*He Kanawai E Ho'opau I Na Hula Kuolo Hawai'i:* The Political Economy of Banning the Hula." *Hawai'ian Journal of History* 34 (2000): 29–48.

Smith, Grant H. "The History of the Comstock Lode, 1850–1920." *University of Nevada Bulletin.* Geology and Mining Series, no. 37, 1943.

Smith, Susan Belasco, and Kenneth M. Price. "Periodical Literature in Social and Historical Context." In *Periodical Literature in Nineteenth-Century America,* 3–16. Charlottesville: University Press of Virginia, 1995.

Spurlock. John C. *Free Love: Marriage and Middle-Class Radicalism in America, 1825–1860.* New York: New York University Press, 1988.

Stanhope, Philip Dormer. "Letter to His Godson, December 12, 1765." In *The Letters of Philip Dormer Stanhope, 4th Earl of Chesterfield,* ed. Bonamy Dobrée, 6:2691–93. London: Eyre and Spottiswoode, 1932.

Stannard, David E. *Before the Horror: The Population of Hawai'i on the Eve of Western Contact.* Honolulu: Social Science Research Institute, University of Hawai'i, 1989.

Sterner, Douglas W. *Priests of Culture: A Study of Matthew Arnold and Henry James.* New York: Peter Lang, 1999.

Stewart, Charles S. *A Residence in the Sandwich Islands.* Boston: Jordan, 1839.

Swain, Barbara. *Fools and Folly during the Middle Ages and Renaissance.* New York: Columbia University Press, 1932.

Tarpley, J. Douglas. "Thomas Bailey Aldrich." In *Dictionary of Literary Biography.* Vol. 79, *American Magazine Journalists, 1850–1900,* 27–33. Detroit: Gale Research, 1989.

Tave, Stuart. *The Amiable Humorist: A Study in the Comic Theory and Criticism of the Eighteenth and Early Nineteenth Centuries.* Chicago: University of Chicago Press, 1960.

Thomas, Amy M. "Literature in Newsprint: Antebellum Family Newspapers and the Uses of Reading." In *Reading Books: Essays on the Material Text and Literature in America,* ed. Michele Moylan and Lane Stiles, 101–16. Amherst: University of Massachusetts Press, 1996.

Turner, Victor. "Liminality and the Performative Genres." In *Rite, Drama, Festival, Spectacle: Rehearsals toward a Theory of Cultural Performance,* ed. John J. MacAloon, 19–41. Philadelphia: Institute for the Study of Human Issues, 1983.

————. "Liminal to Liminoid in Play, Flow, Ritual: An Essay in Comparative Symbology." *Rice University Studies* 60 (1974): 53–92.

Tyrrell, Ian. *Sobering Up: From Temperance to Prohibition in Antebellum America, 1800–1860.* Westport, Conn.: Greenwood Press, 1979.

Tzetzes, John. *First Proem to Aristophanes.* In *Theories of Comedy,* ed. Paul Lauter, 33–34. New York: Doubleday, 1964.

Udall, Nicholas. Prologue to *Ralph Roister Doister.* In *Theories of Comedy,* ed. Paul Lauter, 113. New York: Doubleday, 1964.

Varigny, Charles de. *Fourteen Years at the Sandwich Islands.* Trans. Alfons L. Korn. Honolulu: University of Hawai'i Press and the Hawai'ian Historical Society, 1981.

Walker, Franklin. *San Francisco's Literary Frontier.* New York: Alfred A. Knopf, 1939.

Welsford, Enid. *The Fool: His Social and Literary History.* London: Faber and Faber, 1935.

Wermuth, Paul. *Bayard Taylor.* New York: Twayne Publishers, 1973.

Willeford, William. *The Fool and His Scepter: A Study in Clowns and Jesters and Their Audiences.* Chicago: Northwestern University Press, 1969.

Young, John P. *Journalism in California.* San Francisco: Chronicle Publishing Company, 1915.

Young, Kanalu G. Terry. *Rethinking the Native Hawai'ian Past.* New York: Garland Publishing, 1998.

Zboray, Ronald J. *A Fictive People: Antebellum Economic Development and the American Reading Public.* New York: Oxford University Press, 1993.

Zboray, Ronald J., and Mary Saracino Zboray. "Books, Readings, and the World of Goods in Antebellum New England." *American Quarterly* 48 (1996): 587–622.

# Index